Mosaicos

SPANISH AS A WORLD LANGUAGE

LINGRO 1.0 EDITION

Elizabeth E. Guzmán
University of Iowa, retired

Paloma Lapuerta
Central Connecticut State University

Judith E. Liskin-Gasparro
University of Iowa, Emerita

Acknowledgments of third-party content appear starting on page A-34, which constitute an extension of this copyright page.

1 2024

Access Code & Looseleaf
978-1-63604-095-0

Paperback Print
978-1-63604-109-4

Brief Contents

Scope and Sequence

Scope and Sequence (continued)

CAPÍTULO	LEARNING OUTCOMES	CULTURE
3 ¿Qué hacen para divertirse? 100	• Describe free-time activities and talk about food • Plan your daily activities and express intentions • Identify prices and dates • State what and whom you know • Talk about Peru in terms of products, practices, and perspectives • Share information about free-time activities in Hispanic countries and identify cultural similarities	**Enfoque cultural:** *Perú* **101** **Mosaico cultural:** *Los jóvenes y la vida social* **112** **En acción:** *¡A comer!* **113**
4 ¿Cómo es tu familia? 138	• Talk about family members and their daily routines • Express opinions, plans, preferences, and feelings • Express obligation • Express how long something has been going on • Talk about Venezuela in terms of it's products, practices, and perspectives • Share information about families and family life in Hispanic countries and make cultural comparisons	**Enfoque cultural:** *Venezuela* **139** **Mosaico cultural:** *Las telenovelas venezolanas* **148** **En acción:** *Una fiesta en familia* **149**
5 ¿Dónde vives? 172	• Talk about housing, the home, and household activities • Express ongoing actions • Describe physical and emotional states • Avoid repetition in speaking and writing • Point out and identify people and things • Express when, where, or how an action occurs • Talk about Nicaragua, El Salvador, and Honduras in terms of products, practices, and perspectives • Talk about housing in urban areas	**Enfoque cultural:** *Nicaragua, El Salvador y Honduras* **173** **Mosaico cultural:** *Las viviendas en centros urbanos* **183** **En acción:** *En casa* **184**

Scope and Sequence (continued)

Scope and Sequence (continued)

Scope and Sequence (continued)

CAPÍTULO	LEARNING OUTCOMES	CULTURE
14 **¿Cómo vivimos los cambios sociales? 508**	• Discuss demographics and social conditions • Indicate conditions, goals, and purposes • Express conjecture • Talk about the past from a past perspective • Talk about Chile in terms of products, practices, and perspectives • Talk about social change, gender roles, and migration	**Enfoque cultural:** *Chile* **509** **Mosaico cultural:** *La migración interna en el mundo hispano* **519** **En acción:** *Por un mundo mejor* **520**
15 **¿Qué nos trae el futuro? 544**	• Talk about advances in science and technology • Express wishes and recommendations in the past • Hypothesize and share information about the present and the future • Express unexpected occurrences • Talk about Puerto Rico in terms of products, practices, and perspectives • Talk about technology and scientific research in Spain and Latin America	**Enfoque cultural:** *Puerto Rico* **545** **Mosaico cultural:** *La investigación tecnológica y científica en España e Hispanoamérica* **555** **En acción:** *¡Cuidemos el medio ambiente!* **556**

VOCABULARIO EN CONTEXTO	FUNCIONES Y FORMAS	MOSAICOS
Cambios en la sociedad **511** *Temas de hoy: la emigración* **514** *Las mujeres y el trabajo* **516**	Expressing conjecture: **Adverbial conjunctions that require the subjunctive 521** Expressing conjecture or certainty: **Adverbial conjunctions that take the subjunctive or the indicative 526** Talking about the past from a past perspective: **The past perfect 532**	**Escucha** • Identify the speaker's point of view **538** **Habla** • Organize ideas to present solutions to problems **539** **Lee** • Identify the tone of a text **540** **Escribe** • Write to spark interest **542**
La tecnología en el mundo de hoy **547** *La ciencia y el medio ambiente* **549** *Otros retos del futuro* **551**	Expressing the unexpected: ***Se* for unplanned occurrences 557** Expressing wishes and recommendations in the past: **The imperfect subjunctive 562** Hypothesizing about the present and the future: ***If*-clauses 567**	**Escucha** • Identify the speaker's intention through the main idea and specific information **572** **Habla** • Use drama and humor in telling a personal anecdote **573** **Lee** • Identify the narrator's perspective **575** **Escribe** • Use imagination and humor in writing a narrative **577**

Preface

Why *Mosaicos?*

When ***Mosaicos*** first appeared, it ushered in a new and evolved vision of how the elements that comprise basic language instruction could be combined in a highly communicative, culturally rich language program. Its vision was complete and synthetic, both in the treatment of each element and in how the elements were gathered into an integrated, connected whole. This vision of wholeness has served as the foundation for a sound and compelling approach, reflecting the nature of language and how it is learned. The title was carefully chosen to reflect its founding principles and structure. The most basic elements of the ***Mosaicos*** approach are:

Guided Communication. A **guided communicative approach** based on solid methodological principles combined with years of empirical classroom experience, resulting in an informed and sensible pedagogy that promotes communicative practice.

Context. Learning **language in context** with a **focus on meaning.**

Integrated Culture. The **integration of culture** as an intrinsic part of language and of the experience of language learning.

Four-Skills Synthesis. A **synthetic and focused approach** to listening, speaking, reading, and writing. The ***Mosaicos*** section at the end of each chapter helps students synthesize what they have learned. Four activity clusters that focus on the four skills combine the thematic content (e.g., family, sports, work, travel) of the chapter with the communication modes of the World-Readiness Standards (interpretive, interpersonal, presentational).

The Lingro 1.0 edition of ***Mosaicos*** is more solid and more integrated than ever before, creating for students a multifaceted experience of the intricate mosaic of the Spanish language and its cultures.

Mosaicos *offers instructors the truly communicative, deeply culture-focused approach they seek while providing the guidance and tools students need to be successful using a program with highly communicative goals. With* Mosaicos, *there is no need to compromise.*

This inclusiveness of ***Mosaicos*, 1.0 edition,** extends to the broad range of students often found in many Spanish-language classrooms. Thanks to the multifaceted approach of ***Mosaicos***, students with a range of language-learning backgrounds and learning styles all benefit from the rich program and many opportunities for communication.

What's new in this edition?

- This edition features six new **Integrated Performance Assessments (IPAs)** using authentic sources and focusing on real-life contexts that students will find both engaging and meaningful. The IPAs target each of the three modes of communication: Interpretive, Interpersonal, and Presentational.
- **Exclusive digital content** delivered via LingroHub offers students a fully integrated experience.
- The **Scope and Sequence** has been reorganized to facilitate smooth transitions from familiar or simple grammatical structures to new or more complex ones, both within and across chapters. Also, the number of grammar topics per chapter has been standardized, so that as the structures become more difficult, the number of structures per chapter is reduced. In the 1.0 edition of ***Mosaicos***, Chapters 1–8 each contain five grammar presentations, Chapters 9–12 have four, and Chapters 13–15 each present three.
- A **modern, streamlined design** and clean visual presentation that allows users to easily navigate each chapter.
- Based on user feedback, all **audio** has been revised and newly recorded.
- All new **chapter opener** photos orient students to the chapter theme and country or region of focus. New, contemporary images have been added throughout the chapters to represent the diversity of the Spanish-speaking world and enhance students' learning and cross-cultural reflection.

Capítulo 3

¿Qué hacen para divertirse?

Dos amigos se divierten cerca de Cuzco, Perú.

- All **cultural content,** including ***Enfoque cultural, Mosaico cultural,*** and ***Cultura,*** has been updated. ***Enfoque cultural*** now links to the ***Club cultura*** videos relevant to the country or region of focus.

Cultura

La gastronomía peruana Peruvian food is well known worldwide, due to the variety of its ingredients, the high quality of its dishes, and the originality of its cultural fusion. Peruvian gastronomy is a product of various influences introduced by immigrants from Africa, Italy, Spain, Japan, and China.

Comunidades Do you know of other foods that are the result of cultural fusion? Can you name some in your community?

Ají de gallina en rollo de sushi

- The ***Piénsalo*** self-check activities that accompany the grammar in context have been revised so that they increase students' metalinguistic awareness by linking form to meaning.

Piénsalo. Indica la función de **ser** o **estar** en las siguientes afirmaciones.

	CONDICIÓN	CARACTERÍSTICA
1. El café **está** caliente.	_____	_____
2. ¡La niña **está** muy grande!	_____	_____
3. **Es** muy alta para su edad.	_____	_____
4. **Son** montañas de los Andes.	_____	_____
5. El aire en las montañas **es** muy frío por las noches.	_____	_____

- More **communicative practice** activities have been added to both the vocabulary and the grammar sequences.
- **Instructor resources** have been added for activities that correlate to the ACTFL World-Readiness Standards for Learning Languages. Additionally, a note has been added to each chapter that indicates the activities that require research outside of class.
- The ***Mosaicos*** skills section includes many improvements:
  - ***Escucha*** and ***Habla*** are now thematically connected, so that they can be taught either as linked modules or individually. ***Lee*** and ***Escribe*** are similarly related, so that the ***Escribe*** writing task builds on what students have learned in ***Lee.***
  - ***Escucha*** has updated audio and activity sets.
  - ***Lee*** readings have been updated or replaced in response to instructor feedback, including new authentic literature by Gloria Fuertes and Wilfredo Machado.
  - The interpretive, interpersonal, and presentational activities for each skill area have been revised to maximize the development of students' communication abilities.
  - The ***Comprueba*** self-checks connect directly to the updated **NCSSFL–ACTFL Can-Do Statements.**

Comprueba

I was able to . . .

- use headings and photos to identify the main idea.
- focus on one piece of information at a time.
- identify terms related to technology.

Acknowledgments

Mosaicos is the result of a collaborative effort among the authors, our publisher, and our colleagues. We are also indebted to the members of the Spanish teaching community for their time, candor, and insightful suggestions. Their critiques and recommendations helped us to sharpen our pedagogical focus and improve the overall quality of the program. We gratefully acknowledge the contributions of the following reviewers:

Sissy Alloway, *Morehead State University*
Louise Barbaro-Medrano, *Monmouth College*
Geoffrey Barrow, *Purdue University Northwest*
Zachary Erwin, *Monmouth College*
Katrina Heil, *East Tennessee State University*
Lina Lee, *University of New Hampshire*
Dolores Lima, *University of Pittsburgh*
Frauke Loewensen, *CSU Monterey Bay*
Oswaldo Lucca, *Edmonds Community College*
Ivan Martinez, *Ball State University*
Teresa McCann, *Prairie State College*
Giuditta Monterosso, *Massasoit Community College*
Michelle Orecchio, *University of Michigan, Ann Arbor*
Lynn Pearson, *Bowling Green State University*
Sue Pechter, *Northwestern University*
Dolores Pons, *University of Michigan-Flint*
Laurie Puszczewicz, *University of Toledo*
Pam Ramallo, *Front Range Community College*
Herlinda Ramirez-Barradas, *Purdue University Northwest*
Karen Segura, *Monmouth College*
Virginia Shen, *Chicago State University*
Christine Stanley, *Roanoke College*
Benay W. Stein, *Northwestern University*
Erika Sutherland, *Muhlenberg College*
Assunta Violante, *Caldwell University*
Gabriela Zapata, *Texas A&M University*

We are very grateful to **Sarah Link,** Senior Development Editor, for all of her work, suggestions, attention to detail, and dedication to the text. Her expertise, support, efficiency, and creativity helped us achieve the final product. We are also grateful to **Carolyn Merrill,** Editor in Chief, and **Harold Swearingen,** Managing Editor, for their guidance and encouragement, as well as to many other members of Ohlinger Studios who provided support and fine attention to detail at all stages of the production process: **Helen Alejandra Richardson,** Director of Market Development, **Jorge Arbujas,** Director of Strategies, **Jennifer Feltri-George**, Senior Program Manager, and **Bridget Funiciello**, Product Development Manager. For her diligent work on the digital components, we thank **Julie Allen,** Senior Digital Media Manager. We are very grateful to the team at Lumina Datamatics, especially **Katy Gabel,** for their careful and professional production services.

Finally, we would like to express our sincere thanks to our colleagues at Pearson Education, especially **Amber Chow,** Executive Editor of Courseware Portfolio Management, **Mellissa Yokell**, Senior Field Marketing Manager, and **Charlene Smith**, Digital Studio Course Producer. A special thank you to **Kathryn Foot,** Senior Art Director, and designer **Cate Rickard Barr** for her creative work on the cover.

About the Authors

Elizabeth Guzmán

A native of Chile, Elizabeth Guzmán recently retired after a long teaching and administrative career. She directed Spanish language programs at several universities in the United States and supervised teachers of English in her country. Throughout her career, she designed face-to-face and flipped courses where *Mosaicos, Unidos*, and *Identidades* were used, in addition to overseeing the design and implementation of online Spanish courses. She trained and mentored graduate teaching assistants and has served as a consultant to Spanish programs that were making the transition from face-to-face to flipped models of teaching. Teaching and learning have been at the center of her academic life, and she has shared her energy, passion, and experience with undergraduates and graduate students. Teaching Spanish as a tool for communication to undergraduates taking Spanish courses to fulfill a requirement was one of the challenges that she undertook with love, understanding, and determination during her career.

Paloma Lapuerta

Dr. Paloma Lapuerta is from the Mediterranean city of Castellón, Spain. She holds a *Licenciatura* and a master's degree in Spanish Philology from the University of Salamanca, Spain, and a Ph.D. in Literature from the University of Geneva, Switzerland. She has taught at the universities of Geneva, Kwua-Zulu Natal, in Durban, South Africa, and Central Connecticut State University, where she is currently Professor of Spanish. She has also taught at the Middlebury College School of Spanish, the University of Michigan, and Dartmouth College. Her research interests focus on 19th and 20th century literature, and she has multiple publications on poetry and novels that deal with social and cultural issues. In addition to *Mosaicos*, Dr. Lapuerta is the co-author of *Unidos, Identidades, La escritura paso a paso*, and the author of *Cortos en curso*, all published by Pearson.

Judith Liskin-Gasparro

Judith Liskin-Gasparro (M.A. Princeton University; Ph.D., University of Texas–Austin) is Associate Professor Emerita at the University of Iowa, where she directed the Spanish language program and co-directed the doctoral program in Second Language Acquisition. She taught courses in second language acquisition, applied linguistics and pedagogy, and Spanish language. Her publications and presentations deal with the development of speaking skills, oral proficiency assessment, and program evaluation and outcomes assessment. She is the co-author of *Unidos* and *Identidades*, in addition to *Mosaicos*, and she was the co-editor of Pearson's Theory and Practice in Second Language Classroom Instruction series. She was also a faculty member at Middlebury College, as well as the Middlebury College School of Spanish. While working at Educational Testing Service, she participated in the development of the *ACTFL Proficiency Guidelines*. She also designed and led the first oral proficiency interview workshops in the early 1980s, and she was principally responsible for training the first generation of OPI testers and trainers in Spanish.

Mosaicos

SPANISH AS A WORLD LANGUAGE

Capítulo preliminar

Bienvenidos

Fans del equipo colombiano en un campeonato de fútbol

Enfoque cultural
El español en el mundo

Vocabulario en contexto
Las presentaciones
Los saludos y las despedidas
¿Qué hay en el salón de clase?
Los meses del año y los días de la semana
El tiempo
Expresiones útiles en la clase
El alfabeto

Funciones y formas
Singular forms of **ser**
Estar | location
Numbers 0 to 99
Telling time

En este capítulo...
Vocabulario

Learning Outcomes

By the end of the chapter, you will be able to:

- introduce yourself, greet others, and say goodbye
- identify people and classroom objects and tell where they are in the classroom
- listen to and respond to classroom expressions and requests
- spell names and addresses and share phone numbers
- express dates, tell time, and comment on the weather
- share information about the Spanish language and where it is spoken

Be self-motivated and self-disciplined. As you begin your study of Spanish with *Mosaicos*, you will discover that you will have many online assignments. Most of the activities in the textbook are intended for class time, when you will interact with your classmates in pairs and small groups. With the freedom and flexibility of the online environment comes responsibility. The online process takes commitment and discipline to keep up with the flow of the content and online assignments.

Have regular access to a computer or mobile device and a high-speed internet connection. Key parts of the course content and interaction are engaged through the internet. You must have access to the necessary equipment and meet the system requirements to successfully engage with the online materials.

Use critical thinking in your learning process. All learning involves integrating new information into what you already know. When you read explanations and do homework, you have to use your critical thinking skills to make use of the new information and practice opportunities. Just doing the activities is not enough; you have to think actively to learn.

Enfoque cultural

El español en el mundo

La geografía hispana es inmensa y muy variada:

desde el río Grande al norte de México,

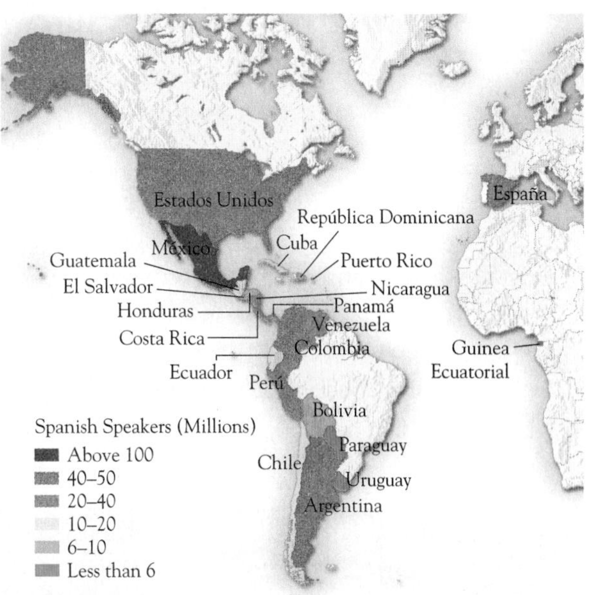

desde la ciudad de Barcelona en España,

hasta Tierra del Fuego al sur de Argentina.

Arte hispano

Island of Many Gods I (2006), by Dominican–American artist Scherezade Garcia

Paradise Redefined exhibition. Acrylic, charcoal, collage on blue silk fabric. 30 x 20 inches. (Collection of Freddy Rodriguez, NY)

Enfoque cultural

¿Qué te parece?

- Like all Romance languages, including French and Italian, Spanish is derived from Latin. It also has Greek, Arabic, and German influences. More recently, Spanish has adopted from English many words related to technology and pop culture.
- Spanish is a highly phonetic language, which means that there is a direct relationship between spelling and sound. In most cases, you can look at a written word in Spanish and know how to pronounce it.
- Some differences exist between the Spanish in Latin America and the Spanish in Spain, but these differences do not interfere with communication.
- Since 1904, the Nobel Prize in Literature has been awarded 11 times to a writer from Latin America or Spain.
- It is projected that by 2050, the United States will become the largest Spanish-speaking country in the world.

Ángeles Mastretta, escritora mexicana

Margarita Salas, científica española

Jennifer López, artista norteamericana

Adrián Beltré, beisbolista dominicano

To learn more about the Spanish-speaking world, go online to view the *Club cultura* videos.

Hablantes nativos de español (en millones)		
México 114,5	**Chile** 18	**El Salvador** 6,1
Colombia 48,6	**Ecuador** 14,7	**Nicaragua** 5,7
España 42,8	**Cuba** 11,4	**Costa Rica** 4,1
Argentina 42	**Guatemala** 10,2	**Paraguay** 4
Estados Unidos 40,5	**República Dominicana** 9,3	**Uruguay** 3,3
Venezuela 30,3	**Honduras** 8,6	**Puerto Rico** 3,3
Perú 26,7	**Bolivia** 6,5	**Panamá** 3

e **¿Cuánto sabes?** Indicate whether each statement is true (**Cierto**) or false (**Falso**).

1. ______ Más de (*More than*) 350 millones de personas en el mundo hablan español.
2. ______ El español deriva del latín.
3. ______ La literatura en español es muy importante.
4. ______ Jennifer López es una artista mexicana.
5. ______ En Estados Unidos más (*more*) personas hablan español que (*than*) en México.

VOCABULARIO EN CONTEXTO

Making introductions and talking about the classroom

Las presentaciones

ANTONIO: **Hola, me llamo** Antonio Martínez. **Y tú, ¿cómo te llamas?**
RAFAEL: Yo me llamo Rafael Sánchez.
ANTONIO: **Mucho gusto.**
RAFAEL: **Igualmente.**

LAURA: María, **este** es **mi amigo** José.
MARÍA: Mucho gusto.
JOSÉ: **Encantado.**

PROFESOR: **¿Cómo se llama usted?**
ISABEL: Me llamo Isabel Contreras.
PROFESOR: Mucho gusto.

- Spanish has more than one word meaning *you.* Use **tú** when talking to someone on a first-name basis (a child, close friend, or relative).
- Use **usted** when talking to someone you address in a respectful or formal manner; for example, **doctor/a; profesor/a; señor/a.** Also use **usted** to address people you do not know well.
- People of college age or younger normally use **tú** when speaking to each other.
- **Mucho gusto** is used by both men and women when they are meeting someone for the first time. A man may also say **encantado,** and a woman, **encantada.**
- You may respond to **mucho gusto** with either **encantado/a** or **igualmente.**

PRÁCTICA

P-1 Presentaciones.

PREPARACIÓN. With a partner, complete the following conversation with the appropriate expressions from the list.

encantado	igualmente	mi amigo Pedro	mucho gusto

ALICIA: Me llamo Alicia. Y tú, ¿cómo te llamas?
ISABEL: Isabel Pérez. ______________.
ALICIA: ______________. Isabel, este es ______________.
ISABEL: Mucho gusto.
PEDRO: ______________.

INTERCAMBIOS. Move around the classroom, introducing yourself to several classmates and introducing classmates to each other.

Lengua

When you talk to people, you address them with various degrees of formality, depending on how well you know the person and the context of the conversation. For example, when you talk to a professor, you probably use more formal language than when you talk to classmates or friends. In Spanish, one way to mark this difference is by using **tú** (informal) and **usted** (formal).

P-2 Escucha y confirma.

PREPARACIÓN. Before you listen to four brief conversations in which people greet each other, indicate the pronoun you think you would use in each case. Compare your answers with those of a classmate and explain why you chose **tú** or **usted.**

WHEN TALKING TO YOUR . . .	TÚ	USTED
1. brother or sister	_____	_____
2. doctor	_____	_____
3. coach	_____	_____
4. parent	_____	_____

ESCUCHA. As you listen to the four conversations, indicate whether the greetings are formal (with **usted**) or informal (with **tú**).

	FORMAL	INFORMAL
1.	_____	_____
2.	_____	_____
3.	_____	_____
4.	_____	_____

Los saludos y las despedidas

SEÑORA GÓMEZ: **Buenos días, señorita** Rivas.
SEÑORITA RIVAS: Buenos días. **¿Cómo está usted, señora** Gómez?
SEÑORA GÓMEZ: **Bien, gracias, ¿y usted?**
SEÑORITA RIVAS: **Muy** bien, gracias.

MARTA: ¡Hola, Inés! **¿Qué tal? ¿Cómo estás?**
INÉS: **Regular,** ¿y tú?
MARTA: **Bastante** bien, gracias. Bueno, **hasta mañana.**
INÉS: **Adiós.**

PABLO: **Buenas tardes, señora** Silva. ¿Cómo está usted?
SEÑORA SILVA: **Mal,** Pablo, mal.
PABLO: **Lo siento. ¡Que se mejore!**

Los saludos

- Use **buenos días** until lunchtime.
- Use **buenas tardes** from after lunch until nightfall. After nightfall, use **buenas noches** (*good evening, good night*).
- **¿Qué tal?** is less formal than **buenos días, buenas tardes,** etc.
- Use **está** with **usted** and **estás** with **tú.**

Las despedidas

- Use the following expressions to say goodbye:

adiós	*goodbye*
chao	*goodbye*
hasta luego	*see you later*
hasta mañana	*see you tomorrow*
hasta pronto	*see you soon*

- **Adiós** is generally used when you do not expect to see the other person for a while. It is also used as a greeting when people pass each other but do not have time to stop and talk.
- **Chao** (also spelled **chau**) is an informal way of saying goodbye and when passing on the street, similar to **adiós.** It is popular in South America.

Expresiones de cortesía

- Here are some courtesy expressions:

por favor	*please*
gracias	*thanks, thank you*
de nada	*you're welcome*
lo siento	*I'm sorry (to hear that)*
con permiso	*pardon me, excuse me*
perdón	*pardon me, excuse me*

- **Con permiso** and **perdón** may be used before the fact, as when asking a person to allow you to go by or when trying to get someone's attention. Only **perdón** is used after the fact, as when you have stepped on someone's foot or have interrupted a conversation.

PRÁCTICA

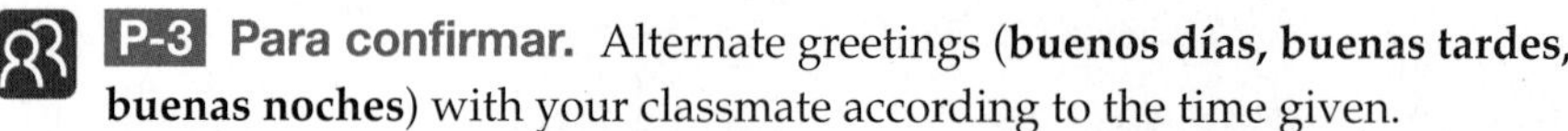

P-3 Para confirmar. Alternate greetings (**buenos días, buenas tardes, buenas noches**) with your classmate according to the time given.

1. 9:00 a.m.
2. 11:00 p.m.
3. 4:00 p.m.
4. 8:00 a.m.
5. 1:00 p.m.
6. 10:00 p.m.

P-4 Despedidas. With a classmate, create short exchanges for the following situations.

MODELO You run into a good friend on campus.
Adiós./Chao.

1. You'll see your friend tomorrow.
2. You arrange to meet your classmate at the library in ten minutes.
3. Your roommate is leaving for a semester abroad.

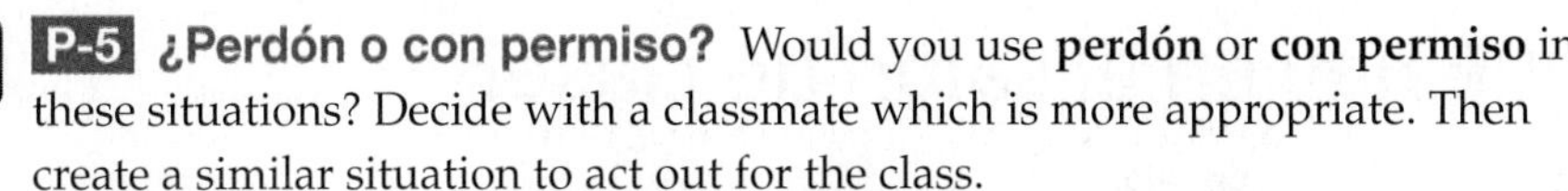

P-5 ¿Perdón o con permiso? Would you use **perdón** or **con permiso** in these situations? Decide with a classmate which is more appropriate. Then create a similar situation to act out for the class.

1.

2.

3.

4.

5.

P-6 Despedidas y expresiones de cortesía. With a classmate, decide which expression is best for each situation. Then create another situation and act it out.

Adiós.	Lo siento.
De nada.	Por favor.
Gracias.	¡Que te mejores!
Hasta luego.	

1. Someone thanks you.
2. You say goodbye to a friend you will see later this evening.
3. You ask if you can borrow a classmate's notes.
4. Your friend tells you that he/she is sick.
5. You receive a present from your cousin.
6. …

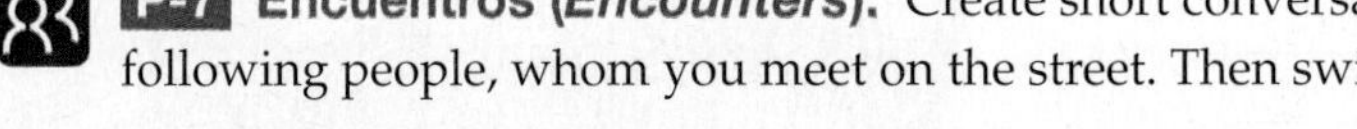

P-7 Encuentros (*Encounters*). Create short conversations with the following people, whom you meet on the street. Then switch roles.

1. tu (*your*) amigo Miguel
2. tu profesor/a
3. tu amiga Isabel
4. tu doctor/a

Cultura

Saludos y despedidas

When saying *hello* or *goodbye* and when being introduced, Spanish-speaking men and women almost always shake hands, embrace, or kiss each other on the cheek. Girls and women most often kiss each other on the cheek, as do men and women who are close friends or acquaintances. In Spain they kiss on both cheeks. Men who are close friends normally embrace and pat each other on the back, and in Argentina, it is common for them to kiss each other on the cheek.

Comparaciones What are common greetings in your culture? Do you greet your family members and your friends in the same way?

¿Qué hay en el salón de clase?

una pantalla
un reloj
una ventana
Hola, ¿cómo estás?
un profesor
una pizarra
una puerta
un marcador / un rotulador
un borrador
un libro
una computadora
una mesa
una tableta
un cesto
una silla
un bolígrafo
una calculadora
un cuaderno
un lápiz
una computadora portátil
una estudiante
un estudiante
un escritorio
una mochila

PRÁCTICA

P-8 Para confirmar. Identify the items on this table and then tell your partner which of the items you have.

MODELO E1: *Hay una mochila.*
E2: *Hay…*

a. ____________________
b. ____________________
c. ____________________
d. ____________________
e. ____________________
f. ____________________
g. ____________________
h. ____________________

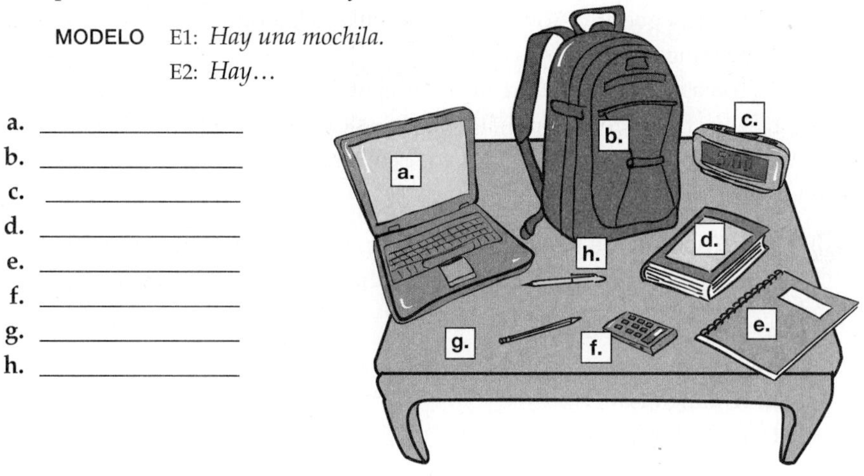

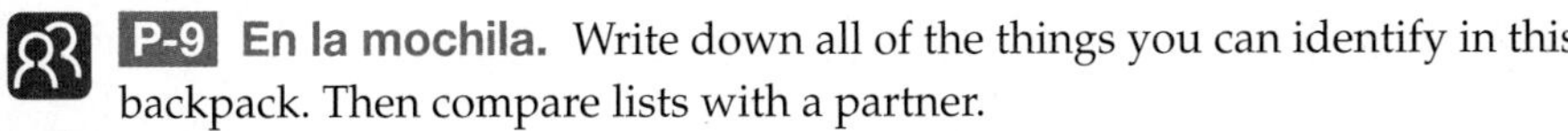

P-9 En la mochila. Write down all of the things you can identify in this backpack. Then compare lists with a partner.

P-10 ¿Qué hay en el salón de clase? Take turns using the clues below to guess the words in Spanish. Then look around the room and ask each other questions about the objects you see.

1. It is essential for your math problems.
2. It has ink and you use it to write.
3. Waste material goes here.
4. You need it to do homework online.
5. You sit on it.
6. You write your notes in it.
7. You pack it every morning to carry your books to campus.
8. It displays the time.

Los meses del año y los días de la semana

Los meses del año

enero	*January*	**mayo**	*May*	**septiembre**	*September*
febrero	*February*	**junio**	*June*	**octubre**	*October*
marzo	*March*	**julio**	*July*	**noviembre**	*November*
abril	*April*	**agosto**	*August*	**diciembre**	*December*

Los días de la semana

lunes	*Monday*	**viernes**	*Friday*
martes	*Tuesday*	**sábado**	*Saturday*
miércoles	*Wednesday*	**domingo**	*Sunday*
jueves	*Thursday*		

- Days of the week and months of the year are not generally capitalized in Spanish, except sometimes in advertisements and invitations.
- To ask what day it is, use **¿Qué día es hoy?** Answer with **Hoy es...**
- To ask about today's date, use **¿Qué fecha es?** or **¿Cuál es la fecha?** Respond with **Hoy es el 14 de octubre.**
- To give a date for an event, say **La fiesta es el 5 de mayo.**
- Express *on + a day of the week* as follows:

el lunes	*on Monday*	**el domingo**	*on Sunday*
los lunes	*on Mondays*	**los domingos**	*on Sundays*

- Cardinal numbers are used with dates (e.g., **el dos, el tres**), except for the first day of the month, which is **el primero.** In Spain, the first day is also referred to as **el uno.**

  Hoy es **el primero** de julio.

Cultura

El calendario hispano In Spanish-speaking countries, the first day of the week on a calendar is Monday. Sunday appears at the end of the week. Some calendars include the saint's name for each day.

Comparaciones
What dates are typically highlighted on your calendar?

Lengua

Here are the numbers you need when giving a date:

1 uno/primero	17 diecisiete
2 dos	18 dieciocho
3 tres	19 diecinueve
4 cuatro	20 veinte
5 cinco	21 veintiuno
6 seis	22 veintidós
7 siete	23 veintitrés
8 ocho	24 veinticuatro
9 nueve	25 veinticinco
10 diez	26 veintiséis
11 once	27 veintisiete
12 doce	28 veintiocho
13 trece	29 veintinueve
14 catorce	30 treinta
15 quince	31 treinta y uno
16 dieciséis	

PRÁCTICA

P-11 Para confirmar. Using the calendar, take turns asking and telling the days of the week that correspond to the following dates. Then tell your partner your favorite day of the week (**Mi día favorito es...**).

9:13 PM

ENERO

lunes	martes	miércoles	jueves	viernes	sábado	domingo
1	2	3	4	5	6	7
8	9	10	11	12	13	14
15	16	17	18	19	20	21
22	23	24	25	26	27	28
29	30	31				

MODELO E1: *¿Qué día de la semana es el 30?*
E2: *El día 30 es martes.*

1. el 2
2. el 5
3. el 22
4. el 18
5. el 10
6. el 13
7. el 28
8. el…

P-12 Preguntas. Take turns asking and answering these questions.

1. ¿Qué día es hoy?
2. Hoy es… ¿Qué día es mañana?
3. Hoy es el… de… ¿Qué fecha es mañana?
4. ¿Hay clase de español los domingos? ¿Y los sábados?
5. ¿Qué días hay clase de español?

Lengua

When dates are written using only numerals, the day normally precedes the month: *11/8* 5 **el 11 de agosto**

P-13 Fechas importantes. Take turns asking your partner the dates on which these events take place.

MODELO la reunión de estudiantes (10/9)
E1: *¿Cuándo es la reunión de estudiantes?*
E2: *(Es) el 10 de septiembre.*

1. el concierto de Manu Chao (12/11)
2. el aniversario de Carlos y María (14/4)
3. el banquete (1/3)
4. la graduación (22/5)
5. la fiesta de bienvenida (24/8)

Lengua

You may have noticed that the word **tú** (meaning *you*) has a written accent mark, and that the word **tu** (meaning *your*) does not. In this book, boxes similar to this one will help you focus on when to use accent marks. You will find all the rules for accentuation in Appendix 1.

P-14 El cumpleaños (*birthday*). Find out when your classmates' birthdays are. Write down their names and birthdays and share with the class.

MODELO E1: *¿Cuándo es tu cumpleaños?*
E2: *(Es) el 3 de mayo.*

El tiempo

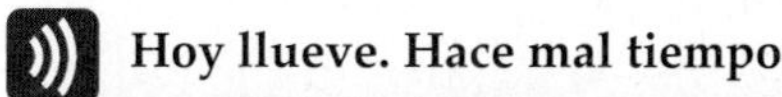

Hoy hace sol. Hace buen tiempo.

Hoy llueve. Hace mal tiempo.

- Use **¿Qué tiempo hace?** to inquire about the weather. To answer, you may use the following expressions that start with **hace:**

Hace buen tiempo.	*The weather is good.*
Hace mal tiempo.	*The weather is bad.*

- To express that it is sunny or that it is raining, use the following:

Hace sol.	*It is sunny.*
Llueve. / Está lloviendo.	*It is raining.*

- The following are the words used for seasons:

Las estaciones

la primavera

el verano

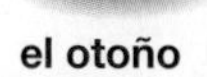

el otoño

el invierno

PRÁCTICA

P-15 ¿Qué tiempo hace hoy? Take turns with your partner asking about the weather in these cities. Then ask about the weather in your city.

MODELO Miami

E1: *¿Qué tiempo hace en Miami?*

E2: *En Miami hace buen tiempo. Hace sol.*

1. Madrid
2. Quito
3. Lima
4. Ciudad de México
5. Bogotá
6. Nueva York

P-16 El hemisferio norte y el hemisferio sur. Look up the weather of one city in the Northern Hemisphere and one in the Southern Hemisphere. Compare the weather in both cities and share your findings with the class.

Cultura

Las estaciones y los hemisferios Seasons in the Northern and Southern Hemispheres are inverted. That is, when it is winter in the United States, it is summer in Argentina. This applies to the school year as well. In Argentina for example, the academic year starts in March and ends in December, right before Christmas. The Christmas holidays are often spent on the beach or enjoying outdoor activities.

Conexiones Why do you think the academic year is arranged in that way in the Southern Hemisphere? Would it be a good idea to change this arrangement?

Expresiones útiles en la clase

La tarea, por favor.

Ve a la pizarra.

Contesta.

Repite.

Levanta la mano.

Escribe.

Lee.

- When asking two or more people to do something, the verb forms are **ve → vayan, contesta → contesten, repite → repitan.**
- Although you may not use all of these expressions, it is useful to recognize them and to know how to respond. Other expressions that you may hear or say in the classroom include the following:

Expressions in plural

Abran el libro.	*Open the book.*
Cierren el libro.	*Close the book.*
¿Comprenden?	*Do you understand?*
Contesten, por favor.	*Please answer.*
Hablen (sobre...)	*Talk (about . . .)*
¿Tienen preguntas?	*Do you have any questions?*
Túrnense.	*Take turns.*
Vayan a la pizarra.	*Go to the board.*

Expressions with *tú*

Abre el libro.	*Open the book.*
Cierra el libro.	*Close the book.*
¿Comprendes?	*Do you understand?*
Contesta, por favor.	*Please answer.*
Dile a tu compañero/a...	*Tell your partner . . .*
¿Tienes preguntas?	*Do you have any questions?*
Ve a la pizarra.	*Go to the board.*

Other useful expressions

¿Cómo se dice... en español?	*How do you say . . . in Spanish?*
¿En qué página?	*On what page?*
Más alto, por favor.	*Louder, please.*
Más despacio, por favor.	*More slowly, please.*
No comprendo.	*I don't understand.*
No sé.	*I don't know.*
Otra vez.	*Again.*
Presente.	*Here.*

PRÁCTICA

P-17 Las expresiones útiles. Match the following expressions with their pictures and compare your answers with those of a classmate. Then take turns telling your partner three things he/she needs to do, and your partner will act them out.

Abre el libro.	Pregúntale a tu compañero.	Siéntate.
Lee.	Repite.	Ve a la pizarra.

1. 7. 8.

9. 10. 11.

 **P-18 Órdenes.** Spend a few minutes reviewing the expressions with **tú.** Then, without reading the expression, tell one of your classmates to do something. If he or she does the task well, he/she gets to give an order to someone else. Later, do the same with the expressions in plural.

El alfabeto

a	a	**j**	jota	**r**	ere
b	be	**k**	ka	**s**	ese
c	ce	**l**	ele	**t**	te
d	de	**m**	eme	**u**	u
e	e	**n**	ene	**v**	uve
f	efe	**ñ**	eñe	**w**	uve doble
g	ge	**o**	o	**x**	equis
h	hache	**p**	pe	**y**	ye, i griega
i	i	**q**	cu	**z**	zeta

- The present-day Spanish alphabet consists of 27 letters.
- The Spanish alphabet includes **ñ,** a letter that does not exist in English. Its sound is similar to the pronunciation of *ni* and *ny* in the English words *onion* and *canyon.*
- The letter combination **rr** (often called the *rolled r*) appears between vowels, in words like **perro** (*dog*) or **carro** (*car*). The letter **r** at the beginning of a word has the same pronunciation.
- The letters **k** and **w** appear mainly in words of foreign origin, but often they are replaced by **qu-** (**quilo**), or by **gü-** (**güisqui**).

En otras palabras

Like English speakers, Spanish speakers have different accents that reflect their region or country of origin. For example, the letter **c** before vowels **e** and **i** and the letter **z** are pronounced like **s** except in certain regions of Spain, where they are similar to the English *th.*

PRÁCTICA

 **P-19 Para confirmar.** Take turns spelling the street in the photo. Then spell the name of the street where you live in Spanish. Check if your partner wrote it correctly.

P-20 Los nombres. You are visiting the admissions office of a Spanish university. Spell your first and last name for the clerk. Take turns.

MODELO E1: *¿Cómo se llama usted?*
E2: *Me llamo Jill Robinson.*
E1: *¿Cómo se escribe Jill Robinson?*
E2: *Jota, i, doble ele, ere, o, be, i, ene, ese, o, ene.*

P-21 Para confirmar. Ask three classmates to spell their first and last names in Spanish. Then write your classmates' names on the board and ask them to confirm if the names are spelled correctly.

FUNCTIONES Y FORMAS

1 Identifying and describing people

CARLOS: **¿Quién es ese chico?**
SANDRA: **Es** Julio.
CARLOS: **¿Cómo es** Julio?
SANDRA: **Es** romántico y sentimental.

LUIS: ¿Quién es **esa chica?**
QUIQUE: Es Carmen.
LUIS: ¿Cómo es Carmen?
QUIQUE: Es activa y muy seria.

Piénsalo. Indicate whether each statement identifies (I) or describes (D) a person.

1. Es Julio. _____
2. Es romántico. _____
3. Es Carmen. _____
4. No es sentimental. _____

Singular forms of *ser*

- The verb **ser** is used to identify and describe.

Esa chica **es** Carmen.	*That girl is Carmen.*
Es activa y muy seria.	*She is active and very serious.*
Julio **es** su amigo.	*Julio is her friend.*
Es romántico.	*He is romantic.*

- Here are the forms of **ser** you will use in this chapter.

SER (*to be*)		
yo	**soy**	*I am*
tú	**eres**	*you are (informal)*
Ud.	**es**	*you are (formal)*
él, ella	**es**	*he, she is*

- To make a sentence negative, place **no** before the appropriate form of **ser.** When responding negatively to a question, say **no** twice.

Ella es inteligente.	Ella **no** es inteligente.
¿Es rebelde?	**No, no** es rebelde.

Cognates

- Cognates (**Cognados**) are words from two languages that have the same origin and are similar in form and meaning. Since English and Spanish have many cognates, you will discover that you already recognize many Spanish words. Here are some cognates that you may use to describe people.
- The following cognates use the same form to describe a man or a woman.

arrogante	**importante**	**optimista**	**popular**
eficiente	**independiente**	**paciente**	**responsable**
elegante	**inteligente**	**perfeccionista**	**sentimental**
idealista	**interesante**	**pesimista**	**tradicional**

- The following cognates have two forms. Use the **-o** form to describe a male, and the **-a** form to describe a female.

activo/a	**creativo/a**	**introvertido/a**	**romántico/a**
ambicioso/a	**dinámico/a**	**moderno/a**	**serio/a**
atlético/a	**extrovertido/a**	**nervioso/a**	**sincero/a**
atractivo/a	**generoso/a**	**pasivo/a**	**tímido/a**
cómico/a	**impulsivo/a**	**religioso/a**	**tranquilo/a**

- Some words appear to be cognates but do not have the same meaning in both languages. These are called false cognates. Some examples are **lectura** (*reading*), **éxito** (*success*), **sensible** (*sensitive*). You will find other examples in future chapters.

e **¿Comprendes?** Describe the following people using the appropriate form of **ser.**

1. Yo _____ inteligente.
2. Usted _____ interesante.
3. Él _____ cómico.
4. Isabel _____ atlética.
5. Tú _____ paciente.
6. Carlos _____ sincero.

PRÁCTICA

P-22 **¿Cómo eres?** Ask your partner about his/her personality. Use the cognates from the list or others that you know.

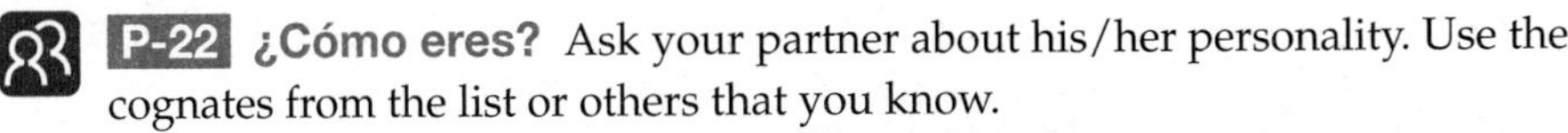

generoso/a	inteligente	optimista	tímido/a
independiente	nervioso/a	responsable	reservado/a

MODELO E1: *¿Eres pesimista?*
E2: *No, no soy pesimista.*
E1: *¿Cómo eres?*
E2: *Soy activo, optimista y creativo.*

P-23 **Descripciones.** Take turns asking each other about your roommate (**compañero/a de cuarto** o **de casa**) or best friend (**mejor amigo/a**). Describe them by using cognates.

MODELO E1: *¿Cómo es tu...?*
E2: *Mi compañero/a de cuarto es... Mi mejor amigo/a es...*

P-24 **¿Cómo es?** Think of the name of someone important to you (your boyfriend or girlfriend, a friend) and four words that describe this person.

MODELO E1: *¿Quién es una persona importante para ti?*
E2: *Es mi… Se llama…*
E1: *¿Cómo es…?*
E2: *Es…, … y…*

2 Locating people and things

La profesora y los estudiantes **están en** la clase. La profesora **está delante de** la pizarra. Los estudiantes **están enfrente de** la profesora. Mercedes **está entre** Juan y María, y Carlos, Ana y Diego **están detrás de** ellos (*them*). ¿Dónde **está** el cuaderno? **Está debajo de** la mesa.

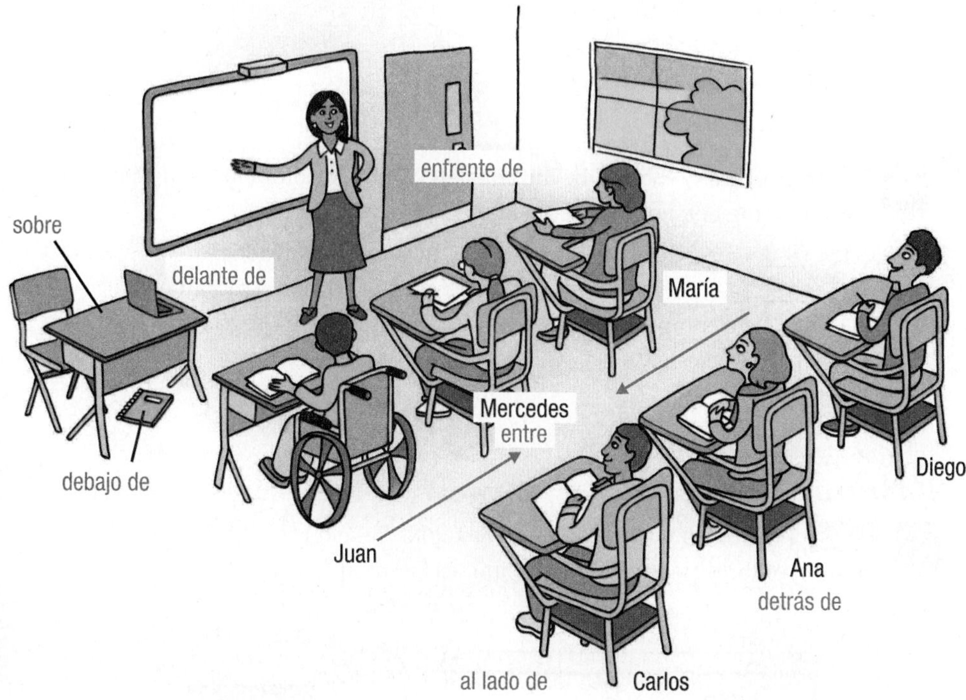

Piénsalo. Complete each sentence with **está** or **están** so that it matches the subject.

1. La computadora _______ sobre la mesa.
2. Los estudiantes _______ en la clase.
3. La profesora _______ enfrente de los estudiantes.
4. Mercedes _______ delante de Ana.
5. ¿Dónde _______ Carlos y Diego?

Estar | location

- To express location, the verb **estar** is used:

La computadora **está** sobre la mesa.	*The computer is on the table.*
María **está** en la clase.	*María is in the classroom.*

- To ask about the location of a person or an object, use **dónde** + **está.**

¿**Dónde está** la profesora?	*Where is the professor?*
Está en la clase.	*She is in class.*
¿**Dónde está** la computadora?	*Where is the computer?*
Está sobre la mesa.	*It is on the table.*

- Here are some expressions that describe location:

al lado de	*next to*
debajo de	*under*
delante de	*in front of*
detrás de	*behind*
encima de	*on, on top of*
enfrente de	*in front of, facing*
entre	*between*
sobre	*on, on top of*

¿Comprendes? Select the appropriate option to complete each sentence based on the position of people in the scene on page 19.

1. _____ La profesora está...
2. _____ Juan está...
3. _____ La computadora está...
4. _____ Ana está...

a. al lado de Mercedes.
b. enfrente de los estudiantes.
c. entre Carlos y Diego.
d. sobre la mesa.

PRÁCTICA

P-25 Personas y lugares. **PREPARACIÓN.** Take turns telling your partner the location of three people or objects in the classroom scene.

ESCUCHA. Listen to the statements about the location of people and objects in the classroom scene. Indicate whether each statement is true (**Cierto**) or false (**Falso**). Compare your answers with those of a classmate.

1. ______
2. ______
3. ______
4. ______
5. ______
6. ______

 **P-26 En la clase.** Look at the student name tags in Professor Gallegos' class. Take turns asking your partner about the location of the people.

MODELO E1: *¿Dónde está Roberto?*
E2: *Está delante de Pedro.*

 **P-27 ¿Dónde está?** Take turns asking where several items in your classroom are. Answer by giving their position in relation to a person or another object.

MODELO E1: *¿Dónde está la mochila?*
E2: *Está debajo de la silla.*

 **P-28 ¿Quién es?** Based on what your partner says about the location of another student in your class, guess who the student is.

MODELO E1: *Está al lado de John. ¿Quién es?*
E2: *Es Amanda.*

3 Using numbers

Los números 0 a 99

0 **cero**	8 **ocho**	16 **dieciséis**	30 **treinta**
1 **uno**	9 **nueve**	17 **diecisiete**	31 **treinta y uno**
2 **dos**	10 **diez**	18 **dieciocho**	40 **cuarenta**
3 **tres**	11 **once**	19 **diecinueve**	50 **cincuenta**
4 **cuatro**	12 **doce**	20 **veinte**	60 **sesenta**
5 **cinco**	13 **trece**	21 **veintiuno**	70 **setenta**
6 **seis**	14 **catorce**	22 **veintidós**	80 **ochenta**
7 **siete**	15 **quince**	23 **veintitrés**	90 **noventa**

Piénsalo. Write the next number word in each sequence.

1. veintiuno, veintidós, ____________
2. treinta y cinco, treinta y seis, ____________
3. cuatro/cuarenta, cinco/cincuenta, seis/____________

Numbers 0 to 99

- Numbers from sixteen through twenty-nine are usually written as one word. Note the spelling changes and the written accent on some forms.

  18: **dieciocho** 22: **veintidós**

- Beginning with thirty-one, numbers are written as three words.

  31: **treinta y uno** 45: **cuarenta y cinco**

- The number *one* has three forms in Spanish: **uno, un,** and **una.** Use **uno** when counting: **uno, dos, tres...** Use **un** or **una** before nouns.

  un borrador
  una mochila
  veintiún libros
  veintiuna mochilas

- Use **hay** for both *there is* and *there are.*

  Hay un libro sobre la mesa. *There is one book on the table.*
  Hay dos libros sobre la mesa. *There are two books on the table.*

e **¿Comprendes?** Indicate the numerals for the following words.

1. diez _____
2. treinta _____
3. noventa y cuatro _____
4. sesenta y seis _____
5. veinticinco _____

PRÁCTICA

P-29 **¿Qué número es?** Your instructor will read a number from each group. Select the number you hear. Then compare your responses with those of your partner.

a.	8	4	3	5
b.	12	9	16	6
c.	37	59	41	26
d.	54	38	76	95
e.	83	62	72	49
f.	47	14	91	56

P-30 **Para la oficina.** You and your partner have to check a shipment of equipment and supplies delivered to the Spanish department. Take turns asking your partner how many of each there are. Then ask each other about the items without a number and respond with your own amount.

MODELO 4 relojes
E1: *¿Cuántos relojes hay?*
E2: *Hay cuatro relojes.*

- 10 tabletas
- 1 computadora
- 20 cestos
- 95 bolígrafos
- 70 rotuladores
- 34 libros
- ...diccionarios
- ...cuadernos

P-31 **Problemas.** Take turns solving the following arithmetic problems. Use **y** (+), **menos** (–), and **son** (=). Then create a new arithmetic problem and ask your partner to solve it.

MODELO 12 – 5 =
Doce menos cinco son siete.

a. 11 1 4 = _____
b. 8 1 2 = _____
c. 13 1 3 = _____
d. 20 2 6 = _____
e. 39 1 50 = _____
f. 80 2 1 = _____
g. 50 2 25 = _____
h. 26 1 40 = _____

Cultura

Direcciones y números de teléfono In Spanish-speaking countries, the name of the street precedes the house or building number. Sometimes a comma is placed before the number.

Calle (*Street*) Bolívar, 132   **Avenida (*Avenue*) de Gracia, 18**

Telephone numbers are generally not stated as individual numbers, but in groups of two, depending on how the numbers are written or on the number of digits, which varies from country to country.

12–24–67: **doce, veinticuatro, sesenta y siete**
2–43–89–07: **dos, cuarenta y tres, ochenta y nueve, cero siete**

Comparaciones How do you say or write a street address in your language? How do you say a phone number?

P-32 **Los números de teléfono y las direcciones (*addresses*).** Take turns asking each other the phone numbers and addresses of the people listed in the directory. Then ask your partner for his/her address and phone number (real or made up for the activity).

Cárdenas Alfaro, Joaquín	General Páez 40	423–4837
Cárdenas Villanueva, Sara	Avenida Bolívar 7	956–1709
Castelar Torres, Adelaida	Paseo del Prado 89	218–3642
Castellanos Rey, Carlos	Colón 62	654–6416
Castelli Rivero, Victoria	Chamberí 3	615–7359
Castillo Montoya, Rafael	Santa Cruz 73	956–3382

MODELO Castellanos Rey, Carlos
E1: *¿Cuál es la dirección de Carlos Castellanos Rey?*
E2: *Calle Colón, número 62.*
E1: *¿Cuál es su* (his) *número de teléfono?*
E2: *(Es el) 6–54–64–16.*

4 Expressing time in Spanish

¿Qué hora es?

Es la una de la tarde.

Son las once.

Son las siete y diez.

Son las ocho y media.

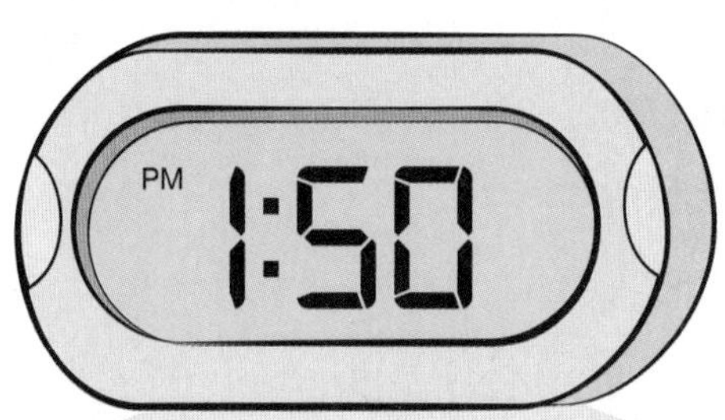

Son las dos menos diez de la tarde. / Es la una y cincuenta de la tarde.

Son las diez menos diecinueve de la mañana. / Son las nueve y cuarenta y uno de la mañana.

Son las tres y veintiséis de la tarde.

Piénsalo. Select the numerical equivalent for each time.

1. _____ las dos y cinco	**a.** 1:30
2. _____ las cinco y cuarto	**b.** 3:50
3. _____ la una y media	**c.** 5:15
4. _____ las cuatro menos diez	**d.** 2:05

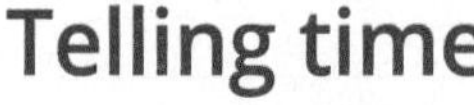

Telling time

- Use **¿Qué hora es?** to inquire about the time. To tell time, use **Es la…** and **Son las…** with the other hours.

  Es la una. — *It is one o'clock.*

  Son las cuatro. — *It is four o'clock.*

- To express the quarter hour, use **y cuarto** or **y quince.** To express the half hour, use **y media** or **y treinta.**

  Es la una **y media.**
  Es la una **y treinta.** } *It is one-thirty.*

  Son las dos **y cuarto.**
  Son las dos **y quince.** } *It is two-fifteen.*

- To express time after the half hour, subtract minutes from the next hour, using **menos.** It is more common, especially in parts of Latin America, to tell time digitally by using **hora + y + minutos.**

Son las cinco **menos** veinticinco.	*It is twenty-five to five.*
Son las cuatro **y** treinta y cinco.	*It is four thirty-five.*

- Add **en punto** for the exact time and **más o menos** for approximate time.

Es la una **en punto.**	*It is one o'clock on the dot / sharp.*
Son las cinco menos cuarto, **más o menos.**	*It is about a quarter to five.*

- To indicate *a.m.* or *p.m.* when expressing time orally, use the following:

de la mañana	(from midnight to noon)
de la tarde	(from noon to nightfall)
de la noche	(from nightfall to midnight)

 **¿Comprendes?** Give the time in numerals.

1. Son las tres y cinco. ______
2. Son las seis y cuarenta y cinco. ______
3. Es la una y cuarto. ______
4. Son las once en punto. ______
5. Son las cinco menos veinte. ______

PRÁCTICA

 **P-33 ¿Qué hora es en...?** Take turns telling your partner what time it is in the following cities. Follow the model. Then draw another time clock and ask your partner to give you the time.

MODELO E1: *¿Qué hora es en Lima, Perú?*
E2: *Son las dos de la tarde.*

Lima, Perú

Cuernavaca, México

San Juan, Puerto Rico

Buenos Aires, Argentina

Madrid, España

Cultura

Decir la hora People in different Spanish-speaking countries have different ways of telling time. Even though digital clocks, watches, and cell phones are common everywhere, in Spain people tend to tell time the traditional way, so at 5:40 most Spaniards say **son las seis menos veinte.** In contrast, in many parts of Latin America, people now usually say **son las cinco (y) cuarenta** or **son/faltan veinte para las seis.**

Comparaciones What is the convention in your culture for telling time? Do you tell time digitally, even if you are looking at a traditional clock? Do people of different ages (e.g., young children, older people) tell time the same way?

Lengua

To ask the time at which an event takes place or something happens, use **¿A qué hora es...?** To answer, use **Es a la(s)...** or simply **A la(s)...**

¿A qué hora es la clase de español?	*At what time is Spanish class?*
(Es) a las nueve y media.	*(It is) at 9:30.*

P-34 El horario de María. Take turns asking and answering questions about María's schedule. Then write down your own Monday schedule, omitting the time each class meets. Exchange schedules with your partner, and find out what time each of his/her classes starts.

MODELO E1: *¿A qué hora es la clase de español?*
E2: *Es a las nueve.*

LUNES	
9:00	la clase de español
10:00	la clase de matemáticas
11:00	la clase de psicología
12:00	el laboratorio
1:00	el almuerzo
2:30	la clase de física
5:00	la clase de tenis

P-35 ¿Qué hora es? ¿Dónde está? Take turns asking what time it is and where the person is in each scene.

MODELO E1: *¿Qué hora es?*
E2: *Son las dos.*
E1: *¿Dónde está Marcos?*
E2: *Está en la clase de física.*

1. 

2. 

3. 

4. 

En este capítulo...

Vocabulario

Las presentaciones	Introductions
¿Cómo se llama usted?	*What's your name?* (formal)
¿Cómo te llamas?	*What's your name?* (informal)
Encantado/a.	*Pleased/Nice to meet you.*
Este/a es…	*This is . . .*
Igualmente.	*Likewise.*
Me llamo…	*My name is . . .*
Mucho gusto.	*Pleased/Nice to meet you.*

Los saludos	Greetings
bastante	*rather*
bien	*well*
buenas noches	*good evening; good night*
buenas tardes	*good afternoon*
buenos días	*good morning*
¿Cómo está (usted)?	*How are you?* (formal)
¿Cómo estás?	*How are you?* (informal)
hola	*hi, hello*
mal	*bad*
muy	*very*
regular	*so-so, not so great*
¿Qué tal?	*What's up? / What's new?* (informal)

Las despedidas	Leave-taking
adiós	*goodbye*
chao/chau	*goodbye*
hasta luego	*see you later*
hasta mañana	*see you tomorrow*
hasta pronto	*see you soon*

En el salón de clase	In the classroom
el bolígrafo	*ballpoint pen*
el borrador	*eraser*
la calculadora	*calculator*
el cesto	*wastebasket*
la computadora	*computer*
la computadora portátil	*laptop*
el cuaderno	*notebook*
el escritorio	*desk*
el lápiz	*pencil*
el libro	*book*
el marcador / el rotulador	*marker*
la mesa (de la computadora)	*(computer) table*
la mochila	*backpack*
la pantalla	*screen*
la pizarra	*board*
la puerta	*door*
el reloj	*clock*
la silla	*chair*
la tableta	*tablet*
la ventana	*window*

Las personas	People
el/la amigo/a	*friend*
el/la chico/a	*boy/girl*
el/la doctor/a	*doctor*
él	*he*
ella	*she*
el/la estudiante	*student*
el/la profesor/a	*professor, teacher*
el señor (Sr.)	*Mr.*
la señora (Sra.)	*Ms., Mrs.*
la señorita (Srta.)	*Ms., Miss*
tú	*you* (informal)
usted	*you* (formal)
yo	*I*

Verbos	Verbs
eres	*you are* (informal)
es	*you are* (formal), *he/she is*
está	*he/she is, you are* (formal)
estás	*you are* (informal)
hay	*there is, there are*
soy	*I am*

Los meses del año	Months of the year
enero	*January*
febrero	February
marzo	*March*
abril	*April*
mayo	*May*
junio	*June*
julio	*July*
agosto	*August*
septiembre	*September*
octubre	*October*
noviembre	*November*
diciembre	*December*

Los días de la semana	Days of the week
lunes	*Monday*
martes	*Tuesday*
miércoles	*Wednesday*
jueves	*Thursday*
viernes	*Friday*
sábado	*Saturday*
domingo	*Sunday*
Hoy es…	*Today is…*
¿Qué día es hoy?	*What day is it?*
¿Qué fecha es? / ¿Cuál es la fecha?	*What is the date?*

El tiempo	Weather
Hace buen/mal tiempo.	*The weather is good/bad.*
Hace sol.	*It is sunny.*
Llueve. / Está lloviendo.	*It is raining.*
¿Qué tiempo hace?	*What's the weather like?*

Las estaciones	Seasons
el invierno	*winter*
el otoño	*fall*
la primavera	*spring*
el verano	*summer*

Palabras y expresiones útiles	Useful words and expressions
a	*at, to*
¿Cómo es?	*What is he/she/it like?*
¿Dónde está…?	*Where is . . .?*
el/la	*the*
ese/a	*that* (adjective)
hoy	*today*
mañana	*tomorrow*
mi(s)	*my*
¡Que se mejore!	*Feel better!*
¿Quién es…?	*Who is . . .?*
tu(s)	*your*
un/una	*a, an*
¿Y tú?	*And you?* (informal)
¿Y usted?	*And you?* (formal)

See page 8 for courtesy expressions.
See page 14 for useful classroom expressions.
See page 16 for the alphabet.
See page 18 for cognates.
See page 20 for expressions of location.
See page 21 for numbers.
See page 24 for telling time.

Capítulo 1
¿Qué estudias?

Edificio universitario en la Plaza de Anaya, Salamanca

Learning Outcomes

You will be able to:

- talk about studies, campus, and academic life
- describe daily routines and activities
- ask and answer questions
- express location and states of being
- specify gender and number
- talk about Spain in terms of products, practices, and perspectives
- share information about student life in Hispanic countries and identify cultural similarities

Enfoque cultural
España

La Universidad de Salamanca, fundada en 1218

La paella, un plato típico de Valencia

El Patio de los Leones en La Alhambra, Granada

Arte hispano

Un fresco del siglo XVI en la Universidad de Salamanca

Enfoque cultural

¿Qué te parece?

- España forma parte de la Unión Europea.
- Muchos turistas visitan España; es uno de los países (*countries*) más visitados del mundo.
- El fútbol es muy popular en España; el Barcelona y el Real Madrid son dos de los equipos (*teams*) más importantes.
- En España se habla castellano (español), catalán, gallego y euskera (vasco).
- España produce mucho vino; es el tercer (3er) productor de vino en el mundo.

El acueducto de Segovia es un monumento romano del siglo II. Tiene 760 metros de largo. Los romanos le dan el nombre de **Hispania** a la península y establecen sus leyes (*laws*) y su idioma (*language*), el latín.

La influencia musulmana es evidente en la Mezquita-catedral de Córdoba. Los árabes vivieron (*lived*) ocho siglos (*centuries*) en la península ibérica.

Madrid es la capital de España. Es una ciudad (*city*) cosmopolita, sede (*headquarters*) de un gobierno democrático y de una monarquía constitucional. Madrid es un importante centro cultural, con grandes teatros, famosos museos y universidades muy buenas.

Barcelona es otra ciudad dinámica y vibrante. Por Las Ramblas pasean todos los días miles de personas. En Barcelona son famosos los edificios (*buildings*) modernistas como la Sagrada Familia o el Hospital de Sant Pau.

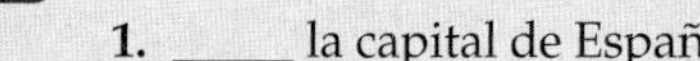

¿Cuánto sabes? Select the place or thing that corresponds with each description.

1. _____ la capital de España
2. _____ un edificio modernista
3. _____ una construcción romana
4. _____ un producto importante
5. _____ un plato típico de Valencia
6. _____ un equipo de fútbol

a. acueducto de Segovia
b. Real Madrid
c. vino
d. Madrid
e. Hospital de Sant Pau
f. paella

To learn more about Spain, go online to view the *Club cultura* videos.

Talking about students, their studies, and their activities

Los estudiantes españoles

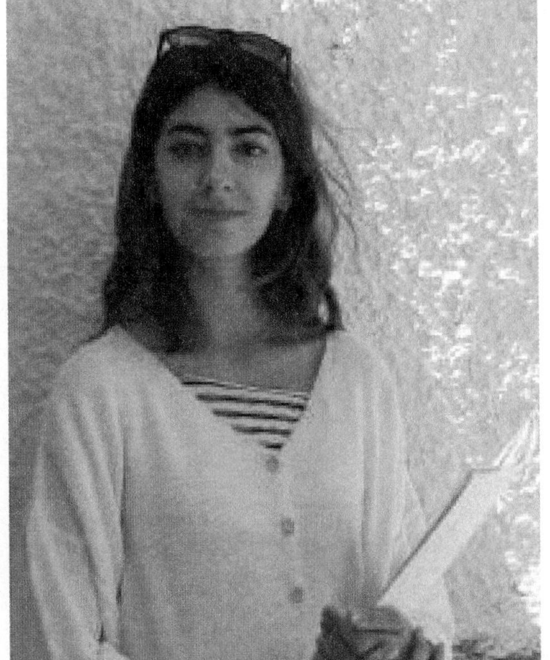

Me llamo Paloma Roldán. **Estudio Administración** y **Dirección de Empresas** en la **Universidad** Autónoma de Madrid. Mis clases son por la mañana. **Llego** a la universidad a las nueve. Este **semestre** mis cursos son **matemáticas, economía, ciencias políticas, estadística** y **análisis financiero.** Mi clase **favorita** es economía. La clase de estadística es **difícil, pero** el profesor es muy **bueno.** La clase de ciencias políticas es **fácil** y muy **interesante. Hablo** español, **francés** e **inglés.**

Lengua

The letter **y** changes to **e** when it precedes a word beginning with the **i** sound (which may include words that start with **hi**): **inglés y español,** but **español e inglés; inteligente y agradable,** but **agradable e inteligente.**

Este chico es mi **primo.** Se llama Daniel y estudia **Humanidades** en la Universidad Pompeu Fabra de Barcelona. Habla castellano (español) y catalán. Sus clases este año son **literatura, historia** y **geografía.** Daniel es muy **responsable** y **estudioso.** Generalmente llega a la universidad a las ocho. Por la tarde, **escribe** sus tareas en el **ordenador**, estudia y **escucha** música o **mira** películas (*movies*) en la televisión. Daniel **practica fútbol todas las semanas con** sus compañeros de clase y sus amigos de la universidad.

En otras palabras

Words related to computers and computing are often borrowed from English (e.g., **software, email**), and they vary from country to country. As you have already learned, one word for *computer* is **la computadora,** used mainly in Latin America, along with **el computador.** *Computer* is **el ordenador** in Spain. *Computer science* is **la informática** in Spain and **la computación** in some countries in Latin America.

PRÁCTICA

1-1 Escucha y confirma. Listen to the statements about Paloma and Daniel. Then, indicate **sí** or **no** based on what you have heard.

1. **a.** sí **b.** no
2. **a.** sí **b.** no
3. **a.** sí **b.** no
4. **a.** sí **b.** no
5. **a.** sí **b.** no
6. **a.** sí **b.** no

1-2 ¿Qué sabes de los estudiantes? Indicate whether the following information refers to Paloma (**P**) or to Daniel (**D**).

1. _____ Llega a las nueve a la universidad.
2. _____ Practica fútbol todas las semanas.
3. _____ Estudia geografía.
4. _____ Escucha música por la tarde.
5. _____ Su clase favorita es economía.
6. _____ Habla catalán.

1-3 Preguntas. Take turns asking and answering the following questions.

1. ¿Quién es Paloma Roldán?
2. ¿Qué estudia Paloma?
3. ¿Cuál es su clase favorita?
4. ¿Cómo se llama el primo de Paloma?
5. ¿Dónde estudia Daniel?
6. ¿Quién habla catalán?

1-4 ¿Qué sabes de tu compañero/a? Use **¿Cuál es...?** to ask each other for the following information.

MODELO E1: *¿Cuál es...?*
E2: *Es...*

1. tu nombre completo
2. el nombre de tu universidad
3. tu clase más difícil
4. tu clase más fácil
5. el nombre de tu profesor favorito / profesora favorita

1-5 Más información. To learn more about your partner, take turns asking him/her the following questions.

1. ¿De dónde eres?
2. ¿A qué hora llegas a la universidad?
3. ¿Dónde está tu universidad?
4. ¿Cómo es la universidad?
5. ¿Cómo es tu profesor favorito / profesora favorita?

La universidad y los cursos

Paloma y su amiga Irene hablan de sus clases.

IRENE: Hola, Paloma. ¿Cómo estás?
PALOMA: Hola, Irene. **¿Cómo te va?**
IRENE: Bueno... bastante bien, pero **tengo** problemas con mi clase de **informática.**
PALOMA: ¿Quién es tu profesor?
IRENE: Se llama Pedro Hernández. Es inteligente y dedicado, pero la clase es **aburrida** y **saco malas notas.**
PALOMA: ¡Vaya! Lo siento. ¿Estudias suficiente?
IRENE: Estudio mucho.
PALOMA: **¡Qué lástima!** Mis cinco clases son **excelentes.** Y tú, **¿cuántas clases tienes?**
IRENE: Tengo **solo** cuatro: **biología, ciencias naturales, química** e **informática.**
PALOMA: ¡Uy! Son las once. Tengo un **examen** de economía **ahora.** Hasta luego.
IRENE: Hasta pronto. **¡Buena suerte!**

Mapa de la universidad

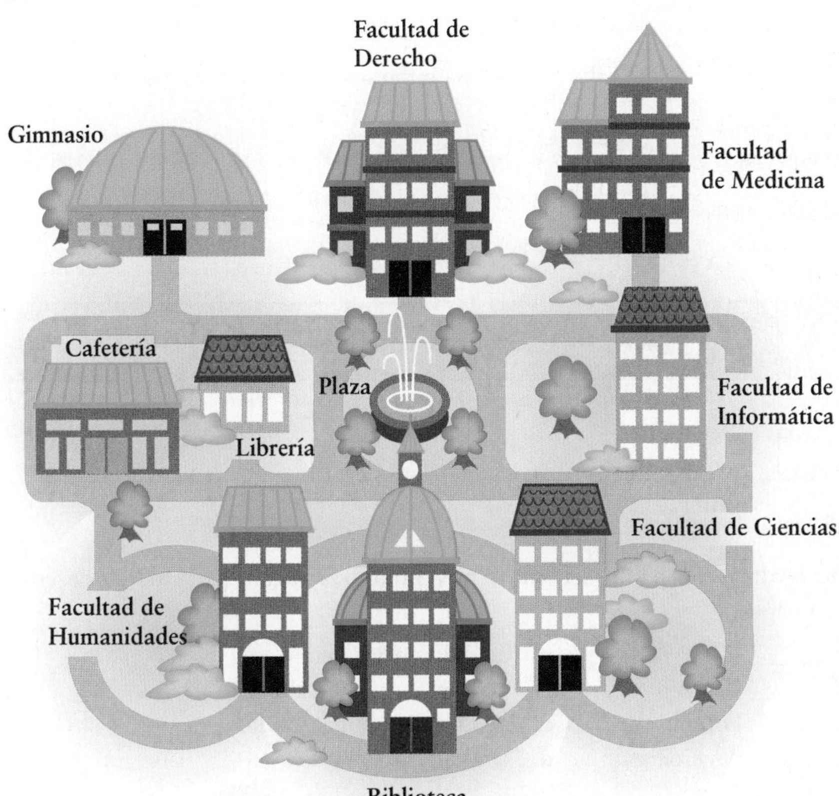

Cultura

La literatura The famous novel *Don Quijote de la Mancha* by the Spanish novelist and playwright Miguel de Cervantes Saavedra (1547–1616) is one of the most important works of world literature. It is a parody of the tales of chivalry, which were popular at the time. The main character is Alonso Quijano, an older man who has read so many of those tales that he believes himself to be a heroic knight. He dubs himself "Don Quijote de la Mancha" and sets off to fight injustice.

Conexiones Name a famous literary character in your culture. In your opinion, who is the most famous writer in your language?

PRÁCTICA

e **1-6 Para confirmar.** Select the subject that corresponds with each idea.

1. _____ *Don Quijote* (Cervantes)
2. _____ números
3. _____ mapa digital
4. _____ animales
5. _____ Freud
6. _____ Napoleón

a. geografía
b. biología
c. literatura
d. historia
e. matemáticas
f. psicología

e **1-7 Cursos.** Match the subjects with the school where they are offered.

Administración electrónica
Anatomía humana II
Biología
Creación de páginas web
Criminología
Derecho romano
Filosofía clásica
Fisiología
Historia medieval
Laboratorio de física
Literatura latinoamericana
Química I

Facultad de Ciencias	Facultad de Humanidades	Facultad de Derecho	Facultad de Medicina	Facultad de Informática

1-8 ¿En qué facultad estudian?

e **PREPARACIÓN.** Select the school where each university student studies, based on the images.

1. _____ Juan
2. _____ Carmen
3. _____ Lorena
4. _____ Álvaro

a. Facultad de Medicina
b. Facultad de Arquitectura
c. Facultad de Humanidades
d. Facultad de Ciencias

Carmen

Lorena

Álvaro

Juan

INTERCAMBIOS. Exchange information with a classmate and indicate two classes that each student is probably taking.

MODELO E1: *¿Dónde estudia Carmen?*
E2: *Carmen estudia en la Facultad de... Probablemente tiene clases de... y de...*

1-9 Mis clases. **PREPARACIÓN.** Make a list of your classes. Indicate the days and time each class meets and whether it is easy or difficult, interesting or boring. Refer to the list of some common courses.

Artes plásticas	Comunicaciones	Filosofía	Negocios
Astronomía	Contabilidad	Física	Seminario de...
Bioquímica	Economía	Historia del arte	Sociología
Cálculo	Estadística	Informática	

Clase	Días	Hora	¿Cómo es?

INTERCAMBIOS. Tell your partner about your classes. Take turns completing the following ideas.

1. Mis clases comienzan (*start*) a la(s)...
2. Mi clase favorita es...
3. El/La profesor/a se llama...
4. La clase es muy...
5. Practico español en...
6. En mi clase de español hay...

1-10 Las clases de mis compañeros/as.

PREPARACIÓN. Use the following questions to interview your partner. Then switch roles.

1. ¿Qué estudias este semestre?
2. ¿Cuántas clases tienes?
3. ¿Cuál es tu clase favorita?
4. ¿Qué día y a qué hora es tu clase favorita?
5. ¿Cómo es tu clase de español? ¿Es fácil o difícil? ¿Es interesante o aburrida?
6. ¿Sacas buenas notas?
7. ¿Tienes muchos exámenes?

INTERCAMBIOS. Introduce your partner to another classmate and state one piece of interesting information about him/her. Your classmate will ask your partner about his/her classes.

MODELO E1: *Él es Pedro. Estudia ciencias políticas y tiene cuatro clases este semestre.*
E2: *Mucho gusto. ¿...?*

Las actividades de los estudiantes

En la biblioteca

Unos **alumnos** estudian en la **residencia estudiantil. Toman apuntes** y **trabajan** en sus tareas. **A veces buscan** palabras en el **diccionario.** Frecuentemente **conversan** sobre sus clases.

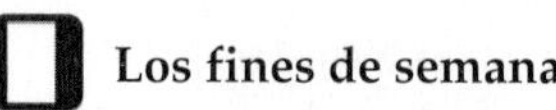

Los fines de semana

Los estudiantes **toman algo** en un **café.**

Miran televisión en **casa.**

Bailan en una **discoteca** con amigos.

Ignacio **camina** por la **playa.**

Luciana **monta en bicicleta.**

En la librería

ESTUDIANTE: Hola, **necesito comprar** unos libros y un cuaderno **para** mi clase de literatura.
DEPENDIENTA: ¿Un cuaderno **grande** o **pequeño?**
ESTUDIANTE: Grande, por favor.
DEPENDIENTA: Este cuaderno es muy **práctico.**
ESTUDIANTE: **¿Cuánto cuesta?**
DEPENDIENTA: Cuatro **euros.**

PRÁCTICA

1-11 Para confirmar. Select the most appropriate option to complete each sentence. Then ask your partner about his/her activities.

MODELO E1: *Los estudiantes buscan palabras en* __el diccionario__. *¿Y tú?*
E2: *Yo, en internet.*

1. Los estudiantes _____ en la biblioteca.
   - **a.** toman café
   - **b.** estudian
   - **c.** hablan
2. Miran televisión en _____.
   - **a.** la biblioteca
   - **b.** la playa
   - **c.** casa
3. Montan en bicicleta _____.
   - **a.** los fines de semana
   - **b.** en el café
   - **c.** en una discoteca
4. Practican deportes (*sports*) como el básquetbol en _____.
   - **a.** el laboratorio
   - **b.** el gimnasio
   - **c.** la Facultad de Artes

1-12 Mis actividades. **PREPARACIÓN.** Indicate the activities that you normally do **durante la semana** (*during the week*) (**DS**), and/or **los fines de semana** (**FS**).

1. _____ Hablo con mis compañeros de clase.
2. _____ Practico deportes.
3. _____ Miro televisión.
4. _____ Estudio en la biblioteca.
5. _____ Compro libros y cuadernos para mis clases.
6. _____ Bailo en una discoteca.

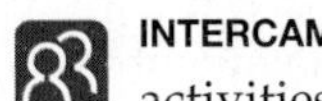

INTERCAMBIOS. Ask each other questions to find out if you both do these activities.

MODELO E1: *¿Hablas con tus compañeros de clase?*
E2: *Sí, hablo con mis compañeros de clase durante la semana.*

1-13 ¿Cuánto cuesta? During your semester in Spain, you go to the university bookstore. Take turns with a partner asking how much the pictured items cost and responding as the salesclerk.

MODELO ESTUDIANTE: *¿Cuánto cuesta el diccionario?*
DEPENDIENTE/A: *Cuesta cuarenta y siete euros.*

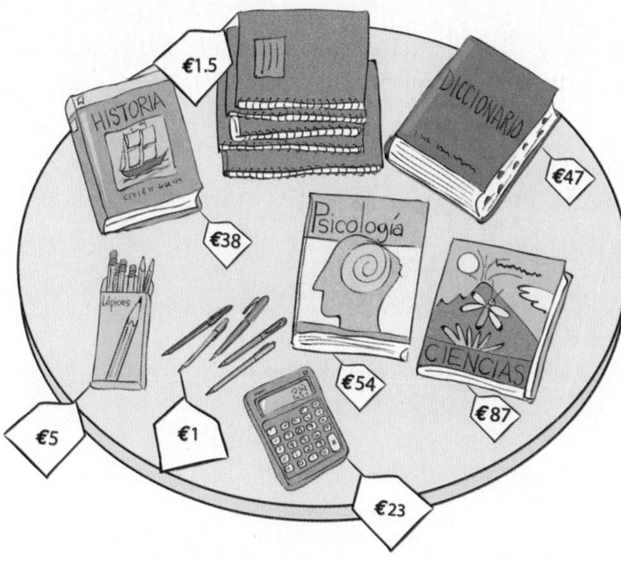

Cultura

El euro Since 2002, the euro has been the official monetary unit of the Eurozone, which includes France, Germany, Greece, Ireland, Italy, and Spain, among others. The euro currency sign is € and the banking code is EUR.

Comunidades What are the advantages and disadvantages of several countries sharing the same currency?

1-14 Entrevista (*Interview*). Ask where and when your classmate does each of the following activities. Then share your findings with the class.

MODELO practicar básquetbol
E1: *¿Dónde practicas básquetbol? ¿Cuándo?*
E2: *Practico básquetbol en el gimnasio por la tarde.*

Actividad	Dónde	Cuándo
1. estudiar para un examen difícil		
2. mirar televisión		
3. tomar café		
4. conversar con tus amigos		
5. escuchar música		
6. comprar unos libros para tus clases		

1-15 Las actividades de tus compañeros.

PREPARACIÓN. Go around the classroom and interview three people. Take notes to report your findings to the class.

1. ¿Qué haces (*do you do*) los fines de semana?
2. ¿Dónde miras tu programa de televisión favorito?
3. ¿Qué compras en la librería?
4. ¿Dónde estudias normalmente?
5. ¿Trabajas los fines de semana? ¿Dónde trabajas?

INTERCAMBIOS. Now share with the class two pieces of information you got from your classmates.

MODELO *María estudia normalmente en casa.*
No trabaja los fines de semana.

1-16 ¿Qué hacen? (*What do they do?*)

PREPARACIÓN. You will hear three people talking about their activities during the week and on weekends. Before you listen, write your own activities in two lists: **Durante la semana** and **Los fines de semana.** Ask your partner if he/she does the same things. What activities do you have in common?

ESCUCHA. Now pay attention to the general idea of what is said in the conversation. Indicate the number of the speaker (**1, 2, 3**) for each topic.

_____ los estudios
_____ el tiempo libre (*free time*)
_____ el trabajo

Mosaico cultural

La vida universitaria en España e Hispanoamérica

En España y Latinoamérica hay universidades muy antiguas y prestigiosas. Normalmente, sus edificios y facultades están en el centro de las ciudades, pero algunas universidades más nuevas tienen un campus en las afueras (*outskirts*).

En la universidad hay residencias para estudiantes, pero muchos jóvenes viven (*live*) en la casa de sus familiares o alquilan (*rent*) un apartamento con otros estudiantes. No es muy común estudiar en universidades lejanas (*far away*), pero muchos participan en programas de intercambio (*exchange*).

Universidad de Viña del Mar, Chile

Universidad de Oviedo, España

En las universidades de España y Latinoamérica no hay fraternidades pero sí hay organizaciones estudiantiles. En general, los deportes no son tan importantes como en las universidades de Estados Unidos. Los estudiantes practican deportes en su tiempo libre y también tienen actividades extracurriculares.

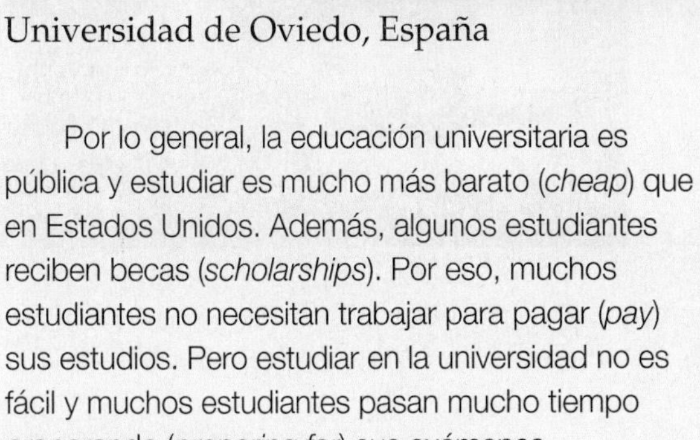

Por lo general, la educación universitaria es pública y estudiar es mucho más barato (*cheap*) que en Estados Unidos. Además, algunos estudiantes reciben becas (*scholarships*). Por eso, muchos estudiantes no necesitan trabajar para pagar (*pay*) sus estudios. Pero estudiar en la universidad no es fácil y muchos estudiantes pasan mucho tiempo preparando (*preparing for*) sus exámenes.

Universidad de Guanajuato, México

Compara

1. ¿Cómo es tu universidad? ¿Tiene un campus grande? ¿Hay residencias para los estudiantes?
2. ¿Qué aspectos son similares o diferentes entre tu universidad y las universidades de España y Latinoamérica?
3. ¿Qué actividades extracurriculares hay para los estudiantes en tu universidad?

En acción

Los saludos

Antes de ver

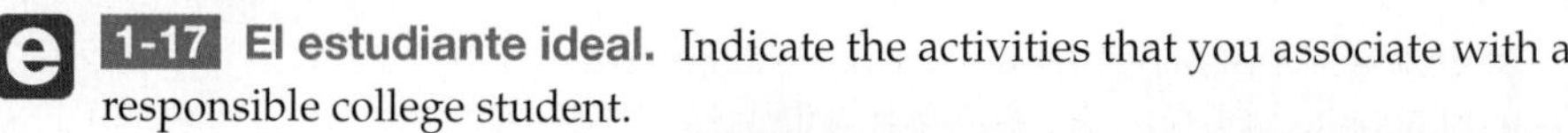

1-17 El estudiante ideal. Indicate the activities that you associate with a responsible college student.

1. _____ Asiste (*attends*) a clase todos los días.
2. _____ Llega tarde a sus clases.
3. _____ Habla con sus profesores.
4. _____ Usa su teléfono en clase.
5. _____ Levanta la mano y participa.
6. _____ Saca buenas notas.
7. _____ Escucha música en clase.
8. _____ Estudia para los exámenes.

Mientras ves

1-18 Un curso de verano. As you watch the video, indicate whether the following statements refer to Esteban (**E**), Yolanda (**Y**), Federico (**F**), or Vanesa (**V**).

1. _____ Es de Costa Rica.
2. _____ Es de Buenos Aires.
3. _____ Es de México.
4. _____ Es de España.
5. _____ Estudia arte.
6. _____ Baila y escucha música.
7. _____ Hace surf.

Después de ver

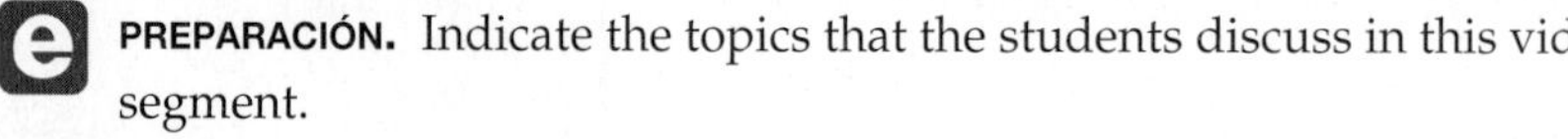

1-19 ¿De qué hablan?

PREPARACIÓN. Indicate the topics that the students discuss in this video segment.

1. _____ la competición por la beca (*scholarship*)
2. _____ los países (*countries*) de origen
3. _____ el profesor de cine
4. _____ los estudios
5. _____ las familias
6. _____ las universidades

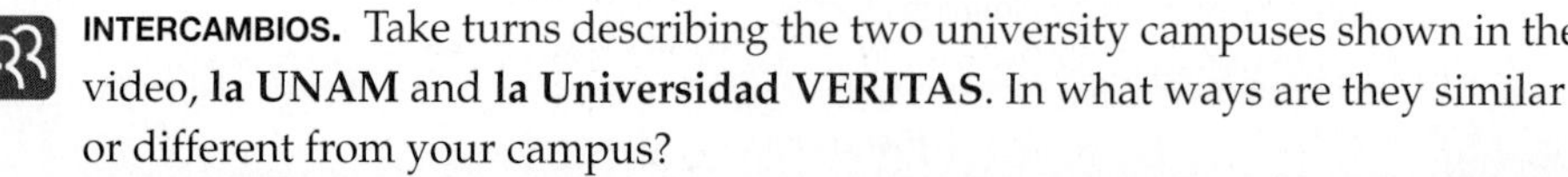

INTERCAMBIOS. Take turns describing the two university campuses shown in the video, **la UNAM** and **la Universidad VERITAS**. In what ways are they similar or different from your campus?

FUNCIONES Y FORMAS

1 Asking and answering questions

Julia López conversa con su consejera (*advisor*) en la Universidad de Salamanca. La consejera debe rellenar (*must fill out*) algunos formularios con información sobre Julia. Estas son algunas de las preguntas de la consejera y las respuestas de Julia.

Consejera	Julia
¿**Cómo** se llama tu residencia estudiantil?	Se llama Residencia Helmántica.
¿**Dónde** está?	Está en la calle San Narciso.
¿**Cuánto** cuesta la habitación doble?	600 euros en pensión completa.
¿**Quién** es tu compañera de cuarto?	Cristina Zapatero.
¿**Por qué** deseas (*want to*) estudiar psicología?	Para ayudar (*help*) a otras personas.
¿**Cuándo** son tus clases?	Por la mañana y por la tarde.

Piénsalo. Select the appropriate question word for each of Julia's responses.

1. _____ Es Cristina Zapatero.
2. _____ Se llama Cristina Zapatero.
3. _____ En la Residencia Helmántica.
4. _____ 600 euros al mes.
5. _____ Por la mañana y por la tarde.

a. ¿Dónde?
b. ¿Cuándo?
c. ¿Quién?
d. ¿Cómo?
e. ¿Cuánto?

Interrogative words

- Interrogative words are used to ask questions or to obtain specific information. You are already using many of these words.

¿(a)dónde?	*where (to)?*	**¿cuántos/as?**	*how many?*
¿cómo?	*how?/what?*	**¿para qué?**	*why? / what for?*
¿cuál(es)?	*which?*	**¿por qué?**	*why?*
¿cuándo?	*when?*	**¿qué?**	*what?*
¿cuánto/a?	*how much?*	**¿quién(es)?**	*who?*

- If a subject is used in a question, it normally follows the verb.

  ¿Dónde trabaja **Olivia?** — *Where does Olivia work?*

- Attach **a** to **dónde** (**adónde**) to signal movement toward a place or target. **Adónde** often requires the use of verb **ir** (*to go*) or another verb that indicates movement toward a target.

  ¿Adónde va Alejandro? — *Where is Alejandro going?*

  ¿Dónde compra sus libros Alejandro? — *Where does Alejandro buy his books?*

- Use **por qué** to ask *why* and **porque** to answer *because.*

  ¿**Por qué** está Pepe en la biblioteca? — *Why is Pepe in the library?*

  Porque necesita estudiar. — *Because he needs to study.*

- Use **qué + ser** when you want to ask for a definition or an explanation.

  ¿**Qué es** la sardana? — *What is the sardana?*

  Es un baile típico de Cataluña. — *It is a typical dance of Catalonia.*

Lengua

All question words have a written accent over the stressed syllable:

cómo, dónde

When these words are used with a non-interrogative function, they do not have a written accent.

¿Dónde está la biblioteca?

Where is the library?

Esta es la biblioteca donde estudio todos los días.

This is the library where I study every day.

- Use **cuál(es) + ser** when you want to ask *which one(s).*

¿**Cuál es** tu mochila?	*Which (one) is your backpack?*
¿**Cuáles son** tus papeles?	*Which (ones) are your papers?*

- Questions that may be answered with **sí** or **no** do not use a question word.

¿Trabajan ustedes los sábados?	*Do you work on Saturdays?*
No, no trabajamos.	*No, we do not.*

- Another way to ask a question is to place an interrogative tag after a statement.

Tú hablas inglés, **¿verdad?**	*You speak English, don't you?*
David es norteamericano, **¿no?**	*David is North American, isn't he?*

Lengua

To request repetition or clarification of a statement, use **¿Cómo?** or **¿Perdón?** The use of **¿Qué?,** the equivalent of English *What?*, may be considered rude in some contexts.

e **¿Comprendes?** Complete the following questions with the appropriate interrogative word.

1. ¿__________ te llamas?
2. ¿__________ es tu clase favorita?
3. ¿__________ es la clase, por la mañana o por la tarde?
4. ¿__________ personas viven (*live*) en la residencia?
5. ¿__________ estudias en esta universidad?
6. ¿__________ vives en la universidad?
7. ¿__________ vas para comprar los libros para las clases?

PRÁCTICA

e **1-20 Preguntas.** First look at the cues and then complete each question with **qué, quién, cuándo, cuántos/as, cuál,** or **por qué** as logical. Use your questions to interview two people as you walk around the room. Take some notes to report later.

1. ¿____________ clases tomas? Tomo…
2. ¿____________ son tus clases? Por la…
3. ¿____________ es tu clase favorita? La clase de…
4. ¿____________ es tu profesor favorito / profesora favorita? El/La profesor/a…
5. ¿____________ estudias español? Estudio español porque es…
6. ¿____________ estudiantes hay en tu clase de español? Hay…

1-21 Entrevista. Take turns asking each other questions to find out the following information. Use appropriate phrases to express disbelief, interest, etc.

MODELO razón para estudiar español
¿Por qué estudias español?

1. número de clases que tomas este semestre
2. tu clase favorita y razón (por qué)
3. número de alumnos en la clase favorita
4. nombre del profesor favorito / de la profesora favorita
5. lugar donde estudias generalmente y número de horas que estudias por (*per*) día
6. lugar donde trabajas

1-22 ¿Qué información me interesa (*interests me*)?

PREPARACIÓN. You recently watched a movie starring the famous Spanish actress Penélope Cruz, and would like to know more about her. Choose four topics from the list that interest you. Then write the questions that you will ask her on social media.

1. características de su personalidad
2. lugar donde está su casa
3. nombre de su pareja (*significant other*)
4. nombre de su película favorita
5. número de autos que tiene
6. lugar donde generalmente toma vacaciones
7. lugar donde toma café con amigos
8. su director favorito / directora favorita

INTERCAMBIOS. In the role of Penélope Cruz, answer your partner's questions. Your partner will expand on answers by asking additional questions as necessary. Then switch roles.

Situación

PREPARACIÓN. Read the following situation with your partner. Then prepare examples of the vocabulary, structures, and other information you will need for your role in the conversation.

Role A. It is the beginning of the term, and you need to add a history class. One of your friends is in a class that looks promising. Ask:
a. who the professor is;
b. where the class is;
c. how much homework there is;
d. when the class meets; and
e. how many exams the class has.

Role B. Your friend wants some information about your history class. Reply as specifically as possible to all of his/her questions. Then offer some additional information about the class.

	ROLE A	ROLE B
Vocabulario	Expressions related to school and people at school Question words	Expressions related to school and people at school
Funciones y formas	Asking questions with appropriate interrogative words Thanking someone for information provided	Answering questions with appropriate information Reacting to what you hear

INTERCAMBIOS. Using the information in **Preparación,** act out the conversation with your partner.

2 Expressing location and states of being

MARIANA: ¡Hola!

FRANCISCO: ¡Mariana! ¡Qué sorpresa! ¿Dónde **estás?**

MARIANA: **Estoy** en el aeropuerto de Barajas, en Madrid. ¿Y tú?

FRANCISCO: Mi padre y yo **estamos** en Nueva York. En este momento, mi padre **está** en una tienda (*store*) de aparatos electrónicos. ¿Y cómo **están** todos en tu familia?

MARIANA: Todos **estamos** muy bien. ¡Qué bueno escucharte! Lo siento, Francisco, pero el vuelo (*flight*) sale (*leaves*) pronto. Hablamos otro día. Adiós.

Piénsalo. Indicate whether the following statements refer to location (**L**) or states of being (**S**).

1. _____ Mariana **está** en el aeropuerto de Barajas.
2. _____ Francisco **está** contento de escuchar a Mariana.
3. _____ Todos (*Everyone*) en la familia de Mariana **están** bien.
4. _____ El padre de Francisco **está** en una tienda probablemente para comprar un aparato electrónico.
5. _____ Francisco y Mariana **están** en dos ciudades diferentes.

Present tense of *estar*

- You have already been using some forms of **estar.** Here are all the present tense forms of this verb.

ESTAR (*to be*)			
yo	**estoy**	nosotros/as	**estamos**
tú	**estás**	vosotros/as	**estáis**
Ud., él, ella	**está**	Uds., ellos, ellas	**están**

- Use **estar** to express the location of persons or objects.

¿Dónde **está** Francisco? *Where is Francisco?*
Está en Nueva York. *He is in New York.*

- Use **estar** to talk about states of health or being.

¿Cómo **está** la familia de Mariana? *How is Mariana's family?*
Está muy bien. Todos **están** contentos. *They are very well. Everyone is happy.*

¿Comprendes? Complete the sentences with the correct forms of **estar.**

1. El profesor _________ en la oficina.
2. Nosotros _________ bien.
3. Yo _________ en el gimnasio.
4. ¿Cómo _________ ustedes?
5. Mis amigos _________ en la biblioteca.
6. Mi compañero _________ bien también.

PRÁCTICA

  **1-23 En la cafetería.** Complete the conversation between José Antonio and Ramón, using the correct forms of **estar.** Then indicate if **estar** signals location (**L**) or a state of being (**S**). Compare answers with a classmate and create a similar conversation.

JOSÉ ANTONIO: Hola, Ramón. ¿Qué tal? ¿Cómo ____________?
RAMÓN: ____________muy bien. ¿Y tú?
JOSÉ ANTONIO: Muy bien. ¿Y cómo ____________ tu hermana (*sister*) Lucía?
RAMÓN: Bien, gracias. Ella y mamá ____________ en España ahora.
JOSÉ ANTONIO: ¡Qué suerte! Y nosotros ____________ en la universidad, ¡y en la semana de exámenes!

1-24 Horas y lugares favoritos. **PREPARACIÓN.** Choose two different times of day and ask your partner where he/she usually is at that time.

MODELO E1: *¿Dónde estás generalmente a las 10:00 de la mañana?*
E2: *Estoy en…*
E1: *¿Y dónde estás a la 1:00 de la tarde?*

INTERCAMBIOS. Compare your responses with those of your partner. Identify the similarities and/or differences in your schedules.

 **1-25 Conversación.** Ask a classmate where any of the people in these scenes are and how they are doing. Then draw where you would like to be and your partner will say where you are and how you are feeling.

MODELO María Luisa
E1: *¿Dónde está María Luisa?*
E2: *Está en la biblioteca.*
E1: *¿Cómo está?*
E2: *Está nerviosa porque tiene un examen.*

María Luisa

1.

Eduardo

Marcelo

2.

Berta Lorena

3.

Carlos el Dr. Núñez

4.

yo

1-26 Adivina (*Guess*). Read the following statements and guess *where* people are and/or *how* people are doing. Use the correct form of the verb **estar.** Compare your responses with those of a classmate.

1. José Pablo estudia para un examen difícil. ¿Dónde está? ¿Cómo está?
2. Los profesores tienen una reunión (*meeting*) urgente. ¿Dónde están? ¿Cómo están?
3. Carmen tiene una competencia importante de básquetbol hoy. Necesita practicar mucho. ¿Dónde está? ¿Cómo está?
4. Tú y tu compañero/a de casa desean (*want*) tomar café. ¿Dónde están ustedes en este momento? ¿Cómo están?
5. El profesor de álgebra no está en clase hoy. ¿Dónde está? ¿Cómo está?
6. Tú necesitas ayuda (*help*) con tu computadora. ¿Dónde estás? ¿Cómo estás?

Situación

PREPARACIÓN. Read the following situation with your partner. Then brainstorm the vocabulary, structures, and other information you will need for both roles in the conversation.

Role A. You are a new student at the university, and you do not know where some of these buildings are located. Introduce yourself to a classmate and ask where the following buildings are:
a. la biblioteca
b. la cafetería
c. la Facultad de Ciencias
d. la Facultad de Humanidades

Role B. You meet a new student on campus. Answer his/her questions about the location of certain buildings.

	ROLE A	ROLE B
Vocabulario	Places on campus Question words	Places on campus Words to express location
Funciones y formas	Introducing oneself Using **estar** to talk about location	Reacting to what you hear Answering questions Giving information about location

INTERCAMBIOS. Using the information in **Preparación,** act out the conversation with your partner.

3 Talking about academic life and activities

REPORTERO: Hola, buenos días, soy Pablo Brito del Canal 6. ¿Su nombre, por favor?

SARA: Yo soy Sara González y mi amiga es Marta Figueroa.

REPORTERO: ¿Tienen ustedes una vida muy activa?

MARTA: Sí, **practicamos** muchos deportes. Sara **participa** en maratones y **practica** tenis. Yo **practico** fútbol y baloncesto.

SARA: Y los fines de semana **montamos** en bicicleta.

REPORTERO: ¡Qué interesante! Muchas gracias.

Piénsalo. Indicate whether each statement refers to **una persona** or to **dos personas.** Use the information in the interview as well as the verb endings to help you decide.

	UNA PERSONA	DOS PERSONAS
1. Soy Sara González.	_____	_____
2. Mi amiga es Marta Figueroa.	_____	_____
3. Practicamos muchos deportes.	_____	_____
4. Participa en maratones.	_____	_____
5. Practico fútbol y baloncesto.	_____	_____
6. Los fines de semana montamos en bicicleta.	_____	_____

Present tense of regular *-ar* verbs

To talk about actions, feelings, and states of being, you need to use verbs. In both English and Spanish, the infinitive is the base form of the verb that appears in vocabulary lists and dictionaries. In English, infinitives are preceded by *to: to speak.* Infinitives in Spanish belong to one of three groups, depending on whether they end in **-ar, -er,** or **-ir.** Verbs ending in **-ar** are presented here, and verbs ending in **-er** and **-ir** are presented in the next section.

HABLAR (*to speak*)			
yo	habl**o**	nosotros/as	habl**amos**
tú	habl**as**	vosotros/as	habl**áis**
él, ella, Ud.	habl**a**	ellos, ellas, Uds.	habl**an**

- Use the present tense to express what you and others do (in general) or are doing (now).

Ana **trabaja** en la oficina.	*Ana works in the office. (This is her job.)*
	Ana is working in the office. (Ana is working there now.)
Luis **practica** el piano todos los días.	*Luis practices the piano every day.*

- Here are some expressions you may find useful when talking about the frequency of actions.

siempre	*always*	**muchas veces**	*often*
todos los días/ meses	*every day/month*	**a veces**	*sometimes*
		nunca	*never*
todas las semanas	*every week*		

- Here are some common **-ar** verbs and expressions.

bailar	*to dance*	**necesitar**	*to need*
buscar	*to look for*	**participar**	*to participate*
caminar	*to walk*	**practicar**	*to practice*
comprar	*to buy*	**sacar buenas/ malas notas**	*to get good/bad grades*
conversar	*to talk*		
escuchar	*to listen (to)*	**tomar apuntes/ notas**	*to take notes*
estudiar	*to study*		
llegar	*to arrive*	**trabajar**	*to work*
mirar	*to look (at)*	**usar**	*to use*
montar (en bicicleta)	*to ride (a bicycle)*		

e **¿Comprendes?** Indicate the person or persons to whom the statements below most likely apply: **yo, tú, usted, ella, nosotros, los estudiantes.**

1. ______________ compran libros para las clases que toman.
2. ______________ necesitamos computadoras para estudiar en internet.
3. Señor, ______________ necesita comprar bolígrafos para tomar apuntes.
4. Y ______________, ¿qué necesitas para el proyecto de química?
5. ______________ compro cuadernos en la librería de la universidad.
6. ______________ necesita hablar de sus problemas de horario con la administración.

PRÁCTICA

1-27 Las rutinas. **PREPARACIÓN.** Indicate the activities that are part of your usual routine.

1. ____ Llego a la universidad a las nueve de la mañana.
2. ____ Llamo a mis amigos por teléfono.
3. ____ Siempre tomo notas en las clases.
4. ____ Uso los medios sociales para hablar con mis compañeros/as.
5. ____ Estudio en la biblioteca.
6. ____ Trabajo en mis tareas todas las noches.
7. ____ Miro películas en la televisión.
8. ____ A veces practico deportes con mis amigos/as.

INTERCAMBIOS. Now compare your answers with those of a classmate. Report your findings to the class.

MODELO *Daniel y yo somos similares. Miramos películas en la televisión.*
Ben y yo somos diferentes. Yo estudio en la biblioteca; él estudia en casa.

 **1-28 A preguntar.** **PREPARACIÓN.** Find four different classmates, each of whom does one of the following activities. Take notes about who does each activity. The **En directo** expressions will help you.

MODELO mirar televisión por la tarde

E1: *Oye, ¿miras televisión por la tarde?*

E2: *No, no miro televisión por la tarde. Miro televisión por la noche.*

Persona	Actividad
	estudiar español todos los días
	llegar a clase a las 9:30 de la mañana
	escuchar música en español
	trabajar en una oficina por la tarde

INTERCAMBIOS. Now report to the class your findings about your classmates' activities.

En directo

To get someone's attention:

¡Oye! *Hey! (informal, to a friend)*

Oiga, por favor. *Excuse me. (formal, to a stranger or a person you are not close to)*

To interrupt to ask a question:

Perdón, tengo una pregunta. *Excuse me, I have a question.*

To respond to a request:

Con mucho gusto. *With pleasure.*

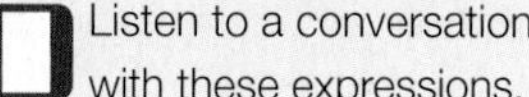 Listen to a conversation with these expressions.

1-29 Mis actividades. **PREPARACIÓN.** Indicate how often you do the following activities.

Actividades	Siempre	Muchas veces	A veces	Nunca
estudiar con amigos				
usar internet para hacer una investigación				
montar en bicicleta los fines de semana				
mirar videos en internet				
bailar los sábados				
tomar café				

 **INTERCAMBIOS.** Now tell each other how often you do these activities, and then ask your partner where he/she does them.

MODELO E1: *Yo estudio con mis amigos a veces. ¿Y tú?*

E2: *Yo siempre estudio con mis amigos.*

E1: *¿Dónde estudian ustedes?*

E2: *Estudiamos en la biblioteca.*

Cultura

Las tapas A popular social activity in Spain is **ir de tapas** (to go out for **tapas**). **Tapas** are small portions of different dishes that are served in most bars with wine or beer. They range from a piece of bread with an anchovy to elaborate appetizers. People often walk from bar to bar to sample different **tapas.**

Comparaciones Do you know of other cultures in which small portions are shared among friends or family in restaurants or bars?

 **1-30 Un día típico.** Take turns describing what Luisa does on a typical day. Then select two of the times and tell your partner what you do at those times.

MODELO *Luisa llega a la universidad a las ocho y veinte.*

1.

2.

3.

4.

Situación

PREPARACIÓN. Read the following situation with your partner. Then brainstorm the vocabulary, structures, and other information you will need for both roles in the conversation.

Role A. Besides studying, your new friend has a job. Ask your friend:
a. where he/she works;
b. the days of the week and the hours he/she works; and
c. if the job (**trabajo**) is interesting/boring/difficult/easy.
Then answer your friend's questions.

Role B. Answer your friend's questions about your job. Then ask similar questions about his/her job (**trabajo**).

	ROLE A	ROLE B
Vocabulario	Routine work activities Places Days of the week and time Adjectives to describe someone's job Question words	Routine work activities Places Days of the week and time Adjectives to describe someone's job Question words
Funciones y formas	Asking and answering questions Giving an opinion Present tense of **ser** Present tense	Asking and answering questions Giving an opinion Present tense of **ser** Present tense

INTERCAMBIOS. Using the information in **Preparación,** act out the conversation with your partner.

4 Talking about academic life and activities

REPORTERA: Hola, buenas tardes. Estoy en el campus para entrevistar (*interview*) a jóvenes estudiantes. ¿Qué hacen ustedes durante el día?

PEDRO: Me llamo Pedro Rodríguez y soy estudiante de arquitectura. Mi amigo Antonio Muñoz estudia ciencias. Antonio **asiste** a sus clases y luego **corre** por (*across*) el campus para llegar al laboratorio donde trabaja todos los días. Habla con el profesor y **aprende** mucho. Los estudiantes de ciencias **leen** mucho, **escriben** trabajos de investigación y sacan buenas notas. Mis compañeros de la Facultad de Arquitectura y yo **leemos** y **escribimos** mucho también. Yo casi (*almost*) **vivo** en la biblioteca cuando estudio para los exámenes.

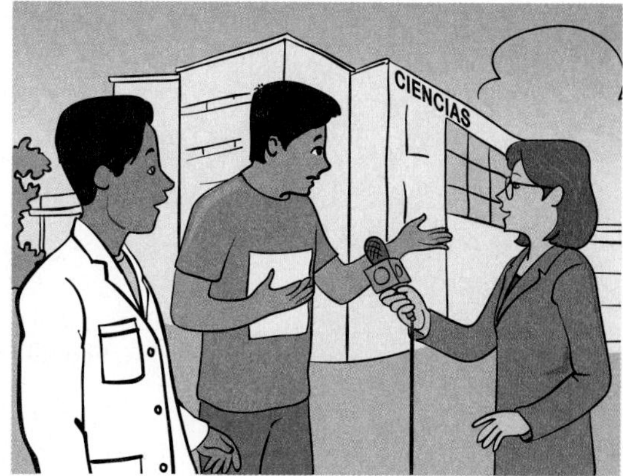

Piénsalo. Indicate whether each statement refers to **una persona** or to **dos o más personas.** Use the information in the interview as well as the verb endings to help you decide.

	UNA PERSONA	DOS O MÁS PERSONAS
1. ¿Qué hacen ustedes durante el día?	_____	_____
2. Asiste a sus clases.	_____	_____
3. Aprende mucho.	_____	_____
4. Leen y escriben mucho.	_____	_____
5. Leemos y escribimos mucho también.	_____	_____
6. Casi vivo en la biblioteca.	_____	_____

Present tense of regular *-er* and *-ir* verbs

- You have learned in this chapter that the present tense is used to express activities and ongoing actions. You have also learned the present tense forms for verbs whose infinitives end in **-ar.** Now you will learn those forms for verbs whose infinitives end in **-er** and **-ir.**

APRENDER (*to learn*)			
yo	aprend**o**	nosotros/as	aprend**emos**
tú	aprend**es**	vosotros/as	aprend**éis**
él, ella, Ud.	aprend**e**	ellos, ellas, Uds.	aprend**en**

- Note that **-er** and **-ir** verbs have the same endings, except for the **nosotros/as** and **vosotros/as** forms.

VIVIR (*to live*)			
yo	viv**o**	nosotros/as	viv**imos**
tú	viv**es**	vosotros/as	viv**ís**
él, ella, Ud.	viv**e**	ellos, ellas, Uds.	viv**en**

- Other common **-er** and **-ir** verbs are:

asistir	*to attend*	**correr**	*to run*
beber	*to drink*	**escribir**	*to write*
comer	*to eat*	**leer**	*to read*
comprender	*to understand*	**responder**	*to respond*

- The verb **ver** has an irregular **yo** form:

VER (*to see*)			
yo	ve**o**	nosotros/as	v**emos**
tú	**ves**	vosotros/as	ve**is**
él, ella, Ud.	**ve**	ellos, ellas, Uds.	**ven**

Veo películas los fines de semana. *I see movies on weekends.*

- Use **deber** +*infinitive* to express that you should/must/ought to do something.

Los atletas **deben beber** mucha agua. *Athletes should drink a lot of water.*

¿Comprendes? Provide the correct forms of **comer** and **escribir** to complete the following sentences.

1. Los estudiantes ____________con sus amigos en un restaurante en el campus todos los días.
2. Yo ____________ en casa porque cuesta mucho dinero comer en los restaurantes.
3. Y tú, ¿____________ tu almuerzo (*lunch*) en casa o en la cafetería de la universidad?
4. La profesora ____________ los exámenes en su computadora portátil.
5. Mis amigos y yo ____________ la tarea de español en la computadora.

PRÁCTICA

1-31 Para pasarlo bien (*To have a good time*). **PREPARACIÓN.** Indicate which of the following activities you do for fun.

1. _____ Leo libros en español todas las semanas.
2. _____ Escribo mensajes de texto.
3. _____ Practico deportes con los amigos.
4. _____ Asisto a clase a las ocho de la mañana.
5. _____ Corro en el gimnasio y en el parque.
6. _____ Veo películas y programas de televisión en casa.
7. _____ Converso con mis amigos y con mi familia por internet.
8. _____ Bebo solo agua con limón en las fiestas.

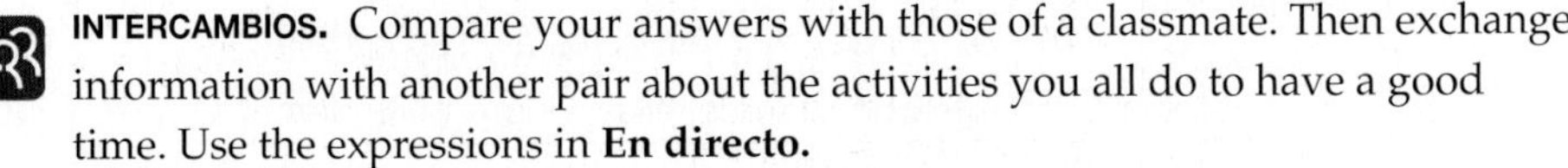

INTERCAMBIOS. Compare your answers with those of a classmate. Then exchange information with another pair about the activities you all do to have a good time. Use the expressions in **En directo.**

MODELO E1: *Nosotros bailamos en discotecas para pasarlo bien. ¿Y ustedes?*
E2: *Bebemos café y conversamos con los amigos.*

En directo

To react to what someone has said:

¡Qué interesante! *That's so interesting!*
¡Qué increíble! *That's unbelievable!*
¡Qué casualidad! *What a coincidence!*
¡Qué divertido! *How funny!*
¡Qué aburrido! *How boring!*
¡Vamos a pasarlo bien! *We're going to have fun / a good time!*
¡Que lo pases bien! *Have fun / a good time!*

Listen to a conversation with these expressions.

1-32 Lugares y actividades. Ask what your classmate does in the following places. He/She will respond with one of the activities listed. Then ask what your classmate does not do in those places.

MODELO en la clase
E1: *¿Qué haces en la clase?*
E2: *Veo películas en español.*
E1: *¿Qué no haces en la clase?*
E2: *No leo mensajes de texto.*

Lugares	Actividades
en la playa	beber cerveza
en un café	caminar
en una discoteca	bailar salsa
en una fiesta	mirar televisión
en el cine	leer las noticias
en la casa	ver películas de terror
en un restaurante	escribir mensajes de texto
en la biblioteca	comer un sándwich y tomar un café

1-33 A preguntar. PREPARACIÓN. Find four different classmates, each of whom does one of the following activities. Take notes about who does each activity.

MODELO ver videos en la computadora
E1: *¿Ves videos en la computadora?*
E2: *Sí, veo videos en la computadora.*

Persona	Actividad
	asistir a conciertos de música rock
	beber café todos los días
	vivir en casa con la familia
	escribir mensajes de texto en clase

INTERCAMBIOS. Now report to the class your findings about your classmates' activities.

1-34 ¿Qué deben hacer? For each situation, take turns saying what the person or people should do. Then create your own situation and your partner will give you advice.

MODELO Olivia desea sacar buenas notas.
Debe estudiar todos los días.

1. Carlos desea aprender sobre cine español.
2. Son las 12:30 y Luisa y Jorge están en la cafetería.
3. Los estudiantes tienen un examen en dos días.
4. Óscar desea aprender a bailar.
5. Son las 9:50. La clase de Camila es a las 10:00 y ella está en casa.
6. …

Situación

PREPARACIÓN. Read the following situation with your partner. Then brainstorm the vocabulary, structures, and other information you will need for both roles in the conversation.

Role A. You see a classmate at a coffee shop with a laptop and books spread out on the table. Ask if he/she:
a. drinks coffee in the coffee shop every day;
b. how often (**con qué frecuencia**) he/she studies there; and
c. whether he/she reads the news there.

Role B. You are sitting at a table with your laptop and books at your favorite coffee shop. A classmate walks over, greets you, and starts a conversation. Answer your classmate's questions about what you usually do there.

	ROLE A	ROLE B
Vocabulario	Greetings After-class activities Question words	Greetings After-class activities
Funciones y formas	Asking questions Present tense Addressing someone you know	Answering questions Present tense Addressing someone you know

INTERCAMBIOS. Using the information in **Preparación,** act out the conversation with your partner.

5 Specifying gender and number

MANUEL: Hola, Rocío. Tengo **un** plan. ¿Por qué no estudiamos español en **la** universidad esta tarde? Necesitamos **un** diccionario para **la** tarea y no tengo wifi en mi apartamento.

ROCÍO: ¡Buena idea! ¿En **la** biblioteca? **El** profesor de español es bueno, pero es **una** clase difícil. ¿Invitamos a Marcos?

MANUEL: Fenomenal. Usamos **la** pizarra y **el** escritorio del salón 12 de la biblioteca.

Piénsalo. Indicate if the words in **bold** refer to something or someone specific (**definido/a**) or not specific (**indefinido/a**). Use the context as clues.

	DEFINIDO/A	INDEFINIDO/A
1. Hola, Rocío. Tengo **un plan.**	____	____
2. ¿Por qué no estudiamos español en **la universidad?**	____	____
3. Necesito **un diccionario.**	____	____
4. ¿Estudiamos en **la biblioteca?**	____	____
5. **El profesor** es bueno.	____	____
6. Es **una clase** difícil.	____	____

Articles and nouns

Gender

- Nouns are words that name a person, place, or thing. In English all nouns use the same definite article *the*, and all singular nouns use the indefinite articles *a* and *an*. Spanish nouns, whether they refer to people or to things, have either masculine or feminine gender. Masculine singular nouns use **el** or **un** and feminine singular nouns use **la** or **una.**
- The terms *masculine* and *feminine* are used in a grammatical sense and have nothing to do with biological gender.

	Masculine	Feminine	
singular definite articles	**el**	**la**	*the*
singular indefinite articles	**un**	**una**	*a/an*

- Generally, nouns that end in **-o** are masculine and require **el** or **un,** and nouns that end in **-a** are feminine and require **la** or **una.**

  el/un libr**o** **el/un** cuadern**o** **el/un** diccionari**o**
  la/una mes**a** **la/una** sill**a** **la/una** ventan**a**

- Nouns that end in **-dad, -ción, -sión** are feminine and require **la** or **una.**

  la/una universi**dad** **la/una** lec**ción** **la/una** televi**sión**

- Nouns that end in **-ma** are generally masculine.

  el/un progra**ma** **el/un** proble**ma**
  el/un dra**ma** **el/un** poe**ma**

- In general, nouns that refer to males are masculine, and nouns that refer to females are feminine. Masculine nouns ending in **-o** change the **-o** to **-a** for the feminine; those ending in a consonant add **-a** for the feminine.

  el/un amigo **la/una** amiga
  el/un profesor **la/una** profesora

- Nouns ending in **-ante** and **-ente** may be feminine or masculine. Gender is signaled by the article (**el/la estudiante**).
- Use definite articles with titles when you are talking about someone. Do not use definite articles when addressing someone directly.

  La doctora García es **la** jefa del Departamento de Lenguas. **El** profesor Campos es **el** director del laboratorio. — *Dr. García is the chair of the Languages Department. Professor Campos is the director of the laboratory.*

  Todos los días, **el** profesor Campos dice: "Buenos días, doctora García". — *Every day, Professor Campos says, "Good morning, Dr. García."*

  Ella contesta: "Buenos días, profesor Campos". — *She responds, "Good morning, Professor Campos."*

Number

	Masculine	Feminine	
plural definite articles	**los**	**las**	*the*
plural indefinite articles	**unos**	**unas**	*some*

- Add **-s** to form the plural of nouns that end in a vowel. Add **-es** to nouns ending in a consonant.

  la silla → las silla**s**   el cuaderno → los cuaderno**s**
  la actividad → las actividad**es**   el señor → los señor**es**

- Nouns that end in **-z** change the **z** to **c** before **-es.**

  el lápiz → los lápi**ces**

- To refer to a mixed group, use masculine plural forms.

  los chic**os**   *the boys and girls*

¿Comprendes? Provide the correct definite article and indefinite article as indicated for the following nouns.

Definite articles: **el, la, los, las**   Indefinite articles: **un, una, unos, unas**

1. _____ compañera
2. _____ escritorio
3. _____ clases
4. _____ profesores
5. _____ mochila
6. _____ mesa
7. _____ señor
8. _____ universidades
9. _____ relojes
10. _____ mapa

PRÁCTICA

1-35 Conversaciones incompletas.

PREPARACIÓN. Complete the conversations on your own, and then compare answers with a classmate.

1. Supply the definite articles (**el, la, los, las**).

   En la universidad

   E1: ¿Dónde está María?
   E2: Está en _____ clase de _____ profesora Sánchez.
   E1: ¡Qué lástima! Necesito hablar con ella. Es urgente. ¿A qué hora llega?
   E2: Llega a _____ dos, más o menos.

2. Supply the indefinite articles (**un, una, unos, unas**).

   En la librería

   E1: Necesito comprar _____ lápices.
   E2: Y yo necesito _____ cuaderno. ¿Qué más compro?
   E1: Para los cursos de español, _____ estudiantes compran _____ diccionario, pero muchos estudiantes usan diccionarios electrónicos.

INTERCAMBIOS. With a partner, select one of the conversations to create and act out a similar situation.

 **1-36 ¿Qué necesitan?** Take turns saying what these classmates need. Then tell your partner what you should do and he/she will tell you what you need.

MODELO E1: *Alicia debe buscar el significado de unas palabras.*
E2: *Necesita un diccionario.*

1. Mónica debe tomar apuntes en la clase de historia.
2. Carlos y Ana deben hacer la tarea de matemáticas.
3. Alfredo debe estudiar para el examen de geografía.
4. Isabel debe escribir una composición para su clase de inglés.
5. Blanca y Lucía deben buscar las capitales de Sudamérica.
6. David debe marcar las partes importantes del libro de texto.
7. Yo debo…

 **1-37 ¿Para qué usamos estas cosas?** With your partner, look at the scenes. For each one, say where the item is located and what you usually do with it. Follow the model.

MODELO E1: *El libro está en la mesa.*
E2: *Leemos el libro para la clase de historia.*

1.

2.

3.

4.

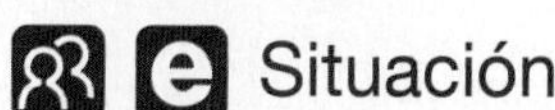

Situación

PREPARACIÓN. Read the following situation with your partner. Then brainstorm the vocabulary, structures, and other information you will need for both roles in the conversation.

Role A. You have missed the first day of class. Ask a classmate:
a. what time the class meets;
b. who the professor is; and
c. what you need for the class.

Role B. Tell your classmate:
a. the time the class meets;
b. the name of the professor and what he/she is like; and
c. at least three items that your classmate needs for the class.

	ROLE A	ROLE B
Vocabulario	Time Question words	Time Class materials Words to describe a person
Funciones y formas	Getting the attention of an acquaintance Asking questions Thanking someone	Answering questions Telling the time Describing someone Definite and indefinite articles

INTERCAMBIOS. Using the information in **Preparación,** act out the conversation with your partner.

MOSAICOS

ESCUCHA

Estrategia

Listen for the gist You can get the gist of what others are saying by relying on what you understand, your knowledge of the topic, and your expectations of what people say in different types of conversations. You will find these techniques helpful when listening to Spanish.

1-38 Preparación. You will hear two college students talking about their classes. Before you listen, think about the topics they may talk about and make a list of the things you may expect to hear, based on your experience as a student.

Comprueba

I was able to . . .
- identify the names of academic subjects.
- recognize places at the university.
- understand actions that refer to students' routines.

1-39 Escucha. Listen to the conversation between Ana and Mario and indicate whether each statement is true (**Cierto**) or false (**Falso**).

1. ______ Mario y Ana estudian en la misma (*same*) universidad este semestre.
2. ______ Mario toma clases de ciencias y humanidades.
3. ______ Ana lee en la biblioteca para sus clases.
4. ______ Mario realmente visita otros países en una de sus clases.
5. ______ Ana toma clases por la tarde.

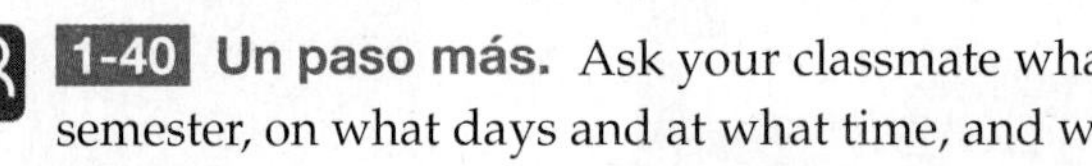

1-40 Un paso más. Ask your classmate what classes he/she is taking this semester, on what days and at what time, and what his/her classes are like. Then switch roles.

MODELO E1: *¿Qué clases tomas este semestre?*
E2: *Tomo…*
E1: *¿Cuándo es tu clase de…? ¿A qué hora es tu clase de…?*
E2: *Mi clase de… es los lunes… Mi clase de… es a las…*
E1: *¿Cómo son tus clases?*

HABLA

Estrategia

Ask questions to gather information Asking questions is a good way to start a conversation, and also to get information. To ask questions, you need to remember question words and common phrases, like **¿Cómo es/son…? ¿Cuándo…? ¿Dónde…? ¿Qué…? ¿Quién…? ¿Por qué?,** and so on.

Comprueba

I was able to . . .
- ask who, what, where, and when questions about academic life.
- answer questions about my classes.
- give information about my study routine.

1-41 Preparación. Listen again to the conversation between Ana and Mario in **Escucha.** Write four questions you hear.

1-42 Habla. Using the questions in **Preparación** as a model, prepare a set of four questions and use them to elicit the following information from your classmates.

- clases que toma este semestre
- cuándo es su clase favorita
- descripción de su clase favorita
- dónde estudia para sus exámenes

1-43 **Un paso más.** Share with the class the information you gathered in your group. Be sure to include the following:

- the classes taken by more than one person in the group
- the most common words the group used to describe their favorite classes

LEE

Estrategia

Identify the format of a text You have lots of reading experience in your first language with different types of texts. Before you start to read a text in Spanish, look at the illustrations, headings, and layout to help you make educated guesses about the content of the text.

Comprueba

I was able to . . .

- make educated guesses about a text based on what I already know.
- understand important information on a university webpage.
- interpret information that is presented visually.

1-44 **Preparación.** Discuss with a classmate which courses students should take for each of these majors: **Medicina, Bellas artes, Psicología, Filología.**

Anatomía	Drogas tóxicas	Historia de la lengua
Conflictos sociales	Estructura del español	Medicinas alternativas
Diseño gráfico	Fisiología	Muralistas mexicanos

1-45 **Lee.** Read the text and look at the photos of this webpage from the **Universidad de Salamanca.** Then choose the option that best completes each statement.

ESCUCHAR

Se imparten hasta 13 idiomas diferentes en formatos presenciales y semipresenciales, con múltiples horarios y niveles. Todo ello compone una oferta para completar tu formación a la que puedes acceder tanto si eres estudiante, como si eres profesor o personal de administración y servicios. Si eres un antiguo alumno, también puedes venir a nuestros cursos consultando nuestra oferta a través de la Asociación Alumni.

CONTACTA CON LA USAL SUGERENCIAS Y QUEJAS PERFIL DEL CONTRATANTE Sede Electrónica TRANSPARENCIA

1. Esta universidad es muy…
   a. nueva. b. antigua.
2. Es posible estudiar una lengua en...
   a. una clase con un/a profesor/a. b. internet.
3. La clase de la foto es...
   a. grande. b. pequeña.
4. Los horarios son...
   a. flexibles. b. fijos (*fixed*).
5. En clase los estudiantes usan...
   a. solamente lápices y cuadernos. b. computadoras y otros dispositivos (*devices*).

1-46 Un paso más. Use an internet search engine to access the website of the **Universidad de Salamanca Servicio Central de Idiomas.** Explain to your classmates: a) what languages you can study there; b) what the address of the office is; and c) why you would or wouldn't like to study at this university in Spain. Your classmates will ask you questions.

ESCRIBE

Estrategia

Brainstorm key ideas before writing Brainstorming helps you come up with good ideas for your writing. To brainstorm, write down a topic or a concept that you want to write about. Then list words and phrases that come to mind. Once you see your ideas laid out on paper, you can start to organize them for your writing.

1-47 Preparación. For your Spanish class, you have to respond to a text message from a university student in Spain. Read the message and write four questions to ask the student about his college life in Spain.

Hola, me llamo Pedro. Estudio francés y portugués en el Centro de Idiomas en la Universidad de Salamanca. Tengo cuatro clases. Mis clases son los lunes, martes y jueves. Los fines de semana practico deportes en el gimnasio o en el parque.
Hasta pronto,
Pedro

1-48 Escribe. Now write Pedro a text message about life at your college or university. Do the following:

- Introduce yourself.
- Describe your school and your classes.
- Describe your daily routine at school, what you do after classes and on weekends, etc.
- Ask some questions about college life in Spain.

Comprueba

I was able to . . .
- introduce myself in a text message.
- give information about my classes and daily routine.
- ask questions about university life in Spain.

1-49 Un paso más. Exchange your text message with a classmate. Then respond with a brief note and ask two additional related questions.

En este capítulo…

Vocabulario

Las materias/ asignaturas	*Subjects*
el análisis financiero	*financial analysis*
las ciencias naturales	*natural sciences*
las ciencias políticas	*political science*
la economía	*economics*
la estadística	*statistics*
el francés	*French*
la geografía	*geography*
la historia	*history*
la informática / la computación	*computer science*
el inglés	*English*
la literatura	*literature*
las matemáticas	*math*
la química	*chemistry*

Las facultades	*Schools, Departments*
de Administración y Dirección de Empresas	*of Business Administration and Management*
de Ciencias	*of Sciences*
de Derecho	*of Law*
de Humanidades	*of Humanities*
de Informática	*of Computer Science*
de Medicina	*of Medicine*

Los lugares	*Places*
la biblioteca	*library*
el café	*cafe, coffee shop*
la cafetería	*cafeteria*
la casa	*house, home*
la discoteca	*dance club*
el gimnasio	*gymnasium*
la librería	*bookstore*
la playa	*beach*
la plaza	*plaza, square*
la residencia estudiantil	*dorm*
la universidad	*university*

Las personas	*People*
el/la alumno/a	*student*
ellos/as	*they*
nosotros/as	*we*
ustedes	*you (plural)*
vosotros/as	*you (plural)*

Las descripciones	*Descriptions*
aburrido/a	*boring*
bueno/a	*good*
difícil	*difficult*
español/a	*Spanish*
estudioso/a	*studious*
excelente	*excellent*
fácil	*easy*
favorito/a	*favorite*
grande	*big*
interesante	*interesting*
pequeño/a	*small*
práctico/a	*practical*
responsable	*responsible*

Verbos	*Verbs*
aprender	*to learn*
asistir	*to attend*
bailar	*to dance*
beber	*to drink*
buscar	*to look for*
caminar	*to walk*
comer	*to eat*
comprar	*to buy*
comprender	*to understand*
conversar	*to talk, to converse*
correr	*to run*
deber	*should*
escribir	*to write*
escuchar	*to listen (to)*
estar	*to be*
estudiar	*to study*
hablar	*to speak*
leer	*to read*
llegar	*to arrive*
mirar	*to look (at)*
montar (en bicicleta)	*to ride (a bicycle)*
necesitar	*to need*
participar	*to participate*
practicar	*to practice*
responder	*to respond*
sacar buenas/malas notas	*to get good/bad grades*
tomar	*to take, to drink*
tomar apuntes/notas	*to take notes*
trabajar	*to work*
usar	*to use*
ver	*to see*
vivir	*to live*

Expresiones de frecuencia	*Expressions of frequency*
a veces	*sometimes*
muchas veces	*many times*
nunca	*never*
siempre	*always*
todas las semanas	*every week*
todos los días/meses	*every day/month*

Palabras interrogativas	*Interrogative words*
¿(a)dónde?	*where (to)?*
¿cómo?	*how?/what?*
¿cuándo?	*when?*
¿cuál(es)?	*which?*
¿cuánto/a?	*how much?*
¿cuántos/as?	*how many?*
¿para qué?	*why? / what for?*
¿por qué?	*why?*
¿qué?	*what?*
¿quién(es)?	*who?*

Palabras y expresiones útiles	*Useful words and expressions*
ahora	*now*
algo	*something*
¡Buena suerte!	*Good luck!*
¿Cómo te va?	*How is it going?*
con	*with*
¿Cuántas clases tienes?	*How many classes do you have?*
¿Cuánto cuesta?	*How much does it cost?*
el diccionario	*dictionary*
el examen	*test*
el euro	*euro*
el fin de semana	*weekend*
el mapa	*map*
para	*for, to*
pero	*but*
porque	*because*
¡Qué lástima!	*What a pity!*
solo	*only*
tengo/tienes	*I have / you have*

Capítulo 2

¿Quiénes son tus amigos?

Un grupo de amigos comparte un momento de *relax*.

Learning Outcomes

You will be able to:

- describe people, places, and things
- express origin and possession
- talk about where and when events take place
- describe what someone or something is like
- express emotions and conditions
- identify what belongs to you and others
- discuss the people, things, and activities you and others like and dislike
- talk about Hispanics in the United States in terms of products, practices, and perspectives
- talk about cultural stereotypes

Enfoque cultural
Estados Unidos

El Parque Dominó en la Pequeña Habana, Miami, FL

Mercado Central, Los Ángeles, CA

El Desfile Nacional Puertorriqueño de Nueva York

Arte hispano

La historia de California, realizado por la artista chicana Judy Baca, es el mural más largo (*long*) del mundo, con 840 metros. Celebra la diversidad y las contribuciones de las diferentes etnias en la historia de la región.

Enfoque cultural

¿Qué te parece?

- Los hispanos en Estados Unidos son el grupo minoritario más grande del país. Hay 58 millones de hispanos. Más del 63% de los hispanos son de origen mexicano.
- El español es la segunda lengua más hablada en Estados Unidos. Muchos jóvenes estudian español para su futuro trabajo, para conversar con otras personas y para los viajes (*trips*) y vacaciones.
- En 1988 el presidente Reagan declaró el período entre el 15 de septiembre y el 15 de octubre el Mes de la Hispanidad, días dedicados a celebrar la herencia y cultura hispanas en Estados Unidos.
- Los hispanos son influyentes en Estados Unidos en todas las áreas: la economía, la política, las artes, las ciencias, los medios de comunicación, la música, la gastronomía, los deportes y la industria del entretenimiento.

María Hojosa es una periodista (*journalist*) de origen mexicano. Trabaja en *Latino USA*.

Robert Rodríguez es un actor y empresario (*enterpreneur*) de origen mexicano. Es un profesional muy importante en Hollywood.

Alisa Valdés-Rodríguez, de origen cubano, es la autora de *The Dirty Girls Social Club*.

Aida Giachello es puertorriqueña. Es fundadora del Midwest Latino Health Research, Training, and Policy Center de la Universidad de Illinois-Chicago.

 **¿Cuánto sabes?** Select the correct option based on **Enfoque cultural.**

1. una periodista de origen mexicano
   a. María Hinojosa **b.** Jennifer López **c.** Robert Rodríguez
2. Se celebra durante las dos últimas semanas de septiembre y las dos primeras de octubre.
   a. el Mes de la Hispanidad **b.** la competencia de dominó en Miami
   c. la fiesta en la Calle Ocho
3. la segunda lengua más hablada en Estados Unidos
   a. el inglés **b.** el chino **c.** el español
4. una escritora latina
   a. Aida Giachello **b.** Alisa Valdés-Rodríguez **c.** Sonia Sotomayor
5. el 63%
   a. el porcentaje de personas que estudian español
   b. el porcentaje de personas bilingües en Estados Unidos
   c. el porcentaje de hispanos en Estados Unidos de origen mexicano

 To learn more about Hispanics in the United States, go online to view the *Club cultura* videos.

Describing yourself and others

Mis amigos y yo

Me llamo Horacio Rivera. Soy de Puerto Rico y **tengo** 22 **años. Me gusta** escuchar música y mirar televisión. Estudio en una universidad de Nueva York y **deseo ser** profesor de historia. Los chicos en estas fotografías son mis amigos. Ellos **también** son **hispanos** y estudian en la universidad. **Todos** somos **bilingües.**

Esta chica es Andrea Salvatierra. Es **alta, delgada** y **morena.** Tiene los **ojos de color café** y el **pelo negro** y muy **largo.** Andrea es una chica muy **agradable.** Estudia **mucho** y desea ser economista. Su familia es **dominicana,** pero vive en Estados Unidos.

Mi amigo Jorge Latorre no es alto **ni bajo.** Es **de estatura mediana,** y usa **lentes de contacto.** Es **pelirrojo** y tiene los ojos **oscuros.** Jorge es **callado, trabajador** y muy inteligente. Sus padres son **cubanos.**

Esta chica es Rosa Fuentes Álvarez. Es **española** y tiene 21 años. Es **rubia,** tiene los ojos **azules** y es muy **divertida.** Este **año** está en Estados Unidos con su familia.

Este chico se llama Antonio Martínez. Antonio es moreno y tiene los ojos **castaños** y el pelo **corto.** Es **guapo, fuerte,** muy **conversador** y **simpático. Le gusta** usar internet para hablar con sus amigos de aquí y de México.

PRÁCTICA

2-1 Escucha y confirma. Listen to people describe their friends. Then, indicate whether the statements are true (**Cierto**) or false (**Falso**).

1. ______ Pedro es callado y estudia mucho.
2. ______ Elena es rubia y alta.
3. ______ Juan y Roberto son muy trabajadores.
4. ______ Patricia es hispana y bilingüe.
5. ______ Rosa María es muy divertida.

2-2 Asociaciones. Select the name of the person that corresponds with each description, according to the information on page 65.

1. _____ Su familia es dominicana.	**a.** Horacio Rivera
2. _____ Tiene 22 años.	**b.** Andrea Salvatierra
3. _____ Es de España.	**c.** Antonio Martínez
4. _____ Le gusta usar internet.	**d.** Jorge Latorre
5. _____ Usa lentes de contacto.	**e.** Rosa Fuentes Álvarez

Lengua

Depending on the region or country, people use **moreno/a** or **negro/a** to refer to African ancestry and skin color. The word **moreno** is also used to refer to dark hair. The word **trigueño/a** (from **trigo,** *wheat*) is used to describe light brown skin color. **Corto/a** generally refers to length (**pelo corto**), while **bajo/a** refers to height (**Ella es baja**).

2-3 ¿Quién es?

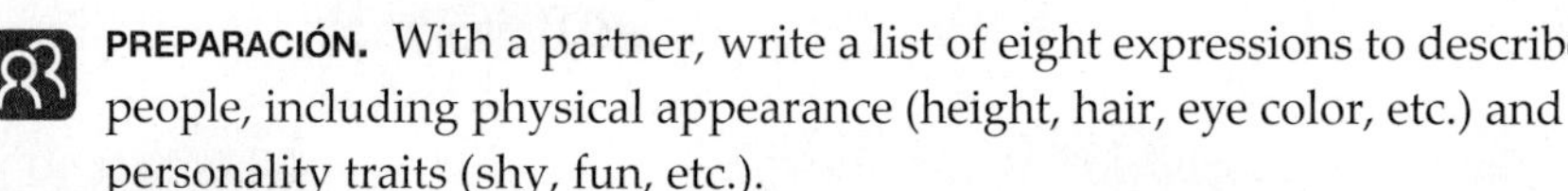

PREPARACIÓN. With a partner, write a list of eight expressions to describe people, including physical appearance (height, hair, eye color, etc.) and personality traits (shy, fun, etc.).

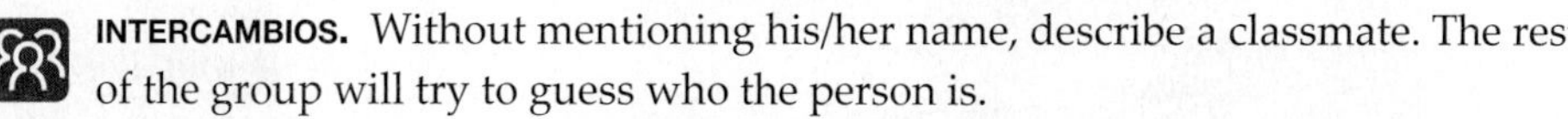

INTERCAMBIOS. Without mentioning his/her name, describe a classmate. The rest of the group will try to guess who the person is.

MODELO E1: *Es delgado y de estatura mediana. Tiene el pelo negro. Es fuerte y callado.*
E2: *¿Es…?*

2-4 ¿Qué me gusta? Tell your classmate if you like each of the following activities. Then compare your responses.

MODELO estar en casa por la noche
E1: *¿Te gusta estar en casa por la noche?*
E2: *Sí, me gusta.*

1. bailar los sábados por la noche
2. comer en restaurantes italianos
3. escribir mensajes de texto
4. estudiar español
5. practicar tenis/fútbol/béisbol
6. tener animales en casa
7. tomar café por la noche
8. trabajar los fines de semana

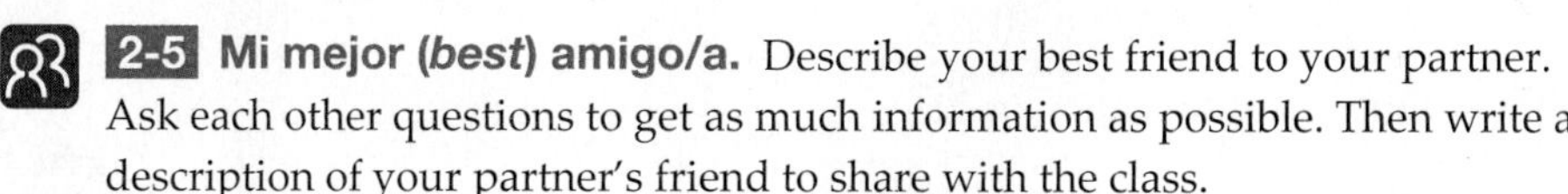

2-5 Mi mejor (*best*) amigo/a. Describe your best friend to your partner. Ask each other questions to get as much information as possible. Then write a description of your partner's friend to share with the class.

Las descripciones

¿Cómo son estas personas?

triste alegre

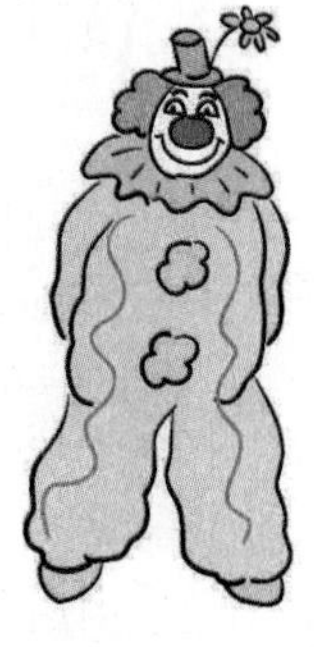

simpático/a antipático/a

trabajador/a perezoso/a

pobre rico/a

fuerte débil

listo/a tonto/a

joven mayor, viejo/a

casado/a

soltero/a

¿Cómo son estos animales?

Este **perro** es **gordo** y **feo,** pero es muy **cariñoso.**

Esta **gata** es **bonita,** pero es muy **delgada.**

Lengua

The word **la pierna** (*leg*) is used with humans. A human foot is **el pie.**

For animals and furniture, **la pata** is used to express both *leg* and *foot.*

¿De qué color son estas cosas?

Este **auto** es **rojo** y es muy bueno.

Esta **flor** es **amarilla** y **blanca.** Es muy bonita.

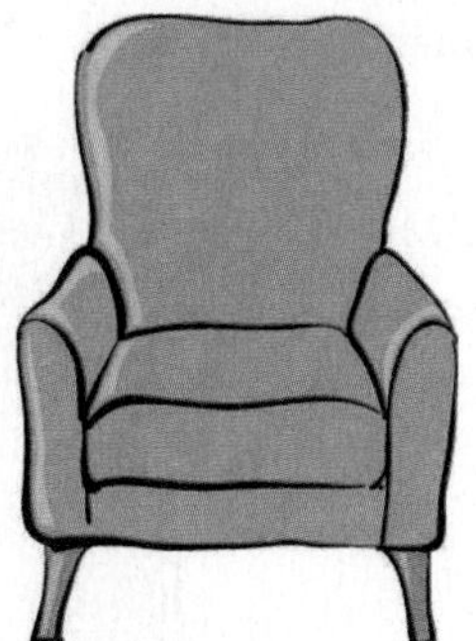

El **sillón azul** es grande.

La silla **verde** es **nueva.**

Otros colores

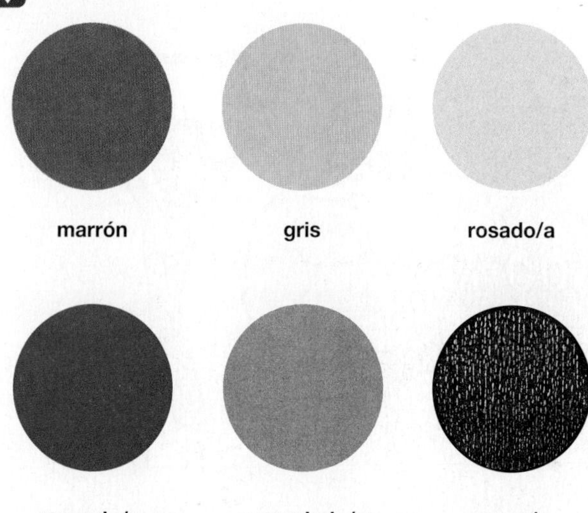

En otras palabras

Depending on the country and what is being described, Spanish has various words to express the color brown: **café, marrón, carmelita, castaño/a,** and **pardo/a.** The words **naranja** and **rosa** are also used instead of **anaranjado/a** and **rosado/a.**

PRÁCTICA

En otras palabras

Depending on the region, Spanish speakers may use **bonita, linda,** or **guapa** to refer to a female. **Bien parecido, buen mozo,** and **guapo** usually refer to a male.

  **2-6 Para confirmar.** Select the logical adjective to complete these descriptions of famous people. Then describe yourself to your partner in two affirmative (**Yo soy...**) and two negative (**No soy...**) statements.

MODELO Shakira no es mayor, es *joven.*

1. _____ Selena Gómez no es gorda, es...	**a.** trabajadora.
2. _____ Sofía Vergara no es perezosa, es...	**b.** lista.
3. _____ Jennifer López no es antipática, es...	**c.** delgada.
4. _____ Lady Gaga no es tonta, es...	**d.** rico.
5. _____ Bill Gates no es pobre, es...	**e.** guapo.
6. _____ Enrique Iglesias no es feo, es...	**f.** simpática.

 **2-7 ¿De qué color son estas banderas (*flags*)?** **PREPARACIÓN.** Read each description and then provide the country name for each flag. Check your answers with a partner.

- La bandera de Bolivia es roja, amarilla y verde.
- La bandera de Estados Unidos es roja, blanca y azul.
- La bandera de España es roja y amarilla.
- La bandera de México es verde, blanca y roja.
- La bandera de Colombia es amarilla, azul y roja.

a. ____________ b. ____________ c. ____________ d. ____________ e. ____________

INTERCAMBIOS. Invent a flag of different colors and describe it to your partner. He/She will draw it based on your description. Write the name of the colors on the flag if you do not have colored pencils.

 **2-8 Vamos a describir.** Take turns describing the people in these photos. Then describe your best friend to your partner.

Eva

Alicia y Raquel

Alejandro

José Luis

2-9 ¿Quién soy? **PREPARACIÓN.** Write a brief description of yourself including at least three physical traits, two personality traits, and two activities you like to do. Do not include your name on the paper.

 **INTERCAMBIOS.** In small groups, collect the descriptions and shuffle the papers well. Take turns reading them aloud so the group can guess who is being described.

El origen

¿De dónde son...?

Shakira

Shakira es de Colombia, es **colombiana.** Su antiguo compañero, Gerard Piqué, no es colombiano, es **español.**

Pitbull y Enrique Iglesias en los Latin Grammys

Pitbull (o Armando Pérez) es de Estados Unidos. La familia de Enrique Iglesias es **española** y la familia de Pitbull es **cubana**. Enrique Iglesias y Pitbull son bilingües; cantan (they sing) en inglés y en español.

PRÁCTICA

2-10 Para confirmar.

PREPARACIÓN. Indicate the origin of the following people. Verify your answers with a partner.

MODELO Luis Fonsi es un cantante (*singer*) famoso de Puerto Rico.
Es *puertorriqueño.*

1. Adrián Beltré es un jugador de béisbol de República Dominicana. Es ___________.
2. Sofía Vergara es una modelo y actriz de Colombia, protagonista de la serie *Modern Family*. Es ___________
3. Rigoberta Menchú es una activista de Guatemala, Premio Nobel de la Paz en 1992. Es ___________.
4. Franklin Chang-Díaz, de Costa Rica, es ingeniero y astronauta. Es ___________.
5. Isabel Allende es escritora, originaria de Chile, autora de *La casa de los espíritus*. Es ___________.
6. Ana Navarro es una comentadora de noticias (*news*) nacida en Nicaragua. Es ___________.
7. Mario Vargas Llosa es un escritor de Perú, autor de *La ciudad y los perros*, Premio Nobel en 2010. Es ___________.
8. Rafael Nadal es un tenista de España. Es .___________

INTERCAMBIOS. Tell your partner why one of the people in **Preparación** is interesting to you.

MODELO *Para mí, Rafael Nadal es un deportista muy interesante. Gana (*wins*) muchos torneos (*tournaments*).*

En directo

To explain why a person might interest you:

Me gustan sus canciones. *I like his/her songs.*
Escribe novelas fascinantes. *He/She writes fascinating novels.*
Me interesa su trabajo. *I am interested in his/her work.*
Baila/Canta/Cocina muy bien. *He/She dances/sings/cooks very well.*

 Listen to a conversation with these expressions.

2-11 Adivina (*Guess*). Think of a well-known person. A classmate will try to guess the person by asking you questions.

MODELO E1: *¿De dónde es?*
E2: *Es de Estados Unidos.*
E1: *¿Cómo es?*
E2: *Es moreno y muy cómico.*
E1: *¿Qué es? / ¿En qué trabaja?*
E2: *Es actor.*
E1: *¿Es Jack Black?*
E2: *¡Sí!*

Lengua

These are other examples of nationalities: **alemán/alemana** (*German*), **canadiense, chino/a, francés/francesa, japonés/japonesa, marroquí** (*Moroccan*), **nigeriano/a, polaco/a, portugués/portuguesa.**

Cultura

Puerto Rico Puerto Rico was a Spanish colony for almost four centuries until it was ceded to the United States following the Spanish-American War in 1898. Puerto Rico is a commonwealth (**estado libre asociado**) of the United States, and its people have been U.S. citizens since 1917. However, Puerto Rico remains geographically and culturally part of Latin America and almost all of its residents speak Spanish as their primary language. English is also widely spoken. Being bilingual opens doors to better economic opportunities in Puerto Rico and on the mainland.

Comunidades What other Hispanic groups have an important presence in the United States? Where is that presence evident—in business, science, music, media, art, food?

2-12 Entrevista. PREPARACIÓN. Prepare at least five questions to interview a classmate to get the following information.

1. his/her name
2. his/her age
3. what he/she is like (his/her personality)
4. the things he/she likes to do
5. where he/she is from

INTERCAMBIOS. Interview your classmate. Then write a short description of your classmate and share it with the class.

2-13 Presentaciones.

PREPARACIÓN. You will hear a student introduce and describe himself to his new classmates. Before you listen, indicate in the **Antes de escuchar** column the information you think you will hear. Then tell your partner what other information you would give about yourself.

	Antes de escuchar	Después de escuchar
1. name		
2. age		
3. parents' names		
4. physical description		
5. nationality		
6. place where he intends to work		

ESCUCHA. As you listen, pay attention to the general idea of what is said. Then, in the **Después de escuchar** column, indicate what information the speaker provided.

Mosaico cultural

Los estereotipos y la cultura hispana

¿Es verdad que los norteamericanos comen hamburguesas todos los días, que todos tienen armas y que no les gusta el ejercicio? Por otra parte, ¿es cierto que muchos españoles son toreros (*bullfighters*), que los mexicanos comen solo tacos y enchiladas o que todos los argentinos bailan tango? La respuesta a estas preguntas es: ¡de ninguna manera (*absolutely not*)!

Una sola característica no define una cultura completamente. Este tipo de comentarios causa conflictos en la comunicación entre las personas. Para comprender la diversidad cultural, es necesario evitar (*avoid*) ideas clichés porque no representan la totalidad de una comunidad o cultura.

Es necesario tener interés por otras culturas para evitar los estereotipos. Recuerda (*Remember*) que existen muchos españoles que no asisten a las corridas de toros (*bullfights*), muchos argentinos que no bailan tango y muchos norteamericanos que no comen hamburguesas todos los días.

¿Comes hamburguesas todos los días?

¿Eres torero?

¿Bailas tango?

Compara

1. ¿Cuáles son algunos estereotipos que se asocian con los norteamericanos? Prepara una lista en español.
2. De tu lista, ¿qué palabras son estereotipos que describen también a un hispano típico?
3. ¿Son siempre negativos los estereotipos? Explica con ejemplos.

En acción

Entre amigos en Los Ángeles

Antes de ver

2-14 La cultura hispana. Indicate the items typically associated with Hispanic cultures in the United States.

1. _____ el guacamole
2. _____ la lasaña
3. _____ la salsa
4. _____ el 4 de julio
5. _____ el festival de la Calle Ocho
6. _____ el lacrosse
7. _____ los tostones
8. _____ el español

Mientras ves

2-15 Dos ciudades. As you watch the video, indicate the qualities that describe Los Angeles, according to the characters. Then make a list of the activities that Blanca likes to do when she is in San Juan, Puerto Rico.

1. _____ Es una ciudad muy grande.
2. _____ Tiene mercados con productos latinos.
3. _____ Es una ciudad colonial.
4. _____ La mitad (*half*) de la población es hispana.
5. _____ Hay muchos puertorriqueños.
6. _____ Tiene edificios muy antiguos.

Después de ver

2-16 ¿Quién es?

e **PREPARACIÓN.** After watching the video, indicate whether the following statements refer to Esteban (**E**), Yolanda (**Y**), Federico (**F**), or Blanca (**B**).

1. _____ Es estudiosa.
2. _____ Es muy hablador.
3. _____ Es listo y simpático.
4. _____ Es vegana.
5. _____ Es puertorriqueña.
6. _____ Está triste.

INTERCAMBIOS. Take turns describing someone you know well or admire. Include two personality traits, two physical characteristics, and at least one activity that he/she likes to do for fun (**para divertirse**).

FUNCIONES Y FORMAS

1 Identifying and describing people, places, and things

Ana, Patricia y Teresa estudian mucho. Son inteligent**es** y trabajador**as.** Son de España.

Eduardo es atlétic**o** y fuert**e.** Es de Colombia. Adriana es muy elegant**e.** Es perua**na.**

Carlos, Luis y Carmen son sociabl**es** y activ**os.** Conversan y bailan mucho en las discotecas.

Piénsalo. Complete the descriptions of the people in the drawings by supplying their names.

1. _________ es pelirroj**a** y joven.
2. _________ es rubi**o** y alt**o.**
3. _________, _________ y _________ son estudios**as** y responsabl**es.**
4. _________, _________ y _________ son simpátic**os** y popular**es.**
5. _________ es colombian**o.**
6. _________, _________ y _________ son español**as.**

Adjectives

As you saw in **Capítulo 1,** adjectives are words that describe people, places, and things. Like articles (**el, la, los, las**) and nouns (**chica, chicas; libro, libros**), they generally have more than one form. In Spanish an adjective must agree in gender (masculine or feminine) and number (singular or plural) with the noun or pronoun it describes. Adjectives that describe characteristics usually follow the noun.

- Most masculine adjectives end in **-o,** and most feminine adjectives end in **-a.** To form the plural, these adjectives add **-s.**

	Masculine	Feminine
singular	el chic**o** alt**o**	la chic**a** alt**a**
plural	los chic**os** alt**os**	las chic**as** alt**as**

- Adjectives that end in **-e** and some adjectives that end in a consonant have the same form for both masculine and feminine. To form the plural, adjectives that end in **-e** add **-s;** those that end in a consonant add **-es.**

	Masculine	Feminine
singular	un libr**o** interesant**e**	una revist**a** interesant**e**
	un cuadern**o** azu**l**	una mochil**a** azu**l**
plural	unos libr**os** interesant**es**	unas revist**as** interesant**es**
	unos cuadern**os** azul**es**	unas mochil**as** azul**es**

- Other adjectives that end in a consonant add **-a** to form the feminine and **-es** or **-as** to form the plurals.

	Masculine	Feminine
singular	el alumn**o** españo**l**	la alumn**a** español**a**
	el alumn**o** hablado**r**	la alumn**a** hablador**a**
plural	los alumn**os** español**es**	las alumn**as** español**as**
	los alumn**os** hablador**es**	las alumn**as** hablador**as**

- For adjectives that end in **-ista,** the masculine and feminine forms are the same. To form the plurals, add **-s.**

Pedro es muy optim**ista,** pero Alicia es pesim**ista.** — *Pedro is very optimistic, but Alicia is pessimistic.*

Ellos no son material**istas.** — *They are not materialistic.*

e **¿Comprendes?** Complete each sentence with the correct form of the adjective.

1. Los habitantes de Puerto Rico son ______________. (puertorriqueño)
2. Ariana vive en Madrid. Es ______________. (español)
3. Los alumnos estudian mucho. Son muy ______________. (trabajador)
4. El color favorito de Javier es el negro. Su mochila es ______________. (negro)
5. Mis clases de economía no son interesantes; son muy ______________. (aburrido)
6. Me gusta mucho mi profesora de historia. Es muy ______________. (inteligente)

Cultura

Hispanos In Spanish-speaking countries, the adjective **hispano/a** emphasizes the common background among peoples, cultures, and countries where Spanish is spoken. In the United States, the word has come to mean somebody with roots in Spain or the Spanish-speaking countries of Latin America. In the Southwest, it refers to people who trace their ancestry to Spaniards who settled there when that area was part of Mexico. **Hispano** is not the same as **español,** which refers either to the Spanish language or to the nationality of people from Spain.

Conexiones Can you name a famous Hispanic person? A famous Spaniard?

PRÁCTICA

2-17 ¿Cómo son estas personas?

PREPARACIÓN. Select the correct option to describe the following people, and then check your answers with a partner.

1. Muchos estudiantes de mi universidad son…
   a. latinoamericano.
   b. hispanos.
   c. norteamericanas.
2. Mi profesora favorita es muy…
   a. jóvenes.
   b. activo.
   c. inteligente.
3. Mi amigo Nicolás es…
   a. español.
   b. dominicana.
   c. peruanos.
4. Las dos chicas más inteligentes de la clase son…
   a. activos y sociables.
   b. trabajadoras y estudiosas.
   c. interesante y optimista.

INTERCAMBIOS. Now take turns telling your partner about: 1) the students at your university; 2) your favorite professor; 3) a friend; 4) the most intelligent people in your class. Use at least three adjectives to describe each person.

Cultura

Bilingüismo Although Spanish is the common language spoken in Spain and most of Latin America, other languages are also spoken. In Spain, people in different regions speak Galician, Basque, or Catalan. In Latin America, large communities speak indigenous languages in Mexico, Guatemala, Peru, and Bolivia. Paraguay is officially a bilingual country, and most people speak both Spanish and Guarani.

Conexiones Do you know somebody who is bilingual? What are the advantages of being bilingual?

Señal (*Sign*) con el nombre de una calle en castellano y en euskera (vasco)

2-18 ¿Qué es? **PREPARACIÓN.** Write brief descriptions of each of the objects below, using the words in the list or other adjectives you know.

aburrido/a	excelente	moderno/a
alto/a	grande	nuevo/a
bajo/a	interesante	pequeño/a
bueno/a	malo/a	viejo/a

las sillas

la computadora

los libros

el concierto

1. Las sillas son…
2. La computadora es…
3. Los libros son…
4. El concierto es…

INTERCAMBIOS. Read one of your descriptions to the class, but without saying what you are describing. Your classmates will guess.

2-19 Cualidades necesarias. Your school has hired some recent graduates who were language majors. Indicate the qualities these new employees have and describe them to your partner. Your partner will mention additional qualities.

MODELO dos empleados bilingües en inglés y español

E1: *Los empleados bilingües hablan bien inglés y español. Son activos y extrovertidos.*

E2: *Sí. Son simpáticos, no son antipáticos. Hablan con los estudiantes y los profesores.*

1. dos especialistas en computadoras para el Centro de Lenguas

_____ activos _____ callados _____ competentes
_____ bilingües _____ agradables _____ trabajadores

2. una recepcionista para la Oficina de Admisiones

_____ imparcial _____ simpática _____ interesante
_____ perezosa _____ habladora _____ perfeccionista

2-20 Personas importantes.

PREPARACIÓN. Take turns reading the descriptions of the people in the photos. Then add one or two more sentences with additional details about them.

Michael Peña es un famoso actor de cine (*movies*). Es mexicoamericano.

Amara La Negra es una cantante y actriz de Miami. Es afrodominicana.

José Altuve es un jugador de béisbol muy bueno. Es venezolano.

Jaquira Díaz es una escritora puertorriqueña. Escribe ensayos (*essays*) y ficción.

INTERCAMBIOS. Now take turns describing someone important in your life. Your classmates will ask questions to get more information about that person.

Cultura

Usar el teléfono: hablar, textear Just like in the United States, smartphone use is increasingly common in Spanish-speaking countries. This means that telecommunication habits are changing also, including a preference for texting over voice phone conversations, and reserving phone calls for more formal purposes. When you talk on the phone or send a text, certain phrases can make the communication more effective.

Comparaciones For what purposes do you use your phone to call someone, rather than send a text message? Are there generational differences between your telecommunication practices and those of people in your family who are significantly older or younger than you?

Lengua

Here are some abbreviations to use in text messages:

hey, cm tas?	Hola, ¿cómo estás?
qtl?	¿Qué tal?
bn, tu?	Bien, ¿y tú?
a2	Adiós
hl	Hasta luego
cdt	Cuídate (*Take care*)

En directo

To address someone you don't know on the phone:

Hola, buenos días / buenas tardes.

To respond:

Buenos días... / Buenas tardes...

To greet someone you know on the phone:

Hola, ¿qué tal?

Soy María... / Habla María...

To respond:

¡Ah, hola!

¿Qué tal, María? / ¿Cómo estás?

 Listen to a conversation with these expressions.

Situación

PREPARACIÓN. Read the following situation with your partner. Then brainstorm the vocabulary, structures, and other information you will need for both roles in the conversation.

Role A. Your friend calls to tell you that he/she is dating someone new. After you greet your friend, ask:

a. where your friend's new boyfriend/girlfriend (**novio/a**) is from;
b. what he/she is like;
c. what he/she studies; and
d. if he/she has a car, what it is like.

Role B. You call your friend to talk about your new boyfriend/girlfriend. Your friend asks a lot of questions. Answer in as much detail as possible.

	ROLE A	ROLE B
Vocabulario	Adjectives of nationality Adjectives to describe people and things Colors School subjects Question words	Adjectives of nationality Adjectives to describe people and things Colors School subjects
Funciones y formas	Asking questions Talking about origin Noun–adjective agreement Present tense Using **tú** to talk to a friend	Giving information Talking about origin Noun–adjective agreement Present tense Using **tú** to talk to a friend

INTERCAMBIOS. Using the information in **Preparación,** act out the conversation with your partner.

2 Identifying and describing; expressing origin, possession, location of events, and time

Prince Royce **es** un artista muy talentoso y versátil. **Es** cantante y compositor. También **es** actor. Su nombre completo **es** Geoffrey Royce Rojas. **Es** de Nueva York y sus padres **son** de República Dominicana. **Es** famoso por sus bachatas, que **son** canciones populares dominicanas. Sus canciones **son** en español y en inglés. Sus conciertos **son** en Estados Unidos y en países latinoamericanos.

Piénsalo. Read the statements about Prince Royce. Select the meaning expressed by **es** in each sentence from the list.

1. _____ Prince Royce **es** de Nueva York.
2. _____ El próximo (*next*) concierto de Prince Royce **es** en California.
3. _____ La bachata **es** muy popular.
4. _____ La canción *Corazón sin cara* **es** de Prince Royce.
5. _____ Su nombre completo **es** Geoffrey Royce Rojas.

a. identificación
b. descripción
c. nacionalidad/origen
d. posesión
e. eventos (localización, hora)

Present tense of *ser*

- You have practiced some forms of **ser** and have used them for identification (**Esta señora es la profesora de historia**) and to tell time (**Son las cuatro**). Here are other uses of this verb.

SER (*to be*)			
yo	**soy**	nosotros/as	**somos**
tú	**eres**	vosotros/as	**sois**
Ud., él, ella	**es**	Uds., ellos/as	**son**

- As you have seen, **ser** is used with adjectives to describe an intrinsic feature of a person, place, or thing.

¿Cómo **es** ella? — *What is she like?*

Es atlética y extrovertida. — *She is athletic and outgoing.*

¿Cómo **es** el apartamento? — *What is the apartment like?*

El apartamento **es** pequeño pero **es** muy cómodo. — *The apartment is small, but it is very comfortable.*

- **Ser** is used to express nationality.

Gonzalo **es** chileno. — *Gonzalo is Chilean.*

Claudia **es** venezolana. — *Claudia is Venezuelan.*

- **Ser + de** is used to express origin.

¿**De** dónde **son** Gonzalo y Claudia? — *Where are Gonzalo and Claudia from?*

Gonzalo **es de** Chile. — *Gonzalo is from Chile.*

Claudia **es de** Venezuela. — *Claudia is from Venezuela.*

- **Ser + de** is used to express possession. The equivalent of the English word *whose?* is **¿de quién?**

¿**De quién es** el apartamento? — *Whose apartment is it?*

El apartamento **es de** Marta. — *The apartment is Marta's.*

- **Ser + de** is also used to express the material of which something is made.

El reloj **es de** oro. — *The watch is (made of) gold.*

Las sillas **son de** madera. — *The chairs are made of wood.*

- **Ser** is also used to express where an event takes place or the time of an event.

El concierto **es** en el estadio. — *The concert is (takes place) in the stadium.*

La clase **es** a las nueve. — *The class is (takes place) at nine.*

e **¿Comprendes?** Complete the sentences with the correct form of the verb **ser**.

1. Muchos jugadores de béisbol _______ de República Dominicana.
2. Nosotros _______ de la Ciudad de Guatemala. ¿De dónde _______ tú?
3. Mi amiga _______ extrovertida y habladora.
4. Las esculturas (*sculptures*) del artista _______ de madera.
5. El concierto de música clásica _______ mañana a las ocho.
6. Estos libros _______ de Jorge.

Lengua

Adjectives of nationality that end in a consonant form the feminine by adding **-a.**

español → español<u>a</u>

Note that the feminine and plural forms do not have a written accent.

francés → frances<u>a</u>

frances<u>es</u> → frances<u>as</u>

alemán → aleman<u>a</u>

aleman<u>es</u> → aleman<u>as</u>

Adjectives of nationality are not capitalized.

Lengua

Note that **de + el** contracts to **del,** but **de + la** and **de + los/las** do not contract.

El diccionario **es del** profesor, no **es de la** estudiante.

The dictionary is the professor's, not the student's.

PRÁCTICA

2-21 ¿Cómo somos? **PREPARACIÓN.** Look at the following statements and indicate if the descriptions are true for you.

	Sí	No
1. Yo soy muy estudioso/a y trabajador/a.	_____	_____
2. También soy callado/a.	_____	_____
3. Soy norteamericano/a.	_____	_____
4. Mis abuelos son de otro (*another*) país.	_____	_____
5. Mi familia es muy religiosa y tradicional.	_____	_____
6. Mi mejor amigo/a es extrovertido/a y conversador/a.	_____	_____
7. Mis amigos y yo somos sociables y activos.	_____	_____
8. Mis clases este semestre son interesantes.	_____	_____

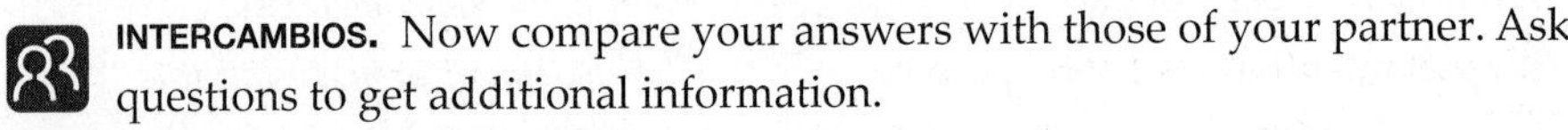

INTERCAMBIOS. Now compare your answers with those of your partner. Ask questions to get additional information.

2-22 ¿Cómo es? Ask what the following people, places, and objects are like.

MODELO tu profesor/a de inglés
E1: *¿Cómo es tu profesor de inglés?*
E2: *Es alto, moreno y muy simpático.*

1. tus amigos
2. tu cuarto (*room*)
3. tu compañero/a de cuarto
4. el auto de tu mejor amigo/a
5. los salones de clase de la universidad

2-23 ¿Qué es esto? Take turns describing an object and its location in the classroom. Your partner will ask you questions and then guess what it is.

MODELO E1: *Es grande, está al lado de la ventana…*
E2: *¿De qué color es?*
E1: *Es roja.*
E2: *¿Es de tela?*
E1: *No, es de plástico.*
E2: *¿Es la silla?*
E1: *Sí.*

> **Lengua**
>
> **Madera** (*wood*), **plástico, tela** (*fabric*), **metal, oro** (*gold*), and **vidrio** (*glass*) are some words used to identify the material things are made of.

2-24 Eventos y lugares. You are working at the university's information desk, and a visitor (your classmate) stops by. Answer his/her questions. Then switch roles.

MODELO la exposición de fotografía
E1: *Perdón, ¿dónde es la exposición de fotografía?*
E2: *Es en la biblioteca.*
E1: *¿Dónde está la biblioteca?*
E2: *Está enfrente de la Facultad de Ciencias.*

1. el concierto de música
2. la conferencia sobre el arte mexicano
3. la fiesta para los estudiantes internacionales
4. la reunión del club de matemáticas
5. el examen final del curso de español

 Situación

PREPARACIÓN. Read the following situation with your partner. Then brainstorm the vocabulary, structures, and other information you will need for both roles in the conversation.

Role A. A friend has invited you to a party at his/her house on Saturday. Ask:
a. where the house is located;
b. what it looks like (so you can find it easily); and
c. the time of the party.

Role B. You have invited a friend to a party at your house on Saturday. Answer your friend's questions. Then explain that the house belongs to your parents (**padres**), and tell your friend why your parents are not at home that weekend.

	ROLE A	ROLE B
Vocabulario	Question words Greetings Adjectives to describe the house	Time expressions Greetings
Funciones y formas	Asking questions **Ser** for where events take place **Estar** to express location Accepting an invitation appropriately	Expressing the time of an event **Ser** for where events take place **Estar** to express location Expressing possession **Ser** to express possession Giving information Extending an invitation appropriately

INTERCAMBIOS. Using the information in **Preparación,** act out the conversation with your partner.

3 Expressing qualities, emotions, and conditions

 La doctora Olivares enseña sociología. **Es** muy inteligente, simpática y amable, pero los estudiantes **están** aburridos en su clase porque la profesora **es** aburrida. La sociología **es** interesante, pero la profesora **es** monótona y sus presentaciones **son** desorganizadas. José, el alumno del suéter verde limón, **está** muy cansado. En general, los alumnos de esta clase **son** estudiosos y trabajadores, pero hoy **están** preocupados porque los exámenes de esta clase **son** difíciles.

e **Piénsalo.** Read the statements and indicate whether they describe **a)** a personality trait or an intrinsic characteristic, or **b)** a feeling or perception.

1. _____ Es muy inteligente.
2. _____ La profesora **es** aburrida.
3. _____ Sus presentaciones **son** desorganizadas.
4. _____ José, el alumno del suéter verde limón, **está** muy cansado.
5. _____ Los estudiantes **son** estudiosos y trabajadores.
6. _____ Pero hoy **están** preocupados.

Ser and *estar* with adjectives

Ser and **estar** are often used with the same adjectives. However, the choice of verb determines the meaning of the sentence.

- **Ser** + *adjective* states the norm—what someone or something is like.

José **es** delgado.	*José is thin.* (He is a thin man.)
La profesora **es** muy aburrida.	*The professor is boring.* (She is a boring teacher.)
Las presentaciones **son** desorganizadas.	*The presentations are disorganized.*

- **Estar** + *adjective* expresses a change from the norm, a condition, or how the speaker feels about or perceives a person, object, or experience.

Jorge **está** delgado.	*Jorge is/looks thin.* (He lost weight recently, or he looks thin in a picture or because of the clothes he is wearing.)
Sara **está** muy aburrida.	*Sara is very bored.* (She is feeling bored.)
El libro **está** nuevo.	*The book is/looks new.* (It is used, but it looks like a brand-new book.)

- The adjectives **contento/a, cansado/a,** and **enojado/a** are always used with **estar.**

Ella **está contenta** ahora.	*She is happy now.*
Los niños **están cansados.**	*The children are tired.*
Carlos **está enojado.**	*Carlos is angry.*

- Some adjectives have one meaning with **ser** and another with **estar.**

Ese señor **es** malo.	*That man is bad/evil.*
Ese señor **está** malo.	*That man is ill.*
La chica **es** lista.	*The girl is clever/smart.*
La chica **está** lista.	*The girl is ready.*
La manzana **es** verde.	*The apple is green.*
La manzana **está** verde.	*The apple is not ripe.*
La profesora **es** aburrida.	*The professor is boring.*
La profesora **está** aburrida.	*The professor is bored.*

e **¿Comprendes?** Complete the sentences with the correct form of **ser** or **estar.**

1. Nosotros ________ aburridos en la clase de física.
2. El profesor de la clase ________ malo. No explica bien el material a los estudiantes.
3. Las manzanas Granny Smith ________ verdes. Es su color natural.
4. Gabriela y Nicolás ________ muy listos. Sacan buenas notas en todas sus materias.
5. Julia, ¿________ cansada o enferma? ________ muy pálida (*pale*) hoy.
6. Mis amigos ________ enojados porque no hablo mucho con ellos.

PRÁCTICA

2-25 ¿Qué pasa aquí? Look at the scenes and then complete the description in each paragraph with the appropriate form of **ser** or **estar.** Check your answers with a partner. Take turns explaining why you chose **ser** or **estar** in each case.

Esteban (1) ______ un joven listo y estudioso. Este semestre saca buenas notas, excepto en la clase de economía. (2) ______ una clase muy difícil. Esteban (3) ______ nervioso porque mañana hay un examen sobre la Unión Europea, pero él no (4) ______ listo. Debe estudiar mucho esta noche.

¡Pobres niños! La fruta (5) ______ buena y saludable (*healthful*), pero estas manzanas (6) ______ verdes, no (7) ______ buenas. Ahora los niños no (8) ______ contentos. Una niña (9) ______ mala porque tiene dolor de estómago (*stomach ache*).

Mis amigos y yo (10) _______ similares. (11) _______ generosos y generalmente relajados (*laid back*). Pero esta semana, Fernando, por ejemplo, (12) _______ estresado (*stressed out*) porque tiene muchos exámenes. En general, yo (13) _______ tranquilo, pero esta semana (14) _______ un poco nervioso porque no (15) _______ listo para mi examen de biología.

2-26 ¿Cómo está ahora? You and your partner know the people mentioned in the table. One of you will describe a person, using an adjective from the list. The other explains how the person has changed and why. Then switch roles.

MODELO Arturo / fuerte / por su enfermedad (*illness*)
E1: *En general, Arturo es fuerte.*
E2: *Pero por su enfermedad, ahora está muy débil.*

Personas	Características	Razones
Ramón	alegre	por sus problemas
Laura y Diego	callado/a	por la dieta
Cristina	conversador/a	por el ejercicio
Andrés	débil	por el exceso de estudio
Sara y Sofía	extrovertido/a	por la falta (*lack*) de motivación
Lupita	feliz	por su depresión
	fuerte	por sus buenas notas
	introvertido/a	por las buenas noticias (*news*) en su familia
	optimista	
	perezoso/a	
	pesimista	
	trabajador/a	
	triste	
	romántico/a	
	responsable	

2-27 Termómetro emocional. **PREPARACIÓN.** Indicate how you feel in each situation.

aburrido/a	preocupado/a
contento/a	relajado/a
interesado/a	tranquilo/a
nervioso/a	triste

Lugar/Situación	Emociones
1. en la cafetería con mis compañeros	
2. durante la semana de los exámenes finales	
3. en la oficina de un/a profesor/a	
4. en un concierto de música *country* con mis amigos	
5. en una fiesta formal	
6. en mi casa por la noche	
7. en una presentación sobre el futuro del mundo	

INTERCAMBIOS. Talk with your partner about how you each feel in the situations given in **Preparación.** Then write a brief paragraph in which you compare your feelings and reactions with those of your partner.

MODELO *Me gusta la música. Estoy contento/a en un concierto de música* country, *pero mi compañero/a está aburrido/a porque le gusta el rock.*

Situación

PREPARACIÓN. Read the following situation with your partner. Then brainstorm the vocabulary, structures, and other information you will need for both roles in the conversation.

Role A. Show your classmate a photo (from your phone or the internet). Identify the people, the place where they are, and give some information about them. Then respond to your friend's questions and react to his/her comments about them.

Role B. After your classmate tells you about the people in the photo, ask and comment about:
a. how they seem to be feeling, based on their facial expressions or what they are doing; and
b. what the place in the photo is like.

	ROLE A	ROLE B
Vocabulario	Adjectives to describe people and places Professions	Question words Adjectives to describe people and places
Funciones y formas	Giving information **Ser** with adjectives to describe people **Ser** to express intrinsic characteristics **Estar** with adjectives to express perceptions about people **Estar** to express location	Asking questions **Estar** with adjectives to express perceptions about people **Estar** to express location Describing a location **Ser** to express intrinsic characteristics

INTERCAMBIOS. Using the information in **Preparación,** act out the conversation with your partner.

4 Expressing ownership

Mis amigos y yo

Mi nombre es Pablo Ramos. En esta foto, soy el chico de la camiseta (*T-shirt*) rosada. Soy estudiante en la universidad. Soy simpático, listo y sincero; por eso tengo muchos amigos. Estos son **mis** amigos. **Mi** mejor amigo se llama Luis. Tiene el pelo corto y es muy guapo. Al lado de Luis está Carmen. Entre Carmen y yo está Teresa, y a **mi** derecha está Ángela, la novia (*girlfriend*) de Luis. Es muy divertida. **Nuestras** amigas son activas y muy trabajadoras. **Sus** notas son excelentes. Y **tus** amigos, ¿cómo son?

Piénsalo. Select the alternative that best replaces the bolded phrases that signal possession.

1. En la foto están **los amigos de Pablo.**
   a. tus amigas   b. sus amigos   c. su amigo
2. Ángela es **la novia de Luis.**
   a. tu novia   b. nuestra novia   c. su novia
3. **La amiga de Teresa** es muy trabajadora.
   a. Su amiga   b. Tu amiga   c. Mi amiga
4. Teresa es **una buena amiga de Pablo.**
   a. mi amiga   b. sus amigas   c. su amiga
5. Pablo dice (*says*): "**Las amigas de Luis y mis amigas** son activas y muy trabajadoras".
   a. Nuestros amigos   b. Nuestras amigas   c. Tus amigas

Possessive adjectives

Possessive adjectives modify nouns to express possession. They always precede the noun they modify.

mi amigo | **tu** familia

POSSESSIVE ADJECTIVES	
mi(s)	*my*
tu(s)	*your* (familiar)
su(s)	*your* (formal), *his, her, its, their*
nuestro(s), nuestra(s)	*our*
vuestro(s), vuestra(s)	*your* (familiar plural)

- Possessive adjectives change number to agree with what is possessed, not with the possessor.
  mi clase | **mis clases**
- The **nosotros/as** and **vosotros/as** forms must agree also in gender.
  nuestro profesor | **nuestra profesora**
  nuestros amigos | **nuestras amigas**
- **Su** and **sus** have multiple meanings. To ensure clarity, you may use **de** + *the name of the possessor* or *the appropriate pronoun* instead of **su/sus.** For example, the multiple meanings of **su compañera** can be expressed as follows:

la compañera +
- **de ella** (la compañera de Elena)
- **de él** (la compañera de Jorge)
- **de usted**
- **de ustedes**
- **de ellos** (la compañera de Elena y Jorge)
- **de ellas** (la compañera de Elena y Olga)

e **¿Comprendes?** Complete the sentences with the appropriate possessive adjective.

1. _______ amigos y yo somos estudiantes.
2. Carla y _______ mejor amiga son muy activas.
3. Oye, Marcos, ¿cuándo es _______ clase de sociología?
4. Marcos y _______ amigos estudian sociología y español.
5. Elena, ¿son difíciles _______ clases este semestre?
6. Nosotros estudiamos en la biblioteca con _______ amigos todos los días.

PRÁCTICA

2-28 **¿De quién es?** Explain to your partner to whom each sentence refers. Follow the model.

MODELO Su libro es muy difícil. (Laura)
El libro de Laura es muy difícil.

1. Sus bicicletas son nuevas. (ellos)
2. Su clase de química es en el laboratorio. (Eva y Rosa)
3. Su auto es viejo pero es muy bueno. (Mario)
4. Su mochila está en el escritorio. (ella)
5. Sus amigas toman café juntas (*together*) todos los días. (ellas)

En otras palabras

The word for *car* varies across the Spanish-speaking world: **el auto** is more common in the southern half of Latin America, and **el carro** is more common in the countries to the north. In Spain, **el coche** is used.

2-29 Mi mundo (*world*). **PREPARACIÓN.** Make a list of two things you own (**pertenencias**) and two people you value. You may use the words from the lists or others.

Pertenencias	Personas
un auto	un/a amigo/a
una computadora portátil	un/a profesor/a ideal
una tableta	un actor / una actriz
dos bicicletas	un hermano / una hermana (*brother/sister*)
muchos libros	un/a compañero/a

INTERCAMBIOS. Take turns describing your selections. Then share with the class the similarities and differences between you and your classmate.

MODELOS **Pertenencias**

E1: *Yo tengo un auto. Es rápido y moderno. ¿Y tú?*
E2: *Yo también tengo un auto. / Yo no tengo un auto, pero tengo una bicicleta.*
E1: *¿Cómo es tu auto/bicicleta?*
E2: *Mi auto es rojo y muy viejo. / Mi bicicleta es liviana (*light*) y rápida.*

Personas

E1: *Mi madre es importante en mi vida (*life*). Es muy alegre. Y tu mamá, ¿cómo es?*
E2: *Mi madre es tranquila y muy inteligente.*

2-30 ¿Cómo es/son...?

PREPARACIÓN. Indicate the statements that apply to you. Then interview a classmate.

	Yo	Mi compañero/a
1. El auto de mi mejor amigo/a es blanco.	_____	_____
2. Mi compañero/a de cuarto es mexicoamericano/a.	_____	_____
3. Mis amigos hablan español.	_____	_____
4. Nuestro deporte (*sport*) favorito es el tenis.	_____	_____
5. Nuestra ciudad es muy grande.	_____	_____
6. Mis amigos son interesantes.	_____	_____

INTERCAMBIOS. Find one similarity and one difference between you and your partner to share with the class.

MODELO *Mi auto es blanco y pequeño. El auto de mi compañero/a es rojo y grande.*

2-31 Nuestra universidad.

PREPARACIÓN. With your group, list some words that describe the aspect of your university assigned by your instructor: **los profesores, las clases, los estudiantes, el campus, los equipos** (*teams*) **de fútbol/baloncesto, la cafetería** and **el laboratorio de computadoras.** Write four sentences about your topic. You must have at least one positive and one negative description.

INTERCAMBIOS. You have been asked to present an appealing view of your university to prospective students. Present your aspect of the university to the class. The class will decide which statements describe the school most accurately and in a more appealing manner.

Situación

PREPARACIÓN. Read the following situation with your partner. Then brainstorm the vocabulary, structures, and other information you will need for both roles in the conversation.

Role A. Call your best friend from high school and tell him/her about your new friends on campus. Describe each of them, including their ages, appearance, personalities, the activities you do together, and your favorite places.

Role B. Your best friend from high school calls you to tell you about his/her new friends in college. Ask questions about them and about their favorite activities and places.

	ROLE A	ROLE B
Vocabulario	Expressions to open, carry out, and close a phone conversation Age Adjectives to describe people Activities (verbs)	Expressions to open, carry out, and close a phone conversation Age Adjectives to describe people Activities (verbs) Question words
Funciones y formas	Making a phone call Describing people **Ser** Talking about age **Tener** Giving information about people, activities, and places	Answering a phone call Asking questions

INTERCAMBIOS. Using the information in **Preparación,** act out the conversation with your partner.

5 Expressing likes and dislikes

Marisa, una estudiante mexicoamericana, chatea con Camila por internet. Camila es venezolana, pero vive en Princeton, Nueva Jersey. Ellas forman parte de un grupo de jóvenes interesados en temas hispanos.

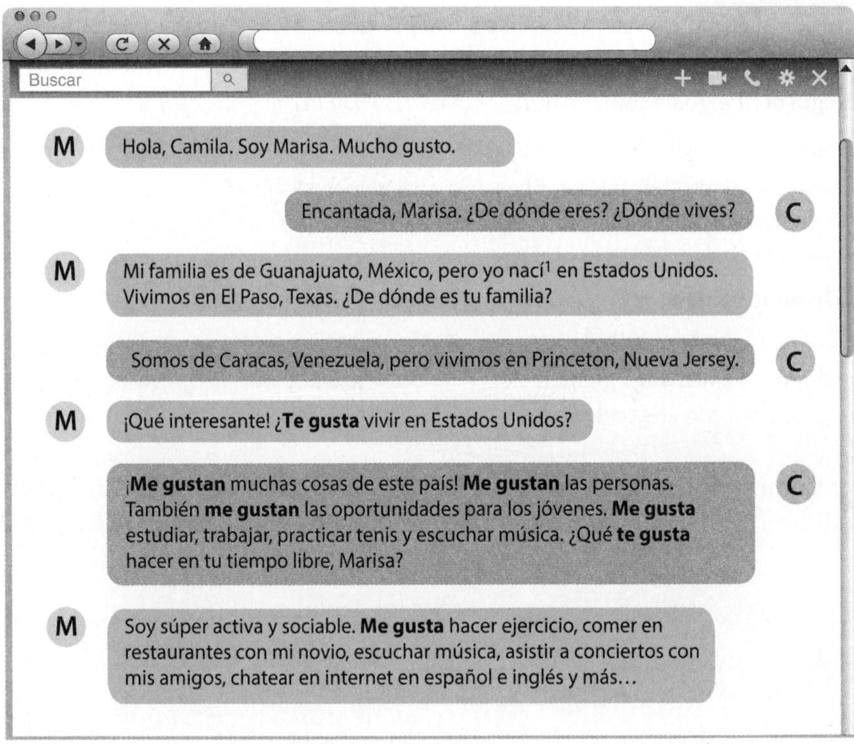

[1] *was born*

Piénsalo. Select the correct option(s) to complete each statement or question, based on Marisa and Camila's conversation.

1. ______ **Me gusta…**
2. ______ **Me gustan…**
3. ______ **¿Te gusta…?**
4. ______ **¿Qué te gusta…?**

a. hacer cuando no tienes tarea
b. el ejercicio
c. vivir en este país
d. las posibilidades que ofrece Estados Unidos
e. ser bilingüe
f. estudiar y trabajar

Gustar

- To express what you like to do, use **me gusta** + *infinitive.* To express what you don't like to do, use **no me gusta** + *infinitive.*

Me gusta hablar español.	*I like to speak Spanish.*
No me gusta mirar televisión.	*I don't like to watch television.*
Me gusta practicar deportes y salir con mis amigos.	*I like to play sports and go out with my friends.*

- To express that you like something or someone, use **me gusta** + *singular noun* or **me gustan** + *plural noun.*

Me gusta la música clásica.	*I like classical music.*
Me gustan las personas alegres.	*I like happy people.*

- To ask a classmate what he/she likes, use **¿Te gusta(n)…?** To ask your instructor, use **¿Le gusta(n)…?**

¿Te gusta / Le gusta tomar café?	*Do you like to drink coffee?*
¿Te gustan / Le gustan los chocolates?	*Do you like chocolates?*

- To state what another person likes, use **a** + *name of person* + **le gusta(n)…** When you are talking about the preferences of more than one person, use **a** + *names* + **les gusta(n)…**

A Diego le gustan las fiestas.	*Diego likes parties.*
A Carlos le gusta el fútbol.	*Carlos likes soccer.*
A Diego y a Carlos les gusta ir de vacaciones con sus padres.	*Diego and Carlos like to go on vacation with their parents.*

e **¿Comprendes?** Complete the mini conversations about people's likes and dislikes with the appropriate phrase: **me gusta(n), te gusta(n),** or **le gusta(n).**

1. LAURA: ¿_________ el básquetbol, Gonzalo?
GONZALO: Sí, _________ todos los deportes.

2. JULIÁN: A Carmen _________ bailar salsa y merengue.
ALEJANDRA: A mí no _________ bailar.

3. FRANCISCO: ¿_________ mirar televisión, Horacio?
HORACIO: Un poco. _________ las comedias y las telenovelas.

PRÁCTICA

2-32 ¿Te gusta...?

PREPARACIÓN. Ask a classmate if he/she likes the following. Be sure to ask follow-up questions as appropriate.

1. el gimnasio de la universidad
2. estudiar informática
3. los autos híbridos
4. los animales, como los gatos, los perros y las serpientes
5. asistir a conciertos de música clásica
6. escuchar la música de Taylor Swift

INTERCAMBIOS. Write a brief note to another classmate in which you share two pieces of information about yourself and two pieces of information you discovered about your partner.

2-33 ¿Qué te gusta más? **PREPARACIÓN.** Take turns asking each other which option you like more. Explain your preferences.

MODELO el verano o el invierno
E1: *¿Qué te gusta más, el verano o el invierno?*
E2: *Me gusta más el verano porque me gusta caminar por la playa.*

1. la música *reggae* o el *jazz*
2. hablar por teléfono o escribir mensajes de texto
3. los Yankees de Nueva York o los Medias Rojas de Boston
4. los restaurantes mexicanos o los restaurantes italianos
5. ver videos cómicos en YouTube o mirar películas (*movies*) de terror en internet
6. los teléfonos inteligentes o las tabletas
7. caminar por el parque o nadar en la playa
8. las hamburguesas o los tacos

INTERCAMBIOS. Tell a different classmate one similarity and one difference regarding your preferences and those of the classmate you interviewed in **Preparación.**

2-34 Mis preferencias. **PREPARACIÓN.** Indicate your preferences for these activities.

Actividad	Me gusta mucho	Me gusta un poco	No me gusta
1. conversar con otras personas en español			
2. comer comida mexicana			
3. cantar karaoke			
4. escuchar música en español y cantar en español			
5. aprender sobre la cultura de otros países			
6. preparar comida en casa			
7. chatear y hablar cara a cara (*face-to-face*) con mis amigos/as			
8. bailar salsa			

INTERCAMBIOS. Compare your answers with those of a classmate. Share with the class one similarity and one difference in your preferences.

2-35 ¿Qué te gusta hacer? **PREPARACIÓN.** Write down some questions that you would ask a classmate to find out the following.

1. what he/she likes to do alone in his/her free time
2. what he/she likes to do with his/her friends

INTERCAMBIOS. Interview two classmates and ask each of them the questions you prepared in **Preparación.** Compare their responses and share your conclusions with the class.

 **2-36 La compatibilidad en la amistad (*friendship*).** **PREPARACIÓN.** With your partner, do the following:

- Write four words related to personality traits that are important to you in a friend (e.g., **honesto/a, amable**) and four activities that you like to do with your friends (e.g., **practicar deportes, comer y bailar**).
- Write five questions that you and your partner would ask to determine if a person is someone you would like to spend time with. For example, if you said that you like to play sports, you may ask: **¿Te gustan los deportes? / ¿Te gusta practicar deportes?**

INTERCAMBIOS. Now ask another classmate the five questions that you and your partner wrote in **Preparación.** Take notes.

Situación

PREPARACIÓN. Read the following situation with your partner. Then brainstorm the vocabulary, structures, and other information you will need for both roles in the conversation.

Role A. You are at a park where you hear someone giving commands to a dog in Spanish. Break the ice and introduce yourself. Ask:
a. the person's name;
b. the dog's name and age; and
c. if the dog is docile (**manso/a**).

Compliment the dog (smart, strong, very pretty, etc.). Tell the person that you like dogs very much and that you also like cats. Answer the questions this person asks.

Role B. You are in the park with your dog and someone approaches. Answer this person's questions and:
a. ask if he/she has a dog, and if so, what it looks like;
b. say that you don't like cats and say why you don't like them; and
c. ask where this person is from and where he/she is studying Spanish.

	ROLE A	ROLE B
Vocabulario	Greetings and introductions Adjectives to describe pets Likes and dislikes Question words	Greetings and introductions Adjectives to describe pets Likes and dislikes Question words
Funciones y formas	Asking questions Giving information Describing animals **Ser** **(No) Gustar** to express likes and dislikes	Asking and answering questions Giving information Describing animals **Ser** **(No) Gustar** to express likes and dislikes

INTERCAMBIOS. Using the information in **Preparación,** act out the conversation with your partner.

MOSAICOS

ESCUCHA

Estrategia

Listen for specific information When someone talks about something of interest to you, he/she may provide not only the information you want to hear, but also additional information. To listen effectively, focus on the information that interests you. This will help you remember it afterwards.

2-37 Preparación. You will listen to a young woman talk about what she and her friends like to do. Before listening, tell a classmate one activity that you like to do alone and one that you like to do with your friends. Then say one activity that your best friend likes to do. Your partner will do the same. Take notes about what you hear.

2-38 Escucha. Listen to Elena talk about what she and her friends like to do. Then indicate who likes to do each activity: **Elena, Pilar,** or **Elena y sus amigos.**

	Elena	Pilar	Elena y sus amigos
1. caminar por la playa			
2. ir (*to go*) al gimnasio			
3. cantar e imitar a cantantes			
4. visitar otros lugares			
5. la música y las películas (*movies*)			
6. leer			

2-39 Un paso más. Use your notes from **2-37** to write a comparison between what your classmate likes to do alone and with his/her friends, and what Elena, the person in **2-38,** likes to do alone and with her friends. Share your comparison with the class.

Comprueba

I was able to . . .

- recognize the names of people.
- associate specific information with each person or group.
- recognize words that refer to likes and preferences.
- recognize words that refer to descriptions of people.

HABLA

Estrategia

Describe a person Descriptions are most effective when they are well organized. For example, you may want to include demographic information (e.g., age, nationality/origin), physical characteristics, personality traits, and accomplishments. A well-organized description presents information by category, beginning with an introductory statement to orient your listener.

2-40 Preparación. Exchange photos of two of your friends. Take notes on the following: a) the place where each friend is, and b) the physical appearance of each friend.

Comprueba

I was able to . . .

- organize my description.
- use a variety of descriptive words.
- talk about my activities alone and with my friends.
- ask clear questions.
- give clear information in response to questions.

 **2-41 Habla.** Take turns asking each other questions about: a) your friends' personalities; b) activities that both of you like to do alone, and c) activities that both of you like to do with your friends. React to your partner's comments and answer questions. Take notes.

En directo

To introduce information about physical characteristics:

En cuanto a lo físico... / Físicamente, es... *In terms of physical appearance . . . / Physically, he/she is . . .*

To introduce information about personality:

Es una persona... / Tiene un carácter... *He/She is a . . . person. / He/She has a . . . character/personality.*

 Listen to a conversation with these expressions.

2-42 Un paso más. Write a paragraph describing your classmate's two friends and yours. Include some similarities and some differences among your friends and those of your classmate. Indicate one or two activities that you and your partner like to do alone, and one or two activities that you and your partner like to do with your friends.

LEE

Estrategia

Scan a text for specific information When you read in Spanish, you can search for particular pieces of information you think will be in the text. Often the comprehension questions after the text will help you decide what information to search for as you read. This approach to reading, called *scanning,* works best if you: a) focus on the information you are seeking, and b) read the text through quickly at least twice, looking for specific information each time.

 **2-43 Preparación.** Read the title of the text in activity **2-44** and examine its format. What type of text is it: a series of e-mail messages, personal ads, or ads for items for sale? Then, with your partner, indicate the qualities that you appreciate most in a partner/friend and say why.

a. _____ sociable
b. _____ simpático/a
c. _____ divertido/a
d. _____ perfeccionista
e. _____ mayor
f. _____ flexible
g. _____ trabajador/a
h. _____ ocupado/a

2-44 Lee. Read the text and scan it for the information about Susana, Ricardo, Pablo, and Valentina that you need to complete the chart. In some cases, it may not be possible to provide all of the information requested.

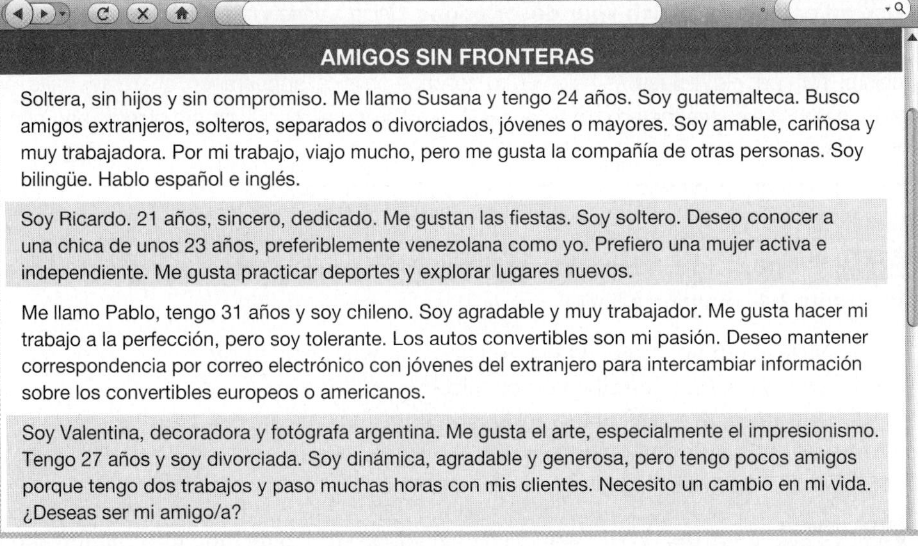

AMIGOS SIN FRONTERAS

Soltera, sin hijos y sin compromiso. Me llamo Susana y tengo 24 años. Soy guatemalteca. Busco amigos extranjeros, solteros, separados o divorciados, jóvenes o mayores. Soy amable, cariñosa y muy trabajadora. Por mi trabajo, viajo mucho, pero me gusta la compañía de otras personas. Soy bilingüe. Hablo español e inglés.

Soy Ricardo. 21 años, sincero, dedicado. Me gustan las fiestas. Soy soltero. Deseo conocer a una chica de unos 23 años, preferiblemente venezolana como yo. Prefiero una mujer activa e independiente. Me gusta practicar deportes y explorar lugares nuevos.

Me llamo Pablo, tengo 31 años y soy chileno. Soy agradable y muy trabajador. Me gusta hacer mi trabajo a la perfección, pero soy tolerante. Los autos convertibles son mi pasión. Deseo mantener correspondencia por correo electrónico con jóvenes del extranjero para intercambiar información sobre los convertibles europeos o americanos.

Soy Valentina, decoradora y fotógrafa argentina. Me gusta el arte, especialmente el impresionismo. Tengo 27 años y soy divorciada. Soy dinámica, agradable y generosa, pero tengo pocos amigos porque tengo dos trabajos y paso muchas horas con mis clientes. Necesito un cambio en mi vida. ¿Deseas ser mi amigo/a?

	Susana	Ricardo	Pablo	Valentina
1. edad				
2. nacionalidad				
3. estado civil				
4. personalidad (uno o dos adjetivos)				
5. le gusta(n)...				

2-45 Un paso más. Find the best match for Susana, Ricardo, Pablo, and Valentina from the following responses received. Share your findings with the class.

1. Tengo 22 años y me gustan todos los deportes. Mis padres viven en Caracas, pero yo vivo en Miami.
2. Enseño (*I teach*) arte en la escuela secundaria. Tengo tiempo para mis amigos los fines de semana.
3. Soy de Nicaragua. Soy muy sociable y deseo perfeccionar mi inglés.
4. Trabajo para *Autos de hoy,* una publicación de internet.

Comprueba

I was able to . . .

- identify the type of text.
- find the information I was looking for in each text.
- recognize important words.

ESCRIBE

Estrategia

Use adjectives to enrich your descriptions Using a variety of adjectives will make your descriptions more vivid and interesting. With objects, use adjectives that describe shapes or colors. With people, adjectives help you to describe physical appearance, character traits, and personality. Make sure the adjectives agree in gender and number with the objects and people they describe.

2-46 Preparación. Prepare to write your own personal ad by rereading the ones in activity **2-44.** Prepare a list of:

1. facts about your age, where you are, and what you study
2. adjectives that describe you physically
3. adjectives that describe your personality
4. activities you like to do

Comprueba

I was able to . . .

- give details about myself.
- describe my interests and activities.
- describe the type of person I am looking for.

2-47 Escribe. Write your personal ad. Be sure to include information about yourself and the type of person you are looking for.

2-48 Un paso más. Exchange personal ads with your partner. Write a brief response to the ad in which you mention things the two of you have in common.

En este capítulo...

Vocabulario

Las descripciones	Descriptions
agradable	*nice*
alegre	*happy, glad*
alto/a	*tall*
antipático/a	*unpleasant*
bajo/a	*short (in stature)*
bilingüe	*bilingual*
bonito/a	*pretty*
callado/a	*quiet*
cansado/a	*tired*
cariñoso/a	*affectionate*
casado/a	*married*
contento/a	*happy, glad*
conversador/a	*talkative*
corto/a	*short (in length)*
de estatura mediana	*average, medium height*
débil	*weak*
delgado/a	*thin*
divertido/a	*funny, amusing*
enojado/a	*angry*
feo/a	*ugly*
fuerte	*strong*
gordo/a	*fat*
guapo/a	*good-looking, handsome*
hispano/a	*Hispanic*
joven	*young*
largo/a	*long*
listo/a	*smart; ready*
mayor	*old*
moreno/a	*dark-haired; dark-skinned*
nuevo/a	*new*
oscuro/a	*dark*
pelirrojo/a	*redhead*
perezoso/a	*lazy*
pobre	*poor*
rico/a	*rich, wealthy*
rubio/a	*blond*
simpático/a	*nice, charming*
soltero/a	*single*
tonto/a	*silly, foolish*
trabajador/a	*hardworking*
triste	*sad*
viejo/a	*old*

Los colores	Colors
amarillo/a	*yellow*
anaranjado/a	*orange*
azul	*blue*
blanco/a	*white*
castaño/a	*brown*
de color café	*brown*
gris	*gray*
marrón	*brown*
morado/a	*purple*
negro/a	*black*
rojo/a	*red*
rosado/a	*pink*
verde	*green*

Las nacionalidades	Nationalities
argentino/a	*Argentinian*
boliviano/a	*Bolivian*
chileno/a	*Chilean*
colombiano/a	*Colombian*
costarricense	*Costa Rican*
cubano/a	*Cuban*
dominicano/a	*Dominican*
ecuatoriano/a	*Ecuadorian*
español/a	*Spanish*
guatemalteco/a	*Guatemalan*
hondureño/a	*Honduran*
mexicano/a	*Mexican*
nicaragüense	*Nicaraguan*
norteamericano/a	*North American*
panameño/a	*Panamanian*
paraguayo/a	*Paraguayan*
peruano/a	*Peruvian*
puertorriqueño/a	*Puerto Rican*
salvadoreño/a	*Salvadoran*
uruguayo/a	*Uruguayan*
venezolano/a	*Venezuelan*

Verbos	Verbs
desear	*to wish, to want*
gustar	*to like, to be pleasing to*
ser	*to be*

Palabras y expresiones útiles	Useful words and expressions
el auto	*car*
la cosa	*thing*
de	*of, from*
¿de quién?	*whose?*
del	*of the (contraction of* **de** + **el**)
el/la esposo/a	*husband/wife*
la flor	*flower*
el/la gato/a	*cat*
los lentes de contacto	*contact lenses*
mucho (*adv.*)	*much, a lot*
mucho/a (*adj.*)	*many*
el ojo	*eye*
el pelo	*hair*
el/la perro/a	*dog*
ni	*nor*
también	*also, too*
Tengo… años.	*I am… years old.*
el sillón	*armchair*
tiene	*he/she has; you (formal) have*
todos/as	*everybody*

See page 88 for possessive adjectives.

Capítulo 3
¿Qué hacen para divertirse?

Dos amigos se divierten cerca de Cuzco, Perú.

Learning Outcomes

You will be able to:

- describe free-time activities and talk about food
- plan your daily activities and express intentions
- identify prices and dates
- state what and whom you know
- talk about Peru in terms of products, practices, and perspectives
- share information about free-time activities in Hispanic countries and identify cultural similarities

Enfoque cultural
Perú

Las islas flotantes de los uros, en el lago Titicaca

El festival Inti Raymi, en el centro de Cuzco

Preparando comida para una boda (*wedding*)

Arte hispano

En este cuadro anónimo del siglo XVIII, vemos la boda entre la princesa inca Beatriz Clara Coya y un noble español, el capitán Don Martín de Loyola.

Enfoque cultural

¿Qué te parece?

- La papa es originaria de Perú. Existen más de 3.000 variedades de este tubérculo.
- Desde la época de los incas hasta ahora, Perú es el principal productor de oro (*gold*) del mundo.
- Inca Kola es el refresco más popular en Perú por su intenso sabor (*flavor*) producido por infusiones de diferentes hierbas naturales, como la verbena o la hierba luisa.
- La llama y la alpaca son animales que viven en los Andes peruanos.

Machu Picchu, fortaleza y santuario de los emperadores incas en el siglo XV, hoy es una ruina arqueológica muy importante. El mundo recibe las primeras noticias (*news*) de este lugar en 1911 por medio del explorador norteamericano Hiram Bingham.

La marinera es uno de los bailes más bonitos y populares de Perú. Todos los años hay un festival de marinera en la ciudad de Trujillo, en la costa norte del país.

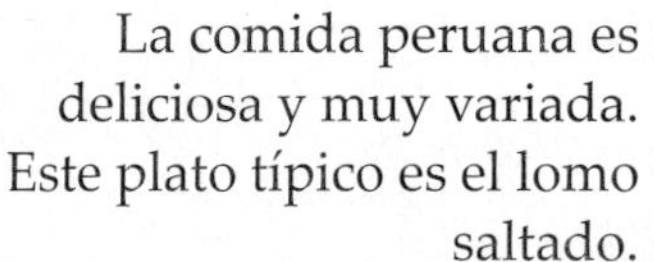

La comida peruana es deliciosa y muy variada. Este plato típico es el lomo saltado.

¿Cuánto sabes? Complete the sentences with the correct word(s), based on **Enfoque cultural.**

1. __________ es uns antigua e importante ciudad de Trujillo.
2. La __________ es un animal que vive en los Andes peruanos.
3. Inca Kola es un __________ con sabor a verbena.
4. En Perú existen más de 3.000 variedades de __________.
5. Inti Raymi es un __________ peruano.

To learn more about Peru, go online to view the *Club cultura* videos.

VOCABULARIO EN CONTEXTO

Talking about free-time activities, plans, and food

Las diversiones

Muchas personas van a la playa en su **tiempo libre** y también **durante** las **vacaciones.** La playa de Punta Hermosa, al sur de Lima, Perú, es buena para **practicar deportes** como el surf. Otras personas **nadan en el mar, toman el sol** y **descansan.**

Estos **jóvenes** están en un **restaurante** peruano y **van a** comer. Les gustan las **reuniones** con los amigos. A veces escuchan **música** y bailan en las **fiestas,** o **tocan la guitarra** y **cantan canciones** populares.

Estos chicos conversan en un café de su **ciudad.** Algunos leen las **noticias en línea** o **comparten** fotos en sus **redes sociales;** otros juegan (*play*) **videojuegos.**

Un **hombre** y una **mujer** miran televisión en casa. También es común ir al **cine para ver películas,** especialmente los fines de semana.

PRÁCTICA

3-1 Escucha y confirma. Listen to the descriptions. Indicate the places where people do the activities you hear.

	(house)	(beach)	(cinema)	(restaurant)
1.				
2.				
3.				
4.				
5.				
6.				

3-2 Asociaciones. Select the activity that corresponds to each place. Compare your answers with those of a classmate and say what other activities you do in those places.

1. _____ la playa
2. _____ la discoteca
3. _____ el cine
4. _____ el restaurante
5. _____ la biblioteca

a. ver una película
b. comer y conversar
c. caminar por la arena (*sand*)
d. estudiar y leer libros
e. bailar y escuchar música

3-3 Nuestro tiempo libre. What do you do in the following places? In small groups, take turns asking one another, and take notes on the responses. Then prepare a report to share with the class about the most popular activities in your group.

MODELO durante tus vacaciones
E1: *¿Qué haces durante tus vacaciones?*
E2: *En mis vacaciones generalmente voy a la playa. ¿Y tú?*

	Compañero/a 1	Compañero/a 2	Compañero/a 3	Yo
1. en la universidad después de clase				
2. en tu ciudad con los amigos				
3. en tu casa el fin de semana				
4. en un parque de tu ciudad				
5. en la playa durante las vacaciones				

3-4 ¿Qué hacen Pedro y Carmen?

PREPARACIÓN. Look at the scenes and take turns explaining what Pedro and Carmen do on weekends.

INTERCAMBIOS. Write a message to an e-pal in Peru explaining what you and your friends do on weekends.

MODELO *Hola, Rafael: ¿Cómo estás? Nosotros estamos muy bien. Los fines de semana mis amigos y yo… ¡Hasta pronto!*

Los planes

Una conversación por teléfono entre Luis y Patricia

PATRICIA: ¿Aló?

LUIS: Hola, mi amor. ¡**Felicidades** por tu **cumpleaños!**

PATRICIA: Ay, gracias, Luis.

LUIS: **¿Qué te parece si vamos** al cine esta tarde y **después** vamos a un restaurante para **cenar?**

PATRICIA: Me parece **fabuloso.** ¿Qué película vamos a ver?

LUIS: **Ponen una película** chilena muy buena: *Una mujer fantástica.*

PATRICIA: Muy bien, ¿y adónde vamos a cenar?

LUIS: Hay un restaurante peruano **cerca** del cine, se llama El Jardín Limeño.

PATRICIA: Estupendo. ¡**Me encanta** la **comida** peruana!

En otras palabras

Telephone greetings vary from country to country. **¿Aló?** is used in Peru and Chile; **¿Hola?** in Argentina; **¡Bueno!** in Mexico; **¡Oigo!** and **¿Qué hay?** in Cuba; **¿Diga?** and **¿Dígame?** in Spain. Different ways expressing agreement with and excitement about a plan are the following: **¡Vale!, ¡De acuerdo!, ¡Perfecto!, ¡Fenomenal!**

En directo

To extend an invitation:

Te llamo/escribo para invitarte a... *I am calling/writing to invite you to . . .*

To accept an invitation:

¡Estupendo! ¿Dónde quedamos? *Great! Where will we meet?*

Sí, gracias. / ¡Ah, qué bien! / ¡Qué buena idea! *Yes, thanks. / How great! / What a great idea!*

¡Fabuloso! *Fabulous!*

To decline an invitation:

Lo siento, pero no tengo tiempo / tengo mucha tarea... *I'm sorry, but I don't have time / I have a lot of homework . . .*

Ese día no puedo, tengo un examen. *I can't on that day, I have an exam.*

Listen to a conversation with these expressions.

PRÁCTICA

Cultura

La puntualidad Many people in Spain and Latin America have a flexible concept of time when it comes to informal settings. Arriving on time for parties and social gatherings is not expected, and it can even be considered rude. Being 30 minutes late, for example, is acceptable. Since parties usually do not end at a set time, people often leave when they feel it is very late, sometimes in the early hours of the morning.

Comparaciones What is considered an acceptable arrival time for a party in your country? What is the host's reaction if you leave a party early?

3-5 Para confirmar. **PREPARACIÓN.** Using the preceding conversation as a model, call a classmate and invite him/her to join you in a weekend activity. He/She should accept or decline the invitation.

INTERCAMBIOS. Repeat the activity with two other classmates. Then explain to the class your weekend plans and who is joining you.

MODELO E1: *El sábado por la tarde, Juan, Verónica y yo vamos al cine para ver la última película de Augusto Tamayo. ¿Quieres venir con nosotros?*

E2: *Lo siento, no puedo porque tengo un examen el lunes.*

3-6 Un plan para el sábado. **PREPARACIÓN.** Write a text message to a classmate inviting him/her to do something fun together on Saturday.

INTERCAMBIOS. Exchange messages and respond to your classmate's message accepting or declining the invitation.

Cultura

El cine Traditionally, Mexico, Spain, and Argentina have had important film industries, but films are made in other Spanish-speaking countries as well. Outstanding Spanish-language film directors like Pedro Almodóvar and Icíar Bollaín in Spain; Alfonso Cuarón, Guillermo del Toro, and Alejandro González Iñárritu in Mexico; Sergio Cabrera in Colombia; and Juan Carlos Tabío in Cuba, among others, are internationally known.

Conexiones What other famous directors (American or from other countries) can you name? What do you like best about their style?

Alejandro González Iñárritu, Guillermo del Toro y Alfonso Cuarón

3-7 ¿Adónde vamos? PREPARACIÓN. Identify three activities from this cultural events listing in Arequipa that you and a classmate would like to do during the month of November. Then complete the chart, including the day and time for each activity.

http://www.agendaculturaldearequipa.pe

Agenda Cultural de Arequipa

Cine

Cine Club Virtuosos presenta: en Auditorio del Centro Cultural Cafae (av. Arequipa 2985 – San Isidro). Entrada general: S/ 12

La vie en rose. (140 min. – Biográfica/Drama – 2007) Dir.: Olivier Dahan, Francia. Domingo, 3 de noviembre, 7:30 p.m.

El diario de Noa. (124 min. – Romance/Drama – 2004) Dir.: Nick Cassavetes, Estados Unidos. Sábado, 16 de noviembre, 5:30 p.m.

Perdona si te llamo amor. (110 min. – Romance – 2008) Dir.: Federico Moccia, Italia. Martes, 19 de noviembre, 7:30 p.m.

Música

Concierto Ensamble de Violines. Artista invitada Estefany Luque, soprano. Biblioteca Regional Mario Vargas Llosa. San Francisco 308. Ingreso libre, viernes, 15 de noviembre a las 6:00 p.m.

Festival cultural: Jueves de Danzas. Presentación regional de folclor de Arequipa. Plaza de Armas. 23 de noviembre, a partir de las 7:00 p.m.

ALL VOICES. Show de música internacional. Ricardo Fernández y Angella Alessandra. Todos los viernes, sábados y domingos, desde la 1:00 p.m.

Exposiciones

Nevados, pintura de Alejandro Jaime, en Sala de Arte del Centro Cultural El Olivar (calle La República 455, El Olivar – San Isidro) de lunes a sábado de 10:00 a.m. a 8:00 p.m. Hasta el 28 de mayo.

Teatro

Evangelina retorna de la Breña. Actuación: Delfina Paredes. Del 17 al 19 de noviembre. Auditorio del Centro Cultural de España (calle Natalio Sánchez 181-185, alt. av. Arequipa, cdra. 6, Urb. Santa Beatriz – Lima). Ingreso libre.

El dolor. Autoría Marguerite Duras (Francia). Actuación: Alejandra Guerra. Dir.: Alberto Isola. Del 22 al 24 de noviembre. Auditorio del Centro Cultural de España (calle Natalio Sánchez 181-185, alt. av. Arequipa, cdra. 6, Urb. Santa Beatriz – Lima). Ingreso libre.

Conferencias

Sábado, 9 de noviembre. Exhibición y debate sobre la película *La educación prohibida*. Organiza: Municipalidad Provincial de Arequipa. Ingreso libre. Cine Auditorio Municipal, a las 10:00 a.m.

¿Adónde vamos?	¿Qué vamos a hacer?	¿Cuándo?	¿Cuánto cuesta?

INTERCAMBIOS. Share your cultural plans with the class.

MODELO *El domingo 3 de noviembre vamos al Centro Cultural Cafae para ver la película* La vie en rose. *Vamos a pagar 12 soles.*

Cultura

Literatura Peruvian author, journalist, and politician Mario Vargas Llosa received the Nobel Prize in Literature in 2010. He published his first novel, *Los jefes,* when he was only twenty-three. He gained worldwide fame with his novel *La ciudad y los perros*. His works are a reflection of Peruvian society and his personal experience.

Conexiones Do you know any other Hispanic writer who has received the Nobel Prize in Literature? Have you read any of his/her work?

3-8 ¿Qué te gusta hacer? **PREPARACIÓN.** From the list provided, choose the activities you like to do and those you don't. Share them with your classmate.

MODELO *Me gusta comer en restaurantes, pero no me gusta beber cerveza.*

aprender lenguas	estudiar para los exámenes
bailar salsa	ir al teatro
caminar con mi perro	jugar videojuegos
cantar canciones	leer libros
comer en restaurantes	llamar por teléfono a mi familia
correr maratones	tocar un instrumento
chatear en línea	ver películas
escribir novelas	viajar a otros países
escuchar música	

INTERCAMBIOS. Take turns explaining where and when you are going to do the activities you like.

MODELO E1: *Voy a caminar con mi perro por el parque mañana por la mañana.*
E2: *Yo voy a comer en un restaurante con mis amigos el viernes por la noche.*

La comida

En el restaurante. Ahora Luis y Patricia están en el restaurante El Jardín Limeño y van a **pedir** comida peruana. Hablan con la **camarera.**

CAMARERA: ¡Buenas tardes y bienvenidos al restaurante El Jardín Limeño!
LUIS: Buenas tardes. Patricia, ¿qué vas a comer?
PATRICIA: Para mí, primero una **ensalada** y después **pollo** con **verduras.**
LUIS: Yo, para empezar, **ceviche** de **pescado.** Y **luego,** un **bistec** con **papas.**
CAMARERA: ¿Y para beber?
PATRICIA: ¿Qué es **chicha morada?**
CAMARERA: Es un **jugo** de **maíz** morado… es muy **rico** y popular aquí.
LUIS: Entonces… ¡una chicha morada!
PATRICIA: Para mí, **vino** blanco y también **agua** con gas, por favor.
CAMARERA: Muy bien.

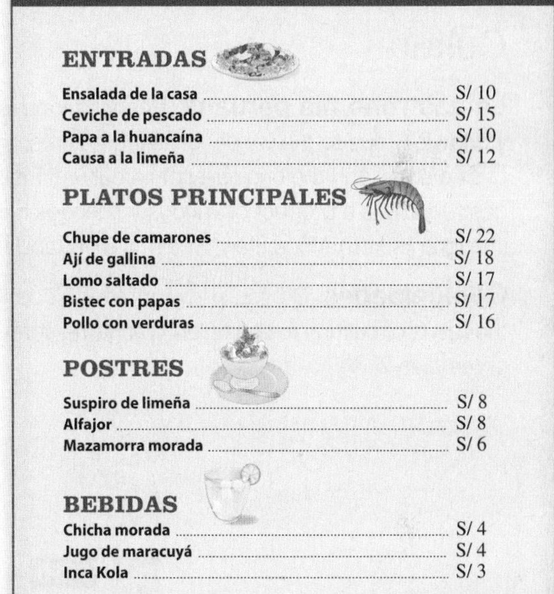

ESPECIALIDADES DE LA CASA

ENTRADAS

Ensalada de la casa	S/ 10
Ceviche de pescado	S/ 15
Papa a la huancaína	S/ 10
Causa a la limeña	S/ 12

PLATOS PRINCIPALES

Chupe de camarones	S/ 22
Ají de gallina	S/ 18
Lomo saltado	S/ 17
Bistec con papas	S/ 17
Pollo con verduras	S/ 16

POSTRES

Suspiro de limeña	S/ 8
Alfajor	S/ 8
Mazamorra morada	S/ 6

BEBIDAS

Chicha morada	S/ 4
Jugo de maracuyá	S/ 4
Inca Kola	S/ 3

Más comidas y bebidas

el desayuno

el almuerzo

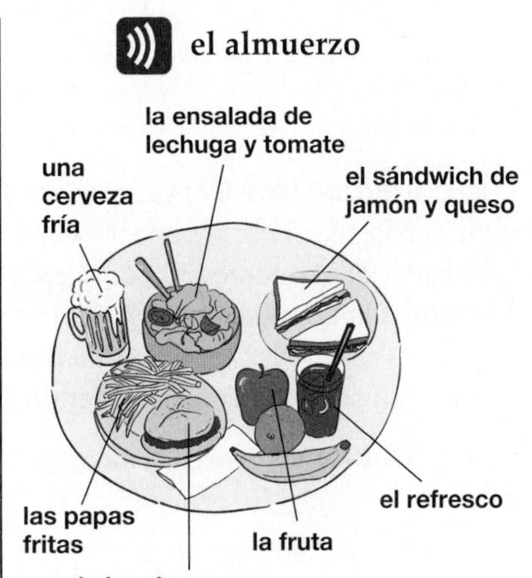

la comida / la cena

PRÁCTICA

3-9 Las calorías.

PREPARACIÓN. Indicate which item in each group contains the most calories.

1. la sopa de tomate, la hamburguesa, la sopa de pollo
2. el pollo frito, el pescado, la ensalada
3. las verduras, las frutas, las papas fritas
4. la cerveza, la leche desnatada (*skim*), el café
5. el helado de chocolate, el cereal, el arroz

INTERCAMBIOS. Compare answers with your partner to see if you agree which foods have the most calories (**¿Qué tiene más calorías?**). Then ask each other about your preferences.

MODELO E1: *Me gusta comer ensaladas y beber cerveza. ¿Y a ti?*
E2: *Yo frecuentemente como hamburguesas con papas fritas y bebo refrescos.*

Cultura

La gastronomía peruana Peruvian food is well known worldwide, due to the variety of its ingredients, the high quality of its dishes, and the originality of its cultural fusion. Peruvian gastronomy is a product of various influences introduced by immigrants from Africa, Italy, Spain, Japan, and China.

Comunidades Do you know of other foods that are the result of cultural fusion? Can you name some in your community?

Ají de gallina en rollo de sushi

3-10 Las comidas.

Discuss with your classmate what you usually eat for breakfast, lunch, and dinner. Then write a paragraph explaining what you and your classmate normally eat.

MODELO E1: *En el desayuno yo normalmente como cereal y bebo café con leche. ¿Y tú?*
E2: *En el desayuno, yo…*

Cultura

Las comidas Meal times vary according to the region but, generally, lunch is the largest and most important meal of the day. In the Hispanic world, people have lunch (**el almuerzo** or **la comida**) between 1:00 and 3:00 p.m. Dinner (**la cena** or **la comida**) is a light meal eaten between 7:00 and 10:00 in the evening. Small meals between breakfast and lunch have different names in different regions, including **la merienda** and **el almuerzo.**

Comparaciones Which is the largest meal of the day in your culture? What is it like?

3-11 ¿Qué debe comer? Look at the dinner menu, and take turns asking each other which dishes are the best options for the following people.

1. Tu amiga Luisa está muy delgada, desea subir de peso (*gain weight*).
2. Tu mamá es alérgica a los mariscos (*seafood*).
3. Tu amigo José necesita bajar de peso (*lose weight*).
4. El profesor Méndez está enfermo (*sick*) del estómago hoy.

MENÚ

SOPAS	
Sopa de pollo	S/ 12
Sopa de tomate	S/ 10
Sopa de vegetales	S/ 10
Sopa de pescado	S/ 16
ENSALADAS	
Ensalada de lechuga y tomate	S/ 12
Ensalada de pollo	S/ 20
Ensalada de atún	S/ 18
PLATOS PRINCIPALES	
Bistec con papas y vegetales	S/ 34
Hamburguesa con papas fritas	S/ 26
Pescado con papas fritas	S/ 42
Arroz con vegetales	S/ 24

3-12 En el café. **PREPARACIÓN.** It is 9:00 on Saturday morning, and you and a friend are in a café in Lima. Look at the breakfast menu and decide what you want to order.

Desayunos

TOSTADAS O PANES Nuestros deliciosos panecillos o tostadas, mermelada o mantequilla.	**S/ 7.00**
FRÍO O CALIENTE Croissant o pan con jamón inglés y queso.	**S/ 11.50**
CROISSANT DE HUEVO FRITO CON JAMÓN INGLÉS	**S/ 13.00**
TAMAL Relleno de pollo y acompañado de salsa criolla.	**S/ 9.00**
HUMITA Rellena de queso y acompañada de salsa criolla.	**S/ 9.00**
TOSTADA FRANCESA Tostadas a la plancha con miel, azúcar, canela y huevo.	**S/ 9.50**
OMELETTE DE JAMÓN Y QUESO Relleno de jamón y queso. Sustituir un ingrediente por champiñones.	**S/ 15.00**

INTERCAMBIOS. Ask your friend what he/she would like to order, and then explain your order to the server.

MODELO E1: *El desayuno es muy bueno aquí. ¿Qué deseas comer?*
E2: *Yo… ¿Y tú?*
E1: *Yo… ¿Y qué vas a tomar?*
E2: *Camarero/a, mi amigo/a… y yo…*

3-13 Nuestro menú. You and your roommate want to have guests over for dinner tonight. Decide who each of you is going to invite and what you are going to serve. Finally, compare your menu with that of another pair of classmates.

Vamos a invitar a...	Vamos a servir...

En directo

Expressions to order food:

Para mí, unas tostadas, café... *For me, some toast, coffee . . .*

Me gustaría / Quisiera comer/tomar... *I would like to eat/drink . . .*

Yo quiero/deseo... *I want . . .*

Listen to a conversation with these expressions.

3-14 ¿Qué hacen estos estudiantes?

PREPARACIÓN. Make a list of three activities you normally do during the week, and three that you plan to do this weekend. Then ask your partner if he/she is going to do the same things.

ESCUCHA. Listen to Carlos and Amanda talk about their activities and weekend plans. Indicate whether they will do the following activities during the weekend.

	SÍ	NO
1. ir a bailar salsa	____	____
2. comer en un restaurante	____	____
3. descansar y tomar el sol	____	____
4. ver una obra de teatro (*play*)	____	____
5. hablar por internet con los amigos	____	____

Mosaico cultural

Los jóvenes y la vida social

En cada país hispano, hay costumbres diferentes y la vida social de los jóvenes es variada. Por ejemplo, los españoles van de tapas, los argentinos y uruguayos organizan grandes asados (*barbecues*) y los colombianos van a fiestas donde bailan toda la noche. Pero en muchas cosas, los jóvenes de todo el mundo son similares.

En los países hispanos es común ver a grupos de amigos pasear, ir al cine, tomar un café o ir a un restaurante después de las clases o del trabajo. Los bares y discotecas son buenos lugares para reunirse, escuchar música o bailar.

Sin duda (*Without a doubt*), internet tiene un impacto muy fuerte en cómo los jóvenes utilizan su tiempo libre. Los jóvenes de hoy pasan mucho tiempo comunicándose por internet, pero también ven películas o juegan videojuegos. Como en todas partes, las redes sociales son una pasión entre los hispanos.

Bar de tapas en Madrid

Asador de carne en Argentina

Compara

1. Y a ti, ¿qué te gusta hacer con tus amigos? ¿Cómo te comunicas con ellos? ¿Cuáles son tus diversiones?
2. Menciona dos semejanzas y dos diferencias de cómo pasan el tiempo los jóvenes en tu país y en algún país hispano.

En acción

¡A comer!

Antes de ver

3-15 Comida típica. Select the country most commonly associated with each food.

1. _____ paella
2. _____ dulce de leche
3. _____ papas a la huancaína
4. _____ hamburguesas con papas fritas
5. _____ arepas
6. _____ tacos

a. Estados Unidos
b. Perú
c. Venezuela
d. España
e. Argentina
f. México

Mientras ves

3-16 En el restaurante. As you watch the video, indicate whether each statement is true (**Cierto**) or false (**Falso**). Correct the false statements.

	CIERTO	FALSO
1. Héctor, Vanesa y Yolanda van a un restaurante para comer el almuerzo.	_____	_____
2. Yolanda está contenta porque hay muchos platos vegetarianos en el menú.	_____	_____
3. Una comida típica de Perú es el arroz chaufa con vegetales.	_____	_____
4. Vanesa va a comer ceviche.	_____	_____
5. Héctor va a beber chicha morada.	_____	_____
6. La cocinera del restaurante es de Lima.	_____	_____

Después de ver

3-17 ¡Qué rico!

PREPARACIÓN. After watching the video, indicate whether the following items are associated with Peruvian food (**P**) or with Mexican food (**M**).

1. _____ el ceviche
2. _____ las frutas y verduras frescas
3. _____ las papas
4. _____ las pastas
5. _____ el tallarín saltado con vegetales
6. _____ los tacos

INTERCAMBIOS. You and several classmates have decided to eat at the restaurant featured in the video. Take turns asking your classmates what they are going to order and why they have made that choice.

FUNCIONES Y FORMAS

1 Expressing movement and plans

Elena, la chica en el centro de la foto, habla de sus amigos.

Mis amigos y yo somos diferentes, pero hacemos muchas cosas juntos (*together*). Por las tardes, nosotros **vamos a** un café para conversar y hacer tareas. Los sábados, yo **voy a** la casa de mi amiga Estela, y luego ella **va** conmigo **al** gimnasio para hacer ejercicio. A veces Rafael, Humberto y Rodrigo también **van al** gimnasio con nosotras. Mi amiga Teresa no sale (*go out*) mucho porque prefiere estudiar. Fernando es muy tranquilo y le fascina el arte. Con frecuencia él y Estela **van a** exposiciones (*exhibitions*) de arte. Generalmente celebramos nuestros cumpleaños (*birthdays*) en un restaurante.

Piénsalo. First, select the correct verb form in parentheses. Then indicate whether each statement is **Cierto** (*true*) or **Falso** (*false*), based on Elena's description.

1. ______ Elena y sus amigos (va/van) a un café para conversar.
2. ______ Fernando (va/vamos) a la casa de Estela durante el fin de semana.
3. ______ Durante el fin de semana, Elena (va/van) a un café para conversar.
4. ______ Elena dice (*says*): Nosotros (va/vamos) a un restaurante para celebrar nuestros cumpleaños.
5. ______ Rafael, Humberto y Rodrigo a veces (vamos/van) al gimnasio con Elena y Estela.

Present tense of *ir* and *ir a + infinitive*

- After the verb **ir,** use **a** to introduce a noun that refers to a place. When **a** is followed by the article **el,** the two words contract to form **al.**

IR (*to go*)			
yo	**voy**	nosotros/as	**vamos**
tú	**vas**	vosotros/as	**vais**
Ud., él, ella	**va**	Uds., ellos/as	**van**

Voy **a la** fiesta de María. — *I am going to María's party.*

Vamos **al** gimnasio. — *We are going to the gym.*

- Use **¿adónde?** when asking *where (to)?* with the verb **ir.**

¿Adónde vas ahora? — *Where are you going now?*

- **Ir a** + the infinitive form of the verb is used to express a future action or condition.

Mis amigos **van a nadar** después. — *My friends are going to swim afterward.*

¿**Van a estar** cansados por la noche? — *Are they going to be tired at night?*

- The expression **vamos a** + *infinitive* can mean *let's.*

Vamos a cenar en mi casa. — *Let's have dinner at my house.*

Vamos a bailar después. — *Let's go dancing afterward.*

Lengua

The following expressions denote future time: **después, más tarde, esta noche, mañana, pasado mañana** (*the day after tomorrow*), **la próxima semana, el próximo mes/año.**

e **¿Comprendes?** Complete the conversation with the correct form of the verb **ir.**

LUIS: Hola, Lorena, ¿adónde (1) ________?
LORENA: Hola, Luis. (2) ________ a la biblioteca porque debo estudiar para el examen de mañana.
LUIS: Ah, pues yo también (3) ________ para allá. ¿Por qué no (4) ________ juntos?
LORENA: Sí, claro. Pero ¿qué tal si primero nosotros (5) ________ a tomar un café a la cafetería?

PRÁCTICA

3-18 ¿Adónde van?

e **PREPARACIÓN.** Josh and Steve are North American students visiting Peru during their summer break. Select the place that corresponds to each description.

a. Machu Picchu

b. las líneas de Nazca

c. la Universidad de San Marcos

d. una peña

1. _____ Steve estudia historia. Por eso, busca una institución prestigiosa. Está en Lima. Va a...
2. _____ Los dos amigos van a visitar uno de los lugares más misteriosos del planeta. Allí hay enormes figuras geométricas trazadas (*drawn*) en la tierra que son visibles solamente desde el aire. Ellos van a...
3. _____ Josh conoce (*meets*) a Susana en Perú. Ella lo invita a un evento folclórico donde las personas escuchan poesía y música tradicional, y también comen y bailan. Josh y Susana van a...
4. _____ Steve y Josh van a un lugar histórico imposible de ignorar. Es considerado el símbolo del Imperio inca. Está cerca de Cuzco. Steve y Josh van a...

INTERCAMBIOS. Now take turns asking your partner where you two will go to do the following in Peru.

1. ¿Adónde vamos para hacer amigos, conversar y bailar ritmos peruanos?
2. ¿Adónde vamos para tomar fotos de un edificio universitario antiguo?
3. ¿Adónde vamos para escalar unas montañas altas de mucha importancia histórica?

3-19 Los horarios. **PREPARACIÓN.** Your classmate's friends Juan, Alicia, and Sofía are busy today. Ask your classmate where each person is and where he/she is going afterward.

MODELO Bob / 8:00 de la mañana / trabajo / cine

E1: *Son las 8:00 de la mañana. ¿Dónde está Bob?*
E2: *Está en el trabajo.*
E1: *¿Adónde va después del trabajo?*
E2: *Va al cine.*

Nombre	Hora	Lugar	Destino
Juan	8:00 de la mañana	gimnasio	clase
Alicia	9:30 de la mañana	laboratorio de computadoras	biblioteca
Sofía	8:30 de la mañana	oficina	cafetería

INTERCAMBIOS. Exchange information with your partner about what each of you does at the times listed in **Preparación.**

MODELO E1: *¿Qué haces a las 8:00 de la mañana?*
E2: *Voy a la universidad.*
E1: *¿Adónde vas después?*
E2: *Voy al gimnasio. ¿Qué haces tú a las 8:00 de la mañana?*

3-20 Mi agenda para la semana. Invite six classmates individually to do the following activities with you. They are going to accept or refuse your invitation.

MODELO estudiar en la biblioteca el lunes por la noche

E1: *¿Vamos a estudiar en la biblioteca el lunes por la noche?*
E2: *Lo siento, Miguel, el lunes por la noche voy a ir al cine con David. Pero, ¿por qué no estudiamos el martes por la mañana?*
E1: *Buena idea. Vamos a estudiar el martes temprano por la mañana.*

1. ir a un concierto el viernes por la noche
2. mirar una buena película en casa el lunes durante el día
3. tomar algo en un café el sábado por la mañana
4. estudiar para un examen difícil el miércoles por la tarde
5. chatear con amigos en internet el jueves por la noche
6. hacer ejercicio el domingo a las 9:00 de la mañana

 **3-21 Los planes de Maribel.** **PREPARACIÓN.** Take turns telling each other what Maribel is going to do at the times indicated.

INTERCAMBIOS. Chat with your classmate about what you are going to do at those times on Friday.

 **3-22 Adivinen (*Guess*) mis planes.** Read this coded text message that your friend Gabriela sent you about her plans for the weekend. Take turns saying what her plans are.

Situación

PREPARACIÓN. Read the following situation with your partner. Then brainstorm the vocabulary, structures, and other information you will need for both roles in the conversation.

Role A. You call to invite a friend to a café tonight where a mutual friend is going to sing. After your friend responds, ask about his/her plans for later in the evening:
a. where he/she is going;
b. with whom; and
c. at what time, etc.

Role B. A friend calls to invite you to a café tonight where a mutual friend is going to sing. Inquire about the event to find out:
a. what time and where it is going to be; and
b. if other friends are going to go.

Accept the invitation and mention your plans for later in the evening.

	ROLE A	ROLE B
Vocabulario	Free-time activities	Free-time activities
Funciones y formas	Making plans Verb **ir** **ir a** + *infinitive* Extending an invitation Asking the time Reacting to what one hears	Verb **ir** **ir a** + *infinitive* Accepting an invitation Telling time Asking questions

INTERCAMBIOS. Using the information in **Preparación,** act out the conversation with your partner.

2 Expressing intention, means, movement, and duration

CARLOS: Papá, necesito tu auto **por** una semana. ¿Está bien?

PADRE: ¿**Por** una semana? ¿**Por** qué?

CARLOS: **Porque** mis amigos y yo vamos **para** la playa durante las vacaciones de primavera.

PADRE: ¡Ni lo pienses! (*Don't even think about it!*)

Piénsalo. Read each statement. Choose **por, para, por qué,** or **porque,** based on the meaning and function of these words in the conversation between Carlos and his father.

	POR	PARA	POR QUÉ	PORQUE
1. Carlos necesita el auto de su padre **durante** siete días.				
2. El padre pregunta **la razón** (*reason*) **de** la petición de Carlos.				
3. Carlos y sus amigos van a ir **en dirección a** la playa.				
4. Carlos explica **la razón de** usar el auto.				

Some uses of *por* and *para*

- **Por** and **para** have different meanings in Spanish, although sometimes they are both translated into English as *for*. The uses presented here include some you have already seen, as well as some new ones.
- **Para** expresses *for* when you mean *intended for* or *to be used for*. It can refer to a person, an event, or a purpose.

  Necesito una computadora **para** la clase. — *I need a computer for the class.*
  Esta computadora portátil es **para** David. — *This laptop is for David.*

- **Para** + *infinitive* means *in order to* and is used to express purpose.

  Tomo el autobús **para** ir a la universidad. — *I take the bus (in order) to go to the university.*
  El restaurante hace publicidad en línea **para** atraer clientes. — *The restaurant advertises online (in order) to attract customers.*

- **Por** and **para** can also be used to express movement in space and time.
- **Para** indicates movement toward a destination.

  Caminan **para** la playa. — *They walk toward the beach.*
  Vamos **para** el túnel. — *We are going toward the tunnel.*

- **Por** indicates movement through or by a place.

  Caminan **por** la playa. — *They walk along the beach.*
  Vamos **por** el túnel. — *We are going through the tunnel.*

- You may also use **por** to indicate length of time or duration of an action. Many Spanish speakers omit **por** in this case, or they use **durante.**

  Necesito el auto **por** tres días. *I need the car for three days.*

- **Por** appears in expressions such as **por favor, por teléfono,** and **por la mañana/tarde/noche.** Other expressions with **por** that you will find useful include the following:

por ciento *percent*	**por fin** *finally, at last*
por ejemplo *for example*	**por lo menos** *at least*
por eso *that is why*	**por supuesto** *of course*

e **¿Comprendes?** Complete the conversation with **por** or **para.**

—Hola, Rubén, ¿(1) _______ dónde vas?

—Hola, Juan, voy a montar en bicicleta (2) _______ el parque.

—Tu bicicleta es muy buena y moderna. Yo necesito una bicicleta (3) _______ ir a mi trabajo. ¿Cuánto cuesta una nueva?

—No sé, pero puedes (*you can*) usar mi bicicleta (4) _______ las mañanas. Yo siempre camino al campus (5) _______ hacer ejercicio.

PRÁCTICA

3-23 *¿Por o para?*

e **PREPARACIÓN.** Read the description, and then select the correct use for each instance of **por** or **para.**

Mis amigos y yo siempre estamos ocupados los fines de semana. Los sábados vamos a un cine de nuestro barrio **por**[1] dos o más horas. Cuando vamos **para**[2] el cine, caminamos **por**[3] el parque. Después del cine, a veces hacemos fiestas en casa. Si es una fiesta de cumpleaños, compro un regalo especial **para**[4] mi amigo. **Para**[5] celebrar, preparo una comida especial.

1. por _____	**a.** *intended for (person)*
2. para _____	**b.** *in order to*
3. por _____	**c.** *length of time*
4. para _____	**d.** *movement toward a destination*
5. Para _____	**e.** *movement through or by a place*

INTERCAMBIOS. Now, ask several different classmates what they do on Saturday nights and what they do to celebrate their birthdays.

3-24 **¿Para dónde van y para qué?** Take turns guessing where these people are going and for what purpose. Then find out where your classmate is going after class, and for what purpose.

MODELO Jorge tiene su guitarra en su auto.
Va para una fiesta. Tiene la guitarra para cantar en el cumpleaños de su amigo.

1. Es la una de la tarde y Pedro camina por la avenida principal.
2. Sebastián lleva una mochila con sus zapatillas de deporte (*athletic shoes*) y su raqueta.
3. Lola y Pepe tienen un examen y necesitan consultar unos libros.
4. Gregorio necesita un libro para su clase de español.
5. Ana María desea ver la nueva película de su actor favorito.
6. Amanda y Clara están muy elegantes y contentas.

 **3-25 Caminante.** You and your classmate like to walk. Take turns asking each other the following questions.

1. ¿Te gusta caminar con amigos o solo/a? ¿Por qué?
2. ¿Por dónde caminas cuando prefieres estar solo/a?
3. ¿Te gusta caminar por la playa o por un parque?
4. Generalmente, ¿caminas por la mañana o por la tarde?
5. ¿Por cuánto tiempo caminas para ir de una clase a otra (*another*)?
6. ¿Usas aplicaciones en tu teléfono? ¿Qué aplicaciones usas? ¿Para qué usas cada aplicación?

 **3-26 ¿Para quiénes son los regalos (*gifts*)?** You are very generous and have bought the following gifts. Your partner asks for whom they are intended.

MODELO la mochila
E1: *¿Para quién es la mochila?*
E2: *Es para mi amigo.*

1. las tres novelas en español
2. las dos entradas (*tickets*) para el cine
3. el teléfono celular
4. la tableta
5. la computadora portátil
6. el buen vino chileno

 **3-27 Mi opinión.** Finish the following statements logically. Be prepared to support your opinion. Then, compare and discuss your responses with your partner.

MODELO Tomar mucho café es bueno para..., pero es malo para...
Tomar mucho café es bueno para estudiar, pero es malo para descansar por la noche.

1. El teléfono con la cámara de alta definición es bueno/malo para... porque...
2. El agua de mar es excelente para..., pero es mala para...
3. Ir a las discotecas es bueno/malo para...
4. Trabajar 50 horas por semana es bueno para..., pero es malo para...
5. Conversar cara a cara (*face-to-face*) con los amigos es ideal para...
6. Hacer fiestas cada fin de semana no es bueno/malo porque...

Situación

PREPARACIÓN. Read the following situation with your partner. Then prepare examples of the vocabulary, structures, and other information you will need to present your role in the conversation.

Role A. You run into a friend who is carrying a big gift box. You ask what it is, whom it is for, and why your friend is going to give this gift to this person.

Role B. You are walking out of a store carrying a big gift box. You run into a friend who asks you about the gift. Answer and explain to whom you are giving the gift and for what occasion.

	ROLE A	ROLE B
Vocabulario	Gifts and gift-giving occasions	Question words
Funciones y formas	Asking questions **Por** and **para**	Answering questions **Por** and **para**

INTERCAMBIOS. Using the information in **Preparación,** act out the conversation with your partner.

3 Talking about things we do

Preparativos para una fiesta

CAROLINA: Bueno, ¿por qué no **hacemos** planes para la fiesta del sábado? Yo **pongo** las decoraciones en la sala. José Manuel, ¿qué música vas a traer para la fiesta?

JOSÉ MANUEL: Voy a buscar buena música para bailar. En las fiestas pongo siempre música para bailar. A ti, Carolina, ¿qué música te gusta?

CAROLINA: Normalmente **oigo** todo tipo de música pero cuando **salgo** con mis amigos me gusta bailar salsa. Tomás, ¿tú **haces** las hamburguesas en la fiesta?

TOMÁS: Sí, yo **hago** las hamburguesas. ¿Y tú, Karen?

KAREN: ¡Estupendo! Pues yo **traigo** las bebidas y pongo la mesa.

Piénsalo. Indicate who said each statement: Carolina (**C**), Tomás (**T**), José Manuel (**JM**), or Karen (**K**). Then provide the infinitive form of the verb in bold.

		INFINITIVO
1.	_____ **Hacemos** planes para la fiesta del sábado.	_________
2.	_____ En las fiestas **pongo** música para bailar.	_________
3.	_____ **Oigo** todo tipo de música.	_________
4.	_____ **Salgo** con mis amigos.	_________
5.	_____ **Hago** las hamburguesas.	_________
6.	_____ **Traigo** las bebidas.	_________

Present tense of *hacer, poner, salir, traer,* and *oír*

- In the present tense, the verbs **hacer, poner, salir, traer,** and **oír** take a **g** in the **yo** form, but not in the other forms.
- **Hacer** means *to do* or *to make.* It is used frequently in questions to ask in a general sense what someone does, is doing, or likes to do.

HACER (*to make, to do*)			
yo	**hago**	nosotros/as	**hacemos**
tú	**haces**	vosotros/as	**hacéis**
Ud., él, ella	**hace**	Uds., ellos/as	**hacen**

¿Qué **haces** para sacar buenas notas? — *What do you do to get good grades?*
Hago la tarea para mis clases todos los días. — *I do the homework for my classes every day.*

- **Poner** generally means *to put,* but it can also have other meanings. **Poner la mesa** means *to set the table;* when used with some electrical appliances, **poner** means *to turn on.*

PONER (*to put*)			
yo	**pongo**	nosotros/as	**ponemos**
tú	**pones**	vosotros/as	**ponéis**
Ud., él, ella	**pone**	Uds., ellos/as	**ponen**

Por la mañana **pongo** mis libros en la mochila. — *In the morning I put my books in my backpack.*
Yo **pongo la mesa** a la hora de la cena. — *I set the table at dinner time.*
Mi abuelo **pone** la televisión después de la cena. — *My grandfather turns on the TV after dinner.*

- **Salir** can be used with several different prepositions. To express that you are leaving a place, use **salir de;** to express your destination, use **salir para;** to express with whom you go out or the person you date, use **salir con;** to express intention, use **salir a.**

SALIR (*to leave*)			
yo	**salgo**	nosotros/as	**salimos**
tú	**sales**	vosotros/as	**salís**
Ud., él, ella	**sale**	Uds., ellos/as	**salen**

Yo **salgo de** mi cuarto a las 7:15 de la mañana. — *I leave my room at 7:15 in the morning.*
Salgo para la cafetería ahora. — *I am leaving for the cafeteria now.*
Mi mejor amiga **sale con** Mario. — *My best friend is dating Mario.*
Ellos **salen a** bailar los sábados. — *They go out dancing on Saturdays.*

- **Traer** means to *bring*. It is used to convey the idea of transporting a person or an object to a place where the speaker or listener is or will be in the near future.

TRAER (*to bring*)			
yo	**traigo**	nosotros/as	**traemos**
tú	**traes**	vosotros/as	**traéis**
Ud., él, ella	**trae**	Uds., ellos/as	**traen**

Yo siempre **traigo** un postre a estas fiestas. — *I always bring a dessert to these parties.*

- **Oír** means *to hear* in the sense of *to perceive sounds*. Note the spelling and the accent marks in the infinitive, **nosotros/as,** and **vosotros/as** forms and the **y** inserted before the ending in the **tú, Ud./él/ella,** and **Uds./ellos/ellas** forms.

OÍR (*to hear*)			
yo	**oigo**	nosotros/as	**oímos**
tú	**oyes**	vosotros/as	**oís**
Ud., él, ella	**oye**	Uds., ellos/as	**oyen**

Yo **oigo** música. — *I hear music.*
—¿**Oyes** la alarma? — *—Do you hear the alarm?*
—No, no **oigo** nada. — *—No, I don't hear anything.*

e **¿Comprendes?** Complete each sentence with the correct form of the verb in parentheses.
Marcos y Victoria son mis mejores amigos. Por lo general, nosotros (1) _________ (hacer) la tarea juntos en mi casa. Ellos (2) _________ (traer) sus libros y apuntes. Yo (3) _________ (poner) música suave. A ellos les gusta la música que yo (4) _________ (oír) normalmente. Los sábados, yo (5) _________ (salir) con ellos y vamos a bailar.

PRÁCTICA

3-28 Los estudios y la diversión. PREPARACIÓN. How do you combine school with fun? Indicate the things that you do regularly.

1. _____ Por las mañanas, **hago** ejercicio y luego **salgo** para la universidad.
2. _____ Yo **hago** toda la tarea antes de salir con mis amigos.
3. _____ Cuando **oigo** que un amigo está triste, lo invito a salir.
4. _____ Siempre **pongo** rock cuando estudio.
5. _____ Generalmente, **traigo** mi teléfono a clase para contestar mensajes de texto.
6. _____ En general, **traigo** mi teléfono al campus para oír música cuando no estoy en clase.

INTERCAMBIOS. Take turns talking about your activities to see what you have in common. Then share the results with the class to find the most and least popular ones.

MODELO E1: *Yo soy organizado/a. Siempre hago ejercicio por la mañana. ¿Y tú?*
E2: *Pues, yo también...*

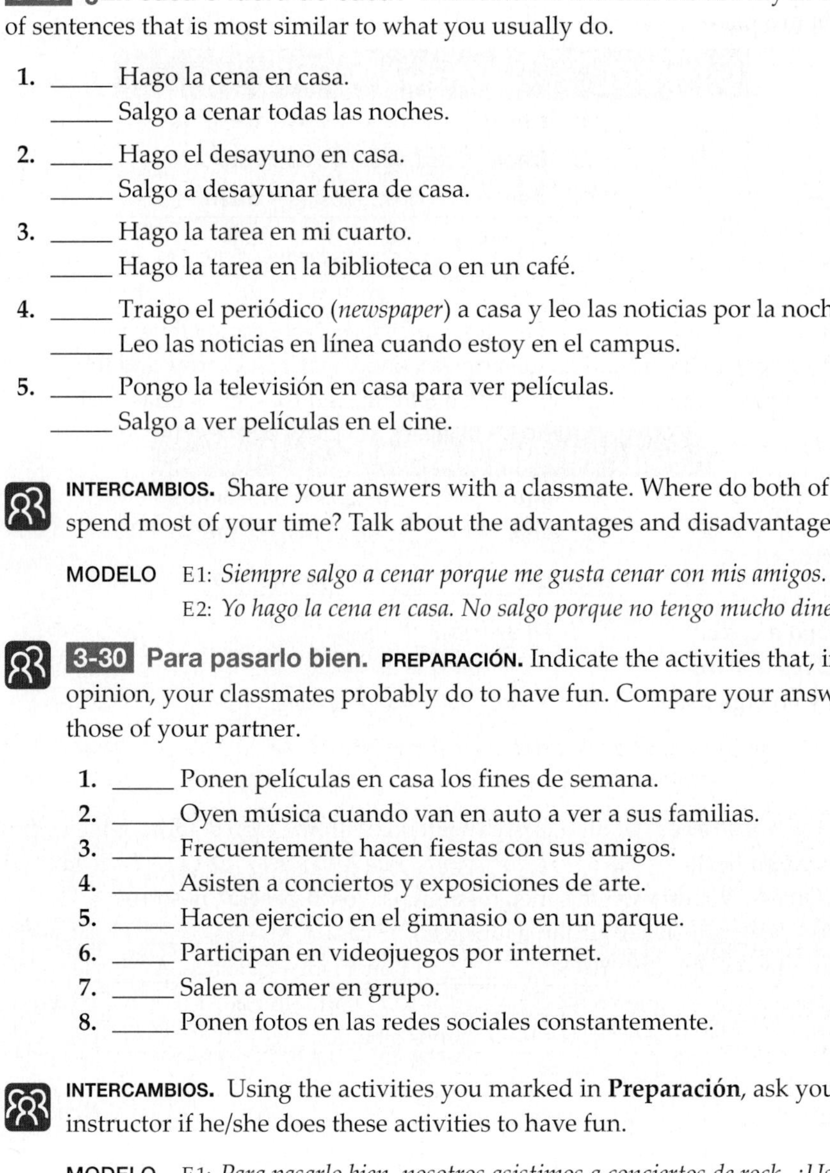

3-29 **¿En casa o fuera de casa?** **PREPARACIÓN.** Indicate the activity in each pair of sentences that is most similar to what you usually do.

1. _____ Hago la cena en casa.
   _____ Salgo a cenar todas las noches.
2. _____ Hago el desayuno en casa.
   _____ Salgo a desayunar fuera de casa.
3. _____ Hago la tarea en mi cuarto.
   _____ Hago la tarea en la biblioteca o en un café.
4. _____ Traigo el periódico (*newspaper*) a casa y leo las noticias por la noche.
   _____ Leo las noticias en línea cuando estoy en el campus.
5. _____ Pongo la televisión en casa para ver películas.
   _____ Salgo a ver películas en el cine.

INTERCAMBIOS. Share your answers with a classmate. Where do both of you spend most of your time? Talk about the advantages and disadvantages.

MODELO E1: *Siempre salgo a cenar porque me gusta cenar con mis amigos. ¿Y tú?*
E2: *Yo hago la cena en casa. No salgo porque no tengo mucho dinero.*

3-30 **Para pasarlo bien.** **PREPARACIÓN.** Indicate the activities that, in your opinion, your classmates probably do to have fun. Compare your answers with those of your partner.

1. _____ Ponen películas en casa los fines de semana.
2. _____ Oyen música cuando van en auto a ver a sus familias.
3. _____ Frecuentemente hacen fiestas con sus amigos.
4. _____ Asisten a conciertos y exposiciones de arte.
5. _____ Hacen ejercicio en el gimnasio o en un parque.
6. _____ Participan en videojuegos por internet.
7. _____ Salen a comer en grupo.
8. _____ Ponen fotos en las redes sociales constantemente.

INTERCAMBIOS. Using the activities you marked in **Preparación**, ask your instructor if he/she does these activities to have fun.

MODELO E1: *Para pasarlo bien, nosotros asistimos a conciertos de rock. ¿Usted asiste a conciertos de rock para pasarlo bien?*
INSTRUCTOR/A: *No, no asisto a conciertos de rock. Para pasarlo bien, escucho conciertos de jazz en la radio.*
E1: *¡Qué interesante!*

3-31 Mi rutina.

PREPARACIÓN. Talk about the activities you routinely do. Then ask your classmate about his/her activities.

MODELO tener clases (por la mañana / por la tarde)
E1: *Yo tengo clases por la mañana y por la tarde. ¿Y tú?*
E2: *¡Qué aburrido! Yo tengo clases por la mañana solamente.*

1. salir de casa (temprano/tarde) por la mañana
2. poner (música / las noticias) por la mañana
3. hacer la tarea (en casa / en la biblioteca)
4. salir a (comer / ver películas) con amigos por la noche
5. traer muchos (libros/amigos) a casa después de las clases

INTERCAMBIOS. Write a brief paragraph comparing your routine with that of your classmate. In your opinion, who has a more interesting routine and why? Provide a few reasons.

En directo

To react to what someone has said:

¡Qué interesante! *How interesting!*
¡Qué divertido! *How fun!*
¡Qué aburrido! *How boring!*
¡Qué lata! *What a nuisance!*

Listen to a conversation with these expressions.

Situación

PREPARACIÓN. Read the following situation with your partner. Then brainstorm the vocabulary, structures, and other information you will need for both roles in the conversation.

Role A. You have made a new friend, and you are asking him/her about the things he/she likes to do in his/her free time. Ask your new friend:
a. if he/she goes out a lot and where;
b. if he/she does any sports;
c. if he/she goes to parties and what he/she brings; and
d. if he/she likes to listen to music and what music he/she listens to.

Role B. You are new in town, and you have just met someone who is interested in knowing more about you. Answer the questions in as much detail as possible and ask some questions of your own.

	ROLE A	ROLE B
Vocabulario	Free-time activities Question words Movies, music, or other forms of entertainment	Free-time activities Question words Movies, music, or other forms of entertainment
Funciones y formas	Asking and answering questions Reacting to what you hear Verbs **hacer, poner, traer, oír**	Asking and answering questions Reacting to what you hear Verbs **hacer, poner, traer, oír**

INTERCAMBIOS. Using the information in **Preparación,** act out the conversation with your partner.

4 Talking about quantity

Adriana compra cinco dólares de lotería. Si gana **dos millones de dólares,** va a comprar un auto deportivo por **cuarenta y dos mil cuatrocientos dólares.** Después va a comprar un billete (*ticket*) para visitar a su familia en Perú por **mil setecientos dólares.** Va a regalar (*give*) a sus padres **mil dólares** todos los meses. Adriana imagina el dinero: **quinientos, seiscientos, setecientos, ochocientos, novecientos...** y las cosas que sus padres van a comprar.

Piénsalo. Look carefully at the numbers that Adriana and her family are mentally counting to figure out which numbers have regular forms (e.g., **doscientos = dos + cientos**) and which have irregular forms. Provide each number in word form, and then indicate if it is regular or irregular.

	REGULAR	IRREGULAR
1. 300 ____________	❏	❏
2. 500 ____________	❏	❏
3. 700 ____________	❏	❏
4. 900 ____________	❏	❏

Numbers 100 to 2,000,000

- You have already learned the numbers up to 99. In this section you will learn the numbers to talk about larger quantities.

100	**cien/ciento**	1.000	**mil**
200	**doscientos/as**	1.100	**mil cien**
300	**trescientos/as**	2.000	**dos mil**
400	**cuatrocientos/as**	10.000	**diez mil**
500	**quinientos/as**	100.000	**cien mil**
600	**seiscientos/as**	150.000	**ciento cincuenta mil**
700	**setecientos/as**	500.000	**quinientos mil**
800	**ochocientos/as**	1.000.000	**un millón (de)**
900	**novecientos/as**	2.000.000	**dos millones (de)**

- Use **cien** to say 100 when used alone or when followed by a noun. Use **ciento** for numbers from 101 to 199.

100	**cien**
100 fiestas	**cien** fiestas
120 películas	**ciento** veinte películas
177 canciones	**ciento** setenta y siete canciones

- Multiples of 100 agree in gender with the noun they modify.

200 libros	**doscientos** libros
1.500 revistas	**mil quinientas** revistas

- Use **mil** for *one thousand.* Multiples of 1,000 are also **mil.**

1.000	**mil** alumnos, **mil** alumnas
12.000	**doce mil** residentes

- Use **un millón** to say *one million.* Use **un millón de** when a noun follows.

1.000.000	**un millón**
1.000.000 de personas	**un millón de personas**
12.000.000 de dólares	**doce millones de dólares**

- In many Spanish-speaking countries, a period is used to separate thousands, and a comma is used to separate decimals.

$1.000	**mil dólares**
$19,50	**diecinueve dólares con cincuenta centavos**

- In dates and street addresses, large numbers are expressed fully, not stated in pairs as they often are in English.

2018 (*twenty eighteen*)	**dos mil dieciocho**
763 (*seven sixty-three*) Colina Street	**calle Colina setecientos sesenta y tres**

e **¿Comprendes?** Select the correct number to complete each sentence.

1. Aproximadamente _____ de personas hablan español.
2. Un dólar tiene _____ centavos
3. El profesor Hiram Bingham llega a Machu Picchu por primera vez (*for the first time*) en el año _____.
4. La Constitución de Estados Unidos tiene más de _____ años.
5. El próximo milenio va a empezar en el año _____.

a. cien
b. mil novecientos once
c. tres mil uno.
d. cuatrocientos cuarenta millones
e. doscientos treinta

PRÁCTICA

3-32 Información sobre Perú. **PREPARACIÓN.** With a classmate, select the correct number to complete each statement. Then read the statements aloud to each other.

1. Perú tiene aproximadamente _____ de habitantes.
2. Unas _____ de personas viven en Lima, la capital de Perú.
3. Lima está a _____ millas de Nueva York en avión.
4. Machu Picchu tiene una altitud de _____ pies (*feet*).
5. Denver, la ciudad más alta de Estados Unidos, está a _____ pies.
6. Los incas abandonan Machu Picchu después del año _____.

a. 1572
b. 7.970
c. 5.280
d. 32.600.000
e. 9.320.000
f. 3.648

INTERCAMBIOS. Ask each other questions about your community.

MODELO E1: *¿Cuántos estudiantes hay en la Universidad de... ?*
E2: *Hay... estudiantes.*

3-33 Cantidades. Alternate asking each other the following questions. Then report the most surprising amounts to the class.

1. ¿Cuántos mensajes de texto envías (*send*) y recibes al día?
2. ¿Cuánto dinero vas a ganar (*earn*) en tu primer trabajo después de la universidad?
3. ¿Qué cantidad máxima puedes gastar (*can you spend*) por un auto usado?
4. ¿Qué cantidad máxima vas a gastar para tu boda (*wedding*)?
5. ¿Cuánto vas a gastar por tu carrera universitaria?
6. ¿Cuántos estudiantes van a graduarse en tu universidad este año?
7. ¿Cuánto dinero vas a gastar en diversiones este semestre?
8. ¿Cuántas personas viven en la ciudad o pueblo donde vive tu familia?

En directo

To call attention to an unusual fact:

¡Fíjate qué noticia! *How about that!*

¡Imagínate! *Imagine that!*

To react to good news:

¡Qué suerte! *How lucky!*

¡Qué maravilla! *How wonderful!*

¡Qué bien! *How nice!*

To convince someone to do something with you:

¡Venga/Anda, anímate! *Come on, let's do it!*

Lo vamos a pasar muy bien. *We are going to have a good time.*

Listen to a conversation with these expressions.

3-34 Unas vacaciones.

PREPARACIÓN. Your classmate has chosen one of the destinations in the ad below for an upcoming vacation. To find out where he/she is going, ask the following questions and react to what you hear. Then switch roles.

1. ¿Adónde vas?
2. ¿Qué lugares vas a ver?
3. ¿Cuántos días vas a estar allí?
4. ¿Cuánto cuesta la excursión?
5. ¿Cuánto dinero vas a necesitar?

AGENCIA MUNDIAL

A SU SERVICIO SIEMPRE *20 años de experiencia, responsabilidad y profesionalidad*

TODOS LOS PRECIOS INCLUYEN PASAJES AÉREOS Y SERVICIOS TERRESTRES POR PERSONA

PERÚ Y BOLIVIA

LIMA, AREQUIPA, CUZCO, MACHU PICCHU, PUNO, LA PAZ, 15 días. La Ruta del Inca. Hoteles de 3 y 4 estrellas. Desayuno incluido.
$4.760

PERÚ

LIMA, CUZCO, MACHU PICCHU, NAZCA, 12 días. Visite fortalezas incas. Vea las misteriosas líneas de Nazca desde el aire. Hoteles de primera. Desayuno y cena incluidos.
$3.950

LIMA, NAZCA, AREQUIPA, LAGO TITICACA, 10 días. Admire la arquitectura colonial de Lima y Arequipa. Vea las líneas de Nazca desde el aire. Navegue en el lago más alto del mundo. Hoteles de primera.
$3.320

ARGENTINA

BUENOS AIRES, BARILOCHE, MENDOZA, 12 días. Disfrute de una gran metrópoli. Esquíe en uno de los lugares más bellos del mundo. Hoteles de 4 y 5 estrellas. Desayuno y cena.
$4.290

CHILE Y ARGENTINA

SANTIAGO, PUERTO MONTT, BARILOCHE, BUENOS AIRES, 12 días. Excursión a Viña del Mar y Valparaíso. Cruce de los Andes en minibús y barco. Hoteles de 3 y 4 estrellas.
$4.875

CARIBE

JAMAICA, 7 días. Happy Inn, todo incluido. Exclusivo para parejas.
$3.180

PUERTO RICO

SAN JUAN, 5 días. Hotel de 5 estrellas. Excursión a Ponce. Visita con guía al Viejo San Juan. Desayuno incluido.
$1.995

MÉXICO

MÉXICO, TAXCO, ACAPULCO, 7 días. Hoteles de 3 y 4 estrellas. Excursión a Teotihuacán. Desayuno bufet incluido.
$2.800

CANCÚN, 5 días. Hotel de 4 estrellas. Excursión a Cozumel. Visita a ruinas mayas. Las mejores playas.
$2.510

Solicite los programas detallados con variantes de hoteles e itinerarios a su agente de viajes.

Tel. 312-785-4455 info@agenciamundial.com

INTERCAMBIOS. Based on your classmate's answers, write a short message to your instructor about your classmate's plans.

Situación

PREPARACIÓN. Read the following situation with your partner. Then brainstorm the vocabulary, structures, and other information you will need for both roles in the conversation.

Role A. You have been working hard, and you would like to splurge on a weekend trip to do some special (but expensive) activities, like rent a car, go to a professional sports event or rock concert, eat out, and go shopping (**ir de compras**). Call and invite your friend to go. Explain your plan and be prepared to answer questions about the cost of the weekend adventure.

Role B. Your friend calls to invite you on a weekend trip. It sounds great, but also very expensive. Ask your friend questions to get an idea of the cost to help you decide whether to go or not. Figure out if you can afford it, and either accept or decline. Thank your friend for the invitation.

	ROLE A	ROLE B
Vocabulario	Food Free-time activities Numbers	Food Free-time activities Numbers
Funciones y formas	Answering questions Extending an invitation Convincing someone to do something	Accepting and declining invitations Asking questions Reacting to what you hear

INTERCAMBIOS. Using the information in **Preparación,** act out the conversation with your partner.

5 Stating what you know

ALFREDO: Me gustan mucho los músicos y ella **sabe** cantar muy bien.
ELENA: Sí, es una cantante fabulosa.

MARIO: Luisa, **conoces** a Liliana, ¿no?
LUISA: Sí, las dos estamos en la clase de arte de la profesora Ruiz.

Piénsalo. Indicate whether each sentence refers to knowing a fact, knowing how to do something, knowing a person, or being familiar with a place, an event, or a thing.

	Know a fact	Know how to do something	Know a person	Be familiar with a place, event, etc.
1. ¿**Conoces** la música afroperuana?				
2. Me gusta mucho la música, pero no **sé** bailar.				
3. ¿**Sabes** los nombres de esos grupos musicales?				
4. ¿**Conoces** a Alfredo Roncal? Toca la guitarra.				
5. ¿**Sabes** si hay un club de música hispana en la ciudad?				

Saber and *conocer*

> **Lengua**
>
> **Sé,** the **yo** form of the verb **saber,** has a written accent to distinguish it from the pronoun **se.**
>
> Yo **sé** que su hermano **se** llama José.

- Both **saber** and **conocer** mean *to know,* but they are not used interchangeably.

	SABER	CONOCER
yo	**sé**	**conozco**
tú	**sabes**	**conoces**
Ud., él, ella	**sabe**	**conoce**
nosotros/as	**sabemos**	**conocemos**
vosotros/as	**sabéis**	**conocéis**
Uds., ellos/as	**saben**	**conocen**

- Use **saber** to express knowledge of facts or pieces of information.

  Él **sabe** dónde está el club. *He knows where the club is.*

- Use **saber** + *infinitive* to express knowing how to do something.

  Yo **sé** tocar la guitarra. *I know how to play the guitar.*

- Use **conocer** to express that you know someone personally or are familiar with a place or a thing. **Conocer** also means *to meet* someone for the first time. Remember to use the personal **a** when referring to people.

  No **conozco a** los músicos. *I don't know the musicians (personally).*
  Pero **conozco** bien su música. *But I know (am very familiar with) their music.*
  Ella va a **conocer a** Luis. *She is going to meet (be introduced to) Luis.*

¿Comprendes? Complete each sentence with the correct form of **saber** or **conocer.**

1. Yo no __________ tocar la guitarra, ¿y tú?
2. Yo no __________ personalmente al presidente de Estados Unidos.
3. Andrés, ¿ __________ París?
4. Emilio y Gustavo __________ mucho de jazz.
5. Nosotros __________ a muchas personas en esta ciudad.
6. La profesora __________ hablar español muy bien.

PRÁCTICA

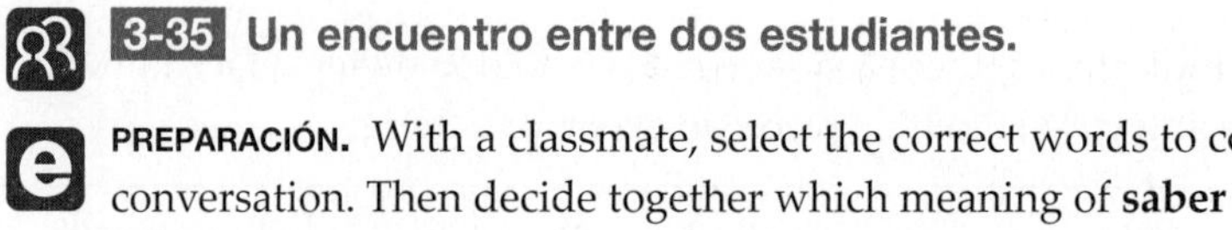

3-35 Un encuentro entre dos estudiantes.

PREPARACIÓN. With a classmate, select the correct words to complete the conversation. Then decide together which meaning of **saber** or **conocer** is expressed in each case: knowing a person, knowing a fact, etc.

RAÚL:	Soy un nuevo estudiante y no (1) _____ dónde está la biblioteca.	**a.** sé	**b.** conozco
SERGIO:	Es muy fácil. Tú (2) _____ dónde está la cafetería, ¿no? Pues, está al lado.	**a.** sabes	**b.** conoces
RAÚL:	Gracias. ¿Y (3) _____ si hay un club de español?	**a.** sabes	**b.** conoces
SERGIO:	Sí, claro, y (4) _____ que esta noche hay una reunión.	**a.** sé	**b.** conozco
RAÚL:	¡Magnífico! Solo (5) _____ a dos o tres personas en la universidad.	**a.** sé	**b.** conozco
SERGIO:	Pues allí vas a (6) _____ a muchos estudiantes.	**a.** saber	**b.** conocer

INTERCAMBIOS. Create a conversation similar to the one between Raúl and Sergio, using what you know about places, people, and events at your school.

 **3-36 ¿Sabes quién es...?** Ask your classmate if he/she knows who is being referred to and say what you know about the person. Take turns asking questions.

MODELO el actor principal de *Rápidos y furiosos*

E1: *¿Sabes quién es el actor principal de* Rápidos y furiosos*?*

E2: *Sí, sé quién es; es Vin Diesel.*

E1: *¿Conoces a Vin Diesel en persona?*

E2: *No, no conozco a Vin Diesel, pero sé quién es y conozco sus películas.*

1. el/la representante de tu distrito en la Cámara de Representantes (*Congress*)
2. el/la decano/a de la Facultad de Humanidades/Ciencias
3. tu profesor/a de español
4. el escritor más famoso de Perú
5. el/la gobernador/a de tu estado
6. el/la vicepresidente/a de Estados Unidos

 **3-37 Adivina, adivinador.** In small groups, take turns reading the descriptions and guessing who is being described. Then, create your own description and ask another group to guess.

MODELO E1: *Es una chica muy pobre que va a un baile. Allí conoce a un príncipe, pero a las 12:00 de la noche la chica debe volver a su casa.*

E2: *Sé quién es. Es Cenicienta (*Cinderella*).*

1. Es un gorila gigante con sentimientos (*feelings*) humanos. En una película aparece en el edificio Empire State de Nueva York.
2. Es una cantante muy famosa. Tiene el pelo largo y rubio. Canta, baila, escribe canciones y también participa en organizaciones benéficas. Es de Colombia.
3. Es una serie de películas de ciencia ficción que pasa en una galaxia lejana (*distant*). Algunos personajes son robots o androides. Un elemento importante es la Fuerza.
4. Es...

 **3-38 ¿Qué sabes hacer?** Ask your classmate if he/she knows how to do the following things. If your classmate says yes, ask more questions to get additional information.

MODELO preparar platos peruanos

E1: *¿Sabes preparar platos peruanos?*

E2: *No, no sé preparar platos peruanos. ¿Y tú?*

1. tocar un instrumento musical
2. cantar karaoke
3. bailar salsa y merengue
4. hablar otras lenguas
5. cantar en español
6. ...

 **3-39 Bingo.** To win this game, you have to fill in three boxes (horizontal, vertical, or diagonal) with the names of classmates who answer the questions correctly.

¿Quién sabe dónde está la ciudad de Cuzco? ____________	¿Quién sabe cuál es la capital de Perú? ____________	¿Quién sabe qué es Machu Picchu? ____________
¿Quién sabe qué océano está al oeste de Perú? ____________	¿Quién sabe cuál es la moneda (*currency*) de Perú? ____________	¿Quién sabe el nombre de un lago importante que está entre Perú y Bolivia? ____________
¿Quién conoce unos platos típicos de Perú? ____________	¿Quién conoce algún país hispanoamericano? ____________	¿Quién sabe cómo se llama la cadena de montañas de Perú? ____________

Situación

PREPARACIÓN. Read the following situation with your partner. Then prepare examples of the vocabulary, structures, and other information you will need to present your role in the conversation.

Role A. You are looking for a new roommate for your apartment. Your partner knows a student from Peru who is looking for a place to live. Ask your partner:
a. the Peruvian student's name;
b. where in Peru he/she is from; and
c. if your partner knows the Peruvian student well.
Also find out if the Peruvian student knows how to cook Peruvian dishes or how to play soccer (**fútbol**).

Role B. Your partner is looking for a new roommate for his/her apartment. Mention that you know a student from Peru who is looking for a place to live. Answer your partner's questions about that person.

	ROLE A	ROLE B
Vocabulario	Food Free-time activities Question words Peruvian food	Food Free-time activities Peruvian food
Funciones y formas	Asking questions Reacting to what you hear Talking about what or whom you know (**saber** vs. **conocer**)	Answering questions Reacting to what you hear Talking about what or whom you know (**saber** vs. **conocer**)

INTERCAMBIOS. Using the information in **Preparación,** act out the conversation with your partner.

MOSAICOS

ESCUCHA

Estrategia

Use background knowledge When you listen to a conversation, you can use your experience and your knowledge of the situation to enhance your comprehension.

 **3-40 Preparación.** Make a list of three enjoyable activities that you do with your family or friends, and three household-related chores that you do but don't always enjoy. Compare your lists with those of your partner.

  **3-41 Escucha.** Listen to José Antonio talk about his leisure activities, and Lidia describe hers and those of her children. Indicate who likes to do each activity, based on the information you hear. Interpretive

	José Antonio	Lidia	Lidia's children	Lidia and her children
1. ir a lugares interesantes				
2. estar cerca de la playa durante el verano				
3. esquiar durante el invierno				
4. limpiar (*to clean*) su apartamento				
5. leer un libro en la playa				
6. nadar				
7. lavar (*to wash*) platos				
8. mirar la televisión				
9. hacer surf				

Comprueba

I was able to . . .

- recognize names of people and places.
- recognize leisure activities.
- associate leisure activities with the people who do the activities.

3-42 Un paso más. Prepare a brief presentation to share with the class. Include the following:

1. your plans for the next holiday season (**verano, invierno,** etc.)
2. two leisure activities that you will do and with whom you will do them
3. the cost of the activities

HABLA

Estrategia

Inform yourself before you do a survey When preparing to do a survey, it is helpful to gather as much information as you can about the topic to ask questions.

3-43 Preparación. Read the tips for having fun with little money. Then, write questions to elicit the following information from a classmate.

Cómo pasarlo bien con poco dinero

Para divertirte con amigos, no necesitas mucho dinero, ¡solo buena disposición e imaginación! Las siguientes son excelentes ideas para pasar momentos memorables con amigos:

- Planificar un maratón de películas. Van a necesitar comida y bebidas.
- Organizar fiestas. Deben pensar en la comida que van a preparar y en algunas actividades divertidas.
- Organizar sesiones de juegos para jugar *Clue*, cartas (*cards*), etc.
- Salir con amigos a caminar y conversar en un parque.
- Practicar deportes con otras personas; por ejemplo, tenis, fútbol, básquetbol.

1. si organiza fiestas en su apartamento o casa
2. qué actividades divertidas prepara para las fiestas
3. frecuencia de sus fiestas
4. si hace maratones de películas
5. si organiza sesiones de juegos

3-44 Habla. In groups of four, use the questions from activity **3-43** to find out what your classmates normally do to have fun with friends and how often they do those activities. Take notes to report your findings later.

MODELO E1: *¿Organizas fiestas en tu apartamento con tus amigos/as?*
E2: *Sí, a veces.*
E1: *¿Cuántas veces por semestre haces fiestas con tus amigos?*
E2: *Hago fiestas una vez / dos veces por semestre.*

En directo

To express frequency:

todos los días *every day*
dos veces por semana *twice a week*
una vez al mes *once a month*
una vez por semestre *once a semester*
cada día *each day*

 Listen to a conversation with these expressions.

Comprueba

I was able to . . .

- ask questions that were easily understood.
- mention enjoyable activities in my questions and responses.
- talk about how frequently I do some activities.

3-45 Un paso más. Analyze the answers you gathered from the classmates you interviewed and present the findings to the class. Include answers to the following questions.

1. Tus compañeros de la clase de español, ¿se divierten de la misma manera (*same way*)? Expliquen.
2. ¿Qué actividades de diversión son más populares entre tus compañeros de la clase de español? ¿Con qué frecuencia hacen las actividades?
3. ¿Necesitan ustedes mucho dinero para divertirse con sus amigos? Expliquen por qué.

LEE

Estrategia

Look for and use key words Even though you may not know all the words when you read a text in Spanish, identifying and focusing on key words can help you understand the main ideas. Look the text over before starting to read to get a sense of what type of text it is and what it may be about.

3-46 Preparación. Look together at the menu for Casa Romano, an Italian restaurant in Trujillo. Identify the words you recognize. Tell each other what Italian dishes you like, what you eat when you go to an Italian restaurant, and if you know how to prepare any Italian dishes at home.

3-47 Lee. Read the menu and the restaurant review. Answer the questions that follow and be ready to share your responses with the class.

Comprueba

I was able to . . .

- identify menu categories.
- understand food vocabulary.
- understand opinions in a restaurant review.

Juana R.

★★★★★ Se escribió una opinión 24 agosto 2018

Buenas pizzas

Vivo cerca de Casa Romano y el restaurante siempre está lleno,[1] especialmente los fines de semana. Nosotros sabemos por qué: las pizzas son muy buenas, la atención[2] es eficiente y el ambiente[3] es agradable. Cuando hace buen tiempo, comemos al aire libre. Vamos todas las semanas porque sus pizzas son adictivas. Mi favorita es la pizza vegetariana. El servicio de entrega a domicilio[4] también es muy bueno: traen la pizza muy rápido y siempre está caliente.

[1]*full* [2]*service* [3]*atmosphere* [4]*delivery*

1. ¿Te gusta la comida italiana en general?
2. ¿Las pizzas de Casa Romano son similares a las pizzas que conoces o son diferentes?
3. Juana R. dice que va mucho a Casa Romano. ¿Por qué?
4. ¿Qué come Juana R. generalmente cuando va a Casa Romano?
5. ¿Puedes (*Can you*) identificar cuatro palabras en el menú de Casa Romano que son similares a palabras en inglés?

 **3-48 Un paso más.** In small groups, read Juana R's review of Casa Romero again. Then list four things she likes about the restaurant. Be ready to share your list with the class.

ESCRIBE

Estrategia

Write for your audience When you write an online review of a restaurant, a hotel, or an entertainment venue, you want to include both positive and negative elements, as well as recommendations. Think about what you would want to know if you were reading reviews before trying a place for the first time.

3-49 Preparación. Choose a restaurant you know well. Find the menu online, and mark the dishes you have tried. Make lists of adjectives that describe the food (**comida**), the service (**atención al cliente**), atmosphere (**ambiente**), and prices (**precios**).

e **3-50 Escribe.** Write a review of the restaurant you selected in activity **3-49.** Make your review as informative as possible, and don't forget to assign a numerical rating.

 **3-51 Un paso más.** Work with a classmate to read each other's reviews. Ask your partner questions to find out more about his/her restaurant.

Comprueba

I was able to . . .

- list foods I like to order at a restaurant.
- write some details about a restaurant, such as service, atmosphere, and prices.
- make recommendations about a restaurant.

En este capítulo...

Vocabulario

Las diversiones y las celebraciones	***Fun and celebrations***
la canción	*song*
el cumpleaños	*birthday*
la fiesta	*party*
la guitarra	*guitar*
la música	*music*
la película	*film, movie*
la reunión	*meeting; gathering*
el tiempo libre	*free time*
las vacaciones	*vacation*
los videojuegos	*videogames*

Las personas	***People***
el/la camarero/a	*server, waiter/ waitress (restaurant)*
el hombre	*man*
el/la joven	*young man/woman*
la mujer	*woman*

La comunicación	***Communication***
en línea	*online*
la noticia	*news*
las redes sociales	*social media*

Los lugares	***Places***
el cine	*movie theater*
la ciudad	*city*
el mar	*sea*
el restaurante	*restaurant*

Las descripciones	***Descriptions***
caliente	*hot*
estupendo/a	*great, wonderful*
fabuloso/a	*fabulous, great*
frío/a	*cold*
frito/a	*fried*
rico/a	*delicious*

En un café o restaurante	***In a coffee shop or restaurant***
la aceituna	*olive*
el agua	*water*
el almuerzo	*lunch*
el arroz	*rice*
la bebida	*drink*
el bistec	*steak*
el café	*coffee*
la cena	*dinner, supper*
el cereal	*cereal*
la cerveza	*beer*
el ceviche	*raw fish marinated in citrus juices*
la chicha morada	*purple corn drink*
la comida	*food; meal; dinner, supper*
el desayuno	*breakfast*
la ensalada	*salad*
los espaguetis	*spaghetti*
los frijoles	*beans*
la fruta	*fruit*
la hamburguesa	*hamburger*
el helado	*ice cream*
el huevo	*egg*
el jamón	*ham*
el jugo	*juice*
la leche	*milk*
la lechuga	*lettuce*
el maíz	*corn*
la naranja	*orange*
el pan tostado / la tostada	*toast*
la papa	*potato*
las papas fritas	*French fries*
el pescado	*fish*
el pollo	*chicken*
el queso	*cheese*
el refresco	*soda, soft drink*
el sándwich	*sandwich*
la sopa	*soup*
el tamal	*tamale*
el té	*tea*
el tomate	*tomato*
el vegetal / la verdura	*vegetable*
el vino	*wine*
la yuca	*yucca*

Verbos	***Verbs***
cantar	*to sing*
cenar	*to have dinner*
compartir	*to share*
descansar	*to rest*
hacer	*to do; to make*
ir	*to go*
nadar	*to swim*
oír	*to hear*
pedir	*to order*
poner	*to put*
poner la mesa	*to set the table*
poner una película	*to show a movie*
practicar deportes	*to practice sports*
salir	*to leave, to go out*
tocar (un instrumento)	*to play (an instrument)*
tomar el sol	*to sunbathe*
traer	*to bring*

Expresiones con *por*	***Expressions with* por**
por ciento	*percent*
por ejemplo	*for example*
por eso	*that is why*
por fin	*finally, at last*
por lo menos	*at least*
por supuesto	*of course*

Palabras y expresiones útiles	***Useful words and expressions***
al (contraction of **a + el**)	*to the*
cerca de	*close to, near*
después, luego	*after, later*
durante	*during*
felicidades	*congratulations*
me encanta...	*I love . . .*
¿qué te parece?	*what do you think?*
si	*if*

See page 114 for expressions that denote future time.
See page 126 for numbers 100 to 2,000,000.

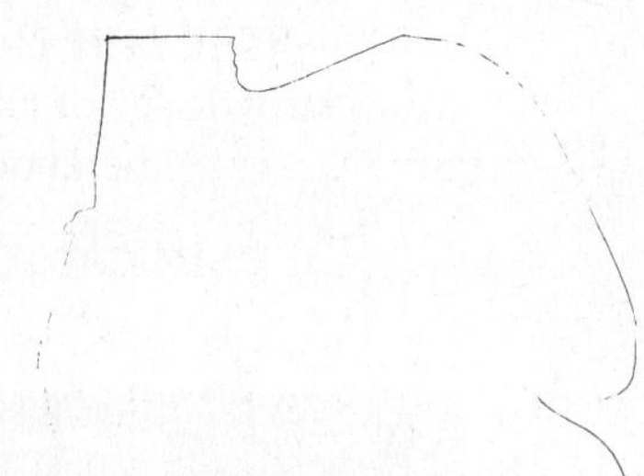

Capítulo 4
¿Cómo es tu familia?

Enfoque cultural
Venezuela

Vocabulario en contexto
Los miembros de la familia
¿Qué hacen los parientes?
Las rutinas familiares

Mosaico cultural
Las telenovelas venezolanas

En acción
Una fiesta en familia

Funciones y formas
Tener que + *infinitive*
Present tense of stem-changing verbs: **e → ie, o → ue,** and **e → i**
Reflexive verbs and pronouns
Reciprocal verbs and pronouns
Hace with expressions of time

Mosaicos
ESCUCHA Listen for a purpose
HABLA Organize information
LEE Use the title and illustrations to anticipate content
ESCRIBE Use your knowledge of the topic when you write

En este capítulo...
Vocabulario

Una familia venezolana se reúne para celebrar un cumpleaños.

Learning Outcomes

You will be able to:

- talk about family members and their daily routines
- express opinions, plans, preferences, and feelings
- express obligation
- express how long something has been going on
- talk about Venezuela in terms of its products, practices, and perspectives
- share information about families and family life in Hispanic countries and make cultural comparisons

Enfoque cultural

Venezuela

Venezuela tiene una de las reservas de petróleo más grandes del mundo.

Caracas es la capital de Venezuela. Está al norte del país, en el valle del río (*river*) Guaire.

Las hallacas, versión venezolana de los tamales, son típicas de la Navidad (*Christmas*).

Arte hispano

Simón Bolívar (1783–1830), nacido en Caracas, Venezuela, es un héroe de la independencia latinoamericana.

Enfoque cultural

¿Qué te parece?

- En el área de los Andes venezolanos hay una gran concentración de personas de origen italiano. Un plato típico es espaguetis con caraotas (frijoles) negras.
- *Venezuela* significa "pequeña Venecia". El italiano Américo Vespucio le dio (*gave*) el nombre al país. Las casas en el lago de Maracaibo le recordaron (*reminded him*) a Venecia, Italia.
- El Salto Ángel es la catarata más alta del mundo, más que las del Niágara. Tiene este nombre porque el aviador norteamericano Jimmie Angel fue la primera persona en verla desde su aeroplano, en 1933.

El turpial es el ave nacional de Venezuela. Es pequeño: entre 15 y 20 centímetros. Tiene un canto muy melodioso. Por eso, de una persona que canta muy bien se dice que "canta como un turpial".

La isla de Margarita está en el mar Caribe, al nordeste de la costa venezolana. La isla tiene playas de arena (*sand*) blanca y es hoy una importante atracción turística.

Las arepas son la base de la cocina y la dieta diaria de los venezolanos. Se preparan con una masa (*dough*) de maíz. Tienen nombres muy variados según sus ingredientes. La reina pepiada tiene pollo, cebolla (*onion*), aguacate (*avocado*) y mayonesa. La arepa tumbarrancho es para el desayuno. Se prepara con queso, repollo (*cabbage*), tomate y mortadela.

El cacao, junto con el petróleo, son los productos más valiosos de Venezuela. Se considera uno de los más exquisitos del mundo. Los conocedores del chocolate y las chocolaterías más exclusivas de Europa importan el cacao de Venezuela para sus productos.

To learn more about Venezuela, go online to view the *Club cultura* videos.

e **¿Cuánto sabes?** Completa estas oraciones con la información correcta.

1. El turpial es un ______________ que se distingue por su canto.
2. Las ______________ forman parte de la dieta básica de Venezuela.
3. ______________ le pone el nombre de Venezuela al país.
4. La influencia ______________ es muy evidente en la comida de la región andina.
5. El Salto Ángel es la ______________ más alta del mundo.
6. Aparte del petróleo, el producto que Venezuela exporta más es el ______________.

VOCABULARIO EN CONTEXTO

Talking about family members, what they do, and their daily routines

Los miembros de la familia

En Venezuela, como en otros países hispanos, las familias generalmente son extensas, y muchas veces varias generaciones conviven en la misma (*same*) casa. Los **abuelos** juegan un papel muy importante y tienen mucho contacto con los **nietos.** ¿Cuántos **niños** hay en esta familia?

El jugador de golf venezolano Jhonattan Vegas celebra con su **esposa** y su **hija** su éxito (*success*) en el Abierto de Canadá.

Patricia Velásquez es una actriz y modelo de Maracaibo. Es la quinta (*fifth*) de una familia de seis **hijos.** Ella tiene una hija, Maya, con su ex **pareja** Lauren, de quien está **separada.** Es fundadora de una organización de ayuda (*assistance*) a los indígenas wayúu de Venezuela.

Gustavo Dudamel también es de Venezuela y es un director de orquesta muy famoso. Su **padre** era (*was*) trombonista y su **madre,** profesora de canto. Está casado con una actriz española, María Valverde. Es su segundo **matrimonio;** tiene un **hijo,** Martín, con su ex esposa, Eloísa.

En otras palabras

Family terms vary from one region to another: **marido** and **mujer** are preferred in Spain, while **esposo** and **esposa** are used in most other countries. Terms of endearment for mother and father also vary: **mamá** and **papá** (Spain), **mami** and **papi** (Caribbean), **mamita** and **papito** (Venezuela).

Rubén habla de su familia.

Me llamo Rubén Gómez Sanhuesa y vivo con mis **padres,** mi **hermana** y mis abuelos en un apartamento en Caracas, la capital de Venezuela. Mi madre se llama Liliana y tiene una hermana, mi **tía** Jennifer, y un **hermano,** mi **tío** Luis. Su esposa es mi tía Daniela. Tienen tres hijos y viven también en Caracas. Mi **primo** Luisito es **el menor.** Mis **primas** Ana y Patricia son **gemelas.** Mis primos son muy simpáticos y **pasamos** mucho tiempo **juntos.** Mis tíos tienen solo dos **sobrinos** en Caracas, mi hermana Fabiana y yo. Su otra sobrina, mi prima Virginia, vive en Maracaibo, al oeste del país. Virginia es **la mayor** de todos los primos. La **nieta** favorita de mis abuelos es mi hermanita Fabiana. Tiene solo tres años y es la menor de todos sus nietos.

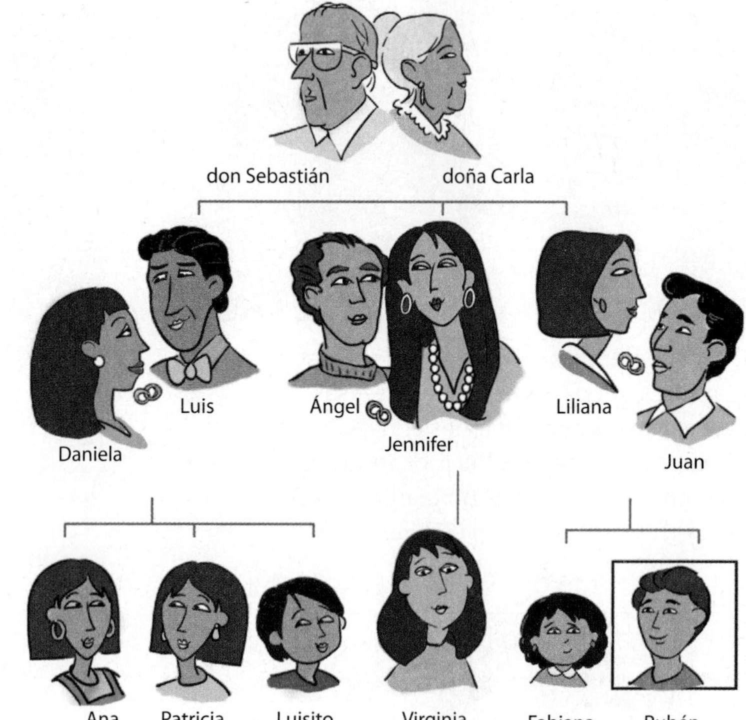

Lengua

The ending **-ito/a** (**Luis → Luisito**) is very common in Hispanic countries. It can express smallness (**hermanito/a, sillita**) or affection and intimacy (**mi primita**). Some names take the ending -**cito/a** (**Carmen → Carmencita**).

Otros miembros de la familia de Rubén

La hermana de mi **mamá** es mi tía Jennifer. Jennifer y Gabriel están **divorciados** y tienen una hija, mi prima Virginia. Ahora la tía Jennifer está casada con Ángel, el **padrastro** de Virginia. Gabriel está casado con Carmen y tienen un hijo, Alberto. Carmen es la **madrastra** de Virginia, y Alberto es su **medio hermano.**

Lengua

Other terms to describe family relationships are: **la familia mixta** (*blended family*), **el matrimonio igualitario** (*same-sex marriage*), **el padre soltero / la madre soltera** (*single parent*), **la pareja del mismo sexo** (*same-sex couple*), **la pareja de hecho** (*domestic partnership*).

PRÁCTICA

4-1 Escucha y confirma. Listen to the questions about Rubén and his family, and select the correct response based on his family tree.

1. **a.** su abuelo **b.** su padre
2. **a.** su prima **b.** su hermana
3. **a.** su hijo **b.** su nieto
4. **a.** Patricia **b.** Daniela
5. **a.** Luis **b.** Juan

4-2 La familia de Rubén. Completa las oraciones según (*according to*) la información que tienes sobre la familia de Rubén.

1. La hermana de Rubén se llama ___________.
2. Don Sebastián y doña Carla son los ___________ de Rubén.
3. Rubén es el ___________ de Juan.
4. Juan es el ___________ de Rubén, y Liliana es su madre.
5. Ana y Virginia son ___________.
6. Ana y Patricia son hermanas ___________.
7. Liliana es la ___________ de Luisito, Ana y Patricia.
8. Jennifer es la ___________ de Luis y Liliana.

4-3 ¿Cierto o falso?

PREPARACIÓN. Indica si cada oración es cierta (**C**) o falsa (**F**), según la información sobre la familia de Jennifer.

1. _____ La tía Jennifer está casada con Ángel.
2. _____ Ángel es el papá de Alberto.
3. _____ Carmen es la madrastra de Alberto.
4. _____ Jennifer es la madre de Virginia.
5. _____ Virginia tiene un medio hermano.

INTERCAMBIOS. Túrnense para hacerse preguntas sobre la familia de Rubén.

MODELO E1: *¿Quién es Ángel?*
E2: *Es el esposo de Jennifer y el…*

Cultura

3 bellezas (3 Beauties) This 2014 film, by Venezuelan director Carlos Caridad Montero, depicts a mother of three—two girls and a boy—and her obsession with beauty pageants. The jealousy and tensions between the two sisters during a cutthroat competition put the family at risk.

Conexiones ¿Qué otras películas centradas en las relaciones familiares conoces? Busca información en internet sobre una de esas películas y describe en clase las relaciones familiares.

4-4 ¿Cómo son?

PREPARACIÓN. Selecciona el miembro de la familia que corresponde a cada descripción. Luego compara tus respuestas con las de tu compañero/a.

1. _____ la esposa de mi padre **a.** mi primo
2. _____ el hermano de mi prima **b.** mi nieto
3. _____ los padres de mi padre **c.** mi madre
4. _____ el hijo de mi hijo **d.** mis abuelos
5. _____ el hermano de mi madre **e.** mi tío

INTERCAMBIOS. Intercambien la siguiente información sobre un miembro de su propia familia.

1. ¿Cómo se llama?
2. ¿Cómo es?
3. ¿Dónde está?

¿Qué hacen los parientes?

Luisito es mi primo favorito. Es **un poco** menor que yo. Jugamos mucho juntos. Los fines de semana montamos en bicicleta por el parque.

Hace dos años que mi prima Ana tiene **novio,** y **frecuentemente dice** que **quiere casarse** muy pronto. Patricia, su hermana gemela, **piensa** que Ana no debe casarse porque es muy joven.

Mis abuelos viven en una casa al lado del parque. Normalmente, ellos **pasean** por las mañanas y **almuerzan** muy **temprano.** Después, **duermen la siesta** y por la tarde **visitan** a sus **parientes.**

Mi tío Luis es un hombre muy **ocupado.** Sale de casa muy temprano y **vuelve tarde** todos los días. Mi tía Daniela, su esposa, dice que él **prefiere** el trabajo a su familia. Pienso que en todas las familias hay problemas. En mi familia también, pero eso es normal.

Lengua

In Spanish, the direct object of a verb is normally introduced without a preposition. However, the preposition **a** is required when the direct object is a person or a specific animal: **los abuelos visitan a sus parientes; la hija pasea al perro.**

PRÁCTICA

4-5 Para confirmar. Indica **Cierto** o **Falso,** según la información adicional sobre la familia de Rubén.

	Cierto	Falso
1. Normalmente, los abuelos pasean por las tardes.	_____	_____
2. Ana tiene novio.	_____	_____
3. Patricia piensa que su hermana es muy joven para casarse.	_____	_____
4. El tío Luis duerme la siesta todos los días.	_____	_____
5. La tía Daniela monta en bicicleta por la mañana.	_____	_____
6. Luisito es un poco menor que Rubén.	_____	_____

4-6 ¿Quién es y cómo es? PREPARACIÓN. Escoge (*Choose*) a un miembro de una familia famosa (los Bush, los Obama, los Jolie-Pitt, los Kardashian, etc.), investiga su familia en internet y prepara su árbol (*tree*) familiar. Usa como modelo el árbol de la familia de Rubén en la página 142. Incluye nombres y apellidos.

INTERCAMBIOS. Intercambien (*Exchange*) los árboles de familia y háganse preguntas (*ask each other questions*) sobre su investigación.

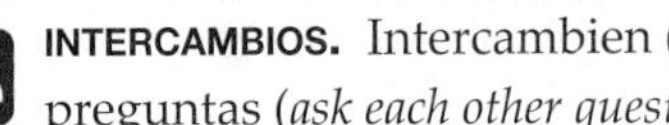

MODELO Carolina Herrera

E1: *¿Quién es Guillermo Behrens Tello?*

E2: *Es el primer esposo de Carolina Herrera.*

E1: *¿Cómo se llaman sus hijas?*

4-7 El arte de preguntar. **PREPARACIÓN.** Escribe las preguntas a estas respuestas.

MODELO Mi madre se llama Dolores.
¿Cómo se llama tu madre?

1. Tengo dos hermanos.
2. Vivo con mi madre y mi padrastro.
3. Mi hermana tiene 12 años.
4. Mis abuelos viven en Caracas.
5. Los fines de semana mi padre monta en bicicleta.
6. Carlos es mi primo favorito.

INTERCAMBIOS. Háganse preguntas para obtener información sobre la familia de su compañero/a. Después, compartan (*share*) esta información con la clase.

Cultura

El matrimonio y la identidad en el siglo XXI

Laws about marriage and gender identity rights are changing in the Spanish-speaking world. Same-sex marriage is now legal in Spain, Argentina, Colombia, Uruguay, and parts of Mexico; Chile and Ecuador recognize civil unions of same-sex couples. Chile, as well as Panama and Costa Rica, are actively considering changes to their marriage laws. Discrimination on the basis of sexual orientation is prohibited by law in Spain and in all countries in Latin America. In a 2018 advisory opinion, the Inter-American Court of Human Rights affirmed that the American Convention on Human Rights requires countries to allow same-sex couples to access civil marriage.

Comparaciones ¿Es legal el matrimonio entre parejas del mismo sexo en tu país, estado o comunidad? ¿Son discriminadas estas parejas? ¿Existe protección legal frente a la discriminación motivada por la orientación sexual o identidad de género?

4-8 Mi familia. Busca fotos de tus parientes en tu teléfono celular. Luego, muéstrale (*show*) las fotos a tu compañero/a y describe a tus familiares.

1. nombre y apellido
2. relación familiar
3. personalidad
4. actividades que compartes con esta persona

4-9 Actividades de la familia. Pídele (*Ask for*) la siguiente información a tu compañero/a sobre su familia.

1. número de personas en la casa, edad (*age*) y parentesco (*kinship*)
2. ocupación y descripción (física y de personalidad) de dos miembros de la familia
3. actividades de estas personas en su tiempo libre
4. nombre del pariente favorito, parentesco y razón (*reason*) de su preferencia

Cultura

Los apellidos In most Hispanic countries, people officially use two surnames: the first is their father's and the second is their mother's. For example, in Rubén's family, his father's name is Juan Gómez and his mother's name is Liliana Sanhuesa. Rubén's official name, then, is Rubén Gómez Sanhuesa.

Comparaciones ¿Cuántos nombres y apellidos tienes? En la cultura hispana, ¿cuál sería (*would be*) tu nombre oficial?

Las rutinas familiares

En casa de Rubén hay mucha actividad por la mañana.

Los niños **se despiertan** a las siete. **Se levantan, se lavan** y luego **desayunan** en la cocina con sus padres. Después salen para la escuela.

Poco después, la madre **se ducha, se seca, se viste** y **se maquilla.**

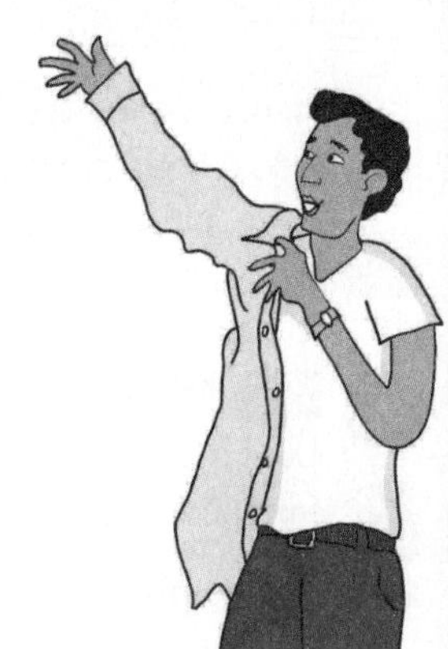

Más tarde, el padre **se afeita, se baña, se pone la ropa** y sale de casa a las nueve.

PRÁCTICA

4-10 Para confirmar. Pon (*Put*) en orden cronológico las siguientes oraciones según las escenas.

_____ La madre se maquilla.
_____ Los niños se despiertan a las siete.
_____ El padre se baña y luego se pone la ropa.
_____ La madre se ducha.
_____ El padre sale de casa a las nueve.
_____ Los niños desayunan y después salen para la escuela.

4-11 Las rutinas diarias. Túrnense para contestar las siguientes preguntas sobre la rutina diaria de la familia de Rubén.

1. ¿Con quién desayunan los niños?
2. ¿Quién se maquilla por las mañanas?
3. ¿A qué hora se despiertan los niños?
4. ¿Quién sale de casa a las nueve?
5. ¿Quién se afeita por las mañanas?
6. ¿Qué hace la madre después de ducharse?

4-12 Mañanas ocupadas. Indica las acciones diarias de los miembros de tu familia. Después, compara la rutina de tu familia con la de tu compañero/a.

	Se despierta temprano	Se ducha por la mañana	Se pone ropa elegante	Desayuna con la familia
mi padre (padrastro)				
mi madre (madrastra)				
mi hermano/a				
mi abuelo/a				
mi tío/a				

4-13 ¿Y tú? **PREPARACIÓN.** Completa las oraciones con las expresiones de la lista para describir tu rutina de los miércoles.

me baño	me ducho	me visto
desayuno	me levanto	salgo para la universidad
me despierto	me maquillo	

Primero, ________________, luego ________________.

Poco después, ________________, más tarde ________________.

Por último, ________________.

Lengua

Use the following expressions to organize time sequentially: **primero, luego, poco después, más tarde,** and **por último.**

INTERCAMBIOS. Compara tus respuestas con las de tu compañero/a para ver qué tienen en común.

MODELO E1: *Los miércoles me levanto a las seis de la mañana. ¿Y tú?*
E2: *Yo me levanto a las siete y media.*

4-14 ¿A qué hora? Túrnense para hacerse las siguientes preguntas sobre la rutina diaria.

1. ¿Te duchas por la mañana o por la noche?
2. ¿Quién se levanta temprano en tu familia?
3. ¿Te vistes antes o después de desayunar?
4. ¿Te pones ropa elegante o informal para ir a clase?
5. ¿A qué hora te acuestas durante la semana?
6. ¿A qué hora te acuestas los fines de semana?
7. ¿A qué hora te levantas los fines de semana?
8. ¿A qué hora tienes la clase de español?

4-15 En la casa de Gloria. Listen as Gloria describes her family's routine and indicate the actions that she mentions.

1. ____ Nos despertamos temprano durante la semana.
2. ____ Desayunamos juntos los fines de semana.
3. ____ Yo me visto y me maquillo.
4. ____ Mi esposo sale tarde de la casa.
5. ____ Mi hija se pone la ropa.

Mosaico cultural

Las telenovelas venezolanas

En muchos países del mundo, la familia ocupa un lugar importante en los programas televisivos. La telenovela *Piel Salvaje* es una de las más famosas de la televisión venezolana. Esta serie es sobre la rivalidad de dos familias poderosas (*powerful*) que compiten por el mercado (*market*) de los cosméticos. Una familia es dueña (*owner*) de la marca Mascarada, y la otra familia es propietaria de Capricho's. Los miembros de las dos familias se odian (*hate each other*), y se perjudican (*harm each other*) mucho. Esta telenovela es muy popular porque tiene mucha acción y suspenso.

En México, Colombia, Argentina y España, este tipo de programa es también muy popular. En España, por ejemplo, la serie *Los Serrano* cuenta la historia de Diego Serrano, un viudo (*widower*) con tres hijos. La historia se complica cuando Diego se casa con Lucía, madre divorciada con dos hijas. Las dos familias tienen que adaptarse para convivir. Al final, como es el caso en muchas familias, la convivencia requiere paciencia y comprensión entre todos los miembros.

Los actores trabajan en el plató (*set*) de una telenovela.

El elenco (*cast*) de la serie *Los Serrano*

Compara

1. ¿Qué familias famosas hay en la televisión de tu país? ¿Cuál es tu favorita?
2. Escoge a una familia de una serie televisiva que te gusta. Describe a esa familia.
3. Compara la familia de la serie televisiva con tu propia familia. ¿Qué tienen en común? ¿Qué diferencias hay entre ellas?

En acción

Una fiesta en familia

Antes de ver

4-16 ¿A solas (*alone*) o en familia? Indica las actividades que haces típicamente a solas (**S**) o en familia (**F**).

1. _____ Celebro mi cumpleaños.
2. _____ Me lavo los dientes (*teeth*).
3. _____ Almuerzo los domingos.
4. _____ Escucho música en mi teléfono.
5. _____ Me visto.
6. _____ Salgo para mis clases.
7. _____ Duermo la siesta en el sofá.
8. _____ Visito a mis parientes.
9. _____ Converso sobre temas (*topics*) políticos.
10. _____ Me ducho.

Mientras ves

4-17 A celebrar. Indica **Cierto** o **Falso**, según el video. Corrige (*Correct*) las afirmaciones falsas.

	Cierto	Falso
1. Blanca prepara un típico desayuno colombiano.	_____	_____
2. Los estudiantes quieren (*want*) conocer a la familia de Blanca.	_____	_____
3. Yolanda habla de la celebración de la independencia colombiana en Nueva York.	_____	_____
4. Esteban muestra (*shows*) un video de sus amigos.	_____	_____
5. El hijo de Blanca llega a la fiesta con su esposa.	_____	_____
6. Yolanda quiere comer la carne que prepara Federico.	_____	_____

Después de ver

4-18 Lejos de casa.

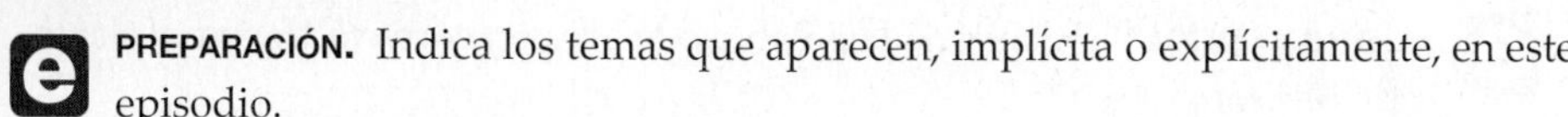

PREPARACIÓN. Indica los temas que aparecen, implícita o explícitamente, en este episodio.

1. _____ la importancia de la familia
2. _____ las oportunidades de trabajo en el extranjero (*abroad*)
3. _____ las tradiciones culturales
4. _____ la separación física entre los padres y los hijos
5. _____ la tecnología como medio de comunicación

INTERCAMBIOS. Comparen sus respuestas de **Preparación** y háganse las siguientes preguntas.

1. ¿Qué fiestas celebras siempre en familia? Describe una fiesta típica con tu familia.
2. ¿Qué fiestas prefieres celebrar con tus amigos/as? ¿Son distintas a las fiestas que celebras con tu familia? Explica.
3. Describan cómo celebra la gente la independencia colombiana en Nueva York. ¿De qué manera es similar a la celebración del 4 de julio? ¿Hay alguna diferencia? Expliquen.

FUNCIONES Y FORMAS

1 Expressing obligation

La Sra. Rojas no está contenta hoy y escribe un mensaje para su familia.

Planes para nuestra familia

De hoy en adelante, todos **tenemos que ser** más organizados. Verónica **tiene que ver** menos televisión. Miguel **tiene que practicar** el piano todos los días. Papá **tiene que hacer** más ejercicio. Agustín y Toño **tienen que terminar** su tarea antes de jugar videojuegos. Finalmente, ¡¡¡TODOS **tenemos que ayudar** con las tareas domésticas!!!

Mamá

Piénsalo. Selecciona la forma de **tener que** que corresponde a cada obligación del mensaje de la Sra. Rojas.

1. _____ Los niños **deben** mirar menos televisión.
2. _____ El padre **debe** hacer ejercicio.
3. _____ Miguel, **debes** practicar el piano todos los días.
4. _____ Todos **debemos** colaborar para mantener la casa limpia (*clean*).
5. _____ Y yo **debo** calmarme (*calm down*).

a. tengo que
b. tienes que
c. tiene que
d. tenemos que
e. tienen que

Tener que + infinitive

- Use **tener que** to express what someone *has to, needs to,* or *must* do.

Eliana, **tienes que estudiar** más.	*Eliana, you have to study more.*
Tengo que visitar a mis abuelos este fin de semana.	*I have to visit my grandparents this weekend.*

¿Comprendes? Selecciona la palabra o expresión correcta para completar cada oración.

1. Tengo que _____ a mis abuelos.
2. Mi madre _____ que trabajar.
3. Nosotros tenemos _____ ir de compras.
4. Mis amigos _____ que estudiar.
5. Y tú, ¿qué tienes _____ hoy?

a. tienen
b. que hacer
c. que
d. visitar
e. tiene

PRÁCTICA

4-19 Mis obligaciones. **PREPARACIÓN.** Indica las tareas que tienes que hacer regularmente. Con tu compañero/a, comparen sus obligaciones.

_____ pasear al perro
_____ hacer ejercicio
_____ comprar comida
_____ hacer la tarea para mis clases
_____ poner los platos sucios (*dirty*) en el lavaplatos (*dishwasher*)
_____ leer y contestar el correo electrónico
_____ asistir a mis clases
_____ trabajar por las tardes
_____ hablar con mi familia

INTERCAMBIOS. Ahora dile a tu compañero/a cuándo tienes que hacer estas tareas. Luego, comparen sus obligaciones. ¿Quién de ustedes tiene más obligaciones?

MODELO E1: *Tengo que pasear al perro todos los días. ¿Y tú?*
E2: *Yo no tengo que pasear al perro porque no tengo un perro, pero tengo que comprar comida para mi gato...*

Cultura

El Parque Nacional Canaima Canaima is a UNESCO World Heritage site in eastern Venezuela near the border with Brazil and Guyana. It is known for its varied flora and fauna, as well as its plateau-like mountains, called **tepuis.** Angel Falls (**Salto Ángel**), the highest waterfall in the world, begins its descent from a **tepui.** This popular tourist destination inspired the Paradise Falls setting in the Disney animated film *Up* (2009).

Comunidades ¿Hay parques en tu región o país dedicados al ecoturismo o al turismo en la naturaleza? ¿Qué hacen los turistas allí?

El Salto Ángel

4-20 Un viaje (*trip*) a Venezuela.

PREPARACIÓN. Tu familia va a viajar a Venezuela. Selecciona la recomendación apropiada para cada persona. Después añade (*add*) algo que deseas hacer tú y explica por qué.

1. _____ Mi hermana desea visitar lugares históricos.
2. _____ A mis abuelos les gustan las vistas panorámicas.
3. _____ Mi prima desea visitar lugares religiosos.
4. _____ Mis padres desean hacer ecoturismo.

a. Tiene que ver la Basílica de Nuestra Señora de Chiquinquirá, en Maracaibo.
b. Tiene que ir a Coro, una ciudad colonial muy antigua.
c. Tienen que hacer una excursión en el teleférico (*cable car*) de Mérida.
d. Tienen que ir al Parque Nacional Laguna de Tacarigua para ver las tortugas (*turtles*).

INTERCAMBIOS. Busquen información en internet y preparen una breve descripción de uno de los lugares o eventos siguientes. Incluyan la ubicación (*location*) y las actividades asociadas con el lugar o el evento. Luego, compartan la información con la clase.

1. la ciudad de Coro
2. el archipiélago Los Roques
3. el carnaval de El Callao
4. el Museo Bolivariano

4-21 Sugerencias. **PREPARACIÓN.** ¿Qué tienen que hacer (o no) las personas en estas circunstancias? Túrnense para responder.

MODELO Luis no tiene dinero (*money*).
E1: *Tiene que buscar trabajo.*
E2: *No tiene que perder el tiempo en las redes sociales.*

1. Mi amigo Juan tiene un examen muy difícil el lunes.
2. Francisco nunca tiene energía. Siempre está cansado.
3. Manuel y Victoria están casados y no se llevan (*get along*) bien.
4. Mi hermana Marta ve televisión todos los días y saca malas notas en sus clases.
5. Luis y Emilia quieren aprender español.
6. Isabel y Lucía desean visitar un país hispano, pero no hablan español.

INTERCAMBIOS. Escribe tres problemas personales. Explícale tus problemas a tu compañero/a y dile qué tienes que hacer.

MODELO *Vivo en un apartamento muy feo. Tengo que buscar un apartamento bonito…*

Situación

PREPARACIÓN. Lean esta situación. Luego, compartan ejemplos de vocabulario, gramática y otra información que necesitan para desarrollar la conversación.

Role A. Your parents are angry at you because you a) stay out late; b) do not study enough; c) prefer to spend all your time with your friends; and d) play on your phone at mealtimes. You ask a friend for advice.

Role B. A friend calls you to discuss family problems. Listen and ask appropriate questions, then tell your friend what you think he/she should do.

	ROLE A	ROLE B
Vocabulario	Family Leisure activities	Family Leisure activities
Funciones y formas	Talking about routines Stem-changing verbs Present tense of verbs	Asking questions Stem-changing verbs Telling someone what to do **tener** + **que** + *infinitive*

INTERCAMBIOS. Practiquen la conversación, incorporando el vocabulario y las funciones de **Preparación.** Luego, represéntenla ante la clase.

2 Expressing opinions, plans, preferences, and feelings

Carmen habla de los planes para el Día de las Familias.

Quiero hablar seriamente con ustedes y les **pido** ayuda. El jueves **vienen** las familias a visitar la universidad y **pienso** que debemos preparar una buena fiesta de bienvenida. Luisa y Ana **pueden** preparar un desayuno o, si **prefieren,** yo preparo el desayuno y ustedes **sirven** el café. Juan **quiere** comprar unos globos (*balloons*) para decorar la residencia estudiantil porque no **cuestan** mucho. El día **empieza** con una visita al campus. Luego, los estudiantes **almuerzan** con sus familias en la cafetería. Por la tarde, vamos al estadio para ver el partido (*game*) de fútbol. Nuestro equipo (*team*) **juega** bien este año y todos pueden divertirse. ¿Qué **piensan** de mis planes? ¿**Tienen** ustedes otras ideas?

Piénsalo. Selecciona el infinitivo que corresponde al verbo en cada oración.

1. _____ Carmen **pide** la ayuda de sus compañeros.		**a.** costar
2. _____ Juan **quiere** decorar la residencia estudiantil.		**b.** jugar
3. _____ Luisa y Ana **pueden** preparar el desayuno.		**c.** pedir
4. _____ Los estudiantes **almuerzan** con sus familias.		**d.** poder
5. _____ El equipo **juega** un partido.		**e.** almorzar
6. _____ Juan dice que los globos no **cuestan** mucho.		**f.** querer

Present tense of stem-changing verbs: *e → ie, o → ue,* and *e → i*

- Some common verbs in Spanish undergo a vowel change in all forms of the present tense except **nosotros/as** and **vosotros/as.**

PENSAR (e → ie) (*to think*)			
yo	pi**e**nso	nosotros/as	pensamos
tú	pi**e**nsas	vosotros/as	pensáis
Ud., él, ella	pi**e**nsa	Uds., ellos/as	pi**e**nsan

VOLVER (o → ue) (*to return*)			
yo	v**ue**lvo	nosotros/as	volvemos
tú	v**ue**lves	vosotros/as	volvéis
Ud., él, ella	v**ue**lve	Uds., ellos/as	v**ue**lven

PEDIR (e → i) (*to ask for*)			
yo	p**i**do	nosotros/as	pedimos
tú	p**i**des	vosotros/as	pedís
Ud., él, ella	p**i**de	Uds., ellos/as	p**i**den

- Other common verbs that have vowel changes in the stem are the following:

e → ie	o → ue	e → i
cerrar *to close*	**almorzar** *to have lunch*	**repetir** *to repeat*
empezar *to begin, to start*	**costar** *to cost*	**servir** *to serve*
entender *to understand*	**dormir** *to sleep*	
preferir *to prefer*	**encontrar** *to find*	
querer *to want; to love*	**poder** *to be able to, can*	

- Use **pensar** + *infinitive* to express what you or someone else is planning to do.

Pienso estudiar esta noche. — *I plan to study tonight.*

Pensamos comer a las ocho. — *We are planning to eat at 8:00.*

- Note the irregular **yo** form in the following **e → ie** and **e → i** stem-changing verbs.

tener (*to have*)	**tengo**, t**ie**nes, t**ie**ne, tenemos, tenéis, t**ie**nen
venir (*to come*)	**vengo**, v**ie**nes, v**ie**ne, venimos, venís, v**ie**nen
decir (*to say, to tell*)	**digo**, d**i**ces, d**i**ce, decimos, decís, d**i**cen
seguir (*to follow*)	**sigo**, s**i**gues, s**i**gue, seguimos, seguís, s**i**guen

- In the verb **jugar** (*to play a game or sport*), **u** changes to **ue.**

Mario **juega** muy bien al tenis. — *Mario plays tennis very well.*

Nosotros **jugamos** todas las semanas. — *We play every week.*

e ¿Comprendes? Completa las oraciones con la forma correcta del verbo.

preferir (e → ie)

1. Yo _________ café.
2. Mis padres _________ té.

dormir (o → ue)

3. Mi perro _________ mucho.
4. ¿_________ mucho tú?

servir (e → i)

5. Nosotros _________ refrescos.
6. Usted no _________ cerveza.

poder (o → ue)

7. ¿_________ ustedes ir al cine?
8. Yo no _________ salir hoy.

PRÁCTICA

4-22 Los planes. **PREPARACIÓN.** Indica tus preferencias y planes.

1. ¿Prefieres tener una familia grande o pequeña?
   _____ Prefiero tener una familia grande.
   _____ Prefiero tener una familia pequeña.
2. ¿Quieres tomar cursos en el verano o prefieres trabajar?
   _____ Quiero tomar cursos en el verano.
   _____ Prefiero trabajar en el verano.
3. ¿Sigues las tradiciones de tu familia o quieres ser más independiente?
   _____ Sigo las tradiciones de mi familia.
   _____ Quiero ser más independiente.
4. Cuando tienes amigos en casa, ¿qué sirves para beber?
   _____ Sirvo vino y cerveza.
   _____ Sirvo agua y refrescos.
5. Al final de las vacaciones, ¿vuelves a la universidad triste o contento/a?
   _____ Estoy triste cuando vuelvo a la universidad.
   _____ Estoy contento/a cuando vuelvo a la universidad.

INTERCAMBIOS. Ahora pregúntale a tu compañero/a sobre sus planes y preferencias. Debes pedir más información.

MODELO E1: *¿Prefieres tener una familia grande o pequeña?*
E2: *Prefiero tener una familia pequeña.*
E1: *¿Cuántos hijos quieres tener? / ¿Por qué prefieres una familia pequeña?*
E2: …

4-23 Planes para la boda (*wedding*).

PREPARACIÓN. Beatriz y Miguel se casan en un mes. Completa la descripción de los planes para la boda con un verbo de la lista y en la forma correcta.

empezar	poder	querer	servir
entender	preferir	seguir	volver

Beatriz y Miguel (1) ______________ tener una boda pequeña, pero elegante. La ceremonia (2) ______________ a las 7:00. Los sobrinos y primos más pequeños de los novios no asisten a la ceremonia. Ellos no (3) ______________ la ceremonia y (4) ______________ jugar en el patio fuera de la iglesia (*church*). Después de la ceremonia, todos van a un restaurante, donde los invitados (5) ______________ bailar y cenar. Los camareros (6) ______________ una cena italiana porque los padres de Miguel son de Italia. Después de la cena, la familia (7) ______________ a la casa de los padres de la novia. Los invitados (8) ______________ en la fiesta, pero Beatriz y Miguel salen para su luna de miel (*honeymoon*).

INTERCAMBIOS. Intercambien información sobre sus preferencias haciéndose las siguientes preguntas.

1. ¿Qué piensas de las bodas grandes? ¿Prefieres las celebraciones pequeñas?
2. ¿Qué fiesta quieres celebrar este año?
3. ¿Puedes invitar a tu familia a esa fiesta o solo a tus amigos?
4. Normalmente, ¿qué comidas sirven en las fiestas de tu universidad?

4-24 ¿Qué pasa en las reuniones (*gatherings*) familiares?

PREPARACIÓN. Descríbele las reuniones de tu familia a tu compañero/a. Deben tomar nota de las semejanzas (*similarities*) y las diferencias.

MODELO preparar la comida
E1: *En las reuniones de mi familia, mi abuela prepara mucha comida.*
E2: *En las reuniones de mi familia, tenemos mucha comida también. Pero mi madre y mi tía preparan la comida.*

1. servir la comida
2. jugar con los niños
3. venir de muy lejos
4. dormir en el sofá
5. preferir hablar de deportes
6. volver a casa para celebrar el Día de Acción de Gracias

INTERCAMBIOS. Hablen de una semejanza y una diferencia entre las reuniones de sus familias. Compartan la información con la clase.

Cultura

Las bodas hispanas
Weddings are important celebrations for Hispanic families. Many relatives and friends attend the ceremony, which can be a religious event or a civil ceremony. When a Hispanic woman marries, she does not take her husband's surname but rather continues to use the name she grew up with.

Comparaciones En tu cultura, ¿qué apellido usan las personas cuando se casan? ¿Qué sistema prefieres y por qué?

Lengua

Pensar de is used to ask for an opinion. **Pensar que** is normally used in the answer.

¿Qué **piensas del** proyecto? *What do you think of the project?*

Pienso que es excelente. *I think it is excellent.*

Pensar en is the Spanish equivalent of *to think about someone or something.*

¿**Piensas en** tu familia cuando estás fuera de casa? *Do you think about your family when you are away from home?*

Sí, **pienso** mucho **en** ellos. *Yes, I think about them a lot.*

 **4-25 Entrevista.** Túrnense para entrevistarse (*interview each other*). Hablen sobre los siguientes temas (*topics*) y después compartan la información con otra persona u otra pareja.

1. las actividades que prefieren hacer con su familia o con sus amigos
2. los deportes que prefieren practicar o mirar en la televisión
3. a qué hora empiezan a hacer la tarea generalmente
4. si duermen una siesta durante el día
5. si vuelven a la casa de sus padres para las vacaciones
6. qué piensan hacer después de graduarse de la universidad

 **4-26 Costumbres y planes familiares.** Piensen en sus familiares y describan sus costumbres o sus planes usando los verbos de la lista.

MODELO E1: *Mi hermano Roberto vuelve a casa todos los fines de semana.*
E2: *Mi prima Julia quiere estudiar español.*

dormir	pensar	querer
jugar	preferir	volver

Situación

PREPARACIÓN. Lean esta situación. Luego, compartan ejemplos de vocabulario, gramática y otra información que necesitan para desarrollar la conversación.

Role A. Your favorite cousin and a friend are planning to visit you at your university. Talk to your cousin on the phone and ask him/her about their plans and preferences. You want to be a good host and need to find out:

a. when they are planning to visit;
b. if they prefer to stay in a hotel or in your dorm room;
c. what places around the university they want to visit and why; and
d. when they plan to return home.

Role B. You and your friend want to visit your cousin at the university. Answer your cousin's questions and explain your preferences.

	ROLE A	ROLE B
Vocabulario	Question words Family members Travel dates	Vocabulary related to travel
Funciones y formas	Discussing plans **pensar** + *infinitive* Expressing preferences **querer** + *infinitive*	Discussing plans **pensar** + *infinitive* Expressing preferences **querer** + *infinitive*

INTERCAMBIOS. Practiquen la conversación, incorporando el vocabulario y las funciones de **Preparación.** Luego, represéntenla ante la clase.

En directo

These expressions help maintain the flow of conversation:

¡Cuánto me alegro! *I am so happy for you!*
Claro, claro... *Of course . . .*
¡Qué bien/bueno! *That's great!*
¡Enhorabuena! *Congratulations!*

Listen to a conversation with these expressions.

3 Talking about daily routines

Me llamo Óscar Torres. Mi esposa Rosa y yo tenemos una vida muy ocupada. **Nos levantamos** a las seis todos los días.

Yo **me ducho** mientras Rosa **se viste** rápidamente.

Después, Rosa **despierta** a Carlitos y a Roberto, nuestros hijos. Roberto **se viste,** y Rosa **viste** a Carlitos.

Desayunamos en familia y luego todos **nos lavamos** los dientes antes de salir de casa a las siete.

Piénsalo. Para cada acción, indica si la persona se hace la acción **a sí mismo/a** (*himself/herself/themselves*) o **a otra persona.**

ACCIÓN	A SÍ MISMO/A	A OTRA PERSONA
1. Óscar **se ducha** por la mañana.	_____	_____
2. Rosa **despierta** a Carlitos.	_____	_____
3. La madre **viste** al niño porque es muy pequeño.	_____	_____
4. Rosa **se viste** rápidamente.	_____	_____
5. Nosotros **nos lavamos** los dientes después de desayunar.	_____	_____
6. Rosa probablemente **se baña** por la noche, porque no tiene tiempo por la mañana.	_____	_____

Reflexive verbs and pronouns

- Reflexive verbs express what people do to or for themselves.

LAVARSE (*to wash oneself*)			
yo	**me lavo**	nosotros/as	**nos lavamos**
tú	**te lavas**	vosotros/as	**os laváis**
Ud., él, ella	**se lava**	Uds., ellos/as	**se lavan**

Reflexive:
Mi hermana **se lava** las manos. — *My sister washes her hands.*

Non-reflexive:
Mi hermana **lava** el auto. — *My sister washes the car.*

- A reflexive pronoun refers back to the subject of the sentence. English sometimes uses the pronouns ending in *-self/-selves* to express reflexive meaning. In many cases, Spanish uses reflexives where English does not.

  Yo **me levanto, me ducho, me seco** y **me visto** rápidamente. — *I get up, take a shower, dry myself, and get dressed quickly.*

- Place reflexive pronouns after the word **no** in negative constructions.

  Rosa **no se levanta** temprano los fines de semana. — *Rosa does not get up early on weekends.*

- The pronoun **se** attached to an infinitive indicates the verb uses the pronouns **me, te, se, nos, os** in its conjugated forms.

  vestir — *to dress (someone else)*

  vestirse — *to get dressed (oneself)*

- With a conjugated verb followed by an infinitive, place the pronoun before the conjugated verb or attach it to the infinitive.

  Yo **me** voy a levantar a las siete.
  Yo voy a levantar**me** a las siete. } *I am going to get up at seven.*

- When referring to parts of the body and articles of clothing, use definite articles rather than possessives with reflexive verbs.

  Me lavo **los** dientes. — *I brush my teeth.*

  Roberto se pone **la** chaqueta. — *Roberto puts on his jacket*

- Some verbs change meaning when they use reflexive pronouns.

dormir	*to sleep*	**dormirse**	*to fall asleep*
levantar	*to raise, to lift*	**levantarse**	*to get up*
llamar	*to call*	**llamarse**	*to be named*
poner	*to put, to place*	**ponerse**	*to put on*
quitar	*to take away*	**quitarse**	*to take off*

- Here is a list of common verbs that are conjugated with reflexive pronouns. Note the stem changes that occur in many of them.

acostarse (ue)	*to go to bed, to lie down*	**lavarse**	*to wash (oneself)*
afeitarse	*to shave (oneself)*	**maquillarse**	*to put on makeup*
bañarse	*to take a bath*	**peinarse**	*to comb (one's hair)*
casarse	*to get married*	**secarse**	*to dry (oneself)*
conectarse a	*to connect to*	**sentarse (ie)**	*to sit down*
despertarse (ie)	*to wake up*	**sentirse (ie)**	*to feel*
divertirse (ie)	*to have fun*	**vestirse (i)**	*to get dressed*
ducharse	*to take a shower*		

e **¿Comprendes?** Completa las oraciones con el pronombre reflexivo o la forma correcta del verbo indicado.

me, te, se, nos

1. Yo____________ baño por la mañana.
2. Los estudiantes ____________ bañan por la noche.
3. Usted ____________ baña después de desayunar.

despertarse

4. Mis abuelos se ____________ temprano.
5. Mi hermana y yo nos ____________ tarde.
6. Y tú, ¿cuándo te ____________?

PRÁCTICA

4-27 ¿Qué hacemos todos los días? Pon estas actividades en el orden más lógico (1 = primero; 6 = finalmente). Luego, comparte tus respuestas con tu compañero/a. ¿Hacen ustedes las actividades en el mismo orden? Comenten las diferencias.

_____ Me duermo.
_____ Me levanto.
_____ Salgo para mis clases.
_____ Me acuesto.
_____ Me lavo los dientes.
_____ Me ducho y me lavo la cara (*face*).
_____ Desayuno.

4-28 ¿Tenemos las mismas rutinas?

PREPARACIÓN. Hablen sobre sus actividades diarias. Toma notas de las respuestas de tu compañero/a.

MODELO despertarse
E1: *Yo me despierto a las siete. ¿Y tú?*
E2: *Generalmente, me despierto a las ocho.*

1. levantarse
2. ducharse
3. vestirse
4. desayunar
5. acostarse
6. dormirse

INTERCAMBIOS. Escribe una semejanza (*similarity*) y una diferencia entre tu rutina y la rutina de tu compañero/a. Comparte oralmente la semejanza y la diferencia con la clase.

MODELO Semejanza: *Mi compañero/a y yo generalmente nos acostamos a las 12:00 de la noche.*
Diferencia: *Mi compañero/a se ducha a las 8:00 de la mañana, pero yo me ducho a las 11:00 de la noche.*

4-29 Los horarios. Usa la información de la actividad **4-28** para completar la tabla. Luego, escribe un párrafo sobre tu horario y el horario de tu compañero/a. ¿Qué tienen en común? ¿Qué diferencias hay entre sus horarios?

	Yo	Mi compañero/a
acostarse		
levantarse		
ducharse		
vestirse		

4-30 **Mi pariente.** **PREPARACIÓN.** Trae a clase una foto de un miembro de tu familia. Luego, indica las actividades que tu pariente hace normalmente.

1. acostarse: _____ temprano _____ tarde
2. despertarse: _____ temprano _____ tarde
3. ducharse: _____ por la mañana _____ por la noche
4. desayunar: _____ en casa _____ fuera de casa
5. para ir a trabajar, ponerse: _____ ropa deportiva _____ ropa formal
6. divertirse mucho: _____ con la familia _____ con los amigos

INTERCAMBIOS. Habla con tu compañero/a de tu pariente (nombre, edad, etc.) y explica su rutina.

Situación

PREPARACIÓN. Lean esta situación. Luego, compartan ejemplos de vocabulario, gramática y otra información que necesitan para desarrollar la conversación.

Role A. You are thinking about working in a summer volunteer program (**programa de voluntariado**) in Mérida, Venezuela. Ask the representative who has come to your campus:
a. where the volunteers (**voluntarios**) live;
b. what time they go to bed and get up; and
c. where and when they eat their meals.

Role B. You work for a non-profit organization and are visiting American colleges and universities to recruit students for a summer volunteer program (**programa de voluntariado**) in Mérida, Venezuela. Answer the questions of a prospective student, giving as much information as possible.

	ROLE A	ROLE B
Vocabulario	Daily routines Question words	Daily routines
Funciones y formas	Asking about routines: Reflexive verbs Stem-changing verbs	Talking about routines: Reflexive verbs Stem-changing verbs

INTERCAMBIOS. Practiquen la conversación, incorporando el vocabulario y las funciones de **Preparación.** Luego, represéntenla ante la clase.

4 Expressing reciprocity

La solidaridad y la reciprocidad son valores (*values*) importantes en las relaciones de amigos y familia. Generalmente, los amigos **se conocen** bien entre ellos y **se demuestran** solidaridad en momentos difíciles. Camilo, mi mejor (*best*) amigo, dice: "Mario y yo somos amigos y compartimos muchas cosas. Pero lo más importante es que **nos respetamos** el uno al otro porque **nos necesitamos"**. Lo mismo ocurre en la familia. Los padres y los hijos **se quieren** mucho; por eso, **se comunican** regularmente, **se ayudan** en todo momento.

Piénsalo. Selecciona la explicación que corresponde a cada afirmación.

1. _____ **Se conocen** entre ellos.
2. _____ **Se demuestran** solidaridad.
3. _____ **Nos necesitamos.**
4. _____ **Nos respetamos** el uno al otro.
5. _____ Los padres y los hijos **se quieren.**

a. Yo respeto a Mario y él me respeta a mí.
b. Los padres quieren a sus hijos y los hijos quieren a sus padres.
c. Mario conoce a Camilo y Camilo conoce a Mario.
d. Camilo ayuda a Mario y viceversa.
e. Yo necesito a Mario y él me necesita a mí.

Reciprocal verbs and pronouns

- You have already learned to use reflexive pronouns to express an action that someone does to himself or herself. The subject can be singular or plural.

Alejandro **se mira** en el espejo.	*Alejandro looks at himself in the mirror.*
Los niños **se visten** solos.	*The children get dressed by themselves.*

- Reciprocal actions are those that two (or more) people do to each other. Use plural reflexive pronouns (**nos, os, se**) to express these reciprocal actions.

Alberto y Gabriela **se abrazan** cuando **se ven.**	*Alberto and Gabriela embrace (hug each other) when they see each other.*
Mi amigo y yo **nos ayudamos** mucho.	*My friend and I help each other a lot.*

- Some statements can be interpreted as either reflexive or reciprocal. You can use the context to figure out the intended meaning.

Carmen y Teresa **se miran** en el espejo.	*Carmen and Teresa are looking at themselves in the mirror.* *Carmen and Teresa are looking at each other in the mirror. (They are looking at each other's reflections.)*

¿Comprendes? Completa las oraciones con **se** o **nos** y la forma correcta del verbo entre paréntesis para indicar reciprocidad.

1. Mónica y Pablo se ayudan (ayudar) con los preparativos para la fiesta.
2. Marcos y Mario se saludan (saludar) en la oficina.
3. Mis amigos y yo nos mandamos (mandar) mensajes de texto.
4. Érica y Luis son novios. Se quieren (querer) mucho.

PRÁCTICA

4-31 Indicaciones de reciprocidad.

PREPARACIÓN. Selecciona la opción apropiada para completar cada oración.

1. _____ Cuando Alicia y Estela no se ven durante el día, ellas...
2. _____ El perro y el gato de Alicia se pelean (*fight*) todo el tiempo. Ellos...
3. _____ Iván y yo somos buenos amigos, pero vivimos en ciudades diferentes. No nos vemos mucho pero...
4. _____ Esteban y Alicia son novios y se quieren mucho. Cuando se ven, ellos...
5. _____ Alicia y Estela dicen que el secreto de su larga amistad es que ellas...

a. nos mandamos mensajes de texto.
b. se llaman por teléfono.
c. se conocen bien y se respetan mucho.
d. se detestan.
e. se abrazan y se besan (*kiss*).

INTERCAMBIOS. Compara tus respuestas con las de tu compañero/a. Explíquense (*Explain to each other*) en otras palabras el significado de las oraciones. Pueden añadir más detalles.

MODELO E1: *Esteban y Alicia se quieren mucho. Esto significa que Esteban quiere a Alicia...*

E2: *...y Alicia quiere a Esteban. Son novios. Pienso que van a casarse.*

 **4-32 El uno al otro.** Miren los dibujos y describan quiénes son, dónde están y qué hacen.

1.

2.

3.

4.

5.

4-33 ¿Qué hacen los buenos amigos?

 **PREPARACIÓN.** Indica las actividades que, en tu opinión, hacen los buenos amigos. Luego, comparte tus respuestas con tu compañero/a y añade información para justificar tu opinión. ¿Están ustedes de acuerdo?

MODELO respetarse

E1: *Los buenos amigos no siempre tienen las mismas opiniones, pero se respetan.*

E2: *Estoy de acuerdo. Mi mejor amigo/a y yo a veces tenemos opiniones diferentes, pero nos escuchamos con respeto.*

1. _____ llamarse o textearse todos los días
2. _____ comprenderse y demostrarse empatía
3. _____ ayudarse cuando tienen problemas
4. _____ insultarse
5. _____ darse consejos (*give advice*)
6. _____ darse regalos (*gifts*) de cumpleaños costosos ($$)
7. _____ decirse la verdad siempre
8. _____ criticarse (constructivamente/continuamente)
9. _____ pedirse perdón después de pelearse (*argue*)
10. _____ prestarse (*lend*) dinero

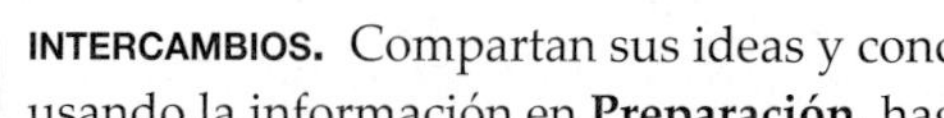 **INTERCAMBIOS.** Compartan sus ideas y conclusiones con otra pareja. Luego, usando la información en **Preparación,** hagan lo siguiente.

1. Escojan dos comportamientos (*behaviors*) que facilitan una buena relación con otras personas. Justifiquen su selección.
2. Escojan dos comportamientos problemáticos en las relaciones con otras personas. ¿Por qué son problemáticos?
3. Compartan sus conclusiones con la clase.

En directo

To express your opinion:

Yo creo que... *I believe that . . .*

En mi opinión... *In my opinion . . .*

A mí me parece que... *It seems to me that . . .*

To react to an opinion:

(No) Estoy de acuerdo. *I (don't) agree.*

 Listen to a conversation with these expressions.

4-34 Las familias.

PREPARACIÓN. Hablen de las relaciones entre las personas de sus respectivas familias. Usen los verbos recíprocos de la lista.

MODELO *Mi hermano y yo… mucho, pero a veces…*

ayudarse	criticarse	llamarse	quererse
comunicarse	hablarse	prestarse	respetarse

INTERCAMBIOS. Hablen con otra pareja sobre sus relaciones con los miembros de su familia. ¿Se relacionan de manera similar o diferente?

4-35 Una relación admirable.

PREPARACIÓN. Trae a clase una foto de una pareja en tu familia o en tu círculo de amigos/as a quienes admiras. Escribe cuatro actividades que hace esta pareja para demostrarse amor, reciprocidad o solidaridad.

INTERCAMBIOS. Comparte la siguiente información con tu compañero/a.

- Nombres de la pareja a quien admiras
- Descripción física y de personalidad de cada uno/a
- Tipo de relación de estas personas: ¿Están casados/as? ¿Son una pareja, pero no están casados/as? ¿Son amigos/as?
- Actividades que cada persona hace para la otra

Situación

PREPARACIÓN. Lean la situación. Luego, compartan ejemplos de vocabulario, gramática y otra información que necesitan para desarrollar la conversación.

Role A. Your brother/sister has just told you that he/she is going to get married in six months. You didn't know that their relationship was this serious, and you want to know if your sibling knows what he/she is doing. You ask:
a. if they know each other (**conocerse**) well enough to get married;
b. how they feel about each other; and
c. how they stay in close communication, since they live in different cities.

Role B. You and your boyfriend/girlfriend have decided to get married in six months. Your brother/sister is surprised when you share the news. Reassure your sibling that you know what you are doing by answering his/her questions about:
a. if you know each other (**conocerse**) well enough to get married;
b. how you feel about each other; and
c. how you stay in close communication, since you live in different cities.

	ROLE A	ROLE B
Vocabulario	Vocabulary related to relationships	Vocabulary related to relationships
Funciones y formas	Asking questions Expressing reciprocity	Answering questions Expressing reciprocity

INTERCAMBIOS. Practiquen la conversación, incorporando el vocabulario y las funciones de **Preparación.** Luego, represéntenla ante la clase.

5 Expressing how long something has been going on

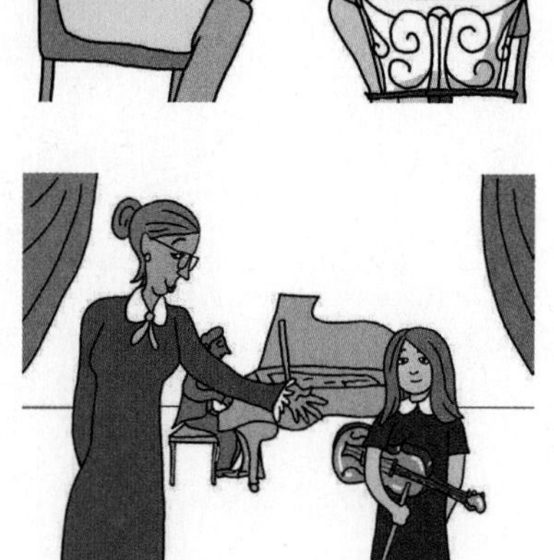

ALEJANDRA: Señora, ¿**cuánto tiempo hace que** practico esta sonata? ¡Estoy muy cansada!

SRA. ESCOBEDO: **Hace dos horas que** trabajas en ella. Pero una vez más, por favor, Alejandra. El recital es en dos días.

El día del recital...

SRA. ESCOBEDO: Les presento a Alejandra Suárez. Estudia el violín conmigo **hace cinco años.** Ahora va a tocar la Sonata número 4 de Mozart.

e Piénsalo. Selecciona la opción correcta para indicar el momento en que comenzó (*started*) cada actividad.

¿Cuándo comenzó?

1. Son las 5:00. **Hace dos horas que** Alejandra practica la sonata.
   a. a las 2:00 **b.** a las 3:00
2. Es el 2019. **Hace cinco años que** Alejandra estudia violín.
   a. en 2014 **b.** en 2016
3. Es el 2019. La Sra. Escobedo enseña (*teaches*) violín **hace veinte años.**
   a. en 2010 **b.** en 1999
4. Es el 2019. **Hace cuatro años que** los padres de Alejandra asisten a los recitales.
   a. en 2014 **b.** en 2015
5. Es noviembre. Alejandra aprende la sonata de Mozart **hace tres meses.**
   a. en agosto **b.** en septiembre

Hace with expressions of time

- To say that an action/state began in the past and continues into the present, use **hace** + *length of time* + **que** + *present tense.*

  Hace diez años que se conocen. — *They have known each other for ten years.*
  Hace dos horas que juegan en el parque. — *They have been playing in the park for two hours.*

- If you begin the sentence with the present tense of the verb, do not use **que.**

  Juegan **hace dos horas.** — *They've been playing for two hours.*

- To find out how long an action/state has been taking place, use **cuánto tiempo** + **hace que** + *present tense.*

  ¿Cuánto tiempo hace que juegan? — *How long have they been playing?*

e **¿Comprendes?** Usa la información en paréntesis para completar las respuestas a la pregunta.

¿Cuánto tiempo hace que estas personas estudian español?

1. (tres semanas) ________________ Juan y Daniel estudian español.
2. (un semestre) ________________ nosotros estudiamos español.
3. (un año) ________________ tú estudias español.
4. (tres días) ________________ mi amigo estudia español.

PRÁCTICA

4-36 Este soy yo. **PREPARACIÓN.** Lee esta descripción de José y completa las oraciones. Compara tus respuestas con las de tu compañero/a.

> Me llamo José Lastra y soy de Valencia, Venezuela. Quiero aprender inglés para poder trabajar en una compañía internacional. Estudio inglés **hace tres años,** pero tengo que estudiar más para hablar correctamente. Siempre miro programas de televisión en inglés. Mi favorito es *The Walking Dead.* **Hace dos años que** miro este programa y me gusta mucho. Tengo una novia **hace un año;** salgo con ella y con mis amigos en un auto que tengo **hace seis meses.** Estamos muy contentos con el auto.

1. José Lastra es de…
2. Hace tres años que Jaime…
3. Hace un año que José…

INTERCAMBIOS. Escribe tu propia descripción, usando el modelo de **Preparación.** Luego, comparte tu descripción con tu compañero/a.

4-37 ¿Cuánto tiempo hace que…? Túrnense para hacerse las siguientes preguntas. Después, compartan la información con otra pareja.

1. ¿Dónde vive tu familia? ¿Cuánto tiempo hace que vive allí?
2. ¿Dónde trabajas? ¿Cuánto tiempo hace que trabajas allí?
3. ¿Cuánto tiempo hace que estudias en esta universidad? ¿Y por qué estudias español?
4. ¿Practicas algún deporte? ¿Cuánto tiempo hace que juegas al…? ¿Juegas bien?
5. ¿Cuánto tiempo hace que conoces a tu mejor amigo/a de la universidad?

4-38 Hablar más del tiempo. **PREPARACIÓN.** Escribe cinco oraciones sobre cuánto tiempo hace que haces (o no haces) **cinco** de las actividades de la lista.

beber café	saber manejar (*to drive*) un auto
conocer a tu mejor amigo/a	tener tu propio (*own*) teléfono
no compartir una pizza con tus amigos/as	tocar un instrumento musical (¿cuál?)
no visitar a tus abuelos o tíos	trabajar durante el verano

INTERCAMBIOS. Compara tu información con la de tu compañero/a.

MODELO E1: *Hace tres años que bebo café. ¿Y tú?*
E2: *Yo no bebo café. No me gusta.*

4-39 **¿Cuánto tiempo hace que...?** **PREPARACIÓN.** Lee las afirmaciones e identifica a pariente(s) o amigo/a(s) con quien(es) asocias las descripciones.

	Pariente(s) o amigo/a(s)
1. Sale con una nueva pareja.	
2. Vive en la misma casa o apartamento de su infancia (*childhood*).	
3. Juega golf, tenis, béisbol o fútbol.	
4. Se ven frecuentemente después de las clases.	
5. Va de vacaciones solo/a.	
6. Usa redes sociales.	
7. No se comunica con su familia.	

INTERCAMBIOS. Comparte con tu compañero/a la información de **Preparación.** Háganse preguntas para saber cuánto tiempo hace que las personas hacen o no hacen estas actividades.

MODELO Toca el piano.
E1: *Mi sobrino Steve toca el piano.*
E2: *¿Cuánto tiempo hace que Steve toca el piano?*
E1: *Hace...*

Situación

PREPARACIÓN. Lean esta situación. Luego, compartan ejemplos de vocabulario, gramática y otra información que necesitan para desarrollar la conversación.

Role A. Your sister/brother studies at a school in another state and is visiting you for the first time. Give him/her a tour and then suggest going to dinner at your favorite restaurant. Give details about the places you visit and answer your brother's/sister's questions.

Role B. You are visiting your brother/sister at school. It is your first visit there, and he/she gives you a tour. Ask your sibling questions: a) how long he/she has lived in his/her current place (**residencia estudiantil, apartamento**); and b) how long the stores, restaurants, and other places you see on the tour have been there.

	ROLE A	**ROLE B**
Vocabulario	Places in town Length of time	Question words Length of time
Funciones y formas	Expressing length of time of an event or condition: **Hace** + *time* + **que** + *present tense verb* Making a suggestion	Asking questions about length of time of an event or condition: **¿Cuánto tiempo** + **hace que** + *present tense verb*? **¿Cuántos años** + **hace que** + *present tense verb*?

INTERCAMBIOS. Practiquen la conversación, incorporando el vocabulario y las funciones de **Preparación.** Luego, represéntenla ante la clase.

ESCUCHA

Estrategia

Listen for a purpose Listening with a purpose in mind will help you focus your attention on the most relevant information. As you focus your attention, you screen what you hear and select only the information you need.

 **4-40 Preparación.** Antes de escuchar el mensaje de Pedro para Julio sobre una fiesta sorpresa (*surprise*), prepara tus ideas sobre la siguiente información. Después, compara tus notas con las de tu compañero/a.

1. el posible propósito (*purpose*) del mensaje
2. la información específica que puede ser importante

  **4-41 Escucha.** First read the incomplete information about a surprise party Pedro is giving. Then, as you listen, complete the sentences. Don't worry if you don't understand every word you hear.

1. La fiesta es para...
2. La fiesta va a ser en la casa de...
3. El día de la fiesta es...
4. Julio debe llevar (*bring*)...
5. Julio tiene que llegar a la casa a las...
6. La dirección es...

Comprueba

I was able to . . .

- recognize the names of people.
- identify specific information about an event.

4-42 Un paso más. Quieres confirmarle a Julio la información sobre la fiesta sorpresa para Gabriela. Escríbele un mensaje de texto con la siguiente información.

1. cuándo y dónde va a ser la fiesta
2. qué van a comer y beber
3. qué música van a escuchar

HABLA

Estrategia

Organize information In *Capítulo 3,* you practiced organizing information for a presentation. Now you will focus on organizing information for a conversation about a specific topic—a family gathering. Follow these steps in organizing your information.

- List the names of family members.
- Indicate the family relationships.
- Decide on possible categories related to organizing and giving a party: invitations, food preparation, decorations, entertainment, cleaning up afterwards, etc.

4-43 Preparación. Vas a organizar una reunión familiar. Primero, escribe una lista con la siguiente información.

- los nombres de unos parientes cercanos (*close*) y unos parientes lejanos (*distant*) y tu relación con ellos, por ejemplo: **David – hermano**
- como mínimo seis actividades relacionadas con organizar y hacer una fiesta, por ejemplo: **comprar comida**

Comprueba

I was able to . . .

- ask who, what, where, and when questions about a party.
- express the purpose of a party.
- provide information about a party.
- use kinship terms appropriately.

 **4-44 Habla.** Háganse las siguientes preguntas relacionadas con la organización y ejecución de la reunión familiar de cada uno/a. Tomen notas.

1. ¿Cuál es el motivo de tu reunión familiar?
2. ¿A qué parientes vas a invitar? ¿Cuántos invitados (*guests*) en total vas a tener?
3. ¿Quiénes en tu familia van a ayudar? ¿Qué tareas van a hacer tus parientes antes de la reunión, durante la reunión y después de la reunión?
4. ¿Qué comida y bebidas vas a servir?
5. ¿Dónde van a sentarse tus parientes mayores o más cercanos? ¿Y los parientes lejanos o más jóvenes? ¿Por qué? ¿Hay problemas entre algunos miembros de tu familia? ¿Qué problemas hay? Explica.

 **4-45 Un paso más.** Usando tus notas sobre la familia y la reunión de tu compañero/a de la actividad **4-44**, prepara un informe para compartir con un/a compañero/a diferente.

MODELO *La fiesta de… es para su hermano/a. Tiene 21 años y la familia quiere celebrar su cumpleaños. Mi fiesta es para mis padres. Es su aniversario. Hace 25 años que están casados.*

LEE

Estrategia

Use title and illustrations to anticipate content Before you start to read, gather as much information about the text as possible. The title, section headings, and illustrations can help you anticipate content, so pay special attention to them. Write down what you think the text is about, and refer to your notes as you are reading, correcting them as necessary. This will help you focus your attention as you read.

4-46 Preparación. Lee el título y los subtítulos del artículo en la actividad **4-47** y observa las fotos. Luego, usa la información del título, los subtítulos y las fotos para contestar las siguientes preguntas. Presenta tus respuestas a la clase.

1. ¿Cuál es la idea principal del artículo?
   a. la violencia que resulta del uso de la tecnología
   b. el efecto de la tecnología en la familia
   c. la comunicación con los colegas en el trabajo
2. En tu opinión, ¿qué ideas puede incluir el artículo? (Hay más de una respuesta posible.)
   a. Hoy en día la comunicación entre padres e hijos es mejor que (*better than*) en el pasado.
   b. Los niños deben leer libros en vez de (*instead of*) jugar en línea.
   c. La tecnología produce tensión y conflicto en las familias.
   d. La tecnología reduce la comunicación entre padres e hijos.
3. En algunas familias es común compartir dispositivos (*devices*). En tu familia, ¿qué dispositivos pertenecen (*belong*) a una persona solamente (*only*)?
   a. _____ el teléfono móvil
   b. _____ la computadora de escritorio
   c. _____ la computadora portátil
   d. _____ el enrutador inalámbrico (*wireless router*)
   e. _____ el control remoto de la televisión
   f. _____ la consola de videojuegos

4-47 Lee. Lee el artículo e indica la siguiente información.

1. algunas palabras asociadas con la tecnología
2. el porcentaje de las familias que tienen una computadora solamente
3. qué pasa cuando varias personas en la familia usan la misma computadora
4. qué pasa cuando todos tienen sus propios dispositivos
5. el porcentaje de adolescentes que son adictos a sus pantallas

Comprueba

I was able to . . .

- use headings and photos to identify the main idea.
- focus on one piece of information at a time.
- identify terms related to technology.

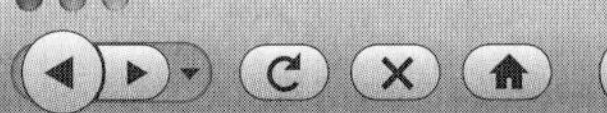

Los efectos de internet en la unión familiar

Un estudio internacional revela[1] el impacto negativo de internet en las relaciones familiares. Los efectos son más distancia y separación entre padres e hijos. Un total de 3.700 familias en siete países participan en este estudio. El 21% de los padres y el 22% de los niños dicen que internet y los dispositivos[2] tecnológicos causan tensiones familiares de varios tipos.

Los virus en los dispositivos compartidos

Cuando toda la familia usa los mismos dispositivos para conectarse a internet, hay conflictos sobre el uso. Casi[3] el 70% de las familias usan la misma computadora, y el 30% de los padres dicen que sus hijos infectan con virus digitales las computadoras compartidas.

Los padres pierden su autoridad

Es difícil para los padres controlar[4] el acceso a internet de sus hijos. Además, los hijos saben más de tecnología que sus padres y usan redes sociales y aplicaciones que los padres no conocen. Usan la tecnología mucho más que sus padres.

Menos tiempo juntos

El uso de los dispositivos electrónicos reduce el tiempo familiar. Los niños mandan mensajes de texto a sus amigos, miran videos o juegan en línea. No hablan mucho con los padres. El 50% de los adolescentes reconocen[5] que son adictos a sus pantallas. Pero muchos padres son adictos a sus dispositivos también, y por eso no son buenos modelos para sus hijos.

[1]*reveals* [2]*devices* [3]*Almost* [4]*monitor* [5]*acknowledge*

 **4-48 Un paso más.** Hablen del impacto de la tecnología en la comunicación familiar. Usen las preguntas como guía (*guide*).

1. En el artículo, hay tres impactos negativos de la tecnología en las relaciones familiares. ¿Existen los mismos efectos negativos en las familias de ustedes?
2. ¿Hay reglas (*rules*) en sus familias sobre el uso de la tecnología? ¿Cuáles son?

ESCRIBE

Estrategia

Use your knowledge of the topic when you write The topic of technology is one you know a lot about, and you can use your knowledge to help you write a well-organized paragraph. Use the words and phrases you know, the language of the reading in **Lee,** and your own experience to organize your ideas and express them simply and clearly. Use the expressions in **En directo** to present your ideas in an organized way.

4-49 Preparación. Revisa (*Review*) los tres efectos negativos de la tecnología en las familias según el artículo en la actividad **4-47.** Luego, escribe una lista de los efectos positivos de la tecnología en las relaciones familiares.

 **4-50 Escribe.** Escribe un párrafo sobre este tema: **El impacto de la tecnología en mi vida.** Incluye tres ventajas (efectos positivos) y tres desventajas (efectos negativos).

En directo

To introduce a list of advantages:

Hay tres ventajas de... son... *The three advantages of . . . are . . .*

...tiene tres ventajas: *. . . has three advantages:*

To put your ideas in a logical order:

Primero..., segundo..., tercero... *First . . . second . . . third . . .*

To make a transition to a list of advantages:

Pero también hay desventajas. *But there are also disadvantages.*

 Listen to an oral presentation with these expressions.

Comprueba

I was able to . . .

- present main ideas clearly with adequate details.
- give information about my use of devices and social media.
- organize my ideas by advantages and disadvantages.

 **4-51 Un paso más.** Compartan sus párrafos y háganse preguntas sobre los siguientes temas.

1. el impacto de la tecnología en su vida familiar
2. los dispositivos electrónicos que usan ustedes y para qué los usan
3. las redes sociales que usan
4. su opinión sobre las ventajas y desventajas de la tecnología

En este capítulo...

Vocabulario

La familia	*The family*
el/la abuelo/a	*grandfather/ grandmother*
los abuelos	*grandparents*
el/la esposo/a	*husband/wife*
el/la hermano/a	*brother/sister*
el/la hijo/a	*son/daughter*
los hijos	*children*
la madrastra	*stepmother*
la madre	*mother*
la mamá	*mom*
el medio hermano / la media hermana	*half-brother/ half-sister*
el/la nieto/a	*grandson/ granddaughter*
los nietos	*grandchildren*
el/la niño/a	*child*
el/la novio/a	*fiancé(e); boyfriend/ girlfriend; groom/ bride*
el padrastro	*stepfather*
el padre	*father*
los padres	*parents*
el papá	*dad*
la pareja	*couple; partner, significant other*
el pariente	*relative*
el/la primo/a	*cousin*
el/la sobrino/a	*nephew/niece*
el/la tío/a	*uncle/aunt*

Las descripciones	*Descriptions*
divorciado/a	*divorced*
gemelo/a	*twin*
ocupado/a	*busy*
separado/a	*separated*

Verbos	*Verbs*
abrazar(se)	*to hug (each other)*
acostar(se) (ue)	*to put to bed; to go to bed, to lie down*
afeitar(se)	*to shave (oneself)*
almorzar (ue)	*to have lunch*
ayudar(se)	*to help (each other)*
bañar(se)	*to bathe; to take a bath*
casarse	*to get married*
cerrar (ie)	*to close*
comunicarse	*to communicate with*
conectarse a	*to connect to*
conocer(se)	*to know (each other)*
costar (ue)	*to cost*
decir (g, i)	*to say, to tell*
demostrar (ue)	*to show, to demonstrate*
desayunar	*to have breakfast*
despertar(se) (ie)	*to wake (someone up); to wake up*
divertirse (ie)	*to have fun*
dormir (ue) la siesta	*to take a nap*
dormir(se) (ue)	*to sleep; to fall asleep*
duchar(se)	*to give a shower to; to take a shower*
empezar (ie)	*to begin, to start*
encontrar (ue)	*to find*
entender (ie)	*to understand*
jugar (ue)	*to play (a game, sport)*
lavar(se)	*to wash (oneself)*
levantar(se)	*to raise, to lift; to get up*
llamar(se)	*to call, to be named*
maquillar(se)	*to put makeup on (someone); to put makeup on (oneself)*
pasar	*to pass; to spend (time)*
pasear	*to take a walk, to stroll*
pedir (i)	*to ask for; to order*
peinar(se)	*to comb (someone's hair); to comb (one's hair)*
pensar (ie)	*to think*
pensar (ie) + *infinitive*	*to plan to* + verb
poder (ue)	*to be able to, can*
poner(se) (g) la ropa	*to put (one's) clothes on*
preferir (ie)	*to prefer*
querer(se) (ie)	*to want; to love*
quitar(se)	*to take away; to take off*
repetir (i)	*to repeat*
respetar (se)	*to respect*
secar(se)	*to dry (oneself)*
seguir (i)	*to follow, to go on*
sentarse (ie)	*to sit down*
sentir(se) (ie)	*to feel*
servir (i)	*to serve*
tener (g, ie)	*to have*
tener que + *infinitive*	*to have to (do something)*
terminar	*to finish*
venir (g, ie)	*to come*
ver(se)	*to see (each other)*
vestir(se) (i)	*to dress; to get dressed*
visitar	*to visit*
volver (ue)	*to return*

Palabras y expresiones útiles	*Useful words and expressions*
frecuentemente	*frequently, often*
juntos/as	*together*
el matrimonio	*marriage*
el/la mayor	*the oldest*
el/la menor	*the youngest*
tarde	*late*
temprano	*early*
un poco	*a little*

See *Lengua* box on page 147 for time expressions.
See *Lengua* box on page 155 for other expressions with **pensar.**
See page 164 for time expressions with **hace.**

Capítulo 5
¿Dónde vives?

Palafitos (*Stilt houses*) en la isla de Roatán, Honduras

Learning Outcomes

You will be able to:

- talk about housing, the home, and household activities
- express ongoing actions
- describe physical and emotional states
- avoid repetition in speaking and writing
- point out and identify people and things
- express when, where, or how an action occurs
- talk about Nicaragua, El Salvador, and Honduras in terms of products, practices, and perspectives
- talk about housing in urban areas

Enfoque cultural

Nicaragua, El Salvador y Honduras

Arrecife de coral en la costa de Roatán, Honduras

Café de Nicaragua recién cosechado (*newly harvested*)

El volcán de Izalco, en El Salvador

Arte hispano

Mural de Fernando Llort, pintor de El Salvador

Enfoque cultural

¿Qué te parece?

- El 90% de la población de Honduras es mestiza (de herencia española e indígena), el 7% indígena, el 2% negra y el 1% blanca. Los lencas son el principal grupo indígena.
- En El Salvador hay más de 1.000 especies de mariposas (*butterflies*) y más de 500 tipos de pájaros (*birds*).
- El café es un producto de exportación importante en esta región.
- El Gran Lago de Nicaragua es el único lago del mundo donde hay tiburones (*sharks*).

La biodiversidad, el clima tropical y la fusión cultural hacen de Nicaragua un importante destino turístico.

Estas mujeres preparan pupusas, unas deliciosas tortillas rellenas (*filled*) típicas de El Salvador.

To learn more about Nicaragua, El Salvador, and Honduras, go online to view the *Club cultura* videos.

En el valle de Copán, en Honduras, se encuentran las ruinas más importantes de la civilización maya. Este antiguo centro de actividad y cultura es ahora el Parque Arqueológico Copán e incluye restos de plazas, templos y un estadio para el juego de pelota. Aquí vemos uno de los marcadores (*scoreboards*).

Suchitoto y Santa Ana son dos ciudades coloniales de El Salvador. Aquí hay casas coloniales, museos, galerías de arte e iglesias.

e **¿Cuánto sabes?** Completa estas oraciones con la información correcta.

1. El Sa lvador tiene frontera con ________ y ________.
2. Hay tiburones en el Gran Lago de ________.
3. Las ________ son tortillas salvadoreñas.
4. El pintor Fernando Llort es de ________.
5. La mayor parte de la población de Honduras es ________.
6. El ________ de esta región se exporta a muchos países.

VOCABULARIO EN CONTEXTO

Talking about housing, the home, and household activities

¿Dónde vives?

En las ciudades de Nicaragua, El Salvador y Honduras hay **viviendas** de diferentes **estilos.** La ciudad de Granada, en Nicaragua, tiene **calles** y plazas como esta, con casas coloniales de colores alegres. En Tegucigalpa, la capital de Honduras, hay **edificios** de **apartamentos.** Algunas personas prefieren vivir cerca del **centro. Creen** que los **barrios** de las **afueras** están muy **lejos** del **trabajo** y de los centros de diversión.

Una calle en el centro de Granada, Nicaragua

En otras palabras

The Spanish word for *apartment* varies according to the country. **El apartamento** is used in Central America, Colombia, and Venezuela, and **el departamento** is common in Mexico, Argentina, Peru, and Chile. The word used in Spain is **el piso.**

¿En qué piso viven?

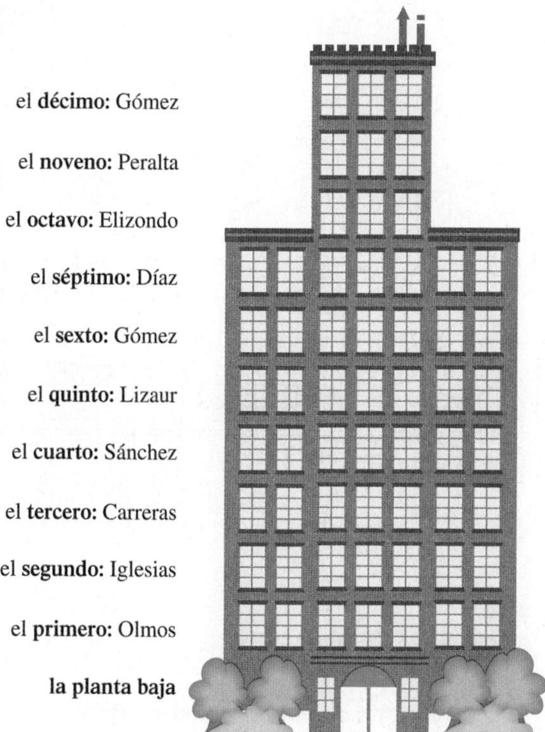

Lengua

Ordinal numbers are adjectives and agree in gender and number with the noun they modify (e.g., **la segunda casa, el cuarto edificio**). **Primero** and **tercero** drop the final **-o** when used before a masculine singular noun.

el **primer** apartamento

el **tercer** piso

Cultura

La planta baja In most Hispanic countries, the term **planta baja** is used for the American first floor or lobby. **El primer piso** or **la primera planta** is usually what in the United States is the second floor, and so on.

Comparaciones Si presionas el botón "1" en un ascensor (*elevator*) en un país hispano, ¿a qué piso llegas? ¿Y en Estados Unidos?

ALQUILERES

Categoría:	Alquiler apartamentos
Ciudad:	Tegucigalpa
Ubicación:	Palmira
Descripción:	Alquiler de apartamento muy amplio, céntrico y accesible, 2 habitaciones, sala-comedor, cocina, 1 baño, área de lavandería, estacionamiento, piscina.
Precio:	L$ 12.000

El apartamento del anuncio

MARTA DÍAZ: Hola, buenos días. Me llamo Marta Díaz. Estoy aquí para ver el apartamento del anuncio.

DIEGO LÓPEZ: Sí, claro. Mucho gusto, señora. Yo soy Diego López. Pase, pase. Como usted puede ver, el apartamento es muy alegre.

MARTA DÍAZ: ¡Ah, sí! Tiene muchas ventanas y **luz** natural.

DIEGO LÓPEZ: Esta es la **sala.** Es un **cuarto** muy grande. Junto a la sala hay un **comedor** pequeño y al lado está la **cocina.**

MARTA DÍAZ: ¡La cocina es lindísima!

DIEGO LÓPEZ: Sí, todos los **electrodomésticos** son **nuevos.** A la izquierda del **pasillo** hay dos **habitaciones** y un **baño.**

MARTA DÍAZ: Esta habitación tiene muy buena **vista** a la **piscina** y al **jardín.** Además, los **muebles** son de buena calidad. Me gusta mucho el apartamento. ¿Cuánto es el **alquiler?**

DIEGO LÓPEZ: Doce mil lempiras al mes.

MARTA DÍAZ: Pues, me encantan el apartamento y esta **zona** céntrica. Y el precio es muy bueno. Voy a decidir esta noche y lo llamo mañana.

DIEGO LÓPEZ: Perfecto. Hasta mañana.

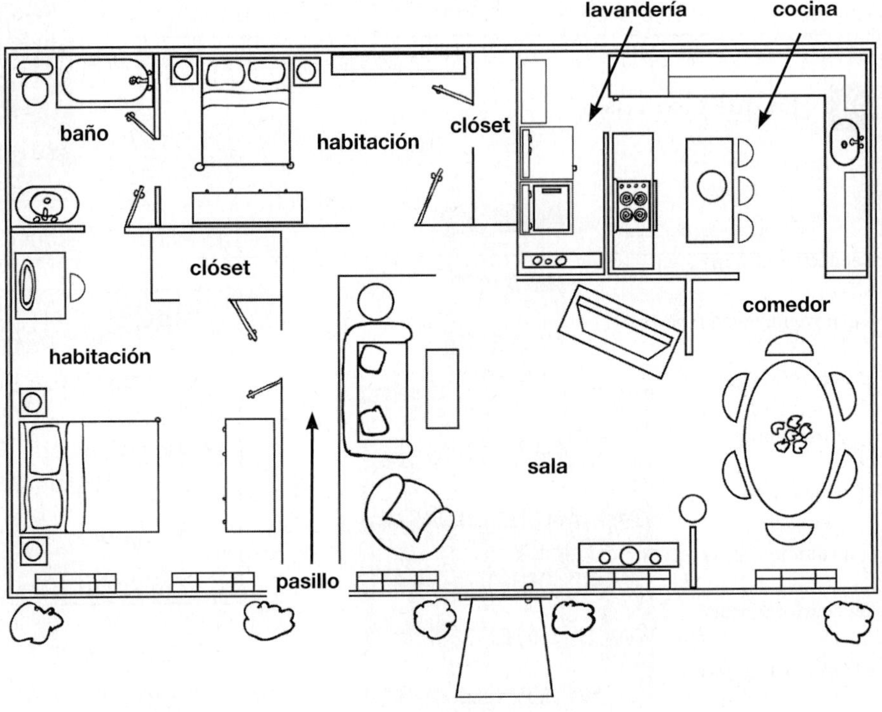

En otras palabras

The expressions **Pase(n)** and **Adelante** invite people to enter a room or a house in many Spanish-speaking countries. In others, like Colombia, the expression **Siga(n)** is preferred.

En otras palabras

Some words for the parts of a house vary from one region to another in the Spanish-speaking world. Here are some examples:

sala → salón, living

habitación → dormitorio, cuarto, alcoba, recámara

piscina → pileta, alberca

PRÁCTICA

5-1 Escucha y confirma. Look at the floor plan of the apartment and indicate whether each sentence you hear is **cierto** (C) or **falso** (F). Correct the false statements.

1. _____
2. _____
3. _____
4. _____
5. _____
6. _____

e **5-2 ¿Cierto o falso?** Indica si las siguientes afirmaciones son ciertas (**C**) o falsas (**F**), según la conversación entre Diego y Marta de la página 176. Corrige las afirmaciones falsas.

1. _____ Marta Díaz quiere comprar el apartamento.
2. _____ La sala es pequeña.
3. _____ El apartamento tiene dos baños.}
4. _____Los electrodomésticos son nuevos.
5. _____ Los muebles son de buena calidad.
6. _____ A Marta no le gusta la zona céntrica.

5-3 ¿En qué piso viven? Túrnense para preguntarse dónde viven las diferentes familias del edificio de apartamentos de la página 175.

MODELO E1: *¿Dónde viven los Sánchez?*
E2: *Viven en el cuarto piso.*

5-4 Un hotel de lujo. Un/a arquitecto/a (tu compañero/a) va a construir un hotel de lujo en la Bahía de Jiquilisco, cerca de San Salvador, y te pide consejos (*advice*) sobre cómo distribuir los siguientes espacios del hotel.

MODELO el restaurante
E1: *¿En qué piso vamos a poner el restaurante?*
E2: *Debe estar en la planta baja.*

1. la discoteca
2. la recepción
3. el gimnasio
4. la oficina de seguridad
5. las habitaciones
6. la piscina
7. la cafetería con vistas a la playa
8. el salón de computadoras

Cultura

Hoteles de lujo In many Hispanic countries, the tourism industry is one of the most important drivers of the economy. As a result, most beach and ski resorts tend to be similar everywhere and, with some exceptions, do not reflect local architecture or building styles. A booming tourism industry also sparks controversy. Although it brings jobs to local communities, most of the economic benefits go to the multinational companies that own the resorts, not to the local communities.

Comparaciones En Estados Unidos, ¿hay zonas de playa donde el turismo es masivo? ¿Dónde están? En general, ¿son zonas ricas o pobres?

5-5 La casa de alquiler.

PREPARACIÓN. Ustedes van a mudarse (*move*) a un apartamento porque la casa donde viven es muy grande y la quieren alquilar. Escriban un anuncio para alquilar su casa. Incluyan la siguiente información:

- número de habitaciones y de baños
- distribución (*layout*) de los cuartos
- color de la sala
- otras características (garaje, jardín, sótano [*basement*], ático, etc.)
- ubicación (*location*) de la casa en relación al centro de la ciudad, a la universidad, etc.
- precio

INTERCAMBIOS. Intercambien su anuncio con otra pareja y háganse preguntas sobre la casa que quieren alquilar: precio, color, número de habitaciones, etc.

Cultura

Desastres naturales Like many cities, Managua, the capital of Nicaragua, has been shaped by its history and economy, as well as by natural disasters. Following the devastating earthquake of 1972, most of the city was rebuilt in the outskirts, which are geographically safer areas. The traditional downtown area was rebuilt as a center for government offices and tourism, but there is little residential space or commercial activity.

Conexiones ¿En qué regiones de tu país ocurren desastres naturales? ¿De qué tipos: huracanes, terremotos (*earthquakes*), tornados, inundaciones (*floods*)? ¿Tienes experiencia directa con algún desastre natural?

5-6 Ventajas y desventajas. Hablen de las ventajas y desventajas (*advantages and disadvantages*) de los temas relacionados con las viviendas. Decidan cuáles son las más importantes y luego compartan sus opiniones con la clase.

	Ventajas	Desventajas
1. vivir en un apartamento		
2. vivir en una casa		
3. tener una piscina		
4. compartir una casa con tres o cuatro compañeros/as		

La casa, los muebles y los electrodomésticos

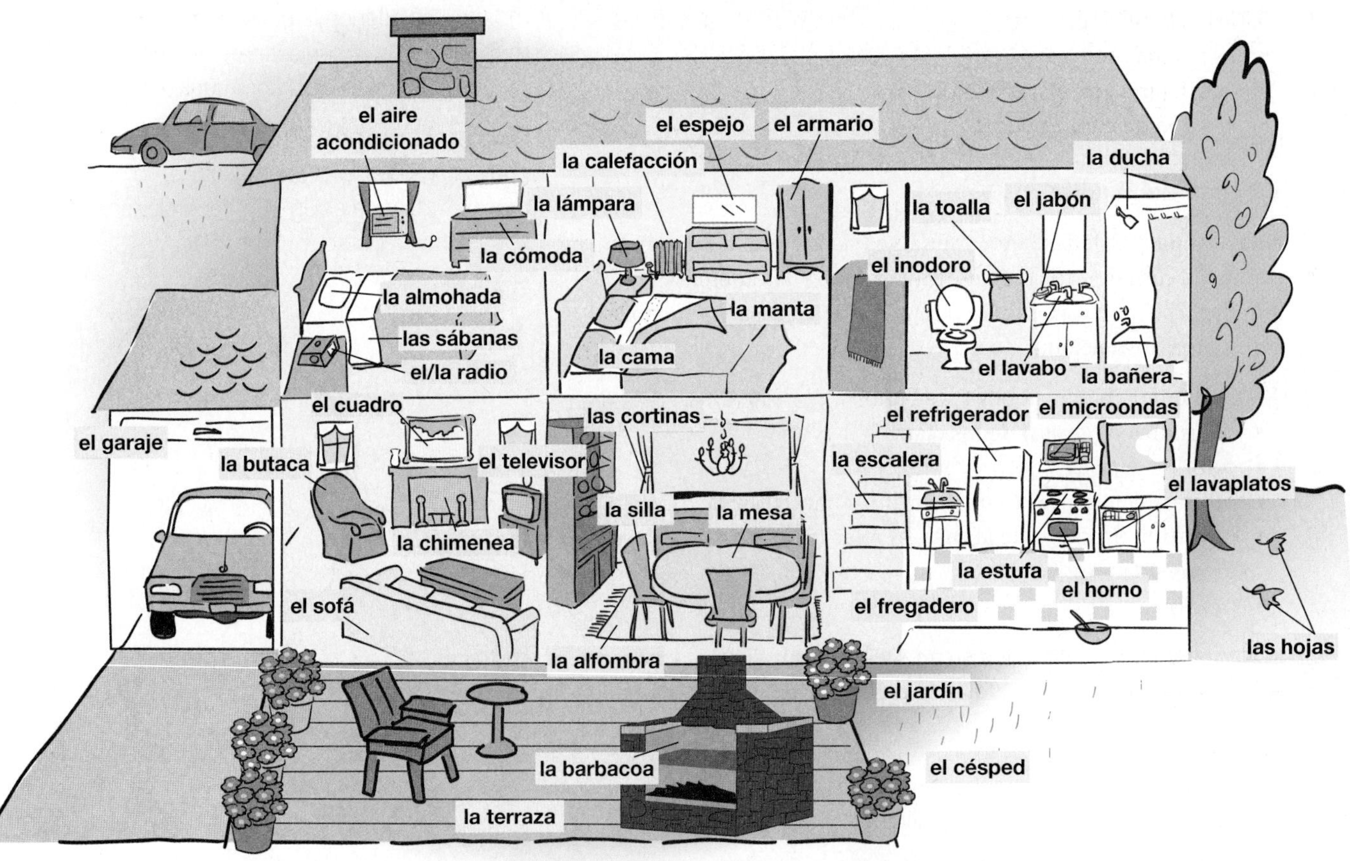

PRÁCTICA

5-7 Para confirmar.

PREPARACIÓN. Pon las siguientes palabras en la categoría apropiada.

la alfombra	las cortinas	el/la radio
el armario	el cuadro	el refrigerador
la butaca	el horno	las sábanas
la cómoda	el lavaplatos	la silla

Aparatos eléctricos	Muebles	Accesorios

INTERCAMBIOS. Contesten las siguientes preguntas relacionadas con **Preparación.**

1. Según ustedes, ¿qué aparato eléctrico cuesta más dinero?
2. ¿Qué muebles necesitan todos los días los estudiantes?
3. ¿Qué accesorios tienen ustedes en sus habitaciones?
4. ¿En qué parte(s) de la casa generalmente están estos accesorios?

5-8 El plano de mi casa.

PREPARACIÓN. Dibuja (*Draw*) un plano de la casa de tu familia. Incluye las habitaciones, la cocina, la sala, etc.

INTERCAMBIOS. Con el plano, descríbanle la casa de su familia a un/a compañero/a y háganse preguntas para obtener la mayor información posible.

MODELO E1: *La sala está en la planta baja, al lado de la cocina.*
E2: *¿Y cómo es la sala?*
E1: *Es pequeña. Hay una alfombra verde y un sofá blanco grande.*

Lengua

Here are some electronics that you may have in your home:

el asistente virtual	*virtual assistant*
el cargador	*charger*
la consola de videojuegos	*games console*
el enrutador inalámbrico	*wireless router*
la impresora multifuncional	*multifunction printer*

En otras palabras

Words for household items often vary from one region to another. For example, **armario** is used in Spain, but **clóset** is preferred in Colombia. The word **bañadera** is preferred in Argentina over **bañera** or **tina**, which are used in many other countries. **Estufa** is preferred in some Latin American countries, but in Spain the word **cocina** is used. **Cobija** and **frazada** are used in Colombia and Venezuela instead of **manta.** Finally, **refrigerador** and **nevera** are preferred in most countries, but **heladera** is common in Argentina and Uruguay.

5-9 Preparativos. **PREPARACIÓN.** Vas a mudarte a una casa muy grande y tienes que comprar muchas cosas. Organiza tu lista de compras según las siguientes categorías.

	Muebles	Accesorios	Electrodomésticos/ aparatos electrónicos
para la habitación			
para la sala			
para el comedor			
para la cocina			

INTERCAMBIOS. Comparte tu lista de compras con tu compañero/a. Él/Ella te va a recordar (*remind you about*) otras cosas que probablemente vas a necesitar.

MODELO E1: *Voy a comprar una cama nueva para la habitación.*
E2: *¿Vas a comprar sábanas y mantas? ¿Necesitas un sofá?*

barato/a	cómodo/a	grande
bonito/a	de buena calidad	práctico/a
caro/a	de color…	pequeño/a

5-10 De compras por internet. Miren la siguiente página web y seleccionen tres productos para comprar. Describan sus preferencias y expliquen dónde van a poner estos accesorios.

MODELO E1: *Voy a comprar un lavaplatos porque es muy práctico. Es para la cocina.*
E2: *Yo necesito unas toallas. Voy a poner las toallas en mi baño.*

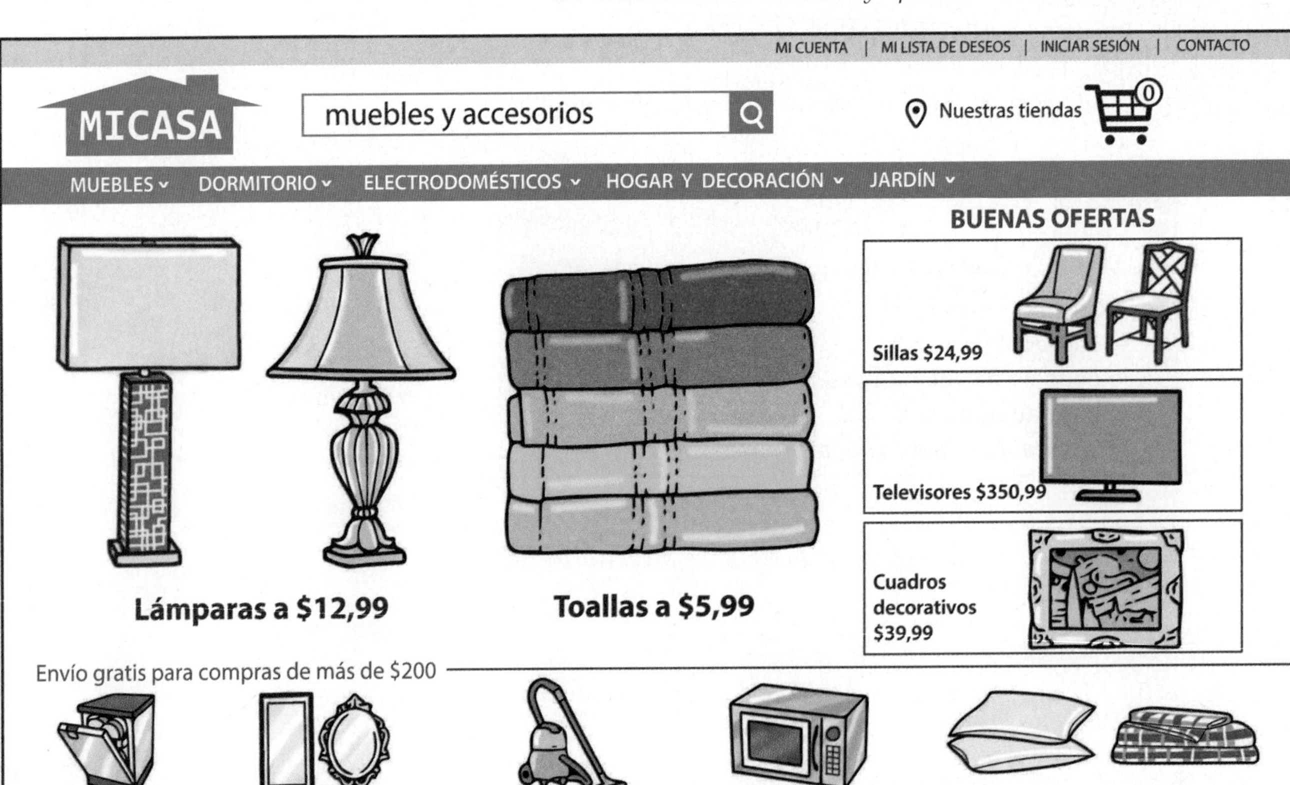

Las tareas domésticas

Hay muchos **platos sucios.** Gustavo los **lava** todos los días.

Cuando los platos están **limpios,** Beatriz los **seca.**

Beatriz **cocina** frecuentemente. Ella usa mucho los electrodomésticos.

Una vez por semana Gustavo **pasa la aspiradora** y **limpia** el baño.

Gustavo **saca** la **basura** todas las noches.

Por las tardes, **barre** la terraza.

Beatriz **tiende** la ropa después de lavarla.

Después la **dobla** cuando está **seca.**

Beatriz **plancha** la ropa los sábados.

Lengua

The following expressions denote frequency:

a veces *sometimes*
una vez por semana *once a week*
los domingos (lunes, martes...) *on Sundays (Mondays, Tuesdays, . . .)*
frecuentemente *frequently*
todas las mañanas (tardes, noches) *every morning (afternoon, night)*
todos los días *every day*

PRÁCTICA

5-11 Para confirmar. Pon estas actividades en el orden que las haces por la mañana. Después, compara tus respuestas con las de tu compañero/a. Usa las siguientes expresiones para indicar el orden: **primero, luego, más tarde, después, finalmente.** ¿Hacen las mismas cosas y en el mismo orden?

_____ lavar los platos
_____ preparar el café
_____ salir para la universidad
_____ desayunar
_____ secar los platos
_____ hacer la cama

MODELO E1: *Primero preparo el café. ¿Y tú?*
E2: *Primero hago la cama.*

5-12 Actividades en la casa. Pregúntale a tu compañero/a dónde hace estas actividades normalmente cuando está en casa.

MODELO E1: *¿Dónde lavas la ropa?*
E2: *Lavo la ropa en la lavandería. ¿Y tú?*

1. dormir la siesta
2. escuchar música
3. ver la televisión
4. pasar la aspiradora
5. estudiar para un examen
6. hablar por teléfono con amigos/as

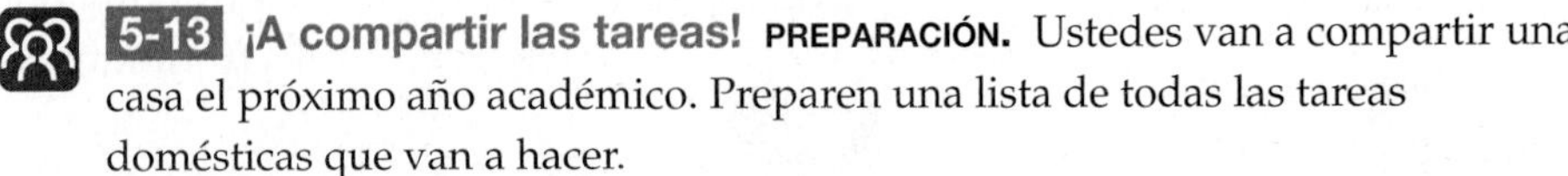

5-13 ¡A compartir las tareas! **PREPARACIÓN.** Ustedes van a compartir una casa el próximo año académico. Preparen una lista de todas las tareas domésticas que van a hacer.

INTERCAMBIOS. Decidan qué tareas va a hacer cada uno/a de ustedes según sus gustos. Finalmente, hagan un calendario de tareas y compártanlo con el resto de la clase.

MODELO *A mí me gusta tener la cocina limpia. Por eso, yo voy a lavar los platos todas las noches.*

5-14 La casa de Alicia. Alicia is talking about her home. As you listen, select the correct option to complete each sentence. Then listen again and check your answers.

1. La casa de Alicia es…
   a. muy grande.
   b. es mediana.
   c. es bastante pequeña.
2. En la sala hay…
   a. un sofá, unas butacas y un televisor.
   b. un sofá, unas butacas y una mesa de comedor.
   c. un televisor y unas butacas.
3. Los electrodomésticos son…
   a. funcionales.
   b. la lavadora y el microondas.
   c. modernos.
4. La habitación de Alicia tiene…
   a. una terraza.
   b. una cama y una cómoda.
   c. un clóset grande.
5. La casa de Alicia está…
   a. fuera de la ciudad.
   b. cerca de la universidad.
   c. cerca del centro.

Cultura

Tareas domésticas Nowadays it is more common in many Spanish-speaking countries for male family members to perform household chores traditionally done by women, such as shopping for groceries, cooking, cleaning the house, and taking care of the children.

Comparaciones ¿Hay tareas domésticas solo para hombres o solo para mujeres en tu familia y en otras familias que conoces? Explica con ejemplos.

Mosaico cultural

Las viviendas en centros urbanos

Las ciudades del mundo hispano son complejas, multiculturales y, a veces, un poco caóticas. Muchas personas viven en apartamentos en las áreas metropolitanas porque no hay mucho espacio. Algunas prefieren vivir cerca del centro para disfrutar de (*enjoy*) la vida cultural de la ciudad: teatros, centros comerciales, centros educativos, etc. En ciudades como Bogotá, Lima, Quito y Buenos Aires existe una tendencia a construir edificios de apartamentos altos para solucionar el problema de la falta (*lack*) de espacio.

Edificios de apartamentos en Bogotá

Con el crecimiento (*growth*) de las ciudades, también crece el costo de vida. Por esta razón, algunas personas deciden vivir en un tipo de vivienda colectiva. En esta vivienda urbana vive una familia o un grupo de amigos, que comparten con otros el baño y la cocina. Estos lugares se llaman **conventillos** en Argentina, **casas de vecindad** en España o **inquilinatos** en Uruguay, Bolivia y Colombia.

En Uruguay y Argentina, por ejemplo, en estos tipos de vivienda residen inmigrantes y trabajadores de pocos recursos. Sin embargo (*However*), los conventillos son importantes centros de cultura popular porque reúnen a personas de diferentes nacionalidades, regiones y clases sociales. En los conventillos del barrio de La Boca de Buenos Aires, por ejemplo, se origina el tango.

Conventillo en el barrio de La Boca en Buenos Aires

Compara

1. ¿Cómo son las ciudades en tu región o estado? ¿Hay problemas de espacio?
2. Generalmente, ¿dónde viven las personas en tu ciudad, en casas o en apartamentos? ¿Hay edificios de apartamentos altos como en Bogotá?
3. ¿Existen viviendas colectivas o algo similar en tu ciudad? ¿Dónde están? ¿Quiénes viven allí?
4. Busca fotos de las viviendas típicas de tu ciudad y describe cómo son.

En acción

En casa

Antes de ver

5-15 ¿Qué es? Selecciona la definición que corresponde a cada palabra.

1. _____ el microondas
2. _____ el barrio
3. _____ la aspiradora
4. _____ el baño
5. _____ la cocina

a. Es el cuarto donde te lavas la cara y te duchas.
b. Lo usas para calentar la comida.
c. Es un área de la ciudad donde vive la gente.
d. Es el cuarto donde preparas la comida.
e. Sirve para limpiar las alfombras.

Mientras ves

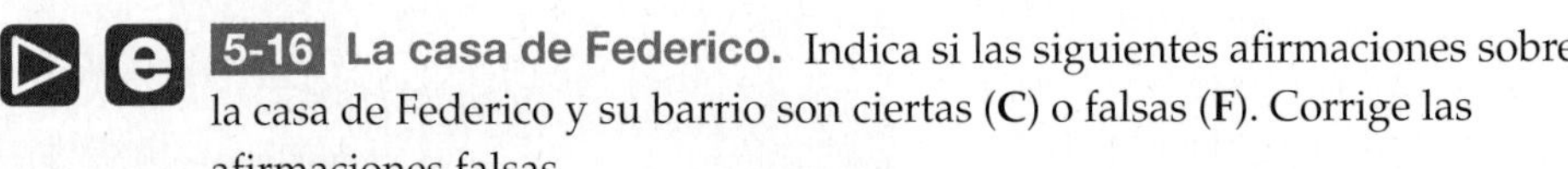

5-16 La casa de Federico. Indica si las siguientes afirmaciones sobre la casa de Federico y su barrio son ciertas (**C**) o falsas (**F**). Corrige las afirmaciones falsas.

1. _____ La casa de Federico está cerca del puerto en un barrio de Buenos Aires.
2. _____ El barrio de Federico es principalmente una zona residencial.
3. _____ El Puente de la Mujer es una obra (*work*) del arquitecto argentino César Pelli.
4. _____ Federico y su familia comen siempre en el comedor.
5. _____ Federico usa el microondas con frecuencia porque siempre tiene hambre.

Después de ver

5-17 ¿Qué hacen?

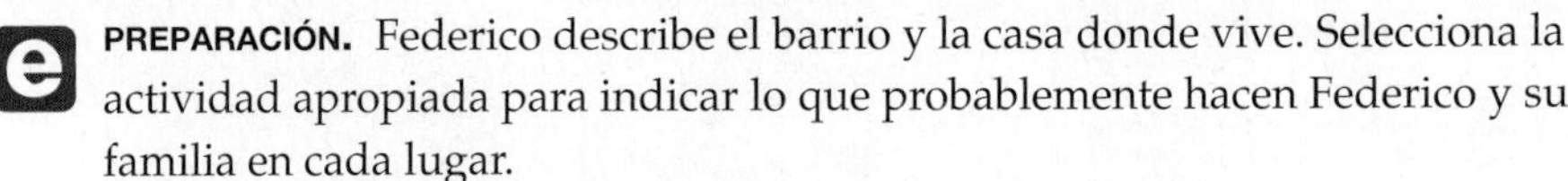

PREPARACIÓN. Federico describe el barrio y la casa donde vive. Selecciona la actividad apropiada para indicar lo que probablemente hacen Federico y su familia en cada lugar.

1. _____ En los restaurantes al aire libre…
2. _____ Frente al Puente de la Mujer…
3. _____ En el salón…
4. _____ En la cocina…
5. _____ En los dormitorios…

a. caminan.
b. miran la televisión.
c. duermen la siesta.
d. disfrutan de la vista y comen.
e. lavan los platos.

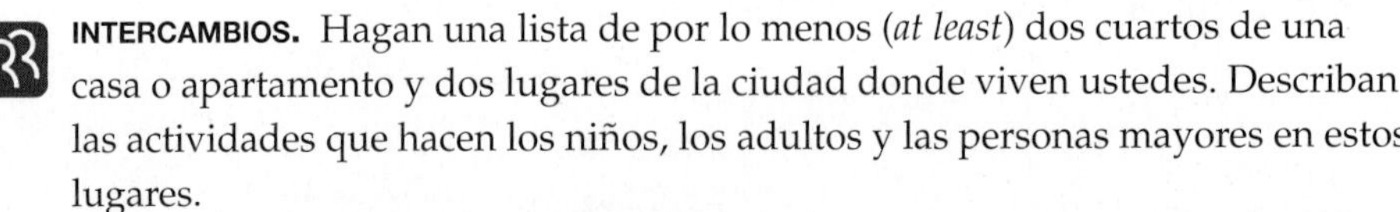

INTERCAMBIOS. Hagan una lista de por lo menos (*at least*) dos cuartos de una casa o apartamento y dos lugares de la ciudad donde viven ustedes. Describan las actividades que hacen los niños, los adultos y las personas mayores en estos lugares.

FUNCIONES Y FORMAS

1 Expressing ongoing actions

ÓSCAR: ¿Aló?
CATALINA: Hola, Óscar. Te habla Catalina. ¿Qué **estás haciendo?**
ÓSCAR: Hola, Catalina. ¡**Estoy trabajando** mucho!
CATALINA: ¿Por qué?
ÓSCAR: Mis padres **están pasando** sus vacaciones en la playa y vuelven mañana. ¡La casa es un desastre total!
CATALINA: ¿Así que **estás limpiando?**
ÓSCAR: ¡Claro! **Estoy barriendo, ordenando** la sala y **recogiendo** cosas. Y tú, ¿qué **estás haciendo?**
CATALINA: ¿Yo?... Nada. **Estoy leyendo** las noticias y **tomando** un café.

Piénsalo. Según la conversación, indica si las afirmaciones se refieren a Catalina (**C**), a Óscar (**O**), a Catalina y a Óscar (**C y O**), o a los padres de Óscar (**P**). Luego, escribe el infinitivo de cada verbo que termina en **-ando/-iendo.**

		Infinitivo
1.	_____ **Está trabajando** mucho.	__________
2.	_____ **Están pasando** sus vacaciones fuera de la ciudad.	__________
3.	_____ **Está bebiendo** algo.	__________
4.	_____ **Está limpiando** la casa de sus padres.	__________
5.	_____ **Están hablando** por teléfono.	__________
6.	_____ **Está descansando** en casa.	__________

Present progressive

- Use the present progressive to emphasize that an action or event is in progress at the moment of speaking, rather than a habitual action.

  Óscar **está limpiando** la casa. *Oscar is cleaning the house.* (at this moment)
  Óscar **limpia** la casa. *Oscar cleans the house.* (habitually)

- Form the present progressive with the present tense of **estar** + *present participle.* To form the present participle, add **-ando** to the stem of **-ar** verbs and **-iendo** to the stem of **-er** and **-ir** verbs.

ESTAR		*Present participle*
yo	**estoy**	
tú	**estás**	habl**ando**
Ud., él, ella	**está**	com**iendo**
nosotros/as	**estamos**	escrib**iendo**
vosotros/as	**estáis**	
Uds., ellos/as	**están**	

- When the verb stem of an **-er** or an **-ir** verb ends in a vowel, add **-yendo.**

  leer S leyendo

  oír S oyendo

- Stem-changing **-ir** verbs (**o → ue, e → ie, e → i**) change **o → u** and **e → i** in the present participle.

dormir (ue)	(**o → u**)	d**u**rmiendo
sentir (ie)	(**e → i**)	s**i**ntiendo
pedir (i)	(**e → i**)	p**i**diendo

- Unlike English, Spanish does not use the present progressive to express future time; Spanish uses the present tense or the **ir** + **a** + *infinitive* construction instead.

Salgo mañana.	*I am leaving tomorrow.*
Voy a salir mañana.	
¿**Te levantas** temprano mañana?	*Are you getting up early tomorrow?*

e **¿Comprendes?** Indica qué están haciendo los estudiantes en este momento. Usa la forma correcta de los verbos en el presente progresivo.

1. Alicia y sus compañeros __________ mucho para su clase de astronomía. (trabajar)
2. Ellos __________ información sobre los planetas. (leer)
3. En este momento Alicia __________ el precio de los apartamentos en internet. (investigar)
4. Pero Cristina no __________ en este momento. (estudiar)
5. Cristina __________ con Alicia. (hablar)
6. Alicia piensa: Nosotros __________ mal el tiempo. ¡Tenemos que terminar este trabajo! (usar)
7. El profesor pregunta: ¿Por qué __________ tú, Bruce? (dormir)

PRÁCTICA

e **5-18 Un día ocupado.** Hoy es un día ocupado para la familia López. Selecciona la explicación que corresponde a cada actividad.

1. _____ La Sra. López está preparando una cena deliciosa y un pastel (*cake*) especial.
2. _____ Su hijo Antonio está barriendo la terraza.
3. _____ Su hija Beatriz está lavando los platos en el fregadero.
4. _____ Su nieta Alicia está poniendo la mesa y decorándola.
5. _____ José está hablando por teléfono.
6. _____ Los músicos están practicando en el jardín.

a. Está llamando al mejor amigo de su padre para invitarlo a la fiesta.
b. El lavaplatos no está funcionando.
c. Necesita poner flores también.
d. Van a tocar *Feliz cumpleaños* y todos van a cantar.
e. Es el cumpleaños de su esposo.
f. Está muy sucia y vienen invitados (*guests*) a celebrar el cumpleaños.

5-19 Tareas para todos. **PREPARACIÓN.** Túrnense para describir cada escena. Incluyan a la(s) persona(s), el lugar y la(s) actividad(es). Tu compañero/a va a identificar la foto.

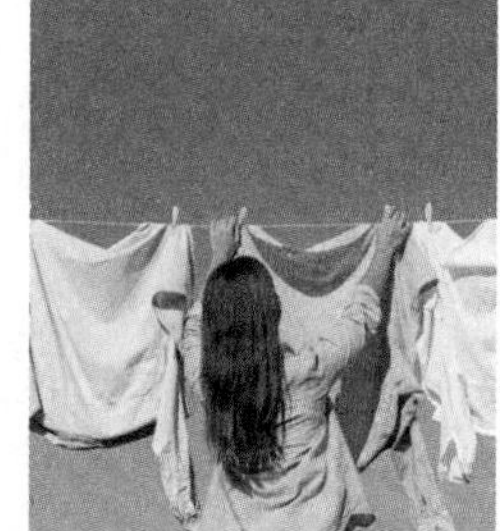

MODELO E1: *En esta foto hay una mujer. Ella está tendiendo ropa en el jardín.*
E2: *Es la foto número…*

1.

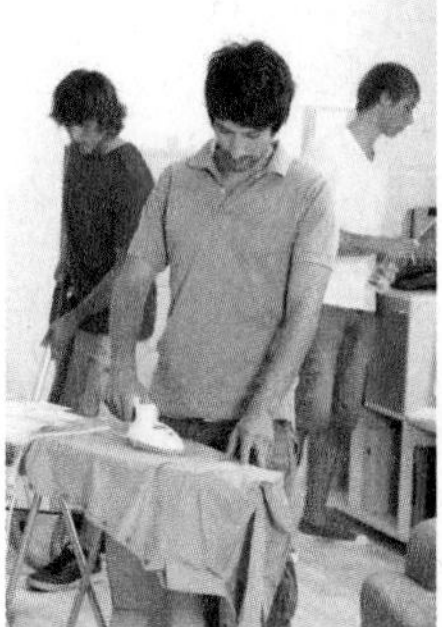

2.

3.

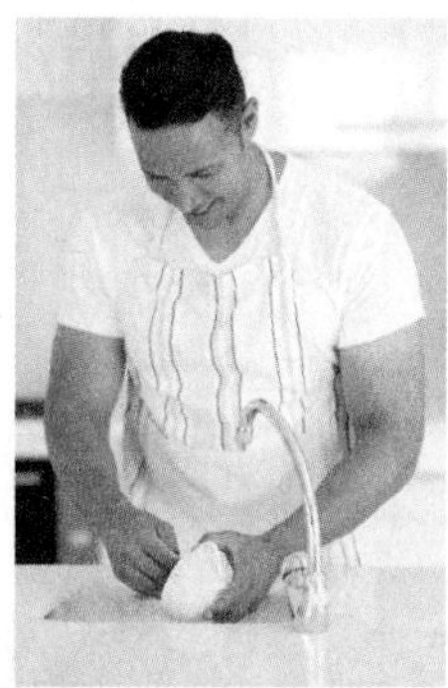

4.

5.

6.

INTERCAMBIOS. Respondan a las siguientes preguntas, según su experiencia personal. Luego, compartan esta información con la clase.

1. ¿Cuál de las tareas domésticas de **Preparación** les gusta más? ¿Cuál les gusta menos?
2. Expliquen sus preferencias.

5-20 La excusa perfecta. Tu compañero/a te pide unos favores. Usa las ideas de la lista para darle (*give him/her*) la excusa perfecta. Indica qué estás haciendo.

celebrar mi cumpleaños	descansar	preparar un examen
cocinar la cena	doblar mi ropa	reparar mi auto
comer con mi familia	estudiar	trabajar
comprar en el supermercado	lavar mi ropa	

MODELO contestar mi teléfono
E1: *¿Puedes contestar mi teléfono, por favor? Estoy ocupado.*
E2: *Lo siento, pero estoy trabajando en un proyecto urgente en este momento.*

1. ayudarme a limpiar mi apartamento
2. cortar el césped esta mañana
3. ir conmigo a comprar una butaca para mi habitación
4. lavar los platos sucios
5. mover mi auto
6. organizar una fiesta sorpresa para mi novio/a

5-21 Lugares y actividades. Miren las siguientes fotografías. Cada uno/a de ustedes debe seleccionar una foto diferente y describir dos o tres actividades que las personas están haciendo. Usen su imaginación. Háganse preguntas para obtener más información.

MODELO E1: *En esta escena hay varios miembros de una familia. Es el cumpleaños de Cristela. Cumple* (She is turning) *tres años. Sus padres, tíos y abuelos están celebrando este día especial. Cristela está escuchando la canción de cumpleaños.*

E2: *¿Tiene hermanos Cristela?*

E1: *Probablemente tiene hermanos o hermanas mayores.*

Coxen Hole, Honduras

La Ceiba, Honduras

Gran Lago de Nicaragua

Situación

PREPARACIÓN. Lean esta situación. Luego, compartan ejemplos de vocabulario, gramática y otra información que necesitan para desarrollar la conversación.

Role A. There is a big family gathering at your aunt's house today, but you are away at school. Call and greet the family member who answers the phone. Explain that you cannot attend, and express your regret for not being there. Ask how everyone is and what each family member is doing at the moment.

Role B. You are at a big family gathering today. A family member calls to say he/she cannot attend. Answer the phone. Greet the caller and answer his/her questions. Finally, tell the caller that everyone says hello (**todos te mandan saludos**) and say goodbye.

	ROLE A	ROLE B
Vocabulario	Words for family relationships Question words	Words for family relationships Activities that people do at family gatherings
Funciones y formas	Observing phone etiquette Expressing regret Asking questions Present progressive	Observing phone etiquette Reacting to what you hear Giving information Present progressive

INTERCAMBIOS. Practiquen la conversación, incorporando el vocabulario y las funciones de **Preparación.** Luego, represéntenla ante la clase.

2 Describing physical and emotional states

Hoy es un día de verano y los Robledo se están mudando a su nueva casa. **Tienen prisa** porque ya son las tres de la tarde. El señor Robledo y su hija Isabel **tienen calor** porque hace cuatro horas que trabajan bajo el sol. Ella **tiene mucha sed** y está bebiendo agua. El bebé, Nicolás, llora (*is crying*) porque **tiene hambre.** La señora Robledo le da de comer mientras la abuelita Rosa duerme la siesta. Después de empacar su ropa y todas sus fotografías, libros y plantas, Rosa **tiene mucho sueño.** ¡Qué día para los Robledo!

Piénsalo. Selecciona la expresión que mejor completa cada oración, según la descripción de los Robledo.

1. Nicolás va a comer porque _____.
2. Isabel está tomando agua porque _____.
3. Los Robledo no _____ porque es verano y hace mucho calor.
4. Rosa está cansada y _____.
5. El señor Robledo e Isabel _____ porque están trabajando bajo el sol.
6. Los Robledo _____. Quieren terminar pronto.

a. tiene sed
b. tiene sueño
c. tienen calor
d. tiene hambre
e. tienen prisa
f. tienen frío

Expressions with *tener*

- Spanish uses **tener** + *noun* for many conditions and states where English uses *to be + adjective.* You have already seen the expression **tener... años: Eduardo tiene 20 años.** Here are some other useful expressions.

TENER + *noun*			
tener	**calor**	*to be*	*hot*
	cuidado		*careful*
	frío		*cold*
	hambre		*hungry*
	miedo		*afraid*
	prisa		*in a hurry/rush*
	razón		*right/correct*
	sed		*thirsty*
	sueño		*sleepy*
	suerte		*lucky*

- With these expressions, use **mucho/a** to indicate *very.*

Tengo **mucho** calor (frío, miedo, sueño, cuidado).	*I am very hot (cold, afraid, sleepy, careful).*
Tienen **mucha** hambre (sed, suerte).	*They are very hungry (thirsty, lucky).*

¿Comprendes? Completa las oraciones con la forma correcta de **tener** y una palabra lógica para describir cómo están Olivia y su familia.

1. Son las 12:00 de la noche. Olivia _________ _________.
2. Hace 100 grados Fahrenheit. Olivia _________ _________.
3. Olivia oye ruidos extraños (*strange noises*) en la casa. Ella _________ _________.
4. El esposo de Olivia le dice que ella imagina los ruidos. Él no _________ _________.
5. Pero los ruidos desaparecen y todo está en silencio. Olivia piensa que ella _________ _________.

PRÁCTICA

5-22 Asociaciones.

PREPARACIÓN. Selecciona la palabra lógica para completar cada afirmación.

1. Mi hermano siempre tiene _____; por eso, está comiendo ahora.
2. Mi hermana duerme a todas horas porque siempre tiene _____.
3. En este momento, mis primos están visitando la Antártida; probablemente tienen mucho _____.
4. Mis abuelos están bebiendo agua en la cocina porque tienen _____.
5. Mi mamá tiene _____; siempre gana (*wins*) cuando juega a la lotería.
6. Amanda está planchando su blusa rápidamente porque sus amigos van a llegar en cinco minutos. Tiene _____.

a. sed
b. prisa
c. suerte
d. sueño
e. frío
f. hambre

INTERCAMBIOS. Túrnense para describir cómo se sienten en cada circunstancia. Pueden usar las ideas de la lista u otras. Tu compañero/a va a hacer una recomendación. Reacciona a su recomendación.

hacer mucho viento
hacer 95 grados Fahrenheit
no dormir mucho en general
recibir una promoción en el trabajo mañana
ser barato el alquiler de un apartamento en esta ciudad
ser excelente la comida en la residencia estudiantil
tener un examen muy difícil hoy
tener una clase en dos minutos
tus padres llegar al campus para visitarte en diez minutos

MODELO hacer 42 grados Fahrenheit
E1: *Hace 42 grados Fahrenheit hoy. Tengo frío.*
E2: *Debes tomar chocolate caliente.*
E1: *Tienes razón.*

5-23 Descripciones. **PREPARACIÓN.** Túrnense para describir qué están haciendo las personas en las escenas. Indiquen dónde están y cómo se sienten.

MODELO *El padre y su hijo están durmiendo en el sofá. Tienen sueño.*

INTERCAMBIOS. Háganse las siguientes preguntas relacionadas con las escenas.

1. ¿Dónde comes normalmente cuando tienes hambre en la universidad?
2. ¿A qué hora tienes sueño por las noches?
3. ¿Qué bebes cuando tienes frío?
4. ¿Tienes miedo alguna vez? ¿Cuándo?
5. ¿Qué haces cuando tienes mucho calor en verano?

5-24 Estados físicos y estados de ánimo (*moods*). **PREPARACIÓN.** Termina las siguientes ideas usando expresiones con **tener.**

1. Por las mañanas no tengo tiempo de desayunar. A mediodía (*noon*), yo...
2. Mi compañero/a de cuarto no puede hacer la tarea por la noche porque...
3. En las mañanas de invierno, yo siempre...
4. Entre clase y clase hay muy poco tiempo. Nosotros siempre...
5. Mi tío gana la lotería todos los años. Él...

INTERCAMBIOS. Usando sus apuntes de **Preparación,** comparen sus ideas.

5-25 Encuesta (*Survey*). **PREPARACIÓN.** Pregunta a tus compañeros/as sobre su experiencia en las siguientes situaciones. Escribe los nombres de las personas que contestan afirmativamente.

MODELO tener calor cuando hace 85 grados Fahrenheit
E1: *¿Tienes calor cuando hace 85 grados Fahrenheit?*
E2: *Sí, tengo calor. / No, no tengo calor.*

	Nombre(s)
1. tener miedo cuando miras películas de terror	
2. tener sed cuando haces ejercicio	
3. tener frío siempre cuando hace 25 grados Fahrenheit	
4. tener prisa para llegar a las clases por la mañana	
5. tener hambre cuando ves una foto de comida	
6. tener suerte de tener un/a compañero/a de cuarto tranquilo/a	
7. tener cuidado de no compartir las contraseñas (*passwords*)	
8. tener siempre razón cuando discutes (*argue*) con un/a amigo/a	

INTERCAMBIOS. Comparte con tu grupo la información de **Preparación.** Luego, preparen un resumen (*summary*) de los resultados del grupo para compartir con la clase.

MODELO *La mayoría de nosotros tenemos miedo cuando miramos películas de terror. Todos tenemos sed cuando hacemos ejercicio y todos tenemos suerte con nuestros amigos. El 30 por ciento de los compañeros tiene hambre cuando ve una foto de comida...*

En directo

To present group results:

Todos tienen/tenemos (*if you include yourself*)... *Everyone / All of us are . . .*

La mayoría de nosotros tenemos... *Most of us are . . .*

La mitad (*half*) **de las personas del grupo tiene/tenemos** (*if you include yourself*)... *Half of the people in the group / Half of us are . . .*

El 20% (por ciento) de las personas del grupo tiene/tenemos (*if you include yourself*)... *Twenty percent of the people in the group / Twenty percent of us are . . .*

Nadie tiene... *No one / Nobody is . . .*

Listen to a report with these expressions.

Situación

PREPARACIÓN. Lean esta situación. Luego, compartan ejemplos de vocabulario, gramática y otra información que necesitan para desarrollar la conversación.

Role A. You are staying at a hotel. You call the front desk and say the following:
a. you are tired and sleepy, and the people in the next room are making a lot of noise (**ruido**);
b. you are cold and need more blankets; and
c. you want to know what time the dining room opens because you are always hungry when you wake up.

Role B. You work at the front desk in a hotel. A guest calls you with two complaints and a question. Be as understanding and helpful as possible in responding to the guest.

	ROLE A	ROLE B
Vocabulario	Words that describe physical states Expressions (**tener** + *noun*)	Words and expressions to express reassurance
Funciones y formas	Observing phone etiquette Using a formal speech style Lodging a complaint	Observing phone etiquette Using a formal speech style Reacting appropriately to a complaint

INTERCAMBIOS. Practiquen la conversación, incorporando el vocabulario y las funciones de **Preparación.** Luego, represéntenla ante la clase.

3 Avoiding repetition in speaking and writing

¿Qué hacen estas personas?

El padre lava los platos y su hija **los** seca.

Los chefs preparan la comida y después los camareros **la** sirven.

La abuela pasa mucho tiempo con su nieta, Susanita. **La** visita todas las tardes.

Piénsalo. Selecciona la opción correcta para indicar a quién(es) se refieren las palabras en negrita (*bold*), según las fotos y descripciones.

1. El padre trabaja y su hija **lo** ayuda.
   a. el padre **b.** la hija
2. El padre está en la cocina con su hija. **La** mira con cariño.
   a. la cocina **b.** la hija
3. Susanita está contenta porque su abuela **la** visita.
   a. la abuela **b.** Susanita
4. La abuela está contenta también. Sabe que Susanita **la** quiere mucho.
   a. la abuela **b.** Susanita
5. Los chefs tienen una cocina enorme. **La** usan todos los días.
   a. los chefs **b.** la cocina
6. Ellos están preparando muchos platos. Después, los clientes van a comer**los**.
   a. los chefs **b.** los platos

Direct object nouns and pronouns

- Direct objects answer the question *what?* or *whom?* in relation to the verb.

¿Qué dobla Pedro?	*What is Pedro folding?*
(Pedro dobla) **las toallas.**	*(Pedro is folding) the towels.*

- Direct objects may be nouns or pronouns. When direct object nouns refer to a specific person, a group of persons, or a pet, the word **a** precedes the direct object. This **a** is called the **a personal** and has no equivalent in English. The **a personal** followed by **el** contracts to **al.**

Amanda seca **los platos.**	*Amanda dries the dishes.*
Amanda seca **al perro.**	*Amanda dries off the dog.*
¿Ves la piscina?	*Do you see the swimming pool?*
¿Ves **al niño** en la piscina?	*Do you see the child in the swimming pool?*

- Since the question word **quién(es)** refers to people, use the **a personal** when **quién(es)** is used as a direct object.

—¿**A quién** vas a ayudar?	*Whom are you going to help?*
—Voy a ayudar **a Pedro.**	*I am going to help Pedro.*

- Direct object pronouns replace direct object nouns and are used to avoid repeating the noun while speaking or writing. These pronouns refer to people, animals, or things already mentioned.

DIRECT OBJECT PRONOUNS			
me	*me*	**nos**	*us*
te	*you* (familiar, singular)	**os**	*you* (familiar plural, Spain)
lo	*you* (formal, singular), *him, it* (masculine)	**los**	*you* (formal and familiar, plural), *them* (masculine)
la	*you* (formal, singular), *her, it* (feminine)	**las**	*you* (formal and familiar plural), *them* (feminine)

- Place the direct object pronoun before the conjugated verb form.

—¿Barre la cocina Mirta?	*Does Mirta sweep the kitchen?*
—No, no **la** barre.	*No, she does not sweep it.*
—¿Cuidas a tu hermanito?	*Do you take care of your little brother?*
—Sí, **lo** cuido.	*Yes, I take care of him.*

- With compound verb forms (a conjugated verb and an infinitive or present participle), a direct object pronoun may be placed before the conjugated verb, or may be attached to the accompanying infinitive or present participle.

—¿Vas a ver a Rafael?	*Are you going to see Rafael?*
—Sí, **lo** voy a ver mañana. / Sí, voy a ver**lo** mañana.	*Yes, I am going to see him tomorrow.*
—¿Están limpiando la casa?	*Are they cleaning the house?*
—Sí, **la** están limpiando. / Sí, están limpiándo**la.**	*Yes, they are cleaning it.*

Lengua

You have seen that words that stress the next-to-the-last syllable do not have a written accent if they end in a vowel: **lavando.** If we attach a direct object pronoun, we are adding a syllable, so the stress now falls on the third syllable from the end and a written accent is needed: **lavándolo.**

¿Comprendes? Completa las oraciones con el pronombre correcto, según la información.

MARIO: Rosario, ¿cuándo vamos a visitar el apartamento?

ROSARIO: Quiero (1) ver___ el jueves. ¿Puedes llamar a la señora del anuncio?

MARIO: Sí, puedo (2) llamar___. ¿Recuerdas si el apartamento tiene lavandería?

ROSARIO: Seguramente (3) __ tiene porque dice el anuncio que los tres apartamentos que alquilan tienen área de servicio.

MARIO: Debemos (4) visitar___ todos para estar seguros.

PRÁCTICA

5-26 En casa. Túrnense para adivinar (*guess*) a qué o a quién se refiere tu compañero/a en el contexto de la casa y la familia.

MODELO Los padres **los** lavan después de comer.
E1: *Los padres los lavan después de comer.*
E2: *Los platos.*
E1: *¡Sí, tienes razón!*

1. El padre **la** plancha cuando está seca.
2. Los hijos **lo** ordenan todos los sábados.
3. Los niños **las** hacen después de levantarse.
4. La madre **los** llama porque necesita ayuda.
5. Cada uno **las** limpia en su habitación para tener más luz natural.
6. El esposo **la** pasa por la alfombra de la sala.
7. El hermano mayor **los** ayuda con su tarea.

5-27 ¿Qué es lógico?

PREPARACIÓN. Selecciona la acción lógica que corresponde a cada situación.

SITUACIÓN	ACCIÓN
1. _____ Las camas están sin hacer (*unmade*).	a. Los hijos las van a ordenar.
2. _____ La ropa está seca.	b. La madre las hace todos los días.
3. _____ Las habitaciones están desordenadas.	c. El padre las va a limpiar.
4. _____ El aire acondicionado no funciona.	d. La hija va a plancharla.
5. _____ Las ventanas están sucias.	e. Los hijos lo van a organizar y limpiar.
6. _____ No pueden poner el auto en el garaje porque hay muchos muebles viejos y cajas con libros.	f. El hijo mayor lo va a reparar.

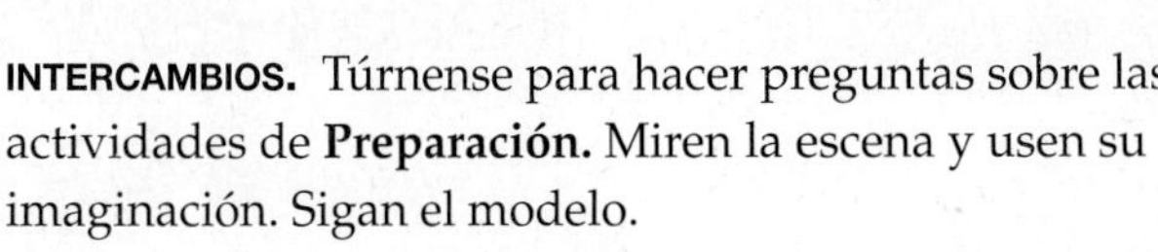

INTERCAMBIOS. Túrnense para hacer preguntas sobre las actividades de **Preparación.** Miren la escena y usen su imaginación. Sigan el modelo.

MODELO hacer la cama
E1: *¿Haces la cama todos los días?*
E2: *No, no la hago porque no es importante.*

5-28 El apartamento de mi compañero/a. Vas a cuidar (*take care of*) el apartamento de tu compañero/a por una semana y quieres saber cuáles van a ser tus obligaciones y qué cosas tu amigo/a te permite hacer allí.

¿Debo o no debo?	¿Puedo o no puedo?
regar (*water*) las plantas	usar los electrodomésticos
pasear al perro	escribir mis ensayos en tu computadora
abrir las cartas (*letters*) que llegan por correo	hacer una fiesta
limpiar el apartamento	ponerme tu ropa

MODELO **Para saber tus obligaciones:**

E1: *¿Debo sacar la basura?*

E2: *Sí, la debes sacar todos los días.*

Para saber qué se permite:

E1: *¿Puedo lavar mi ropa en tu lavadora?*

E2: *Sí, puedes lavarla.*

5-29 Los preparativos para la visita. La familia Granados está muy ocupada porque espera la visita de unos parientes. Túrnense para preguntar y contestar sobre lo que está haciendo cada miembro de la familia.

MODELO E1: *¿Quién está preparando la comida?*

E2: *La madre está preparándola.*

 **5-30 Una mano amiga.** **PREPARACIÓN.** Tu compañero/a te va a hacer preguntas sobre tus relaciones con otras personas. Escoge (*Choose*) a una de las personas de la lista para responder.

mi madre	mi novio/a	mi padre
mi mejor amigo/a	mis abuelos	¿...?

MODELO ayudar económicamente
E1: *¿Quién te ayuda económicamente?*
E2: *Mis padres me ayudan económicamente.*

1. querer mucho
2. escuchar en todo momento
3. llamar por teléfono con frecuencia
4. ayudar con los problemas
5. aconsejar (*advise*) cuando estás indeciso/a
6. entender siempre

INTERCAMBIOS. Dile a tu compañero/a qué haces por las siguientes personas. Indica en qué circunstancias lo haces.

MODELO tu amigo/a
E1: *Lo/La ayudo cuando está cansado/a.*
E2: *Y yo lo/la escucho cuando tiene problemas en el trabajo.*

1. tu papá
2. tu mamá
3. tu novio/a
4. tus vecinos/as (*neighbors*)
5. tu compañero/a de cuarto
6. tu mejor amigo/a

Situación

PREPARACIÓN. Lean esta situación. Luego, compartan ejemplos de vocabulario, gramática y otra información que necesitan para desarrollar la conversación.

Role A. You have to buy a bed for your new apartment. You have picked one out, but you need the store to deliver (**entregar**) it. Arrange a day and time with the salesperson.

Role B. You are a salesperson at a furniture store. A customer has decided which bed to buy and needs to have it delivered (**entregar**). The delivery service is not available on the day and time the customer requests, so negotiate a more suitable time to deliver it.

	ROLE A	ROLE B
Vocabulario	Vocabulary for bedroom items Days and times	Vocabulary for bedroom items Days and times
Funciones y formas	Inquiring about availability of a service Negotiating for a satisfactory outcome Direct object pronouns	Giving information about availability of a service Negotiating for a satisfactory outcome Direct object pronouns

INTERCAMBIOS. Practiquen la conversación, incorporando el vocabulario y las funciones de **Preparación.** Luego, represéntenla ante la clase.

En directo

To assist a customer in a store:

¿Qué desea? *What would you like?* (lit., *What do you desire?*)

¿En qué puedo ayudarlo/la? *How can I help you?*

To request a product:

Quisiera... *I would like . . .*

¿Podría ver...? *Could I see . . .?*

¿Me podría mostrar...? *Could you show me . . .?*

Listen to a conversation with these expressions.

4 Pointing out and identifying people and things

El agente les está presentando diferentes tipos de viviendas a sus clientes.

AGENTE: Bienvenidos a la agencia Casamejor. Estas tres casas están en venta (*for sale*). **Esta** casa blanca es la más grande. Tiene tres habitaciones y dos baños. **Esa** casa amarilla es más pequeña. Solo tiene dos habitaciones y un baño. Y **aquella** casa rosada tiene una habitación y un baño.

CLIENTE: Pero **esa** tiene jardín, ¿verdad?

AGENTE: Es verdad. **Esta** casa y **aquella** no tienen jardín. Por eso, **esa** casa con jardín es más cara.

Piénsalo. Indica si cada descripción se refiere a la imagen de la vivienda que está cerca (**C**), un poco lejos (**P**) o lejos (**L**) del agente.

1. _____ **Esta** casa de dos pisos está en una ciudad. Tiene muchas ventanas en cada piso, pero no tiene jardín.
2. _____ **Aquella** casa donde están la madre y su hija es pequeña, pero muy bonita y de un color alegre.
3. _____ **Esa** casa es de construcción sólida y tiene dos pisos y un garaje. Está en una zona muy verde.

Demonstrative adjectives and pronouns

Demonstrative adjectives

- Demonstrative adjectives agree in gender and number with the noun they modify. English has two sets of demonstratives (*this, these* and *that, those*), but Spanish has three sets.

DEMONSTRATIVE ADJECTIVES			
this	**este** cuadro **esta** butaca	*these*	**estos** cuadros **estas** butacas
that	**ese** horno **esa** casa	*those*	**esos** hornos **esas** casas
that (over there)	**aquel** camión **aquella** casa	*those (over there)*	**aquellos** camiones **aquellas** casas

- Use **este, esta, estos,** and **estas** when referring to people or things that are close to you in space or time.

Este escritorio es nuevo. — *This desk is new.*

Traen el sofá **esta** tarde. — *They will bring the sofa this afternoon.*

- Use **ese, esa, esos,** and **esas** when referring to events, people, or things that are not relatively close to you. Sometimes they are close to the person you are addressing.

Esa lámpara es muy bonita.	*That lamp is very pretty.*
Ese amigo de Lola vende su auto, ¿verdad?	*That friend of Lola's is selling his car, isn't he?*

- Use **aquel, aquella, aquellos,** and **aquellas** when referring to people or things that are more distant, or to events that are distant in time.

Aquel edificio es muy alto.	*That building (over there) is very tall.*
En **aquella** ocasión los niños jugaron en el parque.	*On that (long ago) occasion, the children played in the park.*

Demonstrative pronouns

- Demonstratives can be used as pronouns to mean *this one/these* or *that one/those,* thus avoiding repetition when speaking or writing.

DEMONSTRATIVE PRONOUNS			
this	**este** **esta**	*these*	**estos** **estas**
that one	**ese** **esa**	*those*	**esos** **esas**
that one (over there)	**aquel** **aquella**	*those (over there)*	**aquellos** **aquellas**

- To refer to a general idea or concept, or to ask for the identification of an object, use **esto, eso,** or **aquello.** These forms have no masculine or feminine forms.

Trabajan mucho y **eso** es muy bueno.	*They work a lot, and that is very good.*
¿Qué es **esto?** Es un espejo.	*What is this? It is a mirror.*
Aquello es un edificio de la universidad.	*That (over there) is a university building.*

e **¿Comprendes?** Escribe la forma correcta de los adjetivos demostrativos en cada caso.

este, esta, estos, estas

1. ________ butaca
2. ________ cuarto
3. ________ ventanas
4. ________ sofás

ese, esa, esos, esas

5. ________ sábanas
6. ________ cuadros
7. ________ jardín
8. ________ piscina

aquel, aquella, aquellos, aquellas

9. ________ garaje
10. ________ cortina
11. ________ mesas
12. ________ teléfonos

PRÁCTICA

5-31 Lejos, relativamente cerca o cerca. Decide cuál de las opciones debes usar según el lugar donde están los siguientes objetos. Compara tus respuestas con las de tu compañero/a y explica la razón de tu preferencia.

Lejos de ustedes

1. _____ mesa de madera es de Honduras.

a. Esta **b.** Esa **c.** Aquella

2. _____ cuadros son de artistas hondureños.

a. Estos **b.** Esos **c.** Aquellos

Relativamente cerca de ustedes

3. _____ sofá es muy grande.

a. Este **b.** Ese **c.** Aquel

4. _____ alfombra tiene unos colores muy alegres.

a. Esta **b.** Esa **c.** Aquella

Cerca de ustedes

5. _____ espejo es nuevo.

a. Este **b.** Ese **c.** Aquel

6. _____ lámparas son antiguas.

a. Estas **b.** Esas **c.** Aquellas

5-32 En una mueblería en Managua. Tu compañero/a y tú deciden vivir juntos/as en Nicaragua y van a una mueblería para comprar muebles y accesorios. Usen las y expresiones de la lista para hablar sobre lo que ven. Sigan el modelo.

bonito/a	feo/a
caro/a	me encanta(n)
cómodo/a	(no) me gusta(n)

MODELO E1: *¿Te gusta el sofá?*
E2: *¿Cuál? ¿Aquel sofá verde?*
E1: *No, ese sofá azul.*
E2: *Sí, me encanta.*

5-33 Descripciones. Piensa en tres objetos o muebles y el lugar de la casa donde están. Tu compañero/a va a hacerte preguntas para adivinar qué mueble u objeto es.

MODELO E1: *Este mueble está generalmente en el comedor.*
E2: *¿Es grande?*
E1: *Puede ser grande o pequeño.*
E2: *¿Lo usamos para comer?*
E1: *Sí.*
E2: *Es la mesa.*

 **5-34 ¿Dónde poner los accesorios?** Túrnense para describir los accesorios y decir para qué parte de la casa son. Las flechas (*arrows*) indican si los objetos están cerca (↔), relativamente cerca (⟷) o lejos (⟷) de ustedes.

MODELO ↔

E1: *¿Cómo son estas cortinas y para dónde son?*

E2: *Estas cortinas son azules y cortas. Son para el baño.*

1. 

2. 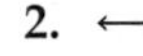

3. 

4. 

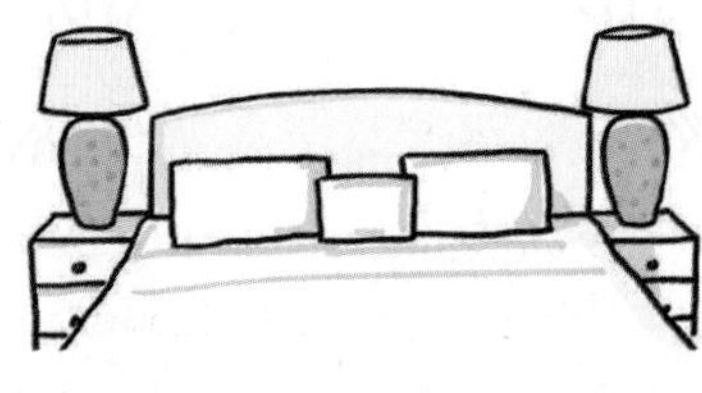

  Situación

PREPARACIÓN. Lean esta situación. Luego, compartan ejemplos de vocabulario, gramática y otra información que necesitan para desarrollar la conversación.

Role A. You and your friend want to rent an apartment together. You are now in the third one you have seen (**este apartamento**), and you are comparing it with the one you saw earlier today (**ese apartamento**) and one you saw three days ago that is farther away from campus (**aquel apartamento**). Tell your friend which apartment you want to rent, including information about the following:

a. the rent for each of the apartments;
b. the number of bedrooms; and
c. the facilities of each apartment, such as the laundry room, balcony (**balcón**), and pool.

Role B. You and your friend want to rent an apartment together. You are now in the third one you have seen (**este apartamento**), and you are comparing it with the one you saw earlier today (**ese apartamento**) and one you saw three days ago that is farther away from campus (**aquel apartamento**). Your friend tells you which apartment he/she wants to rent, but you don't agree. Discuss:

a. the rent for each of the apartments;
b. the number of bedrooms; and
c. the facilities of each apartment, such as the laundry room, balcony (**balcón**), and pool.

	ROLE A	ROLE B
Vocabulario	Rooms of a house/apartment Facilities of a house/apartment Numbers (prices)	Rooms of a house/apartment Facilities of a house/apartment Numbers (prices)
Funciones y formas	Describing an apartment for rent Talking about price of an apartment Talking about apartment amenities Verbs that describe: **ser, tener,** etc. Demonstrative adjectives (**este, ese, aquel**) to refer to apartments	Describing an apartment for rent Talking about price of an apartment Talking about apartment amenities Verbs that describe: **ser, tener,** etc. Demonstrative adjectives (**este, ese, aquel**) to refer to apartments

INTERCAMBIOS. Practiquen la conversación, incorporando el vocabulario y las funciones de **Preparación.** Luego, represéntenla ante la clase.

5 Expressing when, where, or how an action occurs

Los turistas están en la Reserva Natural de Borsawás, al norte de Nicaragua, y tienen que caminar **lentamente** porque la ruta es montañosa y difícil. Si van **rápidamente,** van a tener problemas. Caminan por la montaña **cuidadosamente,** porque no quieren tropezar (*to trip*). Hay muchos animales en esta selva (*forest*) tropical, pero **afortunadamente,** tienen miedo de las personas. **Seguramente** los turistas no van a verlos.

Piénsalo. Escribe los adjetivos que corresponden a las palabras en negrita (*bold*).

MODELO Martina camina **lentamente.** ___*lento*___

	ADJETIVO
1. Estos turistas no visitan la selva **frecuentemente.**	________
2. No pueden ir **rápidamente.**	________
3. Caminan por la montaña **cuidadosamente.**	________
4. **Afortunadamente,** los animales de la selva tienen miedo de las personas.	________
5. **Seguramente** los turistas no van a verlos.	________

Adverbs

- Adverbs are used to describe when, where, and how an action or event takes place. You may already be familiar with adverbs that refer to time (**mañana, siempre, después, más tarde**) and place (**allí, abajo, afuera**), and you have used adverbs to express how you feel (**bien, muy mal, regular**). These adverbs can also be used to express how things are done.

  Diego cocina **bien,** pero yo cocino muy **mal.** — *Diego cooks well, but I cook very badly.*

- Many Spanish adverbs end in **-mente,** which corresponds to the English *-ly*. To form these adverbs, add **-mente** to the feminine singular form of the adjective. With adjectives that do not have different forms for masculine and feminine, add **-mente** to the singular form.

  Mi hermanito come **lentamente.** — *My little brother eats slowly*
  La señora Ramos habla **constantemente.** — *Ms. Ramos talks constantly.*

- When two or more adverbs are used in a series, only the last one has the **-mente** ending. The other adverbs in the series have the same form as the feminine singular form of the adjective.

  El asesor habla **directa** y **claramente.** — *The advisor speaks directly and clearly.*
  Nuestro equipo gana los partidos **rápida** y **fácilmente.** — *Our team wins the games quickly and easily.*

- Some commonly used adjectives ending in **-mente** are:

básicamente	**probablemente**	**simplemente**
frecuentemente	**realmente**	**totalmente**
generalmente	**regularmente**	**tradicionalmente**
inmediatamente	**relativamente**	**tranquilamente**
perfectamente	**solamente**	

Lengua

Adjectives with a written accent mark retain it when forming adverbs ending in **-mente:**

difícil → difícilmente

e **¿Comprendes?** Escribe el adverbio derivado del adjetivo entre paréntesis.

1. En una familia, __________ los padres compran la comida para sus hijos. (tradicional)
2. En el mundo moderno, la familia es __________ una sociedad en la que todos colaboran. (básico)
3. Los miembros de la familia ayudan __________ y __________ en el buen funcionamiento de esta sociedad. (colectivo; eficiente)
4. Los hijos __________ limpian su cuarto y comparten otras tareas domésticas. (frecuente)
5. El trabajo doméstico no es __________ la responsabilidad de los padres. (único)

PRÁCTICA

5-35 ¿Estás de acuerdo o no? **PREPARACIÓN.** La dinámica familiar varía de una familia a otra. Indica si estás de acuerdo (**Sí**) o no estás de acuerdo (**No**) con las siguientes afirmaciones.

En mi familia…

1. _____ yo paso la aspiradora frecuentemente.
2. _____ generalmente lavamos la ropa los fines de semana.
3. _____ normalmente planchamos las sábanas.
4. _____ las habitaciones de los hermanos siempre están perfectamente ordenadas.
5. _____ yo hago la cama rápidamente por las mañanas.
6. _____ solamente los hombres cortan el césped y sacan la basura.

INTERCAMBIOS. Compara tus respuestas con las de tu compañero/a. Expliquen por qué están de acuerdo o no.

MODELO E1: *Estoy de acuerdo con el número 1. En mi familia yo paso la aspiradora con mucha frecuencia porque tenemos tres gatos.*

E2: *Yo no estoy de acuerdo. En mi familia solamente mi madre pasa la aspiradora.*

5-36 ¿Cómo, cuándo y por qué? Túrnense para hablar de cómo hacen las actividades de la lista. Indiquen también el lugar y las circunstancias.

desayunar (lento, rápido)
ducharse (frecuente, ocasional, regular)
escribir ensayos (fácil, perfecto, tranquilo)
estudiar (general, relativo)
hacer la cama (inmediato, regular)
ir a clase (general, solo, tradicional)
levantarse (inmediato, regular, tranquilo)
limpiar el cuarto/apartamento (frecuente, general, total)

MODELO leer las noticias (general, ocasional, total)

E1: *Leo las noticias ocasionalmente cuando no tengo mucha tarea.*

E2: *Yo leo las noticias todos los días, generalmente por la mañana, porque me interesa mucho la política.*

5-37 ¿Cómo o cuándo lo haces? Escribe cómo o cuándo haces las siguientes actividades. Forma adverbios con las palabras de la lista para describir tus actividades. Luego, compara tus actividades con las de tu compañero/a para ver si son similares o no.

difícil	lento
fácil	ocasional
frecuente	perfecto
inmediato	rápido

1. limpiar tu habitación
2. hablar español fuera de clase
3. respirar (*breathe*) durante una carrera (*race*) de bicicleta
4. responder en un examen fácil
5. aceptar una invitación de tu mejor amigo/a

5-38 Actividades frecuentes.

PREPARACIÓN. Háganse estas preguntas y tomen apuntes sobre las respuestas.

1. ¿Qué actividad haces rápidamente?
2. ¿Qué actividad haces frecuentemente?
3. ¿Qué actividad haces lentamente para hacerla bien?
4. ¿Qué actividades haces siempre estupendamente?

INTERCAMBIOS. Conversen con otra pareja sobre lo siguiente. Tomen notas para compartir con la clase.

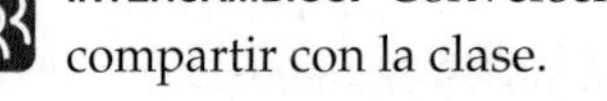

¿Qué hace la mayoría de ustedes…

1. rápidamente/lentamente?
2. frecuentemente en casa durante su tiempo libre?
3. generalmente durante las vacaciones?

Situación

PREPARACIÓN. Lean esta situación. Luego, compartan ejemplos de vocabulario, gramática y otra información que necesitan para desarrollar la conversación.

Role A. Your class is conducting a survey about students' habits and preferences related to household chores. Ask a classmate:

a. how often he/she makes the bed: frequently, occasionally, etc.;
b. whether he/she washes his/her clothes on a regular schedule or not, and why;
c. whether he/she washes dishes after using them, or waits until there are a lot of dirty ones; and
d. what his/her favorite chore is and one chore he/she hates (**detestar**).

Role B. Your classmate is interviewing you for a survey about habits and preferences related to household chores. Answer his/her questions. You are curious about your classmate's preferences, so you ask:

a. how often he/she makes the bed: frequently, occasionally, etc.;
b. whether he/she washes dishes after using them, or waits until there are a lot of dirty ones; and
c. what his/her favorite chore is and one chore he/she hates (**detestar**).

	ROLE A	ROLE B
Vocabulario	Household chores	Household chores
Funciones y formas	Talking about preferences Asking and answering questions Adverbs of frequency	Talking about preferences Asking and answering questions Adverbs of frequency

INTERCAMBIOS. Practiquen la conversación, incorporando el vocabulario y las funciones de **Preparación.** Luego, represéntenla ante la clase.

MOSAICOS

ESCUCHA

Estrategia

Create mental images You have already learned that visual cues can increase your listening comprehension. You can create mental pictures of what a speaker is talking about by using your imagination or by making associations with familiar things or experiences. As you listen, practice creating mental images to help you develop your listening skills in Spanish.

5-39 Preparación. Conversa con tu compañero/a sobre su habitación. Túrnense para preguntar sobre los muebles, aparatos eléctricos/electrónicos o accesorios que hay en sus habitaciones.

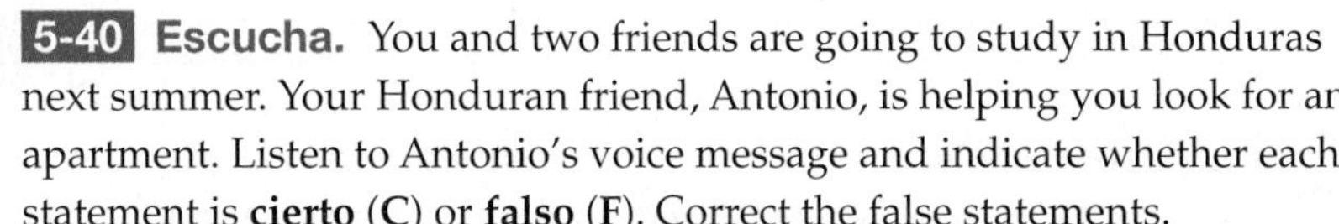

5-40 Escucha. You and two friends are going to study in Honduras next summer. Your Honduran friend, Antonio, is helping you look for an apartment. Listen to Antonio's voice message and indicate whether each statement is **cierto** (C) or **falso** (F). Correct the false statements.

1. _____ El apartamento está en Tegucigalpa.
2. _____ El apartamento tiene dos habitaciones y un baño.
3. _____ En la sala hay unos muebles y un televisor.
4. _____ La cocina no tiene luz natural.
5. _____ Solo un baño tiene bañera.
6. _____ Hay una sala pequeña.
7. _____ La habitación grande tiene ventanas grandes con cortinas.
8. _____ El alquiler cuesta 1.000 lempiras.

Comprueba

I was able to . . .

- understand key words.
- identify the speaker's positive opinion of the apartment.
- create a mental image of the apartment based on my experience.

5-41 Un paso más. Escríbeles un mensaje a los amigos que te acompañan a Honduras para explicarles tus impresiones sobre el apartamento de la actividad **5-40.** Incluye información sobre: a) la zona donde está, b) el tamaño (*size*) y aspecto de las habitaciones y c) los muebles que hay.

HABLA

Estrategia

Plan what you want to say Speaking consists of more than knowing the words and structures you need. You also have to know what you want to say. Planning what you want to say—both the information you want to ask for or convey and the language you will need to express yourself—before you start to speak will make your speech more accurate and also more coherent.

5-42 Preparación. Necesitas alquilar un apartamento en Tegucigalpa, Honduras, para compartir con dos compañeros/as. Tu amigo hondureño te mandó (*sent*) estos anuncios. Léelos y toma notas sobre las características de dos apartamentos que te gustan.

ALQUILERES
1. Se alquila condominio residencial privado, Colonia La Rosa, 3ª planta, 3 habitaciones, 1 baño, cocina con despensa, sala y comedor separados, garaje 2 autos, área recreación niños. (L$ 19.000), vigilancia incluida. Tfno. 22 24 46 30.
2. Alquilamos apartamento cerca de centro comercial, Cerro Brujo. Transporte público a la puerta. Ideal para profesionales. 2 habitaciones, 1 baño con jacuzzi, con muebles y electrodomésticos, terraza, sistema de seguridad, garaje doble. (L$ 15.500) Tfno. 22 65 16 92.
3. Alquilo apartamento, cerca Universidad Nacional Autónoma. 2 habitaciones. 1ª planta. Ideal para estudiantes. (L$ 12.500) Llamar al 22 35 37 83.
4. Alquilo preciosa habitación en casa particular, Barrio El Jazmín. Semi amueblada. Amplia; enorme clóset, internet gratis. Alimentación opcional. (L$ 7.500) Información en Tfno. 22 63 28 07.

Comprueba

I was able to . . .

- convey my preferences.
- express advantages and disadvantages of an apartment.
- ask appropriate questions.

 **5-43 Habla.** Elijan (*Choose*) cada uno/a el apartamento que más les gusta y compárenlos. Hablen sobre las ventajas y desventajas de cada apartamento y por qué lo prefieren.

 **5-44 Un paso más.** Hagan una breve presentación para compartir con la clase.

1. Describan los dos apartamentos que les gustan más. ¿Por qué?
2. Expliquen cuál es el apartamento que van a alquilar. ¿Por qué?

LEE

Estrategia

Inform yourself about a topic before you start to read To get acquainted with a topic, you should think about what you already know, read something about it on the web (in English or in Spanish), talk with people who know about the topic; a combination of these three approaches is the best preparation. The goal is to build your knowledge about the topic before you start to read. Then, when you read the text, try to apply that knowledge to support your comprehension.

5-45 Preparación. ¿Qué sabes sobre el tema (*topic*)? Indica si las afirmaciones son ciertas (**C**) o falsas (**F**). Corrige las afirmaciones falsas. Luego, escribe tu opinión sobre este tema en un párrafo.

1. _____ Hoy en día muchos jóvenes viven con sus padres después de graduarse de la universidad.
2. _____ Los jóvenes de hoy desean independizarse (*become independent*) de sus padres más que hace 10 o 15 años.
3. _____ Vivir en la casa de los padres es un fenómeno norteamericano solamente.
4. _____ El desempleo (*unemployment*) entre los jóvenes es una razón importante para vivir con los padres.
5. _____ Los jóvenes de hoy se casan a una edad mayor que hace 20 o 30 años.

5-46 Lee. El artículo describe un nuevo fenómeno social. Léelo y contesta las preguntas.

1. El primer párrafo presenta el nuevo fenómeno social. Explícalo con tus propias palabras.
2. El segundo y tercer párrafos presentan tres causas del fenómeno. ¿Cuáles son?
3. El tercer párrafo explica una de las causas con más detalles. ¿Cuál es, y qué explicación da?
4. En el artículo se presenta un subgrupo incluido en el fenómeno social. ¿Cuál es?

Comprueba

I was able to . . .

- anticipate content related to the topic.
- identify the three reasons that adults live with their parents.
- use the statistics to confirm my comprehension of the main ideas.
- identify the countries mentioned in the article.

Cultura

Desempleo juvenil In some parts of Latin America, unemployment among young people (ages 18–35) is high. In addition to the social and economic strains caused by unemployment, there are other social consequences, like young adults not being able to move out of their childhood homes and having to postpone marriage and starting a family.

Comparaciones ¿Es el desempleo juvenil un gran problema en tu país o región? ¿Hay muchos universitarios desempleados que tienen que vivir con sus padres después de graduarse de la universidad?

5-47 Un paso más. Hablen sobre los siguientes temas. Usen la tabla para organizar sus ideas.

1. ¿Qué significa para ustedes independizarse de sus padres?
2. ¿Cuáles son las ventajas y desventajas de vivir con los padres después de graduarse? ¿En qué circunstancias es necesario vivir con ellos?

Ser independientes de los padres significa...	Ventajas de vivir con los padres	Desventajas de vivir con los padres
______ no vivir con ellos ______ pagar todos nuestros gastos (teléfono, auto, apartamento, etc.)	1.	1.
______ hablar con ellos solamente una o dos veces por semana	2.	2.
______ depender de los amigos para consejos (*advice*), ayuda, etc. ______ otra idea	3.	3.

ESCRIBE

Estrategia

Consider various perspectives When you write about the advantages and disadvantages of a social practice, it is important to consider the different points of view of the people affected. Doing so adds greater depth to your essay and allows you to adopt a critical perspective on your topic.

5-48 Preparación. El artículo en la actividad **5-46** explica por qué más adultos viven en casa con sus padres ahora que antes. Otro fenómeno relacionado son las familias multigeneracionales, donde tres generaciones viven juntas. ¿Cuáles son las ventajas y desventajas de las familias multigeneracionales? Piensa en las perspectivas diferentes de los abuelos, los padres y los niños. Usa la tabla para organizar tus ideas.

	Para los abuelos	Para los padres	Para los niños
Ventajas			
Desventajas			

5-49 Escribe. Escribe un ensayo breve sobre las ventajas y desventajas de una familia multigeneracional. Adopta una perspectiva diferente de la tuya (*yours*); es decir, la perspectiva de los abuelos o la perspectiva de los padres. Considera la mejor manera de organizar tus ideas. Para las ideas más importantes, incluye también algún ejemplo.

5-50 Un paso más. Habla con tu compañero/a sobre tu ensayo. Para organizar su conversación, consideren lo siguiente:

1. las perspectivas diferentes que tiene cada uno/a
2. su experiencia o conocimiento sobre la vida en una familia multigeneracional
3. otras ideas sobre el tema

Comprueba

I was able to . . .

- express the perspective of another person in my writing.
- present advantages and disadvantages of living in a multigenerational family.
- give reasons to support my statements.

En directo

To represent another person's perspective:

Para los abuelos/padres/niños...

Desde la perspectiva de los abuelos/padres/niños...

To write about advantages and disadvantages:

Hay ventajas y desventajas de...

Una ventaja es... Otra ventaja es...

Pero también hay desventajas. Por ejemplo...

Además... *In addition . . .*

Listen to a report with these expressions.

En este capítulo...

Vocabulario

La arquitectura	*Architecture*
el apartamento	*apartment*
el edificio	*building*
el estilo	*style*
la vivienda	*housing*
En una casa	***In a home***
el aire acondictionado	*air conditioning*
el baño	*bathroom*
la basura	*garbage, trash*
la calefacción	*heating*
la chimenea	*fireplace*
el clóset	*closet*
la cocina	*kitchen*
el comedor	*dining room*
el cuarto	*room; bedroom*
la escalera	*stairs*
el garaje	*garage*
la habitación	*bedroom*
la lavandería	*laundry room*
el pasillo	*corridor, hall*
la piscina	*swimming pool*
el piso	*floor; apartment* (Spain)
la planta baja	*first floor, ground floor*
la sala	*living room*
la terraza	*deck, balcony*
Los muebles y accesorios	***Furniture and accessories***
la alfombra	*carpet, rug*
el armario	*armoire, wardrobe*
la butaca	*armchair*
la cama	*bed*
la cómoda	*dresser*
la cortina	*curtain*
el cuadro	*picture, painting*
el espejo	*mirror*
la lámpara	*lamp*
la mesa	*table*
la silla	*chair*
el sofá	*sofa*
En la cocina	***In the kitchen***
el fregadero	*kitchen sink*
el plato	*dish, plate*
En el baño	***In the bathroom***
la bañera	*bathtub*
la ducha	*shower*
el inodoro	*toilet*
el jabón	*soap*
el lavabo	*bathroom sink*
la toalla	*towel*
En el jardín	***In the garden***
la barbacoa	*barbecue pit; barbecue (event)*
el césped	*lawn*
la hoja	*leaf*
Para la cama	***For the bed***
la almohada	*pillow*
la manta	*blanket*
la sábana	*sheet*
Los electrodomésticos y aparatos eléctricos	***Appliances and electronic devices***
la aspiradora	*vacuum cleaner*
la estufa	*stove*
el horno	*oven*
el lavaplatos	*dishwasher*
el microondas	*microwave*
el/la radio	*radio*
el refrigerador	*refrigerator*
el televisor	*television set*
Los lugares	***Places***
las afueras	*outskirts*
el barrio	*neighborhood*
la calle	*street*
el centro	*downtown, center*
lejos (de)	*far (from)*
la zona	*area*
Las descripciones	***Descriptions***
limpio/a	*clean*
nuevo/a	*new*
seco/a	*dry*
sucio/a	*dirty*
barrer	*to sweep*
cocinar	*to cook*
creer	*to believe*
doblar	*to fold*
lavar	*to wash*
limpiar	*to clean*
ordenar	*to tidy up*
pasar la aspiradora	*to vacuum*
planchar	*to iron*
recoger (j)	*to pick up*
sacar	*to take out*
secar	*to dry*
tender (ie)	*to hang (clothes)*
Palabras útiles	***Useful words***
el alquiler	*rent*
la luz	*light*
el trabajo	*work*
la vista	*view*
Los números ordinales	***Ordinal numbers***
primero/a, primer	*first*
segundo/a	*second*
tercero/a, tercer	*third*
cuarto/a	*fourth*
quinto/a	*fifth*
sexto/a	*sixth*
séptimo/a	*seventh*
octavo/a	*eighth*
noveno/a	*ninth*
décimo/a	*tenth*
Expresiones con *tener*	***Expressions with* tener**
tener...	*to be . . .*
calor	*hot*
cuidado	*careful*
frío	*cold*
hambre	*hungry*
miedo	*afraid*
prisa	*in a hurry*
razón	*right*
sed	*thirsty*
sueño	*sleepy*
suerte	*lucky*

See page 194 for direct object pronouns.
See pages 198–199 for demonstrative adjectives and pronouns.
See page 202 for common adverbs that end in **-mente.**

Capítulo 6
¿Qué te gusta comprar?

Las Bóvedas (*Vaults*), en la antigua fortaleza de Cartagena de Indias, Colombia

Learning Outcomes

You will be able to:

- talk about shopping and clothes
- describe people, objects, and events
- indicate to whom or for whom an action takes place
- express likes and dislikes
- talk about events in the past
- talk about Colombia in terms of products, practices, and perspectives
- share information about shopping practices in Hispanic countries and identify cultural similarities

Enfoque cultural

Colombia

La parte antigua de Cartagena de Indias en primer plano y, al fondo, la moderna

La cordillera de los Andes

Una bandeja paisa con carne molida (*ground*) y aguacate

Arte hispano

Cuadro de la pintora colombiana Beatriz González

Enfoque cultural

¿Qué te parece?

- Medellín, la segunda ciudad más grande de Colombia, recibe en el 2016 el Premio Mundial Lee Kuan Yew por su innovación en el desarrollo (*development*) urbano sostenible.
- El 95% (por ciento) de las esmeraldas del mundo vienen de Colombia.
- Con sus costas en el mar Caribe y el océano Pacífico, sus bosques (*forests*) tropicales y sus altas montañas, Colombia es un país con una gran biodiversidad.
- Colombia produce el 12% del café del mundo. También exporta petróleo, metales, productos farmacéuticos y alimentos (*food*).

El escritor colombiano, ganador (*winner*) del Premio Nobel de Literatura, Gabriel García Márquez, tiene grandes éxitos (*success*) literarios, entre ellos su novela *Cien años de soledad* (*One Hundred Years of Solitude*).

El carnaval de Barranquilla se celebra cada año cuatro días antes de la Cuaresma (*Lent*). Atrae a personas de todas partes que desean disfrutar (*enjoy*) de las tradiciones, la música y el baile colombianos.

La variedad de fauna y flora de Colombia es impresionante. El oso perezoso (*sloth*) es una especie endémica de la región.

Bogotá, la capital de Colombia, está situada en el centro del país, a 2.600 metros sobre el nivel del mar (*sea level*). Es una ciudad moderna y, a la vez, tradicional.

¿Cuánto sabes? Completa las oraciones con la información correcta, según **Enfoque cultural.**

1. La ________________ ciudad más grande de Colombia es Medellín.
2. En Barranquilla se celebra todos los años un ________________.
3. ________________ es una pintora colombiana.
4. El 95% de las ________________ y el 12% del café del mundo vienen de Colombia.
5. El autor de la novela *Cien años de soledad* es ________________.

To learn more about Colombia, go online to view the *Club cultura* videos.

VOCABULARIO EN CONTEXTO

Talking about shopping and clothes

Las compras

Muchas personas **van de compras** a los **mercados al aire libre.** En el Mercado de Pulgas (*flea market*) San Alejo, en Bogotá, **venden telas,** objetos de **artesanía, joyas, ropa** y **bolsos,** pero a veces también hay discos antiguos, aparatos electrónicos y otras cosas para la casa.

En el Museo del Oro de Bogotá venden reproducciones de joyas antiguas, como **aretes, pulseras, anillos** y **collares de oro, de plata** y de otros metales.

En otras palabras

Depending on the country, the words **aros, aretes, pendientes, pantallas, caravanas,** or **zarcillos** are used for *earrings.*

En este **centro comercial** de Medellín venden de todo. Hay **tiendas** de ropa y de **zapatos.** También hay tiendas de muebles y accesorios para la casa, librerías, tiendas de **juguetes** para los niños, **supermercados** y cines.

De compras. José Manuel va a un **almacén** para comprar un **regalo** para su novia. Necesita la ayuda de la dependienta.

DEPENDIENTA: **¿En qué puedo servirle?**

JOSÉ MANUEL: **Quisiera** comprar un regalo para mi novia. Un bolso o una **billetera,** por ejemplo.

DEPENDIENTA: Hay unos bolsos de **cuero preciosos** y no son muy **caros. Enseguida** le **muestro** los que tenemos.

La dependienta trae unos bolsos.

JOSÉ MANUEL: No sé. **Me gustaría** comprar este bolso, pero no puedo **gastar** mucho. ¿Cuánto cuesta?

DEPENDIENTA: Solo **vale** 50.000 pesos. Es bastante **barato.**

JOSÉ MANUEL: Sí, no es mucho **dinero.** Es un buen **precio.**

DEPENDIENTA: Y **están** muy **de moda.** Las mujeres los **llevan** mucho.

JOSÉ MANUEL: Bueno, lo voy a comprar.

DEPENDIENTA: Muy bien, señor. ¿Va a **pagar** con **tarjeta de crédito** o **en efectivo?**

JOSÉ MANUEL: Con tarjeta de crédito.

Lengua

To soften requests, Spanish uses the forms **me gustaría** (instead of **me gusta**) and **quisiera** (instead of **quiero**). English does this with the phrase *would like.*

Me gustaría / Quisiera ir a ese almacén. *I would like to go to that department store.*

PRÁCTICA

6-1 Escucha y confirma. Indicate whether the statement you hear is **cierto** (C) or **falso** (F), according to the conversation between José Manuel and the salesperson.

1. _____ **2.** _____ **3.** _____ **4.** _____ **5.** _____ **6.** _____

Lengua

Names of stores in Spanish are often made by adding the suffix **-ería** to the root of the related noun: **mueble** (*furniture*) → **muebl-** → **mueblería** (*furniture store*).

These are some examples: **heladería** (*ice cream shop*), **joyería** (*jewelry store*), **juguetería** (*toy store*), **zapatería** (*shoe store*).

6-2 ¿Adónde van?

PREPARACIÓN. Las siguientes personas van de compras. Selecciona la tienda apropiada para cada descripción.

1. _____ María necesita unos libros para sus clases.
2. _____ Juan quisiera cocinar comida colombiana.
3. _____ Rosa va a comprar regalos para sus nietos.
4. _____ Felipe necesita una cómoda para su cuarto.
5. _____ Olga necesita unos zapatos.
6. _____ Catalina va a comprar un collar elegante.

a. mueblería
b. juguetería
c. zapatería
d. supermercado
e. joyería
f. librería

INTERCAMBIOS. Dile a tu compañero/a algo que necesitas comprar y pregúntale a qué tienda debes ir.

Cultura

Comprar por internet The use of the internet varies widely across countries and generations. Online shopping is increasingly popular among younger people, particularly for electronics purchases. However, shopping at stores for clothes and shoes is normally preferred, since most people like the personal interaction and the expertise of sales associates.

Conexiones ¿Qué ventajas y desventajas hay en comprar por internet? ¿Qué productos o servicios es mejor comprar en una tienda personalmente? ¿Por qué?

6-3 ¿Qué tienen que comprar? Ustedes van a viajar a Colombia el próximo mes. Hablen de qué necesitan comprar y por qué, y a qué tiendas van a ir.

MODELO unos zapatos cómodos (*comfortable*)
E1: *Necesitamos comprar unos zapatos cómodos porque vamos a caminar mucho.*
E2: *Podemos comprarlos en una zapatería.*

1. unas maletas (*suitcases*) grandes
2. una guía turística
3. un cuaderno para escribir sobre el viaje (*trip*)
4. un regalo para nuestra amiga colombiana
5. un nuevo teléfono celular
6. ropa de verano

Cultura

Mercados tradicionales People in many cultures haggle (**regatear**), which involves a business-like transaction between a customer and a vendor that has rules (usually unspoken) about when, where, and how it is done. In Spanish-speaking countries, haggling is not expected or acceptable in a pharmacy, a supermarket, a restaurant, or a government office, for example. However, people often haggle at outdoor markets.

Comparaciones ¿Se regatea en tu país? ¿En qué situaciones? ¿Regatean tus padres u otros miembros de tu familia? ¿Dónde?

6-4 El mercado tradicional. **PREPARACIÓN.** Túrnense para comprar unos recuerdos (*souvenirs*) en un mercado tradicional en Bogotá. Pregunten el precio y regateen para obtener un precio más barato.

MODELO E1: *Quisiera comprar este collar. ¿Cuánto cuesta?*
E2: *Cuesta 62.000 pesos.*
E1: *¡Uy, qué caro! Lo compro por 55.000.*
E2: *Pero, es muy bonito.*
E1: *Sí, es muy bonito, pero no tengo suficiente dinero.*
E2: *Bueno, está bien. Lo vendo por 60.000.*

INTERCAMBIOS. Muestra tus compras a otro/a compañero/a y explica qué es, para quién lo compras y cuánto cuesta.

En directo

To express displeasure about a high price:
¡Qué caro/a! *How expensive!*
To show pleasure at a bargain:
¡Qué barato/a! *How affordable!*
¡Qué ganga! *What a bargain!*
Listen to a conversation with these expressions.

La ropa

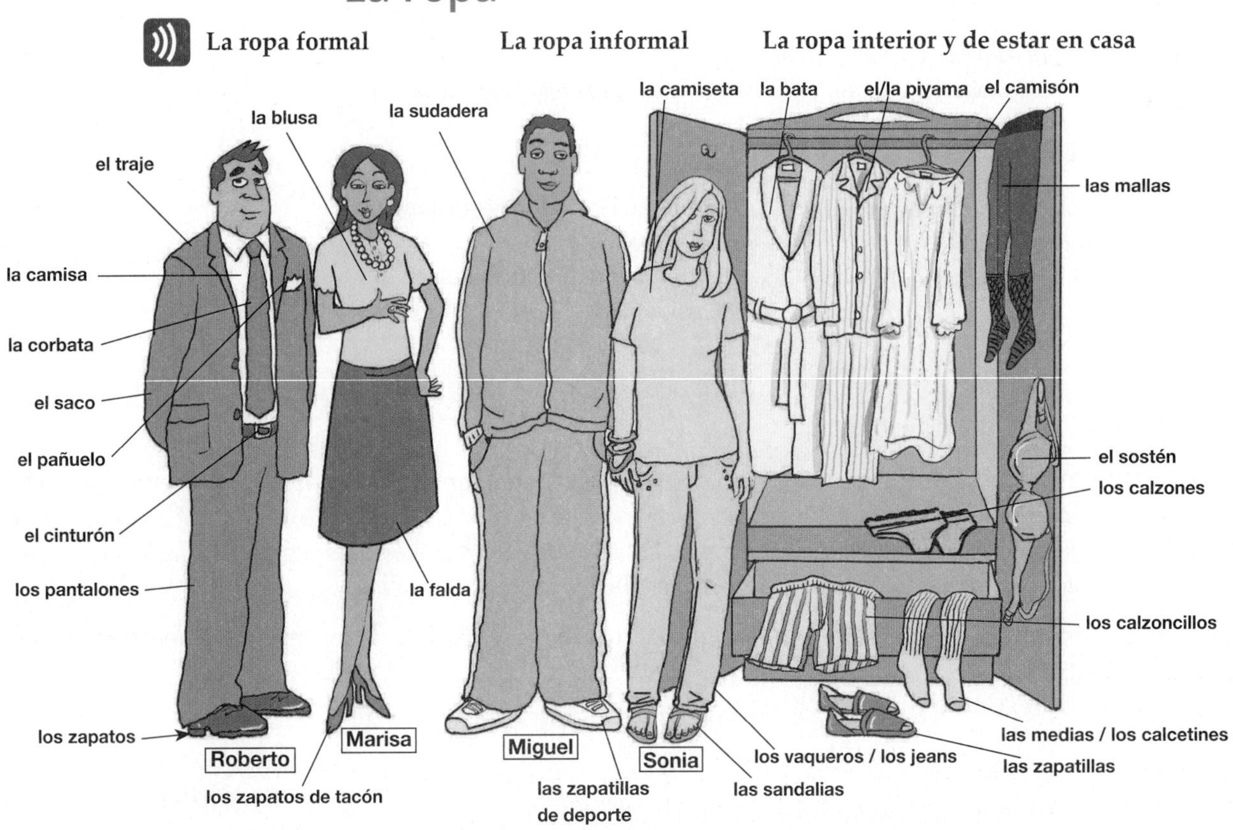

Telas y diseños

Las rebajas. Marta y Ana miran la ropa en el **escaparate** de una tienda.

MARTA: Las **rebajas** son **magníficas.** Mira esa falda de rayas. Parece muy **cómoda,** y está **rebajada** de 68.000 pesos a 45.000.

ANA: Esta falda es de algodón y es preciosa, pero uso la **talla** 6 y a veces es difícil encontrarla.

MARTA: ¿Por qué no vemos si tienen tu talla?

ANA: Sí, y **me pruebo** la falda para ver si **me queda** bien.

MARTA: O te pruebas la falda en casa y si te queda mal, la **cambias.**

Entran en la tienda.

ANA: Buenos días, quisiera probarme la falda de algodón que está en el escaparate en la talla 6.

DEPENDIENTA: Lo siento, pero las únicas (*only*) tallas que **nos quedan** son más grandes, la 8 y la 12.

ANA: ¡Qué lástima! Gracias.

La chaqueta le queda **estrecha.**

La falda le queda **ancha.**

En otras palabras

Some words referring to clothing differ from one region to another. For example, in Spain **el/la piyama** is **el pijama,** and **medias** means *stockings,* but in parts of Latin America it also means *socks.* In Argentina and Uruguay, **pollera** is used instead of **falda,** and in Colombia **vestido** may mean *suit* or *dress.* The words **sostén** or **sujetador** are used for *bra,* but in Argentina **corpiño** is preferred. In Spain, **braga** or **bragas** refer to women's underwear.

PRÁCTICA

6-5 Para confirmar. Selecciona la afirmación que corresponde a cada descripción, según la experiencia de Ana en las rebajas.

1. _____ Ana necesita una falda en la talla 6.
2. _____ La falda no es de color entero.
3. _____ Ana prefiere las telas naturales.
4. _____ En la tienda solo tienen tallas más grandes.
5. _____ La falda no es muy cara.
6. _____ Marta dice que Ana puede probarse la falda en casa.

a. Ana no se prueba la falda.
b. Está rebajada.
c. Sabe que la talla 12 le va a quedar ancha.
d. Puede cambiar la falda si no le queda bien.
e. Es de rayas.
f. Le gusta la falda porque es de algodón.

Lengua

The word **talla** is normally used when talking about clothing size; **número** refers to shoe size. **Tamaño** means size in all other contexts: **¿Cuál es tu número de zapatos?**

The word **calzado** means *footwear* in general: **Las marcas** (*brand-names*) **de calzado colombiano son chéveres.**

The verb **calzar** is also used to ask about someone's shoe size. **¿Qué número calzas? ¿Cuánto calzas?**

6-6 **¿Qué llevas?** **PREPARACIÓN.** Indica qué prendas de vestir (*articles of clothing*) usas en cada situación.

1. Para ir a correr o al gimnasio, me pongo...
2. Para dormir, llevo...
3. Para ir a una fiesta elegante, me pongo...
4. Para comer pizza con mis amigos, llevo...

INTERCAMBIOS. Túrnense para preguntarse qué ropa usan en cada situación.

MODELO venir a clase

E1: *¿Qué usas para venir a clase?*

E2: *Uso unos vaqueros y una camiseta de algodón.*

1. salir los sábados con tus amigos
2. ir a una fiesta de cumpleaños
3. una entrevista (*interview*) de trabajo
4. ir al gimnasio

Cultura

Las compras de ropa In some Spanish-speaking countries, it is still possible to buy clothing that is made locally by artisans. With globalization, however, clothing has become an international product, usually distributed via multinational business networks. As in the United States, people in Latin America and Spain often buy clothes made in other countries or continents. Inditex, a Spanish textile group, is currently the biggest clothing company in the world.

Conexiones ¿En qué tiendas compras ropa generalmente? ¿Dónde manufacturan la ropa que llevas hoy? ¿Dónde se puede encontrar ropa artesanal en tu ciudad? ¿Crees que es necesario pagar más por ropa de marca?

6-7 **¿Qué ropa llevan?** **PREPARACIÓN.** Cuenten (*Count*) cuántas personas de la clase llevan los siguientes accesorios y prendas de vestir. Después, comparen sus resultados.

1. aretes en las orejas
2. camisetas con el nombre de la universidad
3. zapatillas de deporte
4. vaqueros rotos (*ripped*)
5. corbatas
6. collares de oro

INTERCAMBIOS. Túrnense para describir la ropa que llevan algunas personas de la clase para adivinar (*guess*) quiénes son.

Lengua

Here is some useful vocabulary for the body (**el cuerpo**): **la cabeza** (*head*), **la cintura** (*waist*), **el cuello** (*neck*), **las orejas** (*ears*), **la nariz** (*nose*), **los brazos** (*arms*), **las manos** (*hands*), **las piernas** (*legs*), **los pies** (*feet*). You will learn more words related to parts of the body in *Capítulo 11*.

6-8 El regalo. Ustedes van a una tienda para comprarle un regalo a una buena amiga, pero cada artículo que ven presenta un problema. Piensen en la solución.

MODELO collar / Es muy caro. *Debemos buscar uno más barato.*

Artículo	Problema	Solución
1. zapatillas	Le quedan grandes.	
2. vaqueros	Son estrechos.	
3. sudadera	Es pequeña.	
4. blusa	Es de poliéster.	
5. bolso	No es de cuero.	

¿Qué debo llevar?

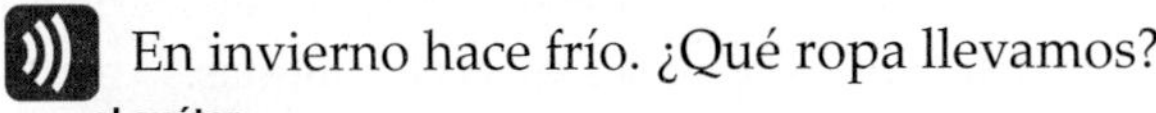

En invierno hace frío. ¿Qué ropa llevamos?

Cuando hace calor en verano, ¿qué nos ponemos para ir a la playa?

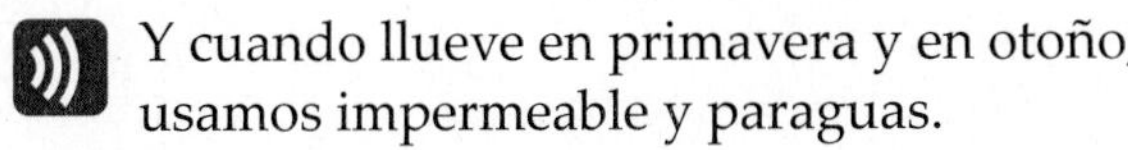

Y cuando llueve en primavera y en otoño, usamos impermeable y paraguas.

PRÁCTICA

 **Para confirmar.**

PREPARACIÓN. Selecciona la descripción que corresponde a cada prenda de vestir.

1. _____ los guantes
2. _____ el traje de baño
3. _____ las botas
4. _____ el suéter
5. _____ los pantalones cortos
6. _____ el sombrero

a. Sirve para protegernos del sol.
b. Los llevamos en las manos cuando hace frío.
c. Son más cómodos cuando hace buen tiempo.
d. Nos lo ponemos para ir a la playa.
e. Es de lana, para llevar cuando hace frío.
f. Las llevamos en los pies en invierno.

INTERCAMBIOS. Túrnense y pregunten qué ropa o accesorios usan ustedes en las siguientes situaciones. Añadan (*Add*) otras opciones en sus respuestas.

MODELO cuando llueve
E1: *¿Qué usas o llevas cuando llueve?*
E2: *Uso un paraguas. ¿Y tú?*
E1: *Llevo un impermeable.*

1. cuando montas en bicicleta
2. para caminar por el parque en invierno
3. para ir a la playa con tus amigos
4. en los pies cuando hace calor
5. cuando hace mucho sol en verano
6. en otoño cuando hace viento (*it's windy*)

 **Vacaciones en Colombia.** Tu amigo/a y tú van a pasar unas vacaciones en Colombia. Escojan (*Choose*) el plan que más les interesa. Busquen información en internet sobre cada lugar (clima, comida típica, lugares de interés) y preparen una breve presentación para la clase incluyendo:

- dos o tres fotos de lugares que van a visitar
- un plato de comida colombiana que quieren probar
- la ropa y accesorios que necesitan

Plan A. Quince días en la ciudad de Cartagena de Indias. Por el día, ir a la playa; por la tarde, pasear por la parte antigua de la ciudad.

Plan B. Tomar un curso de verano en la Universidad de los Andes en Bogotá. Por la mañana, clases de español; por la noche, ir a los mejores restaurantes.

Plan C. Explorar la zona cafetera del Quindío y la ciudad de Cali. Por el día, visitar lugares de interés turístico; por la noche, bailar salsa.

MODELO *Vamos a ir a Cartagena de Indias. Esta es una foto de la muralla (*wall*). Queremos probar el arroz con coco. Yo necesito un traje de baño y mi compañera necesita unos pantalones cortos.*

6-11 Ropa para todos. Cada uno/a debe comprar ropa para hacer unos regalos a tres personas diferentes de la siguiente lista. Explícale a tu compañero/a qué vas a comprar, dónde y para quién.

1. tu sobrina de seis años
2. tu mamá para el Día de la Madre
3. tu amigo/a que necesita ropa informal
4. tu padre para su cumpleaños
5. tu novio/a para el Día de los Enamorados

6-12 Ropa para cada ocasión.

PREPARACIÓN. Tell your classmate what you wear on the following occasions: **una fiesta elegante** and **una fiesta informal.**

ESCUCHA. Listen to the conversation and indicate the clothes and the event mentioned.

1. **a.** ropa elegante **b.** falda y chaqueta **c.** pantalón y blusa **d.** pantalones cortos y camiseta
2. **a.** entrevista (*interview*) de trabajo **b.** reunión de jóvenes **c.** excursión de fin de semana **d.** fiesta formal

Mosaico cultural

Las tiendas de barrio

Productos en una tienda de barrio de Barichara, Colombia

Los centros comerciales son lugares importantes en las ciudades hispanas. Como en Estados Unidos, los centros comerciales son también centros de ocio (*leisure*) y entretenimiento donde se va para comprar, comer o ver películas. Están normalmente en zonas urbanas donde vive mucha gente y, por eso, también tienen grandes supermercados. En algunas ciudades, los supermercados son cadenas (*chains*) nacionales, como Éxito en Colombia y Coto en Argentina. Pero también hay otros de origen europeo, como Carrefour, o norteamericano, como Walmart.

En estos supermercados y centros comerciales, las personas compran comida, ropa, instrumentos musicales, herramientas (*tools*) para el trabajo y productos para sus casas. Sin embargo (*However*), los grandes supermercados compiten con los negocios (*business*) más tradicionales. En América Latina, existen centros de comercio llamados **tiendas de barrio** (o **tiendas de conveniencia** en México, **almacén** en Argentina y Uruguay). Las tiendas de barrio tienen una gran variedad de productos, pero son mucho más pequeñas que los supermercados. Algunas personas prefieren estas tiendas porque son mucho más personales y a veces es posible regatear.

Las tiendas de barrio tienen una gran importancia cultural en los países hispanos. En estos lugares se establecen relaciones de amistad (*friendship*) y solidaridad entre las personas y la comunidad. Las tiendas de barrio también ofrecen otros servicios: recepción y transmisión de mensajes, transferencias de dinero y publicación de información importante.

Compara

1. ¿Qué ofrecen los centros comerciales en tu comunidad?
2. ¿Hay tiendas de barrio o alguna tienda similar donde vives?
3. ¿Cómo se llaman y qué compras allí?
4. ¿Qué importancia tienen las tiendas de barrio en la comunidad?

En acción

De moda

Antes de ver

6-13 ¿Es apropiado? En este episodio, Esteban va a un restaurante muy elegante. Indica la ropa y accesorios apropiados (**A**) y no apropiados (**NA**) para esta ocasión. Si no son apropiados, explica por qué.

1. _____ una camisa
2. _____ una bata
3. _____ unas zapatillas de deporte
4. _____ un traje de baño
5. _____ un saco
6. _____ una sudadera
7. _____ unos zapatos
8. _____ una corbata
9. _____ un cinturón
10. _____ unos calcetines

Mientras ves

6-14 ¿Y después? Los chicos están muy ocupados hoy. Indica el orden (**1–6**) en que ocurren las actividades en el video.

_____ Esteban se prueba la ropa que compra en el centro comercial.
_____ Blanca y Yolanda hablan sobre la ropa de Esteban.
_____ La modelo habla sobre el festival de moda en Los Ángeles.
_____ Llega Amber.
_____ Yolanda y Esteban van al centro comercial.
_____ Vanesa y Yolanda le muestran a Esteban un video sobre un festival de moda.

Después de ver

6-15 La moda hispana en Los Ángeles.

PREPARACIÓN. Indica si las siguientes afirmaciones son ciertas (**C**) o falsas (**F**), según el video. Corrige las afirmaciones falsas.

1. _____ A Yolanda le interesa salir con Esteban.
2. _____ Esteban viste siempre a la moda.
3. _____ La casa Pineda Covalín está en la Ciudad de México.
4. _____ Muchos vestidos de la casa Pineda Covalín están inspirados en diseños árabes.
5. _____ Según la modelo, Suzy Diab, el *Latino Fashion Week* es una buena manera de conectarse con su cultura.
6. _____ Blanca piensa que Yolanda tiene un buen plan.

INTERCAMBIOS. Hablen de la ropa que está de moda entre las personas de su edad. En general, ¿qué ropa llevan los jóvenes todos los días? ¿Y en ocasiones especiales? ¿Dónde compran su ropa los estudiantes? ¿Hay una tienda de ropa de moda en tu campus? ¿Qué tipo de ropa vende?

1 Describing people, objects, and events

ABUELA: Cuidado, Juanita, el café **está** muy caliente.
[*A la madre*] ¡La niña **está** muy grande!

MADRE: Claro, tiene cinco años. **Es** muy alta para su edad.

JUANITA: Abuelita, ¿qué **es** ese cuadro?

ABUELA: **Son** montañas de la cordillera de los Andes en Chile.
El aire en las montañas **es** muy frío por las noches.

Piénsalo. Indica la función de **ser** o **estar** en las siguientes afirmaciones.

	CONDICIÓN	CARACTERÍSTICA
1. El café **está** caliente.	_____	_____
2. ¡La niña **está** muy grande!	_____	_____
3. **Es** muy alta para su edad.	_____	_____
4. **Son** montañas de los Andes.	_____	_____
5. El aire en las montañas **es** muy frío por las noches.	_____	_____

More about *ser* and *estar*

- In *Capítulo 2*, you learned to use **ser** to identify and describe, and to express nationality, ownership, and origin. You also learned to use **ser** to talk about dates and time, and to tell where an event takes place.

Víctor **es** de Colombia.	*Victor is from Colombia.* (nationality)
Es un diseñador de ropa para hombres.	*He is a designer of men's clothing.* (profession)
Es alto y delgado, y **es** muy fuerte.	*He is tall and thin, and he is very strong.* (distinguishing characteristics)
Estas figuras pintadas **son** de Víctor, tiene una colección grande.	*These painted figures belong to Victor; he has a big collection.* (possession)
El próximo desfile de moda con su ropa **es** mañana a las ocho.	*The next fashion show of his clothing is tomorrow at eight o'clock.*
Va a ser en el Teatro El Rey.	*It is going to take place in the El Rey Theater.* (time/location of event)

- **Ser** is also used to talk about what something is made of.

El reloj **es** de oro.	*The watch is (made of) gold.*

- You also learned in *Capítulo 2* that **estar** is used to indicate location, to talk about health and similar conditions, and to describe changes in feelings or perceptions. It is also used to express ongoing actions, presented in *Capítulo 4*.

El Teatro Andrés Bello **está** en el centro.	*The Andrés Bello Theater is downtown.* (location)
Víctor fue al doctor la semana pasada, pero ahora **está** bien.	*Victor went to the doctor last week, but now he is fine.* (health)
Víctor **está** nervioso antes de los desfiles, pero siempre **está** contento después.	*Victor is nervous before fashion shows, but he is always happy (feels good) afterward.* (feelings, condition)
Los modelos se **están** vistiendo ahora.	*The models are getting dressed now.* (ongoing action)

- When describing people or objects, use **ser** to convey an intrinsic characteristic. Use **estar** to convey a feeling or perception. The difference in meaning is sometimes so pronounced that the adjectives have different English translations.

Adjective	With *ser*	With *estar*
aburrido/a	*boring*	*bored*
bueno/a	*good* (character)	*well* (health); *physically attractive*
grave	*serious* (situation)	*seriously ill*
listo/a	*clever*	*ready*
malo/a	*bad* (character)	*ill*
rico/a	*rich, wealthy*	*delicious* (food)
verde	*green* (color)	*unripe*
vivo/a	*lively* (personality)	*alive*

Javier **es** malo, les roba dinero a sus compañeros y dice mentiras.	*Javier is bad; he steals money from his classmates and tells lies.*
Victoria **está** mala. Tiene gripe.	*Victoria is sick. She has the flu.*
Ángela **es** rica. Tiene una casa en California y un apartamento en París.	*Ángela is wealthy. She has a house in California and an apartment in Paris.*
¡Esta sopa **está** riquísima! ¿Usaste una receta diferente?	*This soup is delicious! Did you use a different recipe?*

e **¿Comprendes?** Completa las oraciones con la forma correcta de **ser** o **estar.**

1. Pedro está en cama hoy, ____ malo.
2. Me encanta este postre, ____ muy rico.
3. No comas esa naranja porque ____ verde.
4. Manuel ____ listo y saca buenas notas.
5. La situación ____ grave a causa del incendio (*fire*).
6. Desafortunadamente, Carolina tuvo (*had*) un accidente y ____ grave en el hospital.

PRÁCTICA

6-16 La mañana horrible de Javier.

PREPARACIÓN. Lee el texto sobre la mañana de Javier y complétalo con la forma apropiada de **ser** o **estar.**

Javier se despierta temprano. (1) _____ las seis de la mañana y la casa (2) _____ muy fría. ¡Javier no (3) _____ nada contento! Su reunión con la profesora de historia (4) _____ en su oficina a las 10:00. Quiere desayunar, pero no hay pan, las bananas (5) ____ verdes y (6) _____ demasiado tarde para hacer café. La reunión con la profesora Guzmán no va bien. Le dice a Javier que sus notas no (7) _____ buenas y que tiene que trabajar más. Cuando sale de la reunión, Javier (8) _____ muy preocupado.

INTERCAMBIOS. Compara tus respuestas con las de tu compañero/a. Identifiquen la función de **ser** o **estar** de acuerdo con el contexto.

6-17 Una familia va de compras.

Esta familia colombiana sale de un centro comercial en Bogotá. Túrnense para describir a las personas. Respondan a las preguntas y usen su imaginación para inventar detalles.

1. ¿Quiénes son estas personas? Expliquen su relación.
2. ¿Cómo son?
3. ¿Dónde están?
4. ¿Cómo están?
5. ¿Qué están haciendo?
6. ¿Qué ropa llevan?

6-18 ¿Quiénes son y cómo están?

PREPARACIÓN. Describan qué hacen estas personas, cómo son probablemente y cómo están en estas situaciones.

1. 

2.

3. 

INTERCAMBIOS. Comparen sus respuestas con las de otra pareja.

Situación

PREPARACIÓN. Lean esta situación. Luego, compartan ejemplos de vocabulario, gramática y otra información que necesitan para desarrollar la conversación.

Role A. You can't find your favorite sweater. You think you left it in your Spanish class, so you go to the department office, where they have a lost-and-found box (**una caja de objetos perdidos**). Explain to the receptionist:
a. what you are looking for;
b. where your Spanish class is held; and
c. what your sweater looks like and what it is made of.

Role B. You work as the receptionist in a university Spanish department. A student comes to the office to look for an item in the lost-and-found box (**una caja de objetos perdidos**). Ask the student to:
a. identify himself/herself;
b. say what Spanish class he/she is taking; and
c. describe the sweater.

	ROLE A	ROLE B
Vocabulario	Self-identification Descriptions of items	Interrogative words Descriptions of items
Funciones y formas	Giving personal information Describing items of clothing **Ser** and **estar** Asking and answering questions	Asking about items of clothing **Ser** and **estar**

INTERCAMBIOS. Practiquen la conversación, incorporando el vocabulario y las funciones de **Preparación.** Luego, represéntenla ante la clase.

2 Indicating to whom or for whom an action takes place

LUCÍA: Oye, Miguel, ¿qué **te** compran tus padres para tu cumpleaños: ropa, chocolates o qué?

MIGUEL: Siempre **me** compran libros porque **me** gusta mucho leer. Y tus padres, ¿qué **te** compran a ti, Lucía?

LUCÍA: Mi mamá siempre **nos** compra ropa a mi hermana y a mí. A mí **me** gusta mucho la ropa nueva.

MIGUEL: ¿Y qué **les** das tú a tus padres para sus cumpleaños?

LUCÍA: ¡A mi mamá **le** doy flores y a mi papá **le** doy muchos problemas porque no hago mi tarea!

Piénsalo. Indica a quién se refiere el pronombre en negrita (*bold*).

¿A quién se refiere?

1. Oye, Miguel, ¿qué **te** compran tus padres para tu cumpleaños?
   a. a Miguel **b.** a los padres de Miguel
2. Y tus padres, ¿qué **te** compran a ti?
   a. a Lucía y a Miguel **b.** a Lucía solamente
3. Mi mamá siempre **nos** compra ropa.
   a. a Lucía solamente **b.** a Lucía y a su hermana
4. A mí **me** gusta mucho la ropa nueva.
   a. a Lucía **b.** a la hermana de Lucía
5. ¿Y qué **les** das tú a tus padres para sus cumpleaños?
   a. a Lucía y a su hermana **b.** a los padres de Lucía

Indirect object nouns and pronouns

- Indirect object nouns and pronouns tell *to whom* or *for whom* an action is done; in other words, who is affected by an action.

Indirect Object Pronouns			
me	*to/for me*	**nos**	*to/for us*
te	*to/for you* (familiar)	**os**	*to/for you* (familiar)
le	*to/for you* (formal), *him, her, it*	**les**	*to/for you* (formal), *them*

- Indirect object pronouns have the same forms as direct object pronouns except in the third person: **le** and **les.**

Mi madre **me** compra ropa para mi cumpleaños.	*My mother buys me clothes for my birthday. [My mother buys clothes for me for my birthday.]*
Yo **te** presto mis zapatos para la fiesta.	*I will lend you my shoes for the party. [I will lend my shoes to you for the party.]*
¿El dependiente? Ella **lo** ve todas las mañanas. (*direct object*)	*The salesperson? She sees him every morning.*
¿El dependiente? Ella **le** da los recibos por la mañana. (*indirect object*)	*The salesperson? She gives him the receipts in the morning.*

- Place the indirect object pronoun before a conjugated verb form. It may be attached to a present participle, in which case an accent mark is added, or to an infinitive.

Les voy a vender mi auto. Voy a vender**les** mi auto.	*I am going to sell them my car.*
Juan **nos** está preparando la cena. Juan está preparándo**nos** la cena.	*Juan is preparing dinner for us.*

- Use indirect object pronouns even when the indirect object noun is stated explicitly.

Yo **le** presto mis libros **a Victoria.**	*I lend my books to Victoria.*

- To eliminate ambiguity, **le** and **les** are often used with the preposition **a** + *pronoun.*

Le hablo **a usted.**	*I am talking to you.* (not to him/her)
Siempre **les** cuento mis secretos **a ellos.**	*I always tell my secrets to them.* (not to you/**ustedes**)

- For emphasis, use **a mí, a ti, a nosotros/as,** and **a vosotros/as** with indirect object pronouns.

Pedro **te** habla **a ti.**	*Pedro is talking to you.* (not to someone else)

- Indirect object pronouns are almost always used with the verb **dar** and other verbs of transmission.

DAR (*to give*)			
yo	**doy**	nosotros/as	**damos**
tú	**das**	vosotros/as	**dais**
Ud., él, ella	**da**	Uds., ellos/as	**dan**

Ana **nos** da su libro. — *Ana gives us her book.*

Paco **le** presta su auto a Carmen. — *Paco lends his car to Carmen.*

- Other verbs of transmission (of things, ideas, words) that are generally used with indirect object pronouns include:

decir	*to say, to tell*	**mostrar (ue)**	*to show*
describir	*to describe*	**prestar**	*to lend*
escribir	*to write*	**regalar**	*to give* (a present)
explicar	*to explain*	**vender**	*to sell*
mandar	*to send*		

e **¿Comprendes?** Completa las oraciones con el pronombre correcto según la información entre paréntesis.

1. Yo _____ doy un regalo. (a mi madre)
2. Yo _____ doy un juguete. (a los niños)
3. Los niños ____ dan un beso. (a mí)
4. El profesor _____ da una buena nota. (a ustedes)
5. Mi tía Carla ____ da unos libros. (a mi hermano y a mí)
6. Felisa _____ da las gracias. (a ti)

PRÁCTICA

6-19 Las compras.

e **PREPARACIÓN.** Selecciona la persona que recibe cada acción.

1. _____ Después de probarnos los pantalones de rayas, le preguntamos el precio…
2. _____ Julia está en Colombia y les compra bolsas de café…
3. _____ Para su cumpleaños, pienso regalarle un libro…
4. _____ Los zapatos nuevos me quedan muy bien…
5. _____ Cuando estoy de vacaciones, siempre te mando fotos…
6. _____ Dicen que nos van a comprar unas bufandas muy lindas…

a. a todos sus amigos.
b. a ti.
c. a nosotras.
d. a mi padre.
e. al dependiente.
f. a mí.

INTERCAMBIOS. Compara tus respuestas con las de tu compañero/a. Expliquen su razonamiento (*reasoning*).

6-20 La última moda. Cada uno/a de ustedes desea lo que se indica en la siguiente lista. Explíquense la situación y después háganse recomendaciones.

MODELO Quiero llevar zapatos muy cómodos.
E1: *Quiero llevar zapatos muy cómodos. ¿Qué me recomiendas?*
E2: *Te recomiendo unas zapatillas de deporte. Son buenas para caminar.*

1. Quiero llevar pantalones de moda.
2. Deseo protegerme del sol.
3. Quiero ropa buena y barata.
4. Quiero lucir (*look*) más atlético/a.
5. Me gustaría llevar ropa elegante y fina a la entrevista (*interview*) de trabajo.

Cultura

Trajes regionales y folclóricos de Colombia Most Colombians today wear Western-style clothing, with the expected variations for climate, traditions, and work requirements. In the chilly Andean region of Boyacá, for example, some men wear wool **ruanas,** or ponchos, and women wear long skirts. In the warm coastal areas, people wear loose-fitting clothing and many use bright colors and prints that reflect Caribbean traditions. During major festivals, however, Colombians dress quite differently; each region has traditional clothing that reflects its historic combination of indigenous, European, and African influences.

Trajes típicos de Antioquia

Comparaciones ¿Hay diferencias regionales en la ropa que usan las personas de tu país? ¿Hay otras diferencias, además de las diferencias regionales? ¿Usa ropa tradicional en los festivales la gente de tu región o de tu país?

6-21 Afortunados/as. PREPARACIÓN. Ustedes ganaron (*won*) la lotería ayer y quieren compartir su fortuna con su familia y sus compañeros/as de clase. Hagan una lista de dos o tres personas a quienes desean regalarles algo.

INTERCAMBIOS. Hablen de los regalos que piensan hacer.

MODELO E1: *A nuestros hermanos les vamos a dar tarjetas de regalo porque...*
E2: *A Sara vamos a comprarle una mochila nueva porque...*

6-22 Nuestros hábitos de compras. PREPARACIÓN. Escribe un párrafo contestando las siguientes preguntas.

1. ¿Dónde compras tu ropa normalmente? ¿Tienes una tienda de ropa preferida?
2. ¿A quiénes les compras regalos normalmente? ¿Les compras ropa u otras cosas?
3. ¿Quiénes te dan regalos a ti? ¿Qué regalos te dan?

INTERCAMBIOS. Basándose en los párrafos escritos, pregúntense sobre sus hábitos de compras y los regalos que ustedes dan y reciben de otras personas. Trabajen juntos/as para escribir una comparación entre sus hábitos de compras. Usen las siguientes preguntas como guía (*as a guide*).

1. Sus hábitos de comprar ropa: ¿Similares o diferentes? ¿Tiendas favoritas?
2. Comprar regalos: ¿A quién(es)? ¿De qué tipo(s)? ¿Cuándo?
3. Recibir regalos: ¿De quién(es)? ¿De qué tipo(s)? ¿Cuándo?

Situación

PREPARACIÓN. Lean esta situación. Luego, compartan ejemplos de vocabulario, gramática y otra información que necesitan para desarrollar la conversación.

Role A. You are a customer in a department store. Tell the salesperson:
a. you are looking for a present for a friend (give details about the person and the occasion);
b. you want to buy an article of clothing, but you are not sure what to buy; and
c. the amount you want to spend.

Role B. You are a salesperson. A customer asks you for advice about a gift for a friend. Inquire about the friend's age, taste, size, favorite colors, and other pertinent information. Make suggestions and offer information about the quality of the products, prices, sales (**rebajas**), and so forth.

	ROLE A	ROLE B
Vocabulario	Clothes, shopping, prices	Age, likes and dislikes, sizes, colors, shopping, prices
Funciones y formas	Addressing a salesperson Expressing what you need Asking questions Indirect object pronouns	Addressing a customer Asking questions Giving information Indirect object pronouns

INTERCAMBIOS. Practiquen la conversación, incorporando el vocabulario y las funciones de **Preparación.** Luego, represéntenla ante la clase.

3 Expressing likes and dislikes

DEPENDIENTE: ¿En qué puedo servirle?

JORGE: Necesito ropa, pero hay muchas opciones y estoy indeciso.

DEPENDIENTE: ¿**Le gustan** estas camisas?

JORGE: La verdad, no **me gustan,** pero **me gusta** esta chaqueta.

DEPENDIENTE: Es excelente para el otoño. ¿**Le interesan** los deportes? Tenemos unas zapatillas de deporte muy baratas.

JORGE: **Me encanta** practicar deportes, pero no necesito zapatillas. Ah, ¡pero **me fascina** esta chaqueta!

Piénsalo. Selecciona la opción correcta para completar cada afirmación, según la conversación.

1. A Jorge no _____ las camisas que le muestra el dependiente.
   a. le interesan **b.** le gusta **c.** le fascina
2. A Jorge _____ una chaqueta.
   a. le gusta **b.** no le interesan **c.** le gustan
3. Al dependiente _____ trabajar en la tienda de ropa porque ayuda a los clientes.
   a. le gusta **b.** le gustan **c.** les gusta
4. A Jorge _____ practicar deportes.
   a. le encanta **b.** no le interesan **c.** le encantan
5. Jorge dice que _____ la chaqueta.
   a. no le gusta **b.** le fascinan **c.** le fascina
6. A los amigos de Jorge _____ hablar de fútbol con él.
   a. le interesa **b.** nos interesan **c.** les interesa

Gustar and similar verbs

- In previous chapters you have used the verb **gustar** to express likes and dislikes. You know that **gustar** is not used in the same way as the English verb *to like.* **Gustar** is similar to the expression *to be pleasing* (*to someone*).

Me gusta esta chaqueta.	*I like this jacket.* (lit., *This jacket is pleasing to me.*)

- The subject of **gustar** is the person or thing that is liked. The indirect object pronoun shows to whom the person or thing is pleasing.

me	gusta el traje	*I*	like(s) the suit.
te		*you* (familiar)	
le		*you* (formal), *he/she*	
nos		*we*	
os		*you* (familiar)	
les		*they, you* (formal and familiar)	

- The most frequently used forms of **gustar** in the present tense are **gusta** and **gustan.** If one thing is liked, use **gusta.** If two or more things are liked, use **gustan.**

Me **gusta** ese **collar.**	*I like that necklace.*
No me **gustan los anillos.**	*I do not like the rings.*

- To express what people like or do not like to do, use **gusta** followed by one or more infinitives.

Nos **gusta caminar** por la mañana.	*We like to walk in the morning.*
¿No te **gusta correr** y **nadar?**	*Don't you like to run and swim?*

- Some other Spanish verbs that follow the pattern of **gustar** are:

encantar	*to like a lot, to love*
fascinar	*to like a lot, to love*
interesar	*to interest; to matter*
parecer (zc)	*to seem*
quedar	*to fit; to be left over*

Estoy leyendo la novela y me **encanta.**	*I'm reading the novel and I love it.*
Nos **fascina** la ropa de algodón.	*We love cotton clothes.*
No te **interesan** los blogs sobre la moda.	*You are not interested in fashion blogs.*
El precio me **parece** muy alto.	*The price seems very high to me.*
No me **queda** mucho dinero.	*I don't have much money left.*
No le **quedan** bien los pantalones.	*His/Her pants don't fit well.*

- To express that you or someone else like(s) or dislike(s) a person, use **caer bien/mal,** which follow the pattern of **gustar.**

Les cae bien Miriam.	*They like Miriam.*
Esa dependienta **me cae mal.**	*I do not like that salesperson.*

- To emphasize or clarify to whom something is pleasing, use **a + mí, a + ti, a + él/ella, a usted(es),** etc., or **a** + *noun.*

A mí me gustan esos zapatos, pero **a Pedro** no le gustan.	*I like those shoes, but Pedro does not like them.*

e **¿Comprendes?** Completa las oraciones con la forma correcta del verbo.

1. A Carmen le _________ (interesar) mucho las ciencias.
2. Esta chaqueta nos _________ (parecer) muy cara.
3. Diego es muy simpático. A mí me _________ (caer) muy bien.
4. A mis padres les _________ (encantar) los regalos.
5. A Inés no le _________ (gustar) los vaqueros.

PRÁCTICA

6-23 Preferencias en la ropa y los accesorios.

PREPARACIÓN. Indica si te encanta(n), te gusta(n) o no te gusta(n) la siguiente ropa o accesorios. Luego, compara tus preferencias con las de tu compañero/a.

	Me encanta(n)	Me gusta(n)	No me gusta(n)
1. la ropa con logotipos visibles			
2. la moda retro			
3. los vaqueros ajustados (*skinny jeans*)			
4. las chaquetas de cuero			
5. las zapatillas de deporte			
6. las gorras de béisbol			
7. las gafas de sol			
8. las chaquetas de felpa (*fleece*)			
9. la ropa muy ancha (*oversized*)			
10. las boinas (*berets*)			

INTERCAMBIOS. Explíquenles a sus compañeros/as si coinciden en sus gustos.

MODELO PAREJA 1: *A nosotros/as nos gusta la ropa con logotipos visibles.*
PAREJA 2: *Y a mí me encantan los vaqueros ajustados, pero a mi compañero/a no le gustan.*

6-24 ¿Cuánto dinero o tiempo les queda?

Lean estas situaciones. Túrnense para preguntar y calcular cuánto dinero o tiempo les queda a estas personas.

MODELO Adriana tiene 160.000 pesos. Paga 65.000 pesos por un vestido y 30.000 por unos aretes artesanales.
E1: *¿Cuánto dinero le queda?*
E2: *Le quedan 65.000 pesos.*

1. Daniel y Sebastián tienen 35 días de vacaciones este año. Pasan 12 días en Santa Marta, 5 días en Cauca y 8 días en Medellín.
2. Ernesto tiene 275.000 pesos. Le da 150.000 a su hermano.
3. Érica tiene 592.0000 pesos. Va al cine con una amiga y luego cenan en un restaurante. Una entrada (*ticket*) al cine cuesta 12.500 y la cena para dos personas, 98.000 pesos.
4. Gilberto tiene 128.000 pesos. Compra un suéter por 75.500 pesos.
5. Marco y Luisa tienen 892.000 pesos. Van a la playa en Cartagena y almuerzan en un restaurante por 120.000 pesos por persona.

Cultura

La moda y la industria textil en Colombia Medellín is considered the fashion capital of Latin America today, and Colombia, together with Mexico and Argentina, ranks among the three top Latin American countries in the textile and apparel trade. Colombian designers, such as Adriana Santacruz, Edgar Osorio, and Hernán Zajar, are well known in the fashion world.

As in the rest of Latin America, the Colombian textile and clothing manufacturing industry has undergone decades of hardship since the 1990s. However, today Colombia is becoming the leader in the Latin American garment industry. Approximately 7.5% of Colombia's manufacturing revenue comes from the textile and apparel industry, thanks to significant changes that have improved competitiveness with China and other Asian markets.

Comparaciones ¿Hay una industria textil fuerte en tu país? Tu país, ¿importa o exporta ropa y telas? ¿Existe en tu país una ciudad considerada la capital de la moda? La ropa que compras, ¿se hace en tu país o en otro lugar? ¿Dónde?

6-25 ¿Qué les parece? Describan y expresen su opinión sobre la ropa y los accesorios de estas personas. Expliquen su opinión.

MODELO E1: *No me gustan los vaqueros de Violeta. Son muy estrechos. A mí me fascina la ropa ancha. Pero me gusta mucho su blusa blanca. Es muy simple, pero elegante.*

E2: *Pues a mí me encantan los vaqueros de Violeta. Ella lleva ropa bonita.*

Violeta

Javier

Claudia

María Fernanda

Jorge

 **6-26 ¿Qué te parece?** **PREPARACIÓN.** Entrevista a dos o tres compañeros/as para saber si les gusta, les interesa o les fascina lo siguiente. Toma apuntes.

	¿Te gusta(n)?	¿Te interesa(n)?	¿Te fascina(n)?
1. ponerte ropa estrecha			
2. caminar descalzo/a (*barefoot*)			
3. los relojes caros			
4. tener el último teléfono inteligente			
5. los tatuajes (*tattoos*)			
6. estar a la moda			

INTERCAMBIOS. Hablen con otro grupo sobre los siguientes temas. Expresen sus opiniones con ejemplos y tomen notas para compartir con la clase.

1. la moda actual
2. los accesorios más populares
3. el maquillaje
4. las tiendas de ropa

Situación

PREPARACIÓN. Lean esta situación. Luego, compartan ejemplos de vocabulario, gramática y otra información que necesitan para desarrollar la conversación.

Role A. You are shopping at a community crafts fair where haggling is the norm. You select an item that you plan to give as a gift. In your interaction with the vendor:
a. say how much you like what the vendor is selling;
b. ask the price of the item you are interested in;
c. react to what you hear and offer a lower price;
d. comment on the item, saying whom you plan to give it to; and
e. come to an agreement on the price.

Role B. You are selling your handicrafts and accessories (belts, hats, jewelry, etc.) at a community crafts fair. A customer is interested in one of your items. In your interaction with the customer:
a. respond to his/her compliments;
b. give the price of the item;
c. explain why you cannot accept the customer's offer of a lower price;
d. respond to his/her comments on the item; and
e. come to an agreement on the price.

	ROLE A	ROLE B
Vocabulario	Numbers (prices)	Numbers (prices)
Funciones y forma	Haggling over the price of an item Direct and indirect object pronouns Complimenting an artisan on his/her work	Haggling over the price of an item Direct and indirect object pronouns Refusing an offer

INTERCAMBIOS. Practiquen la conversación, incorporando el vocabulario y las funciones de **Preparación.** Luego, represéntenla ante la clase.

4 Talking about the past

 Camila escribe en su diario.

Ayer Sebastián y yo **gastamos** mucho dinero en ropa para vernos bien en la fiesta de boda (*wedding*) de mi cuñada Laura. Yo **compré** un hermoso vestido de fiesta y un chal de encaje (*lace shawl*). Sebastián **compró** un traje, una camisa y una corbata.

A las 7:00 de la tarde, **empezó** la ceremonia religiosa. La fiesta con la familia y los amigos **comenzó** a las 9:00 de la noche y **terminó** a las 4:00 de la mañana. Todos **comimos**, **bailamos** y **cantamos** mucho. Vamos a recordar este día especial por mucho tiempo. Laura y Andrés son la pareja perfecta.

Ahora voy a dormir. Estoy muy cansada.

 **Piénsalo.** Selecciona la opción correcta para completar cada oración, según Camila.

1. _____ La ceremonia religiosa…
2. _____ La fiesta con la familia e invitados…
3. _____ La cuñada de Camila…
4. _____ Sebastián y Camila…
5. _____ La familia y los invitados…
6. _____ Camila…

a. **se casó** con Andrés.
b. **bailaron** y **comieron** mucho en la fiesta.
c. **terminó** tarde.
d. **ocurrió** antes de la fiesta con la familia y amigos.
e. **gastaron** mucho dinero en ropa para la boda.
f. **compró** ropa elegante.

Preterit tense of regular verbs

- In Spanish, use the preterit (**pretérito**) to talk about past events, actions, and conditions that are viewed as completed or ended.

HABLAR		COMER	VIVIR
yo	habl**é**	com**í**	viv**í**
tú	habl**aste**	com**iste**	viv**iste**
Ud., él, ella	habl**ó**	com**ió**	viv**ió**
nosotros/as	habl**amos**	com**imos**	viv**imos**
vosotros/as	habl**asteis**	com**isteis**	viv**isteis**
Uds., ellos/as	habl**aron**	com**ieron**	viv**ieron**

- Note that the **nosotros/as** forms of the preterit of **-ar** and **-ir** verbs are the same in the present tense and the preterit. Context will help you determine if **nosotros/as** verb forms are present or past.

Llegamos a la tienda a las tres. — *We arrive at the store at three.* / *We arrived at the store at three.*

Salí de la universidad a las dos, y **llegamos** a casa a las tres. — *I left the university at two, and we arrived home at three.*

Lengua

The **yo** and the **usted, él, ella** preterit verb forms are stressed on the last syllable and end in a vowel. Therefore, they carry a written accent: **hablé, comí, viví, habló, comió, vivió.**

- Stem-changing verbs ending in **-ar** and **-er** do not have a stem change in the preterit.
  pensar: pensé, pensaste, pensó, pensamos, pensasteis, pensaron
  volver: volví, volviste, volvió, volvimos, volvisteis, volvieron

- Verbs ending in **-car** and **-gar** have a spelling change in the **yo** form of the preterit that reflects how the word is pronounced. Verbs ending in **-zar** have a spelling change in the **yo** form because Spanish rarely uses a **z** before **e** or **i.**
  sacar: saqué, sacaste, sacó…
  llegar: llegué, llegaste, llegó…
  empezar: empecé, empezaste, empezó…

- The verb **dar** uses the same endings as -**er** and -**ir** verbs in the preterit: **di, diste, dio, dimos, disteis, dieron.**

Jorge le **dio** a Elena una copia de sus apuntes.	*Jorge gave Elena a copy of his notes.*
Mis padres me **dieron** dinero para la matrícula.	*My parents gave me money for tuition.*

- There are some expressions you can use with the preterit to denote when an event took place.

hoy (por la mañana/tarde)	*today (in the morning/afternoon)*
anoche	*last night*
ayer	*yesterday*
ante(a)noche	*the night before last*
anteayer	*day before yesterday*
la semana pasada	*last week*
una semana atrás	*a week ago*
el año/mes pasado	*last year/month*
hace un día/mes/año (que)	*it has been a day/month/year since*

e **¿Comprendes?** Completa las oraciones con la forma correcta del verbo.

1. El año pasado Pablo y Elisa ________ (comer) muchas veces en el restaurante colombiano de la ciudad.
2. La semana pasada Elena y yo _________ (estudiar) juntas para el examen de geografía.
3. Ayer yo _________ (comprar) unos calcetines y una falda en la tienda de ropa Mattelsa.
4. Anoche Luis __________ (escribir) muchos mensajes de texto.
5. Hace un año Carlota __________ (comenzar) a estudiar español.
6. La semana pasada tú __________ (llegar) tarde a clase todos los días.

PRÁCTICA

6-27 Ayer yo... PREPARACIÓN. Indica tus actividades de ayer y añade (*add*) una actividad en cada columna.

Por la mañana	Por la tarde	Por la noche
_____ Desayuné.	_____ Almorcé en la cafetería.	_____ Preparé la cena.
_____ Llegué a tiempo a mis clases.	_____ Saqué libros de la biblioteca.	_____ Miré televisión.
_____ Estudié varias horas.	_____ Lavé mi ropa.	_____ Planché mi ropa.
_____ Llamé por teléfono a un/a amigo/a.	_____ Compré comida para toda la semana.	_____ Salí con mis amigos.

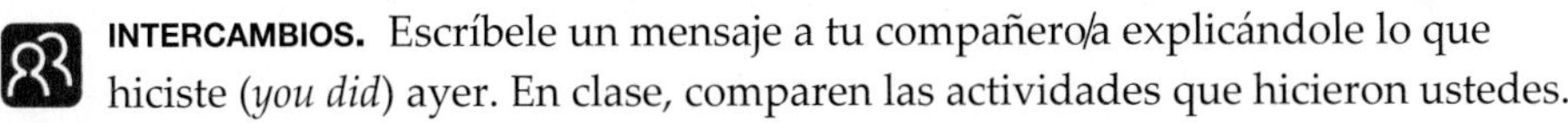

INTERCAMBIOS. Escríbele un mensaje a tu compañero/a explicándole lo que hiciste (*you did*) ayer. En clase, comparen las actividades que hicieron ustedes.

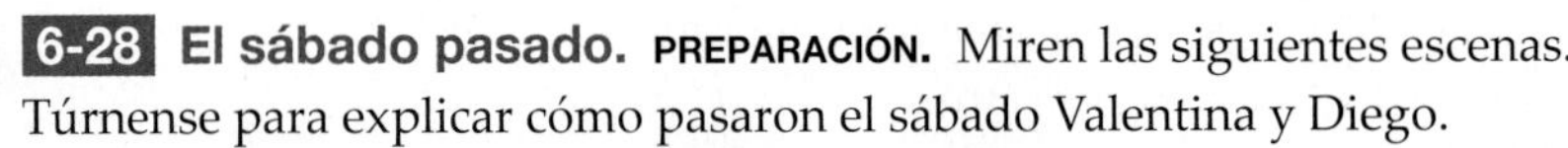

6-28 El sábado pasado. PREPARACIÓN. Miren las siguientes escenas. Túrnense para explicar cómo pasaron el sábado Valentina y Diego.

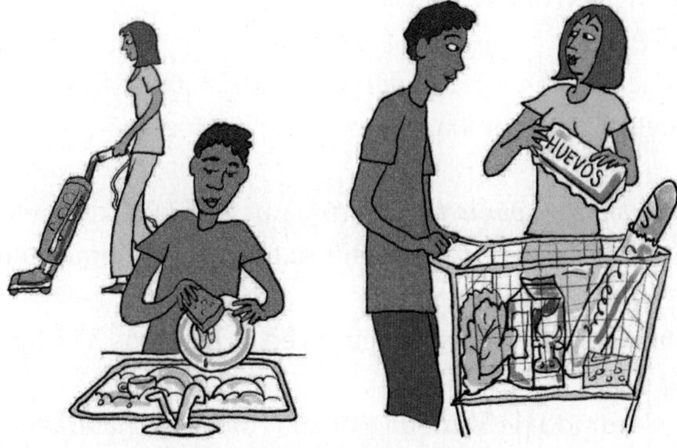

El sábado por la mañana

El sábado por la tarde

El sábado por la noche

INTERCAMBIOS. Escribe un párrafo para comparar las actividades de Valentina y Diego y tus actividades el fin de semana pasado. Después, compártelo oralmente con tu compañero/a.

 **6-29 Un día especial con amigos.** **PREPARACIÓN.** Conversen sobre un día especial que cada uno/a de ustedes pasó con sus amigos/as. Incluyan los siguientes detalles:

- las actividades que hicieron (*did*)
- dónde
- qué día, a qué hora
- un detalle más

INTERCAMBIOS. Determinen quién de ustedes hizo (*did*) las actividades más divertidas o interesantes con sus amigos/as. Luego, compartan sus actividades con la clase.

 **6-30 Adivina quién lo hizo.** Usen su conocimiento o imaginación para adivinar quién hizo lo siguiente. Los nombres de la lista van a ser útiles (*helpful*).

Diana Trujillo	Manuel Patarroyo
Enrique Iglesias y Anna Kournikova	Santiago Calatrava
Fernando Botero	Shakira
Hernán Zajar	Steve Jobs

MODELO crear la Sinfonía número 9
E1: *¿Quién creó la Sinfonía número 9?*
E2: *Beethoven la creó.*

1. empezar a trabajar en la NASA en 2008
2. fundar la compañía Apple
3. diseñar (*design*) el Pabellón Quadracci del Museo de Arte de Milwaukee
4. crear la vacuna sintética para combatir el parásito protozoa que causa la malaria
5. vender su pintura *El domingo por la tarde* (1967) por 1.553.000 dólares
6. comenzar su carrera de cantante y compositora fuera de Colombia en los años 90
7. comprar una mansión de 20 millones de euros en la Bahía de Vizcaya, frente a Miami Beach
8. hacerse famoso en el mundo de la moda por sus colores y materiales

Situación

PREPARACIÓN. Lean la situación. Luego, compartan ejemplos de vocabulario, gramática y otra información que necesitan para desarrollar la conversación.

Role A. Your classmate and a friend went on a shopping spree last weekend. Ask:
a. what store(s) they shopped in;
b. what each of them bought;
c. what time they returned home; and
d. what your classmate's plans are for wearing or using the items.

Role B. Answer your classmate's questions about your shopping spree with a friend over the weekend. Then find out if your classmate went shopping over the weekend, played a sport, or watched a lot of TV.

	ROLE A	ROLE B
Vocabulario	Shopping: clothes, shoes, or other items	Shopping: clothes, shoes, or other items
Funciones y formas	Asking questions Past tense	Recounting events in the past Past tense Talking about future plans Asking questions

INTERCAMBIOS. Practiquen la conversación, incorporando el vocabulario y las funciones de **Preparación.** Luego, represéntenla ante la clase.

5 Talking about the past: *ir* and *ser*

CLIENTA: Compré este vestido aquí el mes pasado. Pero, mire, el vestido encogió (*shrank*).

SUPERVISORA: ¿Quién **fue** el vendedor que le vendió el vestido?

CLIENTA: No sé su nombre, pero **fue** su compañero, un señor alto y delgado.

SUPERVISORA: ¿Qué pasó? ¿Usted lavó el vestido en casa?

CLIENTA: Claro que no. Hay que limpiarlo en seco (*dry clean*). **Fui** a la tintorería (*dry cleaner's*).

SUPERVISORA: Los empleados de la tintorería **fueron** irresponsables. No limpiaron en seco su vestido. Lo lavaron. Usted debe ir a la tintorería para resolver su problema.

CLIENTA: Mi amiga Lucía y yo **fuimos** a la tintorería, pero la respuesta no **fue** satisfactoria.

e **Piénsalo.** Selecciona el verbo correcto para completar las oraciones, según la conversación. Luego, indica si el infinitivo del verbo conjugado en pretérito es **ser** o **ir**.

	¿Ser o ir?
1. La clienta _____ a la tienda para comprar el vestido el mes pasado. **a.** fue **b.** fuiste **c.** fueron	
2. La persona que vendió el vestido _____ el vendedor. **a.** fuiste **b.** fue **c.** fueron	
3. Los empleados de la tintorería _____ quienes lavaron el vestido. **a.** fui **b.** fue **c.** fueron	
4. La clienta dice que ella y su amiga _____ a la tintorería. **a.** fue **b.** fueron **c.** fuimos	
5. Los empleados de la tintorería no _____ amables cuando la clienta se quejó (*complained*). **a.** fueron **b.** fue **c.** fui	
6. La clienta _____ por segunda vez a la tienda donde compró el vestido. **a.** fuiste **b.** fue **c.** fueron	

Preterit of *ir* and *ser*

- The verbs **ir** and **ser** have identical forms in the preterit. They are used often in speaking and writing, and the context will help you to determine the meaning.

IR *and* SER			
yo	**fui**	nosotros/as	**fuimos**
tú	**fuiste**	vosotros/as	**fuisteis**
Ud., él, ella	**fue**	Uds., ellos/as	**fueron**

- You will also be able to differentiate between **ir** and **ser** in the preterit because **ir** is often followed by the preposition **a.**

Ernesto **fue a** la tienda. — *Ernesto went to the store.*

Fue vendedor en esa tienda por dos años. — *He was a salesclerk at that store for two years.*

¿Comprendes? Completa la conversación con la forma correcta del verbo **ser** o **ir** en el pretérito.

ANA: Hola, mamá. ¿Adónde (1) ______ esta mañana?
MAMÁ: (2) ______ a comprar al centro comercial Titán Plaza. Tienen excelentes rebajas.
ANA: ¿(3) _____ papá contigo?
MAMÁ: No, no (4) _____. Invité a tu hermana, prefirió mirar televisión. Ah, encontré unos vaqueros espectaculares y muy baratos.
ANA: ¡Qué bueno! Y, ¿cuál (5) _____ el precio?
MAMÁ: Increíble, pero pagué solo 79.000 pesos, cerca de 22 dólares.
ANA: Fenomenal. Y, ¿qué hiciste después?
MAMÁ: Mi amiga y yo (6) _____ al cine.

PRÁCTICA

6-31 ¿Quién fue a este lugar? Las siguientes personas fueron a Colombia para conocer algunos lugares famosos. Primero, lean cada situación y, luego, indiquen el lugar que cada persona visitó.

1. _____ Andrés fue a un lugar donde los visitantes pueden pasar tiempo al aire libre, rodeados (*surrounded*) de naturaleza y abundante vegetación. Le fascina explorar lugares, caminar por entre los árboles (*trees*) y acampar. ¿Adónde fue Andrés?
2. _____ Decidiste visitar este lugar en la zona central de Colombia. Viste plantaciones de café, escuchaste hablar sobre la historia de la industria cafetera, probaste buen café y disfrutaste de la naturaleza. ¿Adónde fuiste?
3. _____ Los estudiantes del club de español de tu universidad fueron a una isla cerca de Cartagena, Colombia. Nadaron, caminaron mucho y vieron un parque natural que protege uno de los arrecifes (*reefs*) de coral más importantes de la costa del Caribe. ¿Adónde fueron los estudiantes?
4. _____ Los arquitectos Roberto y Angélica Mesa decidieron visitar este lugar turístico construido en el interior de las minas en Zipaquirá. Ellos quieren conocer la historia del lugar. ¿Adónde fueron Roberto y Angélica?

a. La Catedral de Sal

b. El Parque Nacional Los Nevados

c. Las islas Corales del Rosario

d. El Parque Arví

 **6-32 Asociación.** Formen oraciones lógicas para identificar quién(es) fue/fueron, y adónde. Sigan el modelo.

MODELO Sacaron dinero del banco. / mis compañeros de cuarto / un restaurante
Fueron mis compañeros de cuarto. Fueron a un restaurante.

	¿Quién(es)?	¿Adónde?
1. Pidió autorización para celebrar este día especial para su amigo. **2.** Pidieron las llaves (*keys*) del auto deportivo de mi padre para relajarse en la costa. **3.** Por sugerencia de mi tía, se puso un vestido largo muy elegante y joyas finas. **4.** Compraron pantalones y zapatos cómodos y un sombrero. **5.** Robaron (*They stole*) muchas joyas antiguas. **6.** Entramos y tomamos fotos de esta iglesia especial.	los delincuentes mis hermanos mayores mi familia y yo los estudiantes de intercambio la turista el chico de 15 años mi madre	la Catedral de Sal la zona cafetera en Pereira, Colombia el Museo del Oro el cumpleaños de su mejor amigo una boda (*wedding*) Cartagena la playa

 **6-33 ¿Quiénes fueron y adónde fueron?** Completen la información sobre los siguientes famosos. Luego, conversen sobre adónde fue cada persona y por qué. Usen las palabras de la lista para identificar su profesión y las actividades relacionadas con ella. **OJO:** El año marca un evento importante en la vida de estas personas.

antropólogo/a	escritor/a	la Luna	Premio Nobel de Literatura
astronauta	explorador/a	las ruinas	ver
caminar	fundador/a	libertador/a	viajar
descubrir	ganar	pisar (*set foot*)	

MODELO Simón Bolívar, 1819–1830
Simón Bolívar fue un libertador de América. Él fue a muchos países de América Latina para liberarlos. Fue presidente de Colombia de 1819 a 1830.

	¿Qué fue? (actividad/profesión)	¿Adónde fue?	¿Cuándo?
1. Cristóbal Colón			1492
2. Ellen Ochoa			1991
3. Fabian Gottlieb von Bellinghausen			1820
4. Gabriela Mistral			1945
5. Hiram Bingham III			1911
6. Neil Armstrong			1969

6-34 Íconos del arte y de la moda.

PREPARACIÓN. Selecciona la descripción que corresponde a cada persona famosa.

1. _____ Vincent van Gogh fue…
2. _____ Óscar de la Renta fue…
3. _____ Salvador Dalí fue…
4. _____ Frida Kahlo fue…
5. _____ Gustav Klimt fue…

a. el artista que inspiró la creación de las túnicas unisex basadas en los principios del modernismo del siglo XIX.
b. la artista mexicana que, con su estilo de vestir con motivos indígenas, influyó en la moda de hoy.
c. el pintor que inspiró a Jeff Koons en la creación de sus bolsos modelo *Speedy*.
d. el diseñador dominicano que confeccionó ropa para Jacqueline Kennedy en los años 60.
e. el excéntrico pintor español que motivó al multifacético diseñador Paco Rabanne a continuar dibujando (*drawing*).

INTERCAMBIOS. Escojan a uno de estos personajes famosos y preparen una presentación para la clase. Respondan a estas preguntas.

Atahualpa	Frida Kahlo	Pablo Casals
Ernesto Guevara	Manuela Saenz	Roberto Clemente
Eva Perón	Mario Molina	Simón Bolívar

1. ¿Quién fue esta persona?
2. ¿Dónde nació, vivió y murió (*died*)?
3. ¿Por qué fue famoso/a? Indiquen como mínimo dos o tres datos importantes sobre su vida.

Situación

PREPARACIÓN. Lean esta situación. Luego, compartan ejemplos de vocabulario, gramática y otra información que necesitan para desarrollar la conversación.

Role A. A classmate tells you that he/she went to a concert last weekend. Ask:
a. where the concert was;
b. what time it started;
c. with whom he/she went;
d. what time the concert ended; and
e. where he/she went afterwards.
React to the information you hear and answer your classmate's questions about your weekend activities.

Role B. Your classmate wants to know about the concert you went to last weekend. Answer your classmate's questions. Then ask your classmate about his/her weekend activities: if he/she went to a party or concert over the weekend, if he/she went out with friends, and so on. Ask for details about where, when, and with whom he/she went.

	ROLE A	ROLE B
Vocabulario	Time, days of the week, leisure activities	Time, days of the week, leisure activities
Funciones y formas	Asking questions Reacting to what you hear Recounting past events Past tense of **ir** and **ser**	Recounting past events Past tense of **ir, ser,** and other verbs Asking questions Reacting to what you hear

INTERCAMBIOS. Practiquen la conversación, incorporando el vocabulario y las funciones de **Preparación.** Luego, represéntenla ante la clase.

MOSAICOS

ESCUCHA

Estrategia

Take notes to recall information When you want to remember something that you are listening to, like a class lecture, you benefit from taking notes. Taking notes can also be helpful when you want to remember a homework assignment or other instructions.

6-35 Preparación. Prepara una lista de la ropa y los accesorios que compraste este año. Comparte tu lista con la clase.

6-36 Escucha. Listen to the conversation between Andrea and her parents. As you listen, take notes on what she needs. Write at least three items for each category that Andrea mentions.

1. Para ir a clases, Andrea necesita…
2. Para practicar deportes, Andrea tiene que comprar…
3. Para salir con sus amigos, Andrea quiere…

6-37 Un paso más. Túrnense para responder oralmente a las siguientes preguntas y tomen notas de sus respuestas. Después, compartan la información con otra pareja.

1. ¿Qué accesorios, muebles y aparatos electrónicos para tu cuarto compraste antes de comenzar tus clases en la universidad este semestre?
2. ¿Qué libros o artículos compraste para estudiar? ¿Dónde los compraste?
3. ¿Compraste algo más? ¿Qué compraste? ¿Fuiste a las rebajas? ¿Gastaste mucho dinero?
4. ¿Necesitas ropa u otras cosas en este momento?

Comprueba

I was able to . . .

- recognize clothing vocabulary.
- identify the contexts and categories of clothing use.
- connect articles of clothing to their appropriate contexts.

HABLA

Estrategia

Expressing dissatisfaction to achieve a result Written or verbal complaints constitute one way of expressing dissatisfaction with a product or service received that did not meet one's expectations.

Complainants that are successful . . .

a. have a clear idea of what they want to achieve. If you are dissatisfied with a product you bought, you probably want a refund or a replacement of the product.

b. know the facts. The date of your order, the order number, and a detailed description of the product will be necessary.

c. use the right tone and language to achieve their goal. A polite tone and language will lead to better results than an angry one.

6-38 Preparación. Para tu cumpleaños, tu tía te da 200 dólares para comprarte ropa o accesorios. Mira la página web de tu tienda favorita y toma nota en español de las características de tres artículos de ropa o accesorios que quieres, los precios y gastos de envío (*shipping*).

Artículo de ropa / accesorio	Descripción	Precio
	ENVÍO:	
	TOTAL:	

Comprueba

I was able to . . .

- express dissatisfaction with an online purchase.
- identify and explain a problem.
- give clear information in response to questions.
- negotiate a satisfactory solution for the problem.

6-39 Habla. Ayer recibiste la ropa que compraste por internet, pero encontraste varios problemas. Llama al Servicio al Cliente de la compañía para quejarte (*complain*) y pedir un cambio de los productos. Intercambien roles.

En directo

To explain the reason for your call:

Quisiera cambiar... que compré en línea.

I would like to exchange . . . that I bought online.

To discuss a problem related with your purchase:

Compré/Pedí..., pero recibí...

I bought . . ., but I received . . .

... cuesta..., pero cargaron a la tarjeta de crédito...

. . . costs . . ., but they charged . . . to my credit card.

To indicate what you want to resolve the issue:

Quisiera/Necesito devolver/cambiar...

I would like to return/exchange . . .

To apologize for and make up for an error:

Lo siento mucho. Tiene razón. Le enviamos... incorrecto.

So sorry. You're right. We sent you the wrong . . .

Vamos a cambiar/enviarle... por correo expreso.

We are going to exchange/ship . . . overnight.

 Listen to a conversation with these expressions.

6-40 Un paso más. Prepara una presentación para la clase sobre tu experiencia comprando en línea. Incluye lo siguiente:

1. descripción detallada del artículo / de los artículos que compraste con tus $200
2. explicación del problema / de los problemas que tuviste (*you had*)
3. solución del problema

LEE

Estrategia

Use context to figure out the meaning of unfamiliar words When you come across unfamiliar words and phrases while reading, use the context and your understanding of the text so far to figure out the meaning. Reread the line or two that lead up to the problematic part, focusing on overall meaning. In many cases, this strategy will help you understand the unknown word without using a dictionary.

 **6-41 Preparación.** Habla con tu compañero/a sobre lo siguiente:

1. ¿Dónde prefieren hacer sus compras: en tiendas locales, en un centro comercial (*mall*) o por internet? ¿Por qué?
2. ¿Tienen hábitos de compra diferentes para ropa, libros, etc.? Expliquen.
3. ¿Cuáles son las ventajas principales de comprar por internet? ¿Las desventajas?
4. ¿Con qué frecuencia van a un centro comercial? ¿Van allí solamente para comprar o para hacer otras cosas también? Expliquen.

6-42 Lee. Lee el texto completo. Luego, lee las siguientes oraciones. Usa el contexto y tu conocimiento del tema para expresar de otra manera en español el significado de las palabras o frases en negrita.

1. Hay **cada vez más** centros comerciales en América Latina, mientras que **lo opuesto** ocurre en Estados Unidos.
2. Según los expertos, la clase media creció en un 50 por ciento en la **primera década** de este siglo.
3. Además de almacenes grandes, tiendas pequeñas y **zonas de comidas,** es común encontrar supermercados y clínicas de atención médica.
4. Los centros comerciales representan un lugar seguro para comprar y para **disfrutar** con la familia.
5. El problema principal de comprar en línea es la falta de servicio **de entrega a domicilio** seguros y fiables.

Comprueba

I was able to . . .

- use context to decipher meaning of unknown expressions.
- identify specific information correctly.

CENTROS COMERCIALES EN AMÉRICA LATINA

Hoy en día es posible encontrar cada vez más centros comerciales en América Latina, mientras que lo opuesto ocurre en Estados Unidos, donde cada año cierran más centros comerciales. ¿Por qué existe esta diferencia tan grande en los hábitos de compra en las dos regiones? Señalamos tres razones principales.

Primero, el crecimiento de los centros comerciales en América Latina (aproximadamente 100 por año) es el resultado normal de la expansión de la clase media. Según los expertos, la clase media creció en un 50 por ciento en la primera década de este siglo[1]. Más personas ahora tienen suficiente dinero para comprar ropa, muebles, autos y otros productos para uso personal.

Segundo, los centros comerciales en América Latina atraen al público por la gran variedad de tiendas y servicios que ofrecen. Además de[2] almacenes grandes, tiendas pequeñas y zonas de comidas, es común encontrar supermercados, clínicas de atención médica, centros de atención al cliente[3] y espacio para oficinas. En ciudades como Bogotá, los centros comerciales representan un lugar seguro para comprar y para disfrutar con la familia.

Tercero, los centros comerciales en Latinoamérica, por el momento, no tienen que competir tan fuertemente con el comercio por internet, como es el caso en Estados Unidos. El problema principal de comprar en línea es la falta de servicios de entrega a domicilio seguros y fiables[4]. Esto va a cambiar en el futuro. Sin embargo[5], por ahora este es un factor importante para comprender la popularidad de los centros comerciales.

[1]*century* [2]*In addition to* [3]*customer care centers* [4]*reliable* [5]*Nevertheless*

 **6-43 Un paso más.** En grupos, busquen el sitio web de un centro comercial en el mundo hispano. Tomen nota de la información de la lista. Después, presenten el centro comercial a la clase. Sus compañeros/as van a hacerles preguntas.

1. tipos de tiendas
2. otros tipos de negocios (restaurantes, cines...)
3. servicios que ofrece a los clientes
4. otros datos (*facts*) interesantes sobre el centro comercial

ESCRIBE

Estrategia

Recount events in sequence When we tell a story either orally or in writing, we almost always organize the events in chronological order. Using appropriate connectors to indicate the order of the events will make your writing clearer.

6-44 Preparación. Vas a contar una experiencia (buena o mala) de ir de compras. Para prepararte, lee las siguientes oraciones y pon los eventos en orden cronológico.

_____ Javier dejó su chaqueta nueva en la zona de comidas del centro comercial.
_____ Javier se probó una chaqueta de esquí.
_____ Javier fue de compras con su hermano a un centro comercial cerca de su casa.
_____ Compró la chaqueta y salió del almacén.
_____ Javier y su hermano tomaron un café.
_____ Volvieron al centro comercial. Afortunadamente, Javier encontró su chaqueta en la oficina de objetos perdidos.

6-45 Escribe. Escribe una narración sobre una experiencia buena o mala comprando un producto. Debes incluir:

1. adónde fuiste para comprar el producto
2. el producto que compraste y su descripción
3. un recuento en orden cronológico de lo que ocurrió: ¿Qué hiciste (*did you do*) antes de hacer la compra? ¿Qué ocurrió después? ¿Cuánto costó y cómo pagaste? ¿Qué pasó después?
4. cómo terminó la situación

Comprueba

I was able to . . .

- recount the events of the story in chronological order.
- describe an item that was purchased.
- explain why the shopping experience was a positive or negative one.

En directo

To indicate the succession of events or temporal transitions, you may use the following connectors: primero, luego, más tarde, antes de eso, después (de eso), finalmente.

 Listen to a conversation with these expressions.

 **6-46 Un paso más.** Lee la anécdota de tu compañero/a. Luego, túrnense para hacerse preguntas para aclarar (*clarify*) los eventos y para conseguir más información.

En este capítulo...

Vocabulario

La ropa	Clothes
el abrigo	*coat*
la bata	*robe*
la blusa	*blouse*
las botas	*boots*
los calzoncillos	*boxer shorts*
los calzones	*panties*
la camisa	*shirt*
la camisa de manga corta	*short-sleeved shirt*
la camiseta	*T-shirt*
el camisón	*nightgown*
las chancletas	*flip-flops*
la chaqueta	*jacket*
la corbata	*tie*
la falda	*skirt*
el impermeable	*raincoat*
las mallas	*tights; leggings*
las medias / los calcetines	*socks*
los pantalones	*pants*
los pantalones cortos	*shorts*
el/la piyama	*pajamas*
la ropa interior	*underwear*
el saco	*blazer, suit jacket*
las sandalias	*sandals*
el sostén	*bra*
la sudadera	*sweatshirt; jogging suit*
el suéter	*sweater*
la talla	*size* (clothes)
el traje	*suit*
el traje de baño	*bathing suit*
los vaqueros / los jeans	*jeans*
el vestido	*dress*
las zapatillas	*slippers*
las zapatillas de deporte	*athletic shoes*
los zapatos	*shoes*
los zapatos de tacón	*high-heeled shoes*

Los accesorios	Accessories
el anillo	*ring*
el arete	*earring*
la billetera	*wallet*
el bolso	*purse*
la bufanda	*scarf*
el cinturón	*belt*
el collar	*necklace*
las gafas de sol	*sunglasses*
la gorra	*baseball cap*
el gorro	*hat*
el guante	*glove*
la joya	*piece of jewelry*
el pañuelo	*handkerchief*
el paraguas	*umbrella*
la pulsera	*bracelet*
el sombrero	*wide-brimmed hat*

Las telas y los materiales	Fabrics and materials
el algodón	*cotton*
el cuero	*leather*
la lana	*wool*
el oro	*gold*
la plata	*silver*
el poliéster	*polyester*
la seda	*silk*

Los diseños	Designs
de color entero	*solid*
de cuadros	*plaid*
de lunares	*polka-dotted*
de rayas	*striped*

Las compras	Shopping
el almacén	*department store*
el centro comercial	*mall*
el dinero	*money*
en efectivo	*in cash*
el escaparate	*store window*
el mercado	*market*
el precio	*price*
la rebaja	*sale*
el regalo	*present, gift*
el supermercado	*supermarket*
la tarjeta de crédito	*credit card*
la tienda	*store*

Las descripciones	Descriptions
al aire libre	*open-air*
ancho/a	*wide, loose*
barato/a	*inexpensive, cheap*
caro/a	*expensive*
cómodo/a	*comfortable*
estrecho/a	*narrow, tight*
magnífico/a	*great*
precioso/a	*beautiful*
rebajado/a	*marked down*

Verbos	Verbs
caer bien/mal	*to like/dislike* (a person)
cambiar	*to change, to exchange*
dar	*to give*
encantar	*to like a lot, to love*
entrar (en)	*to go in, to enter*
estar de moda	*to be fashionable*
explicar	*to explain*
fascinar	*to like a lot, to love*
gastar	*to spend*
gustar	*to like, to be pleasing to*
interesar	*to interest; to matter*
ir de compras	*to go shopping*
llevar	*to wear; to take*
mandar	*to send*
mostrar (ue)	*to show*
pagar	*to pay (for)*
parecer (zc)	*to seem*
probarse (ue)	*to try on*
quedar	*to fit; to be left over*
regalar	*to give* (a present)
valer (g)	*to be worth*
vender	*to sell*

Expresiones de tiempo	Time expressions
anoche	*last night*
anteayer	*the day before yesterday*
ante(a)noche	*the night before last*
el año/mes pasado	*last year/month*
ayer	*yesterday*
hace un día/mes/año (que)	*it has been a day/month/year since*
una semana atrás	*a week ago*
la semana pasada	*last week*

Palabras y expresiones útiles	Useful words and expressions
la artesanía	*handicrafts*
¿En qué puedo servirle(s)?	*How may I help you?*
enseguida	*immediately, right away*
el juguete	*toy*
Me gustaría…	*I would like . . .*
Quisiera…	*I would like . . .*

Capítulo 7
¿Cuál es tu deporte favorito?

Un escalador se aproxima a la cima (*summit*) del Aconcagua, en Argentina.

Learning Outcomes

You will be able to:

- talk about sports
- talk about the weather
- emphasize and clarify information
- talk about past events
- talk about Argentina and Uruguay in terms of products, practices, and perspectives
- share information about sporting events in Hispanic countries and identify cultural similarities

Enfoque cultural
Argentina y Uruguay

La famosa escultura *La mano*, en una playa de Punta del Este, Uruguay

El glaciar Perito Moreno, Argentina

Bailando tango en el barrio de La Boca, Buenos Aires

Arte hispano

Hamlet y Ofelia (1930), de Juan Carlos Liberti, pintor argentino

Enfoque cultural

¿Qué te parece?

- La influencia italiana en Argentina se nota en palabras como **chau,** en el acento y la entonación, en la comida y en los nombres y apellidos.
- Los habitantes de la capital de Argentina se llaman **porteños** porque Buenos Aires es un puerto.
- La Celeste, el equipo (*team*) nacional de fútbol de Uruguay, ganó (*won*) la Copa América 15 veces.
- Muchos argentinos van en buquebús (*ferry*) de Buenos Aires a Montevideo solo para ver un partido de fútbol. El viaje (*trip*) es menos de tres horas.
- Punta del Este, Uruguay, es un centro turístico muy popular entre los cantantes, actores y diseñadores. Es el Miami de Uruguay.
- La mayoría de los argentinos y uruguayos usan **vos** en vez de **tú.** Por ejemplo, dicen **vos decís** y no **tú dices.**

Al oeste (*west*) de Argentina, junto al lago Nahuel Huapi, está San Carlos de Bariloche, con las mejores pistas de esquí (*ski slopes*) de América del Sur.

Juliana descansa tomando mate, una infusión preparada con hojas de yerba mate. Es una bebida muy popular en Uruguay y Argentina.

La Plaza de Mayo, en Buenos Aires, es un lugar con mucha historia por sus manifestaciones (*demonstrations*) tanto políticas como populares. El pañuelo (*scarf*) blanco es el símbolo de las Madres y Abuelas de la Plaza de Mayo.

La Garganta del Diablo (*Devil's Throat*) es una de las cascadas del Parque Nacional Iguazú, en la frontera (*border*) entre Argentina, Paraguay y Brasil.

¿Cuánto sabes? Completa las oraciones con la información correcta.

1. ________________ es considerado el Miami de Uruguay.
2. ________________ es un glaciar en Argentina.
3. Los habitantes de Buenos Aires se llaman ________________.
4. La influencia ________________ en Argentina se nota en la lengua, en los nombres y en la comida.
5. El ________________ es una bebida típica de Uruguay y Argentina.
6. Una de las cascadas más impresionantes del Parque Nacional Iguazú se llama la ________________.

To learn more about Argentina and Uruguay, go online to view the *Club cultura* videos.

VOCABULARIO EN CONTEXTO

Talking about sports, the weather, and the past

Los deportes

El **fútbol** es el deporte número uno en muchos países hispanos. En España, Argentina, Uruguay, Colombia, México y otros países, hay excelentes **equipos** de fútbol. Los mejores **jugadores** de **cada** país forman la selección nacional. Esta selección representa al país en los **partidos** de los **campeonatos** internacionales y participa cada cuatro años en la Copa Mundial.

En la zona del Caribe, el **béisbol** es el deporte más popular, y hay muy buenos jugadores y **entrenadores.** Algunos **beisbolistas,** como Francisco Lindor, José Altuve, José Ramírez y Freddy Galvis, juegan en equipos de Estados Unidos y son conocidos mundialmente.

El **ciclismo,** el **tenis** y el **golf** son otros deportes muy populares en Hispanoamérica y España. La **tenista** española-venezolana Garbiñe Muguruza es actualmente una de las jugadoras profesionales más importantes, como Rafael Nadal en el tenis masculino. En **natación,** Mireia Belmonte, de Barcelona, es **campeona** olímpica.

Deportes y equipo deportivo

el béisbol

el golf

el tenis

el básquetbol / el baloncesto

el vóleibol

el esquí

En otras palabras

Some Spanish speakers use **básquetbol,** with the stress on the first syllable, rather than **baloncesto. Vóleibol** has several variants, including **volibol,** with the stress on the last syllable.

While the majority of speakers use **jugar al +** ***deporte,*** some omit **al: jugar tenis, jugar golf.**

Cultura

Ídolos del fútbol Soccer stars in Spanish-speaking countries enjoy an unrivaled popularity and importance in everyday life. As celebrities in their countries and beyond, they serve as social role models as well. Some soccer stars, such as Lionel Messi, an Argentinian playing for the Barcelona team, have capitalized on their social status to start nonprofit organizations that address social problems.

Conexiones Piensa en un/a deportista que es un/a ídolo para tu generación. Explica por qué es importante.

Lionel Messi en un partido de su equipo nacional.

PRÁCTICA

7-1 Escucha y confirma. You will hear six sentences about sports. Indicate the number of the sentence you hear that corresponds to each sport.

_____ el básquetbol
_____ el béisbol
_____ el ciclismo
_____ el esquí
_____ el fútbol
_____ el golf
_____ el tenis
_____ el vóleibol

7-2 Deportes: ¿Quién es?

PREPARACIÓN. Selecciona al / a la deportista que corresponde a cada deporte. Compara tus respuestas con las de tu compañero/a.

1. _____ béisbol
2. _____ fútbol
3. _____ natación
4. _____ tenis

a. Mireia Belmonte
b. Lionel Messi
c. Garbiñe Muguruza
d. Fernando Abad

INTERCAMBIOS. Ahora hablen de dos de sus deportistas favoritos/as. Expliquen quiénes son y qué deporte juegan, dónde juegan, qué campeonatos ganaron y por qué son sus deportistas favoritos/as.

7-3 ¿Qué necesitamos para jugar? **PREPARACIÓN.** Indica el equipo que se necesita para practicar cada deporte.

Deporte	Equipo
el balo ncesto	
el béisbol	
el golf	
el tenis	
el vóleibol	

En otras palabras

Different words are used in Spanish for *ball,* depending on the context: soccer: **el balón / la pelota;** basketball, volleyball: **el balón;** golf, tennis: **la pelota;** bowling: **la bola.**

INTERCAMBIOS. Conversa con tu compañero/a sobre deportes.

1. ¿Qué deporte(s) practicas? ¿Dónde y cuándo lo(s) practicas?
2. ¿Qué equipo necesitas para practicarlo(s)?
3. ¿Dónde compras el equipo y la ropa que necesitas?

7-4 ¿Qué deporte es? Túrnense para identificar los siguientes deportes. Después, pregúntale a tu compañero/a cuál es su deporte favorito y por qué.

1. Hay nueve jugadores en cada equipo, y usan un bate y una pelota.
2. Es un juego para dos o cuatro jugadores; necesitan raquetas y una pelota.
3. En este deporte los jugadores no deben usar las manos.
4. Para practicar este deporte, necesitamos una bicicleta.
5. En cada equipo hay cinco jugadores que lanzan (*throw*) el balón a un cesto.
6. Para este deporte, necesitamos una red y una pelota. Mucha gente lo practica en la playa.

7-5 Tu deporte favorito. Háganse preguntas para averiguar lo siguiente.

MODELO el deporte que no te gusta ver en televisión
E1: *¿Qué deporte no te gusta ver en televisión?*
E2: *No me gusta ver el golf en televisión. ¿Y a ti?*

1. el deporte que te gusta practicar
2. el lugar donde lo practicas, con quién y cuándo
3. el deporte que te gusta ver
4. el lugar y las personas con quienes lo ves
5. los nombres de tus equipos favoritos
6. la marca (*brand*) de ropa deportiva que más te gusta

 **7-6 Deportista favorito/a.** **PREPARACIÓN.** En grupos pequeños, escojan a un/a deportista famoso/a y hagan una pequeña investigación.

1. Identifiquen al / a la deportista y su deporte.
2. Digan qué campeonato / torneo (*tournament*) ganó.
3. Mencionen el equipo que necesita para practicar su deporte.
4. Cuenten algún dato personal o profesional de esta persona.

INTERCAMBIOS. Compartan con la clase la información sobre este/a deportista.

El tiempo

En verano generalmente hace buen tiempo y **hace calor.** Es la estación perfecta para practicar vóleibol en la playa o natación al aire libre. Algunos prefieren **hacer surf** en el mar o **deportes de riesgo,** como el **parapente.**

En invierno **hace frío** y a veces **nieva.** Pero la **nieve** es necesaria para **esquiar.** En España y Argentina hay buenas **pistas** para practicar el esquí. Cuando hace mucho frío **se congelan** los **lagos** y es posible **patinar** sobre el **hielo.**

En otoño **hace fresco** y es muy bonito cuando los **árboles** cambian de color antes de **perder** las hojas. Si **está despejado** o **nublado,** el tiempo es perfecto para jugar al **fútbol americano** o al **hockey sobre hierba,** pero no es fácil jugar al golf cuando **hace viento.**

En primavera **llueve** bastante y es difícil practicar **atletismo** u otros deportes al aire libre. Pero la **lluvia** es muy buena para las **plantas** y las flores. Cuando hace mal tiempo, muchas personas **juegan a los bolos** o **levantan pesas** en el gimnasio.

Lengua

Replace **o** with **u** when the word that follows starts with an **o** sound (spelled **o-** or **ho-**).

Pedro u Osvaldo	*Pedro or Osvaldo*
mujer u hombre	*woman or man*

Likewise, **y** is replaced with **e** when the word that follows begins with an **i** sound (spelled **i-** or **hi-**).

Juan e Isabel	*Juan and Isabel*
jugadores e hinchas	*players and fans*

En otras palabras

In some Spanish-speaking countries, the expressions **jugar (al) boliche** or **ir de *bowling*** are preferred to **jugar a los bolos.**

PRÁCTICA

7-7 Para confirmar.

PREPARACIÓN. Selecciona la condición meteorológica que corresponde a cada descripción.

1. _____ Las calles están blancas.
2. _____ Las personas llevan impermeable y paraguas.
3. _____ La casa es un horno y vamos a ir a la playa.
4. _____ Los árboles se mueven (*move*) mucho.
5. _____ Vamos a celebrar mi cumpleaños en el parque porque el clima está perfecto.
6. _____ El cielo (*sky*) está gris y parece que va a llover.

a. Hace muy buen tiempo.
b. Hace mucho viento.
c. Está lloviendo.
d. Hace mucho calor.
e. Está nevando.
f. Está nublado.

INTERCAMBIOS. Túrnense para hablar de los deportes que se pueden practicar en estas situaciones y de los planes que se pueden hacer.

MODELO Hoy hace sol y estamos en la playa. Tenemos una red y una pelota.
E1: *Hoy hace sol y estamos en la playa. Tenemos una red y una pelota.*
E2: *Vamos a jugar vóleibol.*

1. Hace buen tiempo y tenemos unas raquetas.
2. Anoche llovió mucho, pero el césped ya no está mojado (*wet*). Somos 11 jugadores.
3. Está nevando y hace frío, y queremos practicar un deporte en el gimnasio.
4. Está nublado pero no hace frío. Tenemos los palos y muchas pelotas.

7-8 ¿Qué tiempo hace? Tu amigo/a te llama por teléfono desde otra ciudad. Pregúntale qué tiempo hace allí y averigua cuáles son sus planes. Tu amigo/a debe hacerte preguntas también.

MODELO E1: *¡Qué sorpresa! ¿Dónde estás?*
E2: *Estoy en…*
E1: *¿Qué tiempo hace allí?*
E2: *Hace…*

7-9 El tiempo y las actividades. PREPARACIÓN. Túrnense para explicar qué hacen o qué les gusta hacer a estas personas en las siguientes condiciones.

1. Cuando llueve, yo…
2. Cuando hace mucho calor, me gusta…
3. A veces cuando nieva, mis hermanos y yo...
4. Mis amigos y yo… cuando hace mal tiempo.
5. En invierno, mis primos…
6. Los estudiantes… cuando hace buen tiempo.
7. Cuando está nublado, mi amigo Pedro y yo…
8. Hoy hace viento, pero yo…

INTERCAMBIOS. Preparen una breve conversación que incluya al menos (*at least*) una pregunta, tres expresiones de tiempo y un deporte.

MODELO E1: *Hola, Carmen. ¿Vamos a la playa esta tarde? Hace mucho calor.*
E2: *Sí, pero en la televisión dicen que esta tarde va a llover.*
E1: *Está nublado pero pienso que no va a llover.*
E2: *Bueno, pues vamos. Es mejor jugar al vóleibol cuando está nublado.*

En directo

To thank a friend for calling:

Mil gracias por llamar. ¡Fue un gusto escucharte!
Thanks so much for calling. It was great to hear your voice!

Gracias por llamar. ¡Qué placer escucharte!
Thanks for calling. How nice to hear from you!

Listen to a conversation with these expressions.

Cultura

Celsius y Farenheit The Celsius system is used in Hispanic countries. To convert degrees Fahrenheit to degrees Celsius (**grados Celsius** or **grados centígrados**), subtract 32, multiply by 5, and divide by 9.

86 °F − 32 = 54
54 × 5 = 270
270 ÷ 9 = 30 °C

Comparaciones ¿Qué temperatura hace ahora en tu ciudad? ¿Cambia mucho el clima con las estaciones? ¿Cuál es tu estación del año favorita? ¿Por qué? ¿Practicas distintos deportes según la estación del año? ¿Cuáles?

 **7-10 Las temperaturas.** **PREPARACIÓN.** Escojan cada uno/a una ciudad del mapa de Uruguay y túrnense para describir el tiempo y la temperatura.

MODELO E1: *¿Qué tiempo hace en…?*
E2: *Está… Hace… grados centígrados. Su equivalente en grados Fahrenheit es… ¿Y qué tiempo hace donde estás tú?*
E1: *Hace…*

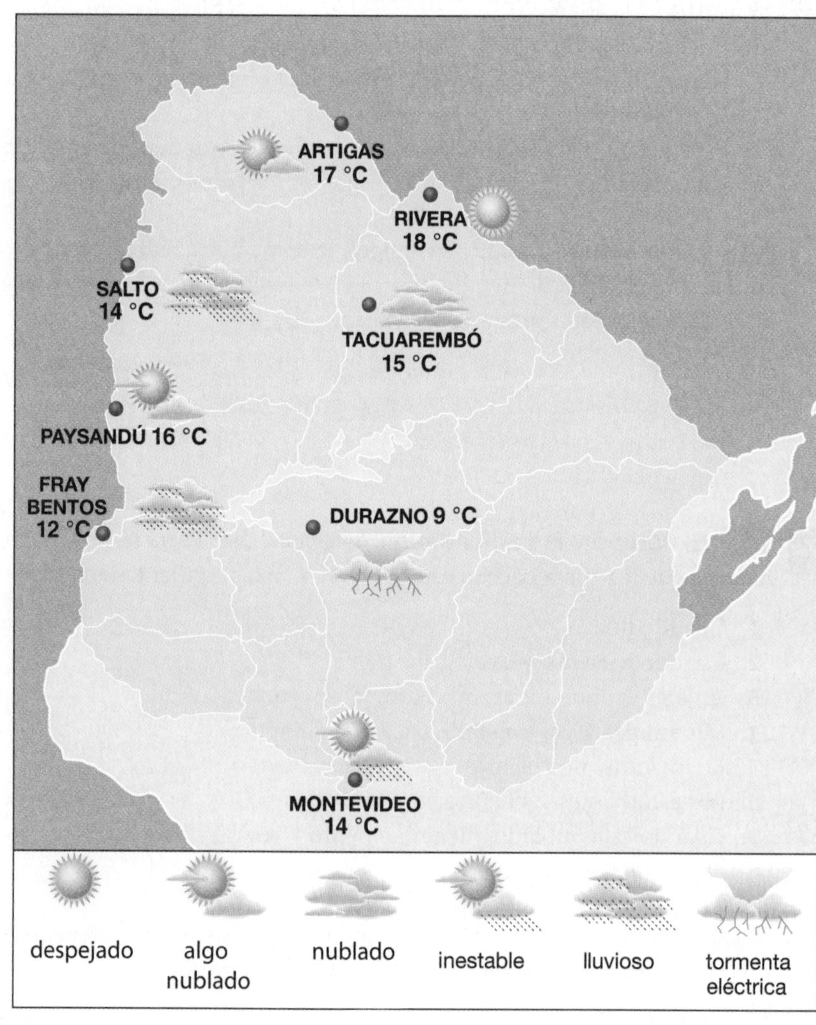

INTERCAMBIOS. Preparen un pronóstico del tiempo (*weather forecast*) de la región donde viven. Indiquen la temperatura de tres ciudades, el tiempo que hace hoy y el tiempo que va a hacer mañana. Después, compártanlo con la clase.

¿Qué pasó ayer?

Un partido importante. Ayer fue el partido decisivo del campeonato de fútbol.

Iván **se despertó** temprano.

Se levantó.

Se vistió.

Se sentó a comer un buen desayuno. Después, **se fue** para el **campo** de fútbol.

Durante el partido, el **árbitro pitó** un **penalti.**

Un jugador del equipo **contrario se enojó** y **discutió** con el árbitro, pero el equipo de Iván **metió un gol** y **ganó.**

Después del partido, Iván **se quitó** el uniforme, **se bañó** y **se puso** ropa limpia.

Luego, fue a una fiesta para celebrar el **triunfo** con los otros **deportistas** y algunos **hinchas.**

Volvió a casa muy tarde, **se acostó** y **se durmió** enseguida.

PRÁCTICA

7-11 Para confirmar.

PREPARACIÓN. Selecciona la definición que corresponde a cada palabra.

1. _____ ganar
2. _____ equipo
3. _____ gol
4. _____ partido
5. _____ árbitro
6. _____ campeón

a. el equipo o deportista que gana
b. la persona que hace el rol de juez (*judge*) en un partido
c. tener más puntos al terminar el juego
d. el juego entre dos equipos o individuos
e. el punto en un partido de fútbol
f. un grupo de jugadores

INTERCAMBIOS. Hazle preguntas a tu compañero/a para ver si sabe las respuestas. Pregúntale sobre las palabras en **Preparación.**

MODELO E1: *¿Cómo se llama el equipo que gana?*
E2: …

7-12 El partido de Iván. Trabajen juntos/as para contestar las preguntas sobre las actividades del día del partido.

1. ¿Qué hizo (*did*) Iván primero?
2. ¿Qué hizo después de levantarse?
3. ¿Qué desayunó Iván?
4. ¿Por qué se enojó un jugador del equipo contrario?
5. ¿Quién ganó el partido?
6. ¿Adónde fue Iván después del partido?

Cultura

Los hinchas descontentos Hispanic sports fans generally do not boo opposing teams or particular players. Instead they show their displeasure by whistling. This behavior may occur at a soccer game, a boxing match, or other popular sports events.

Comparaciones En tu comunidad, ¿cómo demuestran descontento los hinchas con los jugadores o con un partido? ¿Alguna vez viste una escena un poco violenta durante un partido o después? ¿Qué ocurrió? ¿Qué hiciste tú (*did you do*)?

7-13 ¿Las actividades de ayer? PREPARACIÓN. Háganse preguntas para obtener la siguiente información sobre sus actividades de ayer.

MODELO E1: *¿A qué hora te despertaste ayer?*
E2: *Me desperté a las once.*

1. hora de levantarse
2. desayuno que tomó
3. número de horas de estudio
4. deporte(s) que practicó y por cuánto tiempo
5. hora de acostarse

INTERCAMBIOS. Comparen sus actividades.

1. ¿Quién de ustedes se levantó más temprano?
2. ¿Quién comió un desayuno más nutritivo?
3. ¿Quién estudió más?
4. ¿Quién practicó deportes por más tiempo?
5. ¿Quién se acostó más tarde?

7-14 El tiempo y los deportes.

PREPARACIÓN. Write down the information you might hear in a weather forecast in your area in each season. Remember to include temperatures. Then ask your partner what weather conditions he/she listed and if you agree.

MODELO E1: *¿Qué tiempo hace en primavera en…? ¿Qué temperatura hace?*
E2: *Hace…*

ESCUCHA. Focus on the general idea of what you hear. As you listen, indicate whether the forecast predicts good or bad weather for these cities, or if it doesn't say.

	Buen tiempo	Mal tiempo	No se dice
Montevideo			
Buenos Aires			
México			
Quito			

Mosaico cultural

Los hinchas y el superclásico

El fútbol es más que un simple deporte para los hispanos: es una pasión. Es el sueño (*dream*) de muchos niños jugar al fútbol profesionalmente.

Los fines de semana los clubes de fútbol juegan en grandes estadios y miles de hinchas los apoyan (*support*). Existen intensas rivalidades entre los seguidores de los clubes más populares y ganadores. Estos encuentros se llaman clásicos o superclásicos. En México, por ejemplo, los equipos rivales son el Club América y el Deportivo Guadalajara, más conocido como el Chivas. En España son el Real Madrid y el FC Barcelona. En Uruguay, los equipos del clásico son Nacional y Peñarol. Sin embargo (*However*), la experiencia deportiva más intensa ocurre entre Boca Juniors y River Plate, en Argentina. La rivalidad entre estos dos equipos es enorme. Los hinchas de River se burlan de (*make fun of*) los jugadores de Boca y los llaman "chanchos" (*pigs*). En respuesta, los hinchas de Boca llaman "gallinas" (*chickens*) a los jugadores de River.

Cuando Boca y River juegan, la ciudad de Buenos Aires se viste con los colores de los equipos y canta con entusiasmo. Ser hincha de River o del Boca es una tradición familiar. Es normal ver a los niños con camisetas azules cantando: "Boca es entusiasmo y valor, Boca Juniors… a triunfar…". También es común ver a niños y niñas con camisetas rojas y blancas cantando: "Boca: River es tu papá… Olé, olé, River, River…". Por estas razones, el superclásico es más que un evento futbolístico: es también una tradición social. Porque el fútbol es más que un deporte. El fútbol es una parte importante de la identidad de los hispanos.

Compara

1. ¿En tu país hay algún evento deportivo comparable al superclásico? ¿Cuál? ¿Cuándo ocurre? ¿Qué equipos se enfrentan normalmente?
2. ¿Qué rivalidades son famosas en los deportes profesionales o universitarios de tu país?
3. ¿Eres hincha de algún equipo deportivo? ¿Cómo expresas tu apoyo (*support*)? ¿Cómo es tu relación con los hinchas de los equipos rivales?

En acción

Vamos a hacer surf

Antes de ver

7-15 El surf. En este video, Esteban va a enseñarles a hacer surf a sus amigos. Indica las expresiones que asocias con este deporte.

1. _____ el traje de baño
2. _____ el buen tiempo
3. _____ las olas (*waves*)
4. _____ la pelota
5. _____ la pista
6. _____ el equilibrio
7. _____ la playa
8. _____ los palos

Mientras ves

7-16 ¿Qué pasó? Mira el video e indica si las siguientes afirmaciones son ciertas (**C**) o falsas (**F**). Corrige las afirmaciones falsas.

1. _____ Federico llega tarde porque está trabajando en su proyecto.
2. _____ Hace un buen día para hacer surf.
3. _____ Héctor practica el tenis y el béisbol.
4. _____ A Esteban le gusta hacer surf.
5. _____ En Lima hay una playa que se llama Waikiki Beach.
6. _____ En Perú hace buen tiempo durante los meses de junio, julio y agosto.
7. _____ El *sandboard* es un deporte que empezó en Brasil.

Después de ver

7-17 ¡Al agua!

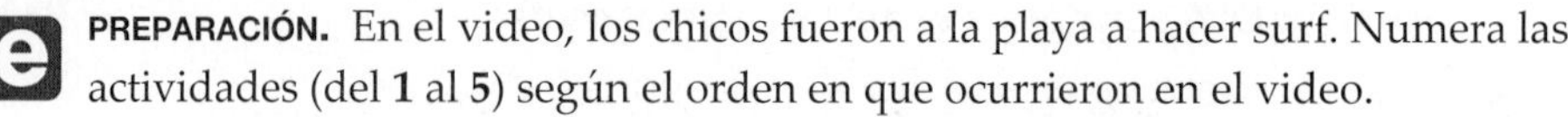

PREPARACIÓN. En el video, los chicos fueron a la playa a hacer surf. Numera las actividades (del **1** al **5**) según el orden en que ocurrieron en el video.

a. _____ Héctor mostró un video sobre las playas de Lima.
b. _____ Los chicos se rieron (*laughed*) mucho de Esteban.
c. _____ Los chicos hablaron de sus deportes preferidos.
d. _____ Esteban corrió hacia (*toward*) el agua con la tabla de surf.
e. _____ Héctor y Esteban esperaron a los otros por mucho tiempo.

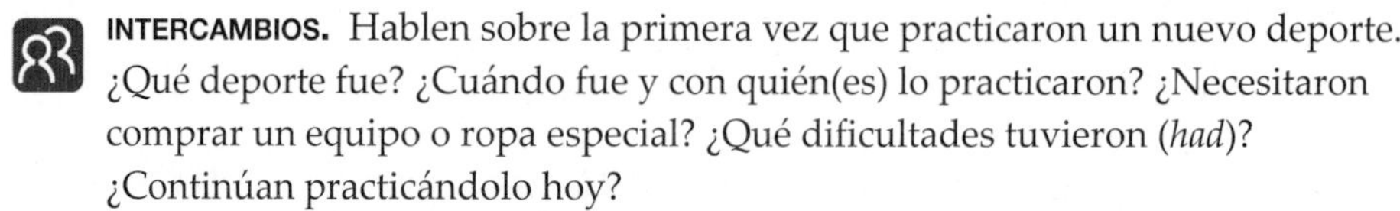

INTERCAMBIOS. Hablen sobre la primera vez que practicaron un nuevo deporte. ¿Qué deporte fue? ¿Cuándo fue y con quién(es) lo practicaron? ¿Necesitaron comprar un equipo o ropa especial? ¿Qué dificultades tuvieron (*had*)? ¿Continúan practicándolo hoy?

FUNCIONES Y FORMAS

1 Talking about the past

REPORTERO: ¡Felicitaciones por el triunfo! ¡Jugaron como campeones!

IVÁN: Gracias. El triunfo es de todo el equipo. Fue un partido difícil, pero **nos preparamos** bien.

REPORTERO: ¿Y cómo empezó este día de victoria para ti, Iván?

IVÁN: Bueno, anoche **me acosté** temprano. Hoy, **me levanté** a las 5:30, **me duché** muy rápido para no llegar tarde al entrenamiento, **me vestí** y **me fui** al campo de fútbol.

REPORTERO: ¿Y cómo **se entrenaron** ustedes para enfrentar al equipo rival?

e **Piénsalo.** Indica si las siguientes afirmaciones se refieren a Iván (**I**) o a los jugadores del equipo (**J**), según la conversación. Luego, escribe el infinitivo del verbo en negrita (*bold*).

		Infinitivo
1.	_____ **Nos preparamos** bien.	__________
2.	_____ **Me acosté** temprano.	__________
3.	_____ **Me vestí** y **me fui** al campo de fútbol.	__________
4.	_____ ¿Y cómo **se entrenaron** ustedes?	__________
5.	_____ Siempre **nos sentimos** ganadores.	__________

Preterit of reflexive verbs

- In **Capítulo 4** you learned about reflexive verbs and pronouns. Now you will use these verbs in the preterit. The rules that apply to reflexive verbs are the same in the past tense as in the present.

  As you have seen, reflexive verbs express what people do *to* or *for themselves*.

LEVANTARSE	
yo	**me levanté**
tú	**te levantaste**
Ud., él, ella	**se levantó**
nosotros/as	**nos levantamos**
vosotros/as	**os levantasteis**
Uds., ellos/as	**se levantaron**

Los jugadores **se levantaron** a las cinco. — *The players got up at five o'clock.*

Yo **me preparé** rápidamente. — *I got ready quickly.*

- With a conjugated verb followed by an infinitive, place the reflexive pronoun before the conjugated verb or attach it to the infinitive.

Yo **me** empecé a preparar a las cinco.
Yo empecé a preparar**me** a las cinco. } *I started to get ready at five.*

- Remember that when referring to parts of the body and clothing, the definite articles are used with reflexive verbs.

  Me lavé **el** pelo. — *I washed my hair.*

  Los jugadores se pusieron **los** zapatos. — *The players put on their shoes.*

- Some verbs that use reflexive pronouns do not necessarily convey the idea of doing something to or for oneself. These verbs normally convey mental or physical states.

  María **se enfermó** gravemente la semana pasada. — *María got seriously sick last week.*

  Nos preocupamos mucho cuando fue al hospital. — *We got very worried when she went to the hospital.*

- The following verbs convey mental or physical states:

arrepentirse	*to regret*
atreverse	*to dare*
disculparse	*to apologize*
divertirse	*to have fun*
enojarse	*to get angry*
quejarse	*to complain*
sentirse	*to feel*

La jugadora **se disculpó** por no asistir a la práctica del viernes pasado. — *The player apologized for not attending last Friday's practice.*

El público **se quejó** del mal desempeño de los jugadores. — *The public complained about the poor performance of the players.*

e **¿Comprendes?** Completa las oraciones con el pretérito de los verbos.

1. Ayer Marta __________ (enfermarse).
2. Pero hoy ella __________ (levantarse) para ir a clase.
3. Los estudiantes no __________ (prepararse) bien para el examen.
4. Yo __________ (disculparse) con el profesor porque no fui a clase.
5. Nosotros __________ (quejarse) ante el profesor porque el examen fue muy difícil.
6. ¿Por qué __________ (sentarse) tú en la última fila (*row*)?

PRÁCTICA

7-18 ¿Cómo te fue (*did it go*) ayer? Pon estas actividades en el orden más lógico, desde la mañana, y compara tus respuestas con las de tu compañero/a. ¿Tienen el mismo orden? Si no coinciden en el orden, presenten sus diferencias a otro grupo.

_____ Me preparé para un examen.
_____ Me dormí.
_____ Me levanté.
_____ Me despedí (*said goodbye*) de mi perro y salí para la universidad.
_____ Me acosté.
_____ Me desperté temprano.
_____ Me senté a desayunar.
_____ Me bañé.
_____ Al final del día, me sentí cansado/a.

7-19 Nuestro último partido. **PREPARACIÓN.** La semana pasada ustedes jugaron un partido importante. ¿Qué hicieron (*did*) antes y durante el partido? Usen por lo menos ocho verbos de la lista, u otros. Tomen apuntes para compartir con la clase.

acostarse	descansar	estresarse	relajarse
bañarse	despertarse	levantarse	vestirse
concentrarse	enojarse	prepararse	

MODELO E1: *Yo me desperté muy temprano el día del partido. ¿Y ustedes?*
E2: *Yo me desperté temprano también.*
E3: *Yo me desperté tarde y me levanté tarde.*

INTERCAMBIOS. Compartan con otro grupo las actividades que hicieron antes y durante el último partido importante que jugaron. Respondan a estas preguntas.

1. ¿Qué deporte jugaron? ¿Ganaron o perdieron el partido?
2. ¿Qué actividades semejantes hicieron ustedes? ¿Y qué actividades diferentes?
3. ¿Qué grupo se preparó mejor para este partido importante? ¿Qué hicieron para prepararse mejor?

7-20 Mis actividades. Para cuidar tu salud, decidiste cambiar tu rutina y empezar a hacer ejercicio cada día antes de ir a clase. Cuéntale a tu compañero/a qué hiciste (*did*) esta mañana. Usa por lo menos cuatro de los siguientes verbos.

caminar	ducharse	nadar
correr	jugar	prepararse
despertarse	levantarse	

7-21 ¿Qué les ocurrió? Lean las siguientes situaciones y digan qué hicieron (*did*) estas personas después. Usen los verbos de la lista. Luego, comparen sus opiniones con las de sus compañeros/as.

afeitarse	maquillarse	quejarse
bañarse	mirarse	quitarse
despertarse	peinarse	relajarse
disculparse	ponerse (la ropa)	secarse
enojarse	prepararse	vestirse
lavarse	probarse	

MODELO Bernardo se despertó cuando sonó la alarma.
E1: *Luego se levantó lentamente. En tu opinión, ¿qué pasó después?*
E2: *Probablemente se afeitó.*

1. Teresa se miró en el espejo.
2. Después del partido, Juan y Tomás entraron al vestuario (*locker room*) del gimnasio.
3. Marisa y Erica salieron de una tienda de artículos deportivos.
4. Ramón salió de la ducha.
5. Marta discutió con la entrenadora.
6. Pablo llegó tarde a la práctica del equipo.
7. Carlos cometió un error y el otro equipo metió un gol.

Cultura

Una actividad física In Spanish-speaking countries, one of the most common physical activities is walking—as light exercise after work or after a meal, as a family activity, or simply to be outside in one's neighborhood. Walking is often a social activity during which friends and neighbors meet and greet each other. As in the United States, professional people with busy work schedules join gyms or sports clubs, especially in metropolitan areas. Biking is also becoming popular in large cities and towns of Latin America.

Comparaciones En tu opinión, ¿andar es una buena actividad física? ¿Por dónde pasea la gente de tu comunidad? ¿Hay ciclovías (*bike lanes*) para los ciclistas en tu ciudad?

 **7-22 El campeonato.** El mes pasado, ustedes representaron a su universidad en un campeonato de tenis en Montevideo. Digan qué hicieron (*did*) para…

1. prepararse físicamente.
2. prepararse mentalmente.
3. cumplir (*to fulfill*) con sus responsabilidades académicas.

 **7-23 Un día de mala suerte.** Observen las siguientes escenas. Túrnense para contar qué ocurrió. Usen su imaginación y los verbos de la lista u otros, si es necesario.

acostarse	ducharse	golpear (*to knock*)	sentarse
despertarse	enojarse	levantarse	sonar
disculparse	explicar	practicar	

Situación

PREPARACIÓN. Lean la situación. Luego, compartan ejemplos de vocabulario, gramática y otra información que necesitan para desarrollar la conversación.

Role A. You are the star player for your university's soccer team. You spend a lot of your free time promoting sports and physical activity for children in your community. A sports reporter for a local TV station interviews you for a special feature on student athletes. Answer the reporter's questions as fully as possible. Remember that you are considered a role model for young athletes.

Role B. You are a sports reporter for a local TV station. Today you are interviewing the star soccer player for the university team who is also a role model for young athletes in the community. After introducing yourself and greeting the athlete, find out:

a. what high school he/she went to;
b. when he/she started to play soccer;
c. what his/her daily routine is to keep in shape (**estar en forma**); and
d. what activities he/she did with young athletes in the community last year.

	ROLE A	ROLE B
Vocabulario	Activities to stay fit Sports routines	Question words Sports-related vocabulary Sports routines
Funciones y formas	Answering questions Present tense Preterit Reflexive verbs Addressing someone formally	Introducing oneself Asking questions Present tense Preterit Reflexive verbs Addressing someone formally

INTERCAMBIOS. Practiquen la conversación, incorporando el vocabulario y las funciones de **Preparación.** Luego, represéntenla ante la clase.

2 Talking about the past

VÍCTOR: Federico, ¿miraste el partido entre la selección de Argentina y la de Colombia?

FEDERICO: No, Víctor. Pero **oí** las noticias por la radio, y mi hermano **leyó** la crónica del partido en las noticias en línea. La selección colombiana ganó dos a uno. Los argentinos no jugaron bien. Y tú, ¿viste el partido?

VÍCTOR: Desafortunadamente no, pero **leí** en internet que los jugadores argentinos no **oyeron** las instrucciones de su entrenador y cometieron muchos errores. Por eso, el árbitro les pitó un penalti.

FEDERICO: Tienes razón, yo **oí** que la estrategia de defensa que **construyeron** (*built*) no fue buena. Ellos **creyeron** que ganarles a los colombianos es fácil, pero los colombianos son muy buenos.

Piénsalo. Indica quién hizo cada actividad de acuerdo con la conversación: Federico (**F**), Víctor (**V**), el hermano de Federico (**HF**) o los jugadores argentinos (**JA**). Luego, escribe el infinitivo del verbo en negrita (*bold*).

		Infinitivo
1.	_____ **Oyó** las noticias del partido por la radio.	________
2.	_____ **Leyó** la crónica en línea.	________
3.	_____ **Leyó** en internet comentarios sobre el partido.	________
4.	_____ No **oyeron** las instrucciones.	________
5.	_____ **Construyeron** una mala estrategia de defensa.	________
6.	_____ **Creyeron** que ganar es fácil.	________

Preterit of *-er* and *-ir* verbs whose stem ends in a vowel

- You have already learned the preterit forms of regular **-er** and **-ir** verbs. For verbs whose stem ends in a vowel (such as **construir, creer, destruir, leer, oír**), the preterit ending for the **usted/él/ella** form is **-yó** and for the **ustedes/ellos/ellas** form, the ending is **-yeron.**

LEER			
yo	leí	nosotros/as	leímos
tú	leíste	vosotros/as	leísteis
Ud., él, ella	le**y**ó	Uds., ellos/as	le**y**eron

OÍR			
yo	oí	nosotros/as	oímos
tú	oíste	vosotros/as	oísteis
Ud., él, ella	o**y**ó	Uds., ellos/as	o**y**eron

¿**Leíste** los comentarios negativos de los reporteros deportivos? — *Did you read the negative comments of the sports commentators?*

Cuando la entrenadora **oyó** el pitazo final, abrazó a las jugadoras. — *When the coach heard the final whistle, she hugged the players.*

Los jugadores del equipo **construyeron** una casa con la ayuda de una organización sin fines de lucro. — *The team members built a house with the help of a nonprofit organization.*

Lengua

Note that **-er** and **-ir** verbs whose stems end in a vowel (**creer, leer, oír**) have an accent mark on the **i** in the infinitive and in the preterit endings that begin with **i.**

No la **oímos** llegar anoche.
We didn't hear her arrive last night.

¿Comprendes? Completa las oraciones con el pretérito de los verbos.

1. Pablo y Miguel ___________ (oír) la noticia en la radio.
2. Ellos no la ___________ (creer).
3. Carmen ___________ (leer) la información en internet.
4. Nosotros no ___________ (creer) lo que Carmen nos contó.
5. Los arquitectos ___________ (destruir) un estadio viejo y ___________ (construir) uno muy moderno.
6. ¿Asististe al partido ayer o ___________ (leer) el libro de historia?

PRÁCTICA

7-24 ¿Cómo se enteraron (*found out*)?

PREPARACIÓN. El fin de semana pasado se jugó la Copa Davis. Indica cómo se enteraron estas personas de los resultados. Usa los verbos **creer, leer** y **oír.**

1. Paula y su novio pasaron el fin de semana en las montañas y ________ los resultados del partido de su equipo favorito en la radio.
2. Mercedes trabajó el fin de semana. Cuando su hermano le contó que su equipo perdió, ella no lo ________.
3. Ricardo ________ los resultados de la Copa Davis en línea.
4. Los Belmar salieron de compras a la hora del partido. ________ los resultados en el periódico (*newspaper*) local al día siguiente.

INTERCAMBIOS. Intercambien una noticia relacionada con los deportes que oyeron en la radio o leyeron en internet. Luego informen a la clase sobre la noticia de su compañero/a.

MODELO E1: *Meghan oyó en la radio que el equipo femenino de baloncesto de la universidad va a jugar en Boston.*
E2: *Lucas leyó que la mejor jugadora de golf se llama…*

7-25 Las noticias.

Dile a tu compañero/a cuándo y cómo te enteraste de lo siguiente. ¿Lo leíste, lo oíste o lo miraste?

MODELO el equipo ganador del Super Bowl
E1: *Lo miré en la televisión. ¿Y tú?*
E2: *Yo lo leí en internet.*

1. el equipo ganador de la última serie mundial de béisbol
2. los resultados de las últimas elecciones presidenciales
3. el matrimonio de Meghan Markle y el Príncipe Harry
4. tu admisión en esta universidad

7-26 ¿Quiénes lo hicieron?

PREPARACIÓN. Entrevista a tus compañeros/as para descubrir quiénes hicieron (*did*) lo siguiente. Escribe los nombres de tus compañeros/as que hicieron la actividad.

MODELO alguna vez leer un artículo sobre el parapente
E1: *¿Alguna vez leíste un artículo sobre el parapente?*
E2: *Sí, leí uno hace un mes. / No, nunca leí un artículo sobre ese deporte. ¿Y tú?*
E3: *Yo leí varios la semana pasada. Me gusta mucho ese deporte.*

	¿Quiénes?
1. leer sobre deportes esta semana	
2. oír música en su teléfono hoy	
3. contribuir al éxito (*success*) de su equipo en un partido	
4. no oír su alarma un día este semestre	
5. construir una amistad (*friendship*) con una persona de otro país	
6. accidentalmente destruir algo en un lugar para practicar deportes	

INTERCAMBIOS. Comparte con tu compañero/a la información que recogiste en **Preparación.** Responde a las preguntas de tu compañero/a y haz (*make*) tus propias preguntas.

MODELO E1: *Para la pregunta número uno, conversé con tres compañeros/as. Dos compañeros/as leyeron sobre deportes esta semana.*
E2: *¡Qué interesante! ¿Quiénes leyeron sobre deportes?*
E1: *John y Stacey leyeron sobre deportes.*

7-27 La semana pasada. **PREPARACIÓN.** Mira la lista de actividades e indica en cuáles participaste la semana pasada. Añade (*Add*) detalles sobre cada actividad.

____ concluir un proyecto importante para la clase de…
____ ir a la biblioteca para…
____ leer el blog de…
____ mirar una película con…
____ oír música de…
____ contribuir con dinero a una organización sin fines de lucro (*non-profit*) para…

INTERCAMBIOS. En grupos de tres o cuatro, comparen sus respuestas para ver quién hizo (*did*) más actividades la semana pasada.

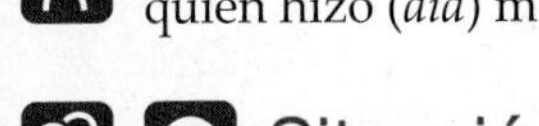

Situación

PREPARACIÓN. Lean la situación. Luego, compartan ejemplos de vocabulario, gramática y otra información que necesitan para desarrollar la conversación.

Role A. Call a friend to invite him/her to go to a sports event with you. Mention:
a. what the event is;
b. that you read about it online; and
c. that you want to see the city's new stadium.

Role B. Your friend calls to invite you to a sports event. Respond to the invitation with questions and comments. Then decide if you want to go and either accept or decline the invitation.

	ROLE A	ROLE B
Vocabulario	Sports events	Question words
Funciones y formas	Inviting someone to do something Preterit	Reacting to what you hear Asking questions Accepting or declining an invitation

INTERCAMBIOS. Practiquen la conversación, incorporando el vocabulario y las funciones de **Preparación.** Luego, represéntenla ante la clase.

3 Talking about the past

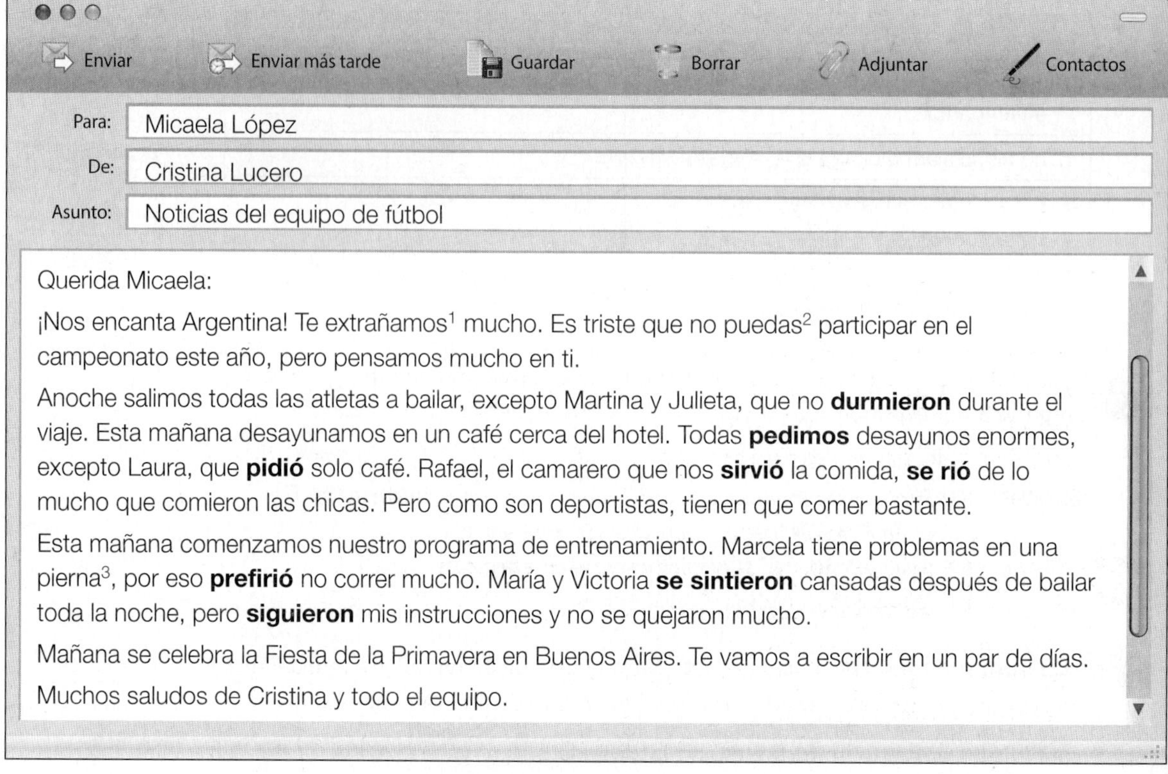

Enviar | Enviar más tarde | Guardar | Borrar | Adjuntar | Contactos

Para: Micaela López

De: Cristina Lucero

Asunto: Noticias del equipo de fútbol

Querida Micaela:

¡Nos encanta Argentina! Te extrañamos[1] mucho. Es triste que no puedas[2] participar en el campeonato este año, pero pensamos mucho en ti.

Anoche salimos todas las atletas a bailar, excepto Martina y Julieta, que no **durmieron** durante el viaje. Esta mañana desayunamos en un café cerca del hotel. Todas **pedimos** desayunos enormes, excepto Laura, que **pidió** solo café. Rafael, el camarero que nos **sirvió** la comida, **se rió** de lo mucho que comieron las chicas. Pero como son deportistas, tienen que comer bastante.

Esta mañana comenzamos nuestro programa de entrenamiento. Marcela tiene problemas en una pierna[3], por eso **prefirió** no correr mucho. María y Victoria **se sintieron** cansadas después de bailar toda la noche, pero **siguieron** mis instrucciones y no se quejaron mucho.

Mañana se celebra la Fiesta de la Primavera en Buenos Aires. Te vamos a escribir en un par de días.

Muchos saludos de Cristina y todo el equipo.

[1]*miss* [2]*are not able* [3]*leg*

e **Piénsalo.** Lee las afirmaciones e indica el infinitivo que corresponde al verbo en negrita (*bold*).

	Infinitivo
1. Martina y Julieta no **durmieron** durante el viaje.	______
2. Laura **pidió** un café solamente.	______
3. El camarero que nos **sirvió** el desayuno se llama Rafael.	______
4. Marcela **prefirió** no correr mucho.	______
5. Martina y Julieta no **se divirtieron** anoche.	______
6. María y Victoria **siguieron** las instrucciones de su entrenadora.	______

Preterit of stem-changing *-ir* verbs

- In the preterit, stem-changing **-ir** verbs change **e → i** and **o → u** in the **usted, él, ella,** and **ustedes, ellos/as** forms. The endings are the same as those of regular **-ir** verbs.

PREFERIR (e → i)			
yo	preferí	nosotros/as	preferimos
tú	preferiste	vosotros/as	preferisteis
Ud., él, ella	pref**i**rió	Uds., ellos/as	pref**i**rieron

DORMIR (o → u)			
yo	dormí	nosotros/as	dormimos
tú	dormiste	vosotros/as	dormisteis
Ud., él, ella	d**u**rmió	Uds., ellos/as	d**u**rmieron

Marta **prefirió** salir temprano. — *Marta preferred to leave early.*
Las jugadoras **durmieron** profundamente. — *The players slept deeply.*

- The following are other stem-changing **-ir** verbs:

despedirse (i)	*to say goodbye*
divertirse (i)	*to have fun*
morir (u)	*to die*
pedir (i)	*to request, to ask for*
reír(se) (i)	*to laugh (at)*
repetir (i)	*to repeat*
seguir (i)	*to follow*
sentirse (i)	*to feel*
servir (i)	*to serve*
vestirse (i)	*to get dressed*

La entrenadora **repitió** sus instrucciones. — *The coach repeated her instructions.*

Todos **se rieron** cuando un perro cruzó el campo. — *Everyone laughed when a dog crossed the field.*

Un hincha **murió** de un ataque al corazón durante el partido. — *A fan died of a heart attack during the match.*

e **¿Comprendes?** Completa las oraciones con el pretérito de los verbos.

1. Durante la recepción, muchos jugadores __________ (preferir) beber agua.
2. Un jugador __________ (pedir) cerveza.
3. El entrenador __________ (seguir) la tradición de dar un discurso divertido.
4. Todos los jugadores __________ (reírse) mucho.
5. Cuando recibieron sus medallas, los jugadores __________ (sentirse) orgullosos.
6. Todos __________ (divertirse) en la recepción.

PRÁCTICA

7-28 Carrera de una campeona. **PREPARACIÓN.** Una famosa deportista recibió muchas medallas durante su carrera. ¿Cómo lo logró (*did she accomplish it*)? Indica la alternativa más apropiada.

1. **a.** ____ Durmió poco antes de cada partido.
   b. ____ Siempre durmió por lo menos ocho horas.
2. **a.** ____ Prefirió evitar (*avoid*) el alcohol.
   b. ____ Prefirió beber alcohol moderadamente.
3. **a.** ____ Se preparó sola.
   b. ____ Prefirió prepararse con una entrenadora.
4. **a.** ____ Siguió las recomendaciones de su entrenadora.
   b. ____ Les pidió consejos a sus amigos.
5. **a.** ____ Cuando no ganó un partido, se sintió deprimida.
   b. ____ Se sintió triste cuando no ganó un partido, pero pidió ayuda para mejorar.

INTERCAMBIOS. Usen su imaginación para hablar de la carrera de la deportista.

MODELO se divirtió…

E1: *Yo creo que no se divirtió mucho durante su carrera. Y tú, ¿qué crees?*

E2: *Yo creo que se divirtió porque le gusta mucho competir.*

1. durmió…
2. siguió una dieta especial de…
3. pidió…
4. se sintió…

7-29 Momentos cruciales.

PREPARACIÓN. Indica lo que hicieron (*did*) las siguientes jugadoras del equipo de básquetbol unos minutos antes del partido.

1. Marta ________ (vestirse) con la camiseta número 3.
2. Ana y Sofía ________ (seguir) los pasos del calentamiento (*warm-up*).
3. Valentina ________ (preferir) no comer antes del partido.
4. Las jugadoras del equipo contrario ________ (reírse) cuando su entrenadora les contó un chiste (*joke*).
5. La entrenadora les ________ (repetir) las instrucciones a todas las jugadoras.
6. El equipo ________ (sentirse) animado (*encouraged*) con los aplausos del público.

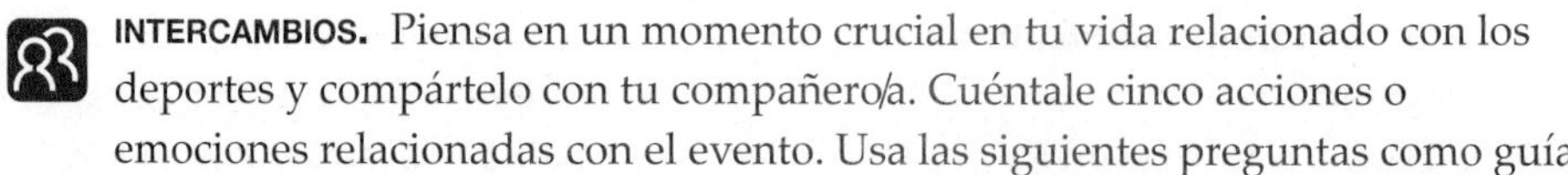

INTERCAMBIOS. Piensa en un momento crucial en tu vida relacionado con los deportes y compártelo con tu compañero/a. Cuéntale cinco acciones o emociones relacionadas con el evento. Usa las siguientes preguntas como guía.

- ¿Qué pasó?
- ¿Cómo te sentiste?
- ¿Con qué número te vestiste?
- ¿Cuántos puntos marcaste?
- ¿Qué tipo de entrenamiento seguiste?

MODELO *Mi momento crucial fue cuando ganamos la final de básquetbol. Me sentí…*

7-30 Celebrando la victoria.

PREPARACIÓN. Uno de los equipos de su universidad ganó un campeonato importante y ustedes organizaron una fiesta en su honor. Usen los verbos de la lista e incluyan los detalles indicados.

despedirse	pedir	repetir	servir
divertirse	reírse	sentirse	vestirse

1. hora y lugar de la fiesta
2. número de personas que asistieron y cómo se vistieron para la fiesta
3. tipo de contribución que ustedes pidieron para cubrir (*cover*) los gastos de la fiesta
4. cómo se divirtieron en la fiesta
5. comida y bebida que sirvieron en la fiesta y tipo de música que escucharon
6. reconocimiento (*recognition*) que les dieron a los jugadores
7. sentimientos de los jugadores durante la fiesta
8. a qué hora se despidieron y se fueron de la fiesta los invitados

INTERCAMBIOS. Ahora explíquenle a otro grupo los detalles de la fiesta.

7-31 Entrevista para el periódico de la universidad.

PREPARACIÓN. Un equipo de su universidad ganó un campeonato importante. Ustedes van a entrevistar a dos jugadores del equipo para el periódico (*newspaper*). Preparen por lo menos cinco preguntas sobre los siguientes temas. Usen los verbos entre paréntesis.

1. instrucciones de su entrenador/a (dar, seguir, dormir, comer, practicar)
2. actividades el día del partido (dormir, levantarse, vestirse, servir)
3. reacciones y actividades después de ganar el campeonato (sentirse, reírse, despedirse, divertirse)

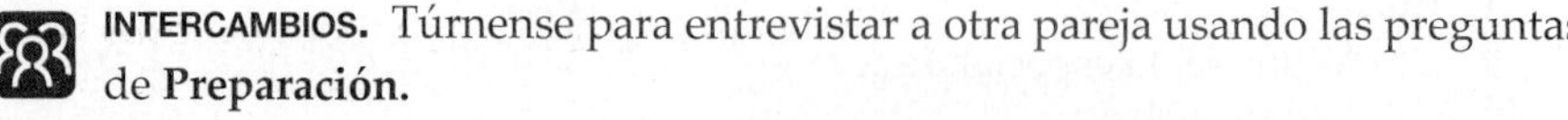

INTERCAMBIOS. Túrnense para entrevistar a otra pareja usando las preguntas de **Preparación.**

Situación

PREPARACIÓN. Lean la situación. Luego, compartan ejemplos de vocabulario, gramática y otra información que necesitan para desarrollar la conversación.

Role A. You had to work late last night and missed an important basketball game. Call a friend who went to the game. After greeting your friend:
a. explain why you did not go;
b. ask questions about the game;
c. answer your friend's questions; and
d. accept your friend's invitation to go to another game next Saturday.

Role B. A friend calls to find out about last night's basketball game. Answer your friend's questions and then:
a. say that there is another game on Saturday;
b. find out if your friend is free that evening; and
c. if free, invite him/her to go with you.

	ROLE A	ROLE B
Vocabulario	Question words	Formulaic expressions related to making an invitation
Funciones y formas	Explaining the reason for something Preterit Asking and answering questions Accepting an invitation Observing phone etiquette	Asking and answering questions Preterit Inviting someone to do something together Reacting to what you hear

INTERCAMBIOS. Practiquen la conversación, incorporando el vocabulario y las funciones de **Preparación.** Luego, represéntenla ante la clase.

4 Emphasizing or clarifying information

ROBERTO: Estas flores son **para ti,** Cristina.
CRISTINA: **¿Para mí?** Gracias, Roberto.

***

ROBERTO: Oye, Cristina. El partido es mañana. ¿Quieres ir **conmigo?**
CRISTINA: No puedo ir **contigo,** Roberto. Mis primos están aquí, y voy al partido **con ellos.**

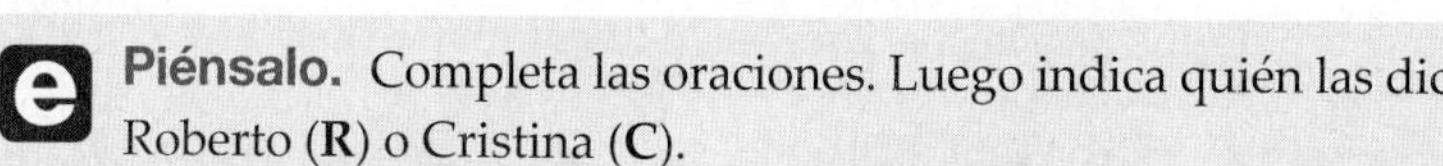

Piénsalo. Completa las oraciones. Luego indica quién las dice: Roberto (**R**) o Cristina (**C**).

1. _____ ¿Quieres ir ________? (with me)
2. _____ Estas flores son ________. (for you)
3. _____ No puedo ir ________. (with you)
4. _____ ¿________? (for me)
5. _____ Voy al partido ________. (with them)

Pronouns after prepositions

- In **Capítulo 6** you used **a** + **mí, a** + **ti,** and so on, to clarify or emphasize the indirect object pronoun: **Le di el suéter a él.** These same pronouns are used after other prepositions, such as **de, para,** and **sin.**

Preposition		Pronoun
a	+	**mí**
de		**ti**
para		**usted, él, ella**
por		**nosotros/as**
sin		**vosotros/as**
sobre		**ustedes, ellos/as**

Siempre habla **de ti.**	*He always talks about you.*
Las raquetas son **para mí.**	*The racquets are for me.*
No quieren ir **sin nosotros.**	*They do not want to go without us.*

- In a few cases, Spanish does not use **mí** and **ti** after prepositions. After **con,** use **conmigo** and **contigo.** After **entre,** use **tú** y **yo.**

¿Vas al partido **conmigo?**	*Are you going to the game with me?*
Sí, voy **contigo.**	*Yes, I am going with you.*
Entre tú y **yo,** ella tiene unos problemas serios.	*Between you and me, she has some serious problems.*

e **¿Comprendes?** Completa las oraciones con los pronombres apropiados.

1. A _______ me gusta el café.
2. Susana no bebe café. A _______ le gustan solamente los jugos.
3. Tenemos vecinos (*neighbors*) muy divertidos. Conversamos mucho con _______.
4. Jorge, no puedo ir al partido _______. Lo siento mucho.
5. Entre _______ y _______, no me gusta la clase del profesor Suárez.
6. Si no estás con ellas, hablan mal de _______.

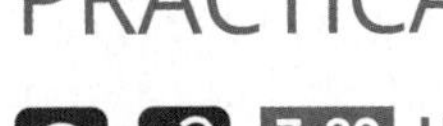

e **7-32 Un amigo preguntón.** Un amigo de Rosario le hace muchas preguntas. Selecciona la respuesta lógica de Rosario a cada pregunta. Luego compara tus respuestas con las de tu compañero/a.

1. _____ ¿Con quién vas a ir al partido de tenis, Rosario?
2. _____ ¿Por qué no vemos la final del campeonato con Sofía?
3. _____ Rosario, ¿para quién es esta raqueta de tenis?
4. _____ ¿Pueden ir mis amigos al partido con nosotros?
5. _____ Después del partido de ayer encontramos una sudadera. ¿Es de Carlos?
6. _____ ¿De quién van a recibir el trofeo los ganadores?

a. La compré para ti.
b. Imposible. No podemos ir con ellos. Tengo solo dos billetes.
c. Contigo, ¡por supuesto!
d. Sí, es de él.
e. De nosotros. De ti y de mí. ¡Qué emocionante!
f. Prefiero verla sin ella. Habla mucho y no puedo concentrarme.

Cultura

Tango y lunfardo en el Río de la Plata The partner dance and music of **tango** originated in the 1880s in the largely immigrant-based, lower class districts of Buenos Aires and Montevideo, along the River Plate (**Río de la Plata**). Both the music and dance are the result of cultural fusion from African, European, and Native American rhythms. **Tango** invites dancers to embrace, lead and follow one another, and connect chest-to-chest or in the upper hip area of the body. According to some, **tango** has also become a source of physical and social activity that promotes relaxation, cures depression, and slows down aging.

The shores of the River Plate are also the birthplace of **lunfardo,** a local dialect derived from the region of Lombardy, in Italy, and mixed with Spanish and some French words. **Lunfardo** began as prison slang at the end of the 19th century and became common in **tango** lyrics.

Conexiones ¿Es el baile considerado una actividad física entre las personas en tu comunidad? ¿Sabes de algún tipo de música o baile que surgió de la fusión de culturas? ¿Qué música en tu país se relaciona en sus orígenes con condiciones de vida difíciles? ¿Conoces algún dialecto derivado de la fusión de otras lenguas?

7-33 ¿Con quién va?

PREPARACIÓN. Completa la siguiente conversación usando pronombres.

CAMILA: Hola, Julia, ¿qué plan tienes para esta noche? Pedro y yo vamos a ir a bailar tango. ¿Quieres venir con (1) ________?

JULIA: No, no puedo ir con (2) ________ hoy. Tengo que entrenar para el partido de tenis de mañana.

CAMILA: ¡Ah, claro! Entonces, ¿nos vemos tú y yo el sábado para ir de compras?

JULIA: Sí, me gustaría ir de compras (3) ________. Necesito una camiseta nueva y hay buenas rebajas en el Centro Comercial Río de la Plata.

CAMILA: Fantástico. Mi hermana está de visita (4) ________ estos días. Voy a hablar con (5) ________ para decirle que vamos las tres juntas.

JULIA: Estupendo. Saludos a Pedro. Que lo pases bien con (6) ________.

CAMILA: Y tú, ¡suerte con el partido mañana!

INTERCAMBIOS. Usen la conversación entre Camila y Julia como modelo para conversar sobre sus propios planes para el fin de semana.

7-34 Fotos de vacaciones.

PREPARACIÓN. Patricia le está mostrando a su prima Kelsey unas fotos de sus vacaciones en Punta del Este. Contesta sus preguntas usando pronombres.

KELSEY: Son tus amigos uruguayos, ¿verdad? ¿Cuándo fueron contigo a la playa?

PATRICIA: ______________________________

KELSEY: ¿Quiénes son las chicas junto (*next*) a ti?

PATRICIA: ______________________________

KELSEY: ¿Y los chicos al lado de ellas?

PATRICIA: ______________________________

KELSEY: ¿Quiénes más fueron a la playa con ustedes?

PATRICIA: ______________________________

KELSEY: ¿Jugaron al vóleibol con aquellos chicos?

PATRICIA: ______________________________

INTERCAMBIOS. Muéstrale a tu compañero/a una foto con tus amigos/as. Háganse preguntas para hablar de las personas y actividades en las fotos.

 **7-35 Haciendo planes.** Escoge una de las actividades de cada grupo e invita a tu compañero/a a hacerla contigo.

MODELO ir al cine / teatro / centro

E1: *Ponen la película… en el Cineplex. ¿Quieres ir a verla conmigo?*

E2: *¡Sí! Me encantaría verla contigo.*

E1: *¿Puedes ir conmigo el sábado?*

E2: *Sí, puedo ir contigo. ¿Invitamos a mi hermana a ir con nosotros?*

1. estudiar español / historia / biología
2. ir al parque / al partido de béisbol / al concierto
3. jugar al golf / al tenis / al vóleibol
4. preparar una fiesta de cumpleaños / una cena para un amigo

Situación

PREPARACIÓN. Lean la situación. Luego, compartan ejemplos de vocabulario, gramática y otra información que necesitan para desarrollar la conversación.

Role A. One of your friends, a basketball player, gave you two tickets for tonight's game, but you have no transportation. Call a friend who has a car. After greeting your friend:
a. explain how you got the tickets;
b. invite your friend to go with you; and
c. explain that you have no transportation.

Role B. A friend calls you to invite you to tonight's basketball game. After exchanging greetings:
a. thank your friend for the invitation;
b. respond that you would be delighted to go with him/her;
c. say that you can pick him/her up; and
d. agree on a time and place.

	ROLE A	ROLE B
Vocabulario	Sports-related expressions	Sports-related expressions
Funciones y formas	Explaining the reason for something Preterit Inviting someone to do something with you Making arrangements to meet	Thanking someone Accepting an invitation Making arrangements to meet

INTERCAMBIOS. Practiquen la conversación, incorporando el vocabulario y las funciones de **Preparación**. Luego, represéntenla ante la clase.

5 Talking about the past

ABUELA: ¡Hola! Pasen, pasen. ¿No **vino** Carmen? ¿Está enferma?

MADRE: Está trabajando en un proyecto para su clase de sociología. **Estuvo** en la biblioteca hasta muy tarde anoche, pero no **pudo** terminarlo. Nos **dijo** que le queda mucho por hacer.

***

CARMEN: ¿Mis padres? **Tuvieron** que ir a la casa de mi abuela, pero yo no **quise** ir a otra cena aburrida. Les **dije** una pequeña mentira (*white lie*) sobre un proyecto…

e **Piénsalo.** Indica si las afirmaciones expresan la verdad (**V**) o una mentira (**M**), según la conversación. Luego, escribe el infinitivo que corresponde a los verbos en negrita.

	¿Verdad o mentira?	Infinitivo
1. Carmen **tuvo** que terminar un proyecto.	_____	_______
2. La abuela pregunta por qué Carmen no **vino** a visitarla.	_____	_______
3. Carmen no **quiso** ir a la casa de su abuela.	_____	_______
4. Carmen **estuvo** en la biblioteca toda la noche.	_____	_______
5. Carmen no **pudo** terminar su proyecto ayer.	_____	_______
6. Carmen les **dijo** la verdad a sus padres.	_____	_______

Some irregular preterits

- Some verbs have irregular forms in the preterit because they use different stems than in the present tense. The preterit endings are added to those stems. Note that the **yo, usted, él,** and **ella** preterit endings of these verbs are unstressed and therefore do not have written accents.
- The verbs **hacer, querer,** and **venir** have an **i** in the preterit stem. Note the **c** changes to **z** in the third person singular form of **hacer.**

INFINITIVE	NEW STEM	PRETERIT FORMS
hacer	**hic-**	hice, h**i**ciste, h**i**zo, h**i**cimos, h**i**cisteis, h**i**cieron
querer	**quis-**	qu**i**se, qu**i**siste, qu**i**so, qu**i**simos, qu**i**sisteis, qu**i**sieron
venir	**vin-**	v**i**ne, v**i**niste, v**i**no, v**i**nimos, v**i**nisteis, v**i**nieron

Felipe **hizo** ejercicio esta mañana. — *Felipe exercised this morning.*

Paula la invitó al cine, pero Sonia no **quiso** ir por exceso de trabajo. — *Paula invited her to the movies, but Sonia refused to go due to her heavy workload.*

- The verbs **estar, tener, poder, poner,** and **saber** have a **u** in the preterit stem.

INFINITIVE	NEW STEM	PRETERIT FORMS
estar	**estuv-**	est**u**ve, est**u**viste, est**u**vo, est**u**vimos, est**u**visteis, est**u**vieron
tener	**tuv-**	t**u**ve, t**u**viste, t**u**vo, t**u**vimos, t**u**visteis, t**u**vieron
poder	**pud-**	p**u**de, p**u**diste, p**u**do, p**u**dimos, p**u**disteis, p**u**dieron
poner	**pus-**	p**u**se, p**u**siste, p**u**so, p**u**simos, p**u**sisteis, p**u**sieron
saber	**sup-**	s**u**pe, s**u**piste, s**u**po, s**u**pimos, s**u**pisteis, s**u**pieron

- The verbs **decir, traer,** and all verbs ending in **-ducir** (e.g., **traducir,** *to translate*) have a **j** in the stem and use the ending **-eron** instead of **-ieron. Decir** also has an **i** in the stem.

INFINITIVE	NEW STEM	PRETERIT FORMS
decir	**dij-**	d**ij**e, d**ij**iste, d**ij**o, d**ij**imos, d**ij**isteis, d**ij**eron
traer	**traj-**	tra**j**e, tra**j**iste, tra**j**o, tra**j**imos, tra**j**isteis, tra**j**eron
traducir	**traduj-**	tradu**j**e, tradu**j**iste, tradu**j**o, tradu**j**imos, tradu**j**isteis, tradu**j**eron

Lengua

- The verb **querer** in the preterit followed by an infinitive normally means *to try (but fail) to do something.*

  Quise hacerlo ayer. *I tried to do it yesterday.*

- **Poder** used in the preterit usually means *to manage to do something.*

  Pude hacerlo esta mañana. *I managed to do it this morning.*

- **Saber** in the preterit normally means *to learn* in the sense of *to find out.*

  Supe que llegó anoche. *I learned (found out) that he arrived last night.*

- In **Capítulo 4,** you learned about **hace** (*ago*) with expressions of time to talk about an action or state that began in the past and continues in the present. To indicate states or actions that were completed in the past, use **hace** + *length of time* + **que** + *preterit verb.*

Hace tres años que **fui** a la Copa Mundial.	*I went to the World Cup three years ago.*
Hace dos semanas que Eva **estuvo** enferma.	*Eva was sick two weeks ago.*

- The same meaning can be expressed without **que.** In this case, **hace** + *length of time* may be moved to the end of the sentence.

Hace tres años que **fui** a la Copa Mundial.	*Three years ago I went to the World Cup.*
Fui a la Copa Mundial **hace** tres años.	*I went to the World Cup three years ago.*
Hace dos semanas que Eva **estuvo** enferma.	*Eva was sick two weeks ago.*
Eva **estuvo** enferma **hace** dos semanas.	*Two weeks ago Eva was sick.*

e **¿Comprendes?** Completa las oraciones con el pretérito de los verbos.

1. Hace dos días que Luis _________ (tener) un accidente de automóvil.
2. Otro auto chocó (*crashed*) con él. Luis no _________ (poder) evitar (*avoid*) el accidente.
3. Las amigas de Luis _________ (pedir) una ambulancia para él.
4. Luis _________ (hacer) los trámites (*paperwork*) para su admisión en el hospital.
5. Las amigas les _________ (decir) a las autoridades cómo pasó el accidente.

PRÁCTICA

7-36 ¿Qué hicieron? **PREPARACIÓN.** Indica las tareas que probablemente hicieron, o no, los jugadores de un equipo de hockey antes del partido.

	SÍ	NO
1. poder lavar las sudaderas	_____	_____
2. ver videos de partidos anteriores	_____	_____
3. ponerse los uniformes nuevos	_____	_____
4. hacer ejercicios de calentamiento (*warm-up*)	_____	_____
5. traer los nuevos cascos (*helmets*) a la cancha	_____	_____
6. tener tiempo para estudiar las nuevas estrategias del partido	_____	_____

INTERCAMBIOS. Háganse las preguntas para compartir sus respuestas.

MODELO traer palos nuevos para jugar

E1: *¿Trajeron palos nuevos para jugar?*

E2: *Sí, probablemente los trajeron.*

7-37 Nuestras actividades. **PREPARACIÓN.** Indica las actividades que hiciste la semana pasada. Añade dos actividades más.

1. _____ jugar al golf
2. _____ hacer ejercicio por lo menos (*at least*) dos días
3. _____ reírse al escuchar un cuento o chiste (*joke*)
4. _____ divertirse con los amigos/as
5. _____ traer comida o bebidas a un evento social
6. _____ tener una conversación interesante
7. _____ poder terminar algún proyecto
8. _____ decir una mentira (*lie*) para no ofender a un/a amigo/a

INTERCAMBIOS. Selecciona de la lista en **Preparación** dos actividades que hiciste la semana pasada y una que no hiciste. Dile las tres actividades a tu compañero/a. Él/Ella tiene que hacerte preguntas para averiguar qué actividad **no** hiciste.

MODELO E1: *divertirme con los amigos, tener una conversación interesante, poder terminar algún proyecto*
E2: *¿Tuviste una conversación interesante?*
E1: *Sí, tuve una conversación interesante con mi prima, Lauren.*
E2: *¿Pudiste terminar algún proyecto?*
E1: *No, no pude terminar el proyecto de biología. ¡Correcto!*

7-38 Unos días de descanso. Tu compañero/a estuvo unos días en Argentina (o Uruguay). Hazle preguntas para saber más de su viaje.

1. lugares adonde fue
2. tiempo que estuvo allí
3. cosas interesantes que hizo
4. los lugares que le gustaron más
5. si pudo hablar español y con quién(es)

7-39 ¿Qué ocurrió? Miren las escenas. Túrnense para narrar con detalles qué le ocurrió a Nicolás el día de su cumpleaños. Después, cuéntale a tu compañero/a lo que hiciste tú el día de tu cumpleaños.

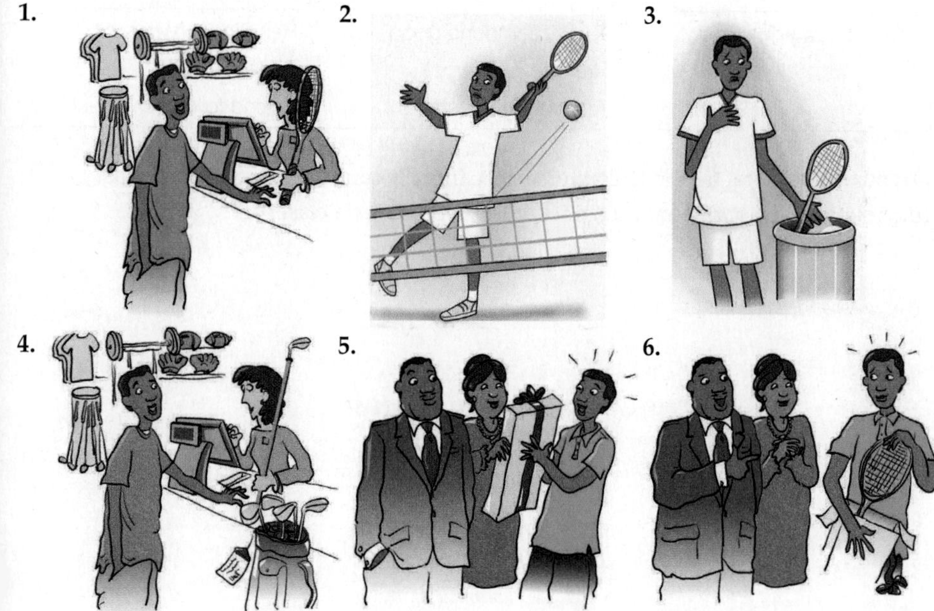

En directo

To express interest and to ask for details:

¡No me digas! ¿Qué pasó? *You don't say! What happened?*

¿Y qué más pasó? *And what else happened?*

¡Cuenta, cuenta! *Tell me more!*

 Listen to a conversation with these expressions.

7-40 Buena y mala suerte. Háganse preguntas para descubrir quiénes tuvieron las siguientes experiencias y cuánto tiempo hace que ocurrieron.

MODELO recibir boletos gratis a un partido de fútbol de la universidad

E1: *¿Quién recibió boletos gratis para el partido de fútbol de la universidad?*

E2: *Mi compañero de cuarto. Está en el equipo.*

E1: *¿Cuánto tiempo hace que los recibió?*

E3: *Hace dos semanas que los recibió. / Los recibió hace dos semanas.*

1. asistir a un partido profesional de fútbol americano
2. ponerse malo/a el día de su graduación
3. celebrar con sus amigos/as un triunfo del equipo de su universidad
4. comprar zapatillas de alta calidad a un precio bajo
5. despertarse con la gripe (*flu*) el día de un partido importante
6. hacer una prueba (*try out*) para un equipo sin éxito (*success*)
7. jugar mal en una competencia importante
8. tomarse una *selfie* con un/a deportista famoso/a

Situación

PREPARACIÓN. Lean la situación. Luego, compartan ejemplos de vocabulario, gramática y otra información que necesitan para desarrollar la conversación.

Role A. Congratulations! You entered a contest (**concurso**) and won an all-expenses-paid trip to attend the World Cup. You are now back from your trip. Tell your classmate that you won the contest and that you went to the World Cup. Answer all of his/her questions in detail.

Role B. Your classmate won a contest and tells you about it. Ask:

a. how he/she found out about the contest;
b. how long he/she was away;
c. how many games he/she attended;
d. with whom he/she went; and
e. details about the last game.

	ROLE A	ROLE B
Vocabulario	Expressions related to a contest and traveling Sports	Expressions related to a contest and traveling Sports
Funciones y formas	Telling someone good news Preterit Answering questions	Reacting to what you hear Preterit Asking follow-up questions

INTERCAMBIOS. Practiquen la conversación, incorporando el vocabulario y las funciones de **Preparación.** Luego, represéntenla ante la clase.

ESCUCHA

Estrategia

Differentiate fact from opinion When you listen to or watch the news or a talk show, you need to distinguish facts from opinions. Facts are provable pieces of information based on statistics, data, and other verifiable evidence. Opinions are personal points of view that combine attitudes and beliefs with factual information.

 **7-41 Preparación.** Hazle preguntas a tu compañero/a para averiguar la siguiente información.

1. si alguna vez fue a otro lugar (ciudad, playa, país, etc.) para practicar o ver un deporte
2. cuándo y con quién fue
3. cómo fue su experiencia en ese lugar

 **7-42 Escucha.** Listen to the interview and write in Spanish three pieces of factual information and three opinions Nicolás offered about the place and/or the people.

 **7-43 Un paso más.** Hagan una lista de los hechos (*facts*) que menciona Nicolás y otra con las opiniones. Compártanlas con la clase.

Comprueba

I was able to . . .

- listen for specific information.
- distinguish facts from opinions.

HABLA

Estrategia

Focus on key information In **Capítulo 6,** you practiced taking notes to understand and remember something you heard. Here you will take the next step: turning your notes into a brief report to present to the class. Follow these steps: 1) decide what aspects of the topic you want to report on; 2) then listen for and take notes on those aspects; and 3) organize your notes for your presentation.

7-44 Preparación. Haz una investigación para averiguar la siguiente información sobre tu deportista favorito/a. Toma notas.

1. nombre, lugar y fecha de nacimiento de tu deportista favorito/a
2. fecha y lugar donde empezó a practicar el deporte, nombre de su primer equipo
3. trofeos o premios (*awards*), cuándo y por qué los recibió

 **7-45 Habla.** Háganse preguntas sobre los/las deportistas que investigaron. Averigüen lo siguiente y tomen notas de las respuestas de su compañero/a.

1. el nombre del / de la deportista favorito/a de su compañero/a
2. dos o tres datos biográficos de este/a deportista
3. información histórica sobre la carrera de este/a deportista
4. contribuciones de este/a deportista a su deporte o equipo

Comprueba

I was able to . . .

- ask comprehensible questions.
- provide relevant information about a well-known sports figure.
- recount biographical facts in chronological sequence.

7-46 Un paso más. Escojan a uno/a de los deportistas que investigaron y preparen una presentación sobre él/ella y su deporte que incluya la información a continuación. Finalmente, preparen una breve prueba (*quiz*) sobre este deportista y su deporte para evaluar cuánto recuerdan sus compañeros/as.

1. nombre y nacionalidad del / de la deportista
2. datos biográficos: fecha y lugar de nacimiento
3. datos sobre la carrera deportiva de este/a deportista: fecha y lugar donde empezó a practicar el deporte, equipo en el que jugó por primera vez
4. contribuciones que hizo a su deporte o equipo
5. su reputación nacional e internacional
6. la reputación de su equipo

En directo

To discuss ideas while working in pairs:

¿Qué te parece si presentamos/destacamos...? *How about if we present/highlight . . .?*

¿Por qué no lees/hablas/miras...? *Why don't you read/say/look at . . .?*

To maintain the interest of listeners:

Hay hechos/datos interesantes sobre... *There are interesting facts about . . .*

La información que tenemos sobre... es increíble. *The information we have about . . . is unbelievable.*

¡Imagínense! Ganó el primer puesto en... *Imagine! He/She won first place in . . .*

Este/a deportista juega al... como nadie. *This athlete plays . . . like no one else.*

Listen to a conversation with these expressions.

LEE

Estrategia

Predict and guess content You may enhance your comprehension of a text by predicting and guessing its content before you start to read. Begin by reading the title and the headings (if any), and looking at the illustrations. Use that information to brainstorm the information you are likely to find in the text and to identify the text format.

7-47 Antes de leer. **PREPARACIÓN.** Mira el texto "Los deportes: una pasión uruguaya". Lee el título y examina las fotos. Busca nombres de lugares y deportes conocidos. Luego, responde a las preguntas.

1. Después de leer el título del texto y mirar las fotos, selecciona el posible tema.
   - **a.** los lugares en Uruguay donde se practican los deportes
   - **b.** los deportistas más famosos de Uruguay
   - **c.** el amor de los uruguayos por los deportes
2. Indica las ideas que probablemente vas a encontrar en el texto.
   - **a.** _____ los deportes más populares de Uruguay
   - **b.** _____ el origen de los deportes de Uruguay
   - **c.** _____ los lugares donde se practican algunos deportes en Uruguay
   - **d.** _____ los campeonatos que ganaron los equipos de fútbol uruguayo
   - **e.** _____ los deportes favoritos de los uruguayos en comparación con los de otros países latinoamericanos

INTERCAMBIOS. Háganse preguntas y compartan la información que recogieron.

1. ¿Te gustan los deportes individuales o prefieres los de equipo? ¿Por qué?
2. ¿Sabes esquiar? ¿Esquías en la nieve o en el agua? ¿Esquías bien o regular?
3. ¿Qué tipos de surf conoces? ¿Alguna vez oíste hablar del surf en la arena (*sand*)? ¿Qué sabes de ese deporte?

7-48 Lee. Lee el artículo y haz lo siguiente:

1. Indica dos razones que explican la popularidad del fútbol en Uruguay.
2. Nombra tres deportes de equipo, dos individuales y uno que no requier una pelota.
3. Explica por qué Punta del Este es un lugar ideal para practicar el surf acuático.

Comprueba

I was able to . . .

- use my knowledge of sports to anticipate the content of the reading.
- distinguish between facts and opinions.
- understand the main ideas and some details in the text.

LOS DEPORTES: UNA PASIÓN URUGUAYA

Uruguay es un país pequeño donde los deportes son fundamentales en la vida de las personas.

Entre las grandes pasiones nacionales está el fútbol. Desde su infancia, muchos uruguayos acompañan con mucha pasión a sus equipos. En varias ocasiones, la selección nacional uruguaya ganó títulos y campeonatos importantes.

Pero los uruguayos también tienen otras pasiones. El básquetbol, el ciclismo, el rugby y el boxeo son otros deportes muy populares. El futsal, o fútbol de sala, es otra pasión nacional. Un profesor en Montevideo lo inventó en 1930, después de ganar Uruguay por primera vez el Campeonato Mundial de Fútbol. Combina aspectos del fútbol, básquetbol y balonmano[1], y se juega en una cancha de básquetbol.

Las playas de Uruguay también favorecen los deportes acuáticos, como la vela[2] y el surf. Uno de los lugares favoritos para practicar el surf es Punta del Este, que está al sureste[3] de Uruguay, a 140 kilómetros de Montevideo. Punta del Este es una península bonita de enormes playas y rocas. Tiene bosques, con árboles de varios tipos y dunas de arena.

Precisamente en estas dunas se practica una variante del surf: el surf en la arena o *sandsurf.* También se llama *sandboard.* Este deporte ganó popularidad hace 40 años para divertirse en las playas cuando no había olas[4] grandes. Es muy popular en Uruguay, ya que tiene muchas playas bonitas con dunas enormes. Las dunas de Valizas, que son las más grandes de Sudamérica, están entre las mejores de todo el planeta para practicar *sandsurf.* La duna conocida como El Gran Vali es la favorita de los *sandsurfers.* Es uno de los puntos más altos del lugar, con unas vistas hermosas.

Sin embargo[5], el tema del *sandsurf* en las dunas es polémico[6]. Las autoridades uruguayas controlan, e incluso prohíben, la práctica de este deporte en algunas dunas por el deterioro ecológico que causa. Pero las prohibiciones no van a afectar el espíritu activo de los uruguayos, quienes van a buscar o inventar otras opciones para entretenerse.

[1]*handball* [2]*sailing* [3]*southeast* [4]*waves* [5]*Nevertheless* [6]*controversial*

 **7-49 Un paso más.** Seleccionen un deporte. Descríbanlo incluyendo la información que se pide en la lista a continuación. Luego, presenten la información a la clase sin mencionar el nombre del deporte. Sus compañeros/as van a adivinar cuál es.

1. lugar donde se practica
2. deporte individual o en grupo (número de personas en el equipo)
3. en qué clima o estación se practica
4. un jugador famoso / una jugadora famosa del deporte
5. otra información relevante

ESCRIBE

Estrategia

Use supporting details Supporting details are facts and examples that follow the topic sentence and make up the body of a paragraph. They should support the main idea of the paragraph and be placed in a logical order. You should then write a closing sentence that summarizes your main point.

7-50 Preparación. Lee otra vez el texto en **7-48** sobre la pasión de los uruguayos por el deporte y responde a estas preguntas.

1. ¿Qué razones se mencionan en el artículo para justificar la pasión de los uruguayos por el fútbol? ¿Cómo se compara esto con tu cultura?
2. ¿Qué dos deportes mencionados en el artículo son menos conocidos en tu cultura? ¿Por qué?
3. ¿Cuáles son los problemas que, según el artículo, se asocian con los deportes de playa? ¿Hay otros problemas que se asocian con los deportes donde tú vives?

 **7-51 Escribe.** Un/a estudiante de Uruguay va a pasar un año en tu universidad y quiere información sobre la relación de los norteamericanos con los deportes. Escribe uno o dos párrafos sobre un deporte popular en tu universidad / país y las pasiones positivas y negativas que provoca. Usa la información de **7-50** para escribir tu informe. Incluye lo siguiente:

1. el deporte y tus razones para elegirlo
2. por qué es popular y si es popular en todas las universidades / regiones
3. cómo muestra la gente su pasión por este deporte
4. tu participación o no participación en estas actividades, y por qué

Comprueba

I was able to . . .

- select a sport and justify my selection.
- describe fan activities related to a sport.
- provide a personal perspective on fan activities related to a sport.

En directo

To explain a concept:

Los expertos afirman que... Dan tres razones: ... *The experts say that . . . They give three reasons: . . .*

Cuando usamos la palabra..., significa... *When we use the word . . ., it means . . .*

To express an opinion:

No comparto la opinión de la mayoría... *I don't share the majority opinion . . .*

En mi opinión... *In my opinion . . .*

A mí me parece que... *It seems to me that . . .*

 Listen to a conversation with these expressions.

 **7-52 Un paso más.** Comparte tu informe con tu compañero/a y háganse preguntas relacionadas.

En este capítulo...

Vocabulario

Los deportes	Sports
el atletismo	*track and field*
el baloncesto / el básquetbol	*basketball*
el béisbol	*baseball*
el campeonato	*championship*
el campo	*field; course* (golf)
la cancha	*court*
el ciclismo	*cycling*
los deportes de riesgo	*extreme sports*
el esquí	*skiing*
el fútbol (americano)	*soccer (football)*
el golf	*golf*
el hockey sobre hierba	*field hockey*
la natación	*swimming*
el parapente	*paragliding*
el partido	*game, match*
el penalti	*penalty* (in sports)
la pista	*ski slope; track* (running)
el tenis	*tennis*
el vóleibol	*volleyball*

Las personas	People
el/la árbitro/a	*umpire, referee*
el/la beisbolista	*baseball player*
el campeón / la campeona	*champion*
el/la deportista	*athlete*
el/la entrenador/a	*coach*
el equipo	*team*
el/la hincha	*fan*
el/la jugador/a	*player*
el/la tenista	*tennis player*

El equipo deportivo	Sports equipment
el bate	*bat*
el balón / la pelota	*ball*
el bastón de esquí	*ski pole*
el cesto / la cesta	*basket, hoop*
los esquís	*skis*
los palos de golf	*golf clubs*
la raqueta	*racquet*
la red	*net*

El tiempo	Weather
está despejado	*it's clear*
está nublado	*it's cloudy*
hace calor	*it's hot*
hace fresco	*it's cool*
hace frío	*it's cold*
hace viento	*it's windy*
el hielo	*ice*
la lluvia	*rain*
la nieve	*snow*

La naturaleza	Nature
el árbol	*tree*
el lago	*lake*
la planta	*plant*

Verbos	Verbs
congelar(se)	*to freeze*
construir	*to build, to develop*
despedirse (i, i)	*to say goodbye*
destruir	*to destroy*
discutir	*to argue*
enojarse	*to get angry*
esquiar	*to ski*
ganar	*to win*
hacer surf	*to surf*
jugar (ue, u) a los bolos	*to bowl*
levantar pesas	*to lift weights*
llover (ue)	*to rain*
meter un gol	*to score a goal*
morir (ue, u)	*to die*
nevar (ie)	*to snow*
patinar	*to skate*
perder (ie)	*to lose*
pitar	*to whistle*
preparar(se)	*to train*
reír(se) (i, i)	*to laugh*
traducir (zc)	*to translate*

Palabras y expresiones útiles	Useful words and expressions
cada	*each*
conmigo	*with me*
contigo	*with you* (familiar)
contrario/a	*opposing*
el triunfo	*triumph*

See page 262 for other reflexive verbs.
See page 269 for other stem-changing **-ir** verbs.

Capítulo 8

¿Cuáles son tus tradiciones?

Día de los Muertos en Guanajuato, México

Learning Outcomes

You will be able to:

- discuss situations and celebrations
- describe conditions and express ongoing actions in the past
- tell stories about past events
- compare people and things
- talk about Mexico in terms of products, practices, and perspectives
- share information about celebrations in Hispanic countries and make cultural comparisons

Enfoque cultural

México

Figura de la princesa Donají, hecha de rábanos (*radishes*), en la celebración de la Noche de Rábanos, en Oaxaca

Entrada al cenote de Kankirixché, en Yucatán, México

El templo maya de Kukulcán, en Chichén Itzá, en la península de Yucatán

Arte hispano

La pintora mexicana Frida Kahlo pintó este cuadro en 1932. Su título es *Autorretrato en la frontera entre México y Estados Unidos*.

Enfoque cultural

¿Qué te parece?

- El nombre completo del país es Estados Unidos Mexicanos. Hay 31 estados más la capital, Ciudad de México.
- Cuando llegaron los españoles a México en 1519, existían civilizaciones indígenas muy avanzadas, como los olmecas, los toltecas, los mayas y los aztecas.
- El Día de la Independencia de México es el 16 de septiembre, no el 5 de mayo como muchos piensan. Este es el día en que un grupo de criollos y campesinos indígenas se rebelaron (*revolted*) contra España en 1810.
- Millones de mariposas (*butterflies*) monarcas migran cada año a México desde Estados Unidos y Canadá.
- Las fiestas y tradiciones de México muestran el mestizaje (*fusion*) y la riqueza (*richness*) de su cultura. Por ejemplo, algunas figuras de la religión católica, como la Virgen de Guadalupe, tienen características indígenas.

Tulum es la única ciudad maya construida en la costa de la península de Yucatán. Al igual que en otras ciudades mayas y aztecas, en Tulum también hay pirámides.

Cabo San Lucas, en la costa del Pacífico, tiene playas que atraen a los turistas a México. Es especialmente popular entre actores y actrices de Estados Unidos y otros países.

San Cristóbal de las Casas es la ciudad más importante de la región de Chiapas, en el centro del país. Es famosa por su arquitectura colonial y por sus festividades, como la Semana Santa (*Holy Week*) y la Feria de la Primavera y la Paz.

El Museo Nacional de Antropología, situado dentro del Bosque de Chapultepec en Ciudad de México, exhibe la mayor colección del mundo de piezas arqueológicas de la cultura precolombina. Dentro de los jardines del museo hay una réplica del templo maya de Hochob.

¿Cuánto sabes? Completa las oraciones con la información correcta.

1. Las ruinas de la ciudad de Tulum se encuentran en la península de ____________________.
2. El 16 de septiembre se celebra la ____________________.
3. La Noche de Rábanos se celebra en ____________________, México.
4. Un lugar del Pacífico que atrae a muchos turistas es ____________________.
5. Los españoles llegaron a lo que hoy es México en ____________________.
6. Cada año llegan a México millones de ____________________.

To learn more about Mexico, go online to view the *Club cultura* videos.

VOCABULARIO EN CONTEXTO

Discussing traditions and celebrations

Las fiestas y las tradiciones

La Alborada

A finales de septiembre se **celebran** las **fiestas** de San Miguel Arcángel en la **hermosa** ciudad de San Miguel de Allende. Estas celebraciones, que culminan con la popular Alborada, **duran** dos días y simbolizan la lucha (*struggle*) entre el Arcángel Miguel y Lucifer, es decir, entre el bien y el mal. Las fiestas **comienzan** a las cuatro de la mañana, con música de mariachis y espectaculares **fuegos artificiales.** A las cuatro de la tarde hay un **desfile** religioso y pagano donde se hacen **ofrendas** de plantas, los *xuchiles.* **Por último, desfilan** las mojigangas, enormes **muñecos** de papel maché.

El Día de los Muertos

El Día de los Muertos, también conocido como el Día de los Difuntos, se conmemora el 2 de noviembre. En México, los **preparativos** para el Día de los Muertos comienzan **con** mucha **anterioridad.** Mucha **gente se reúne** en el **cementerio** para **recordar** a sus familiares y amigos difuntos. Limpian las tumbas y las decoran con flores y **velas.** Algunas familias **acompañan** a sus muertos con comida, cuentos y canciones en el cementerio durante la noche del 1 al 2 de noviembre.

La Diablada

Las fiestas y los bailes que se celebran en diversas partes del mundo ayudan a **mantener** las **costumbres** de los **antepasados.** La Diablada es uno de los **festivales** folclóricos con más colorido en Hispanoamérica. Se celebra durante el **Carnaval** de Oruro en Bolivia y también en el norte de Chile y en otros países, entre ellos, Perú.

El Carnaval

La música, el baile y la **alegría** son características de los carnavales. Hay desfiles de **carrozas** y **comparsas** que bailan en las calles, muchas personas **se disfrazan** y todo el mundo se divierte. El **último** día del Carnaval es el martes antes del **comienzo** de la Cuaresma (*Lent*).

La Semana Santa

En muchos lugares de España y Latinoamérica se celebra la Semana Santa. Una de las **celebraciones** más interesantes es la de Antigua, en Guatemala. En el pasado, esta ciudad fue la capital de Guatemala. Es famosa por su arquitectura colonial y por las **maravillosas** alfombras que se hacen con flores, **semillas** y aserrín (*sawdust*) para el paso de las **procesiones.**

El Día de San Fermín

El 7 de julio, Día de San Fermín, se inicia la celebración de los sanfermines en Pamplona, España. Esta celebración dura del 7 al 14 de julio. Es famosa mundialmente por los encierros, una **tradición** en que los jóvenes corren por las calles seguidos de los **toros.**

> **Lengua**
>
> The words **fiesta, festividad,** and **festival** are often used interchangeably. **Fiesta** may mean a holiday or a party or celebration. **Festividad** normally refers to a public festivity or a holiday. **Festival** often involves a series of events or celebrations of a public nature. Another term for *holiday* is **día festivo. Día feriado** is a legal holiday.

PRÁCTICA

8-1 Escucha y confirma. Indicate whether the descriptions you hear are related to **Carnaval, Día de los Muertos,** or **ninguno de los dos** (*neither*).

	Carnaval	Día de los Muertos	Ninguno de los dos
1.	_____	_____	_____
2.	_____	_____	_____
3.	_____	_____	_____
4.	_____	_____	_____
5.	_____	_____	_____
6.	_____	_____	_____

Cultura

Fiestas El Día de Acción de Gracias (*Thanksgiving*) no se celebra en los países hispanos y tampoco (*neither*) es tradicional el Día de las Brujas (*Halloween*), aunque (*although*) empieza a celebrarse en algunas ciudades de Hispanoamérica y de España. Por la importancia e influencia de la religión católica en los países hispanos, algunas fiestas católicas se consideran también fiestas oficiales y son días feriados. Por otro lado, hay gran diversidad de fiestas locales. Muchas personas trabajan todo el año para garantizar el éxito (*success*) de estas celebraciones.

Comparaciones ¿Hay fiestas religiosas en tu comunidad? ¿Son fiestas oficiales? ¿Cómo se celebran? ¿Hay feriados seculares? ¿Cuáles son?

  **8-2 Definiciones.** Selecciona la descripción que corresponde a cada festividad. Después, compara tus respuestas con las de tu compañero/a y dile a cuáles de ellas te gustaría asistir y por qué.

1. _____ el Día de San Fermín
2. _____ la Diablada
3. _____ la Alborada
4. _____ el Carnaval
5. _____ el Día de los Muertos
6. _____ la Semana Santa

a. Se celebra durante el Carnaval de Oruro en Bolivia. Muchas personas bailan en las calles disfrazadas de demonios.
b. Muchas personas se disfrazan y bailan en comparsas por las calles.
c. Todos van al cementerio a hacer ofrendas a los difuntos.
d. Hay procesiones por las calles y en Antigua, Guatemala, se hacen unas alfombras de aserrín, flores y semillas.
e. Los jóvenes corren por las calles delante de los toros.
f. Comienza a las cuatro de la mañana y hay fuegos artificiales.

 **8-3 Imágenes.** Escojan una de las fotos de las fiestas en las páginas 287–288 y descríbanla detalladamente contestando las siguientes preguntas.

1. ¿Qué están haciendo las personas?
2. ¿Qué llevan? ¿Qué colores hay en la foto?
3. ¿Qué objetos hay? ¿Para qué sirven?
4. ¿Piensan que esta festividad es religiosa? ¿Por qué?
5. Según ustedes, ¿es divertida la festividad? ¿Por qué?

 **8-4 Contextos.** PREPARACIÓN. Hablen sobre las ideas, sentimientos o costumbres que se relacionan con las siguientes palabras.

MODELO el Carnaval
música, baile, alegría, mucha gente por la calle, carrozas…

1. los cementerios
2. los toros
3. los disfraces
4. el baile

INTERCAMBIOS. Escriban por lo menos cuatro oraciones usando las palabras que anotaron en **Preparación.**

MODELO *El Carnaval es una fiesta muy alegre. La gente se disfraza y baila por las calles.*

Otras celebraciones

la Nochebuena

la Navidad

la Nochevieja / el Fin de Año

el Año Nuevo

el Día de la Independencia de México

la Pascua

el Día de la Madre

el Día del Padre

el Día de Acción de Gracias

el Día de las Brujas

el Día de los Enamorados / del Amor y de la Amistad

Cultura

La Navidad En muchos países hispanos, los niños reciben regalos de Papá Noel o del Niño Dios el día de Navidad. Sin embargo, la Nochebuena se considera la fiesta más importante. Muchos católicos van a la iglesia (*church*) a la medianoche para asistir a la Misa del Gallo (*Midnight Mass*). El 6 de enero, Día de la Epifanía o de los Reyes Magos, se celebra la llegada de estos reyes con sus regalos para el Niño Jesús. La noche del 5 de enero, muchos niños se acuestan esperando la visita de los tres reyes que llegan montados en sus camellos con regalos para ellos.

Comparaciones En tu cultura, ¿existen celebraciones en que las personas se dan regalos? ¿Hay alguna tradición especial para los niños? ¿Hay celebraciones infantiles que no son religiosas?

Los Reyes Magos en México

PRÁCTICA

8-5 Para confirmar.

PREPARACIÓN. Selecciona el día festivo que corresponde a cada fecha. Compara tus respuestas con las de tu compañero/a.

1. _____ el 25 de diciembre
2. _____ el 2 de noviembre
3. _____ el 6 de enero
4. _____ el 4 de julio
5. _____ el 24 de diciembre
6. _____ el 31 de diciembre
7. _____ el 14 de febrero
8. _____ el 31 de octubre

a. el Día de la Independencia de Estados Unidos
b. el Día de las Brujas
c. la Nochebuena
d. la Nochevieja / el Fin de Año
e. el Día de los Enamorados / del Amor y de la Amistad
f. el Día de los Reyes Magos
g. el Día de los Muertos
h. la Navidad

INTERCAMBIOS. Compartan sus respuestas a las siguientes preguntas.

1. ¿Cuál(es) de las fiestas de **Preparación** celebran ustedes?
2. ¿Cuál es la fiesta favorita de la mayoría de las personas del grupo, y por qué?
3. ¿En cuál de estas fiestas reciben ustedes regalos? ¿Qué tipo de regalos?
4. ¿En cuál de estas fiestas hay una comida especial?

8-6 Festivales o desfiles. Piensa en algunos festivales o desfiles importantes y completa la información. Tu compañero/a va a hacerte preguntas sobre ellos.

MODELO E1: *¿En qué fiesta o desfile importante estás pensando?*
E2: *En el Día de los Reyes Magos.*
E1: *¿Cuándo lo celebran?*
E2: *El 6 de enero.*
E1: *¿Dónde lo celebran?*
E2: *En México, España y otros lugares.*
E1: *¿Cómo es…?*
E2: …
E1: *¿Qué opinas de…?*
E2: …

Festival o desfile	Fecha	Lugar	Descripción	Opinión

8-7 Unos días festivos. Hablen sobre cómo celebran ustedes estas fechas.

MODELO tu cumpleaños
E1: *¿Cómo celebras tu cumpleaños?*
E2: *Lo celebro con mis amigos. Salimos a cenar o los invito a mi apartamento para ver una película. A veces voy a casa para celebrarlo con mi familia.*

1. la Nochevieja / el Fin de Año
2. el Día de las Brujas
3. el Día de Acción de Gracias
4. el Día de la Independencia
5. el Año Nuevo
6. el Día de la Madre

Cultura

Tradiciones curiosas Existen diferentes tradiciones relacionadas con el último día del año. En España a las 12 en punto de la noche del 31 de diciembre, se comen 12 uvas (*grapes*), una por una, siguiendo cada campanada (*bell strike*). En México, hay personas que salen a la calle con maletas vacías (*empty suitcases*) para simbolizar los viajes (*trips*) que van a hacer durante el nuevo año. Y en Argentina, la gente enciende (*light*) tres velas: verde para la esperanza, roja para espantar (*scare away*) malas energías y amarilla para la abundancia.

Comparaciones ¿Qué tradiciones existen en tu país en la última noche del año? ¿Existe alguna tradición especial en tu familia?

 **8-8 Una celebración importante.** **PREPARACIÓN.** Escojan una celebración importante del mundo hispano (Carnaval, Semana Santa, Año Nuevo, las Posadas, la Diablada, el Día de la Independencia, etc.). Busquen información en internet sobre los siguientes aspectos:

1. el lugar donde se celebra
2. el período del año
3. las actividades
4. los vestidos o disfraces
5. la comida u otro aspecto relevante de la festividad

INTERCAMBIOS. Preparen una presentación breve sobre la celebración que escogieron y preséntenla a la clase.

Las invitaciones

 **¿Quieres salir conmigo?**

LUISA: Hola, Arturo, ¿qué tal?
ARTURO: Bien, Luisa, ¿y tú?
LUISA: **Estupendamente.** ¿Qué planes tienes para Nochevieja? Debemos cenar juntos.
ARTURO: Me gustaría mucho, pero no puedo porque esa noche tenemos la cena familiar.
LUISA: Está bien. ¿Qué tal si hacemos algo después de cenar?
ARTURO: ¡Qué buena idea! Creo que hay fuegos artificiales en la plaza después de las doce. Te **invito** a celebrar el Año Nuevo en mi casa y luego a **dar una vuelta** por la plaza.
LUISA: Sí, **¡cómo no!** Podemos ir a uno de los bares que hay cerca de la plaza. Tienen música **en vivo,** con buenos grupos musicales, y la gente está muy **animada.**
ARTURO: Bueno, **entonces** nos vemos en mi casa el 31 **a eso de** las once y media.
LUISA: Fenomenal, Arturo. **Tengo muchas ganas de** celebrar el Año Nuevo contigo.

PRÁCTICA

 **8-9 Para confirmar.** Con tu compañero/a, lee la conversación entre José y Federico. Después, invita a tu compañero/a a hacer algo juntos/as. Luego, tu compañero/a va a invitarte a ti.

JOSÉ: Hola, Federico, ¿cómo estás?
FEDERICO: Bien, José, ¿y tú?
JOSÉ: Estupendamente. Mira, me gustaría invitarte a mi casa el sábado para ver el partido de fútbol.
FEDERICO: ¡Qué buena idea! ¿A qué hora es el partido?
JOSÉ: A las seis. Voy a invitar a Elena y a Pedro también.
FEDERICO: Perfecto. Yo puedo llevar unas bebidas.
JOSÉ: Muy bien. Entonces, nos vemos el sábado en mi casa.
FEDERICO: Hasta el sábado.

En directo

To accept an invitation:

Gracias. Me encanta la idea. *Thanks. I love the idea.*

Con mucho gusto. *With great pleasure.*

Encantado/a. *Delighted.*

Será un placer. *It will be a pleasure.*

To decline an invitation:

Me gustaría ir, pero... *I would like to go, but . . .*

¡Qué lástima/pena! Ese día tengo que... *What a pity! That day I have to . . .*

No puedo, tengo un compromiso. *I can't, I have plans.*

 Listen to a conversation with these expressions.

8-10 Una invitación de boda. Lean la invitación de boda (*wedding*) y la de la recepción y contesten las preguntas. Luego, preparen una lista con las diferencias que encuentren entre estas invitaciones y las de su país.

Agradecemos su presencia
después de la ceremonia religiosa
en el Club de Golf Chapultepec
Av. Conscripto N° 425, Lomas
Hipódromo

R.S.V.P.
529-99-43
520-16-85

Personal

Pedro Martín Salda
Juana Montoya de Martín

Eduardo Calderón Solís
Elisa Noriega de Calderón

participan el matrimonio de sus hijos

ESTELITA
Y
ALBERTO

y tienen el honor de invitarle a la ceremonia
religiosa que se celebrará el viernes 9 de febrero,
a las diecinueve treinta horas en el Convento de
San Joaquín, Santa Cruz Cocalco N° 15,
Legaria, dignándose a impartir la
bendición nupcial
el R.P. José Ortuno S.J.
Ciudad de México

1. ¿Cómo se llaman los padres de los novios?
2. ¿Cómo se llaman los novios?
3. ¿A qué hora es la boda?
4. ¿En qué país se celebra esta boda?
5. ¿Adónde van a ir los invitados después de la ceremonia?

Cultura

La quinceañera En muchos lugares de Latinoamérica, las jóvenes celebran su 15 cumpleaños con una gran fiesta. La celebración se conoce como **la fiesta de los quince.** Esta celebración marca la transición de la niñez a la juventud. Normalmente, los familiares y amigos se reúnen para compartir comida y para bailar. La niña homenajeada (*honored*) se llama **la quinceañera,** igual que la celebración.

Comparaciones ¿Hay una celebración similar a la fiesta de la quinceañera en tu comunidad o país? ¿Cómo se llama? ¿Y cómo se celebra? ¿Quiénes asisten a esta fiesta?

8-11 Tarjetas digitales. **PREPARACIÓN.** Lee las siguientes invitaciones a las celebraciones. Toma notas de lo siguiente:

1. el tipo de fiesta o celebración
2. la fecha
3. el lugar

Guadalupe Torres Quiero invitarlos a celebrar conmigo y mi familia mis 15 años de vida. 3 de mayo, 20:30 horas Club Campestre Puebla, México	Ana y Eduardo Nos mudamos de casa. Amigos y familia: Queremos invitarlos a la inauguración de nuestra nueva casa. Sábado, 25 de abril. 18:00 horas. Las Amapolas 4, Veracruz	Andrés García Te invito a ti y a tus amigos a mi fiesta de graduación. Baile y música en vivo. Barra libre. A partir de las 21:00 horas Club de Salsa Tolima, en Zona Rosa

INTERCAMBIOS. Invita a tres compañeros/as diferentes a cada una de las fiestas o celebraciones. Tu compañero/a va a aceptar o declinar la invitación.

MODELO E1: *¿Quieres venir conmigo a la fiesta de cumpleaños de Mario?*
E2: *¿Me gustaría. Pero, ¿cuándo es?*
E1: *Es en su casa el viernes a las ocho.*
E2: *Con mucho gusto. ¿Paso a recogerte o me recoges tú? / Pues no puedo. Tengo un compromiso.*

8-12 Una fiesta especial. **PREPARACIÓN.** Piensa en una celebración o fiesta en la que participaste recientemente y descríbele la fiesta a tu compañero/a. Usa las siguientes preguntas como guía.

1. ¿A qué fiesta fuiste? ¿Quién te invitó?
2. ¿Dónde se celebró? ¿Cuántos invitados asistieron?
3. ¿Cuándo fue la fiesta? ¿A qué hora empezó? ¿Cuánto tiempo duró?
4. ¿Qué comida sirvieron?
5. ¿Cómo se divirtió la gente? ¿Qué música tocaron?

INTERCAMBIOS. Ahora compara tu fiesta con la de tu compañero/a y busquen algunas diferencias entre las dos fiestas.

8-13 La fiesta. **PREPARACIÓN.** Before you listen to four short conversations about different holidays, tell your partner one or two things you know about each holiday listed in **Escucha.**

ESCUCHA. You will hear four conversations. Indicate the number of the conversation that corresponds to each holiday. Check answers with a classmate.

_____ el Día del Amor y de la Amistad / de los Enamorados
_____ el Día de los Muertos
_____ el Día de los Reyes Magos
_____ el Día de las Brujas

Mosaico cultural

Las tradiciones y la diversidad cultural

En muchas celebraciones tradicionales, se mezclan (*mix*) costumbres paganas y religiosas. Por ejemplo, en el Carnaval de Barranquilla, en Colombia, se celebra la diversidad cultural del Caribe con sus tradiciones indígenas, africanas y europeas. Esta fusión cultural se ve en los bailes: el **paloteo** es de origen español, pero el **congo** es de origen africano. Este carnaval es el más grande del mundo hispano, y dura una semana entera. Aproximadamente dos millones de personas de todo el mundo se reúnen para ver los desfiles, disfraces, bailes y alegría que llenan las calles cada día.

El Carnaval de Barranquilla es el más grande del mundo después del de Río de Janeiro.

Muchas otras festividades tienen orígenes culturales diversos. Por ejemplo, las cometas o los papalotes (*kites*) fueron inventados en China, así como la pólvora (*gunpowder*) que se utiliza en los fuegos artificiales. En el mundo hispano hay festivales, como el de Tequisquiapán, en México, donde niños y grandes hacen volar (*fly*) cada año sus típicos papalotes decorados. En el festival de Sacatepéquez, en Guatemala, que se celebra el 1 de noviembre, se exhiben cometas gigantes para celebrar el Día de los Muertos.

Cometas en Sacatepéquez, Guatemala

Compara

1. ¿Qué tipo de carnavales o fiestas tradicionales existen en tu país o región? ¿Qué tienen en común con las del mundo hispano? Explica.
2. Cuando eras niño/a, ¿participabas en tradiciones familiares como elevar cometas? ¿Qué tradiciones son importantes en tu cultura?
3. ¿Qué celebración se transmite de generación en generación en tu familia? ¿Cómo es esta celebración?

En acción

Hay que celebrar

Antes de ver

8-14 Las tradiciones. Selecciona las tradiciones que asocias con la cultura hispana. Luego, compara tus respuestas con las de tu compañero/a.

1. _____ el Día de los Muertos
2. _____ el Cinco de Mayo
3. _____ las corridas de toros
4. _____ el Día de las Brujas
5. _____ el Día de Acción de Gracias
6. _____ la Copa Mundial de Fútbol
7. _____ el festival de la Calle Ocho
8. _____ el Cuatro de Julio

Mientras ves

8-15 Unas celebraciones importantes. Indica si las siguientes afirmaciones se refieren a la fiesta de La Mercé (**LM**) o al Día de los Muertos (**DM**), según el video.

1. _____ Es una fiesta en honor a la Virgen.
2. _____ Se celebra el primero y el dos de noviembre.
3. _____ Las familias hacen procesiones hasta el cementerio.
4. _____ Hay espectáculos con música, bailes y desfiles con dragones.
5. _____ Algunas personas forman castillos (*castles*) o torres (*towers*) humanas.
6. _____ Las calaveras de azúcar (*sugar skulls*) son típicas de esta celebración.

Video

Después de ver

8-16 Días festivos.

PREPARACIÓN. Indica las afirmaciones que contienen ideas que aparecen en el video. Después, compara tus respuestas con las de tu compañero/a.

1. _____ Muchas celebraciones de América Latina muestran la fusión de la cultura española y de las culturas precolombinas.
2. _____ Algunas fiestas hispanas se celebran también en Estados Unidos.
3. _____ El Día de los Muertos es una celebración en homenaje (*homage*) a las personas que murieron.
4. _____ Las fiestas del mundo hispano son diferentes según la clase social.

INTERCAMBIOS. Háganse estas preguntas relacionadas con las celebraciones.

1. Piensen en una celebración del mundo hispano. ¿Cómo se celebra? ¿Qué características tiene?
2. ¿Qué diferencias hay entre las celebraciones personales o familiares (cumpleaños, día del santo, bautismo, *Bar Mitzvah,* matrimonio, etc.) y las celebraciones cívicas (carnaval, fiestas de independencia, Día de las Brujas, etc.)?

1 Expressing ongoing actions and describing in the past

ABUELA: Hijita, ¡qué diferentes eran mis tiempos! **Antes** no **había** teléfonos móviles ni internet. La gente **leía** más libros y periódicos. Los amigos **se escribían** cartas (*letters*) y **se mandaban** postales. **Hoy en día** la gente no tiene tiempo para nada, y las personas quieren todo al instante.

NIETA: Abuela, pero antes todo **era** más aburrido. Los amigos no **se comunicaban** por mensajes de texto, ni **se mandaban** fotos. Además, antes **era** más difícil acceder a la información. Hoy en día hacemos muchas cosas a la vez.

Piénsalo. Indica a qué función se refiere cada afirmación.

CONDICIÓN O ACTIVIDAD	DESCRIPCIÓN DE UN ESTADO EN EL PASADO	ACTIVIDAD HABITUAL EN EL PASADO	ACTIVIDAD EN EL PRESENTE
1. Antes no **había** teléfonos móviles.	_____	_____	_____
2. La gente **leía** más libros y periódicos.	_____	_____	_____
3. Los amigos **se escribían** cartas y **se mandaban** postales.	_____	_____	_____
4. Todo **era** más aburrido.	_____	_____	_____
5. **Hacemos** muchas cosas a la vez.	_____	_____	_____

The imperfect

- You have already learned to use the preterit to talk about actions in the past. In these scenes, the grandmother and granddaughter use a different past tense, the *imperfect,* because they are focusing on how things used to be and what usually happened. If they were talking about a specific completed action, they would use the preterit.
- Generally, the imperfect is used to:
  1. express habitual or repeated actions in the past (without focus on the completion of a specific action).

     Nosotros **cenábamos** en casa a las seis todos los días. — *We used to eat dinner at home at six o'clock every day.*
  2. express an action or state that was in progress in the past (not whether the action or state was completed).

     Todos los invitados **hablaban** y **bailaban**. — *All the guests were talking and dancing.*

     Estaban muy contentos. — *They were very happy.*

3. describe characteristics and conditions in the past.

El desfile **era** muy largo y **había** muchos espectadores.	*The parade was very long and there were many spectators.*

4. tell time in the past.

Era la una de la tarde; no **eran** las dos.	*It was one in the afternoon; it was not two.*

5. express a person's age in the past.

Ella **tenía** 15 años entonces.	*She was 15 years old then.*

- Note that the endings for **-er** and **-ir** verbs are the same and have a written accent over the **í** of the ending.

Imperfect			
	HABLAR	**COMER**	**VIVIR**
yo	habl**aba**	com**ía**	viv**ía**
tú	habl**abas**	com**ías**	viv**ías**
Ud., él, ella	habl**aba**	com**ía**	viv**ía**
nosotros/as	habl**ába**mos	com**ía**mos	viv**ía**mos
vosotros/as	habl**aba**is	com**ía**is	viv**ía**is
Uds., ellos/as	habl**aba**n	com**ía**n	viv**ía**n

- Some expressions of time and frequency that often accompany the imperfect to express ongoing or repeated actions or states in the past are:

a veces	*sometimes, at times*
frecuentemente	*frequently*
generalmente	*generally*
mientras	*while*
siempre	*always*

- The Spanish imperfect has several English equivalents.

Mis amigos **bailaban** mucho.
- *My friends danced a lot.*
- *My friends were dancing a lot.*
- *My friends used to dance a lot.*
- *My friends would (usually) dance a lot.* (implying a repeated action)

- There are no stem changes in the imperfect.

Ella no d**ue**rme bien ahora, pero antes d**o**rmía muy bien.	*She does not sleep well now, but she used to sleep very well before.*

- Only three verbs are irregular in the imperfect.

ir	iba, ibas, iba, íbamos, ibais, iban
ser	era, eras, era, éramos, erais, eran
ver	veía, veías, veía, veíamos, veíais, veían

- The imperfect form of **haber** is **había** (*there was, there were, there used to be*). It is invariable.

Había una invitación en el correo.	*There was an invitation in the mail.*
Había muchas personas en la fiesta.	*There were many people at the party.*

¿Comprendes? Completa las oraciones con el imperfecto.

1. Marcos siempre _________ (bailar) en las fiestas.
2. Nosotros siempre _________ (comer) mucho cuando _________ (ir) a la casa de nuestros abuelos.
3. A los niños les _________ (gustar) cantar cuando _________ (estar) en la escuela primaria.
4. Cuando tú _________ (ser) niño, ¿_________ (hacer) tus disfraces del Día de las Brujas o los _________ (comprar)?

PRÁCTICA

8-17 Cuando yo tenía diez años. Marca las actividades que hacías cuando tenías diez años y añade una más. Compara tus respuestas con las de tu compañero/a. ¿Cuántas actividades tienen en común?

1. _____ Jugaba en el parque con mi perro.
2. _____ Invitaba a mis amigos a dormir en mi casa.
3. _____ Salía con mis padres los fines de semana.
4. _____ Iba a la playa en verano.
5. _____ Veía televisión hasta muy tarde.
6. _____ Celebraba el Año Nuevo con mis amigos.
7. _____ Participaba en las fiestas de mi escuela.
8. …

8-18 En mi escuela secundaria. **PREPARACIÓN.** Indica la frecuencia con que tus amigos/as de la escuela secundaria y tú hacían estas actividades. Añade otra actividad y compara tus respuestas con las de tu compañero/a.

MODELO decorar los salones de clase

E1: *Frecuentemente decorábamos los salones de clase.*

E2: *Pues, nosotros los decorábamos solo a veces.*

Actividades	Siempre	Frecuentemente	A veces	Nunca
1. jugar videojuegos				
2. gritar (*to shout*) mucho cuando se reunían para animar a los equipos				
3. ir a los partidos de fútbol y otros deportes				
4. asistir a conciertos y obras de teatro (*plays*)				
5. participar en un equipo, en una banda, etc.				
6. otra actividad: _____________				

INTERCAMBIOS. Hablen de los siguientes temas.

1. ¿Iban con sus amigos/as a los partidos de los equipos de sus escuelas? ¿Qué hacían para divertirse durante los partidos?
2. ¿Cuáles eran las actividades favoritas de cada uno/a de ustedes?

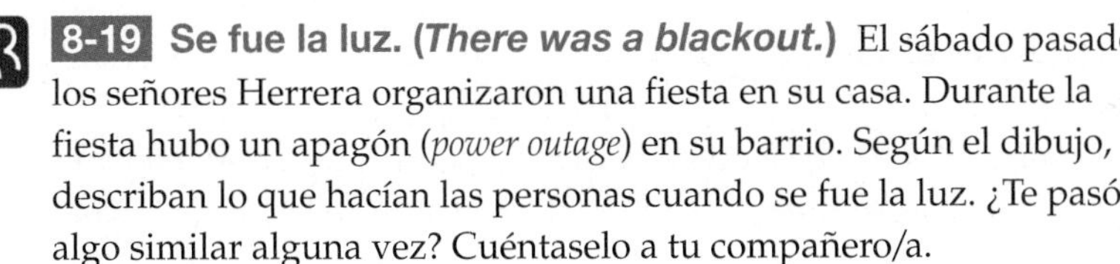

8-19 Se fue la luz. (*There was a blackout.*) El sábado pasado los señores Herrera organizaron una fiesta en su casa. Durante la fiesta hubo un apagón (*power outage*) en su barrio. Según el dibujo, describan lo que hacían las personas cuando se fue la luz. ¿Te pasó algo similar alguna vez? Cuéntaselo a tu compañero/a.

MODELO E1: *Se apagó la luz mientras preparaba un café.*
E2: …

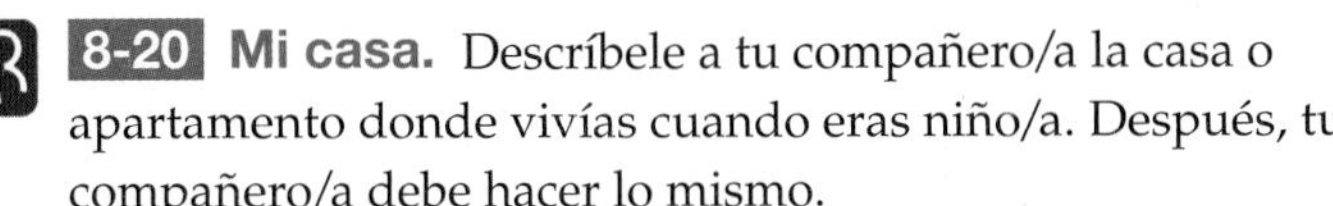

8-20 Mi casa. Descríbele a tu compañero/a la casa o apartamento donde vivías cuando eras niño/a. Después, tu compañero/a debe hacer lo mismo.

8-21 Las fiestas infantiles. Comenten cómo eran las fiestas de cumpleaños cuando ustedes eran pequeños/as. Hablen de los siguientes aspectos y añadan uno más.

1. lugar de las celebraciones
2. horas (comienzo y final)
3. dos o tres actividades que hacían
4. personas que participaban
5. comida y bebida que los padres servían
6. ropa que los niños llevaban
7. …

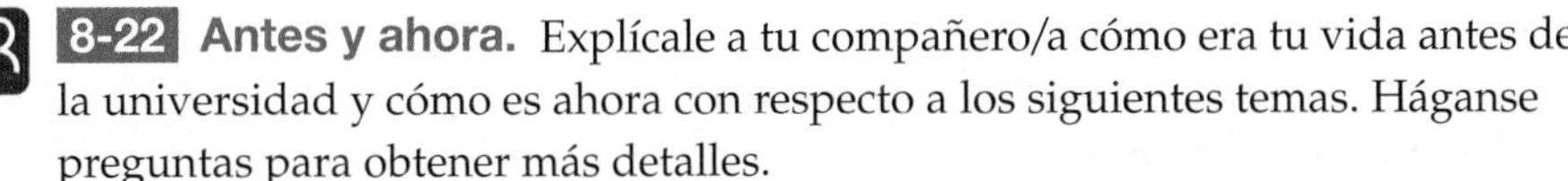

8-22 Antes y ahora. Explícale a tu compañero/a cómo era tu vida antes de la universidad y cómo es ahora con respecto a los siguientes temas. Háganse preguntas para obtener más detalles.

MODELO E1: *Antes yo vivía con mis padres, pero ahora no los veo mucho porque estudio en una universidad en otro estado. ¿Y tú?*
E2: …

1. la relación con tus padres
2. tus relaciones sociales
3. tus estudios
4. tu tiempo libre
5. tus amigos
6. tus vacaciones

En directo

To talk about how things used to be:

Entonces... *Then . . .*
Por aquel entonces... *Back then . . .*
En aquellos tiempos... *In those days . . .*
En esos años... *During those years . . .*

Listen to a conversation with these expressions.

Situación

PREPARACIÓN. Lean la situación. Luego, compartan ejemplos de vocabulario, gramática y otra información que necesitan para desarrollar la conversación.

Role A. You are an international student from Mexico and have become friends with a North American student in one of your classes. Find out about your friend's weekend and summer activities when he/she was in high school. Ask:
a. what activities there were for high school students in the community;
b. what he/she generally did with friends on the weekends; and
c. what he/she usually did in the summer.

Role B. You are a North American student who has become friends with an international student from Mexico (your classmate). Answer his/her questions about your weekend and summer activities when you were in high school. Provide lots of detail to give your new friend a good idea of your activities and life in your community.

	ROLE A	ROLE B
Vocabulario	Free-time and summer activities Question words Expressions to react to what one hears	Free-time and summer activities Expressions to react to what one hears
Funciones y formas	Asking questions Imperfect	Answering questions in detail Imperfect

INTERCAMBIOS. Practiquen la conversación, incorporando el vocabulario y las funciones de **Preparación.** Luego, represéntenla ante la clase.

2 Narrating in the past

Había una vez una chica que **vivía** con su padre, porque su madre **estaba** muerta. La chica **se llamaba** Cenicienta. **Era** muy bella y muy buena, y todos los vecinos (*neighbors*) la **querían** mucho. Pero un día, su vida **cambió.** Su padre **se casó** con una mujer muy mala que **tenía** dos hijas. La mujer y sus hijas **fueron** a vivir a la casa de Cenicienta. Las hijas **eran** muy crueles y **odiaban** (*hated*) a Cenicienta, su hermanastra…

e **Piénsalo.** Lee las afirmaciones e indica su función en la historia de Cenicienta: **contar los eventos** o **dar información de fondo** (*background*).

	CONTAR LOS EVENTOS	DAR INFORMACIÓN DE FONDO
1. La chica **se llamaba** Cenicienta.	____	____
2. **Era** muy bella y muy buena.	____	____
3. Todos los vecinos la **querían** mucho.	____	____
4. Pero un día, su vida **cambió.**	____	____
5. Su padre **se casó** con una mujer muy mala.	____	____
6. La mujer y sus hijas **fueron** a vivir a la casa de Cenicienta.	____	____

The preterit and the imperfect

- The preterit and the imperfect are not interchangeable. They have different meanings and fulfill different functions when telling a story or talking about an event or situation in the past.
- Use the preterit:
  1. to express a sequence of actions completed in the past (note that there is a forward movement of narrative time).

     Oyeron un ruido, **se levantaron** y **bajaron** las escaleras. — *They heard a noise, got up, and went downstairs.*
  2. to report a completed event, action, or condition, including its beginning or end.

     Pepito **aprendió** a leer a los cinco años. — *Pepito learned to read* (began to read) *at age five.*

     El niño **se enfermó** el sábado. — *The child got sick* (became sick) *on Saturday.*

     Marta **comió** el taco. — *Marta ate the taco.* (She finished eating it.)

     El niño **se despertó** temprano. — *The child woke up early.*
  3. to talk about an event, action, or condition that occurred over a specified period of time.

     Vivieron en México por diez años. — *They lived in Mexico for ten years.*

     Fue presidente del club por seis meses. — *She was president of the club for six months.*

- Use the imperfect:
  1. to talk about customary or habitual actions, events, or conditions in the past.

     Todos los días **llovía** y por eso **leíamos** mucho. — *It used to rain every day, and that's why we read a lot.*
  2. to express an ongoing part of an event, action, or condition in the past.

     En ese momento **llovía mucho** y los niños **estaban** muy tristes. — *At that moment it was raining a lot, and the children were very sad.*
  3. to describe people, places, and things in the past.

     El sol **brillaba** y **hacía** mucho calor. — *The sun was shining and it was very hot.*
  4. to express age and time.

     Eran las diez de la mañana. — *It was 10:00 a.m.*

     Martín **tenía** tres años y su hermana **tenía** siete. — *Martin was three years old and his sister was seven.*
- In a story, the imperfect provides the background information, whereas the preterit tells what happened. Frequently an action or situation (expressed with the imperfect) is going on when something else (expressed with the preterit) suddenly happens.

  Era Navidad. Todos **dormíamos** cuando los niños **oyeron** un ruido en el tejado. — *It was Christmas. We were all sleeping when the children heard a noise on the roof.*

e **¿Comprendes?** Completa las oraciones con la forma correcta del verbo en el pretérito o el imperfecto, según el contexto.

1. Cuando yo ________ (tener) diez años, mis padres nos ________ (llevar) a México.
2. Todos los días nosotros ________ (nadar) y ________ (jugar) al vóleibol en la playa.
3. Ese verano mi hermano ________ (aprender) a hacer parapente.
4. Mis padres no me ________ (permitir) tomar lecciones porque yo ________ (ser) demasiado joven.

PRÁCTICA

8-23 ¡Qué día más malo! **PREPARACIÓN.** Ayer iba a ser un día especial para Pedro, pero sus planes terminaron mal. Indica las tres cosas más graves que le ocurrieron a Pedro, según tu opinión. Compara tus respuestas con las de tu compañero/a.

1. _____ Mientras se bañaba por la mañana, se cayó (*fell*).
2. _____ Mientras desayunaba tranquilamente, su hermano vino a la casa para contarle sus problemas.
3. _____ Iba a la joyería para comprarle un anillo a su novia cuando alguien le robó (*stole*) el dinero.
4. _____ Mientras reservaba una mesa en su restaurante favorito, el restaurante se incendió (*caught on fire*).
5. _____ Iba a proponerle matrimonio a su novia cuando su exnovia lo llamó por teléfono.
6. _____ Mientras preparaba una cena deliciosa para celebrar el cumpleaños de su novia, el perro se comió el pastel (*cake*).

INTERCAMBIOS. Túrnense para contar la cosa más terrible que les ocurrió esta semana. Luego, decidan cuál es peor (*worse*) y cuéntensela a la clase.

8-24 La última vez. Túrnense para preguntarse cuándo fue la última vez que cada uno/a de ustedes hizo estas actividades y cómo se sentía mientras las hacía.

MODELO ver un partido

E1: *¿Cuándo fue la última vez que viste un partido?*

E2: *Vi un partido de béisbol la semana pasada.*

E1: *¿Y cómo te sentías mientras veías el partido?*

E2: *Estaba aburrido/a, porque no me gusta mucho el béisbol.*

1. participar en un campeonato
2. asistir a un concierto
3. estar en un desfile
4. llevar un disfraz
5. bailar en una fiesta
6. ...

8-25 ¿Qué les pasó? Miren las fotos y expliquen qué hacían estas personas y qué les pasó. Describan con detalle la situación.

MODELO Meriel: ser verano, caminar por su barrio, empezar a llover, mojarse (*get wet*) mucho, regresar a casa

E1: *Era verano y Meriel caminaba por su barrio cuando empezó a llover.*

E2: *Meriel se mojó mucho. Regresó a casa para secarse.*

1. María: estar sentada, leer noticias, ladrón (*thief*) robar el bolso, darse cuenta

2. Alicia: caminar por el mercado, ver vestidos bonitos, discutir el precio, tomar una decisión

3. José Luis: volver a casa, haber mucho tráfico, otra conductora no verlo, chocar (*hit*), llamar

  **8-26 Una leyenda.** Completa esta narración usando el pretérito o el imperfecto. Compara tus respuestas con las de tu compañero/a y hablen sobre por qué es preferible usar el pretérito o el imperfecto.

> Según una leyenda mexicana, (1) ________ (haber) antiguamente una mujer indígena que (2) ________ (caminar) por las calles. Siempre (3) ________ (vestirse) de blanco. (4) ________ (tener) el pelo negro y largo. (5) ________ (estar) muy triste y (6) ________ (llorar[1]) mucho, por eso muchas personas la (7) ________ (llamar) la Llorona. La leyenda cuenta que ella (8) ________ (enamorarse) de un caballero español. De su romance (9) ________ (nacer[2]) tres hijos. Luego, el caballero (10) ________ (abandonar) a su familia y (11) ________ (casarse) con otra mujer. Entonces, ella (12) ________ (estar) tan desesperada que (13) ________ (matar[3]) a sus hijos. Luego, (14) ________ (arrepentirse) y (15) ________ (vivir) el resto de su vida con mucho sufrimiento. Todavía hoy en día se oye al fantasma[4] de la mujer llorando por sus hijos.

[1]*to cry* [2]*to be born* [3]*to kill* [4]*ghost*

 **8-27 Un evento inolvidable.** Cuéntale a tu compañero/a algo inesperado que te ocurrió en el pasado. Indica qué pasó, dónde y cuándo. Describe la escena y cuenta el evento con detalles.

Situación

PREPARACIÓN. Lean la situación. Luego, compartan ejemplos de vocabulario, gramática y otra información que necesitan para desarrollar la conversación.

Role A. You have just come back from a vacation. Tell your classmate about a particular place you visited. Explain what it was like and what you did there.

Role B. Your classmate has just returned from a vacation. Ask about a particular place he/she visited during the vacation. Find out:
a. what the place looked like;
b. what he/she did there; and
c. what special event he/she can tell you about.

	ROLE A	ROLE B
Vocabulario	Words associated with vacations Words to describe a place	Question words
Funciones y formas	Describing a vacation spot Adjectives Narrating and describing in the past Preterit and imperfect	Asking questions about a past event Preterit and imperfect Reacting to what one hears

INTERCAMBIOS. Practiquen la conversación, incorporando el vocabulario y las funciones de **Preparación.** Luego, represéntenla ante la clase.

3 Comparing people and things

El comité organizador del Carnaval de la Primavera se reúne para hablar del presupuesto (*budget*).

Las estadísticas de los años recientes van a ser útiles para planificar el Carnaval de la Primavera. ¿Vamos a celebrar el carnaval **más de** dos días? El año pasado participaron 1.500.000 personas; 250.000 mujeres y 193.000 hombres fueron parte de las comparsas. El año pasado la asistencia fue **mayor que** el año anterior. Había **más** mujeres **que** hombres. El año pasado participaron **menos** mujeres **que** este año. El año pasado, el presupuesto era **más** pequeño **que** hace dos años. La municipalidad tenía solo 11 millones de pesos. Para tener un **mejor** carnaval **que** en años anteriores, vamos a necesitar **más** dinero **que** en años pasados. Es decir, un **mejor** presupuesto.

	Este año	El año pasado	Hace dos años
Número de días	3	2	2
Asistencia del público	1.600.000	1.500.000	1.450.000
Mujeres	270.000	250.000	240.000
Hombres	195.000	193.000	185.000
Niños	75.000	52.000	45.000
Presupuesto	13.000.000	11.000.000	12.000.000

Piénsalo. Selecciona la opción correcta para completar las afirmaciones, según las estadísticas del Carnaval de la Primavera.

1. _____ En el carnaval de este año participaron... mujeres... hombres.
2. _____ El año pasado, hubo... niños... adultos en el carnaval.
3. _____ El año pasado, el carnaval duró... dos días.
4. _____ Con un buen presupuesto, es posible tener un... carnaval.
5. _____ Hace dos años, el presupuesto era más grande... el año pasado.

a. **más de**
b. **más... que**
c. **menos... que**
d. **mejor**
e. **que**

Comparisons of inequality

- Use **más… que** or **menos… que** to express comparisons of inequality with nouns, adjectives, and adverbs.

COMPARISONS OF INEQUALITY					
Cuando Alina era joven, tenía	**más** **menos**	amigos que Pepe.	*When Alina was young she had*	*more* *fewer*	*friends than Pepe.*
Ella era	**más** **menos**	activa que Pepe.	*She was*	*more* *less*	*active than Pepe.*
Salía	**más** **menos**	frecuentemente que Pepe.	*She went out*	*more* *less*	*frequently than Pepe.*

- Use **de** instead of **que** before numbers.

Hace dos años, hubo **más de** diez carrozas en el desfile. — *Two years ago, there were more than ten floats in the parade.*

En el siguiente año, hubo **menos de** diez carrozas. — *The following year there were fewer than ten floats.*

- Some adjectives have both regular and irregular comparative forms. Use **mayor** to refer to a person's age. **Más viejo/a** is used to refer to the age of nouns other than people; for example, a city, a building, a tree.
- The following adjectives have both regular and irregular comparative forms but with different uses:

FORM	USE	EXAMPLES
más bueno/a *better* **más malo/a** *worse*	refer to a person's moral qualities	Jorge es **más bueno** que su hermano Esteban. *Jorge is a better person than his brother Esteban.*
mejor *better* **peor** *worse*	refer to skills and abilities	Esta orquesta es **mejor** que aquella. *This orchestra is better than that one.*
más viejo/a *older*	generally used with nouns other than people	El cementerio es **más viejo** que la iglesia. *The cemetery is older than the church.*
mayor *older*	refers to a person's age	Soy **mayor** que tú. *I am older than you.*
Exception: **más joven/menor** *younger*	can be used interchangeably	Mi madre es **más joven** que mi tía. / Mi madre es **menor** que mi tía. *My mother is younger than my aunt.*

- **Bien** and **mal** are adverbs. They have the same irregular comparative forms as the adjectives **bueno** and **malo.**

bien S mejor	Yo canto **mejor** que Héctor.	*I sing better than Héctor.*
mal S peor	Héctor canta **peor** que yo.	*Héctor sings worse than I (do).*

¿Comprendes? Completa las oraciones con la forma correcta del comparativo.

1. Mi hermano canta bien, pero Bruno Mars canta _______.
2. Lucía tiene 15 años y su hermana tiene 20. Lucía es _______ _______ su hermana.
3. Yo estudié mucho para el examen. Pasé ______ horas en la biblioteca ______ mis amigos.
4. El auto es muy caro. Cuesta ______ ______ 40.000 dólares.
5. La oficina del rector está en un edificio viejo. Se construyó en 1800. El edificio es ______ viejo ______ los otros edificios de la universidad.

Cultura

Veracruz y Mérida Veracruz y Mérida son dos ciudades mexicanas importantes. Veracruz, que está a 400 kilómetros (250 millas) al sureste de Ciudad de México, fue fundada por el conquistador Hernán Cortés en 1519. Su puerto (*port*) es el más importante del país; por eso, Veracruz es conocida como "la puerta al mundo".

Mérida es la principal ciudad del estado de Yucatán, en el sureste del país. Está a más de 1.550 kilómetros (965 millas) de la capital. En los años 2000 y 2017, Mérida fue nombrada "Capital Americana de la Cultura" por su alta calidad de vida y su extraordinario desarrollo en las artes.

Desfile en Mérida

Comparaciones ¿Cuáles son las ciudades más turísticas de tu país? ¿Por qué? ¿Dónde están los puertos más importantes? ¿Hay ciudades con nombres o títulos especiales en tu país? ¿Cuáles?

PRÁCTICA

8-28 Comparación de dos carnavales.

PREPARACIÓN. Lee la información sobre dos carnavales mexicanos del año pasado. Completa las afirmaciones con **más… que, menos… que, más de** o **menos de**.

	Veracruz	Mérida
habitantes	568.313	870.313
promedio (*average*) de público que participa	1.600.000 personas	1.150.000 personas
bandas	9	7
carrozas	17	12
policías	185	220

1. Mérida tiene ______ habitantes ______ Veracruz.
2. ______ ______ medio millón de personas viven en Veracruz.
3. ______ personas asistieron al Carnaval de Veracruz ______ al Carnaval de Mérida.
4. Las dos ciudades tuvieron ______ ______ diez bandas en total.
5. ______ bandas participaron en el Carnaval de Veracruz ______ en el de Mérida.
6. Veracruz gastó ______ dinero en seguridad (*security*) ______ Mérida.
7. Hubo ______ visitantes en el Carnaval de Mérida ______ en el de Veracruz.
8. ______ ______ 15 carrozas formaron parte de la celebración en Veracruz.

INTERCAMBIOS. Usen su sentido común (*common sense*) para responder a las preguntas.

1. En su opinión, ¿por qué participaron más personas en el desfile del Carnaval de Veracruz que en el de Mérida?
2. ¿Por qué Mérida gastó más dinero en seguridad que Veracruz?
3. Para un carnaval grande, ¿son nueve bandas suficientes? ¿Por qué?

8-29 ¿En qué desfile participar?

PREPARACIÓN. La banda de tu universidad quiere participar en uno de estos desfiles en México. Con tu compañero/a, decidan a qué desfile debe ir y expliquen por qué.

Costo por persona	Desfile de Veracruz	Desfile de Mérida
transporte	11.500 pesos	10.158 pesos
hotel por día	882 pesos	785 pesos
comidas por día	575 pesos	428 pesos

INTERCAMBIOS. Compartan su opinión sobre el desfile en que debe participar la banda de su universidad. ¿Están de acuerdo? Luego, contesten estas preguntas.

1. ¿Es más caro o más barato participar en un desfile en Estados Unidos que en México?
2. ¿Son la comida y el alojamiento (*lodging*) más baratos en México?
3. ¿Qué ventajas tiene ir a un desfile en otro país? ¿Por qué?

Cultura

La Calavera Catrina La Calavera Catrina es un grabado (*etching*) en zinc realizado entre 1910 y 1913 por José Guadalupe Posada. Las calaveras (*skulls*) representaban de manera humorística figuras contemporáneas en forma de esqueletos y a menudo iban acompañadas de un poema. Hoy en día, la imagen se incorpora a las representaciones artísticas del Día de los Muertos en México y, en años recientes, también en Estados Unidos, donde la Catrina es uno de los disfraces más populares de Halloween.

Comparaciones ¿Se usan las calaveras y los esqueletos humorísticamente en tu cultura? Explica tu respuesta.

8-30 La Catrina.

En México se celebra el Día de los Muertos con la imagen de la Catrina y en Estados Unidos celebran el Día de las Brujas con la figura de una bruja (*witch*). Comparen las dos imágenes usando las siguientes características.

MODELO E1: *La bruja es más horrorosa que la Catrina.*
E2: *De acuerdo. Además (*Besides*), la bruja es menos elegante que la Catrina.*

adornado/a	bonito/a	espantoso/a (*scary*)	joven
alegre	colorido/a	feo/a	mayor
alto/a	delgado/a	fuerte	maligno/a (*evil*)
bajo/a	elegante	horroroso/a	misterioso/a

1. la apariencia física
2. los colores
3. el estilo de la ropa
4. lo que más te gusta de una de ellas

La Catrina

La bruja

 **8-31 Personas famosas.** **PREPARACIÓN.** Lean la información personal y profesional de estas hispanas famosas. Luego, compárenlas, según los criterios indicados.

1. edad
2. aspecto físico y ropa
3. éxito (*success*) profesional

ANA DE ARMAS	AMERICA FERRERA
Datos personales	**Datos personales**
30 de abril, 1988	18 de abril, 1984
5' 6"	5' 1"
Datos profesionales	**Datos profesionales**
Películas: 15	Películas: 24
Series de televisón: 3	Series de televisón: 10

INTERCAMBIOS. Escoge a una de estas famosas y compárate con ella. Utiliza los mismos criterios de comparación que usaste en **Preparación.** Tu compañero/a te va a decir si está de acuerdo contigo o no.

8-32 Algunas fiestas populares. PREPARACIÓN. Lean la información sobre algunas fiestas populares de Argentina, Uruguay y Bolivia. Seleccionen **dos** fiestas de países diferentes. Luego, respondan a las preguntas. Tomen apuntes.

1. ¿Representa cada fiesta una tradición histórica, artística, pagana, religiosa, rural, culinaria? ¿Otra tradición?
2. ¿Qué aspecto de cada fiesta les parece más atractivo: la antigüedad, el lugar donde se celebra, las actividades? ¿Otro aspecto? ¿Cuál de las fiestas les gusta más?
3. ¿Qué diferencias hay entre las dos fiestas? Expliquen.

	Comienzo	Duración	Lugar(es)	Actividades
Argentina				
Festival Nacional del Folklore, Cosquín, cerca de Córdoba	1961	9 días (enero)	el escenario giratorio (*revolving*) Atahualpa Yupanqui para 10.000 espectadores	• las peñas: los artistas cantan toda la noche y los espectadores los acompañan y aplauden
Fiesta Nacional de la Vendimia (*grape harvest*), Mendoza	1936	10 días (marzo)	las calles de la ciudad de Mendoza el Teatro Griego	• la bendición (*blessing*) de la fruta • el concurso (*contest*) de las reinas (*queens*) de belleza • el desfile en carrozas de las reinas acompañadas de hombres vestidos de gaucho
Uruguay				
Festival Jazz a la Calle, Mercedes	2006	9 días (enero)	la calle o en edificios donde el público se reúne espontáneamente	• la participación de bandas de jazz improvisadas en las calles • talleres (*workshops*) y conciertos para el público
Festival del Mate, San José y Rocha	2003	3 días (marzo)	el campo escenario Wenceslao Varela el Parque Rodó	• espectáculos de artistas uruguayos y extranjeros • almuerzo con comidas típicas uruguayas (asado, arroz con leche, mate charrúa [uruguayo], etc.) • concurso de bailes folclóricos • concurso de mate para niños
Bolivia				
El Carnaval de Oruro	precolombino	3 días (segunda semana de febrero)	las calles de Oruro	• desfile de los danzarines vestidos con disfraces y máscaras artesanales • representación de la batalla entre el bien y el mal por los danzarines
El Nuevo Año aymara	hace miles de años	1 día (21 de junio)	en todas las ciudades y pueblos de Bolivia	• sacrificio de llamas • rituales al dios del sol a las orillas del lago Titicaca • recibir los primeros rayos del sol (*sunbeams*)

INTERCAMBIOS. Compartan con otro grupo la fiesta que les gustó más y expliquen por qué. Usen expresiones de comparación y palabras de la lista.

MODELO *Nosotros elegimos… en… porque representa… Es más/menos… que…* (nombre de otra fiesta). *Es nuestra opinión, … más… porque…*

Aspectos de la tradición	Características	
el ambiente	artístico/a	inclusivo/a
las actividades	atractivo/a	llamativo/a (*striking*)
el lugar	divertido/a	natural
	educativo/a	pagano/a
	histórico/a	religioso/a

Situación

PREPARACIÓN. Lean la situación. Luego, compartan ejemplos de vocabulario, gramática y otra información que necesitan para desarrollar la conversación.

Role A. You are a student government representative presenting a proposal to the dean to change the graduation ceremony. Compare the current ceremony at your school with one at a rival institution. Say that the other ceremony is better because it is smaller, shorter, better organized, less expensive, and usually has better music and speeches (**discursos**).

Role B. You are the dean. A student government representative is proposing changes to the graduation ceremony. Listen to the presentation and ask questions to compare the advantages of both types of ceremonies.

Then either accept or reject the proposal, and justify your decision.

	ROLE A	ROLE B
Vocabulario	Expressions associated with size, length, organization, cost, and other amenities of a graduation ceremony	Expressions associated with size, length, organization, cost, and other amenities of a graduation ceremony
Funciones y formas	Presenting a group proposal to someone in authority Comparing to highlight better qualities Convincing/persuading Addressing someone in authority with respect and courtesy	Asking questions Drawing conclusions to make a decision

INTERCAMBIOS. Practiquen la conversación, incorporando el vocabulario y las funciones de **Preparación.** Luego, represéntenla ante la clase.

4 Comparing people and things

 **Habla la presidenta del comité organizador.**

Este año tuvimos un carnaval **tan** espectacular **como** el del año pasado. Asistió **tanto** público **como** el año pasado, un total de 1.600.000 personas. Los grupos musicales tocaron música **tan** buena **como** la música del carnaval del año pasado. También el número de paramédicos que ayudaron se mantuvo igual. Además (*Furthermore*), hubo **tantos** doctores **como** el año pasado. Estoy muy agradecida porque ustedes colaboraron **tanto como** en otros años. Vamos a planificar el carnaval del próximo año **tan bien como** el de este año. Vamos a disfrutarlo **tanto como** este año.

e **Piénsalo.** Selecciona la alternativa correcta para completar las afirmaciones con expresiones de igualdad (*equality*).

1. _____ Este año asistió el mismo número de personas que el año pasado. Es decir, asistió... **gente...** el año pasado.
2. _____ Los músicos hicieron un buen trabajo este año. Tocaron... **canciones bonitas...** el año pasado.
3. _____ Este año el comité organizador hizo un trabajo muy bueno, ... **bueno**... el de otros años.
4. _____ Estamos contentos con la planificación del año pasado. Este año, vamos a tener... **éxito** (*success*)... el año anterior.
5. _____ El próximo año, los participantes del carnaval van a **celebrar, cantar** y **bailar**... este año.

a. **tan... como**
b. **tanto... como**
c. **tanta... como**
d. **tantas... como**
e. **tanto como**

Comparisons of equality

- In the previous section, you learned to express comparisons of inequality. In this section, you will learn how to indicate that two people, things, or activities are equal in some way.

COMPARISONS OF EQUALITY	
tan... como	*as . . . as*
tanto/a... como	*as much . . . as*
tantos/as... como	*as many . . . as*
tanto como	*as much as*

- Use **tan... como** with adjectives and adverbs.

La boda fue **tan** elegante **como** la fiesta. — *The wedding was as elegant as the party.*
El padre bailó **tan** bien **como** su hija. — *The father danced as well as his daughter.*

- Use **tanto/a... como** and **tantos/as... como** with nouns.

Había **tanta** alegría **como** en el carnaval. — *There was as much joy as at the carnival.*
Había **tantos** invitados **como** en mi fiesta de graduación. — *There were as many guests as at my graduation party.*

- Use **tanto como** with verbs.

Los invitados bailaron **tanto como** nosotros. — *The guests danced as much as we did.*

¿Comprendes? Completa las oraciones con las expresiones que indican igualdad.

1. El año pasado, el Día de la Independencia fue ______ emocionante ______ el año anterior.
2. En mi casa tuvimos ______ comida ______ en la última celebración.
3. La ciudad organizó ______ desfiles ______ en años anteriores.
4. La gente comió y bebió ______ ______ el año pasado.

Cultura

El peso mexicano La moneda mexicana es el peso. Tanto en los billetes como en las monedas de metal está el escudo (*coat of arms*) nacional, que tiene un águila encima de un nopal (un tipo de cacto) devorando una serpiente.

Comparaciones ¿Sabes cuál es la tasa de cambio (*exchange rate*) entre el peso mexicano y el dólar estadounidense? ¿Qué imágenes hay en los billetes de tu país? ¿Y en las monedas? ¿Qué importancia histórica y simbólica tienen esas imágenes?

PRÁCTICA

8-33 Tradiciones.

PREPARACIÓN. Lee algunos datos de cómo cuatro estudiantes celebraron el Día de la Independencia. Luego, indica si las afirmaciones son ciertas (**C**) o falsas (**F**). Si son falsas, corrige la información.

	Hugo	Martina	Pablo	Valeria
Horas que miraron el desfile en el centro de la ciudad	3	2	3	2
Dinero que gastaron en comida y bebidas	$22	$11	$22	$22
Número de bandas que vieron en el desfile	18	10	18	10
Número de fotos que tomaron	0	26	12	12
Número de amigos que lo/la acompañaron al desfile	8	8	4	4
Hora a la que volvieron a casa	4:00 p.m.	2:00 p.m.	4:00 p.m.	2:00 p.m.

1. _____ Hugo miró el desfile durante **tantas** horas **como** Pablo.
2. _____ Martina gastó **tanto** dinero en comida y bebidas **como** Valeria.
3. _____ Hugo y Pablo vieron **tantas** bandas **como** Martina.
4. _____ Valeria tomó **tantas** fotos **como** Pablo.
5. _____ Pablo fue al desfile con **tantos** amigos **como** Valeria.
6. _____ Valeria volvió a casa **tan** tarde **como** Pablo.

INTERCAMBIOS. Escoge a dos estudiantes de **Preparación** que hicieron las mismas actividades que tú el Día de la Independencia el año pasado. Cuéntale a tu compañero/a qué actividades semejantes (*similar*) hicieron.

MODELO *Valeria y yo hicimos algo semejante el Día de la Independencia. Ella miró el desfile tantas horas como yo. Yo volví a casa tan tarde como Hugo y Pablo.*

8-34 Opiniones. PREPARACIÓN. Prepara una lista de dos personas famosas, dos festividades en tu cultura y dos programas cómicos de la televisión.

INTERCAMBIOS. Ahora, expresen su opinión sobre ellos y compárenlos.

MODELO E1: *Tom Cruise es tan buen actor como Johnny Depp.*
E2: *No estoy de acuerdo. En mi opinión, Johnny Depp es mejor actor que Tom Cruise.*

8-35 Altares en el Día de los Muertos. Tu compañero/a y tú hicieron altares para celebrar el Día de los Muertos, ¡y resultaron casi idénticos! Túrnense para comparar los siguientes aspectos de los dos altares.

MODELO los vasos (*glasses*) / la tela
E1: *Hay tantos vasos en el altar A como en el altar B.*
E2: *Sí, y la tela del altar A es tan bonita como la (tela) del altar B.*

- los esqueletos (*skeletons*)
- las calaveras (*skulls*)
- las fotografías
- la comida (naranjas, limones, panes, etc.)
- las velas
- las flores
- la guirnalda (*garland*)

8-36 Celebración del Año Nuevo. **PREPARACIÓN.** Los Sánchez celebraron el Año Nuevo en casa con una fiesta formal. Identifiquen a las personas que colaboraron con una cantidad igual de trabajo.

MODELO decorar mesas: Juan José, 15 / Pablo, 12 / Marisa, 15
Juan José decoró tantas mesas como Marisa.

Colaboradores	Lavar platos	Recibir a invitados	Cocinar	Decorar mesas	Poner música
Jesús	16	10	4 pavos rellenos (*stuffed turkeys*)	12 velas	10 canciones de música popular
Raúl	18	12	sopa de vegetales para 20 personas	8 floreros (*vases*)	15 rancheras mexicanas
Perla	18	10	4 pavos rellenos	12 velas	8 canciones románticas
Alejandra	16	15	sopa de vegetales para 15 personas	7 floreros	15 rancheras mexicanas

INTERCAMBIOS. Cuéntense (*Tell each other*) cómo celebró cada uno/a de ustedes el Año Nuevo pasado. Respondan a las siguientes preguntas. Pueden inventar respuestas lógicas.

1. ¿Celebraste el Año Nuevo pasado con tantas personas como el año anterior?
2. ¿Quién en tu familia o círculo de amigos/as se vistió tan formal o informalmente como tú esa noche?
3. ¿Qué comiste o bebiste esa noche?
4. ¿Quién comió o bebió tanto como tú?

Situación

PREPARACIÓN. Lean esta situación. Luego, compartan ejemplos de vocabulario, gramática y otra información que necesitan para desarrollar la conversación.

Role A. You are reminiscing about Independence Day celebrations when you were a child. Tell your classmate that you think that:
a. in the past people were more patriotic (**patriótico/a**);
b. the celebrations were less expensive; and
c. the celebrations were more family oriented (**se celebraban en familia**) than today.

Role B. Your classmate argues that today's Independence Day celebrations are less patriotic and family oriented than in the past. You disagree. State that:
a. today people are just as patriotic as they were in the past;
b. people used to spend less money because they made less money; and
c. today families celebrate Independence Day together as much as in the past.

	ROLE A	ROLE B
Vocabulario	Independence Day activities Phrases to express agreement and disagreement	Independence Day activities Phrases to express agreement and disagreement
Funciones y formas	Making comparisons of equality and inequality Expressing agreement and disagreement	Making comparisons of equality and inequality Expressing agreement and disagreement

INTERCAMBIOS. Practiquen la conversación, incorporando el vocabulario y las funciones de **Preparación.** Luego, represéntenla ante la clase.

5 Comparing people and things

PERLA: Lupita, ¿tienes algún plan especial para el Día de los Muertos?

LUPITA: Claro que sí. En mi comunidad, vamos al cementerio para visitar a familiares y amigos muertos. Les llevamos agua, **la mejor** música mexicana y su comida preferida. Es **el** día **más importante del** año para recordarlos. Creemos que ellos vuelven a su tumba el 1 y 2 de noviembre para disfrutar de **la mejor** compañía, la de su familia y amigos.

PERLA: ¡Qué interesante! Para mi familia, **el** acto **más** importante es recordarlos con **las** flores **más** hermosas **de** la estación.

Piénsalo. Selecciona la opción que expresa la calidad superior o la inferior, según la conversación entre Lupita y Perla.

1. _____ Los mexicanos llevan al cementerio… música mexicana.
2. _____ El Día de los Muertos es… día… importante del año para recordar a los familiares y amigos muertos.
3. _____ Los amigos y familiares son… visitas… agradables para los difuntos.
4. _____ Mi familia y yo llevamos la comida que les gustaba… a nuestros difuntos.
5. _____ Ponerles flores en sus tumbas es… regalo que podemos darles a los muertos.

a. **el… más**
b. **las… más**
c. **el mejor**
d. **la mejor**
e. **más**

The superlative

- Use superlatives to express *most* and *least* as degrees of comparison among three or more entities. To form the superlative, use *definite article* + *noun* + **más/menos** + *adjective.* To express *in* or *at* with the superlative, use **de.**

Es **el** disfraz **menos** creativo (**de** la fiesta).	*It is the least creative costume (at the party).*
México es **el** país con **más** fiestas **de** América del Norte.	*Mexico is the country with the most holidays in North America.*

- Do not use **más** or **menos** with **mejor, peor, mayor,** or **menor.**

¿Esos desfiles? Son **los mejores** desfiles **del** país.	*Those parades? They are the best parades in the country.*
Ivonne es **la mejor** bailarina **del** grupo.	*Ivonne is the best dancer of the group.*

- You may delete the noun when it is clear to whom or to what you refer.

Son **los mejores del** país.	*They are the best (ones) in the country.*

- To express the idea of *extremely,* add the ending **–ísimo/a (-os, -as)** to the adjective. If the adjective ends in a consonant, add **-ísimo** directly to the singular form of the adjective. If it ends in a vowel, drop the vowel before adding **-ísimo.**

fácil	Este baile es **facilísimo.**	*This dance is extremely easy.*
grande	La carroza es **grandísima.**	*The float is extremely big.*
bueno	Las orquestas son **buenísimas.**	*The orchestras are extremely good.*

Lengua

A Spanish word can have only one written accent. Therefore, an adjective with a written accent loses the accent when **-ísimo/a** is added.

fácil → facilísimo/a
rápido → rapidísimo/a

¿Comprendes? Completa las oraciones para expresar el superlativo.

1. En mi opinión, los carnavales de la primavera son ______ ______ divertidos. Me encanta verlos, cantar y bailar.
2. Miguel es fenomenal. Es ______ ______ colaborador del comité organizador.
3. Laura tiene 30 años, Marisol tiene 28 y Susana tiene solo 18. Laura es ______ ______ de las tres.
4. Mi abuela hace ______ enchiladas ______ deliciosas del mundo.

PRÁCTICA

8-37 Estadísticas demográficas.

PREPARACIÓN. Lee la información de la tabla. Luego selecciona el país que corresponde a cada descripción. Compara tus respuestas con las de tu compañero/a.

	México	Guatemala	Estados Unidos
Población del país (aprox.)	124.000.000 de habitantes	17.245.000 de habitantes	325.700.000 de habitantes
Población de la capital (aprox.)	Ciudad de México 9.000.000	Ciudad de Guatemala 3.500.000	Washington, DC 700.000
Número de lenguas indígenas (aprox.)	68	23	150
Religión predominante	81% son católicos (100.000.000 de habitantes)	49% son católicos (11.000.000 de habitantes)	45% son protestantes (14.000.000 de habitantes)
Número de estados o departamentos	32 estados	22 departamentos	50 estados

1. _____ Este país tiene **el menor número** de habitantes.
2. _____ La población de la capital de este país es **la más** numerosa.
3. _____ Es el país donde existe **el mayor** número de lenguas indígenas.
4. _____ Este es el país con **menos** lenguas indígenas.
5. _____ Este país tiene **el mayor** número de personas que se identifican con la religión católica.
6. _____ Este país tiene **el menor** número de gobiernos estatales o departamentales.

a. México
b. Guatemala
c. Estados Unidos

INTERCAMBIOS. Escoge un estado o ciudad de tu país y menciona tres cosas en las que se distingue de los demás estados o ciudades. Tu compañero/a tiene que adivinar qué estado o ciudad es.

MODELO E1: *Es la ciudad de Estados Unidos que tiene el mayor número de habitantes.*

E2: *Es Nueva York. Tiene más de ocho millones y medio de habitantes.*

 **8-38 Finalistas y ganadores.** Cada semestre, tu universidad identifica a personas, negocios o grupos destacados (*outstanding*). Comparen a los finalistas y luego decidan el/la ganador/a en cada categoría, según los datos. Indiquen el título del premio (*award*) que va a recibir cada persona o grupo.

Finalistas	Criterio(s) de selección	Premio
ESTUDIANTE DESTACADO/A	**Nota promedio (*average*) en sus clases**	
Carl Einstein Bonita Marín John Vásquez	A+ A A–	
PIZZERÍAS UNIVERSITARIAS	**Precio y calidad del menú**	
Pizzería El Italiano Pizzería Lucas Pizzería El Padrino	\$7,50 Deliciosas \$6,00 De regular sabor \$5,99 Muy deliciosas	
FUTBOLISTA DESTACADO/A	**Goles en temporada de fútbol**	
John Valdés	20	
Susan Curry	38	
Mark Stenson	26	
BANDAS ENTRETENIDAS	**Ritmo y musicalidad**	
Banda de jazz	Buena precisión rítmica y buena musicalidad	
Banda de rock	Precisión rítmica, musicalidad regular	
Banda de marcha	Sobresaliente precisión rítmica, excelente musicalidad	

 **8-39 ¿En qué pueblo o ciudad?** Respondan a las siguientes preguntas y luego comparen sus respuestas con las de otra pareja. ¿Están de acuerdo o tienen opiniones diferentes?

¿En qué pueblo o ciudad de tu país…

1. sirven la mejor comida étnica?
2. comen la comida más picante (*spicy*)?
3. venden el café cubano más fuerte?
4. celebran las mejores fiestas de Año Nuevo?
5. hay el mayor número de desfiles hermosos?
6. tocan la mejor música folclórica?
7. celebran las tradiciones indígenas más antiguas?
8. reciben el mayor número de turistas?

INTERCAMBIOS. Ustedes van a dar unos premios (*awards*) en su comunidad. Pónganse de acuerdo para identificar a las personas, lugares o instituciones que merecen (*deserve*) los siguientes premios.

1. el restaurante con la mejor comida étnica
2. el café que prepara el café más sabroso
3. la institución que organiza las mejores fiestas
4. la banda que toca la mejor música
5. el lugar más interesante para los turistas

8-40 ¿Lo máximo o lo mínimo? PREPARACIÓN. Expresen su opinión sobre las siguientes fiestas o tradiciones. Usen todos los adjetivos de la lista y los superlativos. Expliquen su opinión.

MODELO la Alborada
E1: *Para mí, la Alborada es la fiesta más animada.*
E2: *En mi opinión…*

animado/a	colorido/a	peligroso/a
antiguo/a	divertido/a	popular
caro/a	interesante	religioso/a

Fiestas norteamericanas
- el Día de las Brujas
- el Festival de las Rosas
- Mardi Gras

Fiestas latinoamericanas
- el Festival de la Vendimia
- el Día de los Muertos
- la Alborada

Actividades
- disfrazarse
- visitar a los familiares muertos en el cementerio
- correr con los toros en el Día de San Fermín

INTERCAMBIOS. Individualmente escojan una las fiestas o tradiciones de **Preparación.** Cambien de compañero/a. y háganse las siguientes preguntas, u otras adicionales, para conseguir más información.

1. ¿Cuándo participaste en esta fiesta/tradición por última vez? ¿Fue esa fiesta la mejor celebración hasta este momento? ¿Por qué?
2. ¿Cuál es la peor celebración o fiesta a la que fuiste? ¿Por qué?

Situación

PREPARACIÓN. Lean esta situación. Luego, compartan ejemplos de vocabulario, gramática y otra información cultural que necesitan para desarrollar la conversación.

Role A. You took your traditional trip for spring break and had a great time. Tell your classmate the five most interesting places you saw or activities you did. Provide details about at least one place or activity.

Role B. Ask several questions about your classmate's spring break trip to learn about his/ her interesting and enjoyable activities. Then say where you went during spring break, and share the favorite parts of your trip.

	ROLE A	ROLE B
Vocabulario	Words related to places Expressions associated with trips Descriptive words	Question words
Funciones y formas	Narrating an event Describing in detail: Preterit and imperfect Adjectives Expressing the utmost feature of a place or an experience	Reacting to what you hear Asking follow-up questions Narrating an event Describing an experience Expressing the utmost feature of a place or an experience

INTERCAMBIOS. Practiquen la conversación, incorporando el vocabulario y las funciones de **Preparación.** Luego, represéntenla ante la clase.

MOSAICOS

ESCUCHA

Estrategia

Draw conclusions based on what you know Understanding what someone says involves using the context and the information the speaker provides to draw conclusions that go beyond literal comprehension. This process is called inferencing, or making inferences. For example, if your friend describes in great detail how she is preparing for an upcoming job interview, you will infer that she really hopes she will get the job, even if she never says this directly.

8-41 Preparación. Es el 22 de diciembre y dos amigos conversan sobre las celebraciones de fin de año. Antes de escuchar su conversación, describe en un párrafo cómo celebras tú el fin de año.

  **8-42 Escucha.** First, read the statements below, and then listen as two friends talk about a Mexican holiday. After listening, select the statements that provide information you can infer from what you heard.

1. _____ Daniel es mexicano.
2. _____ Sandra es una persona muy tímida.
3. _____ Sandra no es norteamericana.
4. _____ Daniel está triste porque no va a celebrar la Navidad con su familia.
5. _____ Pedir posada es una costumbre en la que participa solamente la familia.
6. _____ Daniel no conoce algunas costumbres mexicanas.

Comprueba

I was able to . . .

- understand the main idea and key information in a conversation.
- use contextual and factual information to draw conclusions.
- make inferences based on what I understood.

 **8-43 Un paso más.** Comparte tus respuestas a estas preguntas con tu compañero/a.

1. ¿Qué fiesta o tradición te gustaría celebrar en un país hispano? ¿Por qué?
2. ¿Celebras esa fiesta en tu ciudad o país? ¿Cómo se celebra?

HABLA

Estrategia

Conduct an interview To conduct an interview, you need to ask two types of questions: a) questions to open up a topic; and b) follow-up questions to get additional information. Questions that can be answered with **Sí** or **No** are not likely to elicit much information, unless you follow up with **¿Por qué?** Listen carefully to what your interviewee says so that you can ask relevant follow-up questions.

8-44 Preparación. Lee las siguientes afirmaciones y escribe una pregunta de seguimiento (*follow-up*) para cada una.

1. Mi familia siempre organizaba fiestas durante mi infancia.
2. Durante las celebraciones familiares, hacíamos varias actividades.
3. Mis amigos participaban en algunas de las tradiciones de mi familia.
4. Algunas costumbres familiares me gustaban y otras no.
5. En mi adolescencia, me gustaba participar en celebraciones diferentes a las de mi infancia.
6. Durante mi adolescencia, me gustaban algunas tradiciones cívicas, pero detestaba otras.

En directo

To ask someone to talk about or expand on a topic:

¿Me podrías hablar (más) sobre...? *Can you tell me (more) about . . .?*

¿Qué (más) me puedes decir sobre/de...? *What (else) can you tell me about . . .?*

Me gustaría saber... *I would like to know . . .*

To show empathy when responding:

¡Qué lástima! ¡Cuánto lo siento! *How sad! I'm so sorry.*

To share someone's happiness:

¡Qué fabuloso/bueno! *How fabulous/great!*

¡Cuánto me alegro! *I'm so happy to hear that!*

To express interest in what someone said:

¡Qué interesante! *How interesting!*

 Listen to a conversation with these expressions.

Comprueba

I was able to . . .

- request information by formulating topic-opening questions.
- ask follow-up questions to get additional information.

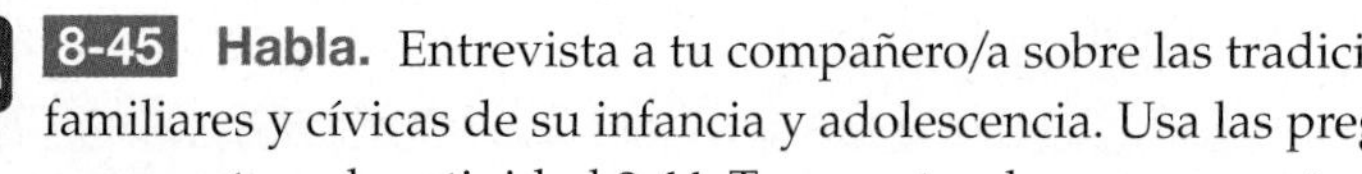

8-45 Habla. Entrevista a tu compañero/a sobre las tradiciones o fiestas familiares y cívicas de su infancia y adolescencia. Usa las preguntas que preparaste en la actividad **8-44.** Toma notas de sus respuestas.

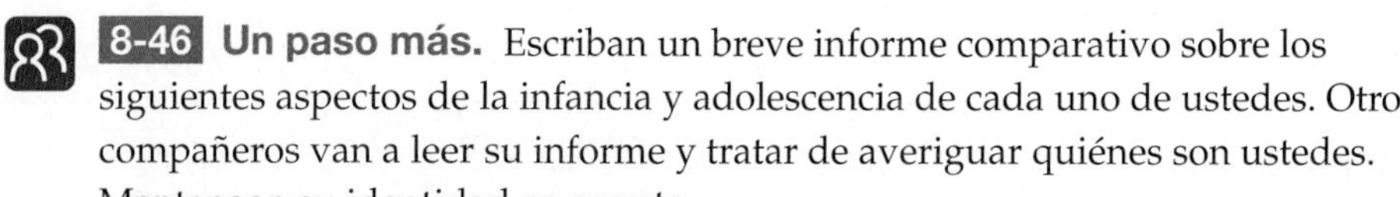

8-46 Un paso más. Escriban un breve informe comparativo sobre los siguientes aspectos de la infancia y adolescencia de cada uno de ustedes. Otros compañeros van a leer su informe y tratar de averiguar quiénes son ustedes. Mantengan su identidad en secreto.

MODELOS *Somos dos almas gemelas (*kindred spirits*). Tanto mi compañero/a como yo participábamos en…*

Somos dos mundos apartes. Mi compañero/a celebraba… Yo celebraba…

1. Durante la infancia/adolescencia, en relación a las costumbres familiares…
2. Con respecto a las fiestas familiares…
3. Con respecto a las fiestas cívicas…
4. Durante la niñez y la adolescencia, mi compañero/a y yo celebrábamos tradiciones familiares y cívicas semejantes/diferentes porque…

LEE

Estrategia

Make inferences Understanding a written text, like listening to a speaker, involves both comprehending the words literally and using the information provided to make inferences. To make inferences when you read, use your knowledge of the topic, understanding of the context, and active thinking skills, as well as your ability to understand the printed words.

8-47 Preparación. Las creencias sobre la muerte varían de una cultura a otra. En base a tus conocimientos generales, indica si las siguientes creencias y prácticas se asocian con la cultura egipcia (**E**), con alguna cultura indígena americana (**I**) o con las dos culturas (**D**). Luego, compara tus respuestas con las de tu compañero/a y comparen la información con su propia cultura.

1. _____ Creían que había vida después de la muerte.
2. _____ Construían pirámides para honrar a los muertos.
3. _____ Vestían a los muertos con ropa funeraria especial.
4. _____ Ponían una máscara sobre la cara del muerto.
5. _____ Enterraban (*They buried*) al muerto en las pirámides, en tumbas o sepulcros, de acuerdo al estatus social de la persona muerta.
6. _____ La familia de la persona muerta depositaba joyas y objetos de valor en la tumba o pirámide.
7. _____ Rociaban (*They sprayed*) el cadáver con un polvo (*powder*) de color rojo para simbolizar el renacimiento (*rebirth*).

 **8-48 Lee.** Lee el texto y determina si las siguientes afirmaciones representan información explícita (**E**) o si son inferencias (**I**) basadas en el contenido del texto. Si es una inferencia, indica la oración o las oraciones del texto en que se basa(n).

1. _____ Los expertos no saben de dónde vinieron los mayas.
2. _____ Los mayas crearon una gran civilización.
3. _____ Las comunidades mayas tenían autoridades que los gobernaban.
4. _____ Como los egipcios, los mayas construyeron edificios magníficos para honrar la memoria de personas de alto estatus en su comunidad.
5. _____ Los mayas, como otros grupos indígenas, pensaban que la vida continuaba después de la muerte.
6. _____ Para los mayas, el tipo de muerte determinaba el destino de una persona.
7. _____ No todos los mayas tenían el mismo destino después de la muerte.
8. _____ La comida, el agua y los amuletos ayudaban al espíritu del muerto a llegar a su destino final.

Comprueba

I was able to . . .

- use contextual knowledge to understand the main idea and key information in the text.
- differentiate between explicit facts and information provided indirectly.
- make inferences based on textual information and my prior knowledge.

CREENCIAS Y COSTUMBRES MAYAS SOBRE LA MUERTE

El origen de los mayas es incierto. Sin embargo[1], se sabe que esta civilización ocupó y se desarrolló[2] en los actuales territorios de Guatemala, México, Belice, Honduras y El Salvador. Durante su período de mayor esplendor, los mayas construyeron ciudades y pirámides, donde enterraban[3] a sus gobernantes[4] y los veneraban[5] después de muertos.

Los mayas compartían con otras culturas mesoamericanas algunas creencias y costumbres. Entre otras cosas, creían en la vida después de la muerte y en la interacción entre el mundo humano y el mundo espiritual. Creían que el destino de una persona después de la muerte dependía de la forma en que moría y no de su conducta mientras vivía. Las tumbas y la ropa de los muertos confirman que los mayas creían que el espíritu se prolongaba más allá de la muerte. La mayoría de los muertos iba a Xibalbá, un lugar en el inframundo[6].

Para llegar a Xibalbá, había que superar numerosos peligros[7]. El espíritu debía comer bien y protegerse. Por eso, los mayas dejaban en la tumba comida, agua y amuletos protectores, de acuerdo al estatus social del muerto.

Los mayas rociaban[8] el cadáver con un polvo[9] rojo que simbolizaba el renacimiento[10]. También lo adornaban con joyas, collares, pulseras y anillos de jade, hueso[11] o concha[12] y un cinturón ceremonial. En muchas tumbas ponían una máscara sobre la cara del muerto para ocultar su identidad. En la boca[13] le ponían una cuenta[14] de jade, símbolo de lo precioso y lo eterno, para preservar su espíritu inmortal.

Algunas de estas creencias y costumbres todavía se conservan, con ciertas variaciones, en algunas comunidades de Guatemala, México y El Salvador.

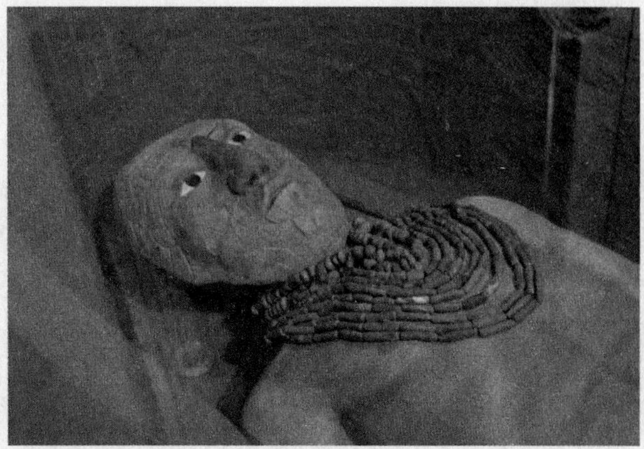

Máscara maya de la muerte del rey Pakal

Mural de Bonampak, un sitio arqueológico maya en Chiapas, México

[1]*However* [2]*developed* [3]*buried* [4]*rulers* [5]*worshipped* [6]*underworld* [7]*dangers* [8]*sprinkled* [9]*powder* [10]*rebirth* [11]*bone* [12]*shell* [13]*mouth* [14]*bead*

8-49 Un paso más. Escribe un párrafo e indica qué objetos probablemente ponían los mayas en la tumba o pirámide de un gobernante con las siguientes características:

- Era físicamente activo.
- Le gustaba mucho el arte.
- Estudiaba astronomía.
- Le fascinaba la guerra.
- Tenía ocho hijas, todas muy bellas.

ESCRIBE

Estrategia

Select and sequence details A description is like a painting—the writer uses words to create a vivid picture of an event or a scene so that readers can imagine it as they are reading. The key to a successful description are the details, which the writer selects and presents in a logical sequence. A description of a custom or a traditional celebration often uses the following structure:

- Introduce custom or traditional celebration by explaining its purpose.
- Present the elements in a logical order, providing ample description of setting, activities, food, clothing, etc.
- Insert brief explanations or stories to highlight the significance of the custom or celebration.
- Conclude by restating the role that the custom or celebration fulfils for the family or community.

8-50 Preparación. Vas a escribir una descripción, real o imaginaria, de una costumbre antigua de tu familia o de tu comunidad. Con tu compañero/a, hagan lo siguiente:

1. Hagan una lista de posibles temas: una celebración o costumbre tradicional de su familia (ej., cumpleaños, el Día de Acción de Gracias), de su comunidad o de su escuela secundaria, etc. Cada uno/a elige su tema (*topic*).
2. Ayúdense a hacer una lista de los elementos que van a incluir en su descripción: propósito (*purpose*) de la celebración o tradición, preparativos, decoraciones, comida, ropa, actividades.
3. Organización. ¿Cómo van a organizar los elementos: en orden cronológico o de otra manera?
4. Preparación lingüística. Individualmente, escribe una lista de verbos que te ayuden a describir los elementos de tu costumbre o celebración. Luego, intercambien sus listas y háganse sugerencias.

8-51 Escribe. Usa la información de la actividad **8-50** y escribe tu descripción.

8-52 Un paso más. Intercambia tu descripción con tu compañero/a. Mientras lees, escribe tres preguntas de seguimiento para hacerle a él/ella sobre su descripción.

En directo

To introduce elements in a description:

Esta tradición tiene su origen en... *This tradition has its origin in . . .*

Comenzó... *It began . . .*

En cuanto a/al... *Regarding . . .*

Otro tema relevante es... *Another relevant (important) topic is . . .*

Para concluir... *In conclusion . . .*

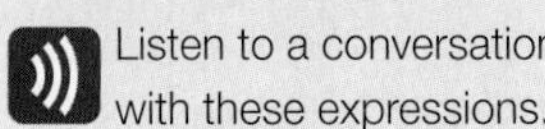

Listen to a conversation with these expressions.

Comprueba

I was able to . . .

- write a description of a celebration or custom that I know well.
- organize the elements of my description logically.

En este capítulo...

Vocabulario

Las fiestas y las tradiciones	Holidays and traditions
la alegría	*joy*
el carnaval	*carnival*
la carroza	*float* (in a parade)
la celebración	*celebration*
el cementerio	*cemetery*
la comparsa	*troupe*
la costumbre	*custom*
el desfile	*parade*
el festival	*festival*
la fiesta	*festivity; holiday; celebration*
los fuegos artificiales	*fireworks*
la ofrenda	*offering*
el/la muñeco/a	*doll, puppet*
el preparativo	*preparation*
la procesión	*procession*
la semilla	*seed*
el toro	*bull*
la tradición	*tradition*
la vela	*candle*

Las personas	People
el/la antepasado/a	*ancestor*
el/la difunto/a, el/la muerto/a	*deceased person*
la gente	*people*

Las celebraciones	Celebrations
el Año Nuevo	*New Year's Day*
el Día de Acción de Gracias	*Thanksgiving Day*
el Día de las Brujas	*Halloween*
el Día de los Enamorados / del Amor y de la Amistad	*Valentine's Day*
el Día de la Independencia de México	*Mexican Independence Day*
el Día de la Madre	*Mother's Day*
el Día de los Muertos/Difuntos	*Day of the Dead*
el Día del Padre	*Father's Day*
la Navidad	*Christmas*
la Nochebuena	*Christmas Eve*
la Nochevieja / el Fin de Año	*New Year's Eve*
la Pascua	*Easter*

Las descripciones	Descriptions
animado/a	*lively*
hermoso/a	*beautiful*
maravilloso/a	*marvelous*
último/a	*last*

El tiempo	Time
a eso de...	*at about . . .*
a finales de...	*at the end of . . .*
antes	*before*
con anterioridad	*in advance*
el comienzo	*beginning*
entonces	*then*
generalmente	*generally*
hoy en día	*nowadays*
mientras	*while*
por último	*finally*

Verbos	Verbs
acompañar	*to accompany*
comenzar (ie)	*to begin*
dar una vuelta	*to take a walk*
desfilar	*to parade; to march*
disfrazarse (c)	*to wear a costume*
durar	*to last*
invitar	*to invite*
mantener (ie)	*to keep, to maintain*
recordar (ue)	*to remember*
reunirse	*to get together, to gather*

Palabras y expresiones útiles	Useful words and expressions
cómo no	*of course*
estupendamente	*wonderfully*
en vivo	*live*
tener muchas ganas de...	*to be very excited to . . .*

See page 299 for other expressions of time and frequency.
See pages 307, 313, and 317 for expressions used to make comparisons.

Capítulo 9
¿Dónde trabajas?

Mujer guatemalteca trabajando en un telar (*loom*)

Enfoque cultural
Guatemala

Vocabulario en contexto
El trabajo
Los oficios y las profesiones
La entrevista de trabajo

Mosaico cultural
¿Trabajas o estudias?

En acción
Buscando trabajo

Funciones y formas
More on the imperfect and the preterit
Review of direct and indirect object pronouns
Use of direct and indirect object pronouns together
Formal commands

Mosaicos
ESCUCHA Use contextual guessing
HABLA Gather information strategically to express a decision
LEE Organize textual information into categories
ESCRIBE Reporting on an interview

En este capítulo...
Vocabulario

Learning Outcomes

You will be able to:

- talk about careers and employment
- describe past events in more detail
- avoid repetition
- give instructions and suggestions
- talk about Guatemala in terms of products, practices, and perspectives
- share information about the causes and consequences of migration from Guatemala to the United States

Enfoque cultural

Guatemala

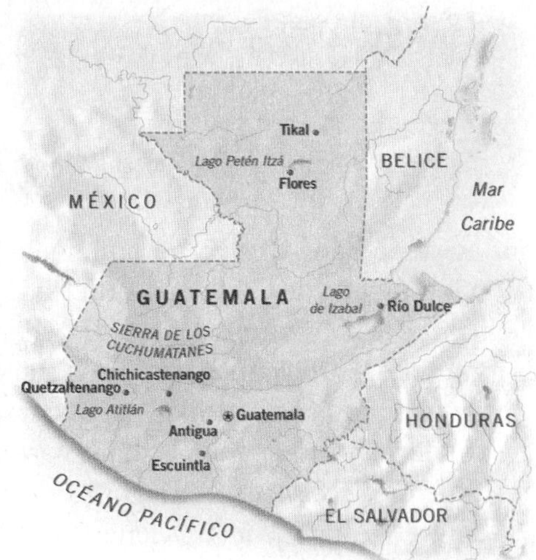

Las ruinas mayas de Tikal, al norte de Guatemala

El mercado al aire libre de Chichicastenango

La histórica ciudad de Antigua

Arte hispano

Café (1991), de Pedro Rafael González Chavajay. El cultivo, la producción y exportación del café tienen una larga tradición en Guatemala. En esta obra se reflejan la vida y las costumbres diarias de los mayas y sus descendientes.

Enfoque cultural

¿Qué te parece?

- El nombre **Guatemala** viene del náhuatl y significa "lugar de muchos árboles".
- En la bandera de Guatemala la franja (*stripe*) blanca con el escudo (*coat of arms*) entre las dos azules representa al país entre el océano Pacífico y el mar Caribe.
- La edad mediana (*median*) de la población de Guatemala es 21,7 años.
- El fiambre es una ensalada típica que puede tener hasta 50 ingredientes. Se come el 1 de noviembre para celebrar el Día de Todos los Santos.

En la ciudad de Cobán, se celebra anualmente la Fiesta Nacional Indígena de Guatemala, un festival folclórico. Este incluye un certamen (*contest*) de belleza para mujeres indígenas. Participan aproximadamente 100 jóvenes que expresan sus ideales en su lengua (*language*) materna y en español. La ganadora es coronada con el título de *Rabín Ajau*, que significa "Hija del Rey" en q'eqchi', una lengua maya.

El quetzal es el ave nacional de Guatemala y tiene un papel mitológico en su historia. El nombre del dios supremo, Quetzalcóatl, está formado por dos palabras de origen náhuatl: *quetzal*, que se refiere a la pluma larga y verde del ave, y *coatl*, que quiere decir "serpiente". Para los mayas, las plumas del quetzal eran sagradas (*sacred*). El quetzal aparece en el escudo nacional y es también el nombre de la moneda (*currency*) nacional.

Rigoberta Menchú es una activista guatemalteca que ha dedicado su vida a defender los derechos (*rights*) de los indígenas. Nació (*was born*) en 1959 en una familia de campesinos y tuvo un acceso limitado a la educación. Durante la Guerra Civil de Guatemala (1960–1996), sus padres y sus hermanos fueron víctimas de las fuerzas armadas de Guatemala que controlaban el país. Ella tuvo que vivir muchos años en el exilio. En 1992 recibió el premio Nobel de la Paz, y en 1998 el premio Príncipe de Asturias. En 2011 fue candidata a la presidencia de su país.

La erupción del volcán de Fuego, cerca de Antigua, el 3 de junio de 2018, es un ejemplo de la actividad volcánica de este país. Guatemala forma parte del llamado "cinturón de fuego del Pacífico", junto con Indonesia y Japón. Por lo menos tres de sus 37 volcanes están activos.

e **¿Cuánto sabes?** Completa las oraciones, según **Enfoque cultural.**

1. _______________ es la capital de Guatemala.
2. El océano _______________ está al oeste del país.
3. El _______________ es una comida típica del Día de Todos los Santos.
4. Una activista famosa es _______________.
5. Las palabras **quetzal** y **Guatemala** vienen de la lengua _______________.
6. La civilización _______________ construyó la ciudad de Tikal.

To learn more about Guatemala, go online to view the *Club cultura* videos.

VOCABULARIO EN CONTEXTO

Talking about careers and employment

El trabajo

El sector más grande en la economía guatemalteca es la **agricultura.** Esta representa dos tercios (*thirds*) de las **exportaciones** y la mitad de la **fuerza laboral** del país. Los productos **agrícolas** principales son el café, la caña de azúcar (*sugar cane*) y las bananas. Antes, los **agricultores** plantaban y **cosechaban** sus cultivos (*crops*) en **terrenos** pequeños. Ahora el café y otros productos agrícolas se **cultivan** en **fincas** grandes.

Antes, los productos del **campo** y los productos artesanales, como las telas, se vendían solo en los mercados locales como en el de Chichicastenango. **Sin embargo,** ahora se exportan a otros países. En concreto, la **industria textil** es una importante **fuente de ingresos** para muchas familias.

El terreno **fértil** es el **recurso natural** más importante de Guatemala. En sus **tierras** también se encuentran minerales como el **hierro,** el **petróleo** y el níquel, que muchas veces **explotan compañías** extranjeras (*foreign*). Antes, los **carpinteros** hacían muebles solamente para el consumo local. Gracias a los abundantes **bosques** de Guatemala, hoy en día se exportan la **madera** y sus productos derivados.

PRÁCTICA

9-1 Escucha y confirma. Listen to the statements and indicate if each one refers to **recursos naturales, agricultura**, or **artesanía**.

1. ____________
2. ____________
3. ____________
4. ____________
5. ____________
6. ____________

> **Lengua**
>
> The suffix **-ero/-era** is often used in Spanish to designate trades and professions, for example, **camarero/a** (*server*), **plomero/a** (*plumber*), **peluquero/a** (*hairdresser*). Another common suffix is **-ista,** for example, **electricista** (*electrician*); **contratista** (*contractor*).

9-2 Los trabajos y los trabajadores. Indica si las siguientes afirmaciones son ciertas (**C**) o falsas (**F**). Corrige las falsas y compara tus respuestas con las de tu compañero/a.

1. _____ Los agricultores hacen los trabajos del campo.
2. _____ Algunos artesanos elaboran telas.
3. _____ Los carpinteros trabajan con los metales.
4. _____ Guatemala exporta muebles y otros productos hechos de madera.
5. _____ El oro y la plata son los minerales más abundantes de Guatemala.
6. _____ Los agricultores plantan y cosechan productos para el consumo local solamente.

9-3 Productos y lugares. Selecciona la palabra o frase que corresponde a cada definición. Luego, compara tus respuestas con las de tu compañero/a.

1. _____ los productos que se venden a otros países
2. _____ las telas que se hacen en fábricas (*factories*) o artesanalmente
3. _____ el conjunto de personas que trabajan
4. _____ el lugar en el campo donde se encuentran los cultivos
5. _____ los depósitos minerales y el terreno fértil
6. _____ el material básico que usan los carpinteros

a. la industria textil
b. la finca
c. los recursos naturales
d. las exportaciones
e. la madera
f. la fuerza laboral

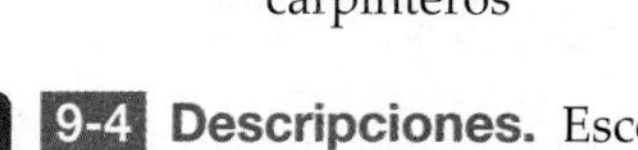

9-4 Descripciones. Escoge una de las fotos de la página 329. Descríbele a tu compañero/a la escena con el mayor detalle posible. Incluye las siguientes ideas.

1. lugar donde están las personas
2. características físicas
3. edad aproximada
4. ropa que llevan
5. qué están haciendo
6. qué están pensando
7. cómo se sienten

Los oficios y las profesiones

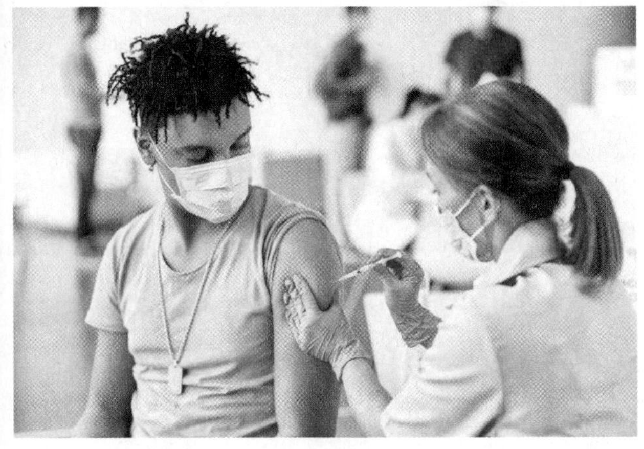

Una **médica** le inyecta un medicamento a un paciente en su **consultorio.**

Una **ejecutiva** llama por teléfono a un **cliente.**

Una **locutora espera** la **señal** para comenzar un programa de noticias en una estación de radio.

Un **técnico** revisa los controles de una compañía petrolera.

Unos **bomberos apagan** un **incendio** en Ciudad de Guatemala.

Un **peluquero** le **corta** el pelo a un cliente.

Otras ocupaciones

PRÁCTICA

> **En otras palabras**
>
> Other words for **contador/a, chofer,** and **plomero/a** are **contable, chófer,** and **fontanero/a**.

9-5 Para confirmar. Lean las siguientes descripciones e indiquen qué profesión u oficio tienen las personas con estas características.

abogado/a	arquitecto/a	médico/a
actor/actriz	ingeniero/a	plomero/a
artista	mecánico/a	psicólogo/a

MODELO A Raúl y a Andrés les fascina diseñar casas y otros edificios.
arquitectos

1. __________ A Pablo le gusta observar y analizar el comportamiento (*behavior*) de las personas.
2. __________ Los hermanos Pedraza siempre resuelven los problemas del auto de su padre. Lo examinan y lo reparan a la perfección.
3. __________ Eva y Ana tienen facilidad para resolver los problemas de otras personas y la habilidad de exponer oralmente ante una corte.
4. __________ A Jaime le encanta desarmar (*take apart*) aparatos electrónicos para estudiar cómo funcionan.
5. __________ Daniela es una chica muy sensible y una gran observadora. Le fascina expresar sus sentimientos y experiencias de manera artística.
6. __________ Adela siempre lee libros sobre anatomía. Ella sabe el nombre de cada parte del cuerpo humano.

Cultura

La mujer y el trabajo Un cambio social importante en los países hispanos en las últimas décadas es la entrada masiva de las mujeres al mercado laboral. Sin embargo, aún (*still*) existen desigualdades. Por ejemplo, los salarios de las mujeres son, en muchos casos, más bajos que los de los hombres. Algunos países, como Perú y Chile, tienen un Ministerio de la Mujer para proteger los derechos (*rights*) de las mujeres.

Conexiones En tu opinión, ¿por qué las oportunidades y condiciones laborales son mejores para los hombres que para las mujeres? ¿Cómo se puede terminar esta desigualdad?

9-6 Las profesiones y la personalidad. **PREPARACIÓN.** Digan cómo deben ser estos/as profesionales. Seleccionen las palabras de la lista para describirlos/las.

autoritario/a	detallista	perezoso/a
calculador/a	estudioso/a	responsable
cuidadoso/a	guapo/a	romántico/a
dedicado/a	inteligente	serio/a
delgado/a	irónico/a	simpático/a
descuidado/a	paciente	valiente

MODELO un/a bombero/a

E1: *Debe ser una persona valiente, seria y responsable.*

E2: *Sí, y no debe ser perezoso o perezosa.*

1. un/a médico/a
2. un actor/una actriz
3. un hombre/una mujer de negocios
4. un/a peluquero/a
5. un/a locutor/a
6. un/a amo/a de casa
7. un/a bibliotecario/a
8. un/a mecánico/a
9. un/a cocinero/a
10. un/a abogado/a

INTERCAMBIOS. Intercambien ideas sobre lo siguiente.

1. ¿Conoces a algún/alguna… (*nombre de la profesión*)? ¿Cómo se llama? ¿Dónde trabaja?
2. ¿Qué características personales o especiales, en tu opinión, lo/la ayudan en su profesión?

9-7 Asociaciones. Asocien una o más profesiones con los siguientes lugares de trabajo. Túrnense y digan lo que hacen estas personas.

Lugar	Profesión	¿Qué hace?
1. el hospital	*enfermero/a, médico/a*	*Ayuda a los pacientes.*
2. el restaurante		
3. la clase		
4. la estación de radio		
5. la tienda de ropa		
6. el consultorio médico		
7. la peluquería		

 **9-8 ¿Cuál es la profesión?** Escribe la ocupación o profesión, y una ventaja y una desventaja de cada descripción en la tabla. Después, túrnense para compartir sus ideas.

MODELO Trabaja en una biblioteca.
E1: *Es un/a bibliotecario/a.*
E2: *Una ventaja de ser bibliotecario/a es tener acceso a muchos libros y una desventaja es trabajar muchas horas frente a la computadora.*
E1: *Para mí, una ventaja es trabajar en un lugar tranquilo y una desventaja es no hacer ejercicio físico.*

	Profesión	Ventajas	Desventajas
1. Escribe artículos para un periódico.			
2. Presenta programas de televisión.			
3. Traduce simultáneamente.			
4. Mantiene el orden público.			
5. Apaga incendios.			
6. Defiende o acusa a personas delante de un/a juez.			

La entrevista de trabajo

SRA. ARCE: Buenos días, Sr. Solano. Soy Marcela Arce, presidenta de la compañía.
SR. SOLANO: Mucho gusto.
SRA. ARCE: Siéntese, por favor. Usted **solicitó** el **puesto** de **gerente de ventas** en línea, ¿verdad?
SR. SOLANO: Así es. Hice una búsqueda en línea y en los **anuncios** vi que había una **vacante.** Así que **llené** una **solicitud** y la **envié** por internet.
SRA. ARCE: Sí, aquí la tengo, y también su **currículum. Por cierto,** es excelente. Veo que tiene mucha **experiencia** como **vendedor** y gerente.
SR. SOLANO: Muchas gracias.
SRA. ARCE: **Actualmente** usted es **empleado** de la **empresa** Badosa. ¿Por qué quiere **dejar** su puesto?
SR. SOLANO: Bueno, **en realidad** estoy muy contento allí, pero a mí me gustaría trabajar en una compañía internacional para poder hablar otras **lenguas.** Como usted ve en mi currículum, hablo español, inglés y francés.
SRA. ARCE: En su solicitud, usted indica que desea un **sueldo** de 25.000 quetzales al mes, con **beneficios.** Sin embargo, para el puesto que tenemos, el sueldo que **se ofrece** es de 20.000 quetzales.
SR. SOLANO: Sí, lo sé, pero la diferencia no es tan importante. **Lo importante** es que aquí puedo tener la oportunidad de comunicarme con los clientes en su **propia** lengua. Creo que esto puede mejorar notablemente las ventas de Computel.
SRA. ARCE: Pues, si le parece bien el sueldo, ¿por qué no pasamos a la oficina del director general para seguir hablando? En unos días, el **jefe** de recursos humanos va a comunicarle nuestra decisión.
SR. SOLANO: ¡Cómo no!

Lengua

In Spanish, **actualmente** means *now, at present.*

Actualmente yo trabajo en Antigua.
At the present time/Now I work in Antigua.

Therefore, **actualmente** is a false cognate of *actually.* The equivalents of *actually* in Spanish are **realmente** or **en realidad.**

Realmente/En realidad yo trabajé en Ciudad de Guatemala solo un mes.
Actually, I worked in Guatemala City for only a month.

PRÁCTICA

9-9 Para confirmar. Busquen la siguiente información en la conversación en la página 334.

1. nombre de la presidenta de la compañía
2. puesto que solicita el Sr. Solano
3. nombre de la compañía donde desea trabajar
4. lenguas que habla
5. sueldo que desea el Sr. Solano
6. sueldo que se ofrece en el nuevo puesto
7. dos motivos para cambiar de puesto

9-10 ¿En qué orden? Cuando alguien busca un trabajo, ¿en qué orden ocurren normalmente las siguientes actividades? Ordénalas de 1 a 8. Después, compara tus respuestas con las de tu compañero/a.

_____ Leo los anuncios de trabajo en internet.
_____ Me llaman de la tienda Rosell para una entrevista.
_____ Les contesto que se cerró el almacén.
_____ Con un clic del ratón, envío mis documentos a la tienda Rosell.
_____ Voy a la compañía para la entrevista.
_____ Me preguntan la razón por la que dejé el trabajo anterior.
_____ Lleno la solicitud en línea para la tienda Rosell y subo (*upload*) mi currículum.
_____ Me ofrecen el puesto de vendedor/a.

9-11 El arte de entrevistarse. **PREPARACIÓN.** Escoge el anuncio que te parece más interesante y solicita ese puesto. Tu compañero/a, en el papel de jefe/a de personal, debe entrevistarte y tomar notas para obtener la siguiente información. Luego, cambien de papel.

1. nombre de la persona que solicita el puesto
2. estudios
3. lenguas que habla
4. lugar donde trabaja y responsabilidades
5. experiencia anterior
6. razones para querer trabajar en esta compañía

INTERCAMBIOS. Ahora informa al/a la presidente/a de la empresa (otro/a compañero/a) sobre las calificaciones de la persona que entrevistaste.

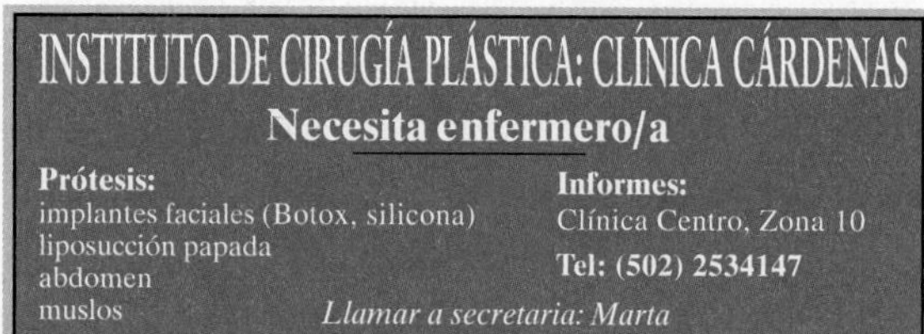

Hotel VILLA ANTIGUA

Necesita

RECEPCIONISTA
- Experiencia
- Bilingüe español-inglés

CAMARERO/A
- Mín. 2 años de experiencia
- Disponible trabajar por las mañanas y tardes

Dirigirse al Hotel VILLA ANTIGUA
Jefe de Personal
9a. Calle Poniente, Carretera a Ciudad Vieja
Antigua, Guatemala
Teléfono: +(502) 78323956 o +(502) 78323955

EMPRESA EXPORTADORA DE ARTESANÍAS
Requiere

CONTADOR/A

Requisitos:
- Experiencia mínima de 5 años
- Graduado del Colegio de Contadores Públicos
- Para cita llamar al Sr. López al (502) 2764532

EMPRESA MINERA

Requiere
Ingenieros/as de sistemas

REQUISITOS:
1. Mayor de 25 años
2. Experiencia en minas de cobre
3. Flexibilidad horaria (incluidos fines de semana)

OFRECEMOS:
1. Ingreso superior a 40.000 quetzales
2. Capacitación profesional
3. Bonos de participación

Interesados enviar currículum a:
Minas de Guatemala S.A.

Oficina de Personal
Diagonal 19, 29-78, Zona 11
Ciudad de Guatemala, Guatemala
Teléfono: (502) 2762147
Email: rh@minasguate.com

9-12 ¿Comportamiento apropiado? Preparen una lista de cinco acciones que se deben hacer antes de una entrevista y cinco que no se deben hacer durante una entrevista. Después, comparen su lista con la de otros/as compañeros/as.

Lo que se debe hacer antes de una entrevista	Lo que no se debe hacer durante una entrevista

Cultura

Documentos a presentar En muchos países hispanos, en una solicitud de trabajo, además de un CV, es común incluir una foto reciente de la persona que solicita el trabajo. Hasta hace poco tiempo, también era necesario agregar en el CV datos como la nacionalidad o el estado civil (*marital status*).

Comparaciones ¿Cuáles son las ventajas y desventajas de incluir una foto junto con el CV y de tener que indicar el estado civil en una solicitud? ¿Qué efecto podría (*could*) tener esta información en una solicitud de trabajo? ¿Es necesario incluir una foto e indicar el estado civil en tu país?

9-13 Mi profesión. **PREPARACIÓN.** Make a list of four professions that have very strict schedules, and four that have flexible hours. Share your answers with a classmate.

ESCUCHA. Pay attention to the general idea of what is said. As you listen, select the appropriate ending to each statement. Check answers with a classmate.

1. Julieta Odriozola es…
   - **a.** artista.
   - **b.** política.
   - **c.** periodista.
2. Julieta tiene un horario…
   - **a.** de 9 a 5.
   - **b.** variable.
   - **c.** de lunes a sábado.
3. Julieta hace casi todo su trabajo en…
   - **a.** su auto.
   - **b.** su casa.
   - **c.** diferentes lugares.
4. Julieta trabaja con…
   - **a.** artistas jóvenes.
   - **b.** personas importantes.
   - **c.** empleados de la comunidad.

Mosaico cultural

¿Trabajas o estudias?

Carlos, un estudiante de publicidad, empezó a hacer malabarismos (*juggling*) en los parques y en las calles de Ciudad de Guatemala a los 18 años. Algunos de sus amigos cantaban en las estaciones de tren y así pagaron sus estudios. El caso de Carlos y sus amigos es bastante común entre los hispanos jóvenes. En general es complicado encontrar un trabajo estable mientras se estudia, o incluso un trabajo a tiempo parcial, especialmente porque los trabajos son escasos y las empresas a veces buscan personas con experiencia laboral.

En Perú y Ecuador, por ejemplo, es posible ver a estudiantes universitarios vendiendo artesanías, collares y pulseras para ganar dinero. Un caso similar es el de Matías, un joven de Buenos Aires, que tuvo este tipo de empleo informal por cinco años, antes de graduarse de dentista. Matías bailaba tango con su novia en las estaciones del metro de Buenos Aires. Dice Matías: "fue una experiencia bonita, hacíamos el espectáculo y la gente nos daba algo de dinero; todos se divertían mucho". En el Cono Sur, este tipo de trabajo se llama **trabajo a la gorra** porque al final del espectáculo, los jóvenes pasan una gorra (o un sombrero) para recolectar el dinero de los espectadores.

Unos estudiantes hacen malabarismos y cantan para ganar dinero.

Este joven toca la guitarra en una estación de tren.

Una pareja de estudiantes baila tango en la calle.

Compara

1. ¿Qué tipo de trabajos son frecuentes entre los estudiantes universitarios en tu país?
2. En general, ¿es fácil encontrar trabajo mientras eres estudiante? ¿Cómo encuentran trabajo los estudiantes?
3. ¿Conoces algún tipo de "trabajo a la gorra" en tu comunidad? Explica.
4. ¿Trabajas para pagar tus estudios? Explica.

En acción

Buscando trabajo

Antes de ver

9-14 Las profesiones. Selecciona la profesión u ocupación que corresponde a cada definición.

1. _____ Trabaja con madera y hace muebles.
2. _____ Sirve comida en un restaurante.
3. _____ Se dedica a cortar el pelo y a peinar a sus clientes.
4. _____ Defiende a un acusado en la corte.
5. _____ Ayuda a otras personas u organizaciones y no recibe sueldo.
6. _____ Planifica y hace películas.
7. _____ Estudia las civilizaciones y culturas del mundo.
8. _____ Atiende a personas que tienen problemas de salud.
9. _____ Recibe el dinero de los clientes.
10. _____ Construye casas y edificios.

a. peluquero/a
b. abogado/a
c. enfermero/a
d. director/a de cine
e. carpintero/a
f. voluntario/a
g. camarero/a
h. antropólogo/a
i. cajero/a
j. arquitecto/a

Mientras ves

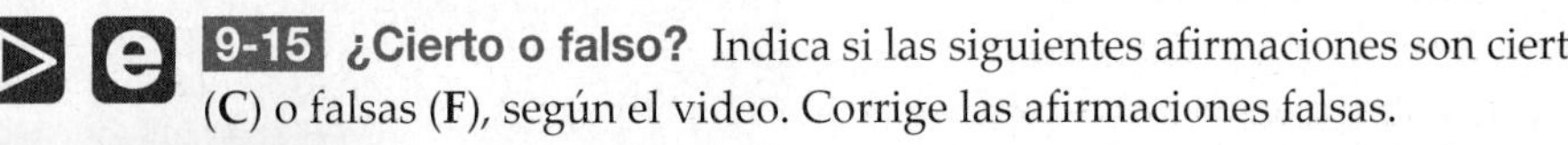

9-15 ¿Cierto o falso? Indica si las siguientes afirmaciones son ciertas (C) o falsas (F), según el video. Corrige las afirmaciones falsas.

1. _____ Pilar recibe un salario muy alto por el trabajo que hace en Guatemala.
2. _____ Las estufas ecológicas son menos peligrosas que las estufas de leña (*firewood*).
3. _____ El lago Atitlán es el lago más profundo de Centroamérica.
4. _____ El café y el maíz son importantes productos de Guatemala.
5. _____ Las ruinas de Tikal son un ejemplo de la arquitectura española en Guatemala.
6. _____ Chichicastenango es un famoso mercado de productos naturales y artesanía.

Después de ver

9-16 ¿Qué dijeron?

PREPARACIÓN. Indica lo que dijeron los personajes en este segmento de video.

1. _____ Vanesa dijo que estaba buscando un trabajo relacionado con la moda.
2. _____ Héctor dijo que él ayudaba a su madre con las cuentas en su peluquería.
3. _____ Héctor le contó a Vanesa que cuando era más joven, él mismo se cortó el pelo.
4. _____ Pilar dijo que estaba haciendo trabajo voluntario en Honduras.
5. _____ Héctor y Vanesa dijeron que iban a pensar seriamente en hacer trabajo voluntario también.

INTERCAMBIOS. Cuéntense alguna anécdota relacionada con un trabajo que tuvieron en el pasado. Usen las siguientes preguntas como guía.

1. ¿Qué trabajo era?
2. ¿Era un trabajo voluntario o pagado?
3. ¿Ocurrió algo interesante en ese trabajo? ¿Qué pasó?

FUNCIONES Y FORMAS

1 Talking about the past

PERIODISTA: Sr. Mario Parada, usted estaba en el Bancafé cuando entraron los ladrones (*robbers*), ¿verdad? ¿Qué **estaba haciendo?**

MARIO PARADA: Yo **estaba hablando** con la cajera. **Iba a** hacer un depósito, pero claro, no **pude** realizar la transacción.

PERIODISTA: ¿Qué hicieron los empleados cuando **supieron** que había ladrones en el banco?

MARIO PARADA: Todo fue muy rápido. En el momento del robo, los cajeros **estaban atendiendo** a los clientes. Los oficiales de seguridad vieron a los ladrones y **quisieron** detenerlos (*stop them*) pero no **pudieron.**

Piénsalo. Indica si cada afirmación representa una **actividad en progreso** o un **evento terminado** en el pasado.

	ACTIVIDAD EN PROGRESO	EVENTO TERMINADO
1. Yo **estaba hablando** con la cajera.	_____	_____
2. No **pude** hacer la transacción.	_____	_____
3. Los empleados **supieron** que había ladrones.	_____	_____
4. Los cajeros **estaban respondiendo** a las preguntas de los clientes.	_____	_____
5. Los oficiales **quisieron** detener a los ladrones.	_____	_____
6. No **pudieron** detenerlos.	_____	_____

More on the imperfect and the preterit

- You have used the imperfect to express an action or event that was in progress in the past. You may also use the imperfect progressive to emphasize the ongoing nature of the activity in the past. Form the imperfect progressive with the imperfect of **estar** and the present participle (**-ndo**).

  Mario **estaba hablando** con la cajera cuando entraron los ladrones. — *Mario was talking to the teller when the robbers came in.*

  Los gerentes del banco **estaban trabajando** en el segundo piso cuando oyeron los gritos. — *The bank managers were working on the second floor when they heard the shouts.*

- To express intentions in the past, use the imperfect of **ir a** + *infinitive.*

  Iba a salir, pero era muy tarde. — *I was going to go out, but it was very late.*

- In **Capítulo 7**, you practiced the preterit of **saber** with the meaning of finding out about something. You also practiced the preterit of **querer** with the meaning of wanting or trying to do something, but failing to accomplish it. In the negative, the preterit of **querer** conveys the meaning of refusing to do something.

  Supe que Jorge consiguió trabajo. — *I found out that Jorge got a job.*

  Quise entrevistarme con el gerente, pero fue imposible. — *I wanted (and tried) to get an interview with the manager, but it was impossible.*

  No quise ir. — *I refused to go.*

- Other verbs that convey a different meaning in English when the preterit is used are **conocer** and **poder.**

IMPERFECT		PRETERIT	
Yo **conocía** a Ana.	*I knew Ana.*	**Conocí** a Ana.	*I met Ana.*
Podía hacerlo.	*I could (was able to) do it.*	**Pude** hacerlo.	*I accomplished (managed to do) it.*
No podía hacerlo.	*I couldn't (wasn't able to) do it.*	**No pude** hacerlo.	*I couldn't do it. (I tried and failed.)*
Quería ir con ellos.	*I wanted to go with them.*	**Quise** ir con ellos.	*I tried to go with them (but didn't go).*
		No **quise** ir con ellos.	*I refused to go with them.*

¿Comprendes? Completa las oraciones con la forma correcta del verbo en el pretérito o el imperfecto.

1. Ellas ____________ (conversar) cuando entró el gerente.
2. Pablo no ____________ (querer) compartir los comentarios del jefe y no dijo nada.
3. El proyecto fue difícil, pero nosotros ____________ (poder) hacerlo.
4. Alfredo y Sandra ____________ (conocerse) en una recepción.
5. Después Alfredo ____________ (saber) que Sandra ya (*already*) conocía a su hermano.

PRÁCTICA

9-17 Las memorias de Arturo.

PREPARACIÓN. Completa el párrafo de Arturo, un profesor de antropología, con el verbo apropiado. Luego, compara tus respuestas con las de tu compañero/a.

El año pasado, yo (1) ________ (conocí/conocía) a mi novia Elizabeth en mi primer viaje (*trip*) a Guatemala. En ese momento, yo solo (2) ________ (conocí/conocía) Antigua y un par de lugares de interés para los turistas. Después de nuestro encuentro, yo inmediatamente (3) ________ (supe/sabía) que mis visitas a Guatemala (4) ________ (fueron/iban) a ser más frecuentes. El año pasado nosotros no (5) ________ (quisimos/queríamos) hacer ningún viaje, pero este año sí. Su familia, ella y yo (6) ________ (pudimos/podíamos) explorar juntos la reserva ecológica Calahuar. Caminamos todo el día por el bosque. Después de caminar tantas horas, yo no (7) ________ (pude/podía) dar un paso más, pero al día siguiente (8) ________ (pudimos/podíamos) continuar el viaje a San Pedro La Laguna en el lago Atlitán.

INTERCAMBIOS. Cuéntense cómo conocieron a su pareja o a su mejor amigo/a. Incluyan la siguiente información:

- cuándo pasó
- dónde estaban
- quién inició la conversación
- cómo se sentían

9-18 Una oficina muy ocupada. Ustedes visitaron la oficina que aparece en la siguiente escena. Túrnense para preguntar qué estaban haciendo las personas cuando cada uno/a de ustedes llegó.

MODELO E1: *¿Qué estaba haciendo Blanca cuando llegaste a la oficina?*
E2: *Estaba conversando con un cliente.*

9-19 ¡A usar la imaginación! Estas descripciones indican lo que estaban haciendo varias personas. Túrnense para identificar la profesión de ellos y qué iban a hacer después.

MODELO Esta persona llevaba un traje espacial, guantes, botas muy grandes y un casco (*helmet*) transparente para poder ver y respirar.
E1: (profesión) *Era un astronauta.*
E2: (hacer después) *Iba a caminar en la Luna.*

1. Un hombre joven tenía un secador en la mano y hablaba con una clienta mientras la peinaba.
2. Unos señores iban en un vehículo rojo con una sirena. El vehículo iba muy rápido y los autos le daban paso (*yielded*).
3. Una joven que llevaba un vestido similar a los que se llevaban en el tiempo de Cleopatra hablaba frente a una cámara. Tenía pelo negro y estaba muy maquillada.
4. Un señor estudiaba los planos de un edificio y decía que ciertas cosas no estaban bien.

9-20 Un día extraño. Trabajen juntos para completar las oraciones, explicando por qué ayer no pudieron hacer lo que hacen normalmente.

MODELO Siempre desayuno bien, pero ayer...
E1: *Siempre desayuno bien, pero ayer no pude desayunar.*
E2: *¿Por qué no pudiste desayunar? ¿Qué pasó?*
E1: *Me desperté a las 8:45 y tuve que pasar por el cajero automático antes de clase.*

1. Mis padres siempre me mandan mensajes de texto, pero ayer...
2. Siempre termino mi tarea antes de las diez de la noche, pero ayer...
3. Generalmente duermo muy bien, pero anoche...
4. Con frecuencia practico deportes por la tarde, pero ayer...
5. Generalmente acepto las invitaciones de mis amigos, pero ayer...
6. Casi siempre hago la tarea de matemáticas sin ningún problema, pero ayer...

9-21 ¡Malas sorpresas! Lean las siguientes situaciones e inventen historias breves: los planes probables de las personas, qué intentaron (quisieron) hacer y qué pudieron (o no pudieron) hacer.

MODELO Martín iba a ir a una fiesta en el parque, pero su bicicleta se descompuso (*broke down*).
E1: *Martín quiso ir al parque, pero no pudo porque su bicicleta se descompuso.*
E2: *Él quiso usar la bicicleta de su hermano, pero no pudo porque...*

1. Cristina tenía que hacer fotocopias, pero su fotocopiadora no funcionaba.
2. Ibas a cenar en tu restaurante favorito, pero el restaurante estaba cerrado.
3. Los empleados tenían una reunión importante, pero comenzó a nevar.
4. Gabriela y Francisco iban a la playa, pero su auto se quedó sin (*ran out of*) gasolina.
5. Esteban tenía una entrevista con el jefe de personal a las nueve, pero llegó a la oficina a las diez.

Situación

PREPARACIÓN. Lean la situación. Luego, compartan ejemplos de vocabulario, gramática y otra información que necesitan para desarrollar la conversación.

Role A. You work as a server at a restaurant near your campus. While you were working last night, there was a power outage (**un apagón**). In the darkness of the crowded restaurant, servers dropped trays (**bandejas**), some customers stole purses, cell phones, and other items from nearby tables, and other people started to fight (**pelearse**). A reporter for the school newspaper interviews you about the incident.

Role B. You are a reporter for your school newspaper, and you are investigating an incident that took place at a restaurant near campus. Ask the server (your classmate) for details:
a. what people were doing when the power went out (**cortarse la luz**);
b. what happened next; and
c. what people tried to do and were able (or not able) to do.

	ROLE A	ROLE B
Vocabulario	Words and expressions related to restaurants	Question words Words and expressions related to restaurants
Funciones y formas	Telling a story in the past Answering questions Preterit and imperfect	Asking questions Preterit and imperfect

INTERCAMBIOS. Practiquen la conversación, incorporando el vocabulario y las funciones de **Preparación.** Luego, represéntenla ante la clase.

2 Avoiding repetition

SILVIA: Emilia, ¿por qué llevas chancletas?
EMILIA: **Le** di mis zapatos al zapatero porque se rompió (*broke*) la suela (*sole*).
SILVIA: ¿Y no tienes frío?
EMILIA: Sí, pero no tengo otra opción. El zapatero va a reparar**los** en una hora. Y tú, Silvia, ¿por qué no trajiste chaqueta? Hace frío.
SILVIA: **La** dejé en casa.
EMILIA: Bueno, yo **te** presto mi suéter.

Piénsalo. Lee las oraciones e indica si las palabras en negrita (*bold*) son objetos directos o indirectos. Escribe tanto los pronombres (*pronouns*) como los sustantivos (*nouns*). Si no hay, escribe una **X.**

	OBJETO DIRECTO	OBJETO INDIRECTO
MODELO El zapatero va a reparar los **zapatos** de Emilia.	*zapatos*	X
1. **Le** di mis **zapatos** al **zapatero.**	________	________
2. El zapatero va a reparar**los.**	________	________
3. ¿Por qué no trajiste **chaqueta?**	________	________
4. **La** dejé en casa.	________	________
5. **Te** presto mi **suéter.**	________	________

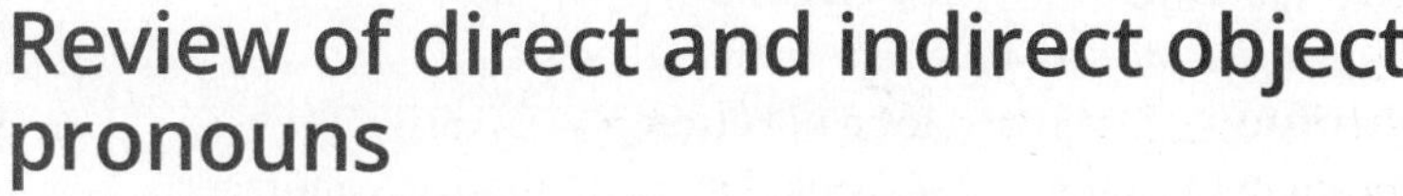

Review of direct and indirect object pronouns

- In **Capítulo 5**, you learned that direct objects answer the question *what?* or *whom?* in relation to the verb. They can refer to people, animals, or objects. When a direct object noun refers to a specific person, a group of people, or a pet, the personal **a** precedes the direct object. To avoid repetition in speaking or writing, direct object pronouns can replace direct object nouns if the noun has already been mentioned.

¿Ves **al chef?**	*Do you see the chef?*
Sí, **lo** veo. Está al lado de la cocina.	*Yes, I see him. He is next to the kitchen.*
La Dra. Martín atiende **a sus pacientes** en la clínica.	*Dr. Martín treats her patients in the clinic.*
Los examina y **los** trata en el hospital.	*She examines them and treats them in the hospital.*

- In **Capítulo 6,** you learned that indirect object nouns and pronouns tell *to whom* or *for whom* an action is done. They most often occur in the context of transferring information or objects, such as giving someone a gift, telling someone a story, or asking someone for something. Indirect object nouns are always preceded by the personal **a.**

El camarero no **nos** trajo la sopa.	*The waiter did not bring us the soup.*
La maestra siempre **les** dice la verdad **a** los niños.	*The teacher always tells the children the truth.*

- Direct and indirect object pronouns are placed before conjugated verbs. When a conjugated verb is followed by an infinitive or present participle, the pronouns can either precede the conjugated verb or be attached to the infinitive or present participle.

¿Las fotos de la casa? La arquitecta está organizándo**las.** La arquitecta **las** está organizando.	*The photos of the house?* *The architect is compiling them.*
Su asistente va a mandar**nos** todos los documentos. Su asistente **nos** va a mandar todos los documentos.	*Her assistant is going to send us all the documents.*

- Direct and indirect object pronouns have the same form, except in the third person. Note that **le/les** refer to either males or females.

DIRECT OBJECT PRONOUNS		INDIRECT OBJECT PRONOUNS	
me	nos	me	nos
te	os	te	os
lo	los	le	les
la	las		

e **¿Comprendes?** Completa las oraciones con el pronombre directo o indirecto correcto.

1. No tengo mi cartera. ____ dejé en casa.
2. Juan ____ dio a Marisol un bolso guatemalteco.
3. Pero Juan no ____ trajo regalos a nosotros.
4. Me encantan tus fotos en Facebook. Estoy mirándo____ ahora.
5. ¿Los intérpretes? ____ voy a llamar ahora.

PRÁCTICA

9-22 Los preparativos para la evaluación.

e **PREPARACIÓN.** Trabajas en la oficina de una arquitecta y mañana empieza la evaluación anual. Indica quién está haciendo estos trabajos: la arquitecta (**A**) o el asistente administrativo (**AA**).

1. _____ Está escribiendo la evaluación de un empleado.
2. _____ Está preparando la versión final de unos planos.
3. _____ Está sacando las fotocopias.
4. _____ Está organizando el horario de la reunión.
5. _____ Está preparando las carpetas (*folders*) con el informe para todos los jefes.
6. _____ Está firmando (*signing*) el contrato.

INTERCAMBIOS. Túrnense para preguntar y responder, siguiendo el modelo.

MODELO Está leyendo cuidadosamente el contrato.
E1: *¿Quién está leyendo cuidadosamente el contrato?*
E2: *La arquitecta está leyéndolo.*
E1: *Y, ¿por qué está leyéndolo?*
E2: *Está leyéndolo porque encontró un error en su último contrato.*

 **9-23 Comunicaciones y transacciones.** Miren las escenas y expliquen dónde ocurren y qué pasa en cada una.

MODELO Pancho/enviar flores/esposa
E1: *Pancho está en la floristería.*
E2: *Sí. Le va a enviar flores a su esposa porque es el Día de los Enamorados.*

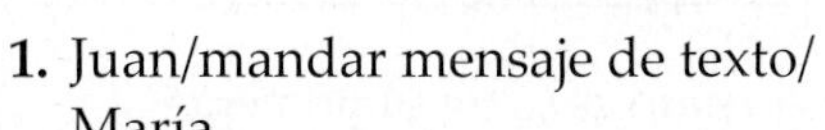

1. Juan/mandar mensaje de texto/ María

2. jefa/dar documentos/asistente

3. artesana/vender telas tradicionales/turistas

 **9-24 El jefe ideal.** **PREPARACIÓN.** Túrnense para hablar sobre lo que hace (o no hace) un/a jefe/a ideal por sus empleados.

MODELO dar las gracias por la calidad de su trabajo a sus empleados
Les da las gracias por la calidad de su trabajo.

1. sugerir estrategias de trabajo eficientes
2. mandar correos electrónicos durante el fin de semana
3. ofrecer ayuda para resolver conflictos
4. subir el salario cada año
5. dar un mes de vacaciones
6. hacer trabajar muchas horas, pero no pagar tiempo extra
7. dar entrenamiento (*training*) para mejorar su eficiencia laboral
8. prometer bonos una vez por año

INTERCAMBIOS. Ahora túrnense para hacerse preguntas sobre lo que ustedes van a hacer por sus empleados cuando sean jefes/as de una empresa. Usen las ideas de **Preparación.**

MODELO E1: *¿Vas a darles las gracias a tus empleados?*
E2: *Sí, les voy a escribir una carta de reconocimiento todos los años.*

 **9-25 Mi primer trabajo.** **PREPARACIÓN.** Marca la información según tu experiencia en tu primer trabajo. Luego, háganse preguntas para comparar sus experiencias.

MODELO una máquina para marcar mis horas de trabajo

E1: *¿Tenías una máquina para marcar tus horas de trabajo?*
E2: *Sí, la tenía. ¿Y tú?*
E1: *Yo también la tenía. ¿La usabas siempre?*
E2: *Por supuesto. Tenía que usarla. ¿Y tú?*
E1: *Yo también la usaba. ¿Te gustaba o la detestabas?*
E2: *Me gustaba. / La detestaba porque a veces me olvidaba de marcar mi hora de llegada o salida.*

	Tenía	Usaba	Me gustaba(n)	Detestaba
1. un casillero (*locker*) para guardar mis objetos personales				
2. un uniforme de la compañía				
3. una computadora para hacer mi trabajo				
4. llaves (*keys*) o tarjeta magnética para entrar en mi lugar de trabajo				
5. acceso a internet				
6. un auto para ir al trabajo				

INTERCAMBIOS. Respondan a las siguientes preguntas sobre su primera experiencia laboral.

1. ¿Cuándo conseguiste tu primer trabajo?
2. ¿Quién te entrevistó para el puesto?
3. ¿Te dieron un contrato escrito? ¿Lo firmaste (*sign*)?
4. ¿Cómo gastaste tu primer cheque? ¿Le compraste algo a alguien? ¿A quién?

 **9-26 Dilemas.** **PREPARACIÓN.** Lean las siguientes situaciones laborales y, luego, túrnense para preguntar y responder. Conjuguen los verbos y usen los pronombres apropiados.

MODELO **Dilema:** Por error, alguien deja un paquete para un compañero de trabajo en tu escritorio.

Soluciones: dar el paquete a la recepcionista/dejar el paquete en el escritorio de tu compañero

E1: *¿Le das el paquete a la recepcionista o lo dejas en el escritorio de tu compañero?*
E2: *No le doy el paquete a la recepcionista. Lo dejo en el escritorio de mi compañero.*

Dilemas	Soluciones
1. Son las 8:00 de la mañana. Las cámaras de seguridad de tu edificio no están funcionando.	desconectar las cámaras / informar del problema al técnico
2. Eres el/la jefe/a de personal. Hay dos empleados que no trabajan porque siempre miran videos en internet.	despedir (*fire*) a los empleados / pedir recomendaciones a la presidenta de la compañía
3. Eres presidente/a de una compañía que necesita ahorrar (*save*) dinero este año. Decides no pagar bonos.	eliminar los bonos permanentemente / suspender los bonos temporalmente a los trabajadores con sueldos altos
4. Tienes un conflicto personal con tu colega de oficina.	discutir el conflicto con tu colega / contar el problema a tu familia
5. Estás descontento/a con el contrato que recibiste.	firmar el contrato / pedir una reunión con tu jefe/a
6. El presidente de tu compañía te ofrece un mejor sueldo, pero con más responsabilidades.	aceptar la oferta / explicar a tu jefe/a por qué no quieres aceptar la oferta
7. Tu jefe debe decidir quién va a recibir el premio al empleado más productivo/a la empleada más productiva. Una de las personas es amigo/a de tu jefe.	dar el premio al / a la mejor trabajador/a / darle el premio a su amigo/a

INTERCAMBIOS. Comparte con tu compañero/a una experiencia que tuviste o algo que viste en el trabajo, similar a las situaciones en **Preparación.** Responde a estas preguntas.

1. ¿Cuándo tuviste esta experiencia o viste esta situación? ¿Cómo reaccionaste? ¿Qué hiciste?
2. ¿Cómo resolvieron la situación las personas involucradas (*involved*)? ¿Llevaron el caso a su jefe/a? ¿Le pidieron ayuda a alguien o lo resolvieron solos/as?
3. ¿Aprendiste algo de esta experiencia? ¿Qué aprendiste?

Situación

PREPARACIÓN. Lean la situación. Luego, compartan ejemplos de vocabulario, gramática y otra información que necesitan para desarrollar la conversación.

Role A. You have come back from a trip to Guatemala and have brought with you the following items that you bought at an outdoor market: blouses, tapestries (**tapices**), and jewelry. With your classmate, decide who in your class will be the recipients of your gifts.

Role B. One of your classmates has come back from a trip to Guatemala, and he/she has a few gifts to distribute among your classmates. Help him/her decide for whom each gift is most appropriate.

	ROLE A	ROLE B
Vocabulario	Handicrafts	Handicrafts Question words
Funciones y formas	Asking and answering questions Direct and indirect object pronouns	Asking and answering questions Direct and indirect object pronouns Giving suggestions

INTERCAMBIOS. Practiquen la conversación, incorporando el vocabulario y las funciones de **Preparación.** Luego, represéntenla ante la clase.

3 Avoiding repetition

CONSEJERA: ¿Ya (*Already*) **le** mandó su currículum al director?
CLIENTE: Sí, **se lo** mandé la semana pasada.
CONSEJERA: ¿Recibió alguna confirmación de la secretaria?
CLIENTE: Sí, ella **me la** mandó rápidamente. **La** recibí hoy.

Piénsalo. Lee las oraciones e indica si las palabras en negrita (*bold*) son objetos directos o indirectos. Escribe tanto los pronombres como los sustantivos (*nouns*). Si no hay, escribe una **X.**

	OBJETO INDIRECTO	OBJETO DIRECTO
MODELO La secretaria **me** programó una **entrevista** para el lunes.	*me*	*entrevista*
1. ¿Ya **le** mandó su **currículum** al **director?**	________	________
2. **Se lo** mandé la semana pasada.	________	________
3. Ella **me la** mandó rápidamente.	________	________
4. **La** recibí hoy.	________	________

Use of direct and indirect object pronouns together

- You have already learned how to use indirect object pronouns or direct object pronouns in sentences. In this section, you will learn how to use both types of pronouns in the same sentence.

INDIRECT OBJECT PRONOUNS		DIRECT OBJECT PRONOUNS	
me	nos	me	nos
te	os	te	os
le (se)	les (se)	lo	los
		la	las

- When direct and indirect object pronouns are used in the same sentence, the indirect object pronoun goes before the direct object pronoun. Place double object pronouns before conjugated verbs.

Ella **me** dio **la solicitud**. (i.o. = me; d.o. = la solicitud) — *She gave me the application.*

Ella **me la** dio. (i.o. = me; d.o. = la) — *She gave it to me.*

- In compound verb constructions, you may place double object pronouns before the conjugated verb or attach them to the accompanying infinitive or present participle.

Él quiere dar**me** **el contrato**. (i.o. d.o.) — *He wants to give me the contract.*

Él quiere dár**melo**. (i.o. d.o.)
Él **me** **lo** quiere dar. (i.o. d.o.) — *He wants to give it to me*

Ella **te** está ofreciendo **el trabajo**. (i.o. d.o.) — *She is offering you the job.*

Ella **te** **lo** está ofreciendo. (i.o. d.o.)
Ella está ofreciéndo**telo**. (i.o. d.o.) — *She is offering it to you.*

- The indirect object pronouns **le** and **les** change to **se** before **lo, los, la,** or **las.**

El director **le** dio **el puesto** a Verónica. (i.o. d.o.) — *The director gave the job to Veronica.*

Él **se** **lo** dio. (i.o. d.o.) — *He gave it to her.*

Verónica **les** va a mostrar **el anuncio**. (i.o. d.o.) — *Verónica is going to show them/you* (ustedes) *the ad.*

Ella **se** **lo** va a mostrar. (i.o. d.o.) — *She is going to show it to them/you* (ustedes).

- When a direct object pronoun and a reflexive pronoun are used together, the reflexive pronoun precedes the direct object pronoun.

María **se** envía **un paquete** (a sí misma). (r.p. d.o.) — *María sends herself a package.*

Ella **se** **lo** envía (a sí misma). (r.p. d.o.) — *She sends it to herself.*

Lengua

You have learned that when the stress falls on the third syllable from the end of a word, a written accent is required. Therefore, you need to add one to the verb when double object pronouns are attached to an infinitive.

¿Va a darme la solicitud?
→ ¿Va a dármela?

When double object pronouns are attached to a present participle, the stress falls on the fourth syllable from the end, and a written accent is also required:

Se la está dando.
→ Está dándosela.
4 3 2 1

e **¿Comprendes?** Completa las oraciones con los pronombres de objeto directo e indirecto.

1. ¿Los informes? La secretaria ____ ____ dio a Javier.
2. ¿Las bebidas? El camarero ____ ____ trajo a nosotros.
3. ¿El collar de plata? Yo ____ ____ regalé a mi hermana.
4. ¿Sus problemas? Laura ____ ____ contó al psicólogo.
5. ¿El puesto? El jefe ____ ____ dio a mí, no a él.
6. ¿La información? ¿Cuándo ____ ____ vas a dar a ellos?
7. ¿La carta de recomendación? El presidente ____ ____ escribió a ti.
8. ¿Mi uniforme? Yo ____ ____ pongo para trabajar.

PRÁCTICA

9-27 Situaciones hipotéticas. **PREPARACIÓN.** La imparcialidad, la amabilidad y la confidencialidad son fundamentales en el trabajo. Lee las siguientes situaciones y selecciona lo que harías (*would do*) tú o harían otras personas.

1. Un cliente te pide el número de teléfono privado del presidente de la compañía.
   a. Se lo doy. **b.** No se lo doy.
2. Alguien quiere leer un documento confidencial en el que estás trabajando.
   a. Se lo muestro. **b.** No se lo muestro.
3. La nueva jefa de personal viene a una reunión en tu departamento. Alguien tiene que presentarla a los empleados.
   a. Se la presento. **b.** No se la presento.
4. Una empleada nueva te dice que quiere dos semanas de vacaciones después de trabajar solo tres semanas.
   a. Voy a dárselas. **b.** No voy a dárselas.
5. Tú les pides los nombres de los clientes nuevos a los contadores.
   a. Me los mandan por correo electrónico. **b.** Rehúsan (*refuse*) dármelos.
6. El gerente y tú envían una propuesta al sindicato (*union*) para aumentarles (*raise*) el sueldo a los empleados más antiguos.
   a. El sindicato nos la acepta. **b.** El sindicato nos la desaprueba.

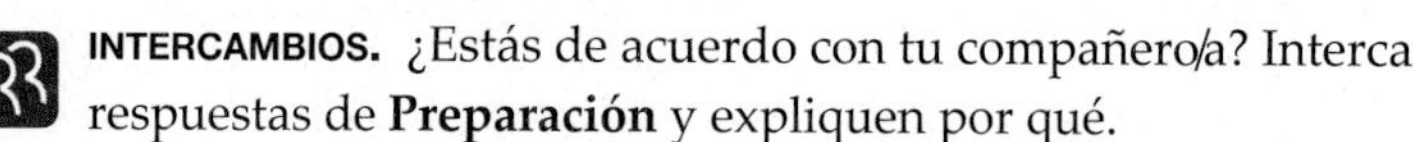

INTERCAMBIOS. ¿Estás de acuerdo con tu compañero/a? Intercambien sus respuestas de **Preparación** y expliquen por qué.

MODELO Un cliente te pide información personal sobre las finanzas de otro cliente. Los dos clientes son hermanos.
E1: *No se la doy porque la información sobre los clientes es confidencial.*
E2: *Yo le recomiendo al cliente pedírsela directamente a su hermano.*

9-28 ¿Qué hizo el supervisor? Eres el/la dueño/a de una compañía. Habla con tu nuevo/a empleado/a (tu compañero/a) para saber si el supervisor le explicó cómo funciona su departamento.

MODELO darle el manual de la compañía
E1: *¿Le dio el manual de la compañía?*
E2: *Sí, me lo dio.*

1. enviarle un mensaje de bienvenida
2. explicarle la campaña de publicidad
3. mostrarle los anuncios en línea
4. traerle el catálogo para escoger muebles para su oficina
5. pedirle un documento que faltaba
6. dejarle las fotos de los nuevos productos
7. describirle los modelos que se necesitan
8. presentarle a la nueva publicista

9-29 El cliente siempre tiene razón. **PREPARACIÓN.** Cada uno/a de ustedes comió recientemente en un restaurante. Comparen su experiencia.

1. ¿Cuándo te sirvieron el agua?
2. ¿Te trajeron pan o algún aperitivo gratis?
3. ¿Te dijo el/la camarero/a cuáles eran los platos especiales del día?
4. ¿Te describió los platos?
5. ¿Te ofreció postre y café?
6. ¿Le dejaste una buena propina al/a la camarero/a?

INTERCAMBIOS. Presenten a la clase un breve resumen del servicio que recibieron en sus respectivos restaurantes.

9-30 Asuntos urgentes. Lee el correo electrónico que recibiste de tu jefe/a (tu compañero/a). Intercambien roles para preguntar, disculparse e indicarle a tu jefe/a cuándo van a resolver cada asunto (*issue*).

MODELO poner mi nombre en la puerta de mi oficina

JEFE/A: *¿Por qué aún* (yet) *no ponen mi nombre en la puerta de mi oficina?*

TÚ: *Lo siento, pero estoy sobrecargado/a de trabajo. Se lo ponemos hoy/esta tarde/mañana, señor/a.*

JEFE/A: *Espero que sí.*

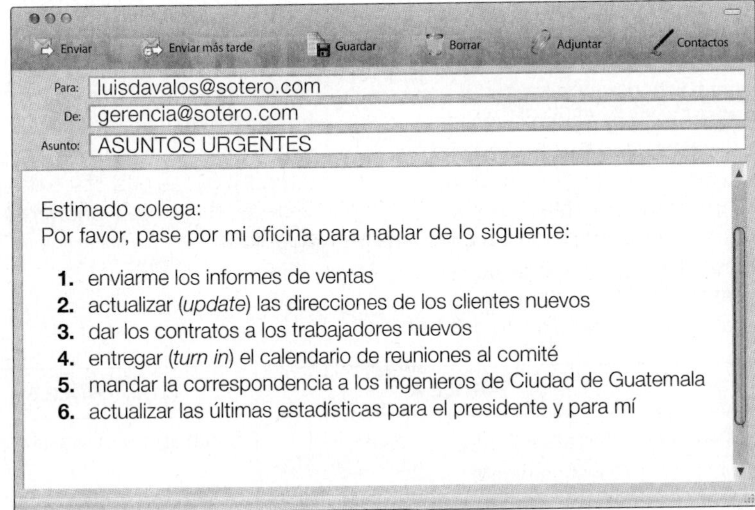

Para: luisdavalos@sotero.com

De: gerencia@sotero.com

Asunto: ASUNTOS URGENTES

Estimado colega:

Por favor, pase por mi oficina para hablar de lo siguiente:

1. enviarme los informes de ventas
2. actualizar (*update*) las direcciones de los clientes nuevos
3. dar los contratos a los trabajadores nuevos
4. entregar (*turn in*) el calendario de reuniones al comité
5. mandar la correspondencia a los ingenieros de Ciudad de Guatemala
6. actualizar las últimas estadísticas para el presidente y para mí

En directo

To give reasons for not doing something:

Lo siento, pero estoy/estamos muy ocupado/a(s). *Sorry, but I am / we are very busy.*

Estoy/Estamos sobrecargado/a(s) de trabajo. *I/We are overloaded with work.*

Tengo/Tenemos un calendario de trabajo muy apretado. *I/We have a very tight work calendar.*

Tengo/Tenemos varios proyectos muy urgentes. *I/We have several urgent projects.*

To acknowledge a reason and to ask for a prompt resolution of issues:

Entiendo, pero espero una solución pronta/rápida. *I understand, but I expect a prompt solution.*

Comprendo perfectamente, pero necesita resolver este asunto pronto. *I totally understand, but you must resolve this issue soon.*

Sí, pero no olvide que esta situación / este asunto es urgente. *Yes, but don't forget that this situation/issue is urgent.*

Comprendo, pero esta situación / este asunto requiere su atención. *I understand, but this situation/issue requires your attention.*

 Listen to a conversation with these expressions.

9-31 Personas muy consideradas. **PREPARACIÓN.** Escribe el nombre de una persona que conoces que hace lo siguiente.

	NOMBRE
1. Les envía tarjetas o regalos a sus amigos/as para su cumpleaños.	________
2. Les presta su auto a sus compañeros/as de apartamento.	________
3. Te enseña temas relacionados con las nuevas tecnologías.	________
4. Les permite a ti y a otras personas usar su computadora.	________
5. Siempre les paga la cena a sus amigos/as cuando van a un restaurante.	________
6. Le da buenas recomendaciones financieras a tu padre/madre.	________

INTERCAMBIOS. Habla con tu compañero/a sobre las personas de **Preparación.** Háganse preguntas para obtener más información.

MODELO Te explica el funcionamiento de las nuevas máquinas.

E1: *Alex me explica el funcionamiento de las nuevas máquinas.*

E2: *¿Por qué te lo explica?*

E1: *Me lo explica porque es experto en tecnología.*

Situación

PREPARACIÓN. Lean la situación. Luego, compartan ejemplos de vocabulario, gramática y otra información que necesitan para desarrollar la conversación.

Role A. It is the end of the day, and you just finished a report for your new supervisor, who has been in meetings all day. You have to leave, so you ask your co-worker to turn it in for you. You call your friend from the car to ask:

a. if he/she gave the report directly to the supervisor;
b. what time he/she turned it in; and
c. what the supervisor said to him/her.

Role B. A co-worker asks you to turn in his/her report to your supervisor because he/she has to leave work early. Your friend wants to make sure that the report is turned in by the end of the day. When your friend calls you, answer all of his/her questions.

	ROLE A	ROLE B
Vocabulario	Greetings Question words Expressions of thanks	Expressions of reassurance
Funciones y formas	Asking questions Direct and indirect object pronouns Opening and closing a phone conversation Expressing gratitude for a favor	Answering questions Direct and indirect object pronouns Opening and closing a phone conversation Acknowledging gratitude

INTERCAMBIOS. Practiquen la conversación, incorporando el vocabulario y las funciones de **Preparación.** Luego, represéntenla ante la clase.

4 Giving instructions or suggestions

RECEPCIONISTA: Auditores y Consultores Méndez. Buenos días. ¿En qué le puedo servir?

RICARDO: Buenos días. Le habla Ricardo Roldán Díaz. Vi en la página web de su compañía que buscan un asistente de contador. Me gustaría solicitar el puesto.

RECEPCIONISTA: Muy bien, Sr. Roldán. Por favor, **busque** la solicitud en nuestra página web, en la sección donde anunciamos los puestos. **Llene** la solicitud y **mándenosla** pronto. Se aceptan solicitudes hasta mañana.

RICARDO: ¿Cómo se la mando?

RECEPCIONISTA: Primero, **llene** la solicitud. Por favor, **asegúrese** de incluir toda la información. Luego, **súbala** a la página web o **envíenosla** por correo electrónico.

Piénsalo. Para cada instrucción, indica con **Sí** o **No** si la recepcionista le dio la instrucción a Ricardo. Luego, escribe el infinitivo del verbo en negrita (*bold*).

	INSTRUCCIÓN DE LA RECEPCIONISTA	INFINITIVO
MODELO **Llene** la solicitud.	*Sí*	*llenar*
1. **Incluya** una foto.	______	______
2. **Busque** la solicitud.	______	______
3. **Asegúrese** de incluir toda la información.	______	______
4. No **deje** ningún espacio en blanco.	______	______
5. **Suba** la solicitud a nuestra página web.	______	______
6. **Envíenosla** por correo electrónico.	______	______

Formal commands

- Commands (los mandatos) are the verb forms used to tell others to do something. Use formal commands with people you address as usted or ustedes. To form these commands, drop the final -o of the yo form of the present tense and add -e(n) for -ar verbs and -a(n) for -er and -ir verbs.

	USTED	USTEDES	
firmar → firmø	**firme**	**firmen**	*sign*
leer → leø	**lea**	**lean**	*read*
abrir → abrø	**abra**	**abran**	*open*

Firme aquí, por favor. — *Sign here, please.*
Lean los informes antes de la reunión. — *Read the reports before the meeting.*
Abra la sesión a las dos en punto. — *Open the session at two o'clock sharp.*

- The stem of the command form is the same as the stem of the yo form of the present tense, even for stem-changing and most irregular verbs.

	USTED	USTEDES	
pensar → piensø	**piense**	**piensen**	*think*
dormir → duermø	**duerma**	**duerman**	*sleep*
repetir → repitø	**repita**	**repitan**	*repeat*
poner → pongø	**ponga**	**pongan**	*put*

- The use of usted and ustedes with command forms is optional. When used, they normally follow the command.

  Pase/Pase **usted.** — *Come in.*

- To make a formal command negative, place no before the affirmative command.

  No salga ahora. — *Do not leave now.*

- Object pronouns and reflexive pronouns are attached to the end of affirmative commands. (Note the written accent over the stressed vowel.) Object pronouns and reflexive pronouns precede negative commands and are not attached.

Cómpre**la.**	*Buy it.*
No **la** compre.	*Do not buy it.*
Léanoslo.	*Read it to us.*
No **nos lo** lea.	*Do not read it to us.*
Siénten**se.**	*Sit down. (to more than one person)*
No **se** sienten.	*Do not sit down. (to more than one person)*

- The verbs dar, ir, ser, and saber have irregular command forms.

  dar: **dé, den**
  ir: **vaya, vayan**
  ser: **sea, sean**
  saber: **sepa, sepan**

- Verbs ending in -car, -gar, -zar, -ger, and -guir have spelling changes in command forms.

sacar	sacø	→ sa**qu**e, sa**qu**en
jugar	juegø	→ jue**gu**e, jue**gu**en
almorzar	almuerzø	→ almuer**c**e, almuer**c**en
recoger	recojø	→ reco**j**a, reco**j**an
seguir	sigø	→ si**g**a, si**g**an

e **¿Comprendes?** Completa las oraciones con la forma correcta del mandato formal.

1. _______ (Leer) el informe, por favor, Sr. Flores.
2. Luego, _______nos (explicar) los puntos principales.
3. No _______ (incluir) información innecesaria.
4. Manuel y Clara, no _______ (salir) antes de las cinco.
5. _______ (Seguir) Uds. mis instrucciones, por favor.
6. Clara, al terminar el proyecto, _______melo (mandar) por correo electrónico.

PRÁCTICA

9-32 Instrucciones a un/a paciente. Un/a paciente preocupado/a habla con su médico/a. Túrnense para representar cada uno/a un rol: el/la paciente que pregunta y el/la médico/a que responde. Añadan una pregunta más.

MODELO E1: *¿Debo tomar los medicamentos antes de comer?*
E2: *Sí, por favor, tómelos con las comidas.*

1. ¿Debo terminar todas las pastillas (*pills*)?
2. ¿Es importante leer las instrucciones?
3. ¿Es necesario seguir la dieta exactamente?
4. ¿Debo beber líquidos cada dos horas?
5. ¿Puedo llamarlo/la a usted si tengo más preguntas?
6. ¿...?

9-33 En el hospital. Un/a enfermero/a entra en la habitación y le hace las siguientes preguntas al/a la paciente. Túrnense para hacer los papeles de enfermero/a y paciente, y añadan una pregunta más.

MODELO E1: *¿Le abro las cortinas?*
E2: *Sí, ábramelas, por favor. Quiero leer.*

1. ¿Le pongo la televisión?
2. ¿Le preparo un café?
3. ¿Le doy otra almohada?
4. ¿Le busco sus zapatos?
5. ¿Le traigo las chancletas?
6. ¿...?

9-34 Mandatos del entrenador. Preparen una lista de sugerencias que el/la entrenador/a puede darles a los miembros de su equipo para lograr los siguientes objetivos. Comparen su lista con la de otra pareja.

MODELO para mantenerse en buen estado físico
E1: *Practiquen todos los días.*
E2: *No se acuesten tarde.*

1. para tener mejor rendimiento (*performance*)
2. para prepararse mentalmente para un partido difícil
3. para evitar (*avoid*) problemas con el árbitro
4. para dormir bien cuando tienen mucho estrés
5. para ser buenos alumnos y también buenos deportistas

9-35 ¿Qué deben hacer estas personas? Busquen una solución a los siguientes problemas y díganle a cada persona qué debe hacer.

MODELO El Sr. Álvarez dice: "No estoy contento en mi trabajo".
E1: *Sr. Álvarez, busque otro trabajo inmediatamente.*
E2: *Hable con su jefe/a y explíquele por qué no está contento.*

1. La Sra. Jiménez dice: "Necesito más vendedores en mi compañía".
2. El Sr. Jiménez se queja: "Tengo que terminar un informe económico, pero mi computadora no funciona".
3. Dos gerentes de una compañía norteamericana, la Sra. Miller y el Sr. Elliott, van a ir a Ciudad de Guatemala, pero no hablan español.
4. La Sra. Peña tuvo un accidente serio con su auto; el chofer que provocó el accidente no quiere darle la información que ella necesita para informar a su compañía de seguro (*insurance*).
5. La Sra. Hurtado entra en su apartamento y ve que hay agua en el piso de la cocina.
6. La Sra. Fernández quiere ir al Festival Folclórico Nacional de Cobán esta noche, pero el Sr. Fernández se enfermó esta mañana.

Cultura

Uso de *tú* y *usted* En Guatemala, los jóvenes se dirigen normalmente a sus padres, a sus profesores y a otras personas mayores con la forma **usted.** El uso de **tú** y de **usted** varía mucho en el mundo hispano. En general la forma **tú,** para dirigirse (*address*) a las personas mayores, es más común en la comunicación con los padres. **Usted** se usa frecuentemente para comunicarse con los mayores fuera del círculo familiar.

Comparaciones No todas las lenguas tienen el equivalente de las formas **tú** y **usted.** ¿Cómo te diriges a otras personas en tu cultura para demostrar respeto?

 **9-36 Escoba nueva barre bien (*A new broom sweeps clean*).** Tienes un trabajo nuevo como director/a de un programa de teatro y quieres hacer muchos cambios. Diles a los actores (tus compañeros/as) lo que deben dejar de hacer. Los actores cuestionan tu autoridad.

MODELO hablar con los músicos

E1: *No hablen con los músicos cuando están trabajando.*
E2: *¿Por qué no? Son nuestros amigos.*
E1: *Esperen hasta el final del ensayo, entonces.*
E3: [a su compañero/a en voz baja] *No me cae bien el nuevo director / la nueva directora.*

1. fumar (*to smoke*) en el teatro
2. sacar fotos de las reuniones del grupo
3. hacer ruido (*noise*) durante los ensayos (*rehearsals*)
4. escribir mensajes de texto durante las sesiones de trabajo
5. traer comida a los ensayos
6. ofrecerles entradas gratuitas (*free*) a sus amigos

Situación

PREPARACIÓN. Lean esta situación. Luego, compartan ejemplos de vocabulario, gramática y otra información que necesitan para desarrollar la conversación.

Role A. Tell your neighbor that you are leaving for three days for a series of job interviews. Ask if your neighbor can do a few things for you. After he/she agrees, tell him/her to:
a. feed (**darle de comer a**) the cat and play with her every day;
b. water (**regar**) the plants;
c. pick up the mail (**correo**); and
d. one other thing that you need done.
Thank your neighbor for helping you out.

Role B. Your neighbor tells you that he/she is going to be away for a few days. Agree to help him/her out. As your neighbor tells you what you will need to do:
a. ask questions about the instructions you receive;
b. get the telephone number of the vet (**veterinario/a**); and
c. ask whom you should call if there is an emergency (**emergencia**).

	ROLE A	ROLE B
Vocabulario	Household chores	Household chores Question words
Funciones y formas	Formal commands Using formal commands politely Answering questions Expressing gratitude	Asking questions Answering questions

INTERCAMBIOS. Practiquen la conversación, incorporando el vocabulario y las funciones de **Preparación.** Luego, represéntenla ante la clase.

ESCUCHA

Estrategia

Use contextual guessing When you have a conversation in a second or foreign language, it is common not to understand everything people say to you. You can figure out the overall message by using contextual cues; that is, by paying attention to the topic or to the words that precede or follow what you did not understand.

9-37 Preparación. Escribe el nombre de una profesión relacionada con los negocios y otra con la salud. Luego, escribe una ventaja y una desventaja para cada una de las profesiones. Comparte tus notas con la clase.

Profesión	Ventaja	Desventaja

9-38 Escucha. First, read the words and phrases in the first column, and indicate the probable meaning of each one in English. Then listen to the conversation between Estela and Susana and write the words and phrases you hear that relate to the given meaning.

	Posible significado en inglés	Palabras relacionadas
1. seguro		
2. médico especialista		
3. una **desventaja** del trabajo de un/a médico/a		

Comprueba

I was able to . . .

- understand the main idea and key information in a conversation between two friends.
- distinguish advantages and disadvantages of two professions.
- use context to figure out the meaning of unknown words.

9-39 Un paso más. Respondan a las siguientes preguntas.

1. En general, ¿cuál de las profesiones mencionadas en la actividad **9-38** te parece más estresante, la de mujer de negocios o la de neuróloga? ¿Por qué?
2. ¿Cuál es la mayor ventaja de esta profesión estresante? ¿Por qué?

HABLA

Estrategia

Gather information strategically to express a decision When you speak to convey a decision, you need to present your decision and the reasons behind it in an organized and convincing way. Lay out your facts and arguments logically (in your mind or in written notes) before you start to speak.

9-40 Preparación. Lee los siguientes anuncios con ofertas de trabajo en Ciudad de Guatemala. Escoge un anuncio y prepara una lista con los requisitos que cumples (*that you meet*).

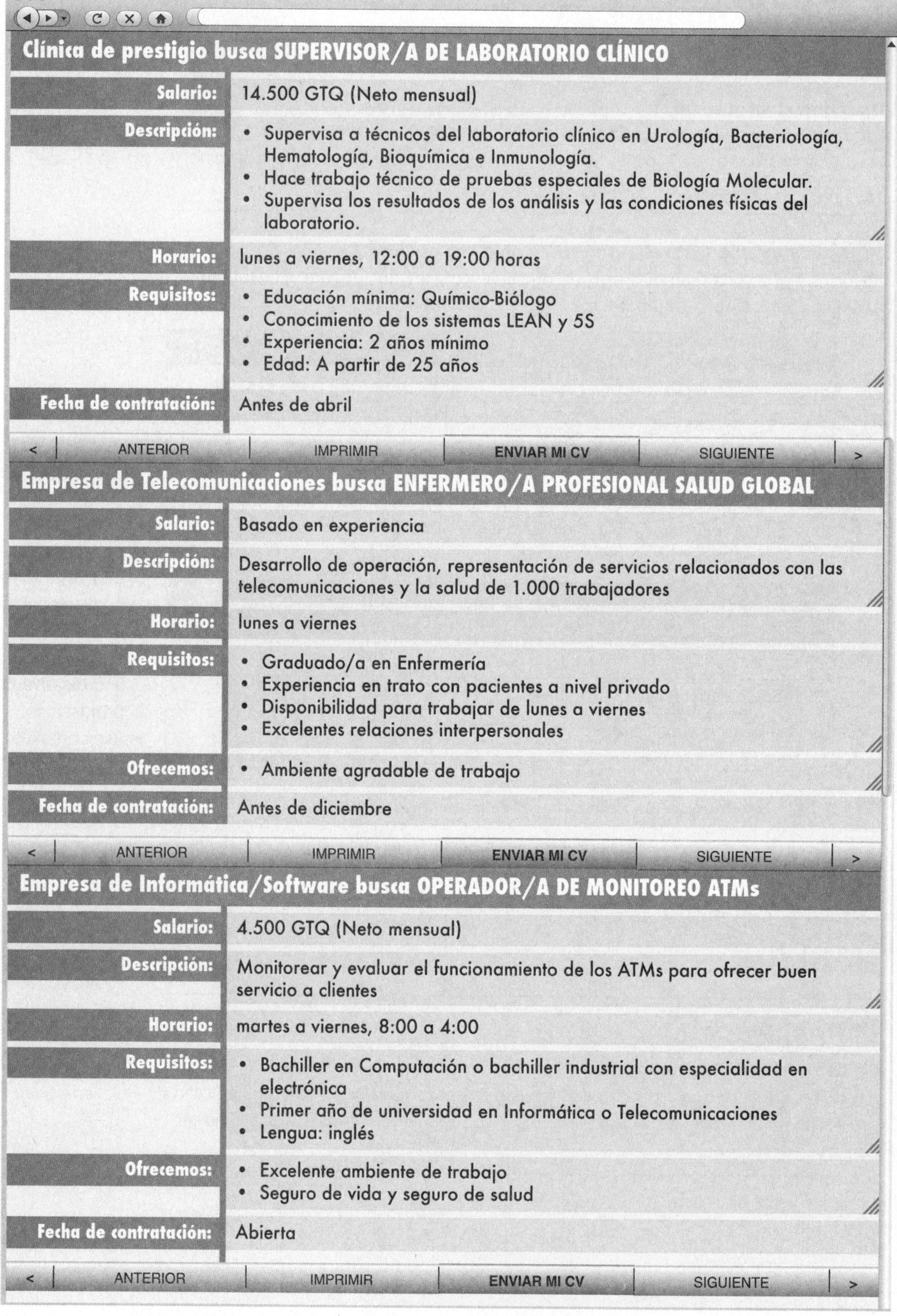

 **9-41 Habla.** Trabajen en grupos de tres. Uno/a de ustedes es el/la jefe/a de personal de una compañía representada en los anuncios de la actividad **9-40.** Los/Las otros/as dos son candidatos/as que solicitan el mismo trabajo.

Jefe/a de personal: Entrevista individualmente a los/las dos candidatos/as. Pregúntales sobre: a) su experiencia, b) sus estudios, c) sus preferencias de sueldo, etc., y decide cuál es la persona seleccionada para el puesto. Toma apuntes para recordar la información.	**Candidatos/as:** Individualmente, respondan a las preguntas del/de la jefe/a de personal y háganle preguntas para obtener información adicional sobre el puesto.

En directo

To welcome someone to your office:

Pase/Adelante, por favor. / Tenga la amabilidad de pasar. *Please come in.*

Por favor, tome asiento. *Please have a seat.*

Siéntese aquí, por favor. *Sit here, please.*

To put someone at ease:

Por favor, póngase cómodo/a. *Please make yourself comfortable.*

To say goodbye at the end of an interview:

Fue un placer conocerlo/la. *It was a pleasure to meet you.*

 Listen to a conversation with these expressions.

Comprueba

I was able to . . .

- conduct a job interview by asking questions relevant to the position.
- provide answers relevant to the questions when I was in the role of job candidate.
- provide explanations to expand on my responses.

9-42 Un paso más. El/La jefe/a de personal y los/las candidatos/as que buscaban trabajo deben informar a la clase sobre lo siguiente.

Informe de los/las candidatos/as:

1. ¿Qué puesto buscabas? ¿Qué requisitos cumples?
2. ¿Qué aspecto de la oferta de trabajo te pareció más atractivo?
3. ¿Crees que van a ofrecerte el trabajo? ¿Por qué?

Informe del / de la jefe/a de personal:

1. ¿Qué puesto ofrecía tu compañía en el anuncio?
2. ¿Qué cualidades debía tener el/la candidato/a?
3. ¿A qué candidato/a vas a contratar? ¿Por qué?

LEE

Estrategia

Organize textual information into categories To understand what you are reading, it is helpful to organize the information into meaningful categories, which helps you connect the information in the text to what you already know. As you read, focus on the main point of each section. Use the subtitles to help you anticipate the content.

 **9-43 Preparación.** Lee el título y los subtítulos del texto en la actividad **9-44.** Basándote en esta información y en lo que sabes sobre la inmigración, anota algunas ideas para compartir con tu compañero/a.

1. En general, ¿por qué emigran (salen de su país) las personas? ¿Conoces algunos inmigrantes? ¿De qué países son?
2. ¿Hay más o menos inmigración a Estados Unidos ahora que en el pasado? ¿Qué grupos de inmigrantes son los más numerosos?
3. ¿Qué efectos puede tener la emigración en la economía del país de origen del emigrante?

Comprueba

I was able to . . .

- use the title and the section headings in the text to anticipate the content.
- organize the content into general categories.
- identify the important ideas and key information in the text.

e **9-44 Lee.** Indica si las siguientes afirmaciones, según el contenido del artículo, son ciertas (**C**) o falsas (**F**). Corrige las afirmaciones falsas.

1. _____ Los países del Triángulo Norte Centroamericano son México, Guatemala y El Salvador.
2. _____ La tasa (*rate*) de inmigración desde México a Estados Unidos aumentó entre 2007 y 2015.
3. _____ Hay inmigrantes de Guatemala en varios países del mundo.
4. _____ Parte de la emigración guatemalteca es consecuencia de la violencia.
5. _____ El dinero que viene del exterior estimula la economía de Guatemala.
6. _____ Para los inmigrantes que vuelven a Guatemala, es imposible encontrar trabajo.

LOS GUATEMALTECOS

EMIGRACIÓN Y REINTEGRACIÓN

¿DÓNDE VIVEN LOS GUATEMALTECOS?

Guatemala, junto con Honduras y El Salvador, forman el grupo de países conocidos como el Triángulo Norte Centroamericano. El número de inmigrantes en Estados Unidos que vienen de estos países aumentó[1] en un 25% entre el 2007 y el 2015, mientras la inmigración desde México declinó, según un informe basado en datos del Censo. De los más de tres millones de inmigrantes del Triángulo Norte Centroamericano que viven en Estados Unidos, casi un millón son de Guatemala. Hay inmigrantes guatemaltecos no solo en Estados Unidos, sino también en México y Centroamérica. Otros viven en Canadá, Europa y Australia.

Guatemaltecos en el mundo (2017)	
País o región	**Población**
Estados Unidos	976.000
México y países centroamericanos	102.000
Canadá y Europa	36.000
Australia	1.000

Source: migrationpolicy.org (2017)

MOTIVOS DE LA EMIGRACIÓN

La migración no es un fenómeno nuevo en Centroamérica. A causa de las guerras[2] civiles, la inestabilidad política y las malas condiciones económicas, muchos guatemaltecos salen de su país a partir de[3] 1980 en busca de seguridad física y mejores oportunidades. En años recientes, hubo un cambio importante: un aumento grande en el número de niños no acompañados de adultos, además de familias enteras, que salen del Triángulo Norte Centroamericano para escapar de la pobreza, de la actividad de las pandillas[4] y de otros tipos de violencia en sus comunidades. Otra razón para emigrar es el deseo de unirse a sus familiares que ya[5] viven en Estados Unidos.

[1]*grew* [2]*wars* [3]*starting in* [4]*gangs* [5]*already*

IMPACTO ECONÓMICO EN GUATEMALA

Un problema añadido a su situación desesperada y al gran número de inmigrantes del Triángulo Norte Centroamericano en este siglo es que el 55% son indocumentados, en comparación con el 24% del total de los inmigrantes indocumentados en Estados Unidos. A pesar de[6] la falta de documentación, casi todos tienen trabajo y pagan impuestos[7]. Los emigrantes guatemaltecos, igual que los de otros países, se comunican frecuentemente con sus familias en Guatemala y les envían remesas[8] para ayudarlos económicamente. Según un estimado reciente, los guatemaltecos en Estados Unidos mandan más de 7.000 millones de dólares a sus familiares por año. Esta cantidad representa el 10,3% de la economía de Guatemala. Es decir, los emigrantes guatemaltecos participan activamente en las economías de ambos países, el país donde viven actualmente y Guatemala, su país natal.

Una consecuencia del estatus indocumentado de tantos inmigrantes guatemaltecos es que muchos no pueden quedarse en Estados Unidos, y tienen que volver a Guatemala. Para muchos el proceso de readaptación es muy difícil, sobre todo si regresan a las áreas rurales donde nacieron[9]. Muchos inmigrantes retornados encuentran trabajo en *call centers* en la ciudad capital. Estas empresas ofrecen servicio de atención a clientes internacionales, mayormente estadounidenses. Los clientes llaman a estos centros porque tienen preguntas o problemas con productos que han comprado. Los inmigrantes retornados son ideales para resolver sus problemas, porque hablan bien inglés y conocen la cultura de Estados Unidos.

[6]*Despite* [7]*taxes* [8]*remittances, money transfers* [9]*they were born*

9-45 Un paso más. En un párrafo, resume las ideas principales del artículo de la actividad **9-44** y compártelo con la clase.

ESCRIBE

Estrategia

Reporting on an interview When you conduct an interview, it is important to design initial and follow-up questions so that you have enough relevant material to write your interview report. Consider the following tips:

- Focus on the purpose of the interview. This will guide you in preparing appropriate questions.
- Take notes. Take brief notes during the interview, so you will remember the important information. If you record the interview, take notes as you listen to the recording.
- As you review your notes, find the theme or story that is embedded in your interview. Everyone has a personal story. In your interview and later in your report, identify the most interesting theme that will tie the details of your interview together.

9-46 Preparación. Vas a entrevistar a una persona (amigo/a, pariente, etc.) de otro país: un/a inmigrante o un/a estudiante internacional. Prepara una lista de preguntas sobre los siguientes temas (*topics*):

- de dónde es; qué recuerdos tiene del lugar
- cuándo vino a Estados Unidos; en qué partes de este país ha vivido (*has lived*)
- motivos de su decisión de venir a Estados Unidos
- cómo se mantiene en contacto con sus familiares y amigos
- otros detalles sobre su experiencia de adaptación a este país

INTERCAMBIOS. Entrevista a la persona que has identificado. Consulta la **Estrategia** para organizar la entrevista de una manera efectiva.

9-47 Escribe. Escribe tu informe sobre la entrevista. Incluye la información importante para presentar de manera interesante la historia de esta persona.

9-48 Un paso más. Comparte tu informe con tus compañeros/as. Comenten las experiencias similares o diferentes de las personas entrevistadas.

Comprueba

I was able to . . .

- write a personal history of a person from another country.
- use my interview notes to give direction to the story.
- include major themes and interesting details in my writing.

En este capítulo...

Vocabulario

Las profesiones, oficios y ocupaciones	*Professions, trades, and occupations*
el/la abogado/a	*lawyer*
el actor/la actriz	*actor/actress*
el/la agricultor/a	*farmer*
el amo/a de casa	*homemaker*
el/la arquitecto/a	*architect*
el/la bibliotecario/a	*librarian*
el/la bombero/a	*firefighter*
el/la cajero/a	*cashier*
el/la carpintero/a	*carpenter*
el/la chofer	*driver*
el/la científico/a	*scientist*
el/la contador/a	*accountant*
el/la ejecutivo/a	*executive*
el/la electricista	*electrician*
el/la empleado/a	*employee*
el/la enfermero/a	*nurse*
el/la gerente (de ventas)	*(sales) manager*
el hombre / la mujer de negocios	*businessman/ businesswoman*
el/la ingeniero/a	*engineer*
el/la intérprete	*interpreter*
el/la jefe/a	*boss*
el/la juez	*judge*
el/la locutor/a	*radio announcer*
el/la médico/a	*medical doctor*
el/la obrero/a	*worker*
el/la peluquero/a	*hairdresser*
el/la periodista	*journalist*
el/la plomero/a	*plumber*
el/la policía	*police officer*
el/la psicólogo/a	*psychologist*
el/la técnico/a	*technician*
el/la vendedor/a	*salesperson*

El trabajo	*Work*
la agricultura	*farming*
el anuncio	*ad, advertisement*
los beneficios	*benefits*
el/la cliente/a	*client*
el currículum	*résumé*
la entrevista	*interview*
la experiencia	*experience*
la exportación	*export*
la fuente de ingresos	*source of income*
la fuerza laboral	*workforce*
el incendio	*fire*
la lengua	*language*
el puesto	*position*
la solicitud	*application*
el sueldo	*salary, wage*
la vacante	*opening*

Los lugares	*Places*
el campo	*countryside*
la compañía, la empresa	*company*
el consultorio	*office* (of doctor, dentist, etc.)
la finca	*ranch, farm*
el terreno, la tierra	*land*

Los recursos naturales	*Natural resources*
el bosque	*forest*
el hierro	*iron*
la madera	*wood*
el petróleo	*petroleum, oil*

Descripciones	*Descriptions*
agrícola	*agricultural*
fértil	*fertile*
propio/a	*own*

Verbos	*Verbs*
apagar	*to extinguish, to turn off*
cosechar	*to harvest*
cortar	*to cut*
cultivar	*to grow, to cultivate*
dejar	*to leave, to quit*
enviar	*to send*
esperar	*to wait (for)*
explotar	*to exploit*
llenar	*to fill (out)*
ofrecer (zc)	*to offer*
solicitar	*to apply (for)*

Palabras y expresiones útiles	*Useful words and expressions*
actualmente	*at the present time*
en realidad / realmente	*in fact, really*
lo importante	*the important thing*
la industria textil	*textile industry*
por cierto	*by the way*
la señal	*signal*
sin embargo	*however, nevertheless*

Capítulo 10
¿Cuál es tu comida preferida?

Algunos platos típicos de la comida ecuatoriana

Learning Outcomes

You will be able to:

- talk about ingredients, recipes, and meals
- state impersonal information
- talk about the recent past
- give instructions in informal settings
- talk about Ecuador in terms of products, practices, and perspectives
- present information, concepts, and ideas about food and public health in Ecuador and other Latin American countries

Enfoque cultural

Ecuador

La ciudad de Quito está a 2.850 metros (9.350 pies) de altura, en la cordillera de los Andes. Su centro histórico es uno de los mejor preservados de Latinoamérica.

Las semillas de tagua (*ivory palm*) se usan para hacer joyas que se pueden comprar en los mercados indígenas, como el de Otavalo.

El volcán Chimborazo, 150 kilómetros al suroeste de Quito, cerca de la ciudad de Riobamba, es la montaña más alta de Ecuador y el punto más alejado del centro de la Tierra.

Arte hispano

Este cuadro del siglo XVIII presenta a un indígena yumbo cerca de Quito, Ecuador. Junto a él hay árboles y frutas típicas de la zona.

Enfoque cultural

¿Qué te parece?

- Charles Darwin visitó las islas Galápagos en 1835. Este viaje influyó en su idea de la evolución mediante la selección natural.
- Ecuador declaró en la Nueva Constitución Ecuatoriana de 2008 que la naturaleza tiene derechos (*rights*) constitucionales. Fue el primer país en reconocer a la naturaleza como sujeto de derecho.
- En Quito, la capital de Ecuador, el punto de ebullición (*boiling point*) del agua es 90 grados centígrados (194 ºF) debido a la altura de la ciudad.
- Ecuador formó parte del Imperio inca. Los diferentes pueblos indígenas de esa zona desarrollaron una agricultura muy productiva. Todavía fabrican textiles y objetos de cerámica y de metal.

Algunos de los platos típicos ecuatorianos son el ceviche de camarones, el cuy (*guinea pig*), los llapingachos (papas con queso), el pan de yuca y el choclo (maíz) con queso. Muchas comidas se sirven con ají criollo, una salsa picante.

Ecuador es uno de los mayores exportadores de bananas y plátanos. El petróleo y otros recursos naturales, además del turismo, han impulsado la economía de Ecuador en los últimos años.

El famoso sombrero Panamá proviene realmente de la ciudad de Cuenca, Ecuador. La artesanía ecuatoriana, como los tejidos (*weavings*), sombreros, joyería y bordados (*embroidery*), es muy apreciada por los turistas que visitan Ecuador.

Las islas Galápagos están situadas a 970 kilómetros (600 millas) al oeste de Ecuador. Este archipiélago está protegido porque durante miles de años no entraron plantas ni animales de afuera. Las tortugas de las islas Galápagos son unos animales vertebrados muy antiguos, que pueden vivir hasta 150 años.

¿Cuánto sabes? Selecciona la opción que corresponde a cada descripción, según **Enfoque cultural.**

1. _____ capital de Ecuador
2. _____ territorio ecuatoriano en el Pacífico
3. _____ llapingachos, cuy y choclo con queso
4. _____ animal protegido
5. _____ ciudad donde fabrican sombreros
6. _____ protección de la naturaleza

a. islas Galápagos
b. Cuenca
c. Nueva Constitución Ecuatoriana
d. tortuga
e. Quito
f. platos tradicionales

To learn more about Ecuador, go online to view the *Club cultura* videos.

VOCABULARIO EN CONTEXTO

Talking about ingredients, recipes, and meals

Los productos y las recetas

a

En Ecuador hay mucha industria relacionada con la **alimentación.** Por ejemplo, se cultiva mucha fruta, sobre todo **piña, limón, melón, papaya, maracuyá** y **banana.** Mucha de esta fruta **se consume** en Estados Unidos y en otros países. Aquí vemos a unas personas trabajando en una compañía de exportación de **plátanos** cerca de Guayaquil. La banana es dulce y normalmente se come **cruda,** como una fruta, pero el plátano **se fríe** o **se asa** al horno.

b

En los mercados ecuatorianos hay **puestos** donde se venden **pasteles** y **dulces** de la región. Los **tenderos** recomiendan los **postres** que se deben **probar.** Uno de los más típicos son las espumillas o suspiros, unos merengues hechos con huevo **batido.**

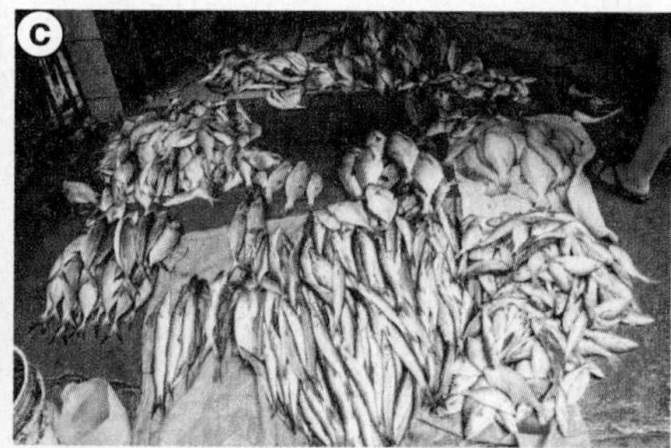
c

El pescado y los **mariscos** son muy importantes en la dieta de algunos países hispanoamericanos como Chile, Perú y Ecuador, y en los mercados hay buenas **pescaderías.** El pescado se puede freír, asar, **hervir** o **marinar.** En la provincia de Esmeraldas, en Ecuador, uno de los platos típicos es el encocado, pescado que se cocina con **leche de coco.**

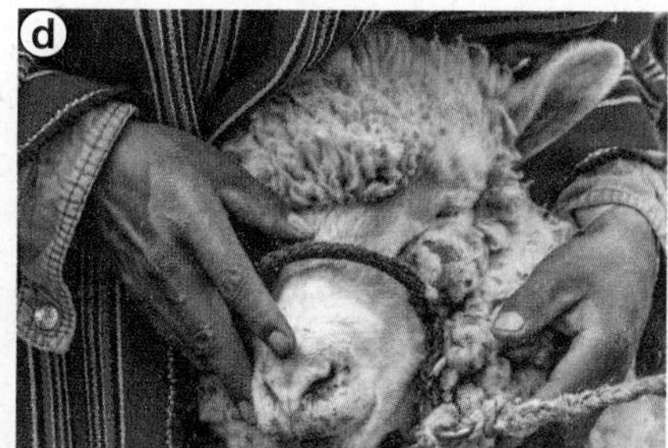
d

Este joven ecuatoriano se ocupa de sus **ovejas** cerca del Parque Nacional Chimborazo. La carne de las ovejas se come y la lana se usa para hacer suéteres y mantas. Además, los **campesinos** usan la leche para hacer queso y **yogur.** Junto a la carne de **cordero,** la de **res** y la de **cerdo** son las que más se usan en la comida de Ecuador y las que más se venden en los mercados y en las **carnicerías.**

e

En el mercado de Zumbahua hay carnes, frutas y vegetales que se usan en muchas **recetas** ecuatorianas. El **cilantro,** el **perejil** y otras **hierbas** y **especias,** como el **achiote, se sofríen** en **aceite** y **se mezclan** con la **cebolla,** el **ajo,** el **pimiento** y el tomate, **agregando sabor** a la gastronomía ecuatoriana.

PRÁCTICA

10-1 Escucha y confirma. Indicate the letter of the photo in **Los productos y las recetas** that best corresponds to the description you hear.

1. _____ 2. _____ 3. _____ 4. _____ 5. _____

10-2 Definiciones. Indica la palabra que corresponde a cada definición, según la información presentada en **Los productos y las recetas.**

1. una lista de ingredientes y de instrucciones para elaborar una comida
2. un animal del que se aprovecha la lana, la leche y la carne
3. una fruta alargada que se pela y que Ecuador exporta mucho
4. un plato ecuatoriano que se cocina con pescado y leche de coco
5. una tienda donde se vende pescado
6. las personas que cultivan productos del campo
7. una tienda donde se venden dulces, pasteles y postres
8. la carne de una oveja joven

Lengua

These are some useful words that appear in the recipe: **paiteña** (*a type of onion*), **diente de ajo** (*clove of garlic*), and **comino** (*cumin*).

Other cooking expressions include: **libra** (*pound*), **cucharada** (*tablespoon*), **taza** (*cup*), **picado/a** (*chopped*), **pelado/a** (*peeled*), **machacado/a** (*crushed*), **añadir** (*to add*), **tapar** (*to cover*).

10-3 Una receta ecuatoriana. PREPARACIÓN. Lean la siguiente receta y clasifiquen sus ingredientes según las categorías.

1. carnes o pescados
2. vegetales
3. condimentos y especias
4. líquidos

PESCADO ENCOCADO

Ingredientes

1 lata de leche de coco
1 libra de camarones crudos, pelados y limpios
2 libras de pescado crudo

Ingredientes para el refrito

4 cucharadas de aceite
1 cebolla paiteña finamente picada
¼ taza de cebolla blanca finamente picada
1 pimiento picado
1 tomate grande rojo, pelado y picado
2 dientes de ajo machacados
4 cucharadas de cilantro picado
4 cucharadas de perejil picado
un poquito de achiote
sal, pimienta, comino al gusto

Elaboración

Haga un refrito con los ingredientes. Agréguele el pescado. Refríalo durante un rato y luego agregue la mitad de la leche de coco. Tape la olla y deje cocinar durante 10 o 15 minutos. Añada los camarones y cocine otros 5 minutos. Después, añada la otra mitad de la leche de coco. Sirva inmediatamente, acompañado de arroz blanco y plátano frito.

INTERCAMBIOS. Después, dile a tu compañero/a cuáles de los ingredientes de este plato te gustan y cuáles no te gustan.

10-4 Cómo hacer una pizza. Ordenen cronológicamente los pasos para preparar una pizza. Luego, hablen de su pizza favorita y de los ingredientes que tiene. Compártanlos con la clase.

_____ Se calienta el horno a 450 °F.
_____ Se pone un poco de aceite en la bandeja de horno y se pone la masa.
_____ Se agrega algún tipo de salchicha o carne cocida, vegetales y especias.
_____ Se ponen la salsa de tomate y el queso.
_____ Se trabaja bien la masa y se extiende para formar un círculo.
__1__ Se compran los ingredientes para la pizza.
_____ Se hornea por unos 20 a 25 minutos.

En el supermercado

Las frutas y las verduras

Los productos lácteos y los huevos

Los pescados, los mariscos y las carnes

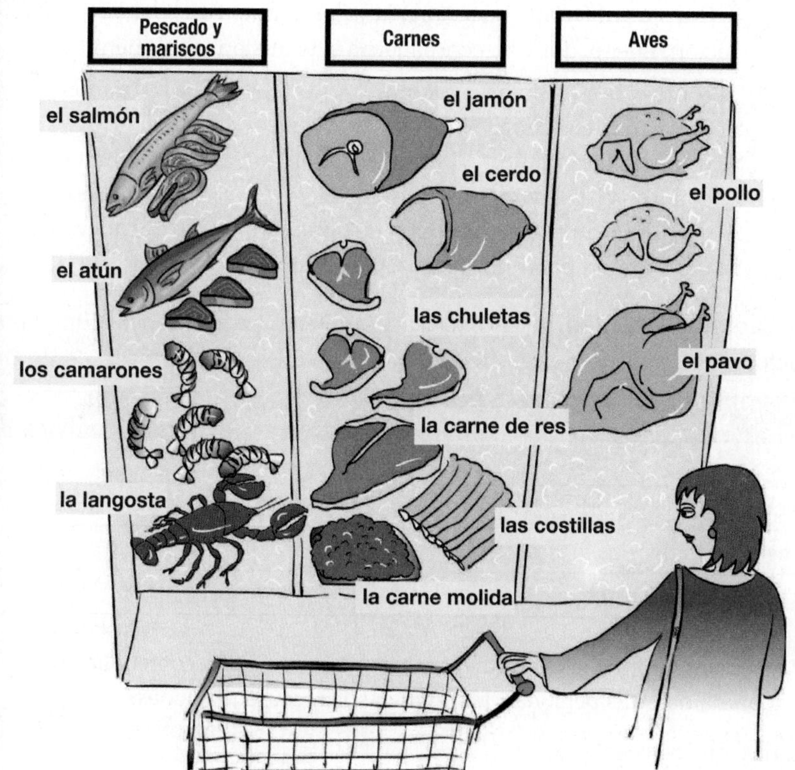

En otras palabras

The words for some vegetables vary by region. **Aguacate** is known as **palta** in some South American countries; **maíz** is known as **elote** in Mexico and in some Central American countries, and as **choclo** in parts of South America.

Names of fruits also vary: **banano** (Colombia) or **banana** (Uruguay) becomes **plátano** in Spain, **cambur** in Venezuela, and **guineo** in the Dominican Republic. Other examples include **durazno** (Latin America) / **melocotón** (Spain); **maracuyá** (Colombia) / **parchita** (Venezuela, Mexico) / **fruta de la pasión** (Spain); and **fresa / frutilla** (Ecuador, Chile, Argentina, Paraguay, Uruguay).

En otras palabras

Other names of foods that vary by country are **pavo,** which is **guajolote** in Mexico, and **camarones,** which are **gambas** in Spain. **Puerco** is also commonly used in place of **cerdo.**

Los condimentos y las legumbres

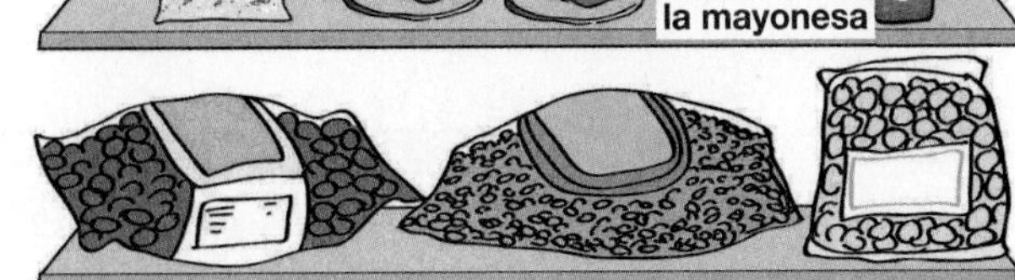

El pan y las bebidas

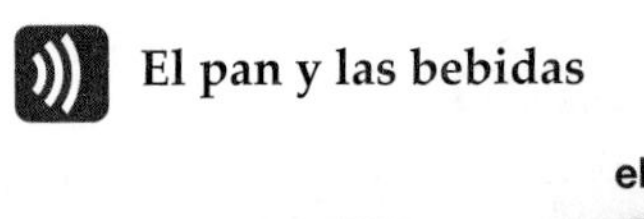

> **Lengua**
>
> **Pimienta** refers to the spice (*ground pepper*) and **pimiento** refers to the vegetable. Therefore, **pimienta roja** refers to cayenne pepper and **pimiento rojo, pimiento morrón**, or **pimentón** is a red bell pepper. The word for hot, spicy peppers is **chile** or **ají,** as in **chile habanero, chile jalapeño,** and so forth.

PRÁCTICA

10-5 Para confirmar. Selecciona la palabra que corresponde a cada descripción. Luego, dile a tu compañero/a si te gustan los alimentos.

1. _____ Se come más cuando hace calor.
2. _____ Se pone en la ensalada.
3. _____ Se usa para hacer vino.
4. _____ Se come en el desayuno con huevos fritos.
5. _____ Se prepara para el Día de Acción de Gracias.
6. _____ Se usa para preparar un sándwich de atún.

a. el jamón
b. la uva
c. la mayonesa
d. el helado
e. el aderezo
f. el pavo

10-6 Dietas diferentes. **PREPARACIÓN.** Completen la tabla con las comidas o productos adecuados para estas dietas.

Dieta	Se debe comer	No se debe comer
vegetariana		
para diabéticos		
para fortalecer (*strengthen*) los músculos		
para bajar de peso (*lose weight*)		

INTERCAMBIOS. Completen las siguientes oraciones con sus recomendaciones para cada una de estas personas. Justifiquen sus recomendaciones.

1. Laura, que es vegetariana, …
2. Mi padre, que es diabético, …
3. Luis, que levanta pesas, …
4. Joaquín y Amalia quieren bajar de peso. Ellos…

Cultura

Comida internacional Muchos hispanohablantes que viven en Estados Unidos mantienen las tradiciones y costumbres alimentarias de su país de origen. Estas tradiciones y costumbres, que varían mucho de un país a otro, se reflejan en las recetas, maneras de cocinar y aun (*even*) en las horas diferentes de comer. Hay productos, como los frijoles, la yuca, el arroz, los chiles, los plátanos y el maíz, que constituyen la base de la dieta de muchos países de Hispanoamérica y que se encuentran en casi todos los supermercados de Estados Unidos.

Comparaciones ¿Qué productos son populares en la comida de tu país o región? ¿Qué platos se preparan con estos productos? ¿Cuáles son los postres especiales? ¿Se comen en una época determinada?

10-7 **¿Qué necesitamos?**

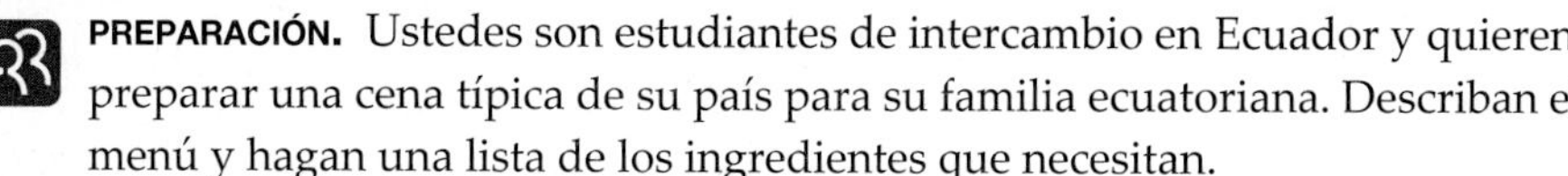

PREPARACIÓN. Ustedes son estudiantes de intercambio en Ecuador y quieren preparar una cena típica de su país para su familia ecuatoriana. Describan el menú y hagan una lista de los ingredientes que necesitan.

INTERCAMBIOS. Compartan su menú con otra pareja.

10-8 **Los estudiantes y la comida.** **PREPARACIÓN.** Responde a las preguntas.

1. ¿Qué comiste hoy?
2. ¿Cuándo y dónde comiste?
3. ¿Cuánto gastaste en comida?

INTERCAMBIOS. Léanse sus respuestas y háganse recomendaciones para una dieta estudiantil más saludable (*healthier*). Compártanla con el resto de la clase.

En directo

To give some general advice:

Debes/Deben + *infinitive* **(comer/beber/etc.)...** *You should* + infinitive *(eat/drink/etc.)...*

Para bajar de peso / comer saludable, recomendamos + *noun* **(las verduras, el agua, etc.).** *To lose weight / eat healthy, we recommend* + noun *(vegetables, water, etc.).*

Para obtener calcio/proteínas/fibra, es bueno + *infinitive* **(comer/beber/etc.)...** *To get calcium/protein/fiber, it's good* + infinitive *(to eat/drink/etc.)...*

Listen to a conversation with these expressions.

La mesa

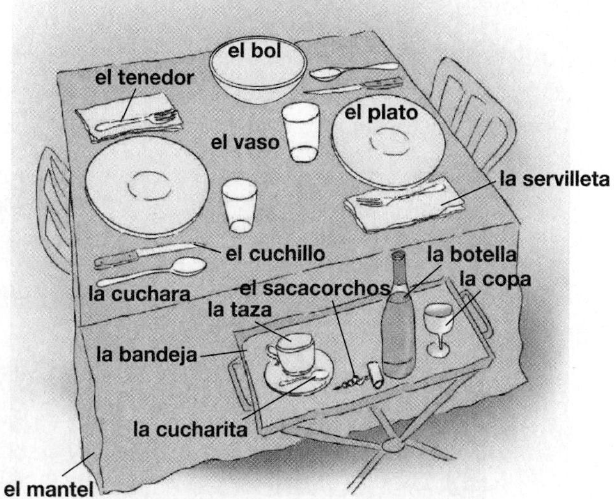

PRÁCTICA

10-9 **Para confirmar.** Indica qué utensilios se necesitan en las siguientes situaciones. Compara tus respuestas con las de tu compañero/a.

1. cortar un bistec
2. comer sopa
3. beber vino
4. poner azúcar en el café
5. llevar comida a la mesa
6. cubrir la mesa
7. limpiarse la boca (*mouth*)
8. abrir una botella de vino

 **10-10 El nuevo camarero.** Ustedes son camareros/as en un restaurante, pero uno/a es nuevo/a. El/La empleado/a con más experiencia debe decirle a la persona nueva dónde debe poner cada utensilio. Después, cambien de papel.

MODELO E1: *Pon el cuchillo a la derecha del plato.*
E2: *Muy bien. ¿Y dónde pongo la copa?*

 **10-11 Los preparativos.** **PREPARACIÓN.** Ustedes deben organizar una fiesta formal para sus mejores amigos que se gradúan de la universidad este año. Primero, decidan cuándo y dónde va a ser la fiesta. Luego, preparen un presupuesto (*budget*), una lista de invitados, un menú y una lista de compras. Hablen también de la decoración del salón y la preparación de la mesa.

INTERCAMBIOS. Informen a la clase sobre sus preparativos, incluyendo la siguiente información.

1. el lugar, la hora, el día
2. los invitados
3. la comida y las bebidas
4. la decoración del salón
5. la preparación de la mesa

Cultura

Platos típicos En Ecuador, al igual que en Perú, el ceviche de pescado o de camarón es muy popular. Otro plato ecuatoriano muy popular es la fritada, una combinación de diversas carnes con plátano maduro, plátano frito y maíz. Pero uno de los platos más típicos de Ecuador es el **locro de papa,** una sopa de papa hecha con cebollas y, frecuentemente, queso. Se sirve con aguacate. Y entre los postres, además de los pasteles y el flan, es muy rico el dulce de higos (*candied figs*).

Comunidades Piensa en los supermercados que hay en tu ciudad. ¿Qué productos típicos de la cultura hispana puedes encontrar en ellos? ¿Cuáles de estos productos se usan en tu casa?

En directo

To express that you had a good time:

Lo pasé/pasamos muy bien. *I/We had a great time.*

Fue estupendo. *It was wonderful.*

Estuvo muy divertido. *It was a lot of fun.*

 Listen to a conversation with these expressions.

 **10-12 Una cena.** Estuviste muy ocupado/a ayer porque tuviste invitados a cenar. Dile a tu compañero/a todas las cosas que hiciste. Él/Ella te va a preguntar dónde hiciste las compras, a quién invitaste, qué serviste y si lo pasaste bien. Después, cambien de papel.

10-13 Una cena perfecta.

PREPARACIÓN. You will listen to a couple talk about their plans for their dinner party tonight. Before you listen, make a list of four ingredients that you will need for a salad and an entrée. Share your list with a classmate.

ESCUCHA. Now listen to the conversation. As you listen, select the appropriate ending to each statement.

1. Rodolfo es (un buen cocinero / muy perezoso / vegetariano).
2. Manuela va a (preparar ceviche / poner la mesa / llamar a los invitados).
3. Rodolfo va a comprar (pescado y maíz / limón y camarones / espinacas y aguacates).
4. Manuela tiene (todos los ingredientes / muchos vegetales y frutas/ casi todos los ingredientes).

Mosaico cultural

Comida callejera

Para María Sanhuesa, encontrar comida en la ciudad de Quito no es nada difícil. "La variedad de restaurantes en la ciudad es increíble", comentó Sanhuesa; pero estas opciones no siempre son económicas para una estudiante, especialmente para alguien que viene de otro país. Por esta razón, ha preferido comer en los puestos de la calle y en los mercados durante los cuatro años que ha vivido en Quito estudiando en la Universidad Internacional de Ecuador.

Un joven probando comida callejera

La mayoría de estos puestos, ubicados en las plazas y en los parques de la ciudad, pero también en las calles cercanas a la universidad y las áreas de negocios, ofrecen una variedad de carnes, verduras, empanadas y pasteles. La comida es más barata que en los restaurantes. Los mercados también ofrecen lugares muy baratos para comer pinchos de carne, fritadas (*different types of fried meat*), hornados (*roasted pork*) y también sopas y ceviche.

En Latinoamérica, los puestos callejeros existen desde la época colonial. En estos puestos de comida callejera, se puede observar la tradición culinaria de cada región y comprar sus productos típicos. En Argentina venden choripanes (pan con chorizo) y empanadas. En Venezuela venden arepas rellenas (*filled*) con carnes y vegetales y en México tacos y tortillas. En todo el mundo hispano se puede conseguir gran variedad de platos típicos. María disfruta mucho de la comida ecuatoriana, pero también extraña (*misses*) la comida de su país.

Un cocinero asando pinchos en la calle

Compara

1. ¿Es común encontrar puestos de comida callejera en tu comunidad? ¿Qué tipo de comida venden? Explica detalladamente.
2. En general, ¿cuáles son las comidas que más consumes en tu vida como estudiante?
3. ¿Se venden comidas de diferentes culturas en tu comunidad?
4. ¿Probaste alguna vez las arepas, los choripanes, los tacos, las empanadas u otras comidas hispanas callejeras? ¿Cómo son en comparación con las comidas callejeras típicas de tu región? Si nunca las probaste, ¿cuál te gustaría probar?

En acción

¡Buen provecho!

Antes de ver

10-14 El restaurante ideal. Indica cuatro sugerencias que tú le harías (*you would make*) a Esteban para elegir el restaurante ideal.

_____ Visita el restaurante antes de hacer la reservación.
_____ Busca un restaurante en el centro.
_____ Acuérdate de que Yolanda es vegana.
_____ Pregunta si tienen descuento para estudiantes.
_____ Habla con los camareros.
_____ Investiga el restaurante en internet.
_____ Consulta el libro de quejas.
_____ Averigua quién es el chef.

Mientras ves

  **10-15 A comer.** Indica si las siguientes oraciones son ciertas (**C**) o falsas (**F**), según la información del video. Corrige las oraciones falsas.

En el restaurante:

1. _____ Yolanda va a pedir dos pupusas.
2. _____ Federico va a pedir bistec con ensalada.
3. _____ Esteban va a probar la yuca con chicharrones y plátanos.

Comidas típicas de Costa Rica:

4. _____ Lo más típico de la comida costarricense es el arroz con frijoles.
5. _____ La soda es un tipo de restaurante caro y elegante.
6. _____ El gallo pinto es un plato que se come en la cena.
7. _____ En los restaurantes de barrio se sirve comida fresca.

Las tapas españolas:

8. _____ Se preparan solamente en casa.
9. _____ El origen de las tapas es muy antiguo.
10. _____ Se sirven en porciones pequeñas.

Después de ver

10-16 La comida.

 **PREPARACIÓN.** Selecciona los temas que aparecen en este episodio, implícita o explícitamente.

1. _____ las comidas tradicionales de algunos países hispanos
2. _____ algunas costumbres asociadas con comidas típicas
3. _____ los peligros del consumo excesivo de carne
4. _____ la importancia de hacer ejercicio
5. _____ el origen de algunas comidas

 **INTERCAMBIOS.** Comparen sus respuestas de **Preparación** y respondan a siguientes preguntas.

1. ¿En qué ocasiones se ve la importancia de la comida como conexión social?
2. Según ustedes, ¿cómo van a cambiar nuestras costumbres alimentarias en el futuro? Expliquen con ejemplos.

1 Stating impersonal information

PROFESOR: En Estados Unidos **se consumen** muchos carbohidratos y mucha grasa. ¿Sabían ustedes que en este país **se comen** aproximadamente 23 libras de pizza por persona al año?

RICARDO: [*piensa*] ¿Cuánta cerveza **se bebe** con 23 pizzas?

PROFESOR: **Se comen** solo 18 libras de manzanas, pero 112 libras de carne roja…

RICARDO: [*piensa*] En esta clase **se aprende** mucho.

Piénsalo. Indica si el verbo en cada afirmación es singular (**S**) o plural (**P**) y si el objeto directo es singular (**S**) o plural (**P**).

	VERBO	OBJETO DIRECTO
MODELO **Se comen** menos vegetales.	*P*	*P*
1. **Se consumen** muchos carbohidratos.	_____	_____
2. **Se comen** aproximadamente 23 libras de pizza.	_____	_____
3. ¿Cúanta cerveza **se bebe** con 23 pizzas?	_____	_____
4. **Se comen** solo 18 libras de manzanas.	_____	_____
5. **Se aprende** mucho.	_____	_____

Se + verb constructions

- Spanish uses the construction **se** + *verb* to emphasize the occurrence of an action rather than the person(s) responsible for that action. The noun (what is bought, sold, offered, etc.) usually follows the verb. The person who buys, sells, offers, and so on, is not mentioned. This is normally expressed in English with the passive voice (is/are + *past participle*).

  Se habla español en este restaurante. — *Spanish is spoken in this restaurant.*

- Use a singular verb with singular nouns and a plural verb with plural nouns.

  Se necesita un horno para hacer galletas. — *An oven is needed to make cookies.*

  Se venden vegetales allí. — *Vegetables are sold there.*

- Use a singular verb when the **se** + *verb* construction is followed by an adverb, an infinitive, or a clause. This is expressed in English with *they, you, one,* and *people.*

  Se trabaja mucho en ese manzanal. — *They work a lot in that apple orchard.*

  Se puede comprar una variedad de manzanas allí. — *You/One can buy a variety of apples there.*

  Se dice que venden sidra también. — *People say they sell cider also.*

¿Comprendes? Completa las oraciones con **se** y la forma correcta del verbo.

1. _________ pasteles en la pastelería. (vender)
2. El ceviche _________ con pescado y mariscos. (preparar)
3. _________ freír o asar la carne de res. (poder)
4. _________ que la comida de ese restaurante es excelente. (decir)
5. En ese restaurante _________ los mejores platos ecuatorianos. (cocinar)
6. _________ beber vino blanco con el pescado. (sugerir)

PRÁCTICA

10-17 Asociaciones.

PREPARACIÓN. Selecciona el lugar donde ocurre cada actividad. Luego compara tus respuestas con las de tu compañero/a.

1. _____ Se cambian cheques en…
2. _____ Se vende ropa en…
3. _____ Se toma el sol y se nada en…
4. _____ Se sirven comidas en…
5. _____ Se ofrece trabajo en…

a. un almacén o una tienda.
b. los anuncios en línea.
c. un banco.
d. una playa.
e. un restaurante.

INTERCAMBIOS. Piensa en un edificio o lugar público que conoces bien y dile a tu compañero/a qué se hace allí.

MODELO *Me gusta mucho la zona peatonal* (pedestrian area) *de mi ciudad. Allí se vende mucha comida callejera y en el verano se escucha la música de grupos locales.*

En otras palabras

The concept of *convenience stores* is expressed differently depending on the country. In Mexico, they are **tiendas de conveniencia,** translated directly from English. In Costa Rica, the term **tiendas de gasolinera** is used. **La tienda de la esquina / del barrio** is frequently used in several Spanish-speaking countries to refer to the small or medium-sized stores located in residential neighborhoods. Convenience stores in Spain that are open 24/7 are called **tiendas de 24 horas.**

10-18 El supermercado y las tiendas pequeñas del barrio.

Indica los productos que se encuentran solo en los supermercados y los que se encuentran en las tiendas de tu barrio. Comparen sus respuestas. Después, dile a tu compañero/a qué productos compras con más frecuencia.

Productos	Supermercado solamente	Tiendas pequeñas del barrio
productos lácteos		
carnes orgánicas		
frutas exóticas caras		
detergente para lavadoras		
alimentos enlatados (*canned*)		
pescado fresco		
flores frescas		

10-19 Adivina.

Túrnense para describir uno de los siguientes productos, ingredientes, especias o platos. Usen varias oraciones en su descripción, pero no den el nombre. Su compañero/a debe adivinarlo.

Ingredientes

el aceite, las aceitunas, el arroz, la carne molida, las cebollas, la crema, los huevos, el maíz, los mariscos, el pescado, el pimiento, el pollo, el queso, los tomates

Condimentos

el ajo, el azafrán, el comino, el curry, el orégano, la pimienta

Platos

el arroz con leche, el ceviche, la fritada, la hamburguesa, el pescado frito, el pollo con arroz, el taco

MODELO el vino

E1: *Estoy pensando en un producto. Generalmente se bebe con la cena, pero no es agua. Se hace de uvas. Se vende en algunos supermercados. Es blanco o tinto.*

E2: *Es el vino, ¿verdad?*

E1: *¡Sí, correcto!*

10-20 Recetas creativas. **PREPARACIÓN.** Lean estas recetas originales. Luego, intercambien opiniones sobre cuáles les gustaría probar y cuáles no.

MODELO Ponche a la romana: Se muele (*grind*) piña. Se mezcla con una botella de champaña y helado de piña. Se agrega azúcar a gusto. Se enfría en el refrigerador antes de servir.

E1: *Me gustaría probar el ponche, pero no bebo alcohol. ¿Se puede preparar sin champaña?*

E2: *Por supuesto, se puede hacer con jugo de piña o con un refresco con sabor a limón.*

1. Banana derretida (*melted*): Se corta un plátano en rebanadas (*slices*). Se agrega azúcar. Se calienta en el microondas entre 30 a 45 segundos.
2. Batido de tarta de manzana (*apple pie*): Se pone en la licuadora (*blender*): media taza de jugo de manzana, tres cucharadas de helado de vainilla y media cucharadita de canela (*cinnamon*). Se bate por un minuto.
3. Hamburguesa y salsa con queso (*nacho cheese sauce*): Se calienta la parrilla (*grill*). Se cocina la hamburguesa. Se pone la salsa con queso en el panecillo y se calienta. Se pone la hamburguesa en el panecillo.
4. Ensalada de pollo: Se abre una bolsa de lechuga prelavada. Se cortan en rebanadas dos pechugas de pollo (*chicken breasts*) cocidas y se corta media libra de queso en cubos pequeños. Se combinan los ingredientes en un bol. Se agrega un aderezo de vinagre balsámico.

INTERCAMBIOS. Escriban juntos/as una receta para compartir con la clase. Si es posible, prepárenla para la clase.

10-21 ¿Cómo se prepara este plato? **PREPARACIÓN.** Tu compañero/a y tú quieren darle una sorpresa a otra persona y deciden prepararle su plato favorito. Primero, seleccionen uno de estos platos. Luego, escriban una lista de los ingredientes que se necesitan para hacerlo.

En directo

To propose an idea:

Tengo una idea. *I have an idea.*

¿Qué te parece esto? *What do you think of this?*

Se me ocurrió una idea. *I just thought of an idea.*

To agree with someone's idea:

Me parece perfecto. *That seems perfect.*

Suena muy bien. *Sounds great.*

¡Qué buena idea! *What a great idea!*

Listen to a conversation with these expressions.

INTERCAMBIOS. Van a cocinar en colaboración. Túrnense para indicar cada paso de la preparación. Los siguientes verbos pueden ser útiles.

agregar	cortar	hornear
asar	dorar (*to brown*)	rallar (*to grate*)
cocinar	freír	sazonar (*to season*)
colar (*to drain*)	hervir	tostar

MODELO E1: *Vamos a preparar pollo asado. ¿Cómo se hace?*
E2: *Primero se lava bien el pollo. Luego se ponen la sal y la pimienta.*
E1: *¿Y después?*
E2: *Se asa en el horno por una hora.*

Situación

PREPARACIÓN. Lean la situación. Luego, compartan ejemplos de vocabulario, gramática y otra información que necesitan para desarrollar la conversación.

Role A. You are an international student who has just arrived in town. A student has offered to help with your orientation. You are not familiar with shopping in the United States, so you ask:

a. where one buys food items like vegetables, sugar, and bread;
b. where on campus one can find a decent meal;
c. where one goes to buy fresh fruit; and
d. where one can get good pizza.

Ask follow-up questions to be sure you understand the answers.

Role B. You have offered to show a new international student around campus. Answer his/her questions about where one goes to buy different things. Offer several options, and be prepared to answer your new friend's questions.

	ROLE A	ROLE B
Vocabulario	Vocabulary related to food Question words	Vocabulary related to food Question words
Funciones y formas	Asking and answering questions Verifying information Thanking someone	Answering questions Giving instructions on how things are done Making comparisons between options

INTERCAMBIOS. Practiquen la conversación, incorporando el vocabulario y las funciones de **Preparación.** Luego, represéntenla ante la clase.

2 Talking about the recent past

CÉSAR: Alicia, ¿**has visto** a Javier? ¡Estoy muy molesto!

ALICIA: ¿Por qué? ¿Qué te pasa?

CÉSAR: Como sabes, el examen de literatura es pasado mañana y yo no **he leído** el libro todavía. ¿Lo **has leído** tú? ¿Lo **ha leído** Javier? ¿Javier te **ha dado** sus notas? No sé qué voy a hacer sin sus notas. ¡Las necesito para estudiar!

ALICIA: Cálmate, César. Yo **he leído** el libro y **he escrito** unas notas. Javi y yo **hemos hablado.** No **ha terminado** el libro todavía, pero va a llamarte esta tarde.

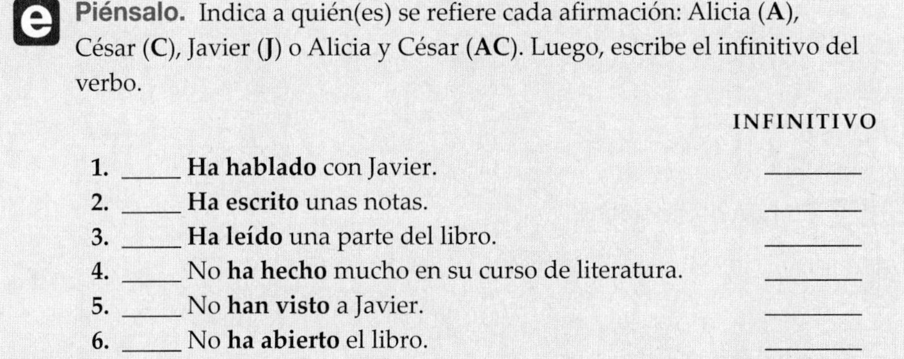

Piénsalo. Indica a quién(es) se refiere cada afirmación: Alicia (**A**), César (**C**), Javier (**J**) o Alicia y César (**AC**). Luego, escribe el infinitivo del verbo.

		INFINITIVO
1.	_____ **Ha hablado** con Javier.	_______
2.	_____ **Ha escrito** unas notas.	_______
3.	_____ **Ha leído** una parte del libro.	_______
4.	_____ No **ha hecho** mucho en su curso de literatura.	_______
5.	_____ No **han visto** a Javier.	_______
6.	_____ No **ha abierto** el libro.	_______

Present perfect

- Use the present perfect to refer to a past event, action, or condition that has some relation to the present.

He lavado los platos.	*I have washed the dishes.*
Cecilia nunca **ha vivido** en otro país.	*Cecilia has never lived in another country.*

- Form the present perfect by using the present tense of **haber** as an auxiliary verb with the past participle of the main verb. In English, past participles are often formed with the endings *-ed* and *-en,* as in *finished* or *eaten.*

PRESENT TENSE OF *HABER* + PAST PARTICIPLE					
yo	**he**	nosotros/as	**hemos**		**hablado**
tú	**has**	vosotros/as	**habéis**	+	**comido**
Ud., él, ella	**ha**	Uds., ellos/as	**han**		**vivido**

Los cocineros **han trabajado** mucho.	*The cooks have worked a lot.*
Ya **hemos traído** los manteles.	*We have already brought the tablecloths.*

- All past participles of **-ar** verbs end in **-ado,** whereas past participles of **-er** and **-ir** verbs generally end in **-ido.** If the stem of an **-er** verb ends in a vowel, use a written accent on the **i** of **-ido** (leer S **leído**).

Paco, ¿ya **has leído** la receta?	*Paco, have you read the recipe yet?*
No, no **he leído** la receta todavía.	*No, I have not read the recipe yet.*

- Some **-er** and **-ir** verbs have irregular past participles. These are common ones:

abrir	**abierto**	morir	**muerto**
cubrir	**cubierto**	poner	**puesto**
decir	**dicho**	romper	**roto**
escribir	**escrito**	ver	**visto**
hacer	**hecho**	volver	**vuelto**

Lengua

To state that something has just happened, use the present tense of **acabar** + **de** + *infinitive*, not the present perfect.

Acabamos de volver del supermercado.
We have just returned from the supermarket.

Acabo de probar la sopa y está deliciosa.
I have just tasted the soup, and it is delicious.

- Place object and reflexive pronouns before the auxiliary **haber.** Do not place any word between **haber** and the past participle.

¿**Le** has dado los vasos a Juan?	*Have you given Juan the glasses?*
No, todavía no **se los** he dado.	*No, I have not given them to him yet.*

e **¿Comprendes?** Completa las oraciones con el presente perfecto de los verbos.

1. Yo ____________ (preparar) la comida.
2. Nosotros ____________ (comprar) los ingredientes.
3. Tú no ____________ (poner) la mesa todavía.
4. El niño ____________ (romper) dos ventanas.
5. Los estudiantes ya ____________ (hacer) su tarea.

PRÁCTICA

10-22 Lo que no he hecho.

PREPARACIÓN. Indiquen las cosas que no han hecho.

1. Yo nunca he estado en (Paraguay/Guatemala/Ecuador).
2. Nunca he visto (las islas Galápagos/un volcán activo/un huracán).
3. Nunca he comido (aguacate/un postre con leche de coco/langosta).
4. Nunca he roto (una taza/un vaso/un plato).

INTERCAMBIOS. Comparen sus respuestas con las de otra pareja.

MODELO PAREJA 1: *Sara ha roto un vaso y yo he roto muchos platos. ¿Y ustedes?*
PAREJA 2: *Nosotros no hemos roto platos. Roberto nunca ha comido langosta, pero yo la he comido muchas veces. Me gusta mucho.*

10-23 Hispanos famosos. **PREPARACIÓN.** Piensen en un hispano famoso o una hispana famosa y preparen una lista de cinco cosas que ha hecho para tener éxito (*to be successful*). Después, compartan su lista con otra pareja.

MODELO E1: *Diego Luna es un actor mexicano.*
E2: *Ha protagonizado la película* Rogue One…

INTERCAMBIOS. Digan tres cosas que ustedes han hecho que los/las han ayudado a tener éxito en su vida personal, académica o profesional.

10-24 Una cena importante. **PREPARACIÓN.** Tú y tu compañero/a de apartamento van a preparar una cena para sus padres. Háganse preguntas para ver qué preparativos ha hecho cada uno/a para la cena.

MODELO comprar la carne
E1: *¿Has comprado la carne?*
E2: *No, no la he comprado todavía.*

1. leer las recetas
2. cortar los vegetales
3. hacer el postre
4. decidir qué música poner
5. poner la mesa
6. decorar el lugar de la cena

INTERCAMBIOS. Digan qué han hecho todos durante la cena y después.

MODELO E1: *Yo he conversado mucho con tus padres. ¡Son muy interesantes!*
E2: *Y mi papá nos ha ayudado a lavar los platos.*

10-25 Justo ahora. Digan qué han hecho estas personas. Den la mayor información posible.

MODELO Maricarmen y sus amigos ya no tienen hambre.
E1: *Han comido toda la comida.*
E2: *Han dejado el refrigerador vacío* (empty).

1. Juan y Ramiro salen del estadio.
2. Alina trae una tarta de manzana caliente a la mesa.
3. Mercedes y Paula traen palomitas de maíz (*popcorn*) para todo el grupo.
4. Un hombre sale corriendo de un banco.
5. Elisa y Rubén salen de un supermercado.
6. Frente a todos sus amigos, Víctor le da una sorpresa a su novia.

10-26 ¿Qué ha hecho este chef famoso? **PREPARACIÓN.** Busquen en internet información sobre José Andrés, un chef español-estadounidense. Luego, túrnense para hacer y contestar preguntas relacionadas con los temas de la lista.

abrir restaurantes	participar en grupos de activismo social
escribir libros	recibir premios (*prizes*)
introducir el concepto de tapas	servir comida a grupos necesitados (*in need*)

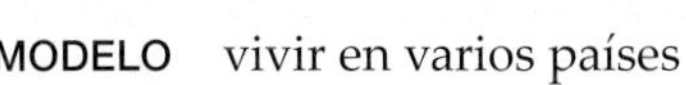

MODELO vivir en varios países
E1: *¿En qué países ha vivido José Andrés?*
E2: *Ha vivido en España y en Estados Unidos. Ahora vive en Washington, DC, pero viaja mucho.*

INTERCAMBIOS. Hablen de lo que han aprendido acerca de José Andrés. Escriban los datos (*pieces of information*) más importantes para ustedes. Presenten sus datos a la clase y justifiquen su selección.

Situación

PREPARACIÓN. Lean esta situación. Luego, compartan ejemplos de vocabulario, gramática y otra información que necesitan para desarrollar la conversación.

Role A. You are a student residence hall assistant at your university. Today you are meeting with a student who lives in the dorm. Explain that other students have complained that:
a. he/she has had parties in the dorm;
b. his/her friends have broken furniture in the public areas; and
c. his/her loud music has bothered everyone on the floor.
Say that you are worried about him/her and ask questions to find out what is prompting this behavior.

Role B. You live in a dorm at your school. The residence hall assistant tells you about complaints that he/she has received regarding your behavior. Respond to his/her comments and questions in detail.

	ROLE A	ROLE B
Vocabulario	University life Furniture Music	University life Furniture Music
Funciones y formas	Talking about the recent past Asking questions Giving advice	Talking about the recent past Stating your case Giving details

INTERCAMBIOS. Practiquen la conversación, incorporando el vocabulario y las funciones de **Preparación.** Luego, represéntenla ante la clase.

3 Describing the result of a previous action

¡Necesito ayuda, por favor! Acabo de llegar a casa, y alguien ha estado aquí. La puerta está **abierta,** la televisión está **puesta** y las dos ventanas de la sala están **rotas.** Además, las cortinas están **destrozadas.** La alfombra y la mesa del comedor están **pintadas** de verde y ¡mi pájaro está **muerto!** Por suerte, mi dinero está **escondido** (*hidden*) en el congelador (*freezer*) y el ladrón (*thief*) no lo ha encontrado. ¿Qué debo hacer?

Piénsalo. Para cada adjetivo en negrita, escribe el sustantivo que describe y el verbo del que se deriva.

	SUSTANTIVO	INFINITIVO
1. La puerta está **abierta.**	__________	__________
2. Las dos ventanas de la sala están **rotas.**	__________	__________
3. Las cortinas están **destrozadas.**	__________	__________
4. La alfombra y la mesa están **pintadas** de verde.	__________	__________
5. Mi pájaro está **muerto.**	__________	__________
6. Mi dinero está **escondido** en el congelador.	__________	__________

Participles used as adjectives

- You have already used past participles with the present perfect tense. Spanish uses **estar** + *past participle* to express a state or condition resulting from a previous action.

ACTION	RESULT
Ella preparó la sopa.	La sopa **está preparada.**
Luego cerró las ventanas.	Las ventanas **están cerradas.**

- When a past participle is used as an adjective, it agrees with the noun it modifies.

una puerta **cerrada** — *a closed door*
los restaurantes **abiertos** — *the open restaurants*
unas botellas **lavadas** — *some washed bottles*

- You have already learned adjectives that convey emotional states or physical conditions as individual vocabulary words. Many of them are past participles.

Luisa está **preocupada.** — *Luisa is worried.* (verb: **preocupar**)
Samuel está **cansado.** Su trabajo le cansa mucho. — *Samuel is tired. His work tires him out.* (verb: **cansar**)

e **¿Comprendes?** Completa las afirmaciones con el adjetivo derivado del verbo entre paréntesis.

1. La comida está __________. (preparar)
2. La ensalada está __________. (hacer)
3. Los libros están __________ en su lugar. (poner)
4. Los niños están __________. (dormir)
5. Los regalos están __________. (esconder)
6. Las ventanas están __________ porque hace calor. (abrir)

PRÁCTICA

10-27 Robo (*Robbery*) en un restaurante.

e **PREPARACIÓN.** El siguiente incidente ocurrió en el restaurante del chef Marco Tovares. Completa el texto con la forma correcta del participio pasado de los verbos entre paréntesis.

El chef Marco Tovares salió de la cocina para asegurarse de que todo iba bien. Vio que el locutor de televisión Jorge Ramos estaba (1) __________ (sentar) en una mesa con otras personas. Marco vio que el bolso de una de las mujeres estaba (2) __________ (abrir) y que un hombre de otra mesa lo miraba. Como la mujer estaba (3) __________ (distraer), llegó el momento (4) __________ (esperar) por el hombre: sacó la billetera del bolso de ella. Marco lo vio todo. Fue a la mesa y le preguntó al hombre: "¿Cómo está la comida esta noche?" El hombre parecía muy nervioso y, curiosamente, tenía las manos (5) __________ (cerrar). Marco le dijo: "Acompáñeme, por favor". El hombre fue con Marco, le dio la billetera (6) __________ (robar) y salió. Marco se acercó a la mesa de Jorge Ramos y les explicó lo ocurrido. Todos estaban muy (7) __________ (sorprender).

INTERCAMBIOS. Usen la imaginación para contarse cómo estaban las personas después del evento de **Preparación.** Usen los adjetivos de la lista u otros.

agradecido/a (*grateful*)	contento/a	nervioso/a	sorprendido/a
avergonzado/a (*embarrassed*)	furioso/a	preocupado/a	triste

MODELO Jorge Ramos

E1: *Me parece que Jorge Ramos estaba contento.*

E2: *Es posible, pero yo creo que estaba triste, porque ahora no quiere volver al restaurante de Marco Tovares. Es su restaurante favorito en Nueva York.*

1. el chef Marco Tovares
2. la amiga de Jorge Ramos
3. el ladrón
4. la esposa del ladrón
5. las otras personas que estaban en el restaurante

10-28 Organizar una reunión. Tú y tu compañero/a han organizado la reunión del CineClub de su universidad, y empieza en media hora. Túrnense para hablar de lo que han hecho.

analizar el presupuesto (*budget*) del club	escoger las películas para el año que viene
arreglar las sillas	escribir la agenda
comprar comida	imprimir (*to print*) la lista de los miembros del club
poner la computadora	poner botellas de agua en la mesa

MODELO mandar las invitaciones

E1: *¿Has mandado las invitaciones?*

E2: *Sí, las invitaciones están mandadas.*

10-29 Hablando de las emociones. Túrnense para hablar de cuándo y por qué han sentido algunas de las emociones de la lista. Cuando uno/a de ustedes habla, la otra persona pide más detalles.

animado/a	fascinado/a
avergonzado/a (*embarassed*)	preocupado/a
enojado/a	respetado/a
estresado/a	sorprendido/a

MODELO E1: *Me siento enojado/a cuando mis amigos no me invitan a salir con ellos.*

E2: *¿Esto te ha pasado recientemente?*

E1: *Sí, la semana pasada. Mis amigos fueron al cine y no me invitaron.*

10-30 ¿Qué ha pasado? Después de limpiar y ordenar tu habitación en la residencia, tu amigo/a se ha quedado allí por unas horas. Al volver, encuentras todo muy desordenado. Habla con tu amigo/a para expresar tu disgusto (*annoyance*). Tu amigo/a va a ofrecerte explicaciones o pedirte perdón.

MODELO las ventanas (cerrar, abrir)

E1: *¿Qué ha pasado con las ventanas? Las he cerrado esta mañana y ahora están abiertas. Ha habido mucho viento y mis papeles están en el piso.*

E2: *Las he abierto porque hace mucho calor…*

1. el espejo (limpiar, romper)
2. la cama (hacer, desordenar)
3. la computadora (apagar, poner)
4. las camisas (colgar [*hang*], tirar [*throw*] al piso)
5. las fotos de mi familia (poner, guardar [*put away*])
6. la comida del refrigerador (tapar [*cover*], destapar)

 **10-31 La fiesta perfecta.** Describan los siguientes elementos de una fiesta. Usen las palabras de la lista.

decorar	poner
hacer	preparar
helar (*to chill*)	servir
ordenar	vestir

MODELO las bebidas
E1: *Las bebidas están heladas, ¿no?*
E2: *Claro que sí. Han estado en el refrigerador por muchas horas.*

1. la comida
2. el lugar
3. la música y otras actividades de diversión
4. los invitados

INTERCAMBIOS. Ahora descríbanse una fiesta muy buena en la que han participado. Háganse preguntas para conseguir más detalles.

MODELO E1: *La mejor fiesta de mi vida fue la boda de mi hermano. La comida estaba muy bien preparada y las mesas estaban decoradas con…*
E2: *¿Qué comida se sirvió en la boda?*

Situación

PREPARACIÓN. Lean esta situación. Luego, compartan ejemplos de vocabulario, gramática y otra información que necesitan para desarrollar la conversación.

Role A. You have been house sitting for your neighbor while he/she was on vacation. You would like the neighbor to hire you again, so you have taken very good care of the house. When your neighbor returns and asks you how things have gone, tell him/her in detail everything you have done and how you have prepared the house for his/her return. You should mention:
a. you have cleaned the house and have washed the windows;
b. the beds are made with clean sheets, the dishes are washed, and the plants are watered (**regar**); and
c. there is a fresh salad already made for him/her in the refrigerator.

Role B. You have just returned from vacation. You ask the house sitter how things have gone. The house sitter tells you in detail what he/she has done in your absence and how the house has been prepared for your return. Respond to his/her account by asking questions, so you know whether to hire him/her again the next time you go on vacation.

	ROLE A	ROLE B
Vocabulario	Activities related to a household Food	Activities related to a household
Funciones y formas	Talking about the recent past Giving details Describing the result of a previous action: Participles used as adjectives	Talking about the recent past Asking questions Describing the result of a previous action: Participles used as adjectives

INTERCAMBIOS. Practiquen la conversación, incorporando el vocabulario y las funciones de **Preparación.** Luego, represéntenla ante la clase.

4 Giving instructions in informal settings

Marcos, la buena alimentación es fundamental para la buena salud. **Desayuna** siempre para no tener hambre por las mañanas. Para tener energía, **consume** carbohidratos y proteínas en las tres comidas. **Come** carbohidratos complejos, como pasta y pan, pero siempre integrales (*whole-grain*). **No olvides** las frutas, las verduras y la leche; son muy buenas para la salud. **Evita** (*Avoid*) comer azúcares en grandes cantidades. **Limita** tu consumo de grasas también y **no comas** muchos dulces.

Piénsalo. Indica si las instrucciones del enfermero para tu amigo Marcos son afirmativas (**A**) o negativas (**N**). Luego, escribe el infinitivo del verbo conjugado.

	¿AFIRMATIVA O NEGATIVA?	INFINITIVO
1. **Desayuna** siempre.	_____	________
2. **Consume** carbohidratos y proteínas.	_____	________
3. **No olvides** las frutas, las verduras y la leche.	_____	________
4. **Evita** comer azúcares en grandes cantidades.	_____	________
5. **Limita** el consumo de grasas.	_____	________
6. **No comas** muchos dulces.	_____	________

Informal commands

- To ask a friend to do or not to do something, use an informal command. Use that form with anyone else you address as **tú,** such as someone your own age or someone with whom you have a close relationship.

Pásame la sal.	*Pass me the salt.*
Mira esta foto.	*Look at this photo.*
Lee las instrucciones.	*Read the instructions.*
Préstame tu lápiz.	*Lend me your pencil.*

- To form the affirmative **tú** command, use the present indicative **tú** form without the final **-s.**

	PRESENT INDICATIVE	AFFIRMATIVE *TÚ* COMMAND
cocinar	cocinas	**cocina**
beber	bebes	**bebe**
consumir	consumes	**consume**

- For the negative **tú** command, use the negative **usted** command form and add the final **-s.**

	NEGATIVE *USTED* COMMAND	NEGATIVE *TÚ* COMMAND
preparar	no prepar**e**	no prepar**es**
comer	no com**a**	no com**as**
subir	no sub**a**	no sub**as**

- Placement of object and reflexive pronouns with **tú** commands is the same as with **usted** commands.

AFFIRMATIVE COMMAND	NEGATIVE COMMAND
Prepáre**lo** (usted).	No **lo** prepare (usted).
Bébe**la** (tú).	No **la** bebas (tú).
Siénte**se** (usted) aquí.	No **se** siente (usted) aquí.
Acuésta**te** (tú).	No **te** acuestes (tú).

- The plural of **tú** commands in Latin American Spanish is the **ustedes** command.

Cocina (tú).	**Cocinen (ustedes).**
Bebe (tú).	**Beban (ustedes).**
Sube (tú).	**Suban (ustedes).**

- Some **-er** and **-ir** verbs have shortened affirmative **tú** commands, but their negative command forms follow the pattern that you have already learned for formal commands.

	AFFIRMATIVE (*tú*)	NEGATIVE (*tú*)
poner	**pon**	**no pongas**
salir	**sal**	**no salgas**
tener	**ten**	**no tengas**
venir	**ven**	**no vengas**
hacer	**haz**	**no hagas**
decir	**di**	**no digas**
ir	**ve**	**no vayas**
ser	**sé**	**no seas**

Sal a las tres si quieres llegar a las cuatro.	*Leave at 3:00 if you want to arrive at 4:00.*
No salgas sin paraguas; va a llover.	*Don't leave without an umbrella; it is going to rain.*
Sé generoso con tus amigos.	*Be generous with your friends.*
No seas impaciente.	*Don't be impatient.*
Dime la verdad.	*Tell me the truth.*
No nos digas mentiras.	*Don't tell us any lies.*

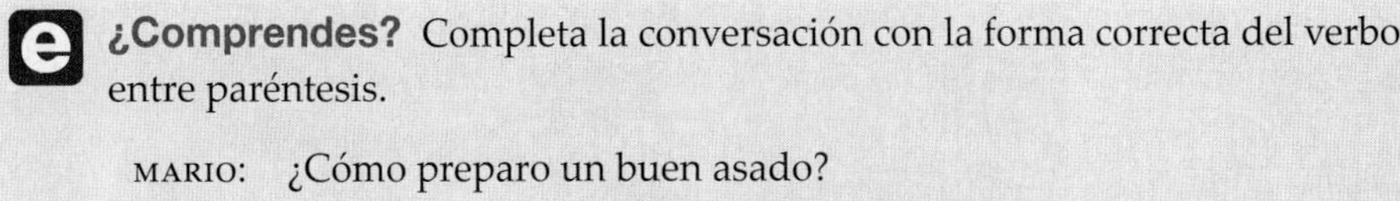

¿Comprendes? Completa la conversación con la forma correcta del verbo entre paréntesis.

MARIO: ¿Cómo preparo un buen asado?

XIMENA: (1) _______ (Comprar) carne blanda (*tender*).
No (2) _______ (comprar) carne barata.

MARIO: ¿Y luego?

XIMENA: (3) _______ (Ponerle) sal y pimienta a la carne.
No (4) _______ (poner) demasiada sal.

PRÁCTICA

10-32 Recomendaciones. Escoge las recomendaciones más adecuadas, según cada situación. Compara tus respuestas con las de tu compañero/a y después añade otra situación. Tu compañero/a te va a dar un consejo.

1. Tu compañero/a comió demasiado en una fiesta de cumpleaños y ahora le duele mucho el estómago.
   - **a.** Come más para recuperarte.
   - **b.** Llama al médico.
   - **c.** Ve a la farmacia y compra medicamentos.
   - **d.** Camina una hora esta tarde.
   - **e.** Practica deportes para olvidarte del dolor de estómago.
   - **f.** No te acuestes.
2. Tu hermana está enferma. Está congestionada y tiene fiebre (*fever*).
   - **a.** Toma sopa de pollo.
   - **b.** Come una hamburguesa.
   - **c.** No duermas mucho.
   - **d.** Bebe jugos y agua.
   - **e.** No bebas vino ni cerveza.
   - **f.** No consumas mucha cafeína.
3. A tu amiga le fascina la comida basura, por eso, subió diez libras en un mes.
   - **a.** Ve a los restaurantes de comida rápida.
   - **b.** Bebe muchos refrescos.
   - **c.** Come en casa, no en restaurantes.
   - **d.** No tomes alcohol.
   - **e.** Evita los helados.
   - **f.** No pidas ensaladas.
4. Tu mamá quiere alimentarse mejor para tener más energía y sentirse sana.
   - **a.** Evita la grasa.
   - **b.** Toma muchos helados.
   - **c.** Come huevos moderadamente.
   - **d.** Compra papas fritas.
   - **e.** Acuéstate y descansa.
   - **f.** Si no tienes energía, consume mucha cafeína.
5. Tu mejor amigo/a quiere preparar una cena espectacular para su novio/a.
   - **a.** Compra pizza.
   - **b.** Haz un plato sofisticado.
   - **c.** No te olvides de comprar un buen vino.
   - **d.** Prepara la mesa el día anterior.
   - **e.** No le pongas chile picante al plato. Ella detesta la comida picante.
   - **f.** Ponle mucha sal a la comida.

Cultura

Las aguas termales de Papallacta En la cordillera de los Andes, a una hora de la capital de Quito, se encuentran las termas de Papallacta. Son famosas por sus características curativas. Además, es un gran centro turístico por su ubicación en un área medioambiental muy diversa e interesante, cercana a reservas ecológicas y a la región amazónica.

Comparaciones ¿Dónde se pueden encontrar baños medicinales en Estados Unidos? ¿Sabes si un/a amigo/a o familiar ha visitado uno de estos lugares? Busca información sobre uno de ellos y descríbeselo a la clase.

10-33 Una cura de reposo. Tu amigo/a estuvo muy enfermo/a. Su médico le recomendó pasar dos semanas de descanso en las termas de Papallacta, en Ecuador. Como tú has visitado este lugar, dile a tu amigo/a qué puede hacer allí. Después, cambien de papel.

MODELO disfrutar de la tranquilidad

E1: *Disfruta de la tranquilidad y no uses tu celular.*

E2: *Y, ¿qué más puedo hacer?*

1. disfrutar del sol
2. respirar aire puro y descansar
3. no hacer la tarea
4. tomar fotos y hacer videos
5. probar un plato típico ecuatoriano en el restaurante Pumamaki
6. salir por las noches y conversar con las personas del lugar
7. tomar baños termales todos los días
8. asistir a un concierto de música andina
9. salir a caminar todos los días
10. llevar ropa apropiada para las noches frías de los Andes

10-34 Tareas pendientes. PREPARACIÓN. Ustedes están a cargo de un restaurante donde se va a celebrar una cena formal. Túrnense para recordarse (*remind each another*) las tareas pendientes.

MODELO lavar la vajilla (*set of dishes*) fina / limpiar el piso

E1: *Lava la vajilla fina.*

E2: *Por supuesto. / Inmediatamente. Y tú, limpia el piso, ¿vale?*

E1: *Vale. / De acuerdo.*

Tareas pendientes: Empleado/a 1	Tareas pendientes: Empleado/a 2
1. comprar temprano los pescados y mariscos frescos	**1.** ser puntual
2. no hacer pan blanco; hacer pan integral (*whole-wheat*)	**2.** sacar las verduras del congelador (*freezer*)
3. tener las mesas puestas a las 4:00	**3.** asar el pescado media hora antes de la cena
4. no poner los manteles plásticos; poner los de lino	**4.** preparar las ensaladas y los platos principales
5. no poner música rock; poner música suave	**5.** imprimir (*to print*) el programa con los nombres de los invitados

INTERCAMBIOS. La cena formal tuvo algunos problemas. Lean las notas del administrador del restaurante. Luego, conversen sobre los problemas y háganse recomendaciones para mejorar la próxima vez.

MODELO Derramaste (*You spilled*) agua en la mesa de los invitados.

La próxima vez, ten cuidado cuando sirves agua.

Problemas con la cena formal	Tus recomendaciones
1. Las ensaladas estaban saladas (*salty*).	
2. El pescado se quemó (*burned*).	
3. Había manchas (*spots*) en las copas.	
4. Nadie imprimió el programa.	
5. Dos camareros llegaron tarde.	
6. Una camarera se cayó con los platos porque el piso estaba mojado (*wet*).	

10-35 Hábitos alimenticios.

PREPARACIÓN. Ustedes están preocupados/as por los hábitos alimenticios de su amigo/a. Lean lo que él/ella come y bebe en un día típico e identifiquen sus hábitos problemáticos.

> Todos los días se levanta tarde. Cuando se levanta, toma varias tazas de café. Una hora más tarde, come tres huevos fritos con tocino (*bacon*) y tostadas. Luego, toma una taza de café cubano con bastante azúcar. Más tarde, lee las noticias en su dormitorio, mira televisión y come chocolate mientras chatea con sus amigos. Para la cena, pide una hamburguesa doble con papas fritas, usando la aplicación de su restaurante favorito; bebe cerveza con su cena. Después, juega videojuegos. Por la noche, tiene problemas para dormir; por eso, toma un batido.

INTERCAMBIOS. Hagan una lista de cinco recomendaciones o instrucciones que su amigo/a debe seguir. Comparen su lista con las de otros grupos.

10-36 Cocina paso a paso (*step by step*). **PREPARACIÓN.** Escojan una receta de un plato que se consume en su país y escriban una lista de los ingredientes.

INTERCAMBIOS. Preparen una presentación de su receta para la clase. Hagan lo siguiente: a) describan el plato; b) presenten sus ingredientes y c) expliquen cómo se prepara.

Situación

PREPARACIÓN. Lean esta situación. Luego, compartan ejemplos de vocabulario, gramática y otra información que necesitan para desarrollar la conversación.

Role A. To improve your health, you call your friend who is studying to become a nutritionist. Explain what you generally eat for breakfast, lunch, and dinner. Ask questions and answer the nutritionist's questions.

Role B. You are studying to become a nutritionist and a friend calls you for help with eating habits. Ask what he/she eats for breakfast, lunch, and dinner. Advise him/her:
a. to eat fruits, vegetables, fish, and chicken;
b. not to drink soft drinks or alcohol;
c. to consume foods with lots of fiber; and
d. to do physical activity daily.
Answer your friend's questions.

	ROLE A	ROLE B
Vocabulario	Food-related vocabulary	Food-related vocabulary
Funciones y formas	Explaining food habits Asking and answering questions Thanking someone for the advice	Asking and answering questions Giving advice Giving instructions Informal commands

INTERCAMBIOS. Practiquen la conversación, incorporando el vocabulario y las funciones de **Preparación.** Luego, represéntenla ante la clase.

MOSAICOS

ESCUCHA

Estrategia

Take notes about relevant details In previous chapters, you have practiced the strategy of focusing on information that is relevant to your purpose for listening. Note-taking is a useful strategy for remembering important information. Listening more than once also helps you to remember relevant details.

10-37 Preparación. Antes de escuchar, prepara una lista de productos que compras regularmente y otra de aquellos que compras solamente en ocasiones especiales. Compártela con la clase.

  **10-38 Escucha.** Andrea, Carolina, Roberto, and Darío have each offered to contribute a dish for their friend's birthday party. As you listen, select the ingredients that each person bought to prepare his/her dish.

Andrea	Carolina	Roberto	Darío
_____ aguacates	_____ ajos	_____ aceite	_____ aderezo
_____ atún	_____ cerdo	_____ aguacates	_____ ajos
_____ cilantro	_____ espinacas	_____ langosta	_____ fruta
_____ lechugas	_____ jamón	_____ pepinos	_____ huevos
_____ pollo	_____ langosta	_____ pavo	_____ jamón
_____ queso	_____ maíz	_____ pimienta	_____ papas
_____ tomates	_____ pollo	_____ sal	_____ pimientos verdes

Comprueba

I was able to . . .

- distinguish between key and secondary information.
- listen for and make note of relevant details.

 **10-39 Un paso más.** Túrnense para hacerse las siguientes preguntas.

1. ¿Con quién celebraste tu último cumpleaños? ¿Qué comiste y bebiste?
2. ¿Preparaste o compraste comida, o alguien organizó la celebración para ti?
3. ¿Fueron saludables la comida y las bebidas en tu cumpleaños?
4. En general, ¿es importante consumir alimentos saludables? ¿Por qué?

HABLA

Estrategia

Give and defend reasons for a decision When you make a decision that you wish to communicate effectively to others, it is important to a) state your decision clearly; b) present and explain your reasons logically; and c) urge your listeners to consider your point of view.

10-40 Preparación. Elige un plato que consideres muy saludable y lee la receta de cómo prepararlo. Luego, haz una lista de los ingredientes que se necesitan y otra lista de los modos de preparación (verbos).

MODELO Plato: *salmón al carbón*
Ingredientes: *salmón, limón, sal, pimienta*
Modos de preparación: *sazonar, marinar, asar, dorar*

Comprueba

I was able to . . .
- exchange information about food preferences.
- describe how to prepare a dish I like.
- talk about healthful foods while referring to an online source for information.

 **10-41 Habla.** Explíquense por qué eligieron el plato en **Preparación.** Respondan a estas preguntas.

1. ¿Cuál es tu plato saludable favorito? ¿Por qué lo elegiste? ¿Por qué es saludable?
2. ¿Con qué frecuencia lo comes?
3. ¿Cómo se prepara? ¿Es sano el modo de preparación?
4. ¿Con qué lo acompañas?
5. ¿Cuál de los dos platos es más saludable: el tuyo o el de tu compañero/a? ¿Por qué? Pueden consultar en internet MiPlato, la guía nutricional del Departamento de Agricultura de Estados Unidos.

 **10-42 Un paso más.** Preparen un informe sobre el plato más sano que escogieron en la actividad **10-41.** Usen las siguientes preguntas como guía. Después, presenten su informe a la clase.

1. ¿De qué platos conversaron?
2. ¿Qué ingredientes tiene el plato más saludable que escogieron? ¿Por qué el plato es más saludable?
3. Expliquen cómo se prepara y con qué se puede acompañar.

LEE

Estrategia

Learn new words by analyzing their connections with known words As you read in a second language, you encounter words that are unfamiliar to you. In some cases, you can skip over a word and still understand the overall meaning of the sentence or paragraph. In other cases, you should focus on the unfamiliar word and guess its meaning. You can figure out the meanings of unfamiliar words and expand your vocabulary by mentally linking them to words you know that are related in meaning or in grammatical form.

 **10-43 Preparación.** Lean el título y los subtítulos del artículo "La fusión culinaria", miren las fotos y lean sus leyendas (*captions*). Luego, hablen de lo que esperan encontrar en el artículo guiándose por las siguientes preguntas. Expliquen sus respuestas.

1. ¿Qué información esperan encontrar en el artículo?
   a. una definición del término "fusión culinaria"
   b. recetas para platos de cocina fusión
   c. información sobre la influencia china en la cocina de un país
   d. información sobre la cocina Tex-Mex
2. Indiquen los elementos que los ayudaron a responder a la pregunta 1.
   a. el título y los subtítulos
   b. las fotos junto con sus leyendas
3. ¿Qué es la fusión culinaria? Indiquen la definición más lógica.
   a. la combinación de la cocina con otras artes, como la decoración de interiores
   b. una cocina que combina la influencia de dos tradiciones culinarias
4. Preparen una lista de platos Tex-Mex que conozcan. ¿Cuáles les gustan más?

LA FUSIÓN CULINARIA

LA FUSIÓN EN LA COCINA CONTEMPORÁNEA

Todos hemos comido platos que combinan la cocina de dos países o culturas. El llamado *California roll* es un ejemplo; la *taco pizza* es otro. La fusión culinaria, o cocina fusión, ejemplifica la mezcla de ingredientes y estilos culinarios de diferentes culturas en el menú de un restaurante o en un mismo plato. Dos ejemplos de este fenómeno en las Américas son la cocina chino-peruana y la cocina mexicano-norteamericana, o Tex-Mex.

EL CHIFA EN PERÚ

La cocina peruana es una mezcla de muchas influencias: indígena, española, africana, china y japonesa. El chifa, o cocina chino-peruana, es el resultado de la combinación de la comida criolla de Lima con la cocina traída por los inmigrantes chinos a mediados del siglo XIX.

Los chinos que se establecieron en Perú se adaptaron a la sociedad y a sus costumbres, pero siempre mantuvieron sus tradiciones culinarias. Con el progreso económico, importaron de China especias y otros productos esenciales para su comida, pero por lo general tenían que cultivar las verduras que necesitaban o sustituirlas por ingredientes locales.

La cultura chino-peruana revolucionó la gastronomía del país. Algunos platos considerados típicamente peruanos, como el arroz chaufa (preparado con carne molida, cebollitas, pimiento, huevos y salsa de soja) y el tacu-tacu (una tortilla hecha de un puré de frijoles, arroz, ajo, ají y cebolla) reflejan la influencia de la cocina china.

Arroz chaufa, un plato chino-peruano

LA COMIDA TEX-MEX

Un ejemplo de la cocina fusión que se conoce en todas partes de Estados Unidos es la cocina Tex-Mex. Se trata de la fusión de los estilos de México y de Texas. La cocina que conocemos hoy en día como Tex-Mex empezó como una mezcla de la comida del pueblo nativo de Texas y la cocina española.

Los indígenas contribuyeron con ingredientes como los frijoles pintos, los nopales (las hojas de un cacto), las cebollas silvestres y el mezquite. La influencia española empezó con la llegada del ganado[1] a la región, traído por los colonizadores al final del siglo XVI. Pero también hay influencias del norte de África. Un grupo de colonizadores de las islas Canarias y de Marruecos inmigraron en el siglo XVIII a lo que es ahora San Antonio, Texas. Trajeron nuevas especias, cilantro y chiles. El *chili con carne* de San Antonio todavía retiene los sabores de la cocina marroquí.

Nachos, un plato popular de la cocina Tex-Mex

En los últimos 30 años se ha intentado separar la cocina mexicana de la cocina mexicana americanizada, o Tex-Mex. La cocina Tex-Mex utiliza más carne y usa las tortillas para envolver mayor variedad de rellenos. Los nachos, los tacos fritos, las chalupas, el *chili con queso* y el *chili con carne* son invenciones Tex-Mex que no se encuentran en la cocina mexicana tradicional.

[1] *cattle*

Comprueba

I was able to . . .

- use words I know to guess the meaning of new words.
- understand the main points of the reading.

10-44 Lee. Lee el artículo "La fusión culinaria" de la página 393. Luego, lee estas oraciones y selecciona el significado de las palabras en negrita.

1. _____ La cocina peruana es una **mezcla** de muchas influencias: indígena, española, africana, china y japonesa.
2. _____ El chifa, o cocina chino-peruana, es el resultado de la combinación de la comida **criolla** de Lima con la cocina traída por los inmigrantes chinos a mediados del siglo XIX.
3. _____ Con el progreso económico, importaron de China **especias** y otros productos esenciales para su comida.
4. _____ La cultura chino-peruana **revolucionó** la gastronomía del país.
5. _____ Los indígenas contribuyeron con ingredientes como los frijoles pintos, los nopales (las hojas de un cacto), las cebollas **silvestres** y el mezquite.
6. _____ La cocina Tex-Mex utiliza más carne y usa las tortillas para envolver mayor variedad de **rellenos.**

a. condimento de origen vegetal
b. cambió
c. combinación
d. algo que está dentro de otra cosa
e. de origen local
f. no cultivado

10-45 Un paso más. **PREPARACIÓN.** Hagan una lista de platos que se sirven en restaurantes y que son ejemplos de la cocina fusión. Luego, seleccionen uno de estos platos.

INTERCAMBIOS. Preparen una presentación sobre algún plato de cocina fusión que conocen y sus antecedentes culinarios, y preséntenla a la clase.

ESCRIBE

Estrategia

Summarize information A good summary maintains the structure of the original text, synthesizes its principal ideas and information, and accurately captures the central meaning of the original. To write a summary:

- Read the text carefully more than once. Locate the thesis (main point) of the text; it is usually in the first or last paragraph. Express the thesis in your own words in one or two sentences.
- Locate the main idea of each section. In your own words, write one or two sentences to summarize the main idea of each section.
- Do not inject your own opinion or add anything not in the original text.

Comprueba

I was able to . . .

- identify the main ideas in each section of the reading in my own words.
- combine the main ideas into a coherent summary of a text.
- focus on factual information rather than my opinion.

10-46 Preparación. Lee una vez más el artículo "La fusión culinaria". Identifica las secciones del artículo y también la idea central de cada sección.

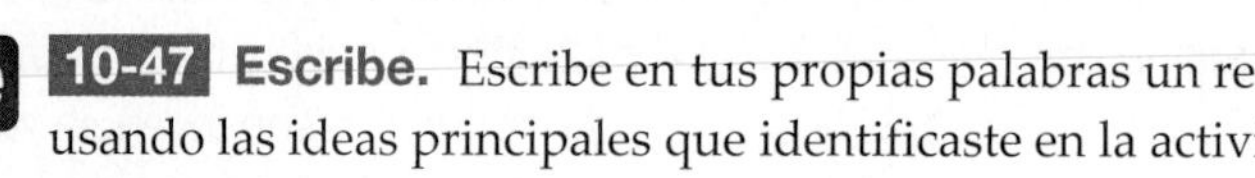

10-47 Escribe. Escribe en tus propias palabras un resumen del artículo, usando las ideas principales que identificaste en la actividad **10-46.** También puedes encontrar sugerencias en **Estrategia.**

10-48 Un paso más. Envíale tu resumen a un/a compañero/a para que te dé su opinión.

En este capítulo...

Vocabulario

Las frutas y las verduras	*Fruits and vegetables*
el aguacate	*avocado*
el ajo	*garlic*
la banana	*banana*
la cebolla	*onion*
la cereza	*cherry*
las espinacas	*spinach*
la fresa	*strawberry*
el limón	*lemon*
el maíz	*corn*
la manzana	*apple*
la maracuyá	*passion fruit*
el melón	*melon*
la papaya	*papaya*
el pepino	*cucumber*
la pera	*pear*
el pimiento	*bell pepper*
la piña	*pineapple*
el plátano	*plantain*
la toronja	*grapefruit*
la uva	*grape*
la zanahoria	*carrot*

Los productos lácteos y los huevos	*Dairy products and eggs*
la crema	*cream*
la crema agria	*sour cream*
el huevo	*egg*
la leche	*milk*
la mantequilla	*butter*
la margarina	*margarine*
el queso	*cheese*
el queso crema	*cream cheese*
el yogur	*yogurt*

Los pescados, los mariscos y la carne	*Fish, shellfish, and meat*
las aves	*poultry, fowl*
el atún	*tuna*
el camarón	*shrimp*
la carne de res	*beef/steak*
la carne molida	*ground beef*
el cerdo	*pork*
la chuleta	*chop*
el cordero	*lamb*
la costilla	*rib*
el jamón	*ham*
la langosta	*lobster*
los mariscos	*shellfish*
el pavo	*turkey*
el pollo	*chicken*
el salmón	*salmon*

Los condimentos, las legumbres y otros productos	*Condiments, legumes, and other products*
el aceite (de oliva)	*(olive) oil*
el achiote	*annatto*
el aderezo	*salad dressing*
el/la azúcar	*sugar*
el cilantro	*cilantro*
las especias	*spices*
los garbanzos	*garbanzo beans*
las hierbas	*herbs*
los frijoles	*beans*
las lentejas	*lentils*
el kétchup	*ketchup*
la harina	*flour*
la leche de coco	*coconut milk*
la mayonesa	*mayonnaise*
la mostaza	*mustard*
el perejil	*parsley*
la pimienta	*pepper*
la sal	*salt*
la salsa de tomate	*tomato sauce*
la salsa picante	*hot sauce*
la vainilla	*vanilla*
el vinagre	*vinegar*

El pan, los dulces y las bebidas	*Bread, sweets, and beverages*
los churros	*fried dough*
el dulce	*candy/sweets*
la galleta	*cookie*
el pan	*bread*
el pan dulce	*bun, small cake*
el pastel	*pastry*
el postre	*dessert*
el refresco	*soda*
el vino blanco	*white wine*
el vino tinto	*red wine*

En la mesa	*On the table*
la bandeja	*tray*
el bol	*bowl*
la botella	*bottle*
la copa	*(stemmed) glass*
la cuchara	*spoon*
la cucharita	*teaspoon*
el cuchillo	*knife*
el mantel	*tablecloth*
el plato	*plate, dish*
el sacacorchos	*corkscrew*
la servilleta	*napkin*
la taza	*cup, mug*
el tenedor	*fork*
el vaso	*glass*

Verbos	*Verbs*
agregar	*to add*
asar	*to roast; to grill*
consumir	*to consume*
freír (i)	*to fry*
hervir (ie, i)	*to boil*
marinar	*to marinate*
mezclar	*to mix, to combine*
probar (ue)	*to try, to taste*
sofreír	*to sauté*

Palabras y expresiones útiles	*Useful words and expressions*
la alimentación	*food, diet*
batido/a	*beaten*
el/la campesino/a	*farm worker*
crudo/a	*raw*
la carnicería	*butcher shop*
la oveja	*sheep*
la pescadería	*fish market*
el puesto	*stall, stand*
la receta	*recipe*
el/la tendero/a	*shopkeeper*
el sabor	*flavor*
todavía	*still, yet*
ya	*already*

Capítulo 11
¿Cómo te sientes?

Practicando *taichí* en La Habana, Cuba

Enfoque cultural
Cuba y República Dominicana

Vocabulario en contexto
Médicos, farmacias y hospitales
Las partes del cuerpo
La salud

Mosaico cultural
La medicina tradicional

En acción
No me encuentro bien

Funciones y formas
Introduction to the present subjunctive
The subjunctive with expressions of influence
The subjunctive with expressions of emotion
Uses of **por** and **para**

Mosaicos
ESCUCHA Listen for the main ideas
HABLA Select appropriate phrases to offer opinions
LEE Focus on relevant information
ESCRIBE Persuade through suggestions and advice

En este capítulo...
Vocabulario

Learning Outcomes

You will be able to:

- discuss health and medical treatments
- express expectations and hopes
- describe emotions, opinions, and wishes
- express goals, purposes, and means
- talk about Cuba and the Dominican Republic in terms of products, practices, and perspectives
- talk about health, the body, and medical practices in Cuba and the Dominican Republic, and identify cultural similarities

Enfoque cultural

Cuba y República Dominicana

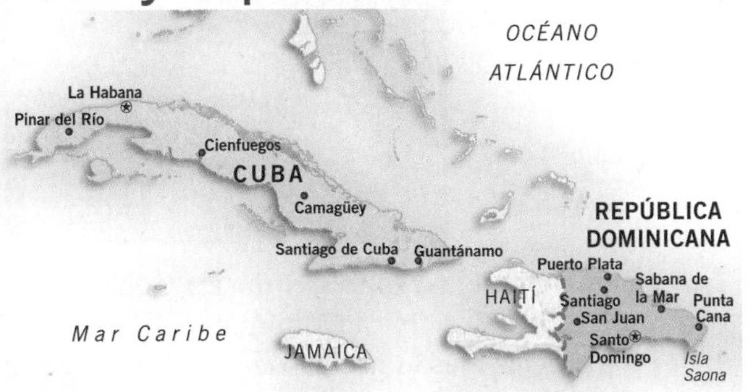

El paseo Malecón en La Habana por la tarde

La ciudad de Santo Domingo en República Dominicana, con la estatua de Cristóbal Colón

Palmeras en una playa de Punta Cana

Arte hispano

Umbral (1950), del pintor cubano Wilfredo Lam

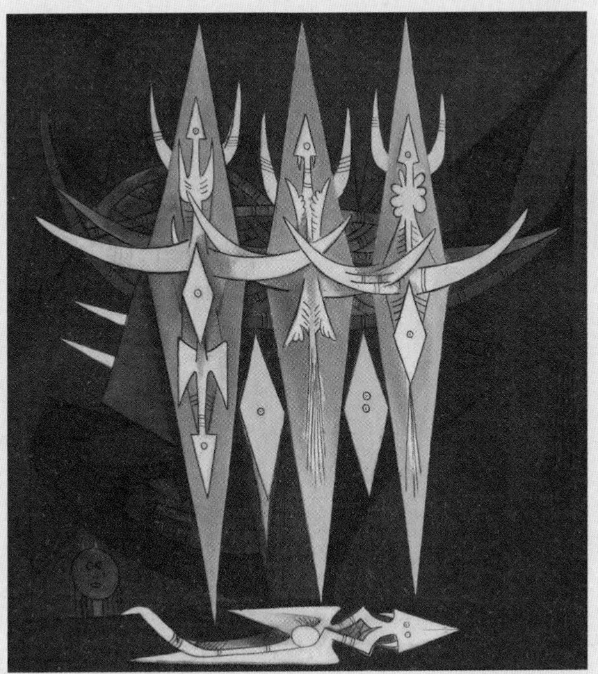

Enfoque cultural

¿Qué te parece?

- Vista desde el aire, la isla de Cuba parece un cocodrilo. Por eso los cubanos la llaman **El Cocodrilo** o **El Caimán.**
- Cristóbal Colón dio el nombre de **La Española** (*Hispaniola*) a la isla que hoy comprende las naciones de República Dominicana y Haití. Esta isla se encuentra en el mar Caribe entre Cuba y Puerto Rico.
- En Cuba, el béisbol y el dominó son actividades de entretenimiento muy populares.
- El tabaco, el ron y el azúcar son productos básicos de la economía cubana. Recientemente las ganancias por el turismo son superiores a los ingresos de la exportación de estos productos.
- Solo en Santo Domingo, la capital de Republica Dominicana, viven más dominicanos que en Nueva York.

El merengue, un estilo de música y de baile, se originó en República Dominicana. Algunos de los artistas más famosos son Juan Luis Guerra, Elvis Crespo (de Puerto Rico) y Los Hermanos Rosario. La bachata también es originaria de este país. Romeo Santos es uno de sus autores más conocidos.

Los deportes acuáticos son un atractivo para los turistas en las playas de Cuba y República Dominicana. Desde los años 90, el turismo se ha convertido en la mayor fuente de ingresos de estos países.

La música cubana evolucionó durante el siglo XVIII a partir de ritmos españoles y africanos. En el XIX tuvo gran repercusión en todo el mundo, influyendo en el jazz de Estados Unidos, a través de Nueva Orleans. Su ritmo y expresividad instrumental son característicos de la rumba y la conga, entre otras variedades.

El sistema de servicios de salud está muy desarrollado (*developed*) en Cuba, tanto para sus ciudadanos como para los extranjeros. Gracias a sus clínicas avanzadas y el costo relativamente bajo de los tratamientos, Cuba cuenta con un próspero negocio de turismo médico. Allí los pacientes encuentran medicina moderna y también alternativa, como el veneno del escorpión azul, que tiene cualidades antiinflamatorias y analgésicas. En años recientes se ha estudiado su posible uso en tratamientos contra el cáncer.

To learn more about Cuba and the Dominican Republic, go online to view the *Club cultura* videos.

e **¿Cuánto sabes?** Escribe las palabras que corresponden a las descripciones.

1. El turismo médico es importante en este país. ____________
2. Esta capital fue la primera ciudad española construida en las Américas. Cristóbal Colón llegó hasta aquí en uno de sus viajes. ____________
3. Juan Luis Guerra es uno de los artistas de este estilo musical. ____________
4. Cuba exporta estos productos: tabaco, ron y ____________.
5. Es una zona turística que se sitúa en el extremo oriental de República Dominicana. ____________
6. Es la capital de Cuba. ____________

VOCABULARIO EN CONTEXTO

Talking about health, medical care, and the body

Médicos, farmacias y hospitales

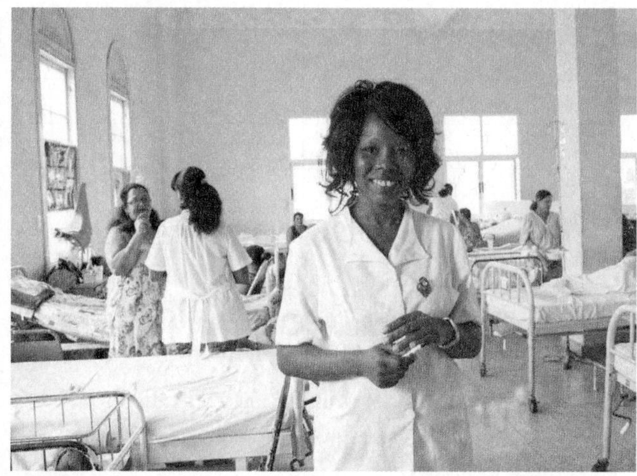

En la mayor parte de los países hispanos existen **hospitales, clínicas** o **sanatorios** y **centros de salud** financiados por el **gobierno,** donde los **enfermos** pueden ir sin tener que pagar nada por los servicios o **medicinas** que reciben.

Esta **enfermera** le toma la **tensión** a una **paciente** en un sanatorio de Las Tunas, Cuba.

En las **farmacias** se vende todo tipo de **medicamentos, remedios** y **productos de belleza.** Al igual que en Estados Unidos, en muchos lugares se necesita tener **receta** médica para comprar **antibióticos.** Estos clientes de la farmacia le preguntan a la **farmacéutica** qué remedio deben comprar para **curar** o **tratar** su **enfermedad.**

Algunas personas prefieren curarse con **hierbas medicinales.** Por ejemplo, para el **dolor** de **estómago,** se recomienda tomar un té de manzanilla (*chamomile*). Otra hierba medicinal muy conocida es la uña de gato (*cat's claw*), que se considera buena para el **tratamiento** de **alergias** y **asma.**

PRÁCTICA

En otras palabras

In some Spanish-speaking countries, the word **sanatorio** is used instead of **hospital;** in others, **sanatorio** is used for a hospital that specializes in pulmonary and respiratory diseases. In some countries, **clínica** refers to a private hospital. **Hospital** usually refers to a government- or church-run facility that may provide free medical care.

11-1 Escucha y confirma. For each word you hear, select the appropriate category.

	Un lugar	Una enfermedad	Una persona
1.			
2.			
3.			
4.			
5.			
6.			

11-2 Definiciones.

PREPARACIÓN. Completa las siguientes oraciones con las palabras apropiadas. Compara tus respuestas con las de tu compañero/a.

1. En las ____________________ se venden medicinas y productos de belleza.
2. El té de manzanilla se recomienda para el ____________________ de estómago.
3. Los/Las ____________________ ayudan a los médicos en los hospitales y cuidan de los enfermos.
4. Según la creencia (*belief*) popular, las ____________________ medicinales pueden curar las enfermedades.
5. Los/Las ____________________ les venden a sus clientes los remedios que necesitan.
6. El ____________________ financia muchos hospitales y centros de salud en los países hispanos.
7. Los/Las ____________________ son las personas que sufren enfermedades.
8. Algunas personas piensan que la uña de gato es buena para el tratamiento contra el ____________________.

INTERCAMBIOS. Háganse las siguientes preguntas.

1. ¿Cuándo y para qué vas generalmente a la farmacia?
2. ¿Qué tomas cuando tienes dolor de estómago?
3. ¿Conoces a alguien que tome hierbas medicinales? ¿Para qué?

Cultura

Los remedios indígenas Los indígenas del continente americano nos han transmitido muchos conocimientos de medicina natural. Conocían los efectos positivos de las infusiones de hierbas y tenían fórmulas para cerrar las heridas (*wounds*) y curar las úlceras. También trataban fracturas de huesos. Acompañaban muchas de estas prácticas con ceremonias en las que invocaban a sus dioses (*gods*), pidiéndoles protección y ayuda.

Comparaciones ¿Qué remedios naturales se usan en tu cultura? ¿Para qué se usan? ¿Recuerdas alguno que se usa en tu familia?

11-3 Conversación. Háganse las siguientes preguntas para intercambiar información.

1. Cuando necesitas una operación o tienes un accidente, ¿adónde vas? ¿Tienes que pagar o no?
2. ¿Hay varios hospitales en tu ciudad? ¿Cómo se llama el más importante?
3. Cuando estás enfermo/a y necesitas medicinas, ¿adónde vas a comprarlas? ¿Qué necesitas del médico / de la médica para poder comprarlas?
4. ¿Qué venden en las farmacias de tu país? ¿Por qué venden muchos otros productos, además de medicinas?
5. ¿Usas hierbas medicinales? ¿Para qué las usas? ¿Las usa alguien de tu familia?
6. ¿Te interesa la medicina alternativa? ¿Alguna vez usaste la acupuntura, la homeopatía o alguna otra? ¿Cómo fue tu experiencia?

11-4 Una emergencia. **PREPARACIÓN.** Ustedes están de viaje en República Dominicana y ambos/as están enfermos/as por algo que comieron. Lean este anuncio y decidan cuál es el número más apropiado para llamar.

CENTRO AGUITA

Servicios Médicos

Santo Domingo

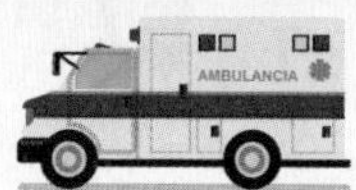

- Badosa Farmacéutica. 563-4230 ➤ Medicina Natural
- Centro de Cirugía Plástica Santo Domingo. 686-7863 ➤ Cirugía
- Clínica Dental. 685-3752 ➤ Odontología
- Clínica Dental Dra. Carmen Gómez. 587-3576 ➤ Odontología
- Consultores en Psicología y Sexualidad. 548-3690 ➤ Psicología
- Dr. Rubén Suárez, MD. 538- 2943 ➤ Medicina General
- Dr. Eliseo Alonso, DDS. 672-3928 ➤ Medicina General
- Farmacia Estrella. 688-4799 ➤ Farmacia
- Óptica Central, CxA. 682-9505; 689-1308 ➤ Óptica
- Productos Naturales. 686-1576 ➤ Productos Farmacéuticos
- Sándalo, 672-3287 ➤ Medicina Aromática

INTERCAMBIOS. En preparación para su consulta médica, escriban las respuestas a las preguntas que les van a hacer.

1. ¿Cuáles son sus síntomas?
2. ¿Cuándo comenzaron a sentirse mal? ¿Cómo se sienten ahora?
3. ¿Saben ustedes qué causó el problema? Explíquenlo.

Las partes del cuerpo

Los órganos y sistemas corporales

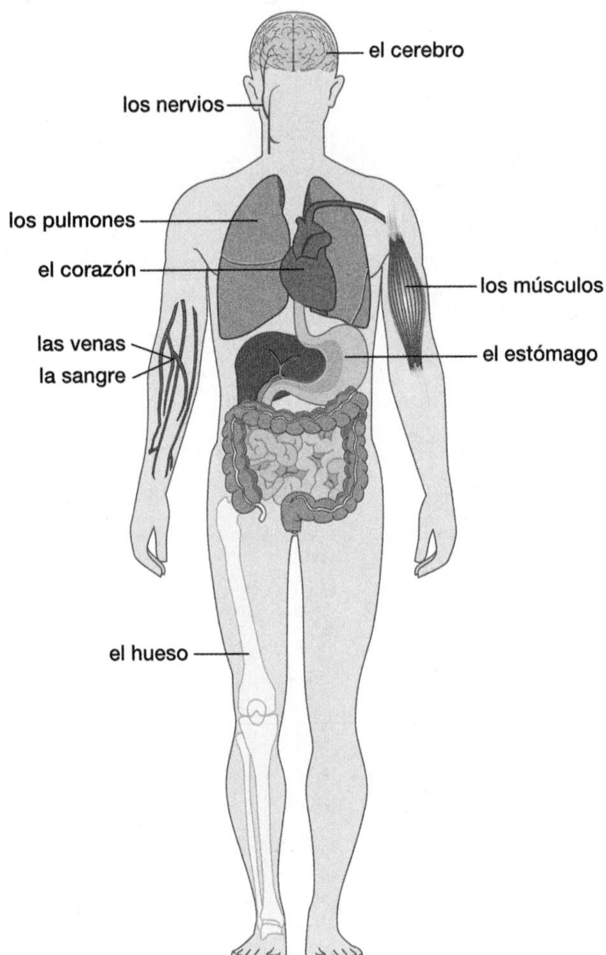

La cabeza

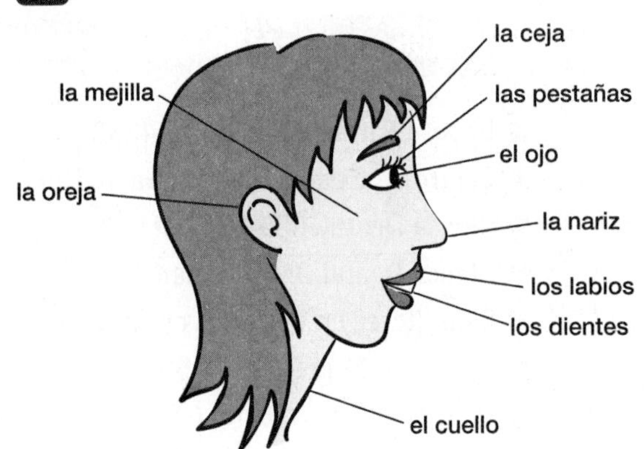

PRÁCTICA

11-5 Para confirmar. Indica en qué parte del cuerpo se ponen estos accesorios y esta ropa.

1. _____ los calcetines
2. _____ los guantes
3. _____ el cinturón
4. _____ el collar
5. _____ los aretes
6. _____ el reloj

a. la muñeca
b. la cintura
c. las orejas
d. el cuello
e. los pies
f. las manos

11-6 ¿Para qué sirve(n)? Túrnense para completar las siguientes definiciones con las palabras de la lista. Luego, indiquen la importancia de estas partes del cuerpo en alguna actividad.

los brazos	la nariz
el cerebro	los ojos
el corazón	las piernas
los dientes	los pulmones
las manos	la sangre

1. ___________ unen las manos con el cuerpo.
2. ___________ permiten que las personas vean.
3. ___________ toman el oxígeno del aire y lo pasan a la sangre.
4. ___________ es un líquido rojo que circula por el cuerpo.
5. ___________ unen el cuerpo con los pies.
6. ___________ se usan para masticar (*chew*) la comida.
7. ___________ están al final de los brazos.
8. ___________ le da órdenes al cuerpo.
9. ___________ impulsa la sangre por las venas del cuerpo.
10. ___________ está entre la frente y la boca.

11-7 Partes del cuerpo.

PREPARACIÓN. Indiquen qué parte(s) del cuerpo se relaciona(n) con cada una de las siguientes situaciones.

Situación	Parte del cuerpo
1. A Felipe le gusta ponerse aretes.	
2. María se maquilla todos los días.	
3. Necesito ponerme gafas porque veo mal.	
4. Un futbolista del Real Madrid le pasa la pelota a un compañero de su equipo.	
5. Se necesitan todos para tocar bien el piano.	
6. Esta mujer ha perdido 30 libras. La falda le queda ancha.	
7. Daniela lleva siempre el mismo collar.	
8. El té de hierbas es muy bueno para la digestión.	

INTERCAMBIOS. Ahora inventen dos adivinanzas para hacer asociaciones con partes del cuerpo.

MODELO E1: *Sirven para besar.*
E2: *Los labios.*

La salud

Jorgito está enfermo.

SRA. VILLA: Jorgito, **tienes muy mala cara.** ¿Estás **enfermo?**

JORGITO: **Me siento** muy mal y **tengo dolor de garganta. Me duele** mucho cuando **toso.**

La Sra. Villa le pone el ***termómetro.***

SRA. VILLA: Tienes 39 grados de **fiebre.** Enseguida voy a llamar a la doctora Bosque. Es posible que tengas **gripe.**

En la clínica…

DOCTORA: Vamos a ver, Jorgito. Cuéntame cómo te sientes.

JORGITO: Ahora me duele la cabeza y también me duelen los **oídos.** Además, **estornudo** y tengo mucha **tos.**

DOCTORA: Vamos a **examinarte** los oídos y la garganta. Abre bien la boca y di "ah". Tienes una **infección.** No es **grave,** solo un **resfriado,** pero es necesario que **te cuides.**

JORGITO: Doctora, no quiero que me ponga una **inyección.**

DOCTORA: ¡No, qué va! Te voy a **recetar** unas **pastillas.** Señora Villa, su hijo debe tomarlas **cada cuatro horas.**

SRA. VILLA: Está bien, doctora.

DOCTORA: Además, Jorgito, debes descansar y beber mucho líquido, pero **evita** los refrescos con azúcar. Aquí está la receta, señora.

SRA. VILLA: Gracias, doctora.

¿Qué les pasó a estas personas?

Juan **se torció** el tobillo.

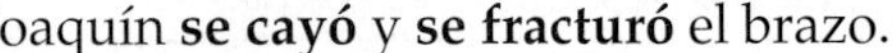

Joaquín **se cayó** y **se fracturó** el brazo.

Lengua

Most words that refer to medical specialists derive from Latin and thus are similar to English: **pediatra** (*pediatrician*), **psiquiatra** (*psychiatrist*), **cirujano/a** (*surgeon*), **radiólogo/a** (*radiologist*), etc. A construction with **de** may also be used: **especialista** or **médico/a del corazón, del estómago,** etc. The primary care doctor is called **médico/a de familia,** or **médico/a de cabecera.**

PRÁCTICA

11-8 Para confirmar. Indica si las siguientes afirmaciones se refieren a síntomas (**S**) o recomendaciones (**R**). Compara tus respuestas con las de tu compañero/a. Después, añade otro síntoma para Jorgito. Tu compañero/a va a darle una recomendación.

1. _____ Jorgito tiene que cuidarse.
2. _____ Tiene dolor de garganta.
3. _____ Debe tomar dos pastillas cada cuatro horas.
4. _____ Estornuda y tose mucho.
5. _____ Tiene que beber mucho líquido.

11-9 Remedios y consejos. Selecciona la mejor recomendación para cada uno de los siguientes problemas. Luego, compara tus respuestas con las de tu compañero/a, y hagan dos sugerencias a cada una de estas personas.

1. Esteban tiene una infección en los ojos. Le recomiendo…
   a. nadar en la piscina.
   b. tomar antibióticos.
   c. leer mucho.
2. Valeria tiene fiebre y le duele el cuerpo. Le aconsejo (*I advise*)…
   a. descansar y tomar aspirinas.
   b. comer mucho y caminar.
   c. ir a su trabajo.
3. Carmen se torció un tobillo. Le sugiero…
   a. correr todos los días.
   b. tomar clases de baile.
   c. descansar y no caminar.
4. Pablo se fracturó un brazo. Le recomiendo…
   a. jugar al tenis.
   b. no usar la computadora por una semana.
   c. hacer ejercicio.

11-10 ¿A quién debo llamar? Explícale a tu compañero/a tus síntomas o necesidades. Él/Ella te va a decir a quién debes llamar, según los anuncios. Después, añadan una situación más.

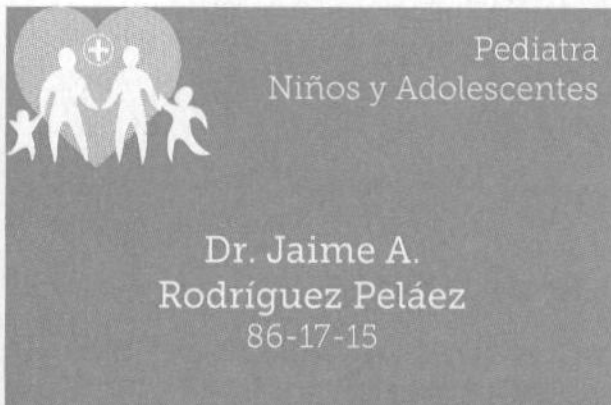

MODELO necesitar un examen médico para el trabajo
E1: *Necesito un examen médico para el trabajo.*
E2: *Debes llamar a la Dra. Corona López.*

1. dolerte la cabeza cuando lees o miras televisión
2. sentirte triste y deprimido/a
3. estar enfermo/a y tener fiebre
4. no poder dormir
5. no poder respirar (*breathe*) bien y tener la piel (*skin*) irritada
6. dolerte los dientes cuando comes
7. buscar un/a médico/a para tu sobrino de cinco años

Lengua

Traditionally, law and medicine were professions dominated by men. Therefore, only the masculine form was used in Spanish: **el médico, el abogado.** Now that more women work in these professions, the feminine forms have entered the language. The feminine article is sometimes used before a masculine noun (**la médico, la abogado, la juez**), but it is increasingly common to use the feminine forms of the nouns: **la médica, la abogada, la jueza.**

11-11 En el consultorio. Tienes un resfriado terrible y vas a ver a tu médico/a. Dile cómo te sientes y pregúntale qué debes hacer. Tu médico/a (tu compañero/a) te dará una recomendación y contestará tus preguntas.

MODELO E1: *Me siento… / Tengo…*
E2: *Creo que usted…*
E1: *¿Es bueno…?*
E2: *Es excelente… / No es recomendable…*

11-12 Me duele mucho.

PREPARACIÓN. You will listen to a teenage boy talk to his father about a sports injury. Before you listen, list two symptoms you think he probably has and compare your answers with those of your partner.

ESCUCHA. Pay attention to the general idea of what is said. As you listen, select the letter that indicates the appropriate ending to each statement.

1. Esteban tiene…
   - **a.** una infección en el dedo.
   - **b.** mucho dolor.
   - **c.** fiebre.
2. El padre de Esteban cree que…
   - **a.** su hijo se ha fracturado el dedo del pie.
   - **b.** Esteban debe acostarse.
   - **c.** es necesario que Esteban se ponga hielo en el pie.
3. El padre de Esteban quiere que su hijo…
   - **a.** descanse y se cuide.
   - **b.** vaya al hospital.
   - **c.** tome una aspirina.
4. El padre de Esteban le dice que…
   - **a.** lo ayuda a caminar para llevarlo al hospital.
   - **b.** decida si prefiere descansar o ir al hospital.
   - **c.** el médico puede verlo esa tarde.
5. Esteban decide…
   - **a.** no escuchar a su padre.
   - **b.** jugar al fútbol al día siguiente.
   - **c.** ir al hospital con su padre.

Mosaico cultural

La medicina tradicional

Carla Martínez y su amiga Julia Macedo deseaban conocer la fascinante cultura cubana, pero, tan pronto como llegaron a La Habana desde Colombia, Carla empezó a sentir molestias (*discomfort*) en la garganta y se sentía cansada.

Sin embargo, decidieron continuar con sus planes de visitar la isla. Cuando llegaron a la ciudad de Santiago, al este del país, a Carla le dolía la cabeza y tosía y estornudaba. Además, tenía fiebre, congestión nasal y escalofríos (*chills*). Quería ir al médico, pero Julia le decía que era un simple resfriado. "Te recomiendo que descanses mucho esta noche y que te tomes una infusión caliente con miel (*honey*)", le decía su amiga.

En Cuba, como en muchos países latinoamericanos, la medicina occidental y los tratamientos que ofrecen en farmacias y hospitales conviven con la medicina alternativa, o medicina verde, cuyo conocimiento ancestral se transmite de generación en generación. En el herbolario (*herbal shop*), Julia compró para Carla una mezcla de hierbas para preparar una infusión. El propietario del herbolario le dijo a Julia que la infusión de malva (*mallow*) blanca es muy buena para la congestión de la nariz, el saúco (*elder*) es bueno para combatir la tos y la manzanilla es un relajante natural. Julia le preparó la infusión a Carla y al día siguiente se sintió mucho mejor. De esta manera pudieron continuar su visita por la isla y disfrutar (*enjoy*) del paisaje (*landscape*) y de la música cubana.

De paseo en La Habana

Este propietario de un herbolario cerca de La Habana vende platas y hierbas.

Compara

1. ¿Te has sentido enfermo/a en algún lugar lejos de casa? ¿Qué tratamientos has seguido en ese caso? Describe tu experiencia con todo detalle.
2. ¿Existe en tu país algún tipo de medicina alternativa? ¿Es importante en tu cultura? Explica con detalles y ejemplos.
3. ¿Qué le recomiendas a un/a amigo/a que tiene gripe?

En acción

No me encuentro bien

Antes de ver

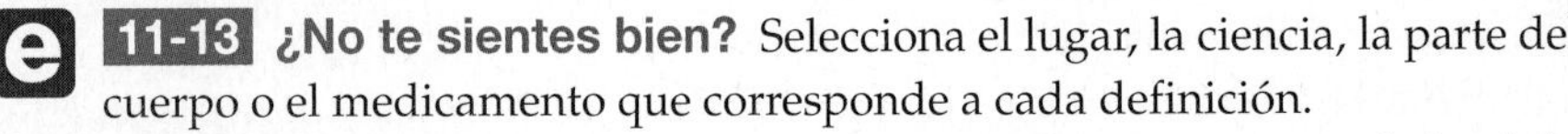

11-13 ¿No te sientes bien? Selecciona el lugar, la ciencia, la parte del cuerpo o el medicamento que corresponde a cada definición.

1. _____ Se venden productos naturales y hierbas medicinales.
2. _____ Vamos a este lugar cuando estamos muy enfermos o en caso de emergencia.
3. _____ Lo tomamos cuando tenemos una infección.
4. _____ Aquí compramos medicamentos con receta médica y también productos de belleza.
5. _____ Es la parte del cuerpo que nos duele cuando comemos demasiado.
6. _____ En México, es un lugar para comprar objetos religiosos y medicinales.

a. la botánica
b. el hospital
c. el estómago
d. la farmacia
e. el herbolario
f. el antibiótico

> **Lengua**
>
> In many Spanish-speaking countries it is common to supplement modern medicine with alternative methods to treat or cure pain, diseases, and certain illnesses. An **herbolario** (Spain) or **herboristería** (Latin America) is a store where medicinal plants and herbs are sold. A **botánica** (Mexico and the Caribbean) is a shop that sells folk medicine, religious candles and objects, amulets, and other products related with spiritual practices.

Mientras ves

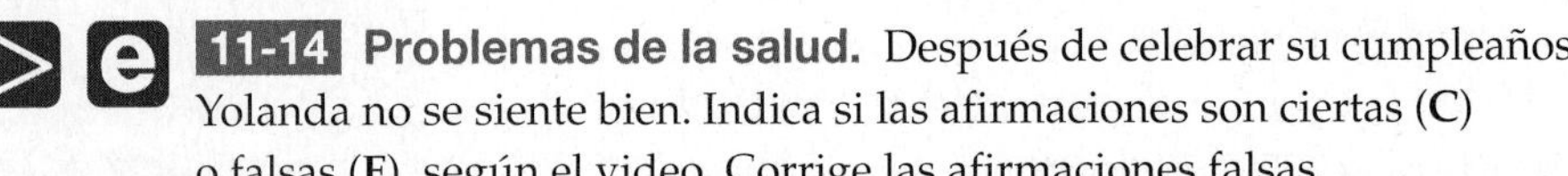

11-14 Problemas de la salud. Después de celebrar su cumpleaños, Yolanda no se siente bien. Indica si las afirmaciones son ciertas (**C**) o falsas (**F**), según el video. Corrige las afirmaciones falsas.

1. _____ A Yolanda le duele el estómago porque comió mucho.
2. _____ Yolanda quiere consultar a su médico.
3. _____ La familia de Yolanda prefiere tomar productos naturales y caseros (*home-based*).
4. _____ El herbolario Morando es uno de los más modernos de Madrid.
5. _____ En México, las botánicas venden medicinas para enfermedades graves.
6. _____ En Los Ángeles no hay botánicas.

Después de ver

11-15 Consejos.

PREPARACIÓN. Selecciona la mejor recomendación para las siguientes situaciones.

1. Yolanda tiene dolor de estómago. Le recomiendo que…
   a. tome un té de manzanilla.
   b. coma solamente pasta por unos días.
   c. beba mucha leche.
2. A Vanesa no le gustan los antibióticos ni las inyecciones. Le recomiendo que…
   a. vaya a la sala de emergencia.
   b. visite un herbolario.
   c. tome el sol todos los días.
3. Muchas personas tienen problemas espirituales. Les recomiendo que…
   a. visiten una botánica.
   b. hagan más ejercicio.
   c. tomen bastante agua diariamente.

INTERCAMBIOS. Cuéntense sobre la última enfermedad que tuvieron. ¿Cuál fue? ¿Qué síntomas tuvieron? ¿Qué hicieron para sentirse mejor?

FUNCIONES Y FORMAS

1 Expressing expectations and hopes

NATALIA: En esta foto estoy con mi madre el día de mi graduación. Ella siempre desea lo mejor para mí: **quiere** que yo **trabaje** mucho, que **tenga** éxito en los estudios y que **piense** en mi futuro.

MATEO: ¿**Espera** que tú **estudies** medicina como ella?

NATALIA: En realidad, no. Solo me **ha dicho** que **tome** buenas decisiones. **Prefiere** que **siga** mis propios sueños.

e **Piénsalo.** En cada oración, indica cuál es el verbo de deseo (**VD**) y cuál es el verbo de acción (**VA**). Luego, indica el sujeto de cada verbo: Natalia (**N**) o la madre de Natalia (**M**).

	VD	SUJETO	VA	SUJETO
1. **Quiere** que yo **trabaje** mucho.	______	_____	_______	_____
2. **Quiere** que **tenga** éxito.	______	_____	_______	_____
3. **Quiere** que **piense** en mi futuro.	______	_____	_______	_____
4. ¿**Espera** que **estudies** medicina?	______	_____	_______	_____
5. **Prefiere** que **siga** mis propios sueños.	______	_____	_______	_____

Introduction to the present subjunctive

- To form the present subjunctive, use the **yo** form of the present indicative, drop the final **-o** and add the subjunctive ending. Notice that just like the endings of the **usted/ustedes** commands, **-ar** verbs change the **-a** to **-e**, while **-er** and **-ir** verbs change the **-e** and the **-i** to **-a.**

	HABLAR	COMER	VIVIR
yo	habl**e**	com**a**	viv**a**
tú	habl**es**	com**as**	viv**as**
Ud., él, ella	habl**e**	com**a**	viv**a**
nosotros/as	habl**emos**	com**amos**	viv**amos**
vosotros/as	habl**éis**	com**áis**	viv**áis**
Uds., ellos/as	habl**en**	com**an**	viv**an**

- The present subjunctive of the following verbs with irregular indicative **yo** forms is as follows:

conocer: cono**zca**, cono**zcas...**
decir: **diga, digas...**
hacer: ha**ga**, ha**gas...**
oír: **oiga, oigas...**
poner: pon**ga**, pon**gas...**
salir: sal**ga**, sal**gas...**
tener: ten**ga**, ten**gas...**
traer: tra**iga**, tra**igas...**
venir: ven**ga**, ven**gas...**
ver: **vea, veas...**

- The present subjunctive of **hay** is **haya.** The following verbs also have irregular subjunctive forms:

dar: **dé, des...**
estar: **esté, estés...**
ir: **vaya, vayas...**
saber: **sepa, sepas...**
ser: **sea, seas...**

> **Lengua**
>
> Remember that you have seen these same orthographic changes in the formal commands:
>
> **Siga las instrucciones.**
> *Follow the directions.*
>
> **Busque las pastillas.**
> *Look for the pills.*

- Stem-changing **-ar** and **-er** verbs follow the same pattern as the present indicative.
  pensar: p**ie**nse, p**ie**nses, p**ie**nse, pensemos, penséis, p**ie**nsen
  volver: v**ue**lva, v**ue**lvas, v**ue**lva, volvamos, volváis, v**ue**lvan
- Stem-changing **-ir** verbs follow the same pattern as the present indicative but have an additional change in the **nosotros/as** and **vosotros/as** forms.
  dormir: d**ue**rma, d**ue**rmas, d**ue**rma, d**u**rmamos, d**u**rmáis, d**ue**rman
  preferir: pref**ie**ra, pref**ie**ras, pref**ie**ra, pref**i**ramos, pref**i**ráis, pref**ie**ran
- Verbs ending in **-car, -gar, -ger, -guir,** and **-zar** have spelling changes.
  sacar: sa**qu**e, sa**qu**es, sa**qu**e, sa**qu**emos, sa**qu**éis, sa**qu**en
  jugar: jue**gu**e, jue**gu**es, jue**gu**e, ju**gu**emos, ju**gu**éis, jue**gu**en
  recoger: reco**j**a, reco**j**as, reco**j**a, reco**j**amos, reco**j**áis, reco**j**an
  seguir: si**g**a, si**g**as, si**g**a, si**g**amos, si**g**áis, si**g**an
  almorzar: almuer**c**e, almuer**c**es, almuer**c**e, almor**c**emos, almor**c**éis, almuer**c**en
- Notice in the examples below that there are two clauses, each with a different subject. When the verb of the main clause expresses a wish or hope, use a subjunctive verb form in the dependent clause (the clause that begins with **que**).

MAIN CLAUSE	DEPENDENT CLAUSE
La doctora **quiere**	que Alfredo **respire** profundamente.
The doctor wants	*Alfredo to breathe deeply.*
Espero	que Alfredo no **tenga** asma.
I hope	*Alfredo doesn't have asthma.*

- When there is only one subject, use the infinitive instead of the subjunctive.

  Lola **necesita llamar** a la farmacia para pedir un medicamento. — *Lola needs to call the pharmacy to order some medication.*
  Ella **quiere recogerlo** esta tarde. — *She wants to pick it up this afternoon.*
  Desea recogerlo antes de las tres. — *She wants to pick it up before three o'clock.*

- Some common verbs that express expectations, wants, and hopes are **desear, esperar, necesitar, preferir,** and **querer.**

  Los vecinos **prefieren** que la clínica **esté** abierta hasta las siete. — *The neighbors prefer that the clinic be open until seven o'clock.*
  La niña **espera** que el enfermero no le **ponga** una inyección. — *The girl hopes that the nurse will not give her a shot.*

- The expression **ojalá (que)** (*I/we hope [that]*) is always followed by the subjunctive.

  Ojalá (que) los invitados **vengan** a tiempo. — *I hope (that) the guests come on time.*
  Ojalá (que) puedas llevarme a la cita con la médica. — *I hope (that) you can take me to the doctor's appointment.*

e **¿Comprendes?** Completa las oraciones con la forma correcta del verbo.

1. ¿Estás enferma? ¿Necesitas que yo ________ (ir) a tu casa para ayudarte?
2. ¿Quieres que Amanda y yo te ________ (hacer) una sopa de pollo?
3. Deseamos que tú ________ ________ (sentirse) mejor pronto.
4. Tus amigos esperan que tú ________ (asistir) al concierto mañana con ellos.
5. Todos dicen: "¡Ojalá que Sofía ________ (poder) ir con nosotros!"

PRÁCTICA

11-16 Comentarios y deseos. Los miembros del Club de Estudiantes de Pre-Medicina están hablando de la fiesta que tiene lugar mañana. ¿Cuáles de las siguientes afirmaciones probablemente son comentarios de ellos? Indíquenlas y justifiquen sus selecciones.

1. _____ Queremos que la fiesta empiece puntualmente.
2. _____ Ojalá que no sirvan comida.
3. _____ Preferimos que pongan música caribeña, porque queremos bailar salsa y merengue.
4. _____ Esperamos que también asistan estudiantes de odontología (*dentistry*) y de enfermería.
5. _____ Necesitamos que la fiesta termine temprano.
6. _____ Deseamos que nuestros profesores vayan a la fiesta.
7. _____ Queremos que todos recojan la basura después de la fiesta.
8. _____ Ojalá que nos divirtamos.

11-17 Trabajo voluntario en el hospital. **PREPARACIÓN.** Unos estudiantes trabajan de voluntarios en el hospital. ¿Qué espera la directora del programa de voluntarios que ellos hagan? Túrnense para hablar sobre cada escena.

MODELO Elena: llevar flores / conversar con los pacientes

E1: *La directora espera que Elena les lleve flores a los pacientes.*

E2: *También espera que Elena converse con los pacientes. Algunos pacientes se sienten muy solos.*

1. José y Camila: jugar con los niños / hablar con los padres de los niños / leerles libros infantiles a los niños

2. Lorena y Julio: conversar con los familiares de los pacientes / ofrecerles café / darles almohadas si quieren dormir mientras esperan

3. Marisa: trabajar en la tienda de regalos / hacerles recomendaciones a los clientes / poner flores frescas en el mostrador (*counter*) de la tienda

INTERCAMBIOS. ¿Qué más esperan los pacientes que hagan los voluntarios en el hospital? Escriban una lista de cuatro cosas más.

MODELO *Los pacientes esperan que los voluntarios les traigan la comida.*

 **11-18 La clínica.** En una semana, se abre una nueva clínica y ustedes están ayudando con los preparativos. Escriban una lista de lo que ustedes tienen que hacer y otra lista de lo que esperan que hagan los empleados.

MODELO E1: *Tenemos que pintar la sala de espera. Espero que los pintores lleguen a tiempo.*

E2: *También tenemos que limpiar los pisos. Espero que los empleados de limpieza hagan bien su trabajo.*

Lo que tenemos que hacer	Lo que esperamos que otras personas hagan
	la médica especialista: los enfermeros: la recepcionista: la chofer de la ambulancia: el anestesista: los empleados de limpieza:

 **11-19 Deseos diferentes.** A veces queremos cosas diferentes de lo que quieren otras personas (por ejemplo, nuestros padres, profesores/as, jefes/as, amigos/as). Túrnense para comentar qué quieren ustedes y qué quieren otras personas que ustedes hagan.

MODELO E1: *Quiero estudiar arte, pero mis padres quieren que estudie medicina.*

E2: *Yo deseo ir a una fiesta esta noche, pero mi profesora desea que estudie.*

11-20 Cómo ayudar a una amiga. **PREPARACIÓN.** Han operado a tu amiga Tania, y va a estar en el hospital por una semana. Escríbele un mensaje. Incluye lo siguiente:

- dos consejos para su estadía (*stay*) en el hospital
- dos preguntas sobre cosas que posiblemente quiera que tú hagas por ella
- dos buenos deseos (**ojalá**)

 **INTERCAMBIOS.** Compara tu mensaje con los de tus compañeros/as. Decidan cuáles son los mejores consejos, ofertas de ayuda y buenos deseos.

Situación

PREPARACIÓN. Lean la situación. Luego, compartan ejemplos de vocabulario, gramática y otra información que necesitan para desarrollar la conversación.

Role A. You are sick today, so you will miss the review session for your Spanish midterm. Call a classmate and tell him/her:
a. you need him/her to take notes for you;
b. that you hope it is not too much trouble;
c. when you want your friend to bring you the notes; and
d. thank you.

Role B. When a friend from your Spanish class calls to ask a favor, say that you will be happy to take notes for him/her.
a. Ask how your friend is feeling and what illness he/she has;
b. ask when your friend wants you to bring over the notes; and
c. say that you hope he/she feels better.

	ROLE A	ROLE B
Vocabulario	Expressions related to health and parts of the body	Expressions related to health and parts of the body
Funciones y formas	Describing symptoms Making polite requests Subjunctive with verbs of volition Thanking someone	Replying to requests Asking questions Subjunctive with verbs of volition

INTERCAMBIOS. Practiquen la conversación, incorporando el vocabulario y las funciones de **Preparación.** Luego, represéntenla ante la clase.

2 Expressing requests

ERNESTO: ¿Qué me recomienda, doctor?

MÉDICO: Le **recomiendo** que **tome** agua y sopa de pollo. **Quiero** que **duerma** mucho y que no **vaya** a clase.

Más tarde…

CLAUDIA: ¿Qué dice el médico?

ERNESTO: **Dice** que **me quede** en cama. También **quiere** que tú me **prepares** una sopa de pollo y que **limpies** mi apartamento. Finalmente, **insiste** en que me **traigas** helado…

e **Piénsalo.** Para cada afirmación, indica quién recomienda la acción y quién va a hacer la acción: **el médico, Ernesto** o **Claudia.**

	RECOMIENDA LA ACCIÓN	VA A HACER LA ACCIÓN
1. Le **recomiendo** que **tome** agua y sopa de pollo.	____________	____________
2. **Quiere** que tú me **prepares** una sopa de pollo.	____________	____________
3. **Deseo** que **duerma** mucho.	____________	____________
4. **Dice** que **me quede** en cama.	____________	____________
5. **Quiere** que **limpies** mi apartamento.	____________	____________
6. **Insiste** en que me **traigas** helado.	____________	____________

The subjunctive with expressions of influence

- Verbs that express an intention to influence the actions of others (**aconsejar, insistir [en], pedir, permitir, prohibir, recomendar**) also require the subjunctive in the dependent clause. With these verbs, Spanish speakers often use an indirect object.

El médico **le** recomienda a Carlos que no **salga** por unos días.	*The doctor recommends to Carlos that he not go out for a few days.*
La enfermera **me** aconseja que no **coma** por una hora.	*The nurse advises me not to eat for an hour.*

- You may also try to impose your will or express your influence, wishes, and hopes through these impersonal expressions, followed by **que.**

es aconsejable	**es malo**	**es preferible**
es bueno	**es mejor**	**es recomendable**
es importante	**es necesario**	

Es necesario que los niños **duerman** diez horas por noche.	*It is necessary that children sleep ten hours a night.*
Es mejor que no coman caramelos porque no son buenos para los dientes.	*It is better that they not eat candy because it isn't good for their teeth.*

- If you are not addressing or speaking about someone in particular, use the infinitive.

Es mejor **comer** pescado y pollo.	*It is better to eat fish and chicken.*

- With the verb **decir,** use the subjunctive in the dependent clause when expressing a wish or an order. Use the indicative when reporting information.

María José les dice a sus amigas que **llega** a las tres. (*report information*)	*Mary Jo tells her friends that she will arrive at three o'clock.*
María José les dice a sus amigas que **lleguen** a las tres. (*give a directive*)	*Mary Jo tells her friends to arrive at three o'clock.*

e **¿Comprendes?** Completa las oraciones con el infinitivo o la forma correcta del subjuntivo.

1. El médico te aconseja que __________ (beber) menos café y más agua.
2. Es necesario que nosotros __________ (cuidarse) si queremos vivir muchos años.
3. La enfermera le dice que __________ (hacer) más ejercicio.
4. Es importante __________ (comer) bien.
5. El especialista le aconseja al paciente que __________ (descansar) mucho.
6. Es bueno __________ (dormir) siete horas por noche.

PRÁCTICA

11-21 ¿Qué me recomiendas? **PREPARACIÓN.** Tu amigo/a va a estudiar en República Dominicana por un semestre y quiere recomendaciones sobre qué hacer en su tiempo libre. Indica tus recomendaciones.

Actividades de ocio	Recomiendo	No recomiendo
1. comunicarse en inglés todos los días con amigos en Estados Unidos		
2. ver un partido de béisbol en el estadio local		
3. pasar los fines de semana estudiando español en casa		
4. conocer los museos y monumentos de la Ciudad Colonial de Santo Domingo		
5. salir a bailar los fines de semana		
6. hacer una excursión con amigos a las playas de Punta Cana		
7. comprar regalos en los mercados de artesanías		
8. ir a los restaurantes de las cadenas americanas		

INTERCAMBIOS. Compara tus respuestas con las de tu compañero/a y digan qué le van a recomendar a su amigo/a y qué no le van a recomendar.

MODELO leer un periódico local

E1: *Le voy a recomendar que lea un periódico local.*

E2: *También le voy a recomendar que asista a los eventos locales anunciados en el periódico.*

11-22 Normas de conducta en el trabajo. **PREPARACIÓN.** Tu amiga Rebeca tiene un trabajo nuevo como recepcionista en un consultorio. Te pide consejos sobre qué hacer con respecto a los temas de la lista. Escribe cinco recomendaciones para ella y compáralas con las de tu compañero/a.

MODELO usar el celular
Te recomiendo que no uses tu celular en el trabajo. Es importante que no hagas llamadas personales.

- llegar al trabajo unos minutos antes
- llevar chancletas
- almorzar en la oficina
- conversar con los pacientes
- traer galletas para los pacientes
- escribir mensajes de texto a los amigos durante las horas de trabajo

INTERCAMBIOS. Escríbanle un mensaje a Rebeca combinando sus recomendaciones. Léanlo a la clase.

MODELO *Juan y yo te aconsejamos que…*

11-23 Consejos y sugerencias. Estás organizando un nuevo programa para estudiantes que quieren trabajar en programas de salud en República Dominicana. Explícales a dos compañeros/as los aspectos del programa que todavía no están resueltos. Ellos/as te van a hacer recomendaciones.

MODELO viajar a República Dominicana
E1: *Hay varias opciones: podemos viajar a República Dominicana en grupo, o cada estudiante puede hacer su propia reservación.*
E2: *Es preferible que viajen en grupo para conseguir un mejor precio.*
E3: *Y también es bueno que todos los estudiantes lleguen juntos.*

1. organizar clases de español
2. establecer conexiones con las clínicas de la capital
3. buscar alojamiento (*lodging*)
4. escoger actividades de ocio (*free time*)
5. investigar opciones para tener seguro (*insurance*) médico en República Dominicana
6. averiguar el costo del programa

11-24 ¿Apropiado o inapropiado? **PREPARACIÓN.** Indica si consideras apropiada (**A**) o inapropiada (**I**) cada una de las siguientes actividades.

1. _____ llevar ropa deportiva a clase
2. _____ leer mensajes de texto cuando estás con amigos en un restaurante
3. _____ copiar las respuestas de otro estudiante en un examen
4. _____ pedir permiso para interrumpir una conversación
5. _____ escribirles una nota de agradecimiento a las personas que te dan regalos
6. _____ presentarte a los vecinos (*neighbors*) del edificio donde vives
7. _____ cantar en voz alta en la biblioteca
8. _____ llegar diez minutos tarde al trabajo de vez en cuando

INTERCAMBIOS. Túrnense para hacerse recomendaciones, usando sus respuestas de **Preparación.**

MODELO gritarle (*shout*) a tu amigo/a si hace algo que no te gusta
E1: *Te recomiendo que no le grites a tu amigo/a si hace algo que no te gusta.*
E2: *Estoy de acuerdo. Es preferible hablarle del problema.*

Cultura

La industria turística República Dominicana es un país que en los últimos años ha desarrollado (*developed*) una próspera industria turística, gracias en parte a su clima ideal y sus extraordinarias playas. Boca Chica es la playa familiar más famosa de República Dominicana por su arena blanca, agua cristalina y proximidad a la capital. Otras playas conocidas son las de Punta Cana, al este del país, donde predominan los centros turísticos privados (*resorts*). Sin embargo, quedan muchas otras zonas de interés cultural y ambiental relativamente poco exploradas.

La playa de Boca Chica

Conexiones En tu opinión, ¿es bueno hacer turismo en centros turísticos privados? ¿Por qué? ¿Cuáles son las ventajas y desventajas de organizar tus propios viajes?

11-25 Excursión a la playa.

PREPARACIÓN. Ustedes van a pasar un día en la playa de Varadero, en Cuba. Escriban una lista de todo lo que hay que preparar y llevar para pasarlo bien.

MODELO E1: *Es importante que tengamos/compremos unas toallas.*
E2: *Sí, y es necesario que llevemos botellas de agua.*

INTERCAMBIOS. En grupos de tres o cuatro, decidan qué quieren que haga cada persona de su grupo. Compartan la información con la clase.

MODELO E1: *Queremos que David busque toallas para todo el grupo.*
E2: *Sí, y esperamos que Alicia lleve unas botellas de agua.*
E3: *Necesitamos que…*

e Situación

PREPARACIÓN. Lean la situación. Luego, compartan ejemplos de vocabulario, gramática y otra información que necesitan para desarrollar la conversación.

Role A. You are allergic (**alérgico/a**) to cats, and you just spent the weekend with your friend who has two cats. Now you have a headache, your eyes itch (**me pican los ojos**), your lungs hurt, and it is hard to breathe (**respirar**). Call the clinic and talk to a nurse:
a. explain your situation;
b. describe your symptoms; and
c. ask what the nurse recommends that you do.
Ask questions to be sure you understand.

Role B. You work as a nurse at the clinic, and someone calls for advice about an allergic reaction. Ask about the person's symptoms, when they started, and what caused them. Offer advice about what he/she should do.

	ROLE A	ROLE B
Vocabulario	Health symptoms	Health symptoms and remedies
Funciones y formas	Explaining health conditions Asking for recommendations Present subjunctive with expressions of influence Asking clarification questions	Asking clarification questions Making recommendations Present subjunctive with expressions of influence

INTERCAMBIOS. Practiquen la conversación, incorporando el vocabulario y las funciones de **Preparación.** Luego, represéntenla ante la clase.

3 Expressing emotions, opinions, and attitudes

Mateo Sara

MATEO: **Me molesta** que **fumen.** Además, no **me gusta** que **hablen** tan alto.

SARA: **Estoy contenta de** que **se vayan** pronto. Ya han terminado de comer. **Me frustra** que la gente no **respete** el espacio que comparte con otras personas.

MATEO: **Es malo** que el camarero no les **diga** nada.

Piénsalo. Clasifica los verbos o frases en negrita (*bold*) según lo que expresan: un **sentimiento** o una **acción o estado.**

	VERBO DE SENTIMIENTO	VERBO DE ACCIÓN/ESTADO
1. **Me molesta** que **fumen.**		
2. No **me gusta** que **hablen** tan alto.		
3. **Estoy contenta de** que **se vayan** pronto.		
4. **Me frustra** que la gente no **respete** el espacio que comparte con otras personas.		
5. **Es malo** que el camarero no les **diga** nada.		

The subjunctive with expressions of emotion

- When the verb of the main clause expresses emotion (e.g., fear, happiness, sorrow), use a subjunctive verb form in the dependent clause. Note that the subjects of the two clauses must be different.

Sentimos mucho que el niño **tenga** fiebre.	*We are very sorry (that) the child has a fever.*
Me alegro de que **estés** con él.	*I am glad (that) you are with him.*

- Some common verbs that express emotion are:

alegrarse (de)	*to be glad (about)*	**molestar**	*to bother, to be bothered by*
encantar	*to love*	**preocupar**	*to worry*
estar contento/a (de)	*to be happy (about)*	**sentir (ie, i)**	*to feel sorry*
frustrar	*to frustrate*	**temer**	*to fear*
gustar	*to like*		

- Impersonal expressions and other expressions that show emotion or point of view are also followed by **que** + *subjunctive.*

Es triste que el niño **esté** enfermo.	*It is sad that the child is sick.*
¡**Qué lástima que** no **pueda** ir a la fiesta!	*What a shame that he cannot go to the party!*
Es fastidioso que no **vaya** a la escuela.	*It's frustrating that he does not go to school.*
Es necesario que tome los medicamentos a tiempo.	*It's necessary that he take his medication on time.*
Es malo que el niño **tenga** una fiebre tan alta.	*It's bad that the child have such a high fever.*

e **¿Comprendes?** Completa las oraciones con la forma correcta de los verbos indicados.

1. Juan, yo ________ (alegrarse) mucho de que tú ________ (venir) a verme durante las próximas vacaciones.
2. Yo también ________ (estar) contento de que nosotros ________ (poder) pasar tiempo juntos.
3. A mi madre le va a gustar que tú ________ (visitar) a tus primos durante las vacaciones.
4. Sí, ya sé, es una lástima que nosotros ________ (vivir) tan lejos.
5. A todos en la familia nos encanta que tú y tu novia ________ (estar) comprometidos/as (*engaged*).

Cultura

Fumar es malo para la salud Tradicionalmente, los países hispanos eran más permisivos en el consumo del tabaco en lugares públicos, dada (*given*) la importancia de los cafés, bares y restaurantes en la vida de las personas. Sin embargo, recientemente la mayor parte de los países han creado leyes que prohíben o limitan el uso del tabaco en lugares públicos. Esto ha producido una gran reducción del consumo del tabaco entre los jóvenes y una mayor concienciación sobre sus efectos peligrosos.

Comparación ¿Qué dicen las leyes relacionadas con el uso del tabaco en tu país? ¿Te parecen suficientes? ¿Son excesivas? Explica.

PRÁCTICA

11-26 Estoy enfermo/a. Seleccionen la reacción apropiada para cada comentario. Después, túrnense para añadir nuevos comentarios y reacciones.

1. _____ Estoy muy enfermo/a.
2. _____ Mis padres llegan hoy para estar conmigo.
3. _____ Creo que el doctor Pérez me va a operar.
4. _____ Dicen que es una operación seria.
5. _____ No voy a poder participar en el campeonato.

a. Me alegro de que vengan.
b. Siento mucho que estés tan mal.
c. ¡Qué bueno que sea ese el médico!
d. Es una lástima que no puedas jugar.
e. Ojalá que no tengas complicaciones.

11-27 Una visita. PREPARACIÓN. Visitas a tu compañero/a que está operado/a de la rodilla. Él/Ella te cuenta sobre su experiencia en la clínica. Escoge diferentes expresiones de **En directo** para responderle. Intercambien papeles.

MODELO E1: *No me gusta la comida del hospital.*
E2: *Siento que la comida no sea buena. ¿Qué te sirven?*
E1: …

1. Me duele bastante la rodilla.
2. Tengo fiebre y dolor de cabeza.
3. Estoy mal del estómago porque las medicinas son muy fuertes.
4. Mis amigos me mandan mensajes de texto y tarjetas digitales.
5. Detesto estar en cama tanto tiempo.
6. Hay demasiado ruido (*noise*) y no puedo dormir.
7. Las enfermeras vienen a verme cada media hora.

INTERCAMBIOS. Escríbele un mensaje de texto o correo electrónico a tu compañero/a que está en la clínica para…

- expresarle tus sentimientos sobre tu visita a la clínica y sobre uno o dos de los problemas que te mencionó.
- desearle una pronta recuperación.

En directo

To express empathy:

Siento que… *I feel sorry that . . .*

Me alegro de que… *I'm glad that . . .*

Temo que… *I'm afraid that . . .*

Espero que… *I hope that . . .*

No me gusta que… *I don't like that . . .*

¡Qué (des)agradable que…! *How (un)pleasant that . . .!*

Listen to a conversation with these expressions.

11-28 Reacciones. Luisa desea tener una vida con menos estrés y Rafael quiere bajar de peso (*lose weight*). Túrnense para indicar si están de acuerdo o no con los planes de Luisa y Rafael para la próxima semana.

MODELO Rafael / no desayunar
E1: *Rafael no va a desayunar.*
E2: *No me gusta / Es malo que Rafael no desayune.*
E1: *Y yo siento/lamento que… / (No) es bueno que…*

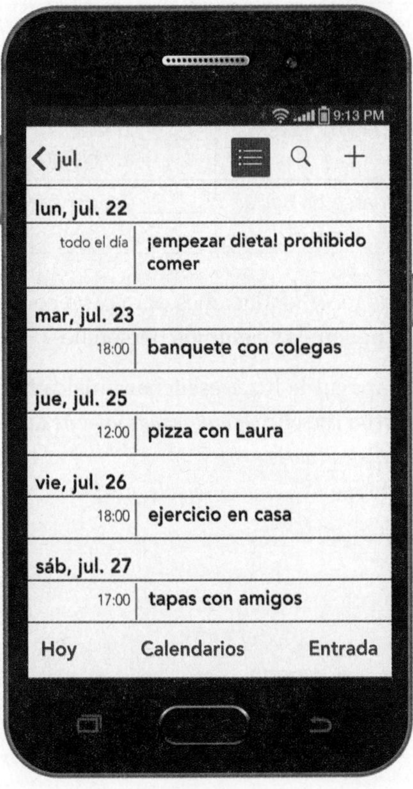

Rafael

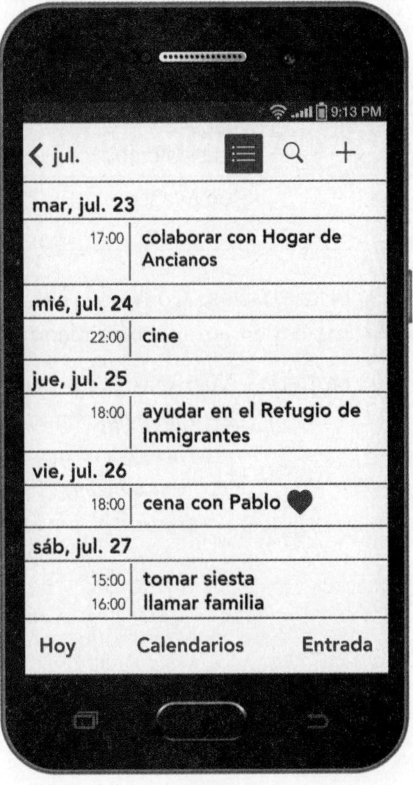

Luisa

 **11-29 ¿Qué te molesta?** **PREPARACIÓN.** Haz una lista de cinco hábitos o comportamientos que te molestan de otras personas. Usa las ideas de la lista u otras. Compara tus ideas con las de tu compañero/a.

MODELO llegar tarde
Me molesta que mis amigos lleguen tarde.

beber demasiado alcohol	no respetar las opiniones de otros	ser inflexible
fumar	no ser sincero/a	ser irresponsable
mentir (*lie*) frecuentemente	ser desconsiderado/a (*inconsiderate*)	ser tacaño/a (*stingy*)
no demostrar solidaridad	ser desleal (*disloyal*)	tener una visión pesimista de la vida
no gustarle las fiestas		

 **INTERCAMBIOS.** Comparen sus listas. Escojan los seis hábitos o comportamientos que les molestan más a todos en su grupo y expliquen por qué. Compartan sus conclusiones con la clase.

11-30 ¿Qué recomiendas? **PREPARACIÓN.** Selecciona las recomendaciones apropiadas para una persona con las siguientes condiciones, según lo que tú sabes.

Migrañas	Acidez estomacal (*heartburn*)	Gripe	Bronquitis
_____ evitar situaciones de estrés que las causan	_____ comer comida con muchos condimentos	_____ comer sopa de pollo	_____ mantenerse en un lugar frío
_____ estar en un lugar con mucha luz	_____ beber leche	_____ beber un té de infusión de hierbas	_____ comer miel
_____ mantenerse en la oscuridad	_____ tomar antiácido	_____ dormir bastante	_____ tomar antibióticos
_____ evitar el ruido (*noise*) y los olores (*odors*) fuertes	_____ consumir alcohol	_____ tomar pastillas antigripales	_____ fumar
_____ tomar analgésicos (*pain killers*)	_____ hacer musicoterapia	_____ consumir whisky	_____ inhalar antihistamínicos
_____ relajarse al aire libre	_____ tomar agua	_____ bañarse en agua fría	_____ descansar mucho

 **INTERCAMBIOS.** Conversen sobre algunas recomendaciones para cada condición. Expliquen por qué recomiendan eso. Pueden dar ejemplos personales.

MODELO Migrañas: jugar deportes / apagar la luz / escuchar música fuerte
E1: *En mi opinión, es mejor que la persona con migrañas apague la luz. / No es bueno que escuche música fuerte.*
E2: *Tienes razón. / Estoy de acuerdo. No es aconsejable que practique deportes al aire libre.*

 **11-31 ¿Qué te parece?** Eres médico/a y te preocupan tus pacientes. Explícale tus preocupaciones a tu colega (tu compañero/a) y expresa tus sentimientos u opinión sobre cada situación. Tu colega te va a dar su opinión. Intercambien papeles.

MODELO Una paciente sufre de gastroenteritis, pero le fascina comer comida picante. Frecuentemente va a tu consulta para pedirte medicamentos. Tú estás preocupado/a.

E1: *Una paciente viene a mi consultorio frecuentemente porque se enferma cuando come comida picante. Me pide medicamentos para sentirse mejor. Me preocupa que ella coma comida picante con frecuencia.*

E2: *¡Qué lástima que coma comida picante! Es mejor que la evite.*

1. Un señor siempre te pide una receta diferente para tratar su diabetes, pero no toma los medicamentos con regularidad. Te molesta su comportamiento.
2. Una paciente de muchos años necesita operarse una rodilla. Tú siempre le recomiendas cuidar la dieta para evitar la cirugía (*surgery*), pero ella no quiere hacer dieta ni ejercicio. A ti no te gusta su irresponsabilidad.
3. Una señora viene a tu consulta para contarte sus problemas familiares y quejarse de su mala salud. Tú la examinas para averiguar si realmente tiene alguna enfermedad, pero ella habla constantemente de su familia. Tú crees que la señora no tiene una enfermedad física.
4. Un paciente joven sufre de depresión. Bebe demasiado alcohol y no quiere vivir más. Tú piensas que para su depresión y su dependencia del alcohol, el joven necesita consultar a un/a médico/a especialista. Tienes esperanzas de que él pueda tener una vida mejor.

Situación

PREPARACIÓN. Lean la situación. Luego, compartan ejemplos de vocabulario, gramática y otra información que necesitan para desarrollar la conversación.

Role A. You and your housemate disagree about almost everything. You exercise regularly, ride your bike, and hike on the weekends, and want only healthful foods in the refrigerator. Your housemate buys a lot of junk food (**comida basura**), leaves a mess in the living room and bathroom, and disturbs you with loud music at all hours. You have a serious conversation to tell him/her what is bothering you.

Role B. Your housemate is uptight and conventional and doesn't know how to enjoy life. When he/she tells you what is bothering him/her about your behavior, you should:

a. react to his/her complaints;
b. respond with your complaints about his/her excessive tidiness; and
c. regret that you do not agree on anything.

	ROLE A	ROLE B
Vocabulario	Activities for a healthy lifestyle Household chores Verbs of emotions, likes, and dislikes	Household chores Verbs of emotions, likes, and dislikes
Funciones y formas	Expressing emotion about someone's actions Subjunctive with expressions of emotion	Expressing emotion about someone's actions Subjunctive with expressions of emotion

INTERCAMBIOS. Practiquen la conversación, incorporando el vocabulario y las funciones de **Preparación.** Luego, represéntenla ante la clase.

4 Expressing goals, purposes, and means

Vive más.

- **Para** vivir más, no necesitas más dinero. No pagues miles de pesos **por** aparatos de ejercicio. ¡Mantente activo/a!
- Sube a tu clase u oficina **por** las escaleras; no tomes el ascensor (*elevator*).
- Cuando vayas **para** una tienda cerca de tu casa, no manejes (*drive*) tu auto. Caminar es mejor **para** tu salud.
- Si caminas 30 minutos **por** día, vivirás más. Pasea **por** el parque con tus amigos o tu familia.
- Relájate mientras caminas al aire libre y vive con menos estrés **por** ti y **para** ti.

Piénsalo. Selecciona el significado de **por** o **para** en cada afirmación. Luego, indica si la afirmación es cierta (**C**) o falsa (**F**).

1. ______ **Para** vivir más, no necesitas más dinero.
2. ______ Debes subir a tu clase **por** ascensor (*elevator*).
3. ______ Cuando vayas **para** una tienda, no manejes.
4. ______ Si caminas 1 minuto **por** día, vivirás más.
5. ______ Caminar es mejor **para** tu salud.
6. ______ Debes vivir con menos estrés **por** ti.

a. en beneficio de alguien o algo
b. objetivo o propósito
c. en dirección a un lugar
d. a causa de alguien o algo
e. medio de transporte
f. duración

Uses of *por* and *para*

- As you learned in *Capítulo 3*, the prepositions **por** and **para** have several meanings and uses. You have used them easily in some contexts in which they are similar to *for* in English:

  Compré estas vitaminas **para** Anita. *I bought these vitamins for Anita.*

- Other uses of **por** and **para** that are not similar to English can be learned by grouping them into functional categories: expressions of movement, time, purpose, and means.

POR		PARA
• **through or by a place** Caminaron **por** el hospital. *They walked through the hospital.*	**MOVEMENT**	• **toward a destination** Caminaron **para** el hospital. *They walked toward the hospital.*
• **duration of an event** Estuvo con la médica **por** una hora. *He was with the doctor for an hour.*	**TIME**	• **deadline** Necesita el antibiótico **para** el martes. *He needs the antibiotic by Tuesday.*
• **reason or motive** Ana fue al consultorio **por** el dolor de garganta. *Ana went to the doctor's office because of a sore throat.*	**PURPOSE**	• **for whom something is intended or done** Compró el antibiótico **para** Ana. *He bought the antibiotic for Ana.*

- **Por** is also used to express the following:

means of transportation

Mandaron los órganos del trasplante **por** avión.	*They sent the transplant organs by plane.*

exchange or substitution

Irma pagó 120 dólares **por** las pastillas.	*Irma paid 120 dollars for the pills.*
Cambió los tranquilizantes **por** los analgésicos.	*She exchanged the tranquilizers for pain killers.*

unit or rate

Yo camino cinco kilómetros **por** hora.	*I walk five kilometers per hour.*
El seguro médico cubre el 60 **por** ciento de las cuentas.	*The health insurance covers 60 percent of the bills.*

object of an errand

Sara fue a la farmacia **por** los antibióticos.	*Sara went to the drugstore for the antibiotics.*
Pasamos **por** ti a las 5:00.	*We'll come by for you at 5:00.*

- **Para** is also used to express the following:

judgment or point of view

Para nosotros, este es el mejor consultorio.	*For us (in our opinion), this is the best doctor's office.*
Es un caso difícil **para** un médico joven.	*It is a difficult case for a young doctor.*

intention or purpose, when followed by an infinitive

Fueron a la farmacia **para** recoger los antibióticos.	*They went to the drugstore to pick up the antibiotics.*
Evita las grasas **para** tener mejor salud.	*Avoid fats (in order) to have better health.*

e **¿Comprendes?** Completa las oraciones con **por** o **para.**

1. Te llamo ______ pedirte un favor.
2. Paso ______ la farmacia después de ir al médico.
3. ¿Puedes pasar _____ mi casa mañana a las cinco?
4. Todos los días camino _____ el parque, pero hoy no puedo _____ mis migrañas.
5. Caminar _____ una hora es demasiado ejercicio _____ mí.
6. Mi colega siempre trabaja _____ mí cuando estoy enferma.
7. _____ mis compañeros de oficina, ella es la persona más solidaria.

PRÁCTICA

11-32 Un episodio.

PREPARACIÓN. Selecciona la preposición correcta, según el significado entre paréntesis.

1. Salimos **por / para** el consultorio médico a las nueve de la mañana. (*toward a destination*)
2. Fuimos **por / para** el túnel para llegar más rápido. (*through*)
3. Ana fue a ver al médico **por / para** su gripe y bronquitis. (*reason or motive*)
4. El médico escribió una receta de antibióticos **por / para** Ana. (*for whom it is intended*)
5. Yo fui a la farmacia **por / para** los antibióticos. (*object of an errand*)
6. Pagué ochenta dólares **por / para** los antibióticos. (*exchange or substitution*)
7. **Por / Para** Ana, los antibióticos ayudan a recuperarse rápidamente, pero dañan (*damage*) el cuerpo. (*point of view*)

INTERCAMBIOS. Túrnense para hablar de lo siguiente.

1. ¿Cuándo fue la última vez que fuiste al médico?
2. ¿Por qué fuiste?
3. ¿Qué te recomendó el médico y para qué?
4. ¿Por cuántos días seguiste el tratamiento?
5. ¿Cuánto pagaste por la consulta?
6. ¿Cuánto pagaste por los medicamentos?

11-33 La graduación de un nuevo médico.

PREPARACIÓN. Completa estos párrafos sobre la graduación de Fernando con **por** o **para,** según el contexto. Luego, selecciona la función de la lista que corresponde a cada uso de **por** o **para.**

El 14 de junio es la graduación de Fernando en la Facultad de Medicina de la Universidad Católica Madre y Maestra de Santiago de los Caballeros, en República Dominicana. Sus padres, el señor y la señora Rovira, viven en Puerto Plata, pero van a Santiago (1) _______ asistir a la graduación. Quieren llevarle un regalo. El lunes pasado fueron a una tienda y pagaron 150 pesos (2) _______ un regalo muy bonito (3) _______ Fernando. Graciela, su hermana gemela, vive en Miami y no puede ir (4) _______ su trabajo. Ella también le compró un regalo y se lo envió (5) _______ correo expreso porque quiere que llegue (6) _______ el día de la graduación.

El día 14, los padres de Fernando salieron (7) _______ la universidad. Estaba lloviendo, y (8) _______ eso salieron temprano. Normalmente, ellos pueden estar en la universidad en aproximadamente una hora y media, pero (9) _______ la lluvia, el viaje duró casi dos horas. (10) _______ ellos, que son mayores, el viaje fue un poco largo, pero al final pudieron pasar ese día con su hijo.

To express or indicate . . .

- **a.** intention or purpose (with infinitive)
- **b.** judgment or point of view
- **c.** means of transportation
- **d.** exchange or substitution
- **e.** toward a destination
- **f.** deadline
- **g.** for whom something is intended or done
- **h.** reason or motive

INTERCAMBIOS. Respondan a las siguientes preguntas.

1. Mientras estudia, Fernando vive en Santiago de los Caballeros. Sus padres viven en Puerto Plata, a una hora y media de distancia. ¿Es mejor que Fernando viaje por auto o por avión (*plane*) cuando los visita? ¿Por qué?
2. ¿Qué tipo de regalo de graduación es bueno que los padres les den a sus hijos? ¿Por qué?
3. Para ustedes, ¿qué es más importante: recibir un regalo de graduación o contar con la compañía de la familia y amigos en la ceremonia? ¿Por qué?

11-34 Exámenes, resultados y medicamentos. Consulten la información de la tabla para hablar de lo siguiente sobre cada paciente:

1. cuándo van a estar listos los resultados del examen
2. el propósito (*purpose*) del examen
3. cuándo van a estar listos los medicamentos de la farmacia

MODELO Paciente: Alfredo Benítez
Resultados: la prueba intradérmica / 2:00 p.m. / detectar posibles alergias
Medicamentos: los antihistamínicos / 4:00 p.m.

E1: *¿Cuándo van a estar listos los resultados de la prueba intradérmica de Alfredo Benítez?*
E2: *Para las dos de la tarde.*
E1: *¿Para qué le hicieron la prueba intradérmica?*
E2: *Para detectar posibles alergias.*
E1: *¿Y para cuándo van a estar listos los antihistamínicos?*
E2: *Para las cuatro de la tarde.*

Paciente	Resultados	Medicamentos
Yaritza Corvalán	la broncoscopía 11:00 a.m. detectar inflamación de los pulmones	las pastillas antiinflamatorias al mediodía
Luis González	el examen de glucosa esta tarde monitorear el nivel (*level*) de azúcar en la sangre	las inyecciones de insulina 6:00 p.m.
Joel Pérez	el análisis de la prueba de esfuerzo (*stress test*) 3:15 p.m. diagnosticar su enfermedad coronaria	las píldoras de agua mañana por la mañana
Aleida Miranda	el examen de resonancia magnética (*MRI*) mañana por la tarde identificar una posible enfermedad del abdomen	los analgésicos (*pain killers*) 3:00 p.m.
Óscar Villegas	el estudio de sueño martes diagnosticar el insomnio	los medicamentos para dormir esta noche

Cultura

Nuestra Señora de Altagracia En un país profundamente católico como República Dominicana, la devoción a Nuestra Señora de Altagracia ocupa un lugar preeminente. Los dominicanos consideran a esta virgen como la protectora de la nación. El 21 de enero celebran con devoción y emoción el día de su festividad. Ese día no se trabaja en República Dominicana y muchas personas peregrinan (*make a pilgrimage*) al templo de Higüey para rezar, dar gracias y pedirle protección.

Comparación ¿Hay lugares espirituales en tu país donde la gente va para reflexionar y dar las gracias? ¿Dónde? ¿Hay fechas en el calendario cuando la gente agradece (*gives thanks*) por algo? ¿Qué agradece la gente?

Peregrinación de Nuestra Señora de Altagracia, en Higüey

 **11-35 Una cura para el estrés.** **PREPARACIÓN.** Por el exceso de trabajo y el estrés de sus clases, ustedes decidieron hacer un viaje a República Dominicana en sus próximas vacaciones. Primero, seleccionen el propósito que corresponde a cada actividad. Luego, túrnense para hacerse recomendaciones usando las actividades de la lista e indicando el propósito de cada actividad. Sigan el modelo.

MODELO caminar por el Jardín Botánico de Santo Domingo / ver la gran variedad de plantas
Camina por el Jardín Botánico de Santo Domingo para ver la gran variedad de plantas.

Actividad en República Dominicana	Propósito
1. _____ participar en la fiesta nacional de Nuestra Señora de Altagracia en Higüey	a. escuchar música y bailar merengue
2. _____ visitar la Bahía (*Bay*) de Samaná	b. visitar el santuario de las ballenas jorobadas (*humpback whales*)
3. _____ ir a un club en la Zona Colonia de la capital	c. conocer el significado de esta figura espiritual del pueblo dominicano
4. _____ explorar la Cueva de las Maravillas cerca de La Romana	d. nadar, hacer kayak y tomar el sol
5. _____ salir a cenar al Mesón de la Cava en Santo Domingo	e. entrar en las cavernas y ver unas pinturas antiguas hechas por los indígenas taínos
6. _____ pasar unos días en las playas de Punta Cana	f. comer comida típica dominicana

INTERCAMBIOS. Completen individualmente las siguientes ideas relacionadas con el estrés. Luego, comparen sus respuestas y den recomendaciones si es necesario.

1. La última vez que me sentí estresado/a fue… (explica la causa o razón).
2. Hice lo siguiente:

   ____________________ (actividad) ____________________ (propósito)

   ____________________ (actividad) ____________________ (propósito)
3. Después de hacer estas dos actividades, me sentí…

11-36 En la sala de emergencia. Trabajas en la sala de emergencia y llega un/a paciente joven que está desorientado/a. Averigua si la memoria de tu paciente está funcionando bien después de una mala caída (*fall*). Pregúntale sobre los objetos que encontraste en su mochila. Intercambien papeles.

MODELO E1: *¿Qué traes en tu mochila?*
E2: *Traigo varias cosas. Un sándwich, por ejemplo.*
E1: *¿Para qué lo traes? / ¿Para quién es?*
E2: *Para almorzar con mi novio/a. / Para mi novio/a.*
E1: *¿Qué más traes?*

11-37 ¿Mito o realidad? **PREPARACIÓN.** Indica si las siguientes afirmaciones son un mito (**M**) o una realidad (**R**). Luego, compara tus respuestas con las de tu compañero/a.

1. _____ El té de manzanilla alivia el dolor de estómago.
2. _____ Algunas verduras como el brócoli y las espinacas proveen calcio.
3. _____ La sopa de pollo ayuda a curar el resfriado.
4. _____ Las pastillas para adelgazar no tienen efectos secundarios.
5. _____ El uso de laxantes es excelente para perder peso.
6. _____ El estrés provoca dolores musculares.
7. _____ La salvia (*sage*) es un buen remedio para tratar el estrés.
8. _____ Los jugos naturales son buenos para darle energía al cuerpo.

INTERCAMBIOS. Identifica las condiciones de salud mencionadas en **Preparación.** Luego, selecciona dos enfermedades o condiciones que tú o alguien que conoces experimenta frecuentemente. Intercambien roles para describir cada condición y sugerir qué hacer.

MODELO E1: *Mi compañero/a de cuarto siempre tiene dolor de estómago.*
E2: *Para el dolor de estómago, es bueno que tome un té de manzanilla.*

Situación

PREPARACIÓN. Lean la situación. Luego, compartan ejemplos de vocabulario, gramática y otra información que necesitan para desarrollar la conversación.

Role A. You hurt your ankle while playing soccer, so you go to the health center at your college or university. Tell the doctor that:
a. you fell during the game;
b. your ankle is swollen (**hinchado**); and
c. you cannot walk because of the pain.
Ask questions and answer your doctor's questions.

Role B. A patient comes to see you with a sports injury. After you hear how the injury happened, ask:
a. what the coach did for him/her, and;
b. how he/she got to the health center.
After determining that the ankle is not broken, recommend that the patient:
a. rest for three or four days;
b. take a pain killer (**analgésico**); and
c. put ice on his/her ankle to reduce the swelling (**reducir la hinchazón**).
Add that because of the injury, he/she should not play soccer for a month.

	ROLE A	ROLE B
Vocabulario	Health and injuries Parts of the body	Means of transportation Possible treatment for injuries Medication and remedies
Funciones y formas	Explaining reason for a condition Describing symptoms Asking and answering questions: **por/para**	Asking and answering questions Giving advice: **por/para** Subjunctive / Formal commands

INTERCAMBIOS. Practiquen la conversación, incorporando el vocabulario y las funciones de **Preparación.** Luego, represéntenla ante la clase.

MOSAICOS

ESCUCHA

Estrategia

Listen for the main ideas You can focus your attention listening for the main ideas by following these tips:

1. Rely on knowledge of the topic to make connections.
2. Think about the specific words or concepts you may hear.
3. Pay attention to the introduction and the conclusion, where the main ideas are usually stated.
4. Listen for transitional phrases that signal main ideas, such as **Lo importante es..., Recuerde(n)..., Otro punto importante/central...**

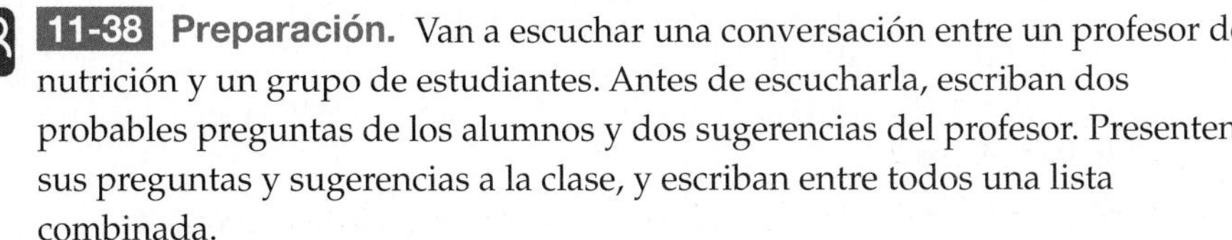

11-38 Preparación. Van a escuchar una conversación entre un profesor de nutrición y un grupo de estudiantes. Antes de escucharla, escriban dos probables preguntas de los alumnos y dos sugerencias del profesor. Presenten sus preguntas y sugerencias a la clase, y escriban entre todos una lista combinada.

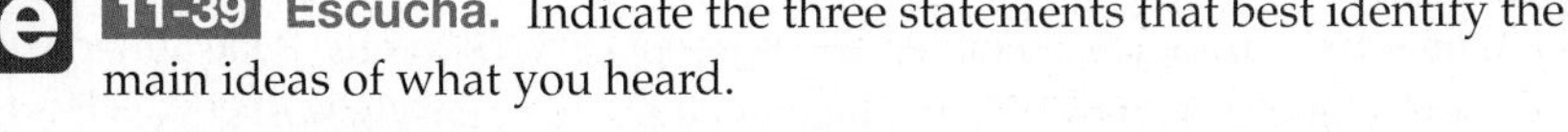

11-39 Escucha. Indicate the three statements that best identify the main ideas of what you heard.

1. _____ Consultar al médico una vez por año es importante para evitar enfermedades.
2. _____ El consumo de tomates, lechugas, uvas, naranjas, cerveza y carne de res es recomendable para tener energía.
3. _____ La buena alimentación y el ejercicio tienen un efecto positivo en la salud.
4. _____ Se recomienda comer bastante y hacer muchísimo ejercicio para mantener una vida saludable.
5. _____ Bajar de peso afecta positivamente la salud y la apariencia de las personas.
6. _____ La buena salud requiere disciplina.

Comprueba

I was able to . . .

- use my knowledge of the topic to anticipate what I might hear.
- listen for parts of the conversation where main ideas are about to be presented.
- identify the main ideas and some details.

11-40 Un paso más. Háganse las siguientes preguntas. Comparen sus respuestas y puntos de vista.

1. ¿Tienes buenos hábitos alimenticios y de actividad física? ¿Qué hábitos son buenos y cuáles son malos para tener una vida saludable?
2. ¿Estás de acuerdo con la afirmación "eres lo que comes"? ¿Por qué?
3. ¿Qué aspectos de tu vida puedes cambiar para mejorar tu salud física y emocional? ¿Cómo los cambiarías (*would you change*)?

HABLA

Estrategia

Select appropriate phrases to offer opinions When you are talking with someone, it is natural to offer opinions and evaluations of what the other person has said and to express agreement or disagreement. An effective way to do this is to acknowledge the value of what the other person has said and then express your reaction to it.

11-41 Preparación. Indica los hábitos o condiciones que ayudan a prolongar la vida de las personas, según tu opinión.

1. _____ hacer ejercicio físico regularmente
2. _____ estresarse en el trabajo
3. _____ reducir el consumo de calorías
4. _____ consumir comida saludable
5. _____ beber una copa de vino tinto con el almuerzo o la cena
6. _____ llevar una vida sedentaria
7. _____ curar los dolores y enfermedades con remedios caseros (*home*)
8. _____ evitar las grasas
9. _____ ser optimista

Comprueba

I was able to . . .

- exchange information about the exercise and eating habits of a person I know well.
- express concerns and opinions about my friend's exercise and eating habits.
- offer advice and recommendations.

11-42 Habla. Entrevístense para hablar sobre una persona que cada uno/a de ustedes conoce bien. Hablen sobre los siguientes temas. Reaccionen y opinen según lo que escuchen y hagan recomendaciones cuando sea necesario.

1. el nivel (*level*) de actividad física de esta persona
2. sus hábitos de comida y bebida
3. cómo cuida su salud emocional

En directo

To express concern:

Me preocupa que no haga ejercicio. *I am concerned that he/she doesn't exercise.*

Creo que debe cuidarse. *I believe that he/she should take care of himself/herself.*

To express happiness:

¡Qué bueno que consuma comida saludable! *It's great that he/she eats healthy food!*

¡Qué fantástico que se mantenga activo/a! *How great that he/she stays active!*

Es fabuloso que no fume ni beba. *It's wonderful that he/she doesn't smoke or drink.*

To introduce a contrasting opinion:

Lo que dices es interesante, pero mi perspectiva es diferente. / Yo lo veo diferente. *What you say is interesting, but I have a different perspective. / I see it differently.*

Entiendo tu punto de vista, pero no estoy de acuerdo contigo. *I understand your viewpoint, but I disagree with you.*

 Listen to a conversation with these expressions.

 **11-43 Un paso más.** Usa la información de la conversación con tu compañero/a en la actividad **11-42** para escribir un informe que incluya lo siguiente:

1. las actividades y hábitos de la persona de quien habló tu compañero/a
2. una comparación de sus hábitos con los tuyos (*yours*)
3. tu opinión y tus recomendaciones para tener una vida más saludable

LEE

Estrategia

Focus on relevant information Identifying the relevant information in a text and disregarding what you think is irrelevant helps you read faster and understand more. Techniques that help you identify what is important include a) reading the titles and subtitles; b) looking at the visuals and reading the captions; c) brainstorming possible content by using your knowledge of the topic; and d) comparing those ideas with what you find as you read.

 **11-44 Preparación.** De la siguiente lista, identifica las enfermedades que conoces. Después, habla con tu compañero/a sobre las ideas que probablemente encuentren en el artículo que van a leer.

1. la tuberculosis
2. la malaria
3. el virus del ébola
4. el virus del zika
5. la gripe H1N1

 **11-45 Lee.** Lee el artículo "Las enfermedades y la globalización". Según el contenido del artículo, selecciona las palabras que se relacionan con cada tema.

Temas	Palabras relacionadas
1. Enfermedades	_____ las pandemias _____ el virus del Nilo occidental _____ la tuberculosis _____ el virus del Ébola
2. Desafíos (*Challenges*) de las enfermedades para los expertos	_____ las infecciones _____ la resistencia _____ los pueblos remotos _____ la evolución _____ la migración
3. Medidas (*Measures*) que los expertos toman para enfrentar estas enfermedades	_____ las campañas _____ las vacunas _____ la incubación _____ la prevención

Comprueba

I was able to . . .

- use the titles, subheadings, and visuals/captions to predict the content of an informational text about a topic of general interest.
- understand the main message and supporting details of the text.

LAS ENFERMEDADES Y LA GLOBALIZACIÓN

La globalización significa la tendencia de los mercados y de las empresas a extenderse más allá[1] de las fronteras nacionales. Además de los productos comerciales, incluye también el constante movimiento de personas entre los continentes por motivos de turismo, inmigración y trabajo. Pero las personas y los productos no viajan solos de un continente a otro; los acompañan virus y enfermedades infecciosas. Algunas de estas enfermedades pandémicas que ya casi no existían, como la malaria y la tuberculosis, ahora reaparecen y se extienden por todo el mundo. Hay otros virus, como el ébola, el zika y la gripe H1N1, anteriormente limitados a un solo país, que en años recientes han aparecido en otros continentes.

BACTERIAS, PARÁSITOS Y VIRUS VIAJEROS Y RESISTENTES

Un buen ejemplo de la adaptabilidad de las enfermedades infecciosas es la tuberculosis. Los científicos pensaban que estaba controlada en los países desarrollados. Sin embargo, ahora sabemos que esta enfermedad ha evolucionado y ha retornado.

Además, la Organización Mundial de la Salud (OMS) expresa gran preocupación por la malaria. El mosquito que la provoca puede sobrevivir largos viajes interoceánicos. Por eso, hay personas enfermas de malaria en muchas partes del mundo. La malaria es peligrosa si no se detecta a tiempo. Los médicos sin experiencia en este tipo de enfermedades la pueden confundir con la gripe y tratarla con medicamentos inadecuados.

LAS ENFERMEDADES MIGRATORIAS

La globalización implica también el movimiento de personas y, con ellas, las enfermedades. Una persona infectada que viaja de un continente a otro por avión puede propagar[2] la enfermedad a muchas otras personas, antes de manifestarse[3] los primeros síntomas. Es decir, podemos llevar un virus en nuestros cuerpos y, sin saberlo, dispersarlo por el mundo.

Un técnico aplica un insecticida contra los mosquitos que propagan el virus del zika.

El brote[4] del ébola en África en 2014 fue enorme porque empezó en una zona de Guinea que está cerca de Liberia y Sierra Leona. Rápidamente pasó a esos países y terminó matando a más de 11.000 personas. Los brotes anteriores ocurrieron en pueblos pequeños muy remotos. Allí nacía el virus y también moría. Solo infectaba a residentes de otros pueblos durante los funerales.

De igual manera, el zika, un virus transmitido por la picadura[5] de un mosquito, tiene un alcance[6] global también. Empezó en Uganda y luego viajó a Asia. Entonces, en 2007, pasó a las islas del Pacífico, donde miles de personas se enfermaron. De allí, pasó a América del Sur, donde en 2016, unos 20 países reportaron la detección del zika en su territorio. También llegó al estado de Florida en Estados Unidos.

Finalmente, en 2009, surgió la nueva cepa[7] H1N1 del virus de la gripe. Apareció en cerdos en México, pasó a los humanos con un cambio genético que permite el contagio entre nosotros. Afectó a más de 35.000 personas en 76 países en menos de tres meses. En total, más de 200.000 personas murieron de esta gripe entre 2009 y 2010.

Las enfermedades infecciosas ya no tienen límites geográficos. Frente a la expansión, los científicos inventan mejores vacunas y los profesionales de salud pública producen campañas de información y educación antes del próximo virus pandémico. Dicen los científicos que es necesario protegernos contra la gripe, que es la amenaza[8] global número uno entre las enfermedades infecciosas.

[1]*beyond* [2]*spread* [3]*show up* [4]*outbreak* [5]*bite, sting* [6]*reach* [7]*strain* [8]*threat*

 **11-46 Un paso más.** Hagan una lista de la información en el artículo que ustedes no sabían antes de leerlo. Seleccionen los tres datos (*pieces of information*) más importantes o más interesantes. Compartan su lista con la clase y expliquen por qué han escogido esos datos.

ESCRIBE

Estrategia

Persuade through suggestions and advice Well-structured suggestions and advice are important for effective persuasion in writing. Remember to . . .

- decide whether to address your reader as **tú** or **usted,** based on your relationship (e.g., friend vs. supervisor at work).
- select suggestions that match the nature of your relationship.

11-47 Preparación. Lee este mensaje de tu amigo Tomás. Después, escribe tres problemas que tiene Tomás y algunas ideas para ayudarlo a resolver cada uno. Tomás probablemente tiene una enfermedad infecciosa, y tú acabas de leer un artículo sobre este tema.

Hola.

Perdón por no escribirte antes. Como sabes, estoy en un programa de antropología en República Dominicana este verano, y la verdad es que no me siento bien. No puedo concentrarme en las clases y no tengo energía para participar en el trabajo de campo (*field work*). Vivo en un apartamento con dos estudiantes dominicanos, pero no tengo energía para cocinar, así que muchas noches como solo pan o sopa. Otras veces voy a un restaurante de comida rápida. Tomo café constantemente, porque necesito la cafeína para sobrevivir, pero luego no puedo dormir. Mis compañeros son amables, pero no los veo mucho. Me siento muy solo. Mi vida es una pesadilla (*nightmare*). ¿Qué me aconsejas?

Bueno, escríbeme para saber de ti.

Tu triste amigo,
Tomás

Problemas de Tomás	Recomendaciones
1.	
2.	
3.	

En directo

To express concern or sympathy:

Me preocupa (mucho) que... *It concerns me (a lot) that . . .*

Siento/Lamento que... *I am sorry that . . .*

Qué lástima que... *It's too bad that . . .*

To persuade a friend through suggestions:

Te recomiendo/sugiero/aconsejo que... *I recommend/suggest/advise that . . .*

Es importante/necesario/urgente/mejor que... *It is important/necessary/urgent/better that . . .*

Ojalá (que)... *I hope that . . .*

 Listen to a conversation with these expressions.

Comprueba

I was able to . . .

- use a familiar tone to express concern to a friend.
- give information that may be relevant to a friend's situation.
- offer suggestions and recommendations.

e **11-48 Escribe.** Responde al mensaje de Tomás. Incluye lo siguiente:

- Exprésale tus sentimientos o tu preocupación por sus problemas.
- Haciendo referencias al artículo en la actividad **11-45,** explícale lo que sabes acerca de las enfermedades infecciosas.
- Hazle preguntas sobre sus síntomas y lo que ha hecho para tratarlos.
- Dale recomendaciones y sugerencias para resolver sus problemas. Usa tus ideas de la actividad **11-47** y las expresiones de **En directo.**

En directo

To put ideas together coherently:

Por un lado... *On one hand . . .*

Por otro (lado)... *On the other (hand) . . .*

En primer/segundo lugar... *In the first/second place . . .*

Además... *Besides / In addition . . .*

To contrast ideas:

No obstante, ... *However, . . .*

Sin embargo, ... *Nevertheless, . . .*

 Listen to a conversation with these expressions.

 **11-49 Un paso más.** Lee el mensaje que tu compañero/a le escribió a Tomás. Luego, comenten juntos/as lo siguiente.

1. ¿Qué problemas de Tomás les parecen más serios? ¿Por qué?
2. ¿Qué soluciones le proponen ustedes? ¿Por qué?

En este capítulo...

Vocabulario

El cuerpo humano	*The human body*
la boca	*mouth*
el brazo	*arm*
la cabeza	*head*
la cadera	*hip*
la cara	*face*
la ceja	*eyebrow*
el cerebro	*brain*
la cintura	*waist*
el codo	*elbow*
el corazón	*heart*
el cuello	*neck*
el dedo	*finger*
el dedo del pie	*toe*
el diente	*tooth*
la espalda	*back*
el estómago	*stomach*
la frente	*forehead*
la garganta	*throat*
el hombro	*shoulder*
el hueso	*bone*
el labio	*lip*
la mano	*hand*
la mejilla	*cheek*
la muñeca	*wrist*
el músculo	*muscle*
la nariz	*nose*
el nervio	*nerve*
el oído	*(inner) ear*
el ojo	*eye*
la oreja	*(outer) ear*
el pecho	*chest*
el pelo / el cabello	*hair*
la pestaña	*eyelash*
el pie	*foot*
la pierna	*leg*
el pulmón	*lung*
la rodilla	*knee*
la sangre	*blood*
el tobillo	*ankle*
la vena	*vein*

Los proveedores de salud	*Healthcare providers*
el centro de salud / la clínica / el sanatorio	*clinic*
el/la enfermero/a	*nurse*
el/la farmacéutico/a	*pharmacist*
la farmacia	*pharmacy*
el gobierno	*government*
el hospital	*hospital*

Los tratamientos médicos	*Medical treatments*
el antibiótico	*antibiotic*
la hierba medicinal	*medicinal herb*
la inyección	*injection*
el medicamento / la medicina	*medicine*
la pastilla	*pill*
la receta	*prescription*
el remedio	*remedy, medicine*
el termómetro	*thermometer*
el tratamiento	*treatment*

La salud	*Health*
la alergia	*allergy*
el asma	*asthma*
el dolor	*pain, ache*
la enfermedad	*illness*
el/la enfermo/a	*ill/sick person*
la fiebre	*fever*
la gripe	*flu*
la infección	*infection*
el/la paciente	*patient*
el resfriado	*cold*
la tensión (arterial)	*(blood) pressure*
la tos	*cough*

Verbos	*Verbs*
aconsejar	*to advise*
alegrarse (de)	*to be glad (about)*
caer(se)	*to fall*
cuidar(se) (de)	*to take care (of)*
curar	*to cure*
doler (ue)	*to hurt, to ache*
esperar	*to hope; to expect*
estar contento/a (de)	*to be happy about*
estornudar	*to sneeze*
evitar	*to avoid*
examinar	*to examine*
fracturar(se)	*to fracture, to break*
frustrar	*to frustrate*
fumar	*to smoke*
insistir (en)	*to insist*
molestar	*to bother, to be bothered by*
pedir (i, i)	*to ask for, to request*
permitir	*to permit, to allow*
preocupar	*to worry*
prohibir	*to prohibit, to forbid*
recetar	*to prescribe*
recomendar (ie)	*to recommend*
sentir(se) (ie, i)	*to feel; to feel sorry*
temer	*to fear*
torcer(se) (ue)	*to twist*
toser	*to cough*
tratar	*to treat*

Palabras y expresiones útiles	*Useful words and expressions*
cada… horas	*every . . . hours*
enfermo/a	*sick*
grave	*serious*
ojalá (que)…	*I/we hope (that) . . .*
el producto de belleza	*beauty item*
¿Qué te/le(s) pasa?	*What's wrong (with you/them)?*
tener dolor de…	*to have a(n) . . . ache*
tener mala cara	*to look terrible*

See pages 413 and 418 for impersonal expressions used with the subjunctive.

Capítulo 12
¿Te gusta viajar?

Una joven admira una cascada en Costa Rica.

Learning Outcomes

You will be able to:

- talk about travel arrangements and preferences
- express affirmation and negation
- express possession and clarify what belongs to you and to others
- express doubt and uncertainty
- talk about travel experiences
- talk about Costa Rica and Panama in terms of products, practices, and perspectives
- share information about low-cost travel in Latin America and make comparisons

Enfoque cultural

Costa Rica y Panamá

La moderna Ciudad de Panamá, con sus múltiples rascacielos (*skyscrapers*)

Un paseo por el río Tárcoles, en Costa Rica

La playa de Manuel Antonio, en Puntarenas, Costa Rica

Arte hispano

Una mola tradicional de los gunas, indígenas de las islas San Blas en Panamá

Enfoque cultural

¿Qué te parece?

- El ecoturismo es muy popular en Costa Rica. Las reservas naturales y la tierra protegida forman el 26% del país.
- Para muchos norteamericanos, Costa Rica y Panamá son países populares para jubilarse (*retire*).
- Panamá, también llamada "la nueva Suiza", es uno de los centros bancarios del mundo.
- Panamá es el país natal de varios cantantes de reguetón, como Flex (Félix Danilo Gómez), Eddy Lover (Eduardo Mosquera) y Makano (Ernán Enrique Jiménez).
- Costa Rica es el único país latinoamericano sin ejército (*army*).

La mola es un tejido (*fabric*) artesanal hecho de varias piezas de tela superpuestas. Los gunas las usan para hacer blusas y cojines (*cushions*). Algunas molas son verdaderas obras (*works*) de arte.

El canal de Panamá tiene aproximadamente 80 kilómetros (48 millas) de largo. El viaje dura entre ocho y diez horas y los barcos (*boats*) pasan por tres esclusas (*locks*). El canal de Panamá une el océano Atlántico y el océano Pacífico.

Costa Rica tiene casi cinco millones de habitantes. Muchos de ellos son mestizos (*mixed race*) y tienen origen africano. Esta mujer celebra la cultura afrocaribeña en la provincia de Puerto Limón.

Costa Rica tiene montañas, volcanes activos, playas espectaculares, lagos y mucha diversidad de flora y fauna. Muchos monos araña (*spider monkeys*), osos perezosos (*sloths*) y caimanes, como el de la foto, viven en los numerosos parques nacionales.

¿Cuánto sabes? Completa las oraciones con la información correcta, según **Enfoque cultural.**

1. Un tipo de turismo popular en Costa Rica es el ______________.
2. Un reptil que vive en los parques nacionales de Costa Rica es el ______________.
3. Los miembros de una tribu indígena que vive en Panamá se llaman los ______________.
4. Las ______________ se usan para hacer blusas y cojines.
5. El ______________ conecta el océano Atlántico y el océano Pacífico.
6. Un tipo de música popular en Panamá es ______________.
7. El único país latinoamericano sin ejército es ______________.

To learn more about Costa Rica and Panama, go online to view the *Club cultura* videos.

VOCABULARIO EN CONTEXTO

Talking about travel arrangements and modes of travel

Los medios de transporte

Mucha gente usa el **transporte** público. Los **autobuses** son populares en las ciudades y también para los **viajes** de larga distancia. Son la solución perfecta para las personas que no tienen **carro,** o para quienes simplemente no les gusta **manejar** en las **carreteras** y **autopistas.** El **metro** es otra forma de transporte eficiente en los centros urbanos, como Madrid, Barcelona, Santiago, Buenos Aires, Caracas y Ciudad de México.

Gracias al turismo, se ha recuperado en Costa Rica la antigua tradición de **recorrer** el país en **tren.** Algunas **agencias de viajes** organizan **excursiones** desde San José a la costa este. En España, la RENFE (Red Nacional de Ferrocarriles Españoles) es tan importante como las **líneas aéreas** en Estados Unidos. El AVE es el tren español de alta **velocidad** que conecta Madrid con otras grandes ciudades españolas y **viaja** a unos 300 kilómetros por hora.

El **crucero** es otra forma de viajar para hacer turismo. En **barcos** modernos con una capacidad de 400 hasta más de 2.000 **pasajeros,** se puede hacer de todo. En las **escalas** en los diferentes puertos hay excursiones organizadas y oportunidades para ir de compras. De noche, la diversión continúa en la discoteca, el casino o el teatro.

En el avión

Aunque (*Although*) más cara, la manera de viajar rápidamente de un lugar a otro es el **avión.** Hoy en día, se ofrecen **vuelos** domésticos entre muchas ciudades de los países hispanos. Se puede **volar** en **clase turista** o en **primera clase.** En esta foto, el **auxiliar de vuelo** les sirve bebidas a los **viajeros.**

> **En otras palabras**
>
> Other words for **auxiliar de vuelo** are **azafato/a,** used especially in Spain, and **aeromozo/a,** used mostly in Latin America. To buy a ticket in Latin America, you will most likely hear people use the terms **pasaje** or **boleto,** whereas in Spain the word **billete** is more common.

En el aeropuerto

Antes de **subir** al avión, los pasajeros **hacen cola** frente al **mostrador** de la **aerolínea** para **facturar** el **equipaje.** Muchos prefieren pedir el **asiento** y conseguir la **tarjeta de embarque** por internet.

En el mostrador de la línea aérea

EMPLEADA: Buenos días. Su **pasaporte** y su **boleto,** por favor.

VIAJERO: Aquí están. Y si es posible, prefiero un asiento cerca de una **salida de emergencia.**

EMPLEADA: Muy bien. ¿Prefiere usted un asiento **de ventanilla** o **de pasillo?**

VIAJERO: De pasillo. Por favor, ¿me puede decir dónde hay un **cajero automático** aquí en el aeropuerto?

EMPLEADA: Sí, hay una oficina del Banco Popular enfrente, a la derecha.

VIAJERO: Gracias. ¿Me acreditó las millas a mi programa de viajero frecuente?

EMPLEADA: Sí, y su **pasaje** es **de ida y vuelta,** así que va a tener bastantes millas. Su asiento a San José es el 10F. Aquí tiene su tarjeta de embarque. La **puerta de salida** es la C20. ¡Que tenga un buen viaje!

PRÁCTICA

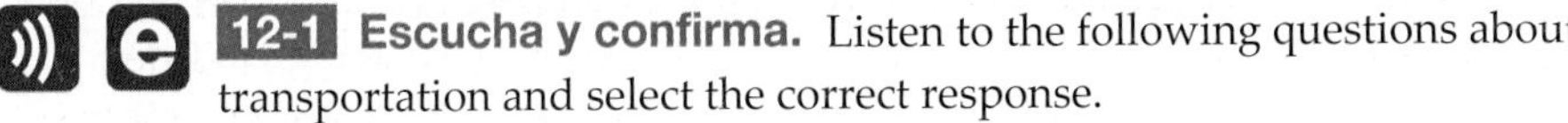

12-1 Escucha y confirma. Listen to the following questions about transportation and select the correct response.

1. **a.** el metro — **b.** el autobús
2. **a.** el AVE — **b.** la RENFE
3. **a.** el crucero — **b.** el avión
4. **a.** facturar el equipaje — **b.** hacer escalas
5. **a.** en el mostrador — **b.** en el cajero automático
6. **a.** el boleto de ida y vuelta — **b.** el pasaporte

En otras palabras

Depending on the region, different words for **autobús** are used: **camión** (Mexico), **ómnibus** (Peru), **bus, guagua** (Puerto Rico, Cuba), **colectivo** (Argentina), **micro** (Chile), and **chiva** (Colombia).

12-2 Asociaciones. Selecciona la palabra o frase que corresponde a cada descripción. Luego, compara tus respuestas con las de tu compañero/a y dile qué medio de transporte prefieres y por qué.

1. _____ transporte público para viajar por las calles de la ciudad
2. _____ viaje en un barco grande de pasajeros
3. _____ persona que atiende a los pasajeros en un vuelo
4. _____ transporte subterráneo
5. _____ lugar de inspección al llegar a otro país
6. _____ identificación necesaria para viajar al extranjero
7. _____ pasaje para ir y volver
8. _____ se viaja en un asiento cómodo y se come bien

a. auxiliar de vuelo
b. pasaporte
c. primera clase
d. autobús
e. metro
f. aduana
g. boleto de ida y vuelta
h. crucero

 **12-3 Salidas y llegadas.** Miren los horarios y la puerta de salida de los siguientes vuelos y háganse preguntas.

MODELO E1: *¿A qué hora sale el vuelo para San José?*
E2: *Sale a las tres y media por la puerta 1A.*

NÚMERO DE VUELO FLIGHT NUMBER	SALIDA DEPARTURE	ABORDAR BOARDING	PUERTA GATE	DESTINO DESTINATION
AA 652	3:30	2:45	1A	SAN JOSÉ
AV 30	3:50	3:05	4	MANAGUA
IB 993	4:10	3:25	6	GUATEMALA
AA 743	4:25	3:40	10	PANAMÁ
DL 78	4:45	4:00	8	LIMÓN
B6 55	5:10	4:25	5	MÉXICO
DL 46	6:00	5:15	5	KINGSTON

 **12-4 Problemas en los viajes.** Túrnense para completar las conversaciones y resolver los problemas.

MODELO E1: *Estoy en Madrid y tengo que ir a Barcelona inmediatamente.*
E2: *Te recomiendo que tomes el AVE. El tren va muy rápido.*

Estudiante 1	Estudiante 2
1. No me gusta manejar en las ciudades grandes. ¿Qué hago?	No hay problema. En las ciudades grandes, hay… Te recomiendo que tomes…
2. No pude imprimir mi tarjeta de embarque en casa porque no tengo internet. ¿Qué hago?	No te preocupes. Al llegar al aeropuerto, tienes que… Si tienes móvil, te aconsejo que…
3. Tengo miedo de viajar por avión, pero quiero ir de Chicago a Seattle.	Si te gustan los paisajes espectaculares pero no quieres manejar, te sugiero que…
4. Dejé mi pasaporte en casa y mi vuelo para San José sale en cuatro horas.	¡Ay, qué problema! Te aconsejo que…

Cultura

Parque Nacional de Isla del Coco El Parque Nacional Isla del Coco se encuentra en el océano Pacífico a unos 550 kilómetros de la costa costarricense. Es un espacio protegido y una reserva natural con numerosas especies animales y vegetales endémicas. Los visitantes llegan atraídos por la naturaleza salvaje (*wild*) y limpia con el deseo de descansar. La isla está llena de bosques y cascadas donde se puede pescar y caminar. Solo se puede llegar a la isla por barco en un viaje que dura unas 36 horas. Por su interés natural, viven allí numerosos biólogos e investigadores del medio ambiente (*environment*). El turismo está muy regulado para proteger el ecosistema.

Comparaciones ¿Existe en tu país un parque nacional de características similares a las del Parque Nacional Isla del Coco? ¿Qué parque nacional de tu país te gusta más? ¿Por qué? ¿Qué hay en este parque?

12-5 Haciendo turismo en Costa Rica o Panamá. Tu compañero/a y tú quieren viajar a Costa Rica o Panamá. Seleccionen su destino y usen la información cultural del capítulo para planear su itinerario. Incluyan la información de la lista. Después, presenten su itinerario a la clase y digan por qué eligieron ese destino.

Itinerario:

1. destino y por qué lo seleccionaron
2. lugares que van a visitar
3. fechas de viaje (número de días)
4. tipo de boleto aéreo (primera clase o clase turista) y asiento (ventanilla, etc.) y por qué lo seleccionaron
5. medio de transporte que prefieren utilizar en el lugar
6. sus actividades

El alojamiento y las direcciones

En la recepción

EMPLEADA: Buenas tardes. ¿En qué les puedo servir?

SRA. CANO: Buenas tardes. Tenemos dos **habitaciones** reservadas a nuestro nombre, señor y señora Cano.

EMPLEADA: Sí, señora. Aquí veo que **reservaron** una **doble** y una **sencilla.**

SRA. CANO: Muy bien. Una es para nosotros y la otra para nuestro hijo. Quisiera dejar los pasaportes en un lugar seguro. **¿Podría** usted**...?**

EMPLEADA: ¿Por qué no los deja en la **caja fuerte** de su habitación?

SRA. CANO: Muy bien.

EMPLEADA: Bueno, aquí tiene sus **tarjetas magnéticas.** Ya no usamos **llaves.** Sus habitaciones están en el segundo piso.

SR. CANO: Y... ¿nos puede indicar cómo llegar a la Plaza de la Independencia?

EMPLEADA: Sí, cómo no. Mire, salgan del edificio y **doblen a la derecha. Sigan derecho** por esta calle hasta la próxima **esquina.** Allí, doblen **a la izquierda** y caminen una **cuadra** hasta la plaza que está a la derecha. No pueden **perderse.**

SR. CANO: Muchísimas gracias.

PRÁCTICA

12-6 Para confirmar. Estás perdido/a en Ciudad de Panamá. Usando el plano, pregúntale a una persona en la calle (tu compañero/a) cómo ir a ciertos lugares. Tu compañero/a debe explicarte cómo llegar.

MODELO Estás en el Palacio de las Garzas. Deseas ir al Teatro Nacional.
E1: *¿Me podría decir cómo llegar al Teatro Nacional, por favor?*
E2: *Sí, cómo no. Salga del Palacio de las Garzas y doble a la derecha. Siga derecho por dos cuadras. Doble a la derecha. Camine una cuadra y doble a la izquierda. El Teatro Nacional está en la Avenida B, esquina Calle 3ª (Tercera) Este.*

Estás en...	Deseas ir a...
la Plaza de la Independencia	el Palacio de las Garzas
el Palacio de las Garzas	la Plaza Simón Bolívar
la Plaza Simón Bolívar	el Museo del Canal Interoceánico de Panamá

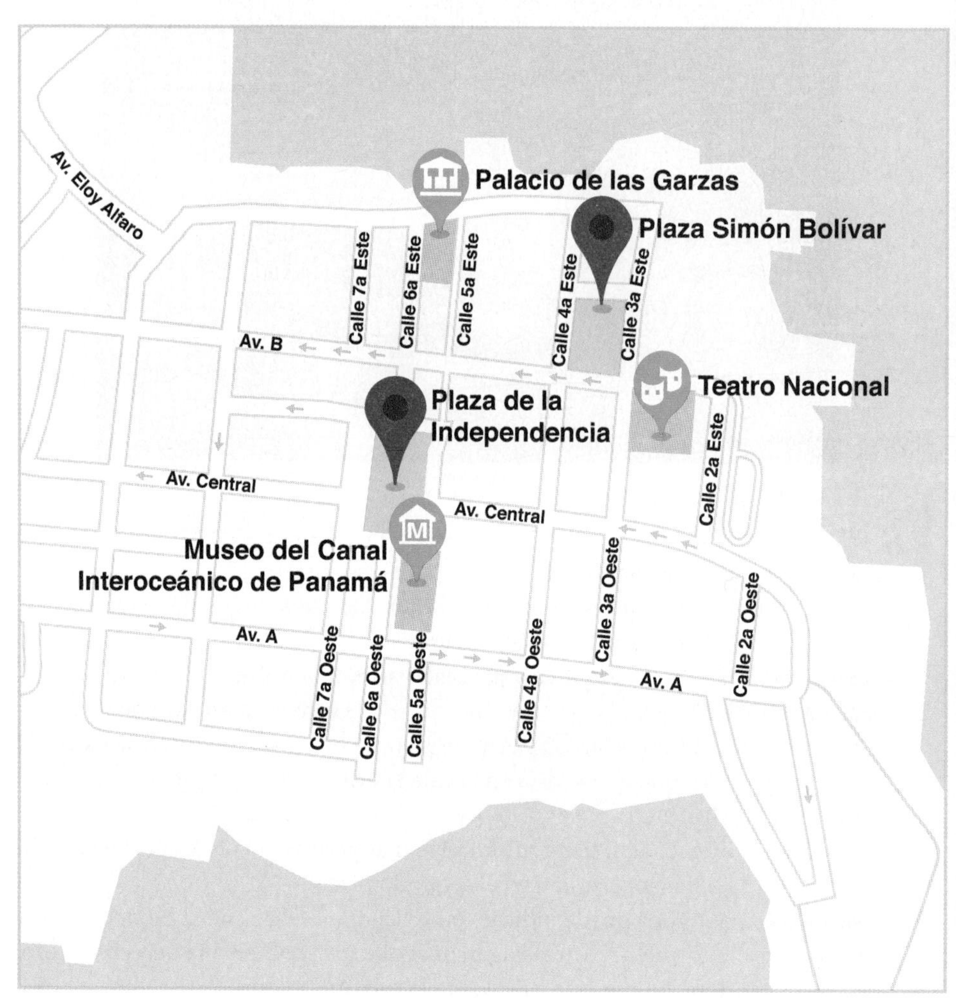

12-7 En el hotel. Túrnense para hacer el papel de recepcionista de hotel y cliente/a en las siguientes situaciones. Usen el vocabulario y las expresiones de la lista. Después, escojan una situación y preséntenla a la clase.

la caja fuerte	¿Dónde...?
el equipaje	¿Podría...?
una habitación doble/sencilla	Quisiera...
una reservación	
la tarjeta magnética	

	Cliente/a	Recepcionista
Situación 1	Llega al hotel y necesita una habitación.	Hace muchas preguntas.
Situación 2	Necesita una habitación con dos camas para él/ella y su amigo/a, pero no tiene reservación.	Solo tiene una habitación sencilla.
Situación 3	Quiere reservar una habitación por teléfono, pero no quiere dar su número de tarjeta de crédito.	Para garantizar la reservación, debe dar el número de tarjeta de crédito.

Cultura

Bocas del Toro Isla Colón es la isla principal del archipiélago de Bocas del Toro en el noroeste de Panamá. La ciudad principal lleva el nombre del archipiélago. Esta ciudad es uno de los centros turísticos más importantes de Panamá. Se puede llegar a ella por barco o avión, pues tiene un aeropuerto internacional. Los turistas viajan a Isla Colón durante todo el año atraídos por las playas y el buen clima. Una atracción turística importante es el surf y la práctica de deportes acuáticos.

Comparaciones ¿Prefieres pasar tus vacaciones cerca del mar o en otro lugar? Compara las ventajas o desventajas de pasar las vacaciones en la playa, en la montaña o en otro lugar.

12-8 Un correo electrónico. Estás en Panamá y le envías un mensaje a tu compañero/a. Cuéntale algunos aspectos especiales de tus experiencias. Tu compañero/a contesta tu mensaje y te hace preguntas para obtener más detalles.

1. lugar(es) que visitaste
2. lugar donde te quedaste y el tipo de alojamiento
3. personas que conociste
4. experiencias divertidas o especiales que viviste
5. comida nueva que probaste
6. regalos que compraste

Los viajes en coche

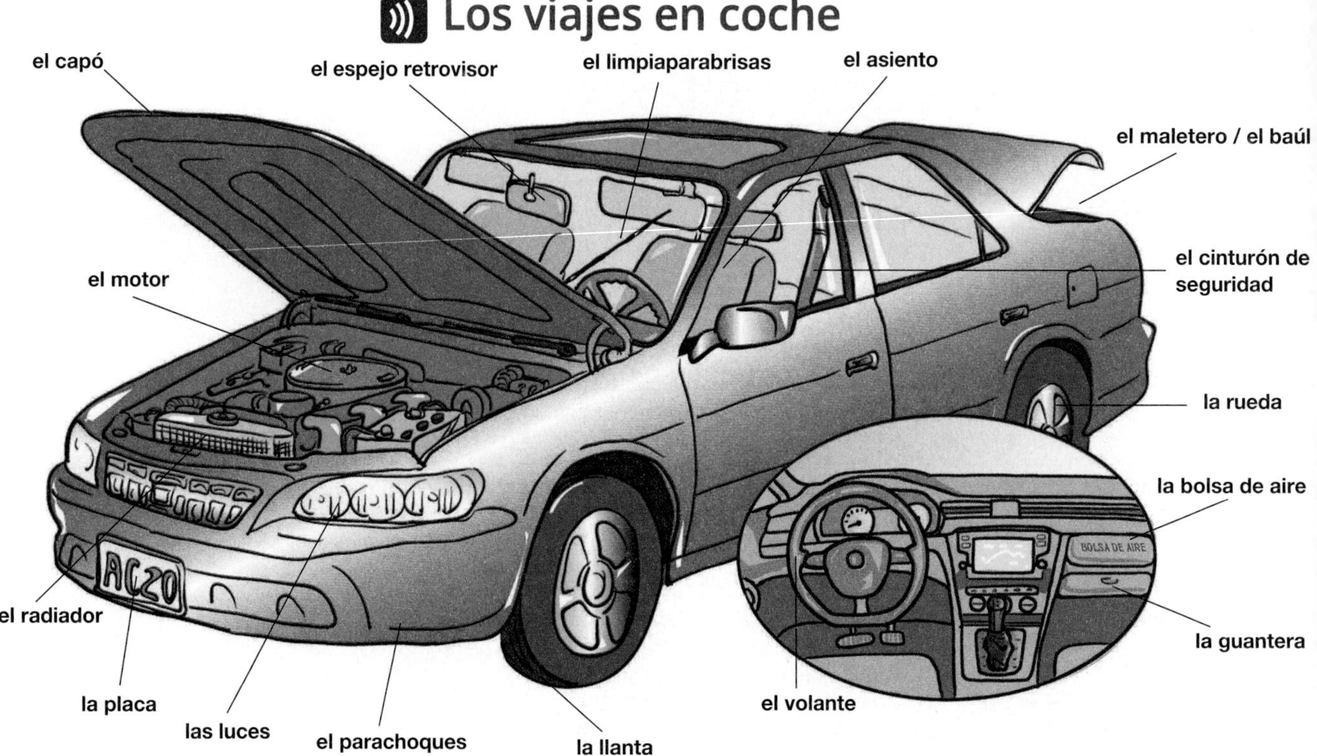

Un episodio desafortunado

Cuando estaba en la calle Losada, mi auto **se descompuso.** Por las **luces** de la consola, pensé que era el **radiador** o el **motor.** Puse las manos al **volante** y quise limpiar el **parabrisas,** pero el **limpiaparabrisas** no funcionaba y el motor se apagó. Saqué el manual de la **guantera.** Traté de **bajarme** del carro, pero por el **espejo retrovisor** vi que venía una larga fila de vehículos. Puse las **luces intermitentes.** Me bajé para abrir el **capó** y vi un carro patrulla de la policía. Sin decirme una palabra, el policía tomó nota de la **placa** de mi carro. Luego, me pidió la **licencia de conducir.** Intenté explicarle que tenía problemas eléctricos con el carro, pero me puso una **multa** por estar **mal aparcado.**

> **En otras palabras**
>
> The word for *license plate* differs from one region to another. **La placa** is used in Mexico, Central America, and parts of South America. In Chile and Argentina, **la patente** is used. In Cuba it is **la chapa**, and in Puerto Rico it is **la tablilla**.

PRÁCTICA

12-9 Para confirmar. Identifiquen la palabra que corresponde a cada descripción. Después, describan otras partes del coche para ver si otra pareja sabe cómo se llama cada una.

1. Es para poner el equipaje.
2. Permite ver bien cuando llueve.
3. Son negras y llevan aire por dentro.
4. Controla la dirección del coche.
5. Tiene letras y números, y sirve para identificar el coche.
6. Le permite al conductor ver los carros que vienen detrás.
7. Se abre para ver el motor, el radiador, etc.
8. Protege al coche en caso de accidentes.
9. Se activan durante un choque o accidente para proteger al conductor y a los pasajeros.

12-10 Mi auto favorito. Averigüen qué medio de transporte usa cada uno/a de ustedes con más frecuencia. Después, pregúntense cuál es el auto favorito de cada uno/a y por qué. Cada persona debe decir cuatro características del auto para explicar su preferencia.

Cultura

Los autos y el transporte público Aunque en los países hispanoamericanos se usa mucho el transporte público, el tráfico y la contaminación son problemas serios en las ciudades grandes. Además, cada vez es más difícil encontrar estacionamiento. Por eso, se usan mucho las motos y los carros pequeños. En ciudades como Bogotá, en Colombia, se han establecido medidas (*measures*) como el "pico y placa", que limita el acceso de los carros a la ciudad según el último número de la placa.

Comunidades ¿Qué medios de transporte hay en tu comunidad? ¿Cuáles son más populares entre los jóvenes? ¿Cuáles son más populares entre los mayores? ¿Qué problemas se asocian con el transporte en tu comunidad y tu región?

12-11 Para evitar accidentes. Escriban un anuncio con recomendaciones para evitar accidentes de tráfico. El anuncio debe tener la siguiente información:

1. un título o eslogan
2. el nombre de la compañía o grupo que patrocina (*sponsors*) el anuncio
3. tres recomendaciones para evitar accidentes

12-12 Antes de viajar.

PREPARACIÓN. You will listen to a conversation between a woman who is checking in at the airport and an airline employee. Before you listen, write two questions you think the employee will ask her and the answers you think the woman will provide. Compare your answers with those of your partner.

ESCUCHA. Now listen to the exchange, and choose the appropriate ending for each statement.

1. El empleado le pide a la viajera…
   a. su boleto de ida y vuelta.
   b. su tarjeta de embarque.
   (c.) su pasaporte y su pasaje.
2. La viajera va a facturar…
   a. tres maletas.
   b. equipaje de mano.
   (c.) dos maletas.
3. La viajera prefiere un asiento…
   a. al lado de la ventanilla.
   (b.) de pasillo.
   c. en la parte posterior del avión.
4. El empleado le puede conseguir un asiento…
   (a.) de pasillo, el 28C.
   b. de centro, entre la ventanilla y el pasillo.
   c. de la ventanilla, en primera clase.
5. El empleado le dice a la pasajera que…
   (a.) debe pasar por seguridad rápidamente.
   b. no va a tomar mucho tiempo pasar por seguridad.
   c. no tiene que pasar por seguridad.

Mosaico cultural

El mochilero

Cuando Sebastián celebró su cumpleaños número 22 —al mismo tiempo que terminó la universidad— decidió hacer un viaje por los lugares más atractivos del mundo hispano. En junio, Sebastián tomó su mochila, que estaba cargada con poca ropa y sus utensilios de *camping,* y se fue de viaje con poco dinero.

Sebastián decidió hacer algo común entre los jóvenes hispanos: ser mochilero. El plan de mochilero significaba viajar sin muchas complicaciones, adaptándose a las circunstancias inmediatas. Sebastián tomaba el transporte disponible (*available*) y dormía en los lugares donde le permitían usar su tienda (*tent*), o en hoteles baratos. "Fue un periodo muy bonito, conocí a mucha gente linda y aprendí mucho de la cultura de varios lugares que no conocía", dijo Sebastián.

Hotel barato en Bocas del Toro, Panamá

Para empezar, Sebastián tomó un autobús que lo llevó desde su casa en San José de Costa Rica hasta Bocas del Toro, en Panamá. Allí se alojó por dos días en un hostal donde conoció a un par de mochileros norteamericanos que estaban de visita. Luego de dos días y muchas experiencias, Sebastián salió para Colombia. Este viaje le tomó cuatro días, porque lo hizo haciendo dedo (haciendo autostop). Sebastián se ponía al lado de las autopistas y esperaba que alguien lo llevara hasta su destino. Es una forma arriesgada (*risky*) de viajar porque no es muy eficiente y puede ser peligrosa, pero es mucho más económica que comprar boletos de avión. Cuando llegó a Colombia, Sebastián le envió una postal a su mamá: "Mami, estoy en Cartagena de Indias y ¡me encanta! Monté en bus, canoa, bicitaxi y ¡en un burro (*donkey*)!". Después de recorrer Colombia, viajó hasta Perú. En Perú, caminó 43 kilómetros por el Camino Inca, la ruta más famosa del continente americano, que va desde Cuzco hasta Machu Picchu. Esta ruta va entre bosques y montañas espectaculares. La recompensa (*reward*) por este esfuerzo fueron las espléndidas vistas de las ruinas incaicas.

Subiendo a la cima de Machu Picchu

Compara

1. ¿En tu cultura hay una palabra equivalente a **mochilero?** ¿En qué contextos se usa?
2. ¿Es algo común hacer dedo/autostop en tu país? ¿Lo has hecho? Explica con detalles.
3. En tu cultura, ¿existe un viaje simbólico que hacen los jóvenes para marcar la transición a la edad adulta? Explícalo con ejemplos.
4. ¿Te gustaría tener la experiencia de viajar como mochilero/a? ¿Qué lugares te gustaría visitar y qué precauciones es importante que tomes?

En acción

Lugares fantásticos

Antes de ver

12-13 De viaje. Vas de vacaciones a un lugar que nunca has visitado. Indica las tres actividades más importantes que debes hacer antes de llegar allí.

1. _____ hacer una reservación de hotel
2. _____ comprar un mapa del lugar
3. _____ buscar información en internet sobre los sitios más representativos
4. _____ hablar con alguien que viva allí
5. _____ hacer las maletas
6. _____ despedirte de tus amigos
7. _____ comprar ropa para el viaje

Mientras ves

12-14 Lugares inolvidables. En este segmento, se describen tres lugares de interés turístico. Mira el video e indica si las siguientes afirmaciones se refieren a las cataratas del Iguazú (**I**), Costa Rica (**CR**) o San Francisco (**SF**).

1. _____ Vanesa siempre ha querido visitar este lugar.
2. _____ Hay un río que pasa por tres países distintos.
3. _____ Es muy popular por su ecoturismo.
4. _____ Las corrientes (*currents*) son muy fuertes.
5. _____ Una de sus atracciones más conocidas es un enorme puente que cruza la bahía.
6. _____ Muchas personas van a este lugar para hacer surf.
7. __I__ Su nombre viene de una palabra guaraní que significa "agua grande".

Después de ver

12-15 Lugares y preferencias.

PREPARACIÓN. Indica si las siguientes afirmaciones se refieren a Esteban (**E**), a Vanesa (**V**) o a Federico (**F**).

1. _____ Prefiere los sitios que tienen vida nocturna.
2. _____ Le encantan los sitios donde se puede hacer surf.
3. _____ Muestra mucho orgullo (*pride*) al hablar de la industria turística en su país.

INTERCAMBIOS. Tienen la oportunidad de hacer un video para promocionar un lugar especial. Escojan el lugar y digan por qué es especial. Indiquen qué actividades pueden hacer las personas allí. Escriban un eslogan para promocionarlo.

1 Expressing affirmation and negation

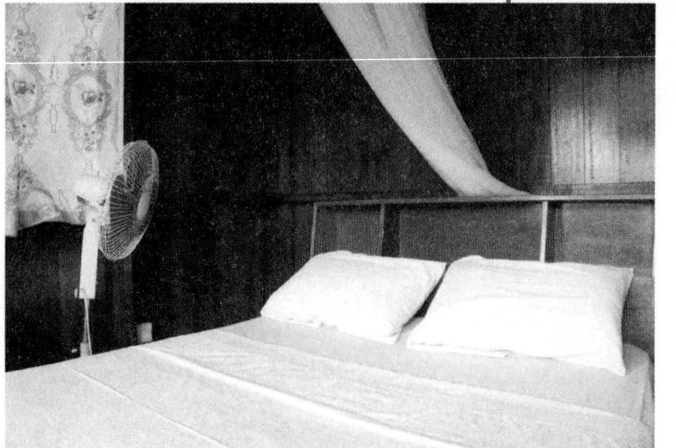

JOSEFINA: Elián, tenemos que hablar de nuestro viaje a Costa Rica. **Siempre** intento buscar alojamiento económico, pero no me gusta **ningún** hotel de pasalobienconpoco.com. **Todos** parecen viejos y malos. Muy pocas veces encuentro **algo** bueno en ese sitio web. No voy a usarlo más.

ELIÁN: A mí **tampoco** me gusta ese sitio. **Nunca** encuentro **nada** que me guste. ¿Por qué no le pedimos una recomendación a tu amiga Marisela? Es de San José, ¿no?

JOSEFINA: Buena idea. Seguramente tendrá **algunas** recomendaciones.

Piénsalo. Indica quién dice las afirmaciones: Josefina (**J**) o Elián (**E**). Luego, indica si cada palabra en negrita (*bold*) es una expresión afirmativa (**A**) o negativa (**N**).

	¿QUIÉN LO DICE?	¿AFIRMATIVA O NEGATIVA?
1. **Siempre** intento buscar alojamiento económico.	_____	_____
2. No me gusta **ningún** hotel de pasalobienconpoco.com.	_____	_____
3. **Todos** parecen viejos y malos.	_____	_____
4. A mí **tampoco** me gusta ese sitio.	_____	_____
5. **Nunca** encuentro **nada** que me guste.	_____	_____
6. Seguramente tendrá **algunas** recomendaciones.	_____	_____

Affirmative and negative expressions

- You have already seen and used some affirmative and negative expressions in previous chapters. In this section, you will study the most frequently used expressions.

AFFIRMATIVE		NEGATIVE	
algo	*something, anything*	**nada**	*nothing*
todo	*everything*		
alguien	*someone, anyone*	**nadie**	*no one, nobody*
todos/as	*everybody, all*		
algún, alguno/a/os/as	*some, any, several*	**ningún, ninguno/a**	*no, not any, none*
o... o	*either . . . or*	**ni... ni**	*neither . . . nor*
siempre	*always*	**nunca/jamás**	*never, (not) ever*
una vez	*once*		
alguna vez	*sometime, ever*		
algunas veces	*sometimes*		
a veces	*at times*		
también	*also, too*	**tampoco**	*neither, not*

- Negative words may precede or follow the verb. If they follow the verb, use the word **no** before the verb.

Nadie va a ese museo. **No** va **nadie** a ese museo.	*No one / Nobody goes to that museum.*

- **Alguno** and **ninguno** shorten to **algún** and **ningún** before masculine singular nouns.

¿Ves **algún** monumento interesante?	*Do you see any interesting monuments?*
No veo **ningún** monumento interesante.	*I do not see any interesting monuments.*

- Use the personal **a** when **alguno/a/os/as** and **ninguno/a** refer to persons and are the direct object of the verb. Use it also with **alguien** and **nadie** since they always refer to people. Note that negative statements are expressed in the singular.

¿Conoces **a alguno** de los guías?	*Do you know any of the guides?*
No, no conozco **a ninguno.**	*No, I do not know any (of them).*
¿Conoces **algunas** agencias de turismo?	*Do you know any tourism agencies?*
No, no conozco **ninguna.**	*No, I do not know any (of them).*

¿Comprendes? Completa las afirmaciones para expresar lo contrario.

1. Josefina **siempre** intenta buscar alojamiento económico. Pero Daniel y Nora _______ buscan alojamiento económico. Prefieren los hoteles de lujo (*luxury*).
2. No me gusta **ningún** hotel de este sitio web porque son feos y malos. Pero a Marcos le gustan _______ porque no tiene mucho dinero.
3. **Nunca** encuentro **nada** que me guste. Marisela tiene mejor suerte. Ella _______ encuentra _______ hoteles que le gustan.
4. **Algunos** de mis amigos se alojan en albergues juveniles (*youth hostels*) cuando viajan. Pero _______ amigo de mis padres se aloja allí. _______ prefieren los hoteles.

PRÁCTICA

12-16 Nada de nada.

PREPARACIÓN. Selecciona la respuesta que corresponde a cada pregunta. Luego, compara tus respuestas con las de tu compañero/a.

1. _____ ¿Has visitado Panamá alguna vez?
2. _____ ¿Conoces a alguien en Costa Rica?
3. _____ ¿Bailas algún baile típico de la región?
4. _____ ¿Conoce alguien de tu familia al autor de la novela *El último tango de Salvador Allende?*
5. _____ ¿Conoces alguna canción de Maribel Guardia?

a. No, ninguna.
b. No, ninguno.
c. No, nadie.
d. No, a nadie.
e. No, nunca.

INTERCAMBIOS. Preparen tres preguntas similares a las de **Preparación.** Luego, háganselas a otra pareja.

 **12-17 ¿Con qué frecuencia?** Indica con qué frecuencia haces cada una de las siguientes actividades y explica por qué las haces. Después conversa con tu compañero/a sobre sus actividades.

MODELO ver una película en español

E1: *Veo una película en español todas las semanas porque me gusta escuchar la lengua. ¿Y tú qué haces?*

E2: *Yo nunca veo películas en español porque no me gustan los subtítulos.*

Actividad	Yo: Frecuencia/Razón	Compañero/a: Frecuencia/Razón
1. viajar a otros países		
2. comprar pasajes de avión o tren en internet		
3. ir de vacaciones con amigos/as		
4. usar transporte público		
5. hacer reservaciones usando una aplicación (*app*)		
6. manejar un carro		
7. ver películas extranjeras		

Cultura

Ecoturismo Costa Rica y Panamá han decidido apostar por (*bet on*) un ecoturismo de calidad en vez de un turismo de masas. Apoyado en una estabilidad política y económica singular dentro de la zona, Costa Rica fue el país pionero, uno de los primeros en crear una extensa red (*network*) de parques naturales y áreas protegidas donde se respetan la biodiversidad y el equilibrio medioambiental (*environmental*). Hoy en día esta red ocupa casi el 25% de la superficie total del país gracias a las decisiones del gobierno costarricense en los años 80.

Comparaciones ¿Prefieres hacer ecoturismo o turismo convencional? Compara las ventajas y desventajas de cada uno.

Haciendo senderismo (*hiking*) en un bosque tropical

 **12-18 Una excursión de ecoturismo.** Estás en Costa Rica para hacer una excursión de ecoturismo. Tu compañero/a ya hizo la excursión y piensa que fue un desastre. Él/Ella va a contestar tus preguntas negativamente. Añade una pregunta más.

MODELO ofrecer excursiones

E1: *¿Ofrecieron excursiones para ver la fauna y la flora?*

E2: *No, no ofrecieron ninguna excursión.*

1. poder observar tortugas en la playa
2. tomar fotos de las vistas panorámicas
3. comer un almuerzo típico costarricense
4. permitirte entrar a algunas áreas protegidas
5. hablar con un/a experto/a en ecología de la zona

12-19 ¡La negatividad es contagiosa! Después de pasar unas vacaciones con tu amigo/a, su negatividad te ha contagiado y contestas a todo negativamente. Túrnense para preguntarse y añadan alguna actividad más.

MODELO llamar a un amigo

E1: *¿Vas a llamar a un amigo?*

E2: *No, no voy a llamar a nadie. ¿Y tú vas a…?*

1. visitar Panamá alguna vez en el futuro
2. ver alguna película latinoamericana este fin de semana
3. leer un artículo sobre los siete pueblos indígenas de Panamá
4. invitar a alguien a ver un documental sobre Costa Rica
5. hacer algo divertido en las próximas vacaciones

Cultura

Comarca Guna Yala Guna Yala, conocida como San Blas hasta 1998, es una región de Panamá que incluye parte de la costa caribeña de Panamá y numerosas islas pequeñas a las que se accede en barco. Es la tierra de los gunas, un pueblo indígena que ha luchado por sus derechos sobre la tierra. En estas islas se mantienen activas tradiciones locales relacionadas con la agricultura y la pesca, y se ha desarrollado también una industria turística basada en el ecoturismo.

Comunidades ¿Existen en tu país comunidades como las de Guna Yala? ¿Qué tradiciones tienen? ¿Qué actividades se asocian con esta comunidad?

Casas de Guna Yala

12-20 Planeando un viaje.

PREPARACIÓN. Quieren hacer un viaje a Panamá para conocer su cultura. Comenten qué van a hacer allí.

MODELO pasar unos días en la capital

E1: *Quiero pasar unos días en la capital.*

E2: *Yo también. Es una ciudad interesante.*

1. conocer la comarca Guna Yala
2. comprar unas molas, hechas por artesanas gunas
3. hacer una excursión al canal de Panamá
4. tomar una clase de cumbia, un baile folclórico
5. asistir a un partido de fútbol

INTERCAMBIOS. Conversen sobre dos o tres actividades que quieren hacer en Panamá. Después, reúnanse con otros dos estudiantes para explicarles sus planes y escuchar los planes de ellos. Respondan negativamente a los planes de la otra pareja.

MODELO pasar cuatro días en la capital

E1: *Daniel y yo vamos a pasar unos días en la capital primero.*

E2: *Eva y yo no vamos a pasar ningún día en la capital. Preferimos conocer el resto del país. Todas las capitales son similares.*

Situación

PREPARACIÓN. Lean esta situación. Luego, compartan ejemplos de vocabulario, gramática y otra información que necesitan para desarrollar la conversación.

Role A. You are planning a trip to Panama. You call a travel agency to purchase tickets for an all-day excursion in Panama City (**Ciudad de Panamá**). When the clerk answers, ask:
a. if sometimes they offer free tickets for students;
b. if they have any tickets for Friday or Saturday; and
c. whether lunch at a restaurant is included in the price.
You may express your annoyance at all the negative answers you receive when you thank the clerk for his/her help.

Role B. You work in a travel agency. A customer calls to ask about tickets for an excursion in Panama City (**Ciudad de Panamá**). Reply that:
a. they never give free tickets to anyone (not students, not young children);
b. there aren't any tickets for the days the customer is inquiring about; and
c. there will be two breaks for snacks (**meriendas**), but not a restaurant meal.
You are annoyed and you let it show during the conversation.

	ROLE A	ROLE B
Vocabulario	Question words Travel vocabulary	Travel vocabulary
Funciones y formas	Asking questions Expressing annoyance in a business setting Expressions of negation	Giving information Expressing annoyance in a business setting Expressions of negation

INTERCAMBIOS. Practiquen la conversación, incorporando el vocabulario y las funciones de **Preparación.** Luego, represéntenla ante la clase.

2 Expressing possession

MADRE: Ramiro, mi maleta casi está lista. ¿Y **la tuya?**

RAMIRO: ¡**La mía** no! Después del programa la empaco. ¿Ya empacaste tus libros, mamá?

MADRE: **Los míos** ya están en mi equipaje de mano. ¿Y las muñecas (*dolls*) de Susana?

RAMIRO: **Las suyas** están en su mochila, pero **las de** Laurita no sé dónde están.

Piénsalo. Lee las siguientes afirmaciones de la conversación de Ramiro y su madre. Indica a qué se refieren las palabras en negrita (*bold*).

1. "¡**La mía** no!" **La mía** se refiere…
   a. al programa de Ramiro. **b.** a la maleta de Ramiro.
2. "**Los míos** ya están en mi equipaje de mano". **Los míos** se refiere a…
   a. los libros de la madre. **b.** las muñecas de Susana.
3. "**Las suyas** están en su mochila". **Las suyas** se refiere…
   a. al equipaje de mano. **b.** a las muñecas de Susana.
4. "**Las de Laurita** no sé dónde están". **Las de Laurita** se refiere a…
   a. sus libros. **b.** sus muñecas.

Possessive pronouns

- Possessive pronouns express ownership or possession. They are used to avoid repetition of the noun to which they refer.

SINGULAR				PLURAL			
	Masculine		Feminine		Masculine		Feminine
el	mío	la	mía	los	míos	las	mías
	tuyo		tuya		tuyos		tuyas
	suyo		suya		suyos		suyas
	nuestro		nuestra		nuestros		nuestras
	vuestro		vuestra		vuestros		vuestras

- The definite article precedes the possessive pronoun, and both article and pronoun agree in gender and number with the noun to which they refer.

¿Tienes la mochila de Mario? — *Do you have Mario's backpack?*
Sí, tengo **la suya** y **la mía** también. — *Yes, I have his and mine too.*

- After the verb **ser,** the article is usually omitted.

Esa maleta es **mía.** — *That suitcase is mine.*

- To be clearer and more specific, the following structures may be used to replace any corresponding form of **el/la suyo/a.**

la de usted	*yours* (singular)
la de él	*his*
la de ella	*hers*
la mochila suya → **la suya**	
la de ustedes	*yours* (plural)
la de ellos	*theirs* (masculine, plural)
la de ellas	*theirs* (feminine, plural)

Lengua

Stressed possessive adjectives, which have the same forms as possessive pronouns, emphasize to whom a particular object belongs. Because they are adjectives, they always immediately follow the noun to which they refer. They are often used to emphasize a contrast.

El cuarto mío es grandísimo. — *My room is very big. (but someone else's is not)*
La maleta tuya está en la recepción. — *Your suitcase is at the front desk. (and other suitcases are in a different place)*
Las llaves nuestras están encima del escritorio. — *Our keys are on the desk. (but someone else's keys are not)*
Los primos míos llegan hoy. — *My cousins arrive today. (but someone else's cousins arrive on a different day)*

e **¿Comprendes?** Indica el pronombre posesivo correcto.

1. mi maleta: _____ _______
2. los pasajes de ustedes: _____ _______
3. nuestras llaves: _____ _______
4. el viaje de ellos: _____ _______
5. tus planes: _____ _______
6. el equipaje de Daniela y Sara: _____ _______

PRÁCTICA

12-21 ¿De quién(es) son estas cosas?

PREPARACIÓN. En la clase de español hacen un viaje a Costa Rica. En este momento van a tomar el bus para ir al aeropuerto. Contesta las preguntas y compara tus respuestas con las de tu compañero/a.

1. Miguel, ¿es tuya esta mochila?	**a.** Sí, es mía.	**b.** Sí, es tuya.
2. ¿Son estas maletas de Paco?	**a.** Sí, son suyas.	**b.** Sí, son mías.
3. ¿El equipaje rojo es de Alicia?	**a.** No, es tuya.	**b.** No, no es suyo.
4. Este mapa de San José, ¿es tuyo?	**a.** Sí, es mía.	**b.** Sí, es mío.
5. ¿Son nuestros estos boletos?	**a.** Sí, son suyos.	**b.** Sí, son suyas.

INTERCAMBIOS. Ve por la clase y pregunta a varios compañeros/as de quién son algunos de los objetos que ves o encuentras.

MODELO E1: *Esta mochila, ¿es tuya?*
E2: *No, es suya.*
E1: *¿De quién es?*
E2: *Es de Miguel.*

12-22 ¿Quién tiene auto? **PREPARACIÓN.** Entrevístense para saber quién(es) tiene(n) auto. Hablen de sus autos: marca, modelo, año y color. Tomen apuntes sobre la información.

MODELO E1: *Mi auto es un Toyota Corolla rojo del 2015. ¿Y el tuyo?*
E2: *El mío es un Ford Focus azul del 2012.*
E3: *Yo no tengo carro, pero mi hermana me presta el suyo a veces. Es muy viejo, pero funciona bien.*

INTERCAMBIOS. Combinen la información de todos los grupos y preparen un informe sobre las características más comunes de sus autos.

12-23 Preparándose para un viaje. Van a hacer un viaje en auto y deben tomar varias decisiones antes de salir. Háganse preguntas para decidir lo que van a hacer y den una razón.

MODELO usar mi coche o tu coche
E1: *¿Vamos a usar mi coche o el tuyo?*
E2: *Prefiero usar el tuyo porque es más nuevo.*

1. llevar tus maletas o las de mi hermano
2. llevar tu cámara o mi cámara
3. usar tu GPS o usar el GPS de mi teléfono
4. escuchar mi música o tu música en el auto
5. quedarnos en casa de mis primos o en la de tus primos

12-24 Recuerdos. **PREPARACIÓN.** Túrnense para hablar de sus experiencias favoritas. Compartan aspectos similares y diferentes de sus experiencias.

MODELO E1: *Mi viaje favorito fue a… ¿Y el tuyo?*
E2: *El mío fue a…*

1. un viaje que hiciste
2. una película que viste
3. un/a famoso/a a quien conociste
4. un hotel donde te alojaste
5. una comida que probaste

INTERCAMBIOS. Cuéntale a un/a compañero/a diferente las semejanzas y las diferencias entre el viaje tuyo y el de tu compañero/a en **Preparación.**

12-25 Objetos perdidos. Después del vuelo, tu compañero/a y tú no encuentran su equipaje. Vayan a la oficina de reclamaciones y descríbanle al agente cómo son sus maletas.

MODELO E1: *Nuestras maletas no llegaron.*
E2: *La mía es… / En la mía traigo…*
E1: *Sí, la suya es…, pero la mía…*
E3: *La suya viene en el próximo vuelo. La de… llega mañana.*

Situación

PREPARACIÓN. Lean esta situación. Luego, compartan ejemplos de vocabulario, gramática y otra información que necesitan para desarrollar la conversación.

Role A. On the plane home from an ecotourism trip to Costa Rica, you sit next to a student returning from a similar trip. Ask your seatmate:
a. why he/she went on an ecotourism trip;
b. what national park he/she liked best, and why;
c. one thing he/she learned from the trip; and
d. whether he/she has plans to return to Costa Rica.
Answer your seatmate's questions about your trip.

Role B. On the plane home from an ecotourism trip to Costa Rica, you sit next to a student returning from a similar trip. After answering your seatmate's questions, ask him/her similar questions about his/her trip. Comment on how your experience was similar to that of your seatmate.

	ROLE A	ROLE B
Vocabulario	Greetings Question words Vacation activities Ecotourism activities Future plans	Greetings Question words Vacation activities Ecotourism activities Future plans
Funciones y formas	Asking and answering questions about a past experience: Possessive pronouns Preterit Making small talk Talking about future plans	Asking and answering questions about a past experience: Possessive pronouns Preterit Making small talk Talking about future plans Comparisons of equality and inequality

INTERCAMBIOS. Practiquen la conversación, incorporando el vocabulario y las funciones de **Preparación.** Luego, represéntenla ante la clase.

3 Expressing doubt and uncertainty

ANGELINA: ¡Qué buenos son! Es evidente que **son** músicos talentosos. Es seguro que **ganan** el premio.

VÍCTOR: No estoy de acuerdo. No me parece que la cantante **sepa** cantar bien. Dudo que **lleguen** a la final del concurso.

ANGELINA: Son mejores que el grupo anterior. Es posible que **tengan** éxito, ¿no crees?

VÍCTOR: Creo que no. Tienen ritmo, pero no melodía. Es dudoso que **salgan** ganadores en la final.

Piénsalo. Indica si las siguientes afirmaciones expresan certeza (*certainty*) o duda (*doubt*). Luego, indica si el verbo en negrita (*bold*) es una forma del indicativo (**I**) o del subjuntivo (**S**).

	CERTEZA	DUDA	INDICATIVO O SUBJUNTIVO
1. Es evidente que **son** músicos talentosos.	_____	_____	_____
2. Es seguro que **ganan** el premio.	_____	_____	_____
3. No me parece que la cantante **sepa** cantar bien.	_____	_____	_____
4. Dudo que **lleguen** a la final del concurso.	_____	_____	_____
5. Es posible que **tengan** éxito.	_____	_____	_____
6. Es dudoso que **salgan** ganadores en la final.	_____	_____	_____

Subjunctive with expressions of doubt

You learned in *Capítulo 11* to use the subjunctive to express emotions, opinions, expectations, and wishes. In this chapter, you will learn to use the subjunctive for a related communicative function: to express doubt and uncertainty.

- When the verb in the main clause expresses doubt or uncertainty, use a subjunctive verb form in the dependent clause (the clause that begins with **que**).

Dudo que **vendan** periódicos en inglés aquí.	*I doubt (that) they sell English-language newspapers here.*
Es dudoso que el guía **llegue** tarde a la excursión.	*It's unlikely (that) the guide will arrive late to the tour.*

- Use the subjunctive with impersonal expressions that denote doubt or uncertainty, such as **es dudoso que, es difícil que, es probable que,** and **es posible que.**

Es dudoso que **encontremos** artesanías panameñas en ese mercado.	*It is doubtful that we will find Panamanian handicrafts in that market.*
Es posible que **tengan** telas.	*It is possible that they have textiles.*

- Use the indicative with impersonal expressions that denote certainty: **es cierto/verdad/evidente que, es seguro que,** and **es obvio que.** When these expressions are negative, the following verb is in the subjunctive.

Es verdad que el tamborito y la cumbia **son** bailes populares en Panamá.	*It is true that tamborito and cumbia are popular dances in Panama.*
No es cierto que los bailes panameños se **conozcan** mucho en Estados Unidos.	*It is not true that Panamanian dances are well known in the United States.*

- When the verbs **creer** and **pensar** are used in the negative, the subjunctive is used in the dependent clause. In questions with these verbs, the subjunctive may be used to express uncertainty or to anticipate a negative response.

SUBJUNCTIVE	
Hace sol. No creo que **llueva.**	*It is sunny out. I don't think it will rain.*
¿Piensas que **llueva** esta tarde?	*Do you think it will rain this afternoon?*
¿Crees que **haga** calor en San José?	*Do you think it is / will be hot in San José?* (I am not sure.)

- Since the expressions **tal vez** and **quizá(s)** convey uncertainty, the subjunctive is normally used.

Tal vez el conjunto **toque** un tamborito panameño.	*Perhaps the group will play a Panamanian tamborito.*
Quizás todos **empiecen** a bailar.	*Perhaps everyone will start to dance.*

e **¿Comprendes?** Completa las oraciones con la forma correcta de los verbos.

1. Es seguro que el avión _________ (llegar) tarde.
2. Es posible que _________ (llover) el día de la excursión.
3. Dudo que la compañía nos _________ (dar) boletos para otro día.
4. Creo que los autobuses _________ (tener) un horario diferente los domingos.
5. No es cierto que los choferes _________ (trabajar) siete días a la semana.
6. Quizás _________ (ser) mejor tomar un taxi.
7. Es verdad que los turistas _________ (divertirse) mucho en Costa Rica.

PRÁCTICA

12-26 ¿Están de acuerdo? **PREPARACIÓN.** Indica si estás de acuerdo o no con las siguientes opiniones. Luego, compara tus respuestas con las de tu compañero/a. Explíquense las razones de sus respuestas.

	SÍ	NO
1. Yo creo que los bailes folclóricos son fáciles de aprender.	_____	_____
2. Yo dudo que el transporte público sea más popular en Estados Unidos que en América Latina.	_____	_____
3. Creo que los parques nacionales de Costa Rica son muy importantes para la ecología del planeta.	_____	_____
4. Es posible que viajar por avión sea más caro que viajar por barco.	_____	_____
5. Es obvio que el precio de la gasolina en Estados Unidos afecta al turismo.	_____	_____
6. No creo que los estudiantes de hoy viajen menos a otros países que los estudiantes de hace 20 años.	_____	_____

INTERCAMBIOS. Contesten las siguientes preguntas relacionadas con los viajes. Compartan sus respuestas con la clase.

1. ¿Qué dos características básicas es importante que tenga el lugar adonde van de vacaciones?
2. ¿Qué prioridad dan a los siguientes factores al escoger un lugar para pasar las vacaciones? (1 = más importante, 6 = menos importante) ¿Por qué?

_____ el costo del viaje
_____ las costumbres del lugar
_____ la lengua que se habla
_____ las atracciones turísticas que ofrece
_____ la protección de la naturaleza
_____ la seguridad del lugar

En directo

To report agreement:

Todos creemos/pensamos que... *We all believe/think that . . .*

Nosotros estamos de acuerdo con que... *We all agree that . . .*

To report different opinions:

No hay consenso entre nosotros/ellos. Unos piensan que..., otros creen que... *We/They do not agree. Some think that . . ., others believe that . . .*

Listen to a conversation with these expressions.

12-27 Opinión, duda y certeza. Intercambien opiniones sobre las vacaciones, usando expresiones de duda y certeza. Después, comparen sus respuestas con las de otra pareja y compartan sus conclusiones con la clase. Usen las expresiones de la lista u otras.

(No) Creer que...	Es difícil/mejor/más... que...
Dudar que...	Es (im)posible/(im)probable que...
(No) Es cierto/verdad/evidente que...	

MODELO el lugar ideal para ir de vacaciones: la playa / las montañas / una ciudad

E1: *En tu opinión, ¿cuál es el lugar ideal para ir de vacaciones?*

E2: *Creo que el lugar ideal para ir de vacaciones es la playa. Es relajante caminar por la arena, nadar y tomar el sol. También es divertido conocer a otras personas. Y tú, ¿qué opinas?*

E3: *No creo que la playa sea mejor que las montañas. Yo prefiero estar cerca de los árboles y los animales. Para mí, es evidente que hay menos ruido en las montañas que en la playa.*

1. la compañía ideal para salir de vacaciones: los amigos / la familia / la pareja
2. la manera ideal de viajar: hacer dedo / hacer un crucero / viajar por avión, tren o auto
3. las actividades más entretenidas: mirar televisión / hacer deportes / ver espectáculos o exposiciones de arte / hacer ecoturismo

12-28 Un golpe de fortuna (*stroke of luck*). **PREPARACIÓN.** Ustedes ganaron un viaje de una semana a uno de los siguientes lugares. Escojan el lugar y hagan una lista de tres cosas que posiblemente ocurran y tres cosas que dudan que ocurran durante la semana.

MODELO Puntarenas, Costa Rica

E1: *Es posible que alguien nos invite a un club nocturno porque nos gusta mucho escuchar música y bailar.*

E2: *También es posible que vayamos de excursión al volcán Arenal porque es impresionante. Es importante que no llueva, porque queremos explorar el lugar.*

E3: *Dudamos que llueva, porque hace buen tiempo casi todo el año. Es probable que volvamos otra vez; nos encanta la naturaleza de Costa Rica. Es evidente que las personas la protegen mucho.*

América del Sur	América Central	El Caribe
Cusco, Perú	Islas San Blas, Panamá	La Habana, Cuba
Isla de Pascua, Chile	Península de Osa, Costa Rica	Punta Cana, República Dominicana

INTERCAMBIOS. Reúnanse con otro grupo para: a) contarles qué ciudad escogieron para ir de vacaciones y por qué; y b) compartir por lo menos tres expectativas y tres dudas que tienen antes de su viaje. Sus compañeros/as van a opinar sobre sus expectativas y dudas. Intercambien roles.

MODELO GRUPO 1: *Nosotros escogimos… porque… Creemos que es posible que… porque… Dudamos que… porque…*

GRUPO 2: *¡Qué interesante/aburrido/sorprendente* (surprising)*! Pero, ¿es verdad/cierto que…?*

12-29 Circunstancias imprevistas (*unforeseen*). Túrnense para explicarse cada situación que ocurre durante un viaje. Luego, intercambien opiniones y expresen incertidumbre y duda.

MODELO Te han robado (*stolen*) el pasaporte y solo te das cuenta (*realize*) cuando la policía te lo pide en un puesto de control (*checkpoint*).

E1: *¿Qué debo hacer si me han robado el pasaporte y solo me doy cuenta cuando la policía me lo pide?*

E2: *Creo que debes explicarle tu situación a la policía. Dudo que no te crea. Es evidente que no puedes viajar sin tu pasaporte. Es posible que la policía te sugiera ir pronto al consulado de tu país para obtener otro.*

E1: *¿Debo pagar por el nuevo pasaporte?*

E2: *Es seguro que tienes que pagar.*

Estudiante 1	Estudiante 2
1. Mientras haces ecoturismo, te atacan insectos que causan enfermedades. En minutos, tienes fiebre. **2.** Por un problema mecánico, tu vuelo no puede salir. La aerolínea te informa que debes esperar 18 horas en el aeropuerto hasta el próximo vuelo. **3.** Al facturar tu equipaje para regresar a tu país, te dicen que tus maletas pesan demasiado y que debes pagar una multa de 500 dólares, pero no tienes dinero.	**1.** Compraste comida en la calle y ahora estás muy enfermo/a. No hablas la lengua del lugar donde estás; por eso, tienes problemas para explicar cómo te sientes. **2.** El hotel donde te alojas es malísimo. Las habitaciones son feas y están sucias, y el servicio es muy malo. **3.** Tu vuelo se cancela en el último momento porque no hay suficientes pasajeros; no puedes llegar a una celebración importante.

12-30 Mensajes misteriosos. Ustedes están de vacaciones en Costa Rica y su amigo Felipe decide salir solo por dos días. Durante su ausencia, reciben estos mensajes de texto de Felipe. Para cada mensaje, indiquen lo que a ustedes les parece evidente y otro aspecto que, en su opinión, es dudoso. Las palabras clave pueden ser útiles.

Palabras clave
la ballena *whale*
el gallo pinto *rice and beans dish*
el mono *monkey*
el pájaro *bird*
la piscina termal *hot spring*
la soda *informal restaurant in Costa Rica*

MODELO Amigos, acabo de pedir tres gallos pintos. ¿Mucha comida? Tal vez... pero definitivamente esta es la mejor soda de Costa Rica.
E1: *Es evidente/seguro/obvio que Felipe tiene mucha hambre.*
E2: *Dudo / No creo / Es dudoso que Felipe pueda comer tres platos de gallo pinto.*

1. Chicos, ¡las rutas por el bosque son muy estrechas y es difícil caminar!
2. El guía dijo "antrópico". ¡¿Qué significa "antrópico"?!
3. ¡Impresionante! Los turistas tienen sus cámaras listas para tomarle fotos a este enorme animal marino.
4. Amigos, el mono está feliz con la botella en la mano. Jajaja. ¡Qué mono tan loco!
5. El volcán es altísimo y muy hermoso. Hay un lugar donde uno se puede bañar en agua muy caliente que viene del volcán.
6. ¡La vista del bosque! ¡Los pájaros y otros animales! La playa es hermosa. Envídienme. Voy a dormir un rato.

Situación

PREPARACIÓN. Lean esta situación. Luego, compartan ejemplos de vocabulario, gramática y otra información que necesitan para desarrollar la conversación.

Role A. A friend borrowed your car and brought it back a whole day later than the two of you had agreed, which caused you a lot of inconvenience. Ask your friend for an explanation. Express doubt about at least three reasons your friend gives you. To avoid ongoing conflict with your friend, make sure the situation is resolved.

Role B. You borrowed your friend's car, and you brought it back a whole day later than the two of you had agreed, which caused your friend a lot of inconvenience. Now you have to explain yourself. You don't want to tell the real reason, so you make up a detailed story of what happened. Your friend is skeptical, so you have to try hard to be convincing. To avoid ongoing conflict with your friend, make sure the situation is resolved.

	ROLE A	ROLE B
Vocabulario	Words and expressions related to travel	Words and expressions related to travel
Funciones y formas	Expressing doubts or disbelief: Subjunctive with expressions of doubt and disbelief Resolving a problem with a friend	Telling a story: Preterit and imperfect Making excuses Apologizing Resolving a problem with a friend

INTERCAMBIOS. Practiquen la conversación, incorporando el vocabulario y las funciones de **Preparación.** Luego, represéntenla ante la clase.

4 Talking about things that may not exist

MUJER: Perdón, ¿de qué andén (*platform*) **sale** el tren de las 9:00?

AGENTE: No hay trenes que **salgan** por la noche. El último tren salió a las 6:00 de la tarde.

MUJER: ¡Ay, Dios mío! ¿Hay un tren que **salga** temprano por la mañana?

AGENTE: Claro que sí. El primer tren sale a las 7:00.

MUJER: Bueno, voy a tener que esperar hasta mañana, entonces. ¿Me puede recomendar un hotel que **esté** cerca? Prefiero un hotel que no **sea** caro.

AGENTE: Sí, cómo no. Le recomiendo el Hotel Trópico. Es un buen hotel que **tiene** precios módicos (*reasonable*).

Piénsalo. Indica si las siguientes afirmaciones expresan algo que existe (**E**), algo que no existe (**NE**) o algo que posiblemente exista (**PE**). Luego, indica si el verbo en negrita (*bold*) es una forma del indicativo (**I**) o del subjuntivo (**S**).

	EXISTE	NO EXISTE / POSIBLEMENTE EXISTA	INDICATIVO O SUBJUNTIVO
1. ¿De qué andén **sale** el tren de las 9:00?	____	____	____
2. No hay trenes que **salgan** por la noche.	____	____	____
3. ¿Hay un tren que **salga** temprano por la mañana?	____	____	____
4. ¿Me puede recomendar un hotel que **esté** cerca?	____	____	____
5. Prefiero un hotel que no **sea** caro.	____	____	____
6. Es un buen hotel que **tiene** precios módicos.	____	____	____

Subjunctive in adjective clauses

As you have learned, the subjunctive in Spanish is used primarily in sentences that have two clauses. In this section, you will learn about using the subjunctive in adjective clauses.

Lengua

Que introduces a dependent clause, and it may refer to persons or things.

El cuarto **que** reservé es muy caro.	*The room I reserved is very expensive.*
Ese es el agente **que** me alquiló el coche.	*That is the agent who rented the car for me.*

When referring to people, use **quien(es)** after a preposition, such as **con, en, de, para, por,** etc.

Allí está el recepcionista **con quien** hablé esta mañana.	*There is the receptionist with whom I spoke this morning.*

- Both adjectives and adjective clauses provide descriptive information about a noun in the independent clause.

Vamos a ir a un hotel muy **moderno.** (ADJECTIVE)

Vamos a ir a un hotel **que es muy moderno.** (ADJECTIVE CLAUSE)

- Use the indicative in an adjective clause that refers to a person, place, or thing (antecedent) that exists or is known. Use the subjunctive in an adjective clause that refers to a person, place, or thing that does not exist or whose existence is unknown or in question. Study the examples to see the differences.

INDICATIVE	SUBJUNCTIVE
Hay un buen hotel que **queda** cerca de la playa. *There is a good hotel that is near the beach.* (You are familiar with the hotel.)	Busco un buen hotel que **quede** cerca de la playa. *I am looking for a good hotel that is near the beach.* (The existence of such a hotel is uncertain or unknown to you.)
Visité el museo que **tiene** una exposición de molas. *I visited the museum that has a molas exhibit.* (You went there, so there is such a museum.)	Aquí no hay ningún museo que **tenga** una exposición de molas. *There is no museum here that has a molas exhibit.* (There is no such museum.)

Lengua

Use the personal **a** before specific persons or animals that function as direct objects. If the person or animal is unknown or specific, use the subjunctive and do not use the personal **a.** Always use the personal **a** before **alguien** and **nadie.**

Busco **a** la auxiliar que trabaja en ese vuelo.
I am looking for the (specific) flight attendant who is working on that flight.

Busco **una** auxiliar que **trabaje** en ese vuelo.
I am looking for a (any) flight attendant who is (happens to be) working on that flight.

Busco **a** alguien que me **acompañe** al museo.
I am looking for someone who will go with me to the museum.

¿Comprendes? Completa las oraciones con el indicativo o el subjuntivo de los verbos.

1. Buscamos un guía que (ofrece/ofrezca) excursiones a las pirámides.
2. Buscamos a alguien que (trabaja/trabaje) los sábados.
3. No conozco a nadie que (visita/visite) Costa Rica este año.
4. El año pasado encontramos un hotel que (está/esté) en el centro.
5. Hay tres itinerarios que me (gustan/gusten).
6. José, ¿hay algún itinerario que te (gusta/guste)? Te veo indeciso (*indecisive*).
7. Necesito un restaurante que (sirve/sirva) comida vegetariana.

PRÁCTICA

12-31 ¿Existe o no existe? Selecciona el verbo correcto para completar cada oración. Luego, indica la razón: existe o es conocido (**E/C**), o no existe o es desconocido (**NE/D**).

RAZÓN

1. No hay ningún vuelo que… por la noche. _____
   a. sale **b.** salga
2. Pero hay un vuelo que… a las 7:00 de la mañana. _____
   a. sale **b.** salga
3. Me interesa encontrar un hotel que… en el centro. _____
   a. queda **b.** quede
4. Hay un hotel que no es muy caro que… en el centro. _____
   a. queda **b.** quede
5. Busco al empleado que… inglés. _____
   a. habla **b.** hable
6. ¿Hay algún empleado en este departamento que… inglés? _____
   a. habla **b.** hable

12-32 Por casualidad (*By any chance*). **PREPARACIÓN.** Túrnense para hacerse preguntas sobre la familia y amigos de cada uno/a. Respondan con detalles adicionales. Tomen apuntes de las respuestas de su compañero/a.

MODELO en tu familia / dormir mucho durante los viajes largos en auto

E1: *Por casualidad, ¿hay alguien en tu familia que duerma durante los viajes largos en auto?*

E2: *Sí, mi hermano siempre duerme mucho en el auto. El año pasado fuimos a la casa de mis abuelos y él durmió durante todo el viaje. / No, no hay nadie que duerma. Todos nos divertimos mucho durante los viajes.*

1. en tu familia / viajar frecuentemente en primera clase
2. entre tus amigos / trabajar incluso (*even*) durante las vacaciones
3. entre tus amigos / conocer los lugares más interesantes de Costa Rica
4. entre tus familiares / saber pilotear un avión
5. entre tus amigos / ir a esquiar en sus vacaciones
6. en tu familia / ser viajero/a frecuente de una aerolínea
7. en tu familia / tener acceso a las salas VIP de los aeropuertos
8. entre tus amigos de la universidad / sentir pánico de viajar en un avión

INTERCAMBIOS. Identifica dos datos sobre la familia o los amigos de tu compañero/a de **Preparación** que te parecieron interesantes o sorprendentes. Explica por qué. Compártelos con otro/a compañero/a.

MODELO *Conversé con… Me dio dos respuestas interesantes/sorprendentes. Primero, en su familia / entre sus amigos… Me pareció interesante/sorprendente porque… Segundo, en su familia / entre sus amigos… Es interesante/ sorprendente que…*

12-33 El hotel ideal. **PREPARACIÓN.** Indica las características mínimas y deseables de tu hotel ideal. Añade otra si es necesario. Prepárate para explicar por qué.

_____ botones (*bellhop*)
_____ buen servicio
_____ buena ubicación
_____ desayuno gratis
_____ empleados bilingües
_____ estacionamiento gratis
_____ gimnasio
_____ lavandería
_____ limpio
_____ peluquería
_____ piscina
_____ restaurante abierto 24/7
_____ servicio al cuarto
_____ transporte gratis al aeropuerto
_____ wifi rápido
_____ otra idea:

INTERCAMBIOS. Descríbanse su hotel ideal. Comenten las características esenciales y no esenciales. Expliquen por qué.

MODELO Esencial: *Para mí, es esencial que un hotel tenga cuartos cómodos y limpios. Para descansar, necesito una cama cómoda y limpia.*

No esencial: *No es esencial/necesario que tenga una piscina. Generalmente no uso la piscina de los hoteles.*

 **12-34 ¡A dar una mano!** Túrnense para explicar cada situación imprevista (*unexpected*) y para ofrecer ayuda. Las expresiones de la lista pueden ser útiles.

MODELO Ves que un pasajero se cae y está inconsciente en el piso.

E1: *¿Hay alguien que pueda llamar al número de emergencia? Es importante que venga un médico.*

E2: *No tengo el número de emergencia. ¿Hay alguien que pueda buscar el número rápidamente?*

E3: *Yo lo busco y llamo inmediatamente. Es importante que vengan pronto.*

Posibles acciones

avisar a…	llevar
ayudar	pedir ayuda a…
consultar	tomar
llamar	traer

Personas clave

agente de la aerolínea
agente de seguridad
chofer del carro de cortesía
intérprete

Equipo clave

ascensor (*elevator*)
camilla (*stretcher*)
diccionario en línea
equipo médico
silla de ruedas

1. Un pasajero furioso le grita a un agente de la aerolínea que no le permite subir al avión porque llegó muy tarde a la puerta de salida.
2. Una madre con un bebé enfermo olvidó su equipaje de mano en el avión. El bolso tiene los medicamentos y la ropa del bebé.
3. Un niño que juega por el aeropuerto encuentra un bolso en un rincón (*corner*). El niño corre hacia el bolso para abrirlo. A ti te parece que el bolso tiene un aspecto sospechoso (*suspicious*).
4. Trabajas en el mostrador de información del aeropuerto. Una persona te hace preguntas en japonés. Tú no hablas ni entiendes japonés.
5. Una persona que tiene problemas para caminar quiere subir una escalera mecánica en el aeropuerto, pero tú vas de prisa a tomar tu vuelo y no puedes ayudarla.
6. Una pareja que está cargando (*charging*) su teléfono en un enchufe (*outlet*) a tu lado se levanta y corre a otra puerta para tomar su vuelo. Después de unos segundos, te das cuenta (*realize*) que olvidaron su teléfono.

12-35 ¡Qué afortunado/a! **PREPARACIÓN.** Tus abuelos te regalan un viaje. Elige un lugar de esta lista e identifica las características mínimas (**M**) y las deseables (**D**) del lugar. Luego, busca en internet la información indicada por tu profesor/a.

Posibles lugares	Características	
islas San Blas, Panamá	_____ playas limpias _____ museos _____ restaurantes elegantes de comida típica	_____ eventos culturales _____ ¿otra?
Parque Nacional Volcán Poás, Costa Rica	_____ áreas de conservación _____ senderos (*trails*) para explorar _____ transporte cómodo	_____ caballos (*horses*) para montar _____ ¿otra?
desierto de Atacama, Chile	_____ un lugar donde observar las estrellas _____ playas _____ tiendas donde hacer compras	_____ un/a guía para hablar sobre el lugar _____ ¿otra?
Ciudad de Panamá, Panamá	_____ museos _____ ruinas	_____ recorrido de lugares históricos _____ ¿otra?

INTERCAMBIOS. Túrnense para describirle a otra pareja el lugar de vacaciones que escogieron. Indiquen dónde está y qué condiciones mínimas y deseables cumple (*fulfills*).

MODELO E1: *Quiero visitar San José, Costa Rica. Es importante que sea segura y que tenga buenos restaurantes y áreas verdes. ¿Sabes si existe lo que busco en San José?*

E2: *Sé que San José es una ciudad muy segura. Evidentemente, hay buenos restaurantes, varios parques y plazas donde puedes caminar. Yo quiero ir a una ciudad que esté cerca de un lago o un río. También quiero que ofrezca lugares donde hacer esquí acuático. Elegí la ciudad de Varaguas de Santiago en Panamá. ¿Sabes si existe lo que busco en Varaguas de Santiago?*

E3: *En Varaguas de Santiago hay una playa que se llama Santa Catalina. Allí puedes practicar deportes acuáticos. También hay montañas y bosques donde puedes ver animales y plantas. Yo quiero visitar…*

Situación

PREPARACIÓN. Lean esta situación. Luego, compartan ejemplos de vocabulario, gramática y otra información que necesitan para desarrollar la conversación.

Role A. Your family owns a small inn that houses international faculty who visit the campus. You need to hire two people for your staff, so you call an employment agency. Explain that you are looking for:

a. a receptionist who speaks Chinese, French, or Spanish (preferably two of those languages) and who has experience as a secretary; and

b. a chef who is familiar with several culinary styles and who is able to work nights and weekends.

Role B. You work at an employment agency, and you receive a call from an innkeeper who is looking for a receptionist and a chef. Listen to the innkeeper's requirements and ask about any other qualifications that may be desired. Tell the innkeeper you will start looking right away.

	ROLE A	ROLE B
Vocabulario	Question words Employment qualifications Words and expressions related to cooking Time and schedules	Question words Employment qualifications Words and expressions related to cooking Time and schedules
Funciones y formas	Asking questions Giving information Subjunctive with adjective clauses to express uncertainty	Asking questions Giving information Subjunctive with adjective clauses to express uncertainty Expressing reassurance and guarantee of assistance

INTERCAMBIOS. Practiquen la conversación, incorporando el vocabulario y las funciones de **Preparación.** Luego, represéntenla ante la clase.

ESCUCHA

Estrategia

Use background knowledge to support comprehension When you listen to a conversation or a presentation in Spanish, your experience may lead you to expect certain content. To support your comprehension, do the following:

Before you listen . . .

- brainstorm a list of ideas you expect to hear about the topic;
- read about the topic on the internet if you are not familiar with it.

As you listen . . .

- use your prior knowledge to help you understand. For example, when you hear numbers announced at an airport, they probably refer to flight or gate numbers.

12-36 Preparación. El señor Hernández llama a una agencia de viajes para pedir información sobre un hotel en San José para él y su familia. Escribe tres características que el señor Hernández probablemente desea que tenga el hotel y tres preguntas que probablemente le va a hacer la agente. Compártelas con la clase.

Comprueba

I was able to . . .

- understand the main points of the conversation and some supporting details.
- use experience and logic to confirm what I understood.

12-37 Escucha. As you listen to the conversation between Mr. Hernández and the travel agent, indicate the statements that best report what was said.

1. _____ La agente tiene varias posibilidades y le describe tres hoteles para que escoja.
2. _____ El señor Hernández prefiere que sus hijos y esposa estén cómodos aunque él tenga que tomar un taxi o manejar mucho.
3. _____ El señor Hernández finalmente decide hacer la reservación en el hotel que no está en el centro de la ciudad.
4. _____ La agente le dice al cliente que su elección no es buena porque el hotel es muy caro y está muy lejos del centro de la ciudad.

12-38 Un paso más. Háganse las siguientes preguntas.

1. Cuando haces un viaje, ¿haces las reservaciones de tu hotel por internet, o buscas alojamiento de otra manera? Explica tus preferencias.
2. ¿Alguna vez te has alojado en un hotel de cinco estrellas? Describe el mejor hotel en que te has alojado. Da ejemplos de las comodidades que tenía.

HABLA

Estrategia

Use visuals to make your presentations engaging When you give a presentation, visual aids can help your audience be more engaged with what you are saying. Here are some tips to keep in mind:

- Referring to photos, drawings, and animation will help you to speak directly to your audience, rather than read from your notes or from text on your slides.
- Visual material will attract the attention of your audience, so that they focus on the connection between the sentences they hear and the images you see.

12-39 Preparación. Ustedes quieren viajar de vacaciones a un lugar de Hispanoamérica o España. Busquen lo siguiente en internet y tomen notas para compartir con la clase más adelante.

Un lugar con...	¿Cómo se llama el lugar? ¿Dónde está?
1. buen transporte (frecuente y seguro) a lugares de interés para ustedes. Seleccionen por lo menos dos lugares posibles.	
2. alojamiento cómodo y precios módicos para estudiantes. Indiquen específicamente el tipo de alojamiento que buscan (cuartos simples, dobles, comodidades, etc.).	
3. actividades (sociales, culturales, deportivas, etc.) individuales o grupales para los gustos e intereses de ustedes. Encuentren ejemplos específicos.	

12-40 Habla. Hagan una breve presentación sobre el lugar que escogieron, usando fotos o breves fragmentos de video para mantener el interés de sus compañeros/as de clase. Incluyan como mínimo la siguiente información:

1. lugar que quisieran visitar, ubicación (país y región) y descripción
2. características que para ustedes son importantes o interesantes
3. características que son inconvenientes o que el lugar no ofrece
4. actividades que es posible o improbable que se puedan hacer en el lugar

Comprueba

I was able to . . .

- select visuals that coordinated well with the main points of my presentation.
- refer to the visuals as I spoke.

12-41 Un paso más. Decidan cuál de los lugares presentados por sus compañeros/as es el más interesante. Expliquen por qué.

LEE

Estrategia

Focus on logical relationships Magazine articles often address current issues, such as identity theft, sedentary lifestyles, or travel tips. When you read an article of this type, you can take advantage of its structure to maximize your comprehension. As you read, look for the issues or problems that the author introduces, and then focus on the logical relationships, such as between problems and their causes, or between problems and their solutions. The story of a particular person often appears at the beginning of the article as an example of the problem, and then returns to the person at the end to illustrate a possible solution.

 **12-42 Preparación.** Hablen de lo siguiente.

1. ¿Prefieren los viajes en avión o por tierra? ¿Por qué?
2. ¿Les gusta organizar sus propios viajes o prefieren usar los servicios de una compañía de turismo? ¿Por qué?
3. ¿Qué problema serio ha tenido cada uno/a de ustedes en un viaje?
4. ¿Han tenido problemas semejantes o diferentes?

Comprueba

I was able to . . .

- understand the main message and most supporting details in the text.
- following the chronological sequence of the travelers' problems and how they were resolved.

 **12-43 Lee.** Indica los problemas que tuvieron los viajeros, según el artículo "Vacaciones o pesadilla". Después, busca en el artículo ejemplos de lo que se indica.

Problemas

1. _____ agencias de viajes deshonestas
2. _____ maletas perdidas
3. _____ vuelos cancelados
4. _____ hotel con habitaciones pequeñas y malas
5. _____ robo (*theft*) de tarjetas de crédito
6. _____ servicios prometidos que no se cumplieron (*honored*)
7. _____ comida de mala calidad
8. _____ enfermedades causadas por la comida

Ejemplos

1. tres problemas que tuvieron Isabel y Mario en sus vacaciones
2. la causa principal de la situación desagradable de Isabel y Mario
3. recomendaciones para evitar o minimizar problemas

VACACIONES O PESADILLA[1]

CÓMO RESCATAR[2] UN VIAJE PROBLEMÁTICO

Isabel y Mario, una pareja norteamericana de origen uruguayo, decidieron celebrar su aniversario de boda en Costa Rica. Después de investigar algunas opciones en internet, se pusieron en contacto con la agencia TravelTour. La agencia ofrecía un paquete que incluía boleto de avión, hotel y auto de alquiler por un precio bastante módico. Las fotos prometían una visita relajada en un hotel de ambiente auténtico en el noroeste del país. La variedad de piscinas, la cercanía al mar, la deliciosa gastronomía local y las bebidas refrescantes que se veían en mesitas junto a las hamacas[3] de los afortunados clientes confirmaban que se trataba de un verdadero paraíso. Además, las excursiones de ecoturismo ofrecían una variedad de oportunidades para conocer los famosos parques nacionales costarricenses.

Isabel y Mario pagaron la cantidad requerida y no dudaron ni un momento su decisión. Pero al llegar a su destino, comprobaron que las fotos no se correspondían para nada con la realidad. El hotel no tenía ni vista al mar ni jardines de plantas locales. Las habitaciones eran pequeñas e incómodas y la comida dejaba mucho que desear. Lo peor[4] fueron las excursiones: no había ni programa organizado ni guía experto en ecología, solo unos folletos turísticos e instrucciones sobre cómo llegar a algunos sitios cercanos.

¿Por qué vivieron esta pesadilla Isabel y Mario? Su experiencia, y la de otros turistas, nos enseña a ser prudentes y prever los riesgos[5]. Cuando viajamos internacionalmente, es preferible dirigirse a una agencia del país de destino para que los especialistas de viajes nos ayuden a elegir las mejores opciones. Frecuentemente es más caro hacerlo así, pero se puede economizar el tiempo y evitar sorpresas desagradables. Por suerte, las vacaciones de Mario e Isabel resultaron ser muy agradables. Después de dos días bastante mediocres, hicieron causa común[6] con otra pareja que estaba en la misma situación. Llamaron a la agencia Viajes Reales para quejarse. Por suerte, la agencia les canceló todo y les devolvió dinero suficiente para organizar su propio viaje. En grupo con la otra pareja, fueron primero a la zona del activo volcán Arenal, donde pudieron ver una erupción acompañada de humo[7] y gases. Luego visitaron las aguas termales de Baldi, que provienen del fascinante volcán. Allí se bañaron en las piscinas de agua mineral y sacaron fotos de las cataratas naturales de agua caliente.

El volcán Arenal en erupción

El mono capuchino es el primate más común en el Parque Nacional Manuel Antonio.

Los cuatro comentaron que lo mejor del viaje fueron los dos días que pasaron en el Parque Nacional Manuel Antonio, uno de los parques más bellos del mundo y el más visitado de Costa Rica. Como muchos de los 161 parques nacionales del país, está dedicado a la conservación, la investigación y el turismo ecológico orientado hacia la educación sobre el medio ambiente. Tiene de todo: playas de arena blanca, grandes montañas y bosques que llegan hasta las playas. Tiene una gran biodiversidad terrestre y marina con maravillosos arrecifes coralinos[8]. Mario, Isabel y sus nuevos amigos pasaron muchas horas recorriendo el parque, donde vieron monos, iguanas y perezosos[9]. Por suerte, la otra pareja era aficionada a los pájaros[10]. Con la ayuda de sus binoculares y una guía con fotos, pudieron identificar a más de 20 de las 184 especies de pájaros que se encuentran en el parque.

Al final, Isabel y Mario volvieron a casa felices y también aprendieron una lección. Como dice un conocido refrán[11]: Más vale prevenir que curar.

[1]*nightmare* [2]*rescue* [3]*hammocks* [4]*the worst part* [5]*risks* [6]*joined forces* [7]*smoke* [8]*coral reefs* [9]*sloths* [10]*birds* [11]*proverb*

12-44 Un paso más. Después de llegar a casa, Isabel y Mario escriben una evaluación negativa en el sitio web de la agencia Viajes Reales. Escribe la respuesta de la agencia. Debes:

1. asumir responsabilidad (o no) de la mala experiencia de los clientes
2. justificar o explicar la falsa publicidad
3. prometerles mejor servicio en el futuro

ESCRIBE

Estrategia

Use facts to offer advice In your academic work, you are often expected to provide reliable support for your argument, such as statistics and expert opinions. When talking to a friend, you also need to use facts about different options to provide convincing support for the advice you give. However, not all sources of information are helpful. Always be sure to . . .

- consult reliable sources;
- acknowledge your sources;
- make it clear how your facts are connected to other sources of information, such as your knowledge about your friend, or your own experiences.

12-45 Preparación. Tu amigo/a acaba de ganar un concurso: un viaje de ecoturismo a Costa Rica. Te ha pedido ayuda para elegir una de estas dos opciones: siete días en la costa del Caribe, o siete días en la costa del Pacífico. Luego, necesita tu ayuda para planificar el viaje. Para ayudarlo/la, haz lo siguiente:

1. En internet, investiga las dos opciones. Toma nota de las actividades y atracciones para explicarle a tu amigo/a cuál es la mejor opción.
2. Basándote en el texto de la actividad **12-43,** prepara una lista de consejos sobre cómo escoger una buena compañía de ecoturismo.
3. Usa información de tu investigación y de tus conocimientos previos para escribir otra lista de consejos para tu amigo/a: dinero, documentos, ropa, salud, etc.
4. Organiza la información y las ideas en orden de importancia.
5. Selecciona las palabras adecuadas para lograr (*achieve*) el tono apropiado.

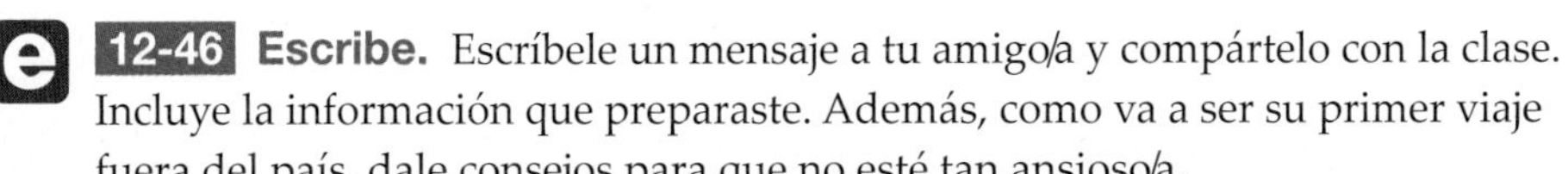

12-46 Escribe. Escríbele un mensaje a tu amigo/a y compártelo con la clase. Incluye la información que preparaste. Además, como va a ser su primer viaje fuera del país, dale consejos para que no esté tan ansioso/a.

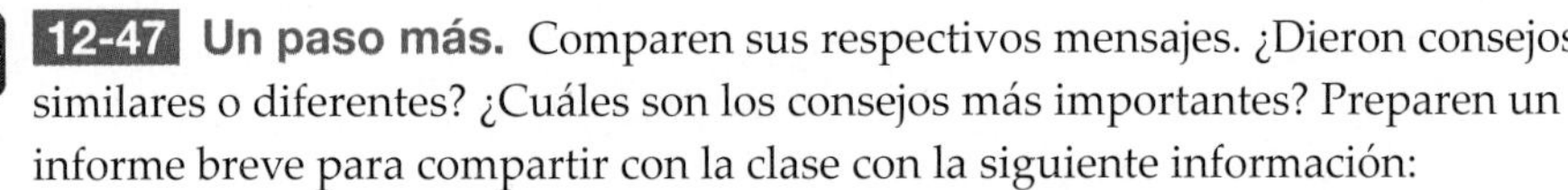

12-47 Un paso más. Comparen sus respectivos mensajes. ¿Dieron consejos similares o diferentes? ¿Cuáles son los consejos más importantes? Preparen un informe breve para compartir con la clase con la siguiente información:

- una semejanza y una diferencia entre sus consejos
- el consejo más importante que mencionaron

Comprueba

I was able to . . .

- state my viewpoint on a topic I have researched.
- give advice based on factual information.
- present my recommendations logically and coherently.

En este capítulo...

Vocabulario

Los medios de transporte	Means of transportation
el autobús / el bus	*bus*
el avión	*plane*
el barco	*ship; boat*
el carro / el coche	*car*
el metro	*subway*
el tren	*train*

Los viajes	Trips
la agencia de viajes	*travel agency*
la autopista	*freeway*
el boleto / el pasaje	*ticket*
la carretera	*highway*
el crucero	*cruise*
el equipaje	*luggage*
el equipaje de mano	*carry-on luggage*
la escala	*stopover*
la excursión	*outing, trip*
la maleta	*suitcase*
el pasaporte	*passport*
el transporte	*transportation*
la velocidad	*speed*

En el aeropuerto	At the airport
la aduana	*customs*
la aerolínea / la línea aérea	*airline*
el asiento (de pasillo/ ventanilla)	*(aisle/window) seat*
la clase turista	*tourist class*
el mostrador	*counter*
la primera clase	*first class*
la puerta (de salida/ llegada)	*(departure/arrival) gate*
la salida	*departure*
la sala de espera	*waiting room*
la salida de emergencia	*emergency exit*
la tarjeta de embarque	*boarding pass*
el vuelo	*flight*

En el hotel	In the hotel
el alojamiento	*lodging*
la caja fuerte	*safe*
la habitación doble/ sencilla	*double/single room*
la llave	*key*
la recepción	*front desk*
la tarjeta magnética	*key card*

Las personas	People
el/la auxiliar de vuelo	*flight attendant*
el/la inspector/a de aduana	*customs agent*
el/la pasajero/a	*passenger*
el/la viajero/a	*traveler*

Los carros	Cars
la bolsa de aire	*airbag*
el capó	*hood*
el cinturón de seguridad	*seatbelt*
el espejo retrovisor	*rearview mirror*
la guantera	*glove compartment*
la licencia de conducir	*driver's license*
el limpiaparabrisas	*windshield wiper*
la llanta	*tire*
la luz (las luces)	*light(s)*
las luces intermitentes	*flashers, hazard lights*
el maletero / el baúl	*trunk*
el motor	*motor*
la multa	*fine*
el parabrisas	*windshield*
el parachoques	*bumper*
la placa	*license plate*
el radiador	*radiator*
la rueda	*wheel*
el volante	*steering wheel*

Las direcciones	Directions
a la derecha	*(to the) right*
a la izquierda	*(to the) left*
la cuadra	*city block*
la esquina	*corner*

Verbos	Verbs
bajarse (de)	*to get off/out (of); to go down*
descomponerse (g)	*to break down*
doblar	*to turn*
facturar	*to check (luggage)*
hacer cola	*to stand in line*
manejar	*to drive*
perderse (ie)	*to get lost*
recorrer	*to cover, to travel*
reservar	*to reserve*
seguir (i, i) derecho	*to go straight*
subir (a)	*to get on/in(to); to go up*
viajar	*to travel*
volar (ue)	*to fly*

Palabras y expresiones útiles	Useful words and expressions
el cajero automático	*ATM*
bien/mal aparcado/a	*well/badly parked*
de ida y vuelta	*round-trip*
¿Podría...?	*Could you...?*

See page 450 for affirmative and negative expressions.
See page 455 for a list of stressed possessive adjectives and pronouns.

Capítulo 13
¿Qué es arte para ti?

Entre fanáticos y detractores, el arquitecto Freddy Mamani está marcando estilo en Bolivia con su nueva arquitectura andina.

Learning Outcomes

You will be able to:

- talk about art and culture
- talk about the future
- hypothesize
- talk about past events
- talk about Bolivia and Paraguay in terms of products, practices, and perspectives
- share information about art and culture in Hispanic countries and identify cultural similarities

Enfoque cultural

Bolivia y Paraguay

El Palacio de los López, en Asunción, es la sede (*headquarters*) del gobierno paraguayo.

El Salar de Uyuni, al suroeste de Bolivia, es el desierto de sal más grande del mundo y posee una gran reserva de litio (*lithium*).

La ciudad de Sucre hoy en día es la capital constitucional y la sede del poder judicial de Bolivia.

Arte hispano

Detalle de tabla de madera pintada (siglo XVI). Está en el Museo Casa de Murillo, La Paz, Bolivia.

Enfoque cultural

¿Qué te parece?

- El Salar de Uyuni es visitado por más de 60.000 turistas cada año y tiene varios hoteles de lujo (*luxury*) construidos de sal.
- El lago Titicaca, entre Bolivia y Perú, es el lago comercial navegable más alto del mundo, con una altura de 3.812 metros (12.500 pies). Es el lago más grande de Sudamérica.
- Paraguay y Bolivia son los únicos países de Sudamérica sin salida directa al mar.
- El español y el guaraní son los dos idiomas oficiales de Paraguay. El guaraní es también el nombre de su moneda.
- El 95% de la población de Paraguay es mestiza, es decir, de ascendencia europea e indígena.

Este árbol de piedra (*stone*) está en el desierto Siloli, al suroeste de Bolivia. Siloli forma parte del desierto de Atacama, compartido con Chile, que es uno de los desiertos más áridos del mundo. Sus formaciones rocosas, a causa de los fuertes vientos, son espectaculares.

La Santísima Trinidad de Paraná forma parte de una serie de misiones fundadas por los jesuitas en el siglo XVII. Siete de estas misiones se establecieron en Paraguay. Hoy en día, solo quedan las ruinas de estos centros urbanos y espirituales.

La ciudad de Santa Cruz de la Sierra, en el este de Bolivia, era un puesto fronterizo insignificante de menos de 30.000 habitantes hasta mediados del siglo XX. Hoy en día es la ciudad más grande de Bolivia, con 1.749.000 habitantes, incluyendo el área metropolitana, y produce el 80% de la agricultura del país. Es una ciudad tradicional y sofisticada a la vez, con una multitud de cafés, museos, boutiques y grandes centros comerciales.

La Represa (*dam*) Hidroeléctrica de Itaipú en el río Paraná, entre Paraguay y Brasil, suministra (*provides*) el 90% de la energía de Paraguay y el 25% de la energía de Brasil. En 1994, fue nombrada una de las Siete Maravillas del Mundo Moderno por la *American Society of Civil Engineers.*

To learn more about Bolivia and Paraguay, go online to view the *Club cultura* videos.

¿Cuánto sabes? Indica si las siguientes afirmaciones son ciertas (**C**) o falsas (**F**), según lo que sabes sobre Bolivia y Paraguay. Corrige las falsas.

1. _____ El río Paraná está en la frontera entre Paraguay y Brasil.
2. _____ El guaraní es una de las lenguas oficiales de Paraguay.
3. _____ La capital de Bolivia es Santa Cruz.
4. _____ Paraguay no produce suficiente energía hidroeléctrica para exportarla a sus países vecinos (*neighboring*).
5. _____ Bolivia tiene grandes depósitos de sal y litio.
6. _____ Los jesuitas establecieron misiones en Paraguay en el siglo XVII.

Discussing the arts: literature, film, art, music, and dance

La literatura y el cine

Uno de los **novelistas** más importantes de Hispanoamérica es el paraguayo Augusto Roa Bastos (1917–2005). Su novela *Yo, el supremo* (1974) **trata** del **tema** de las dictaduras (*dictatorships*). Su **personaje principal** se basa en la figura de José Rodríguez de Francia, dictador de Paraguay en las primeras décadas del siglo XIX. Este **escritor** fue uno de los iniciadores del movimiento literario conocido como el *realismo mágico,* que combina elementos mágicos o irracionales con situaciones de aparente normalidad.

La **poesía** tiene nombres **destacados** en las letras hispanas. La chilena Gabriela Mistral (1889–1957) fue la primera persona de Hispanoamérica en recibir el Premio Nobel de Literatura, en 1945. Algunos de los temas de su obra son el **amor,** la **amistad,** la **maternidad,** la **muerte** y el **mestizaje** como característica de la identidad latinoamericana. Otros **poetas** universalmente conocidos son el chileno Pablo Neruda, el peruano César Vallejo y el español Federico García Lorca.

El cine hispano ha dado numerosos ejemplos de **calidad** en películas de muchos países; tiene una buena **representación** en las películas de Hollywood. El **director** mexicano Guillermo del Toro ganó un Óscar en 2018 por su película *La forma del agua* (*The Shape of Water*). El mismo año, ganó el Óscar a la mejor película extranjera la chilena *Una mujer fantástica,* de Sebastián Lelio, que trata de los problemas de una mujer **transgénero** enfrentada a una sociedad tradicional. Una directora de cine española conocida internacionalmente es Isabel Coixet, que ganó el premio Goya a la mejor película en 2018 con *The Bookshop,* una **adaptación** de la novela del mismo nombre.

La escritora mexicana Elena Poniatowska fue **galardonada** con el prestigioso **Premio** Cervantes en 2013 por su brillante **carrera literaria.** Algunas de sus **novelas** y **cuentos** tratan de **asuntos** sociales y políticos y se basan en la investigación histórica. Una de sus **obras** más **conocidas** es *La noche de Tlatelolco* (1971), **traducida** al inglés como *Massacre in Mexico,* donde **narra** la represión que sufrieron los estudiantes en 1968 en Ciudad de México como consecuencia de su protesta en oposición al gobierno.

PRÁCTICA

13-1 Escucha y confirma. Listen to the descriptions. Then select the writer or artist each one refers to.

	Augusto Roa Bastos	Elena Poniatowska	Gabriela Mistral	Isabel Coixet
1.				
2.				
3.				
4.				
5.				
6.				

Cultura

Óscares y otros premios Las nominaciones y los premios son muy codiciados (*sought-after*) en el mundo del cine. Las películas que compiten en los festivales de cine adquieren más publicidad y tienen más éxito (*success*) económico. Ganar un Óscar a la mejor película extranjera es una de las aspiraciones de muchos directores de todo el mundo, pero hay otros premios, como los Goya, y otros festivales de cine internacionales que tienen gran tradición y repercusión en el mundo hispano, como los de Valladolid (Seminci) y de San Sebastián, en España.

Conexiones Busca información sobre la Semana Internacional de Cine de Valladolid (Seminci) y el Festival de Cine de San Sebastián. ¿Qué películas fueron premiadas en los últimos festivales? ¿Te parecen interesantes estas películas? ¿Conoces algún director o actor entre los ganadores?

13-2 Cineastas (*Filmmakers*) y escritores.

PREPARACIÓN. Completen la tabla con la información que leyeron sobre ciertos hispanos prominentes en la página 477.

Nombre	Profesión	Lugar de origen	Datos interesantes
	director de cine	México	Ganó un Óscar en 2018.
	poeta	Chile	
Isabel Coixet			
Augusto Roa Bastos	novelista		
	escritora		Ganó el Premio Cervantes en 2013.

INTERCAMBIOS. Comparen su tabla con la de otra pareja, y entre todos hagan una lista de otros artistas o escritores hispanos famosos. Pueden incluir a gente del cine, la música, la pintura, el periodismo, la arquitectura, el diseño de ropa, etc. Incluyan el nombre y la siguiente información:

1. profesión **2.** lugar de origen **3.** algunos datos interesantes de su carrera

13-3 ¿De qué trata? **PREPARACIÓN.** Intercambien información sobre un libro que han leído o una película que han visto. Usen las preguntas como guía.

1. ¿Quién escribió el libro o dirigió (*directed*) la película?
2. ¿Cuál es el tema?
3. ¿Quién es su personaje principal? ¿Cómo es?
4. ¿Te gustó la película / el libro? ¿Por qué?

INTERCAMBIOS. Comparte con la clase la información que has obtenido.

13-4 Un poema. **PREPARACIÓN.** Busquen en internet el poema "Las puertas" de la escritora paraguaya Josefina Plá y contesten las preguntas.

1. En su opinión, ¿qué representan las puertas en el poema?
2. ¿Qué significa una puerta que se cierra "a destiempo"?
3. ¿Cómo se describe la última puerta en el poema? ¿Qué simboliza esta puerta?
4. ¿Qué expresiones de este poema se refieren al espacio? ¿Y al tiempo?
5. ¿De qué trata este poema probablemente?

INTERCAMBIOS. En sus propias palabras, expresen su interpretación y su opinión sobre este poema.

Cultura

Josefina Plá Aunque nació en las islas Canarias, España, en 1909, esta escritora vivió la mayor parte de su vida en Paraguay hasta su muerte en 1999. Fue una autora prolífica. Publicó más de 60 libros, principalmente obras de teatro, poemas y cuentos breves. También fue periodista y escribió ensayos sobre el bilingüismo. Además, fue artista plástica e hizo murales y piezas de cerámica explorando motivos y técnicas populares e indígenas.

Comparaciones ¿Conoces a alguien famoso que practique distintos tipos de arte a la vez? ¿A qué debe su fama principalmente? ¿Cómo se compara con la poeta Josefina Plá?

13-5 Escritores famosos. Busquen información en internet sobre uno de estos poetas hispanos y preparen una breve presentación incluyendo la siguiente información.

Federico García Lorca
Dulce María Loynaz
Pablo Neruda
Alejandra Pizarnik
César Vallejo
Adela Zamudio

1. datos biográficos
2. explicación de uno de sus poemas (tema y características de estilo)

La pintura y el arte

Vieja friendo huevos (1618), de Diego Velázquez

Diego Velázquez, del siglo XVII, es uno de los grandes **pintores** españoles. Uno de sus cuadros más importantes es *Las Meninas,* donde **retrata** una **escena** en el palacio real. En cambio (*However*), el cuadro *Vieja friendo huevos* es una escena popular. El **estilo** de Velázquez es **realista** y usa mucho el **contraste** de **luces** y **sombras.**

Francisco de Goya, del siglo XVIII, **pintó** muchos **retratos** y **paisajes,** pero también tiene obras con escenas impactantes, como la serie de las **pinturas** "negras", donde usa la imaginación para protestar contra la sociedad y enfatizar lo grotesco de la experiencia humana. Muchas de sus obras están en el Museo del Prado, en Madrid.

Saturno devorando a su hijo (circa 1819), de Francisco de Goya

La persistencia de la memoria (1931), de Salvador Dalí

Algunos de los mejores pintores del siglo XX, como Pablo Picasso y Salvador Dalí, también son españoles. En este cuadro vemos el estilo **surrealista** de Dalí, con sus relojes blandos (*soft*) y su obsesión por los insectos. Este paisaje, con el mar **al fondo,** es un **recuerdo** del pueblo del Mediterráneo donde él vivió, y se repite en muchos de sus cuadros. Picasso **desarrolló** el estilo **cubista** y fue muy original en el uso de los colores y las **formas.**

Fulang-Chang y yo (1937), de Frida Kahlo

Los mexicanos Frida Kahlo y Diego Rivera muestran en sus pinturas las costumbres y las condiciones sociales de su país. Kahlo combina elementos surrealistas con situaciones íntimas. Rivera es muy famoso por sus grandes **murales.** Algunos de ellos se pueden ver en México, Detroit y San Francisco. En Bolivia, Roberto Mamani, conocido como Mamani Mamani, es un **artista** que incorpora **símbolos** de la tradición aymara y usa mucho **colorido.** Sus cuadros se **exhiben** por todo el mundo.

La **escultora** argentina Lola Mora (1866–1936) destacó en la **escultura,** la minería y el urbanismo, áreas reservadas **hasta** entonces a los hombres. Su obra más conocida es la *Fuente de Las Nereidas,* que tuvo mucha oposición por sus figuras **desnudas.** Otro escultor y pintor latinoamericano famoso es el colombiano Fernando Botero, conocido por sus voluminosas figuras humanas, que critica con humor a una sociedad infantilizada o inmadura en la que **abundan** los símbolos de la autoridad y del poder, como clérigos, presidentes y burgueses (*wealthy*).

Fuente de Las Nereidas (1903), en Buenos Aires, de la escultora argentina Lola Mora

PRÁCTICA

13-6 Para confirmar. Selecciona el/la artista que corresponde a cada descripción.

1. _____ Hace esculturas y pinturas de figuras voluminosas.
2. _____ Sus cuadros son de estilo surrealista.
3. _____ Es famoso por sus murales.
4. _____ Fue un pintor español del siglo XVIII.
5. _____ Es el pintor de *Las Meninas* y de muchos cuadros de estilo realista.
6. _____ Es una pintora mexicana que retrata las costumbres de su país.
7. _____ Su estilo cubista muestra formas muy originales.

a. Diego Velázquez
b. Francisco de Goya
c. Pablo Picasso
d. Salvador Dalí
e. Frida Kahlo
f. Diego Rivera
g. Fernando Botero

Cultura

Los aparapitas Enrique Arnal (1932–2016) es uno de los artistas bolivianos más importantes a nivel internacional. Es muy conocido por una serie de pinturas que se enfoca en la figura del aparapita, cargador indígena contratado para llevar objetos y productos en los mercados de La Paz. La palabra, que proviene de la lengua aymara, significa "el que carga". De origen rural, los aparapitas se encuentran en una sociedad moderna, desorientados y marginados socialmente. Arnal presenta esta alienación en sus cuadros, y pone a estos personajes entre portales donde parece que pasan de una dimensión a otra. Para expresar su anonimidad ante el público, Arnal borra los rasgos (*traits*) de las caras. Al mismo tiempo que los aparapitas están presentes, pasan sin ser percibidos (*noticed*).

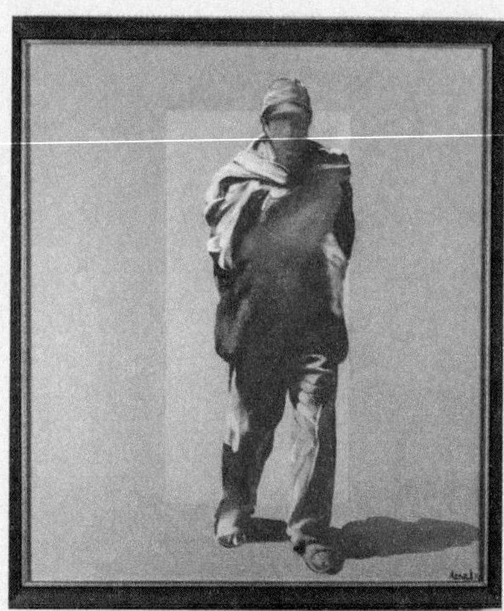

Doble recinto, de Enrique Arnal

Conexiones ¿Qué otras personas en la sociedad moderna están marginadas? ¿Has visto alguna fotografía o cuadro que muestre sus condiciones de vida? ¿Puedes compartir alguna fotografía, cuadro, canción u otra forma artística que critique la alienación de estas personas?

Aparapita en un mercado boliviano

13-7 Otros artistas. Busquen información en internet sobre algún pintor, escultor o muralista de Bolivia o de Paraguay. Luego, preparen una presentación visual para la clase que incluya lo siguiente:

1. lugar y fecha de nacimiento
2. título y descripción de una de sus obras más famosas
3. algún acontecimiento (*event*) notable de su vida

13-8 Comparación. Comparen *Las Meninas* de Velázquez con *Las Meninas* de Picasso. Analicen los siguientes aspectos de los cuadros y expliquen cuál de los dos cuadros les gusta más y por qué.

1. el color
2. la ubicación de los personajes
3. las formas
4. el estilo

Detalle de *Las Meninas* (1656), de Diego Velázquez

See **https://www.pablopicasso.org/las-meninas.jsp** for a picture of *Las Meninas* (1957), de Pablo Picasso.

La música y la danza

El boliviano Piraí Vaca es uno de los **guitarristas** más famosos de **la actualidad.** Aparte de su **repertorio clásico,** Vaca **interpreta** la música popular tradicional, como el tango argentino y el chopi paraguayo. Entre sus muchas distinciones, Vaca ha sido honrado con la *Fellowship of the Americas* por el *John F. Kennedy Center for the Performing Arts* y declarado el Boliviano más Destacado en el Exterior por las Naciones Unidas para la Juventud. Sus conciertos son **inolvidables** por su talento musical y su carismática presencia sobre el **escenario.**

La impresionante variedad de la música hispanoamericana, que va **desde** la música afrocaribeña hasta la polca paraguaya, ha proporcionado grandes **intérpretes** y **voces,** como la de Carlos Gardel, famoso **cantante** y compositor de tangos. La música instrumental también tiene mucha importancia en América Latina. Por ejemplo, en los países andinos, los pueblos quechua y aymara interpretan melodías evocativas con **flautas**, **charangos** y otros instrumentos de la región.

Los cantantes son a menudo los protagonistas de las **revistas del corazón.** Los medios de comunicación hablan de sus **éxitos** y de sus **fracasos,** de sus relaciones y de la ropa que llevan. El multifacético Enrique Iglesias forma parte de una familia de artistas y famosos, pero se ha convertido en una **estrella** por sus propios méritos. Canta en inglés y en español y ha vendido más de 170 millones de **discos** en todo el mundo. Lo llaman el "rey del pop latino".

La **danza** latinoamericana tiene una larga tradición, en su manifestación tanto clásica como **contemporánea.** Alicia Alonso de Cuba, Julio Bocca de Argentina y Laura Rocha de México fueron **bailarines** y directores de sus propias **compañías** y han tenido mucha influencia en las nuevas generaciones de artistas. La tradición de la danza continúa con excelentes bailarines jóvenes, como el mexicano Isaac Hernández, la española Tamara Rojo y el cubano Carlos Acosta.

Cultura

Los instrumentos musicales La música de Hispanoamérica incluye una gran variedad de instrumentos, desde los tambores y trompetas de la música del Caribe hasta las quenas y los charangos característicos de los Andes. La quena es una flauta tradicional, generalmente de bambú, y el charango es parecido a una guitarra, pero más pequeño. El instrumento típico del tango argentino es el bandoneón, que es como un acordeón con botones a los lados. La música típica de Paraguay incluye en ocasiones el arpa (*harp*).

Comparaciones ¿Cuáles son los instrumentos más importantes en la música folclórica de tu cultura? Selecciona uno y descríbelo.

PRÁCTICA

e **13-9 Para confirmar.** Selecciona a la persona o cosa que corresponde a cada descripción.

1. _____ lo contrario del éxito
2. _____ un/a artista muy famoso/a
3. _____ una persona cuya (*whose*) profesión es la danza
4. _____ un grupo de artistas que hace un espectáculo
5. _____ un espectáculo de música
6. _____ una publicación sobre la vida privada de los artistas

a. un bailarín/una bailarina
b. una compañía
c. un concierto
d. una revista del corazón
e. el fracaso
f. una estrella

Cultura

El flamenco El flamenco es un tipo de música que se originó en Andalucía, en el sur de España, hacia el siglo XV. Inicialmente eran canciones breves (*brief*), sin acompañamiento instrumental, que los gitanos (*gypsies*) cantaban para lamentarse de sus malas condiciones de vida. A través de (*Through*) los siglos, el flamenco ha continuado su desarrollo y ha añadido instrumentos musicales, principalmente la guitarra. A partir del siglo XVIII, adquirió gran popularidad el baile flamenco, que es uno de los más emocionantes y variados del mundo.

Comparaciones Investiga el origen del *blues* y compáralo con lo que sabes del flamenco. ¿Qué semejanzas (*similarities*) encuentras?

13-10 Personajes célebres. **PREPARACIÓN.** Elige a uno de los artistas mencionados en la página 483. Investiga los siguientes aspectos de su vida. Luego escribe un breve artículo sobre él/ella incluyendo esta información.

1. su lugar de origen
2. su familia
3. algún recuerdo o anécdota de su vida
4. los inicios de su carrera artística
5. sus mayores éxitos y sus fracasos
6. sus planes

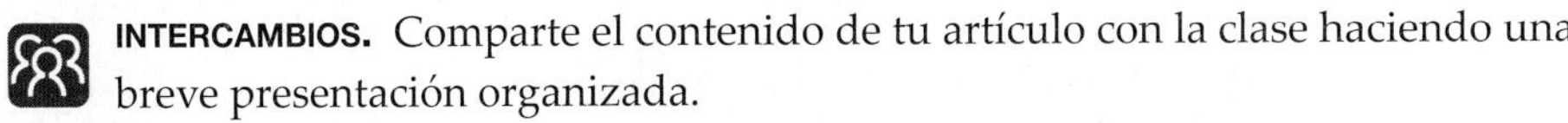

INTERCAMBIOS. Comparte el contenido de tu artículo con la clase haciendo una breve presentación organizada.

13-11 La cultura en los medios de comunicación. **PREPARACIÓN.** Busca en internet un artículo en español sobre algún concierto o película que te interese. Lee el artículo y resúmelo.

INTERCAMBIOS. Comparte con tu grupo el resumen del artículo que leíste. Incluye la siguiente información:

1. el sitio web donde encontraste el artículo
2. el/la autor/a del artículo
3. el tema del artículo
4. las ideas centrales del artículo
5. por qué lo escogiste

13-12 ¿Adónde vamos?

PREPARACIÓN. You will listen to a young couple trying to decide where to go on a Friday evening. With your partner, list three places where you think they might want to go.

ESCUCHA. As you listen, focus on the general idea of what is said. Then select the appropriate ending for each statement.

1. Uno de los eventos culturales a los que Sergio y Dalia consideran ir es…
   a. una exposición de arte precolombino.
   b. una lectura de poemas.
   c. un concierto de música popular.
2. Dalia prefiere ir al…
   a. concierto de la orquesta sinfónica.
   b. Museo de Arte Latinoamericano.
   c. lugar que sea más barato.
3. Para averiguar si hay entradas, Sergio va a…
   a. llamar por teléfono a todos los lugares.
   b. buscar información en internet.
   c. ir personalmente al centro.
4. Mañana ellos van a…
   a. ir al Centro Boliviano de las Artes.
   b. comprar ropa barata.
   c. visitar el Museo de Arte Latinoamericano.

Mosaico cultural

El grafiti y la identidad urbana

El grafiti es una manifestación cultural que ha adquirido mucha fuerza en el mundo hispano. Para Oz Montania, un reconocido artista urbano paraguayo, el grafiti es libertad de expresión y es espacio público. Desde los 12 años, Montania ha llevado esta forma de arte hasta la gente de una manera absolutamente democrática, como dice él. Históricamente, el grafiti —que es una parte del arte urbano— ha tenido inicios políticos: en los periodos de dictadura (*dictatorship*) militar, el grafiti fue una de las formas de expresión ideológica más fuerte, especialmente en Argentina, Chile y México. Desde entonces, el grafiti ha ganado importancia entre las otras artes populares, como la música y la danza.

Grafiti en el barrio La Boca, de Buenos Aires

Sin embargo, este arte popular es todavía relativamente joven y no es comprendido por algunos sectores de la población. Sartos, un grafitero chileno, ha tenido problemas con la policía porque a veces lo han considerado un criminal y no un artista. "Es posible que la gente no entienda el mensaje político de mis grafiti o el humor que contienen. Deben pensar que soy un inconformista", comentó Sartos.

Es obvio que esta manifestación artística ha comenzado a definir la identidad de las ciudades. Desde hace años se celebra en Valparaíso el Festival Mundial del Grafiti. En este encuentro se reúnen artistas urbanos de todo el mundo y pintan gran parte de la ciudad de forma colaborativa. Dice Sartos sobre este proceso creativo: "Lo interesante del grafiti es la integración de lo visual en el contexto urbano. El resultado es un producto cultural que beneficia a todo el mundo".

Un mural en el barrio La Candelaria, de Bogotá

Compara

1. ¿Conoces a algún artista urbano de tu ciudad? ¿Qué tipo de grafiti hace?
2. ¿Piensas que el grafiti es una manifestación artística y que tiene importancia cultural? Justifica tu respuesta.
3. ¿Piensas que los grafitis en los países hispanos son diferentes de los de Estados Unidos? Explica tu opinión con ejemplos.

En acción

¡No te lo pierdas!

Antes de ver

13-13 Artistas del mundo hispanoamericano. Selecciona el/la artista que corresponde a cada obra.

1. _____ *Fulang-Chang y yo* a. Gabriel García Márquez
2. _____ *Cien años de soledad* b. Miguel de Cervantes
3. _____ *Danza en Tehuantepec* c. Diego Velázquez
4. _____ *Don Quijote de la Mancha* d. Frida Kahlo
5. _____ *Las Meninas* e. Diego Rivera

Mientras ves

13-14 Manifestaciones artísticas. Selecciona el nombre de la persona interesada en cada tema, según el video.

1. _____ obras de pintores latinoamericanos a. Vanesa
2. _____ música puertorriqueña b. Yolanda y Federico
3. _____ teatro infantil c. Héctor
4. _____ muralistas latinoamericanos d. Esteban

Después de ver

13-15 Preferencias artísticas.

PREPARACIÓN. Indica si las siguientes afirmaciones son ciertas (**C**) o falsas (**F**), según el video. Corrige las afirmaciones falsas.

1. _____ El Museo de Arte Latinoamericano tiene una importante colección de obras de artistas hispanos del siglo XIX.
2. _____ A Héctor le interesan mucho los artistas que hacen un comentario social a través de (*through*) sus obras.
3. _____ Federico y Yolanda salen a la calle para entrevistar a un novelista hispano.
4. _____ En el festival que grabó (*recorded*) Vanesa, se celebra la cultura y herencia de todos los latinos en Estados Unidos.
5. _____ Según Choco Orta, la música salsa representa la voz de la gente pobre e invisible.

INTERCAMBIOS. En el video que muestra Héctor se dice que algunos artistas hispanos enfocan su arte en la realidad política o económica de su país. ¿Hay artistas en su país que se enfoquen en la política o la economía? Expliquen con ejemplos de una obra de algún artista que ustedes conozcan.

FUNCIONES Y FORMAS

1 Talking about the future

PROFESORA: Según los expertos, el arte del futuro **será** una expresión popular; **tendremos** la posibilidad de crear obras de arte usando una combinación de técnicas tradicionales y programas de computadoras. Es decir, **manipularás** tus imágenes ilimitadamente para crear obras digitales en tercera dimensión.

JULIA: Pero, ¿cómo **ocurrirá** esto?

PROFESORA: Los artistas **sustituirán** el mundo real por el virtual. **Se conectarán** a unas gafas de realidad virtual que les **permitirán** tener un espacio tridimensional. **Podrán** usar su habitación como un lienzo (*canvas*) blanco, donde **dibujarán** y **pintarán** en el aire usando un pincel de inclinación (*tilt brush*).

JULIA: Entonces, ¿quiere decir que en el futuro **habrá** millones de pintores y que todos **seremos** famosos con la ayuda de la tecnología?

PROFESORA: Todos **tendremos** acceso a la tecnología para hacer arte. Pero, nuestro talento e imaginación **dirán** si somos famosos o no.

Piénsalo. Escribe el sujeto del verbo en negrita (*bold*) en cada afirmación. Luego, indica el infinitivo de los verbos en negrita.

	SUJETO	INFINITIVO
1. El arte del futuro **será** una expresión popular.	________	________
2. **Tendremos** la posibilidad de crear obras de arte.	________	________
3. **Manipularás** tus imágenes ilimitadamente para crear obras digitales en tercera dimensión.	________	________
4. ¿Cómo **ocurrirá** esto?	________	________
5. **Se conectarán** a unas gafas de realidad virtual.	________	________
6. Nuestro talento e imaginación **dirán** si somos famosos o no.	________	________

The future tense

You have been using the present tense and **ir a** + *infinitive* to express future plans. Spanish also has a future tense. Although you have other ways to express a future action, event, or state, it is important to be able to recognize the future tense in reading and in listening.

- The future tense of regular verbs is formed by adding the endings **-é, -ás, -á, -emos, -éis,** and **-án** to the infinitive. All verbs, **-ar, -er, -ir,** regular or irregular, use these endings.

FUTURE TENSE			
	HABLAR	**COMER**	**VIVIR**
yo	hablar**é**	comer**é**	vivir**é**
tú	hablar**ás**	comer**ás**	vivir**ás**
Ud., él, ella	hablar**á**	comer**á**	vivir**á**
nosotros/as	hablar**emos**	comer**emos**	vivir**emos**
vosotros/as	hablar**éis**	comer**éis**	vivir**éis**
Uds., ellos/as	hablar**án**	comer**án**	vivir**án**

Rafael **visitará** Bolivia el mes próximo. *Rafael will visit Bolivia next month.*
Él y sus colegas **volverán** después de dos semanas. *He and his colleagues will return after two weeks.*
Se reunirán con sus clientes bolivianos en La Paz. *They will meet with their Bolivian customers in La Paz.*

- Some verbs have irregular stems in the future tense and can be grouped into three categories. The first group drops the **-e** from the infinitive ending.

IRREGULAR FUTURE—GROUP 1		
Infinitive	**New Stem**	**Future Forms**
haber	**habr-**	habrá
poder	**podr-**	podré, podrás, podrá, podremos podréis, podrán
querer	**querr-**	querré, querrás, querrá, querremos, querréis, querrán
saber	**sabr-**	sabré, sabrás, sabrá, sabremos, sabréis, sabrán

Este mes **habrá** muchos conciertos. *This month there will be many concerts.*
Podrás escuchar música folclórica. *You will be able to listen to folk music.*

- The second group replaces the **e** or **i** of the infinitive ending with a **-d.**

IRREGULAR FUTURE—GROUP 2		
poner	**pondr-**	pondré, pondrás, pondrá, pondremos, pondréis, pondrán
salir	**saldr-**	saldré, saldrás, saldrá, saldremos, saldréis, saldrán
tener	**tendr-**	tendré, tendrás, tendrá, tendremos, tendréis, tendrán
venir	**vendr-**	vendré, vendrás, vendrá, vendremos, vendréis, vendrán

Pondremos este cuadro en el comedor. *We will put this painting in the dining room.*
Vendrán a cenar el jueves. *They will come over for dinner on Thursday.*

- The third group consists of two verbs whose stems in the future tense are quite different from their respective infinitives.

IRREGULAR FUTURE—GROUP 3		
decir	**dir-**	diré, dirás, dirá, diremos, diréis, dirán
hacer	**har-**	haré, harás, hará, haremos, haréis, harán

El profesor nos **dirá** las preguntas del examen.	*The professor will tell us the exam questions.*
Nosotros **haremos** muchos exámenes de práctica.	*We will do many practice tests.*

e **¿Comprendes?** Completa las siguientes ideas sobre el futuro, usando los verbos entre paréntesis.

1. En 20 años, _______ más artistas visuales. (haber)
2. Los artistas _______ mucha competencia porque muchas personas _______ dedicarse al arte. (tener; querer)
3. Las exposiciones de arte _______ presenciales (*in person*) y virtuales. (ser)
4. Los piratas (*hackers*) cibernéticos no _______ robar (*steal*) obras fácilmente. (poder)
5. Nosotros _______ cursos para aprender a crear arte en tercera dimensión. (hacer)

Cultura

La protección de la Madre Tierra Bolivia, uno de los ocho países con más diversidad biológica del mundo, posee 66 de los 112 ecosistemas existentes. Las áreas protegidas por las leyes bolivianas incluyen parques nacionales, monumentos naturales, reservas de vida silvestre (*wildlife*), santuarios nacionales y reservas naturales. En las áreas protegidas se puede ver una enorme riqueza de flora y fauna. De hecho, Bolivia ocupa el quinto lugar entre los países más ricos en aves del mundo y el décimo lugar entre los países con el mayor número de especies de plantas, particularmente en los Andes. Los indígenas bolivianos piensan que "la Madre Tierra podrá vivir sin nosotros, pero nosotros no podemos vivir sin ella".

Comparaciones ¿Se protege la naturaleza en tu región o país? ¿Cómo? ¿Hay reservas naturales en tu región o país? ¿Dónde están y qué se protege? ¿Qué piensan los pueblos indígenas de tu país sobre la protección de la Tierra?

PRÁCTICA

13-16 ¿Qué harán en Bolivia? Selecciona la opción correcta para completar cada oración.

1. A Juana y a Mario les gusta comer bien. _____ a un restaurante especializado en la cocina de Santa Cruz.
2. A doña María y a su hija les fascinan los parques con una gran variedad de especies animales. _____ un viaje juntas al Parque Nacional Madidi cerca del Amazonas.
3. Don Jorge y yo leímos sobre las seis misiones jesuitas fundadas en los siglos XVII y XVIII. _____ la misión que está en San José de Chiquitos.
4. A ti te interesa aprender sobre la historia y la arquitectura de los lugares que visitas. _____ por las calles de la ciudad de Potosí, el lugar donde los conquistadores buscaban oro.
5. En la clase de historia prehispánica, voy a estudiar Tiwanaku, la ciudad capital de una de las civilizaciones más importantes anteriores a los incas. _____ leer sobre las ruinas del imperio y el lago Titicaca.

a. Podré
b. Irán
c. Harán
d. Visitaremos
e. Caminarás

13-17 ¿Qué hará en Santa Cruz? PREPARACIÓN. Mario pasará una semana en Santa Cruz para ver la cultura y el arte del lugar. Para matar (*kill*) su curiosidad, háganse preguntas y contesten según la agenda que preparó Mario.

MODELO E1: *¿Qué hará Mario el jueves al mediodía?*
E2: *Irá al Museo de Arte Contemporáneo. ¿Y cuándo/(a)dónde/qué…?*

PLANIFICACIÓN SEMANAL

LUNES	MARTES	MIÉRCOLES	JUEVES	VIERNES
8:00 a.m. salir para Santa Cruz	9:00 a.m. visitar el Jardín Botánico Santa Cruz	8:00 a.m. hacer senderismo (*hiking*) guiado	10:00 a.m. visitar el Zoológico Santa Cruz	7:00 a.m. empacar las maletas
12:00 p.m. registrarse (*check in*) en el hotel	2:00 p.m. ver las pinturas rupestres (*cave paintings*) en las Cavernas de Mataral	3:00 p.m. ver artesanías del altiplano boliviano (cuero, madera, piedras preciosas)	12:00 p.m. ir al Museo de Arte Contemporáneo	11:00 a.m. dejar (*check out*) el hotel
2:00 p.m. ir al paseo artesanal La Recova UNARCRUZ		6:00 p.m. escuchar música boliviana en vivo en Meraki Teatro Bar		12:00 p.m. almorzar en restaurante El Aljibe
10:00 p.m. acostarse				6:00 p.m. regresar a Estados Unidos

INTERCAMBIOS. Díganse cinco actividades que Mario probablemente hará al regresar a su país. Expliquen por qué.

13-18 Nuestro próximo viaje.

PREPARACIÓN. Ustedes le pidieron recomendaciones a su agente de viajes sobre qué actividades hacer en Asunción. Lean su correo electrónico y decidan un lugar que visitarán individualmente y tres que visitarán juntos/as. Tomen notas. Usen los verbos de la lista u otros.

aprender	conocer	leer	preguntar	recorrer
comprar	hablar	observar	probar	tomar

Actividades	
Individualmente	**Juntos/as**
MODELO *Visitaré el Palacio de Gobierno...*	*Iremos al Museo de la Estación de Ferrocarril. Veremos los primeros trenes de Paraguay. Tomaremos fotos del carro-comedor. Nos sentaremos en...*

Enviar | Enviar más tarde | Guardar | Borrar | Adjuntar | Contactos

Para: estudiante1@gmail.com, estudiante2@gmail.com

De: agente@agenciaguarani.com

Asunto: Qué hacer en Asunción

Estimados clientes:

Unas líneas para recomendarles algunas actividades en Asunción.

- Paseo La Galería: grandes almacenes donde hacer compras y comer
- Museo del Barro: entrada gratis; muestra diversidad cultural
- Cerro Lambaré: vista panorámica de la ciudad
- Plaza de los Desaparecidos: honra la memoria de las víctimas de la dictadura militar de Alfredo Stroessner

Con respecto a museos y arte...

- El Cántaro, Almacén de Arte: venta de artesanía
- Museo de Sillas: gran colección de sillas antiguas y vanguardistas; algunas diseñadas por indígenas
- Museo de Bellas Artes: arte nacional (guaraní) y arte universal

Edificios históricos...

- El Panteón Nacional de los Héroes
- El Banco Nacional de Fomento: antiguo edificio de estilo neoclásico
- El Palacio de Gobierno

INTERCAMBIOS. Cuéntenle a otra pareja qué harán individualmente y juntos/as en Asunción. Luego, identifiquen una semejanza y una diferencia entre las actividades de las dos parejas.

Cultura

El arte al servicio de la historia El Centro de Artes Visuales Museo del Barro fue creado a fines de la década de los 70. Posee una gran colección de piezas de cerámica precolombina de arcilla (*clay*) y barro (*mud*), hechas por indígenas. También exhibe platería (*silversmithing*), encajes (*lace*) y otras obras artísticas grabadas (*engraved*) en madera. De particular importancia histórica es la colección de xilograbados (*woodcuts*) de los periódicos bilingües (español–guaraní) sobre la guerra (*war*).

Santos tallados (*carved*) en madera

Comparaciones ¿Existen museos que muestren el arte indígena en tu comunidad o país? ¿Alguna vez viste palabras (o textos más largos) grabadas en madera? ¿Conoces textos escritos en otros materiales?

13-19 Nuestro futuro. **PREPARACIÓN.** Para el proyecto final de su clase de arte popular, tendrán que crear un póster en el que expresarán su preocupación o entusiasmo por el futuro. Tomen notas mientras hacen lo siguiente:

1. Comenten el tema de su póster: ¿Se referirá a la política, la economía, la ciencia, la tecnología, la antropología, el arte o una mezcla de temas?
2. Hagan una lista de palabras clave para expresar su mensaje.
3. Discutan sus estrategias para llamar la atención del público: ¿Usarán la ubicación del póster, el color, la forma y tamaño de las letras, las imágenes, el relieve? ¿Otras?
4. Escriban por lo menos tres afirmaciones y tres preguntas en su póster. Por ejemplo, para el tema de la economía: ¿Habrá trabajos para todos en el futuro? Seremos felices sin trabajo.

INTERCAMBIOS. Compartan con otro grupo el proyecto de su póster. Luego, háganse las siguientes preguntas. Tomen notas para compartir con la clase.

1. Según ustedes, ¿cuál de los pósteres creados por ustedes llamará más la atención del público del futuro? ¿Por qué?
2. ¿Cómo reaccionará el público a cada una de las preguntas o afirmaciones que hicieron? ¿Cómo responderá a sus preguntas?

13-20 Un acróstico. **PREPARACIÓN.** Escoge a una persona a quien le escribirás un acróstico relacionado con su futuro. Usa tu imaginación y tu sentido del humor.

MODELO *Mantendrás una actitud positiva. Te reirás incluso de los problemas.*
Ayudarás a muchos en tu trabajo y en la comunidad, pero pocos te ayudarán a ti porque pensarán que eres una supermujer.
Resolverás todos tus problemas porque eres inteligente y positiva.
Y tendrás una larga y exitosa vida.

INTERCAMBIOS. Intercambien sus acrósticos y lean el suyo. Luego, hablen sobre el contenido, respondiendo a las siguientes preguntas.

1. ¿Cómo es el tono del acróstico que recibiste cómico, trágico, positivo, negativo...? ¿Por qué?
2. ¿Te gustó el acróstico? Explica.

Situación

PREPARACIÓN. Lean esta situación. Luego, compartan ejemplos de vocabulario, gramática y otra información que necesitan para desarrollar la conversación.

Role A. You and your friend (your classmate) are speculating about what your lives will be like ten years from now. Describe your vision of your future to your friend. Answer your friend's questions. Say:

a. where you and the people important to you will live ten years from now;
b. what you will do for a living and how you will probably feel about your life then;
c. at least two activities that you will want to do ten years from now; and
d. if you will go to new places, where you will go, and with whom.

Role B. You and your friend (your classmate) are envisioning your own personal futures ten years from now. As your friend shares his/her vision of his/her future, ask questions. Then, switch roles and answer your friend's questions.

	ROLE A	ROLE B
Vocabulario	Vocabulary related to future life: job, places to go, dream activities	Vocabulary related to future life: job, places to go, dream activities
Funciones y formas	Talking about the distant future Asking and answering questions Future tense	Talking about the distant future Asking and answering questions Future tense

INTERCAMBIOS. Practiquen la conversación, incorporando el vocabulario y las funciones de **Preparación.** Luego, represéntenla ante la clase.

2 Hypothesizing

MANUEL: Aquí veo solo dos de los instrumentos para el concierto de esta noche. ¿Dónde están los otros?

MÓNICA: Siempre grabamos (*record*) digitalmente la música de los otros instrumentos. Yo los **traería** todos, pero **sería** carísimo. **Gastaríamos** demasiado para transportar los tambores, las guitarras y las quijadas (*jawbones*), por ejemplo.

MANUEL: ¿Cuánto **costaría** transportar los otros instrumentos?

MÓNICA: Bueno, yo **tendría** que pagar 200 dólares solo para transportar mi guitarra. Para traer todos los instrumentos, **pagaríamos** una fortuna.

Piénsalo. Indica en la columna correspondiente si cada una de las siguientes afirmaciones se refiere a la **realidad** o a una **hipótesis.**

	REALIDAD	HIPÓTESIS
1. Aquí **veo** solo dos de los instrumentos para el concierto.	_____	_____
2. Siempre **grabamos** digitalmente la música de los otros instrumentos.	_____	_____
3. ¿Cuánto **costaría** transportar los otros instrumentos?	_____	_____
4. **Sería** carísimo.	_____	_____
5. **Tendría** que pagar $200 solo para transportar mi guitarra.	_____	_____
6. **Pagaríamos** una fortuna.	_____	_____

The conditional

- You have used the expression **me gustaría...** to express what you would like. **Gustaría** is a form of the conditional.
- The conditional in Spanish is similar to the English construction *would* + *verb*. It is used to hypothesize about a situation that is not part of the speaker's present reality.

Yo **saldría** temprano para el concierto, pero trabajo hasta tarde. — *I would leave early for the concert, but I work late. (and therefore I can't leave early)*

- The conditional is easy to recognize. The conditional tense of regular verbs is formed by adding the endings **-ía, -ías, -ía, -íamos, -íais, -ían** to the infinitive.

CONDITIONAL			
	HABLAR	**COMER**	**VIVIR**
yo	hablar**ía**	comer**ía**	vivir**ía**
tú	hablar**ías**	comer**ías**	vivir**ías**
Ud., él, ella	hablar**ía**	comer**ía**	vivir**ía**
nosotros/as	hablar**íamos**	comer**íamos**	vivir**íamos**
vosotros/as	hablar**íais**	comer**íais**	vivir**íais**
Uds., ellos/as	hablar**ían**	comer**ían**	vivir**ían**

- Verbs with an irregular stem in the future have that same stem in the conditional.

IRREGULAR CONDITIONAL VERBS		
INFINITIVE	**NEW STEM**	**CONDITIONAL FORMS**
haber	**habr-**	habría
poder	**podr-**	podría, podrías, podría...
querer	**querr-**	querría, querrías, querría...
saber	**sabr-**	sabría, sabrías, sabría...
poner	**pondr-**	pondría, pondrías, pondría...
salir	**saldr-**	saldría, saldrías, saldría...
tener	**tendr-**	tendría, tendrías, tendría...
venir	**vendr-**	vendría, vendrías, vendría...
decir	**dir-**	diría, dirías, diría...
hacer	**har-**	haría, harías, haría...

Yo **pondría** el cuadro sobre la chimenea. — *I would put the painting over the fireplace.*

¿**Podrías** escribir un poema de amor en español? — *Would you be able to write a love poem in Spanish?*

- When English *would* implies *used to*, the imperfect is used in Spanish.

Cuando era chica, mi papá me **llevaba** a conciertos al aire libre en el parque. — *When I was little, my father would (used to) take me to open air concerts in the park.*

e **¿Comprendes?** Completa las oraciones con el condicional de los verbos.

1. De ser el líder del grupo, yo __________ (pagar) para llevar todos los instrumentos a mis conciertos.
2. El público __________ (preferir) escuchar la música en vivo a escucharla digitalizada.
3. Nosotros __________ (ganar) más dinero porque __________ (asistir) más público.
4. Los conciertos __________ (ser) un éxito rotundo.
5. Los músicos __________ (tener) más oportunidades de dar conciertos.

PRÁCTICA

13-21 ¿Qué harías? **PREPARACIÓN.** Lee las siguientes situaciones y escoge lo que probablemente harías.

1. Tu amigo Jeremy se especializa en español y le fascina la literatura. Es su cumpleaños y le quieres regalar algo útil.
   a. Le compraría la novela más famosa del autor paraguayo Roa Bastos traducida al inglés.
   b. Le regalaría *El Quijote* de Cervantes.
   c. Le daría un buen diccionario.
2. El grupo musical boliviano Tupay va a dar un concierto en tu ciudad este fin de semana.
   a. Como mi amiga Ángela conoce su música, la invitaría al concierto.
   b. Llamaría a mis amigos para ir juntos al concierto.
   c. Llevaría mi guitarra para tocar con ellos durante el concierto.
3. Van a estrenar (pasar por primera vez) una nueva película de Guillermo del Toro.
   a. Iría a ver la película la noche del estreno.
   b. No vería la película porque no me interesa ese director.
   c. Leería las reseñas (*reviews*) antes de ir a verla.
4. Vas a pasar unos días en Asunción, pero tienes poco tiempo para visitar el Museo Nacional de Bellas Artes. ¿Qué harías?
   a. Pasaría algunos minutos en el museo para conocerlo.
   b. Me informaría sobre lo que se puede ver en el museo.
   c. Solo visitaría las salas donde están las obras de mis pintores favoritos.

INTERCAMBIOS. Comparen sus respuestas y después digan qué harían ustedes realmente en esas situaciones.

Cultura

Museo Nacional de Bellas Artes El Museo Nacional de Bellas Artes de Asunción es el museo más importante de Paraguay. En él se puede apreciar la historia del país, caracterizada por la importancia de la cultura indígena y por su aislamiento (*isolation*) de corrientes artísticas y emigraciones de influencia europea hasta el siglo XX. Hoy en día, tiene una importante colección de arte indígena y también obras de los principales artistas paraguayos del siglo XX que siguieron tendencias (*trends*) cosmopolitas. También tiene una colección de artistas internacionales.

Comparaciones ¿Con qué frecuencia visitas museos de arte? ¿Qué tipo de obras se pueden ver en el museo de bellas artes de tu ciudad o estado?

13-22 ¿Cómo deberíamos gastar el dinero? **PREPARACIÓN.** Tu universidad ha recibido 100.000 dólares para promover el interés de los alumnos en las artes y las letras. Estás en un comité cuya (*whose*) misión es decidir qué hacer con el dinero y por qué. Escribe algunas ideas relacionadas con los siguientes temas.

1. promocionar la pintura
2. despertar el interés por las artes populares
3. organizar proyectos de pintura, escritura, etc. para la comunidad
4. ...

INTERCAMBIOS. Comenten y comparen sus planes hipotéticos. Luego, seleccionen el mejor plan y explíquenle a la clase por qué lo escogieron.

13-23 Buscar soluciones. Primero di qué harías en las siguientes situaciones. Después, compara tus respuestas con las de otros/as estudiantes.

1. Estás en un restaurante y ves que los miembros de tu conjunto musical favorito están en otra mesa.
2. Una amiga tuya es pintora y necesita dinero para montar su primera exposición.
3. Acabas de descubrir que alguien en el campus está vendiendo entradas falsas y muy baratas para un concierto de un grupo famoso.
4. Alguien acaba de contarte que la persona que pintó grafiti en las paredes de la residencia donde vives es uno de tus mejores amigos.

13-24 ¿Qué harían en estas situaciones? Túrnense para comentar qué harían en los siguientes casos.

MODELO Te gustaría estudiar arte en Italia. El programa es carísimo.
E1: *Mis padres me pagarían todo porque les gusta mucho el arte.*
E2: *¡Qué suerte tienes! Yo tendría que trabajar mucho para pagarlo todo.*

1. Un amigo te invita a un concierto. No te gusta mucho la banda.
2. Quieres asistir a una lectura (*reading*) de poesía esta noche. Ninguno de tus amigos quiere acompañarte.
3. Te gustaría aprender a tocar el piano, pero no tienes tiempo para practicar.
4. Paco tiene ganas de ver una exposición de arte en otra ciudad, pero no tiene auto.
5. Invitaste a tus padres a visitarte este fin de semana. Ahora no quieres que vengan porque tienes que terminar un proyecto importante.
6. Tienes que tocar el violín en un recital dentro de una semana y estás muy nervioso/a.

13-25 Músicos aficionados.

 **PREPARACIÓN.** Tienen un grupo de amigos que han creado una banda de música muy buena, pero no saben promocionarse. Denles ideas de lo que ustedes harían en su lugar.

MODELO hacer calcomanías (*bumper stickers*) con el nombre de la banda

E1: *Yo haría calcomanías con el nombre de la banda.*

E2: *¡Buena idea! Yo se las regalaría a sus seguidores para poner en sus autos. Sería buena publicidad para la banda.*

compartir algunas canciones por medios sociales
contactar (*network*) con otras bandas
contratar a una compañía de promoción
diseñar un buen sitio web para la banda
escribir un blog sobre las actividades de la banda
hacer publicidad tradicional: pósteres, comunicados de prensa (*press releases*), etc.
ofrecer conciertos gratuitos (*free*) al aire libre
relacionarse con sus seguidores en los medios sociales

 **INTERCAMBIOS.** Compartan sus ideas con otra pareja y escojan las mejores para compartir con la clase.

Situación

PREPARACIÓN. Lean la situación. Luego, compartan ejemplos de vocabulario, gramática y otra información que necesitan para desarrollar la conversación.

Role A. You are considering visiting Paraguay next summer so you call a Paraguayan friend who goes there regularly. Include the following in your conversation:
a. ask how much money you would need for food and lodging for a month in Paraguay;
b. tell your friend that you are really interested in seeing and studying the indigenous art of Paraguay;
c. ask your friend to recommend some Paraguayan folk music; and
d. find out how long it would take to learn Guarani, the indigenous language of Paraguay.

Role B. Your friend is thinking of visiting Paraguay, your native country. Tell your friend the following:
a. he/she would probably need around U.S. $1,500 for food and lodging for a month if he/she stays at youth hostels (**albergues juveniles**);
b. you would recommend the **Museo Nacional de Bellas Artes** in Asunción for indigenous art; and
c. the **Teatro Nacional** for concerts of Paraguayan folk music;
d. he/she would probably be able to learn some basic expressions in Guarani during the trip, but it's totally different from Spanish.

	ROLE A	ROLE B
Vocabulario	Expressions related to traveling and popular art, such as handicrafts Question words	Expressions related to traveling and popular art, such as handicrafts
Funciones y formas	Asking questions about hypothetical situations The conditional	Answering questions Giving suggestions about hypothetical situations The conditional

INTERCAMBIOS. Practiquen la conversación, incorporando el vocabulario y las funciones de **Preparación.** Luego, represéntenla ante la clase.

3 Talking about the past

JOSEFINA: Alberto, ¿qué piensas de esta obra?
ALBERTO: Es una expresión magnífica del arte abstracto.
JOSEFINA: ¿Ah, sí? ¿Quién la **pintó?**
ALBERTO: **Fue** un artista que en todas sus obras **pintaba** un ojo abstracto. **Tenía** mucho talento, pero **murió** joven. **Empezó** a pintar a los 15 años y **vendió** su primer cuadro a los 17 años. Poca gente lo **conocía.** Sin embargo, **era** uno de los favoritos de los críticos.
JOSEFINA: ¿Qué le **pasó?**
ALBERTO: **Tuvo** un accidente de moto cuando **viajaba** por los Andes. ¡Muy trágico!

Piénsalo. Indica si cada una de las oraciones se refiere a un evento que ocurrió en el pasado (**E**), o si es una descripción en el pasado (**D**).

1. _____ ¿Quién lo **pintó?**
2. _____ En todas sus obras **pintaba** un ojo abstracto.
3. _____ **Tenía** mucho talento.
4. _____ **Murió** joven.
5. _____ **Vendió** su primer cuadro a los 17 años.
6. _____ Poca gente lo **conocía.**

Review of the preterit and the imperfect

- In previous chapters, you learned two ways to express the past in Spanish: the preterit (**el pretérito**) and the imperfect (**el imperfecto**). You used the preterit to talk about past actions or conditions that are viewed as completed or ended. You used the imperfect to describe situations, characteristics, and conditions in the past; to express habitual or repeated actions, or activities in progress at a particular time in the past; and to tell the time and someone's age in the past. In this section, you will gain further experience using the preterit and imperfect to narrate and describe in the past.

REGULAR PRETERIT ENDINGS			
	-ar	**-er**	**-ir**
yo	-é	-í	-í
tú	-aste	-iste	-iste
Ud., él, ella	-ó	-ió	-ió
nosotros/as	-amos	-imos	-imos
vosotros/as	-asteis	-isteis	-isteis
Uds., ellos/as	-aron	-ieron	-ieron

REGULAR IMPERFECT ENDINGS			
	-ar	**-er**	**-ir**
yo	-aba	-ía	-ía
tú	-abas	-ías	-ías
Ud., él, ella	-aba	-ía	-ía
nosotros/as	-ábamos	-íamos	-íamos
vosotros/as	-abais	-íais	-íais
Uds., ellos/as	-aban	-ían	-ían

Refer to *Capítulos 6* through *9* for more information about the past tense.

 **¿Comprendes?** Escoge entre el pretérito y el imperfecto en cada oración.

1. Durante nuestra visita a La Paz, Marcos y yo (fuimos/íbamos) al Museo Nacional de Arte Contemporáneo.
2. (Fue/Era) temprano cuando el museo (abrió/abría) sus puertas.
3. (Hubo/Había) un guardia en cada sala del museo.
4. Toda la gente (caminó/caminaba) en silencio y (admiró/admiraba) las hermosas obras de arte.
5. Marcos y su familia siempre (fueron/iban) al museo cuando él y sus hermanos (fueron/eran) pequeños.

PRÁCTICA

 **13-26 El arpa de Paraguay.** Lee la siguiente historia sobre el arpa en la música paraguaya. Completa las oraciones con la forma correcta del pretérito o el imperfecto de los verbos. Luego, compara tus respuestas con las de tu compañero/a.

Los historiadores afirman que los españoles (1) __________ (traer) el arpa a América. Cuando este instrumento (2) __________ (llegar) a Paraguay, a los habitantes indígenas del lugar les (3) __________ (encantar) la música que (4) __________ (tocar) el español don Martín Niño. El contacto de la cultura europea y la indígena (5) __________ (resultar) en la fusión de dos culturas. De esa unión (6) __________ (nacer) el arpa paraguaya. Los guaraníes (7) __________ (adoptar) el arpa y la (8) __________ (remodelar), usando materiales americanos, como la madera. También (9) __________ (crear) su propio repertorio musical. (10) __________ (Ser) obvio para los jesuitas y los franciscanos españoles que los mestizos (11) __________ (tener) gran talento musical. Con cada perfeccionamiento del instrumento musical, los clérigos (12) __________ (observar) una mejor sonoridad y claridad en la ejecución del arpa paraguaya. Por ejemplo, (13) __________ (usar) las uñas (*fingernails*) de la mano derecha para crear la melodía. El acompañamiento lo (14) __________ (hacer) con la mano izquierda. Con los años, el arpa (15) __________ (pasar) a ser parte de diversos tipos de música de México, Venezuela, Perú, Chile y Argentina.

13-27 Un espectáculo inolvidable.

 **PREPARACIÓN.** Piensa en un espectáculo emocionante al que asististe en el pasado. Habla con tu compañero/a sobre el espectáculo e incluye la siguiente información.

1. lo que sabías acerca del espectáculo y los artistas antes de ir
2. lo que esperabas ver allí
3. algo nuevo que descubriste después de ver el espectáculo y los artistas
4. dos actividades que hiciste y dos actividades que no hiciste
5. lo que más recuerdas del espectáculo

 **INTERCAMBIOS.** Determinen cuál de los dos espectáculos fue el más interesante y por qué. Compartan con la clase sus experiencias en el espectáculo.

13-28 Nuestro viaje a Bolivia. Visiten virtualmente las salas del Museo Nacional de Etnografía y Folklore de Bolivia y seleccionen un objeto que les interese. Presenten un informe breve a la clase con la siguiente información.

1. qué tipo de objeto es
2. cuándo y dónde se encontró
3. quiénes lo usaban y para qué lo usaban
4. qué importancia tenía
5. otros detalles interesantes que ustedes descubrieron en su investigación

13-29 No hay mal que por bien no venga (*Every cloud has a silver lining*). **PREPARACIÓN.** Observen las escenas. Tomen apuntes sobre lo que pasó en cada escena y cómo se sentían Diego y Carla.

Eventos	Detalles descriptivos
1.	1.
2.	2.
3.	3.
4.	4.
...	...

INTERCAMBIOS. Luego, túrnense para contar la historia de Diego y Carla. Usen sus apuntes de **Preparación** para enfocarse (*concentrate*) en los eventos y para incorporar muchos detalles descriptivos. Las expresiones de la lista les ayudarán a contar una historia coherente.

A las cuatro de la tarde... / A las nueve menos cinco de la noche...
Entonces... / Luego...
Todo terminó bien porque...

13-30 Investigación de un robo en la universidad. **PREPARACIÓN.** Durante la noche alguien entró en el museo de su universidad y robó (*stole*) un objeto de cerámica de la colección de arte latinoamericano. Ustedes tienen que averiguar quién lo hizo. Túrnense para preguntarle a una persona de su grupo sobre sus actividades de la noche anterior: dónde estaba, con quién estaba y qué hizo entre las ocho y las doce de la noche.

INTERCAMBIOS. Hagan un resumen de las actividades de los miembros de su grupo para presentar a la clase.

Situación

PREPARACIÓN. Lean la situación. Luego, compartan ejemplos de vocabulario, gramática y otra información que necesitan para desarrollar la conversación.

Role A. Last week you travelled to La Paz, Bolivia and, on the plane, you happened to be seated next to a well-known actor. Call your best friend and tell him/her:
a. who the famous person was;
b. what he/she looked like;
c. what he/she was wearing; and
d. if you spoke to him/her and what you talked about.

Role B. Your best friend calls you to tell you that he/she met a well-known actor on his/her flight to Bolivia. Listen to his/her descriptions and information about the encounter. Ask him/her additional information:
a. what the famous actor did during the flight;
b. what he/she ate;
c. why he/she was sitting in economy class; etc.

	ROLE A	ROLE B
Vocabulario	Physical descriptions Clothes	Airplane and travel expressions Food
Funciones y formas	Using the imperfect to describe Using the preterit for actions	Using the imperfect to describe Using the preterit for actions

INTERCAMBIOS. Practiquen la conversación, incorporando el vocabulario y las funciones de **Preparación.** Luego, represéntenla ante la clase.

MOSAICOS

ESCUCHA

Estrategia

Identify the speaker's intentions When you listen to a speaker, you can frequently infer his or her intentions from the context. Let's imagine that you get this message: "I have a couple of tickets to a recital. Please give me a call." You immediately know the caller wants to invite you to the recital, even though the word *invitation* has not been uttered.

To identify correctly a speaker's intention, follow these tips:

- Hypothesize about what the speaker probably means, making logical connections based on what you hear.
- As you listen, see if you can confirm your hypothesis.
- If you get information that does not fit, form a new hypothesis.

13-31 Preparación. Cuatro estudiantes universitarios hablarán sobre actividades culturales. Antes de escuchar lo que dicen, haz una lista de tres actividades culturales que te interesan a ti. Compártela con la clase.

  **13-32 Escucha.** Read the following statements, and then listen to the students. Write the number of the speaker (1–4) associated with each statement.

_____ Miguel probablemente quiere escuchar a los artistas latinoamericanos o conversar con ellos para decidir sus estudios de posgrado.
_____ Joaquín es el pintor a quien le gusta más la pintura mexicana.
_____ Rosa María piensa ir a ver las obras de teatro este año.
_____ Eugenia es pianista y quiere convencer a otra persona de las ventajas de aprender a tocar el piano.

Comprueba

I was able to . . .

- understand descriptions of cultural interests and activities.
- make logical connections between interests and activities.

 **13-33 Un paso más.** Comparte tu opinión con tu compañero/a.

1. ¿Es importante que los jóvenes aprendan a apreciar las diversas expresiones artísticas (la pintura, la música clásica, el teatro o la escultura)? ¿Por qué?
2. ¿Qué manifestación artística prefieres?
3. ¿Cuándo fue la última vez que asististe a un evento cultural o artístico? ¿Qué tipo de evento fue? ¿Qué viste o escuchaste? ¿Te gustó? ¿Por qué?

HABLA

Estrategia

Make your presentations comprehensible and interesting When you give a presentation in your Spanish class, your two challenges are a) to make it understandable to your classmates; and b) to make it interesting. The following guidelines will help you:

- Keep it simple. If you consulted sources for your presentation, present content in your own words. Look up new words in the dictionary and simplify your speech.
- Practice your presentation, so you can talk, not read, to your audience.
- Use visuals and props to make your presentation more lively and interesting.
- Involve your audience. Make eye contact, ask questions, check that they understand you, and invite them to ask questions.

 **13-34 Preparación.** Escojan a una de las siguientes personas relacionadas con las artes. Busquen la información sugerida sobre ella e incluyan otra información pertinente.

Eduardo Caba	Carlos Colombino	Jaime Laredo
Luis Cañete	Susy Delgado	Marina Núñez del Prado
Luzmila Carpio	Efrén Echeverría	María Luisa Pacheco
Pablo Casals	Alfonso Gumucio Dagron	Cayo Sila Godoy

1. datos personales: fecha y lugar de nacimiento/muerte
2. profesión: contribución a su profesión, obras destacadas
3. logros: premios, reconocimientos

Comprueba

I was able to . . .

- present the main contributions of an important person.
- give biographical information about this person.
- use visuals and props to make my presentation interesting.

 **13-35 Habla.** Hagan una breve presentación sobre la persona que escogieron en la actividad **13-34.** Tengan en cuenta las estrategias para hacer una presentación. Incluyan la mayor cantidad de información posible.

En directo

To support a decision:

Elegimos a... porque... *We chose . . . because . . .*

Lo que más influyó en nuestra decisión fue/fueron... *What most influenced our decision was/were . . .*

Nuestra decisión se basó en lo siguiente... *Our decision was based on the following . . .*

 Listen to a conversation with these expressions.

 **13-36 Un paso más.** Entrevisten a otra pareja sobre el/la artista que eligieron. Háganle al menos tres preguntas. Intercambien roles.

LEE

Estrategia

Focus on multiple meanings when reading poetry When you read a narrative or journalistic text in Spanish, you have learned to increase your comprehension by going for the main ideas and using your prior knowledge to guess what the text is about. When you read poetry in Spanish, you need different strategies. Start by looking up the meanings of unfamiliar words. Then, with a pencil in your hand, read the poem aloud several times. Circle important, unusual, or repeated words. Draw lines to connect related ideas. Try to unfold the language of the poem by paraphrasing it in straightforward sentences: subject, verb, object. This will help you answer the question: "What is this poem about?"

 **13-37 Preparación.** Organiza las siguientes palabras en dos listas: **Conceptos positivos** y **Conceptos negativos.** Luego, compara tus listas con las de tu compañero/a. ¿Son iguales o diferentes? Añadan otras palabras.

la alegría	el egoísmo	la pobreza
la armonía	el entusiasmo	la tranquilidad
la crueldad	la felicidad	la tristeza
el dolor	la injusticia	la violencia
la educación	el optimismo	

13-38 **Lee.** Lee la siguiente nota biográfica sobre la autora. Después, lee el poema y relaciona los conceptos con las categorías: característica o emoción personal, o problema social.

Gloria Fuertes, poeta española (1917–1998), nació en Madrid. Era de una familia pobre: su madre era costurera (*seamstress*) y sirvienta, y su padre limpiaba edificios comerciales. Fuertes comenzó a una edad temprana a escribir cuentos y poemas. De adolescente, leía sus poemas en Radio España, de Madrid. En 1961, recibió la beca Fulbright para dar clases de poesía española en la Universidad de Bucknell, en Pensilvania. Los temas principales de su poesía son el amor, la muerte y los derechos humanos. Le interesaba mucho la capacidad de la poesía de revelar el significado profundo de la vida cotidiana (*everyday*). Además de sus poemas para adultos, también escribió cuentos y poemas para niños.

Comprueba

I was able to . . .

- understand what the poem is about.
- understand the emotional impact of words in the poem.

POEMA AL NO

No a la tristeza.
No al dolor.
No a la pereza[1].
No a la usura[2].
No a la envidia.
No a la incultura[3].
No a la violencia.
No a la injusticia.
No a la guerra[4].
Sí a la paz[5].
Sí a la alegría.
Sí a la amistad.

[1]*laziness* [2]*usury (lending money at excessively high interest rates)* [3]*ignorance* [4]*war* [5]*peace*

Concepto	¿Personal o social?
1. la tristeza	
2. el dolor	
3. la pereza	
4. la usura	
5. la envidia	
6. la incultura	
7. la violencia	
8. la injusticia	
9. la guerra	
10. la paz	
11. la alegría	
12. la amistad	

 **13-39 Un paso más.** Comparen sus respuestas a la actividad **13-38** y respondan a las siguientes preguntas. Luego, presenten sus conclusiones a la clase.

1. ¿Están de acuerdo en su clasificación de los conceptos? ¿Por qué piensan que un concepto es social o personal? Den ejemplos.
2. De los problemas sociales que se mencionan en el poema, ¿cuáles son los más urgentes, en su opinión? ¿Por qué?

ESCRIBE

Estrategia

Use language to express emotions Poetry is well suited to the expression of emotions. Poets use words to paint experiences or feelings of heroism, beauty, love, sadness, loss, or injustice. To compose an effective poem, it is important to think carefully about the feelings we want to convey. Because poetry is a reflection of human experience, it is available to everyone both as readers and writers.

13-40 Preparación. Lee otra vez el poema en la actividad **13-38** y revisa (*review*) tus respuestas a las actividades **13-38** y **13-39.** Haz una lista de las palabras y oraciones que expresan algunas de tus ideas sobre la sociedad en que vives.

 **13-41 Escribe.** Escribe tu propio "Poema al No", siguiendo el formato del poema de Fuertes en la actividad **13-38:** unos versos (*lines*) que comienzan **No a...** y luego unos versos que comienzan **Sí a...**

 **13-42 Un paso más.** Lee el poema que escribió tu compañero/a. Luego, hazle preguntas sobre sus ideas y las palabras que seleccionó para expresarlas.

Comprueba

I was able to . . .

- imitate the structure of a poem when writing my own poem.
- use single words and short phrases to represent concepts and ideas.

En este capítulo...

Vocabulario

Las personas	*People*
el/la artista	*artist*
el bailarín / la bailarina	*dancer*
el/la cantante	*singer*
la compañía (de danza/teatro)	*(dance/theater) company*
el/la directora/a	*director*
el/la escritor/a	*writer*
el/la escultor/a	*sculptor*
el/la estrella	*star*
el/la guitarrista	*guitarist*
el/la intérprete	*performer, artist*
el/la novelista	*novelist*
el/la pintor/a	*painter*
el/la poeta	*poet*

Las obras de arte	*Works of art*
la adaptación	*adaptation*
el asunto	*issue, topic*
el colorido	*coloring*
el contraste	*contrast*
el cuento	*story*
la danza	*dance*
el disco	*album*
la escena	*scene*
el escenario	*stage*
la escultura	*sculpture*
el estilo	*style*
la forma	*shape, form*
la luz	*light*
el mural	*mural*
la novela	*novel*
la obra	*work*
el paisaje	*landscape*
el personaje principal	*main character*
la pintura	*painting*
la poesía	*poetry*
el repertorio	*repertoire*
la representación	*representation*
el retrato	*portrait*
el símbolo	*symbol*
la sombra	*shadow*
el tema	*topic; theme*
la voz	*voice*

Las descripciones	*Descriptions*
clásico/a	*classical*
conocido/a	*well-known*
contemporáneo/a	*contemporary*
cubista	*cubist*
destacado/a	*prominent*
desnudo/a	*naked*
galardonado/a	*awarded*
inolvidable	*unforgettable*
realista	*realist*
surrealista	*surrealist*
traducido/a	*translated*
transgénero	*transgender*

Verbos	*Verbs*
abundar	*to abound*
desarrollar	*to develop*
exhibir	*to exhibit*
interpretar	*to perform, to play*
narrar	*to narrate*
pintar	*to paint*
retratar	*to portray*
tratar	*to deal with, to be about*

Palabras y expresiones útiles	*Useful words and expressions*
la actualidad	*the present time*
al fondo	*in the background*
la amistad	*friendship*
el amor	*love*
la calidad	*quality*
la carrera literaria	*literary career*
el charango	*guitar-like instrument*
desde	*from; since*
el éxito	*success*
la flauta	*flute*
el fracaso	*failure*
hasta	*until, (up) to*
la maternidad	*motherhood*
el mestizaje	*fusion*
la muerte	*death*
el premio	*award, prize*
el recuerdo	*memory*
la revista del corazón	*gossip magazine*

Capítulo 14

¿Cómo vivimos los cambios sociales?

Manifestación contra la violencia de género en Concepción, Chile

Enfoque cultural
Chile

Vocabulario en contexto
Cambios en la sociedad
Temas de hoy: la emigración
Las mujeres y el trabajo

Mosaico cultural
La migración interna en el mundo hispano

En acción
Por un mundo mejor

Funciones y formas
Adverbial conjunctions that require the subjunctive
Adverbial conjunctions that take the subjunctive or indicative
The past perfect

Mosaicos
ESCUCHA Identify the speaker's point of view
HABLA Organize ideas to present solutions to problems
LEE Identify the tone of a text
ESCRIBE Write to spark interest

En este capítulo...
Vocabulario

Learning Outcomes

You will be able to:

- discuss demographics and social conditions
- indicate conditions, goals, and purposes
- express conjecture
- talk about the past from a past perspective
- talk about Chile in terms of products, practices, and perspectives
- talk about social change, gender roles, and migration

Enfoque cultural

Chile

En el desierto de Atacama, situado en el norte de Chile, se encuentran riquezas minerales como el cobre (*copper*), el hierro, el oro y la plata.

Santiago, la capital de Chile, tiene más de seis millones y medio de habitantes. Es una de las ciudades más importantes de Sudamérica por el comercio y por su alta calidad de vida.

Punta Arenas, frente al estrecho (*strait*) de Magallanes, es la ciudad más al sur del país. En verano, el sol sale (*rises*) antes de las seis de la mañana y se pone (*sets*) después de las 10:00 de la noche.

Arte hispano

Este mural de la artista argentina Elisa Algranati se titula *Al centro de la injusticia*. Se encuentra en la ciudad de Osorno, en Chile, y denuncia la opresión y el sufrimiento de los chilenos durante la dictadura militar entre 1973 y 1990.

Enfoque cultural

¿Qué te parece?

- Muchos han especulado que el nombre de Chile proviene de la palabra quechua *chiri*, que significa "frío, helado". Sin embargo, otros piensan que el nombre probablemente viene de Tili, un cacique picunche, quien gobernó la región de Aconcagua antes de la llegada de los españoles. Hasta hoy no existe consenso sobre el origen del nombre de Chile.
- El pueblo indígena más numeroso de Chile son los mapuches. Los índices de pobreza de este pueblo son superiores a la media nacional chilena, debido a la discriminación racial y social que sufren.
- Al sur de Chile, compartida con Argentina, se encuentra la Patagonia. La parte chilena tiene una geografía muy variada, con gran diversidad de ecosistemas, con islas y fiordos (*fjords*) formados por el hundimiento (*sinking*) de los Andes.
- Los recursos económicos más importantes de Chile son el cobre, el vino, la fruta y el pescado, los cuales Chile exporta a muchos países en todos los continentes.

A aproximadamente 3.670 kilómetros del puerto de Valparaíso, está la isla de Pascua, que forma parte del territorio chileno. Aparte del español, en la isla se habla el rapanui, una lengua indígena. En la isla hay unas esculturas gigantes, los moáis, que son muy antiguas y tienen forma humana. Por su historia y su atractivo cultural, la isla de Pascua es un lugar visitado por muchos turistas de todo el mundo. En 1996, el Parque Nacional Rapa Nui fue declarado Patrimonio de la Humanidad por la UNESCO.

El pastel de choclo y las empanadas son dos platos típicamente chilenos. Preparado con choclo, o maíz, carne y huevos, el pastel de choclo usualmente se come durante el verano. Las empanadas son normalmente de carne o de mariscos. Tanto el pastel de choclo como las empanadas se acompañan con vino tinto o blanco.

En los últimos 20 años, Chile se ha convertido en uno de los principales países exportadores de vino de todo el mundo. Los mercados de China, Estados Unidos y Gran Bretaña son los destinos principales de este vino de excelente calidad y precios competitivos. Desde 2015, cada 4 de septiembre se celebra en Chile el Día Nacional del Vino.

e **¿Cuánto sabes?** Completa las siguientes oraciones con la información correcta.

1. El desierto de ______________, uno de los desiertos más áridos del mundo, está en el norte de Chile.
2. En ______________, la capital de Chile, viven más de seis millones de habitantes.
3. El ____________ se prepara con maíz, carne y huevos.
4. Punta Arenas es la ciudad más al sur de Chile. Está junto al estrecho de ______________.
5. En la isla de Pascua hay unas ____________ gigantes llamadas moáis.

To learn more about Chile, go online to view the *Club cultura* videos.

VOCABULARIO EN CONTEXTO

Talking about social change, gender roles, and migration

Cambios en la sociedad

Aunque existe una gran **diversidad** social, económica y demográfica en América Latina, la crisis de finales de 2008 en Estados Unidos y Europa afectó al **comercio** internacional. Además, **frenó** el **flujo** de **capital** y el **crecimiento económico** de toda la región. Sin embargo, desde 2010, la mayoría de estos países ha registrado una **recuperación** económica que hace de Latinoamérica una de las regiones con mayor crecimiento del mundo. Países como Chile, Uruguay, Colombia y Panamá están **invirtiendo** en proyectos de **infraestructura** y abriendo mercados nuevos para la **exportación.** Por otro lado, países de gran importancia económica, como México y Argentina, **luchan** por resolver los problemas de **corrupción** que han frenado su **desarrollo.**

Las mujeres representan un **cambio** social importante en los últimos tiempos. La **desigualdad** y la **pobreza** han **disminuido** entre las mujeres **debido a** la **escolarización** y a un mayor acceso al trabajo **remunerado.** También hay ahora más mujeres en posiciones de **poder.** Sin embargo, todavía hay diferencias **salariales** y muchas mujeres tienen la doble carga del trabajo fuera y dentro de la casa. Además, aunque el **analfabetismo** ha disminuido, es mayor entre las mujeres que entre los hombres. Por otro lado, se han establecido **leyes** en contra de la **discriminación** sexual en muchos países, aunque varían de un país a otro, y el matrimonio entre personas del mismo sexo es un **derecho** civil en Uruguay, Colombia y Argentina, entre otros.

Uno de los mayores **desafíos** sociales de nuestra época son los flujos **migratorios.** La violencia, la pobreza y los desastres naturales obligan a muchas personas a **desplazarse** a otros países más **seguros** o económicamente más estables. La ventaja de la lengua común y una cultura similar hace que muchas personas prefieran **emigrar** a España, Colombia, Uruguay y Chile, que reciben cada año miles de **inmigrantes** hispanohablantes.

2017 (Est.)	Chile	Bolivia	Colombia	Guatemala
Población	17.789.267	11.138.234	45.698.234	15.460.732
Tasa de crecimiento económico o PNB (*GDP*)	1,2%	4,2%	1,7%	3,2%
PNB per cápita en US$	$24.600	$7.500	$14.500	$8.200
Años de escolarización	16 años	14 años	14 años	11 años
Índice de alfabetización (mujeres)	97,4%	88,6%	94,1%	76,3%
Índice de alfabetización (hombres)	97,6%	96,5%	94,4%	87,4%
Tasa de desempleo	7%	4%	9,3%	2%
Población bajo línea de pobreza	14,4%	38,6%	27,8%	59,3%
Tasa de fertilidad (número de hijos por mujer)	1,8	2,6	2	2,7
Mortalidad infantil (por cada mil nacimientos)	6,6	35,3	13,6	21,3
Esperanza de vida (años)	78,9	69,5	75,9	72,6

Fuente: CIA, *The World Factbook*

Estos **datos** muestran y comparan algunos de los problemas sociales de Hispanoamérica. Por ejemplo, **a pesar de** ser un país **emergente,** la **tasa** de **desempleo** de Colombia es bastante alta. El **índice** de pobreza en algunos países, como Guatemala y Bolivia, es muy alto, debido a la **precariedad** del **empleo** y los salarios bajos. El **porcentaje** de hombres **alfabetizados** es más alto que el de las mujeres en casi todos los países. El índice de escolarización es menor en Guatemala que en Chile. Las mujeres guatemaltecas tienen el **promedio** más alto de hijos. La **esperanza de vida** es más alta en Colombia que en Guatemala, y Bolivia tiene la tasa más alta de **mortalidad infantil.**

PRÁCTICA

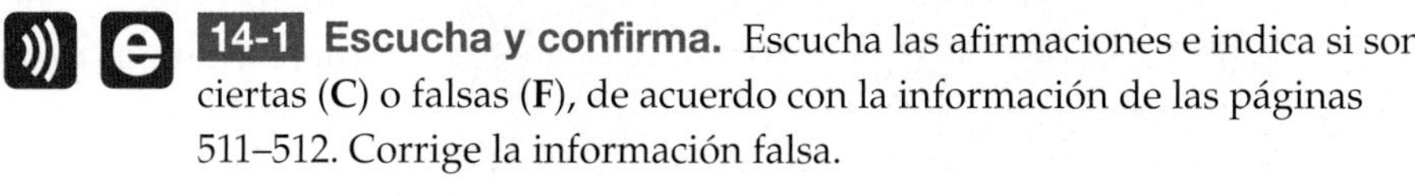

14-1 Escucha y confirma. Escucha las afirmaciones e indica si son ciertas (**C**) o falsas (**F**), de acuerdo con la información de las páginas 511–512. Corrige la información falsa.

1. _____
2. _____
3. _____
4. _____
5. _____

Cultura

La natalidad El índice de natalidad en los países hispanos ha descendido de manera espectacular en los últimos 30 años. Este descenso parece ser la tendencia (*trend*) general, a pesar de las circunstancias particulares de cada país. En Perú y Bolivia, por ejemplo, los gobiernos han apoyado (*supported*) campañas para mostrar las ventajas de los planes familiares y el control de la natalidad. En otros países, sin embargo, el promedio de hijos ha bajado también aun sin campañas por parte de los gobiernos. Esto se debe a varios factores, como la crisis económica, la escasez (*shortage*) de vivienda y el mayor acceso de las mujeres al trabajo y a la educación. Pero tal vez el caso más extremo de esta tendencia es el de España, que ha pasado de ser el país de Europa con más hijos por pareja en los años 60 a ser, junto con Italia, el país europeo con el índice de natalidad más bajo en la actualidad, con un promedio de 1,3 hijos.

Comparaciones Piensa en el número de hijos en tu familia en las últimas dos o tres generaciones. Después compara el caso de tu familia con el de tus compañeros/as. ¿Qué tendencia de natalidad se puede observar? ¿Creen ustedes que hay una crisis de natalidad en Estados Unidos?

14-2 Los datos demográficos. **PREPARACIÓN.** Busquen en la tabla de la página 512 la información necesaria para contestar las siguientes preguntas. Después comparen sus respuestas con las de otros/as compañeros/as.

1. ¿Qué país en la tabla es el más poblado?
2. ¿Cuál tiene menos habitantes?
3. ¿En qué país vive más años la gente?
4. ¿Qué país tiene la mayor tasa de desempleo?
5. ¿De dónde son las mujeres que tienen más hijos?
6. ¿En qué país estudian más años los jóvenes?
7. ¿En qué país hay menos desempleo?
8. ¿En qué país mueren más niños cuando son bebés?
9. ¿En qué país crece más rápido la economía?
10. ¿Qué país probablemente les ofrece más oportunidades educativas a las mujeres?

INTERCAMBIOS. Investiguen y comparen los datos de los países hispanos en las siguientes áreas con los datos de su propio país.

1. escolarización
2. desempleo
3. promedio de hijos
4. mortalidad infantil
5. esperanza de vida

14-3 Una encuesta sobre las familias. **PREPARACIÓN.** Hazle preguntas a tu compañero/a para obtener los siguientes datos sobre su familia.

1. número de personas que forman el núcleo familiar
2. número de hombres y de mujeres
3. edad promedio de los miembros de la familia
4. número de personas que estudian
5. número de personas que trabajan

INTERCAMBIOS. Recopilen (*Compile*) la información obtenida de todos los estudiantes. Con estos datos, preparen una tabla con lo siguiente:

El porcentaje de familias en su clase...

- con menos de tres miembros o con más de tres
- con mayoría de mujeres o de hombres
- con edad promedio de más o menos 40 años
- con más de dos personas con títulos (*degrees*) universitarios
- donde trabajan más de dos miembros

Temas de hoy: la emigración

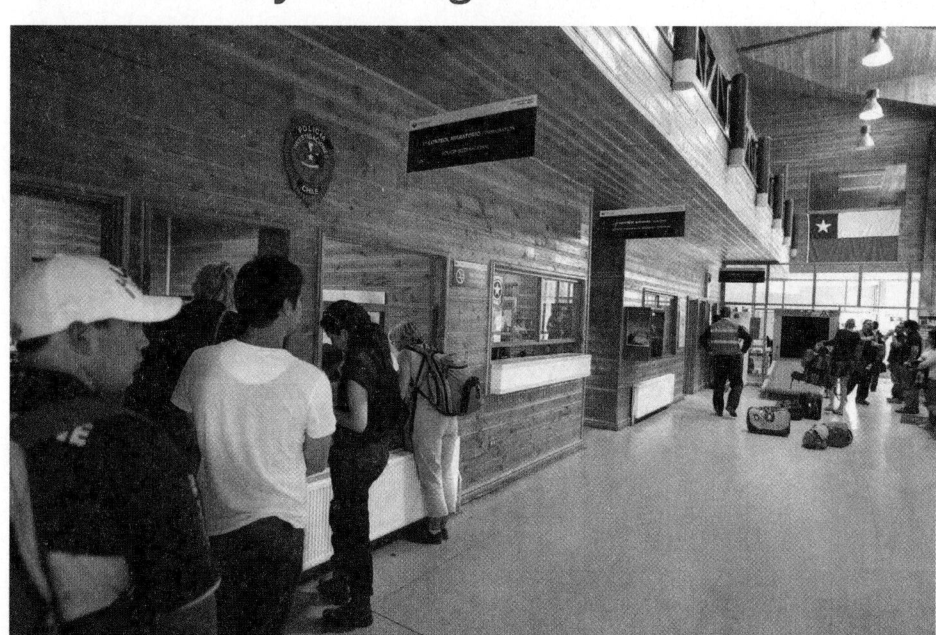

Control de inmigración en la frontera (*border*) de Chile

El **desplazamiento** de personas de un país a otro es un fenómeno muy común en los últimos tiempos. En general, las personas que emigran de sus países lo hacen por motivos económicos o políticos. Muchos tienen la esperanza de **mejorar** sus **condiciones** de vida. Entre los países hispanos, Chile y España son los que más **emigrantes** reciben, aunque debido a la crisis económica, la **inmigración** a España ha disminuido en los últimos años.

Lengua

La emigración refers to the act of *leaving* one's country to settle somewhere else. **La inmigración** refers to *entering* another country for the purpose of setting up permanent residence there. In general, we may use the expression **flujos migratorios** to refer to the movement of people from one country to another.

País de origen de los extranjeros en Chile

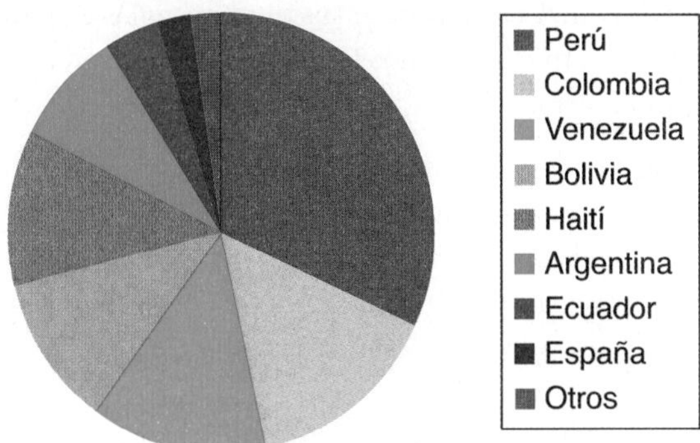

En Chile, los peruanos, colombianos y venezolanos son los grupos de **extranjeros** más numerosos. En España las comunidades dominicana, colombiana y argentina son muy numerosas, solo superadas por los inmigrantes de origen ecuatoriano. La ventaja de estas **migraciones** interhispanas es que todos hablan la misma lengua y esto hace que las dificultades de **adaptación** sean menores. También es más fácil para ellos conseguir la **nacionalidad** del **país de acogida.**

Muchos hispanoamericanos, especialmente mexicanos y caribeños, prefieren emigrar a Estados Unidos **en vez de** a Europa en busca de oportunidades económicas y una mayor **proximidad** con sus países. Los jóvenes por lo general se adaptan más fácilmente que sus padres porque aprenden inglés rápidamente. Además, hoy en día las ventajas de ser bilingüe en Estados Unidos son evidentes. Sin embargo, las leyes migratorias de Estados Unidos dificultan el acceso a los **permisos** de trabajo y de residencia.

PRÁCTICA

14-4 Para confirmar. Selecciona la palabra que mejor completa cada oración.

adaptación	emigración	nacionalidad
condiciones	inmigrantes	proximidad

1. En España hay muchos habitantes de ___________ ecuatoriana.
2. Una ventaja para los caribeños que emigran a Estados Unidos es la ___________ a los países del Caribe.
3. La ___________ al país de acogida es más fácil cuando se habla la misma lengua.
4. Frecuentemente las personas se desplazan para mejorar sus ___________ de vida.
5. La ___________ es un fenómeno de nuestros días que está relacionado con la globalización.
6. Chile es uno de los países de Hispanoamérica que más __________ recibe.

14-5 Los habitantes de su comunidad. Preparen preguntas para entrevistar a un/a compañero/a sobre sus orígenes y las costumbres de su comunidad o grupo étnico. Usen los temas a continuación como guía para elaborar su cuestionario.

MODELO E1: *¿Cuál es el origen de tu familia?*
E2: *Mis abuelos eran italianos.*
E1: *¿Cuándo llegaron a este país?*
E2: *Emigraron de Italia cuando mi padre tenía cinco años.*

- origen de tu apellido
- grupo(s) étnico(s) que asocias con tu familia
- área de concentración en Estados Unidos
- costumbres y lengua
- fiestas o celebraciones
- productos que consumen
- comida típica

14-6 Noticias. **PREPARACIÓN.** Selecciona una noticia en internet o en la televisión sobre el tema de la inmigración y toma notas para resumirla en clase. Ten en cuenta lo siguiente:

1. Asunto principal: ¿Qué pasó? ¿Cómo pasó?
2. Contexto de la noticia: ¿Dónde pasó? ¿Cuándo pasó? ¿Por qué?
3. Consecuencias y posible resolución: ¿Cuáles son las consecuencias? ¿Qué va a pasar? ¿Qué medidas se van a tomar?

INTERCAMBIOS. Comparte tu noticia con tu compañero/a y háganse preguntas. Tomen notas de la noticia de su compañero/a para compartirla con la clase.

Las mujeres y el trabajo

En 2015, las Naciones Unidas adoptaron la llamada *Agenda 2030 para el Desarrollo Sostenible*[1]. Según este informe, la desigualdad entre mujeres y hombres persiste en los mercados **laborales** mundiales. A pesar de los **logros** educativos y económicos de los últimos años, la posición laboral de la mujer no ha mejorado, ya que la **calidad** de los empleos de la mujer es peor que la de los hombres. Además, la desigualdad en la distribución de las tareas domésticas no remuneradas es un **factor** que dificulta el progreso profesional y personal de las mujeres.

[1]*Las mujeres y el trabajo. Tendencias de 2016.* Resumen ejecutivo. Organización Internacional del Trabajo. Ginebra, Suiza.

A escala mundial, el sector de servicios emplea a un mayor número de mujeres que el de la agricultura. En los países de **ingresos altos,** las mujeres consiguen empleo principalmente en los sectores de la salud y de la educación. En cambio, en los países de ingresos **bajos,** la agricultura sigue siendo la fuente de ingresos más importante para ellas.

La desigualdad es aún más preocupante entre las mujeres jóvenes. Las tasas mundiales de desempleo son del 5,5% para los hombres y del 6,2% para las mujeres. Como consecuencia de la crisis **financiera** de los años 80, muchas mujeres se han incorporado al mercado laboral para compensar la pérdida de ingresos a consecuencia del desempleo masculino.

No obstante, según este estudio, si las tendencias de discriminación salarial y calidad laboral continúan, se necesitarán al menos 70 años para disminuir la **brecha** salarial. Lo peor es que la discriminación laboral produce una menor protección social para las mujeres, que afecta a las **prestaciones** de maternidad y de **vejez.**

PRÁCTICA

14-7 Para confirmar.

PREPARACIÓN. Basándote en la información sobre las mujeres y el trabajo, indica si las siguientes afirmaciones son ciertas (**C**) o falsas (**F**). Corrige las afirmaciones falsas.

1. _____ Según las Naciones Unidas, no hay desigualdad entre mujeres y hombres en el mundo laboral.
2. _____ La calidad de los empleos de las mujeres es normalmente mejor que la de los hombres.
3. _____ Normalmente las mujeres no reciben dinero por hacer las tareas en su casa.
4. _____ El sector que emplea a más mujeres a escala mundial es la agricultura.
5. _____ En los países de ingresos bajos, muchas mujeres se dedican a los sectores de salud y educación.
6. _____ Las mujeres jóvenes tienen más problemas para encontrar trabajo que los hombres jóvenes.
7. _____ Debido a la crisis económica, más mujeres trabajan fuera de casa.
8. _____ La consecuencia de tener peores trabajos es que las mujeres tienen menos ventajas sociales.

INTERCAMBIOS. Elijan un país hispanohablante para preparar un informe sobre la situación de la mujer. Luego compártanlo con la clase. Tengan en cuenta los siguientes puntos y compárenlos con la situación de los hombres:

1. educación de las mujeres
2. salud de las mujeres
3. condiciones laborales
4. participación en la vida política y social

14-8 Mujeres importantes. **PREPARACIÓN.** Cada uno/a de ustedes debe hacer una lista de cinco mujeres que ocupan puestos importantes en países hispanos o en su país. Hablen sobre estas mujeres, basándose en lo siguiente:

1. puesto que ocupan y responsabilidades que tienen
2. su personalidad y rasgos (*traits*) de carácter
3. obstáculos que cada una ha tenido que superar (*overcome*) en su área de trabajo

INTERCAMBIOS. Ahora, comenten lo siguiente:

1. ¿Qué rasgos de personalidad y carácter tienen en común estas mujeres?
2. ¿Hacen estas mujeres trabajos tradicionalmente femeninos, o han entrado en un sector típicamente masculino del mundo laboral?
3. ¿Son similares los obstáculos que estas mujeres han tenido que superar? ¿Cuáles son esos obstáculos? ¿Cómo han podido superarlos?

14-9 Los tiempos cambian. Conversen sobre los logros de la mujer en este siglo (*century*) y en el pasado. Hagan una lista de los cambios que han afectado a la mujer en las siguientes áreas en los últimos 50 años.

1. la familia
2. el trabajo
3. la casa
4. el gobierno / la política
5. la educación

14-10 La mujer en los países hispanos. **PREPARACIÓN.** You will listen to a conversation between a reporter and a professor of sociology at the Universidad de Santiago de Chile about the status of women in the Hispanic world. Before you listen, write two questions the reporter may ask the professor and the answers that you think she may provide.

ESCUCHA. As you listen, focus on the main ideas of what is said. Indicate the appropriate ending to each statement.

1. La doctora Gómez dice que la situación de la mujer ha mejorado porque...
   a. más mujeres son jefas de empresas.
   b. ahora hay más leyes que las protegen.
   c. hay muchas mujeres que no tienen hijos.
2. Según la doctora Gómez, en comparación con los hombres, las mujeres...
   a. no tienen que trabajar tanto.
   b. tienen que estar mejor preparadas.
   c. no estudian tanto.
3. Las mujeres hispanas ganan...
   a. más dinero que los hombres.
   b. tanto dinero como los hombres.
   c. menos dinero que los hombres.
4. En los hogares (*homes*) hispanos, el trabajo de la casa y el cuidado de los hijos...
   a. son la responsabilidad de los empleados domésticos.
   b. son compartidos por todos los miembros de la familia.
   c. están principalmente en manos de las mujeres.

Mosaico cultural

La migración interna en el mundo hispano

Emilia Sepúlveda vive en Santiago, la capital de Chile, hace siete años. Emilia nació en Ercilla, una pequeña ciudad en la región de Araucanía, donde vivía con tres hermanos en una familia campesina (*farming*). "Tan pronto como terminé mis estudios secundarios, supe que quería ir a la universidad", comenta Emilia. Las oportunidades de educación superior son limitadas en las ciudades pequeñas, por eso muchas mujeres como Emilia prefieren ir a las ciudades principales. "Cuando mi madre tenía mi edad, ya había tenido a mis hermanos. Yo sabía que si no salía de Ercilla a estudiar, mi futuro sería similar", dice Emilia. Emilia tuvo que dejar a su familia y pasar momentos difíciles adaptándose a la vida de la ciudad. Como muchos otros jóvenes, Emilia trabajaba mientras estudiaba, y después de los tres años de carrera universitaria, consiguió un trabajo estable como auxiliar de dentista.

Emilia Sepúlveda

Esta decisión de Emilia demuestra un cambio de mentalidad en los jóvenes hispanos: tener menos hijos y tomarse más tiempo para educarse. Sin embargo, las oportunidades en educación y seguridad social son estables, principalmente en las ciudades grandes. El rápido progreso económico de algunas ciudades capitales no es igual al de las ciudades más pequeñas. Por esta razón, muchas personas deciden buscar suerte en la gran ciudad, en un proceso que se conoce como migración interna. Pero llegar a la ciudad no siempre asegura mejores condiciones; en ocasiones, estas personas enfrentan desafíos de adaptación demasiado grandes y terminan en situaciones de pobreza. Afortunadamente para Emilia, este no fue su caso: "Venir a Santiago fue muy difícil, pero tenía que salir de Ercilla para encontrar el desarrollo personal y profesional y la estabilidad económica que buscaba".

La región de Araucanía en Chile

Compara

1. En promedio, ¿cuántos hijos por familia tienen las personas en tu país? ¿Este número ha variado en las últimas décadas? ¿Piensas que esta tendencia varía dependiendo de la región geográfica?
2. ¿Qué importancia social tiene la educación en tu país? Piensa en las regiones que no son predominantemente universitarias. Compara las grandes ciudades con otras zonas más pequeñas.
3. ¿En tu país existe un fenómeno similar a la migración interna? ¿Cuáles son las razones principales de esta migración? Incluye detalles en tu respuesta; piensa en tendencias demográficas que han cambiado en los últimos años.
4. En tu opinión, ¿qué implicaciones sociales tiene la migración interna para las grandes ciudades? ¿Qué ocurre con la economía?

En acción

Por un mundo mejor

Antes de ver

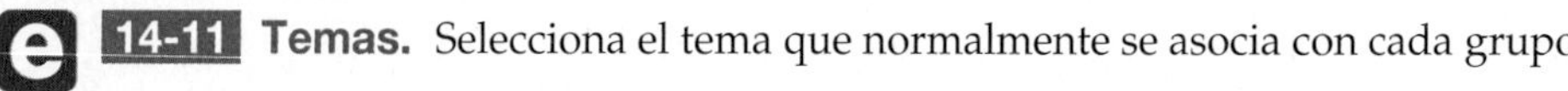

14-11 Temas. Selecciona el tema que normalmente se asocia con cada grupo.

1. _____ los techos (*roofs*) verdes
2. _____ los refugiados
3. _____ los indocumentados
4. _____ los indígenas
5. _____ los homosexuales
6. _____ los veganos

a. la persecución política
b. la protección de animales
c. el medio ambiente (*environment*)
d. la reforma migratoria
e. las minorías étnicas
f. la discriminación por orientación sexual

Mientras ves

14-12 Cambios y más cambios. Indica si las afirmaciones son ciertas (**C**) o falsas (**F**) según el video. Corrige las afirmaciones falsas.

1. _____ Yolanda ya ha terminado su proyecto de video.
2. _____ El proyecto de Yolanda está relacionado con problemas del medio ambiente.
3. _____ Esteban cree que la pobreza y el analfabetismo ya no existen.
4. _____ El video de Esteban trata de la inmigración.
5. _____ La organización Chirla lucha por los derechos (*rights*) de los homosexuales.
6. _____ Chirla promociona actividades para que haya una sociedad más justa.
7. _____ El proyecto de Federico trata de la legalización de la marihuana en Argentina.
8. _____ Argentina fue el primer país latinoamericano en legalizar el matrimonio entre personas del mismo sexo.

Después de ver

14-13 Un mundo mejor.

PREPARACIÓN. Selecciona el final apropiado para cada afirmación incompleta.

1. _____ Para que (*So that*) haya más conciencia sobre los problemas del medio ambiente…
2. _____ Chirla intentará influir en el congresista de Los Ángeles…
3. _____ Yolanda hablará con Federico sobre los derechos de los animales…
4. _____ Los chicos van a presentar proyectos sobre problemas sociales…

a. para que deje de consumir carne y otros productos derivados.
b. para que aumente (*raise*) la conciencia social sobre ellos.
c. para que vote a favor de la reforma migratoria.
d. la organización Techos Verdes busca cambiar la actitud de las personas en México.

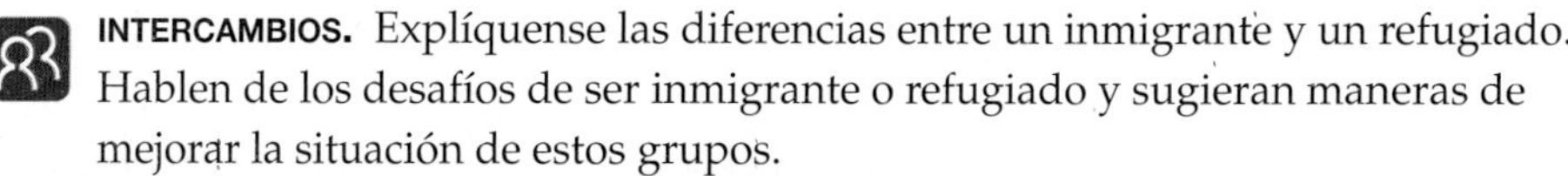

INTERCAMBIOS. Explíquense las diferencias entre un inmigrante y un refugiado. Hablen de los desafíos de ser inmigrante o refugiado y sugieran maneras de mejorar la situación de estos grupos.

1 Expressing conjecture

Muchos inmigrantes dejan su país de origen **para que** sus familias tengan una vida mejor. Otros emigran **antes de que** la violencia en sus países destruya sus vidas. Según la ley, los inmigrantes pueden trabajar en Estados Unidos **con tal de que** tengan estatus legal en el país y permiso para trabajar. Frecuentemente, los inmigrantes realizan trabajos difíciles **sin que** sus empleadores les paguen sueldos justos. Después de años de sacrificio, muchos vuelven a su país **a menos que** su familia pueda ir a Estados Unidos también.

Piénsalo. Indica si cada expresión en negrita (*bold*) requiere el uso del indicativo (**I**) o el subjuntivo (**S**).

	¿INDICATIVO O SUBJUNTIVO?
1. Muchos inmigrantes dejan su país de origen **para que** sus familias tengan una vida mejor.	_____
2. Otros emigran **antes de que** la violencia en sus países destruya sus vidas.	_____
3. Los inmigrantes pueden trabajar en Estados Unidos **con tal de que** tengan estatus legal en el país y permiso para trabajar.	_____
4. Frecuentemente, los inmigrantes realizan trabajos difíciles **sin que** sus empleadores les paguen sueldos justos.	_____
5. Muchos vuelven a su país **a menos que** su familia pueda venir a Estados Unidos también.	_____

Adverbial conjunctions that require the subjunctive

- Conjunctions are words or phrases that function as connectors in sentences. Some conjunctions introduce dependent clauses known as adverbial clauses, which indicate relationships of time, purpose, and cause and effect between the two parts of a sentence.
- Some conjunctions always require the subjunctive when followed by a dependent clause.

a menos que	*unless*
antes (de) que	*before*
con tal (de) que	*provided that*
para que	*so that*
sin que	*without*

Las mujeres tendrán una reunión **antes de que** sus abogados hablen con ellas. — *The women will have a meeting before their attorneys speak with them.*

Los enfermeros votarán por sus representantes **con tal de que** implementen los cambios mencionados en la petición. — *The nurses will vote for their officials provided that they implement the changes mentioned in the petition.*

Las representantes negocian con la compañía **para que** todos los niños tengan acceso a servicios médicos. — *The representatives negotiate with the company so that all children have access to medical services.*

- Use an infinitive after the prepositions **antes de, en, para,** and **sin** when there is no change of subject.

Algunas organizaciones están interesadas **en preparar** a los inmigrantes para su trabajo. — *Some organizations are interested in preparing immigrants for their work.*

Los inmigrantes toman clases de inglés **para aprender** la lengua rápidamente. — *Immigrants take English classes to learn the language quickly.*

Lengua

You have already learned several uses of the infinitive: after a preposition, as in **antes de llegar** or **para comprar.** The expression **al +** *infinitive* is the equivalent of **cuando** + *verb:* **llámanos al llegar a la estación** (*call us when you get to the station*). The infinitive is also used as a command form, usually on signs, such as **No fumar** or **No tocar.** The infinitive has other uses as well. It is the only verb form that may be used as the subject of a sentence: **Nadar es bueno para el dolor de espalda.** Sentences with infinitives as subjects express indirect advice or statements of belief: **ver es creer** (*seeing is believing*).

e **¿Comprendes?** Completa las afirmaciones a continuación con las conjunciones más lógicas en cada contexto.

1. Pagamos impuestos (*taxes*) ________________ todos los niños tengan acceso a la educación.
2. Tenemos que organizar la oficina ________________ lleguen los miembros del comité.
3. Votaremos por los candidatos ________________ nos gusten sus planes para la ciudad.
4. No publicaremos el panfleto ________________ el presidente lo apruebe (*approves*).

PRÁCTICA

14-14 Predicciones.

PREPARACIÓN. Seleccionen el final apropiado para cada afirmación. Presten atención al contexto y también a la forma verbal correcta.

1. _____ Muchos empleados trabajarán en casa sin…
2. _____ Las compañías de limpieza programarán los robots para que…
3. _____ Podremos jubilarnos (*retire*) antes de…
4. _____ La mayoría de los cursos universitarios se ofrecerán en internet sin que…
5. _____ Los jóvenes no tendrán que trabajar a menos que…
6. _____ Habrá computadoras de uso gratis en todos los lugares públicos para…
7. _____ Los empleados de las compañías multinacionales podrán comunicarse en cualquier lengua con tal de que…
8. _____ Después de nacer (*be born*) sus hijos, los padres no volverán a trabajar antes de que los niños…

a. los profesores ni los alumnos tengan que ir a la universidad.
b. tengan aparatos de interpretación simultánea.
c. tener que comunicarse cara a cara con los clientes o colegas.
d. facilitar la comunicación entre las personas.
e. cumplan cinco años de edad.
f. limpien los edificios sin intervención de los seres humanos.
g. les interese hacer trabajo de voluntariado.
h. los 50 años.

INTERCAMBIOS. Escojan dos afirmaciones incompletas de **Preparación** y termínenlas, según sus propias ideas. Luego, comparen en grupos sus respuestas.

14-15 La entrevista de una ingeniera.

Martina Rojas se entrevista hoy con la gerente de Tecnofarma, una compañía farmacéutica. Descubre qué pasa en la entrevista, completando el texto con la forma correcta del verbo apropiado de la lista. Usa cada verbo solo una vez.

considerar	ofrecer
decir	pasar
entrevistarse	pensar
hacer	saber

Martina llega temprano a la cita; la secretaria le pide que espere unos minutos antes de (1) __________ con la gerente. Martina trata de tranquilizarse para que nadie (2) ____________ que está muy nerviosa. Piensa que podrá dar una buena impresión con tal de que la gerente le (3) __________ preguntas relevantes sobre su experiencia. Finalmente, la gerente la invita a (4) __________ a su oficina. Martina responde a las preguntas sin que la gerente (5) __________ una palabra. Al final de la entrevista, la gerente le ofrece el puesto. Martina dice que no puede aceptar la oferta a menos que la compañía le (6) _________ seguro (*insurance*) médico. La gerente acepta esta condición después de (7) __________ la petición de Martina.

14-16 ¿Estudio en Chile o no? Quieres estudiar en Chile el próximo semestre, pero no sabes si será posible. Analiza tus opciones, usando las expresiones adverbiales de la lista. Tu compañero/a va a responderte de forma lógica.

a menos que	antes de que	con tal (de) que	para que	sin que

MODELO el precio del programa: caro/razonable

E1: *Voy a estudiar en Chile, a menos que el programa sea muy caro.*

E2: *Buen punto. No vayas a menos que te den ayuda económica.*

1. el fin del semestre: el 1 de junio / el 30 de junio
2. clases de español: grupos grandes / pequeños
3. alojamiento: con una familia / en una pensión (*boarding house*)
4. autorización de visitas durante el semestre: visita de mi familia / visitas prohibidas
5. viajes: oportunidades de viajar dentro del país / a países vecinos (*neighboring*)
6. acceso a la cultura local: conocer la cultura mapuche en el sur / la cultura aymara en el norte
7. diversión durante los fines de semana: esquiar en los Andes / hacer surf en el desierto de Atacama

14-17 Temas sociales sin resolver.

PREPARACIÓN. Individualmente, describe los problemas sociales en tu comunidad, ciudad o país. Luego, compara tus ideas con las de tu compañero/a. ¿Están de acuerdo o no?

1. Hay desigualdad entre… (Indica el tipo de desigualdad.)
2. Persisten las confrontaciones entre… (Indica entre quiénes.)
3. La educación universitaria cuesta… (Especifica en qué áreas de estudio.)
4. Existe discriminación contra algunos grupos… (Especifica contra qué grupos.)
5. Hay violencia contra algunas personas… (Especifica contra qué personas.)
6. La inflación en nuestro país es… (Indica si es alta, baja, normal, mayor o menor que…)
7. ¿Otro?

INTERCAMBIOS. Expresen su opinión sobre los problemas de **Preparación** y den soluciones usando las expresiones adverbiales y los verbos de la lista. Tomen notas para compartir con la clase.

a menos que	aceptar	haber	respetar
antes de que	aprender	hacer	ser sensible
con tal de que	coexistir	legislar	tener empatía
para que	comprender	rechazar (*to reject*)	valorar (*to value*)
sin que			

MODELO Habrá pobreza…

E1: *Habrá pobreza a menos que haya trabajo para todos.*

E2: *De acuerdo. Las compañías deben crear empleos para que todos puedan trabajar y tener una vida digna.*

E3: *Las compañías crearán empleos con tal de que los empleados sepan usar la tecnología.*

1. Habrá desigualdad entre…
2. Persistirán las confrontaciones entre… y…
3. La educación costará menos…
4. Existirá discriminación contra…
5. Habrá violencia contra…
6. La inflación continuará…
7. …

14-18 Plan de acción. **PREPARACIÓN.** Selecciona dos temas de los que aparecen a continuación. Para cada tema, escribe qué harás, usando tres expresiones adverbiales diferentes de la lista.

a menos que	antes de que	con tal de que	para que	sin que

MODELO luchar contra la desigualdad

Seré parte de un comité para luchar contra la desigualdad con tal de que participen tantas mujeres como hombres en el grupo.

Lucharé en las cortes para que las mujeres tengan los mismos derechos que los hombres.

Educaré a mis hijos en la igualdad a menos que no tenga hijos.

1. aumentar (*increase*) la participación de la mujer en las ciencias
2. dar acceso a la educación a todos
3. eliminar la explotación infantil
4. luchar contra el tráfico de personas

INTERCAMBIOS. Escribe un resumen de tus ideas de **Preparación.** Luego, en parejas, leánse sus textos y háganse dos preguntas relacionadas con el tema de su resumen.

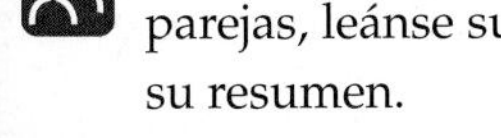

Situación

PREPARACIÓN. Lean la situación. Luego, compartan ejemplos de vocabulario, gramática y otra información que necesitan para desarrollar la conversación.

Role A. You are an exchange student who has recently arrived in the United States. Ask your classmate a) how students in the United States can pay the high cost of attending college; b) if in big lecture classes students can use their cell phones without their professors' knowledge; and c) what he/she hopes to accomplish before graduating.

Role B. You have become acquainted with an international student at your university. Answer his/her questions about university life in the United States and ask about university life in his/her country.

	ROLE A	ROLE B
Vocabulario	Academic subjects Technology	Academic subjects Technology
Funciones y formas	Formulating questions Adverbial conjunctions with subjunctive	Answering questions Adverbial conjunctions with subjunctive

INTERCAMBIOS. Practiquen la conversación, incorporando el vocabulario y las funciones de **Preparación.** Luego, represéntenla ante la clase.

2 Expressing conjecture or certainty

SRA. LÓPEZ: ¿Qué te interesa hacer **cuando te gradúes?**

VICENTE: **Después de terminar** mis estudios, me gustaría trabajar en otro país para una organización sin fines de lucro (*nonprofit*).

SRA. LÓPEZ: Muy bien. **Tan pronto como terminemos** de hablar, te mandaré una lista de organizaciones. No esperes **hasta que te gradúes** para empezar a buscar trabajo. Familiarízate con las posibilidades ahora, **mientras eres** estudiante. Solicita el puesto **cuando cumplas** (*fulfill*) con los requisitos. Algunas organizaciones contratan a jóvenes como tú **cuando tienen** proyectos que requieren originalidad y dedicación.

Piénsalo. Indica si cada afirmación se refiere al presente (**P**) o al futuro (**F**). Luego, indica si la expresión en negrita requiere el uso del subjuntivo (**S**) o del indicativo (**I**).

	PRESENTE/ FUTURO	SUBJUNTIVO/ INDICATIVO
1. ¿Qué te interesa hacer **cuando te gradúes?**	________	________
2. **Tan pronto como terminemos** de hablar, te mandaré una lista de organizaciones.	________	________
3. No esperes **hasta que te gradúes** para empezar a buscar trabajo.	________	________
4. Familiarízate con las posibilidades ahora, **mientras eres** estudiante.	________	________
5. Solicita el puesto **cuando cumplas** con los requisitos del trabajo.	________	________
6. Algunas organizaciones contratan a jóvenes **cuando tienen** proyectos que requieren originalidad y dedicación.	________	________

Adverbial conjunctions that take the subjunctive or the indicative

- Earlier in this chapter you learned about conjunctions that are always followed by the subjunctive. Here you will learn about conjunctions that are followed by a verb in the subjunctive to express that an event has not yet occurred or is unknown. You will use the same conjunctions followed by a verb in the indicative to indicate that an event has already occurred.
- The following conjunctions require the subjunctive when the event in the adverbial clause has not yet taken place. Note that the main clause expresses future time.

cuando *when*
después (de) que *after*
en cuanto *as soon as*
hasta que *until*
mientras *while, as long as*
tan pronto (como) *as soon as*

La sociedad será justa **cuando haya** igualdad.
Society will be just when there is equality.

Nos reuniremos **después de que comiencen** las clases.
We will meet after classes start.

Los sueldos subirán **en cuanto aumente** la producción.
Salaries will go up as soon as productivity increases.

Va a insistir **hasta que** la comunidad **ofrezca** clases gratis para los nuevos inmigrantes.
She is going to insist until the community offers free classes for new immigrants.

Lucharemos por nuestros derechos **mientras vivamos.**
We will fight for our rights as long as we live.

Llamaré a los representantes **tan pronto reciba** la aprobación del alcalde.
I will call the representatives as soon as I receive approval from the mayor.

- These conjunctions require the indicative when the event in the adverbial clause has already taken place, is taking place, or usually takes place.

Fuimos de vacaciones **después de que** nuestro padre **se recuperó** de la operación.
We went on vacation after our father recovered from surgery.

Me llamó **tan pronto como recibió** la aprobación del alcalde.
She called me as soon as she received approval from the mayor.

La organización apoya a los inmigrantes **hasta que se establecen** en la comunidad.
The organization supports the immigrants until they become established in the community.

- **Donde** and **según** require the indicative when they refer to something definite or known, and the subjunctive when they refer to something indefinite or unknown.

Vamos a reunirnos **donde** ella **dice.**
We are going to meet where she says. (She has already announced the place.)

Vamos a reunirnos **donde** ella **diga.**
We are going to meet wherever she says. (She has not yet announced the place.)

Llena el formulario **según dice** el consejero.
Fill out the form according to what the adviser says. (Instructions have already been given.)

Vamos a seguir el procedimiento **según diga** el alcalde.
We will follow the procedure in line with whatever the mayor may say. (Instructions have not yet been given.)

- **Aunque** also requires the subjunctive when it introduces a condition not regarded as fact.

Siempre lo compro, **aunque es** caro.	*I always will buy it, although it is expensive.*
Lo compro, **aunque sea** caro.	*I will buy it, although it may (turn out to) be expensive.*

e **¿Comprendes?** Completa las oraciones con la forma del subjuntivo o indicativo del verbo.

1. El secretario siempre distribuye los informes después de que yo los ________ (aprobar).
2. Comenzaremos la reunión tan pronto como Sandra ________ (llegar).
3. No importa la hora; iré a las protestas aunque ________ (empezar) a la medianoche.
4. Voy a las recepciones de mi oficina cuando ________ (poder).
5. Voy a ir a la próxima recepción cuando ________ (poder).
6. Iremos al concierto después de que ______ (llegar) los niños.
7. Tendremos la próxima reunión donde el grupo _______ (querer).

Cultura

Acceso a la educación universitaria en Chile La educación universitaria chilena, gratuita para todos hasta 1981, sufrió un cambio radical con la dictadura de Augusto Pinochet (1973–1990). Basándose en un modelo de economía neoliberal, se estableció un sistema de pago de la educación universitaria según los ingresos de las familias. Como los estudiantes de familias pobres no podían pagar las cuotas que les correspondían, el sistema creó más desigualdad en el acceso a la educación entre los jóvenes de las familias pobres y los de las familias ricas.

En 2006, los estudiantes de la escuela secundaria comenzaron la llamada Revolución Pingüina (*penguin*). Su objetivo era conseguir un acceso más justo e igualitario a la educación universitaria. En 2015, los estudiantes chilenos consiguieron educación universitaria gratuita parcial. Es decir, para acceder a este beneficio, los estudiantes deben pertenecer al 70% de la población con menos recursos, según la escala socioeconómica. Los alumnos que provienen de familias modestas, cuyos (*whose*) ingresos no alcanzan los 251.000 pesos mensuales (aproximadamente 380 dólares) por persona, tendrán educación gratuita.

Conexiones ¿Es tu educación cara o barata? ¿Es la educación universitaria de tu país gratuita o pagada? En tu opinión, ¿la educación universitaria gratuita debe ser un derecho para todos, o solamente una opción para los estudiantes de bajos recursos financieros? ¿Es posible la educación gratuita parcial en tu país?

PRÁCTICA

14-19 ¿Cuáles serán los cambios?

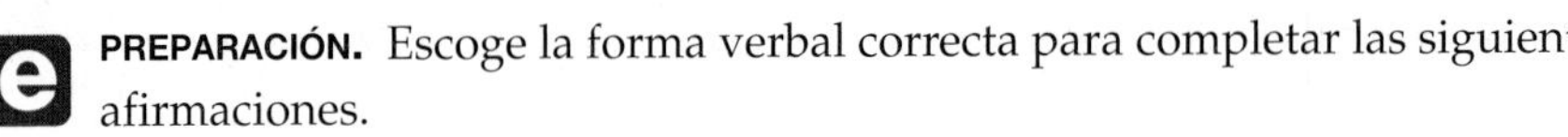

PREPARACIÓN. Escoge la forma verbal correcta para completar las siguientes afirmaciones.

1. Hasta que (hay/haya) elecciones limpias y democráticas, un país no puede considerarse democrático.
2. En un régimen dictatorial, se suprime (*suppress*) el derecho de libre expresión según (ordene/ordenó) la Junta Militar.
3. Las personas que tenían familiares desaparecidos demandaron justicia cuando (se recupere/se recuperó) la democracia.
4. La Corte Suprema dictaminó que los casos de los desaparecidos deben ser resueltos, aunque los militares (se opongan/se oponen).
5. Muchas personas dicen que no creerán en la justicia hasta que los culpables (estén/están) en prisión.

INTERCAMBIOS. Completen las siguientes ideas, según su opinión o conocimiento personal.

1. En nuestro país siempre tendremos elecciones democráticas, aunque...
2. Tendremos derecho de libre expresión hasta que...
3. La libertad se pierde cuando...
4. Lograremos completa igualdad tan pronto como...
5. Lucharemos por una sociedad justa según...

14-20 ¿Qué harás? **PREPARACIÓN.** Tu compañera del curso Historia de Chile te envió un correo electrónico con varias preguntas. Escribe tus respuestas, usando una conjunción diferente y las expresiones de la lista u otras.

aunque cuando después de que en cuanto hasta que tan pronto como	escribirme mi compañero/a virtual leer unos correos electrónicos de la profesora llegar el día del examen final ser las 12:00 ser muy tarde tener sus horas de consulta tener tiempo terminar de leer sobre los regímenes dictatoriales

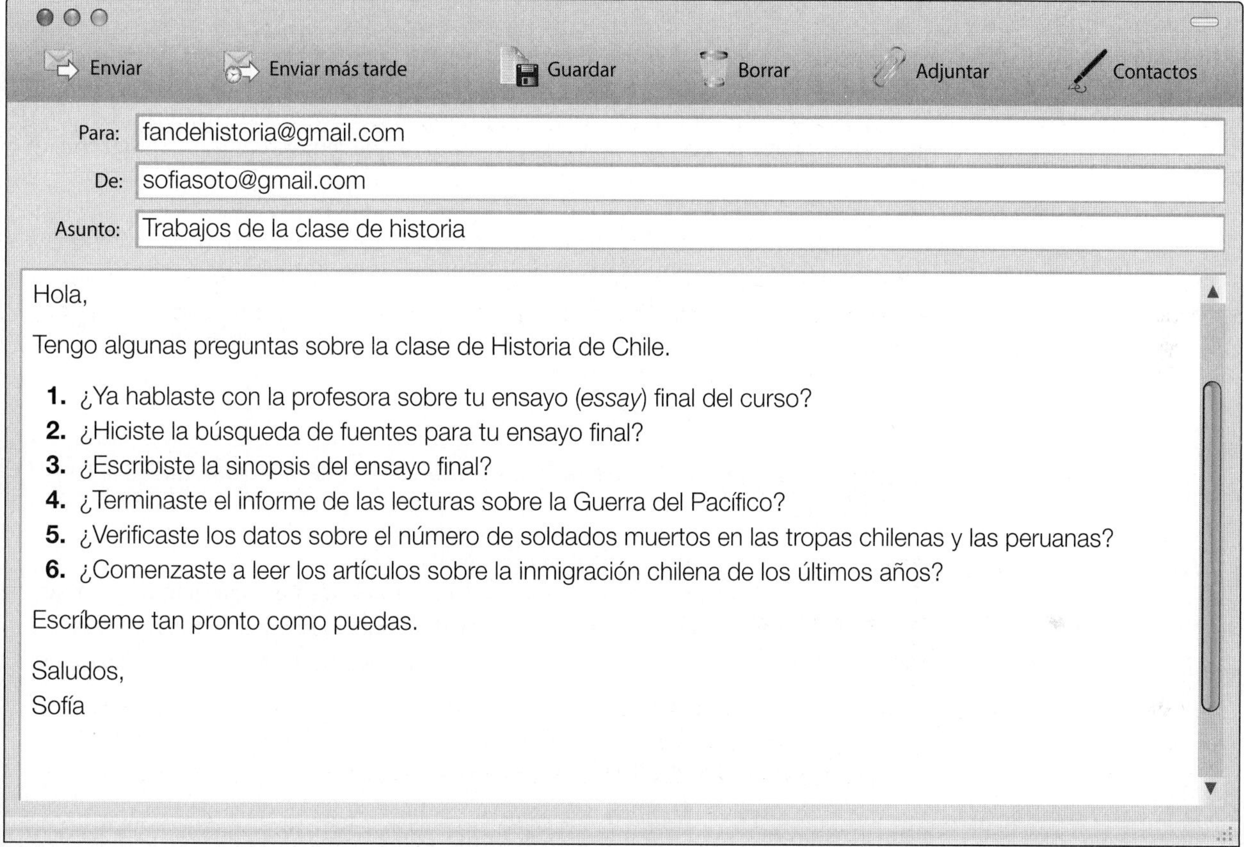

INTERCAMBIOS. Comparen sus respuestas de **Preparación.** Luego, hablen sobre dos trabajos o proyectos que cada uno/a de ustedes aún no ha hecho para sus clases este semestre. Digan cuándo los harán. Tu compañero/a te hará preguntas adicionales.

MODELO E1: *No he estudiado para el examen final de mi clase de historia. Comenzaré a estudiar tan pronto como termine el ensayo para mi clase de inglés.*

E2: *¿Y ya hiciste la tarea en línea para la clase de español?*

E1: *No, pero la haré después de que mi profesor me explique la gramática durante sus horas de oficina.*

14-21 Después del fin del año escolar.

PREPARACIÓN. Quieres descansar y divertirte después del fin de las clases, pero también quieres hacer algo por tu comunidad. Selecciona las dos opciones que más te interesen en cada columna y complétalas con tus propias ideas. Luego, añade una más en cada columna. Después, comparte tus planes con tu compañero/a.

Diversión	Ayuda comunitaria
1. Quiero dormir hasta que...	**1.** Trabajaré de voluntario/a donde...
2. No voy a abrir los libros, aunque...	**2.** Ayudaré en la biblioteca después de que...
3. Haré un crucero por... tan pronto como...	**3.** Les serviré comida a los sin techo (*homeless people*) cuando...
4. Iré a la playa todos los días cuando...	**4.** No organizaré juegos infantiles en el parque hasta que...
5. ...	**5.** ...

INTERCAMBIOS. En grupos, preparen un plan que tendrá un impacto significativo y duradero (*long lasting*) en su comunidad. Indiquen lo siguiente:

1. sector de la comunidad: ¿Los ancianos, los niños, los veteranos de guerra, las personas abusadas, los inmigrantes? ¿Otro grupo?
2. objetivo de su plan: ¿Para qué?
3. tipo de ayuda y cuándo la darán: ¿Apoyo financiero, físico, espiritual, laboral? ¿Otro tipo de ayuda?
4. resultados que esperan obtener

14-22 ¿Somos tratados de la misma manera?

PREPARACIÓN. Indica si las siguientes afirmaciones son ciertas (**C**) o falsas (**F**) en tu comunidad o país hoy en día.

1. _____ Todos los niños reciben la misma educación.
2. _____ Independientemente de su raza (*race*), todas las personas son respetadas.
3. _____ Las mujeres y los hombres ganan el mismo sueldo por el mismo trabajo.
4. _____ Todas las personas pueden acceder a un seguro (*insurance*) médico de la misma calidad.
5. _____ Las personas LGBT tienen los mismos derechos que los heterosexuales.
6. _____ No existe violencia en la sociedad.

INTERCAMBIOS. Compara tus respuestas con las de tu compañero/a. Defiende tus opiniones y di cuándo o bajo qué condiciones crees que ocurrirán los cambios necesarios.

MODELO No existe discriminación de salario en contra de la mujer.

E1: *No estoy de acuerdo. Los hombres siempre ganan más que las mujeres por el mismo trabajo.*

E2: *Tienes razón. Además, los hombres ocupan la mayoría de los puestos importantes en las compañías y en el gobierno. Esto no va a cambiar hasta que todos luchemos por la igualdad de género.*

En directo

To make a request or a proposal:

Pido/Pedimos/Queremos (que)... *I/We ask (that)...*

Para que..., es necesario (que)... *So that..., it is necessary (that)...*

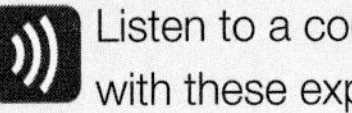

Listen to a conversation with these expressions.

 **14-23 Tira y afloja (*Give and take*).** Vas a negociar algunos conflictos con tu compañero/a de cuarto. Explíquense qué le molesta a cada uno/a y negocien posibles cambios. Usen las conjunciones de la lista.

aunque	en cuanto
cuando	hasta que
después de que	tan pronto como

MODELO Tu compañero/a de cuarto usa tu cargador (*charger*) de teléfono, pero no te lo devuelve.

E1: *Jorge, me molesta que no me devuelvas el cargador de mi teléfono cuando lo usas.*

E2: *Lo siento, Pablo. Te devolveré el cargador tan pronto como se cargue mi teléfono. / Te devolveré el cargador después de que termine de cargar mi teléfono.*

Estudiante 1	Estudiante 2
• Tu compañero/a escucha música a todo volumen mientras estudia. A ti te molesta. • Nunca recoge su ropa del suelo. • Come en el cuarto y el espacio que comparten huele (*smells*) mal. • No te da privacidad para conversar confidencialmente con tu familia.	• Tu compañero/a habla por teléfono mientras tú estudias. No puedes concentrarte. • Trae plantas al cuarto. Tú eres muy sensible a los olores (*smells*) de las plantas. • Prepara café, pero nunca lava la cafetera. • Nunca hace su cama.

e Situación

PREPARACIÓN. Lean la situación. Luego, compartan ejemplos de vocabulario, gramática y otra información que necesitan para desarrollar la conversación.

Role A. You make a presentation to the city council (**concejo municipal**) about starting an adult literacy program. Explain how the lives of participants will improve when they know how to read and write well. In response to questions, say that you will a) organize the program; b) hold classes wherever the council says; and c) decide on class schedules according to the needs of the participants.

Role B. You are the president of the city council (**concejo municipal**). After listening to a presentation by a specialist in adult literacy who wants to start a program in the community, ask a) where and when the classes will be held; and b) who will pay for the program.

	ROLE A	ROLE B
Vocabulario	Social problems Dates and time	Social problems Dates and time
Funciones y formas	Expressing conjecture or certainty Adverbial conjunctions that take the subjunctive or indicative	Asking questions Expressing conjecture or certainty Adverbial conjunctions that take the subjunctive or indicative

INTERCAMBIOS. Practiquen la conversación, incorporando el vocabulario y las funciones de **Preparación.** Luego, represéntenla ante la clase.

3 Talking about the past from a past perspective

VIOLETA: Oye, mamá, hoy mi profesora habló un poco de Gabriela Mistral. ¿Tú sabes algo de ella?

MADRE: ¡Claro que sí! Gabriela Mistral fue una gran poeta chilena que ganó el Premio Nobel de Literatura en 1945. Antes de recibir el premio, Gabriela ya **había hecho** muchas cosas importantes.

VIOLETA: ¿Qué **había hecho?** Me gustaría saber más de ella.

MADRE: Gabriela tuvo una vida muy difícil. Su padre **había abandonado** a la familia cuando Gabriela era muy joven. Antes de ser famosa, Gabriela, su hermana y su madre **habían pasado** muchas necesidades por la ausencia del padre. Vivió fuera de Chile por muchos años y murió en Nueva York en 1957.

VIOLETA: ¡Qué triste la vida de Gabriela!

MADRE: Sí y no. Ella utilizó su sufrimiento positivamente para lograr mucho. Por ejemplo, a los 15 años, ya **había escrito** sus primeras poesías y **se había graduado** de profesora. Además, antes de ella, ningún escritor latinoamericano **había ganado** el Premio Nobel.

VIOLETA: ¡Qué impresionante esta mujer, mamá!

MADRE: La verdad es que fue un buen ejemplo para las mujeres.

Piénsalo. Indica si cada una de las siguientes experiencias pasó antes (**A**) o después (**D**) de 1945, cuando Gabriela Mistral ganó el Premio Nobel. Luego escribe el verbo relacionado con cada evento.

	ANTES O DESPUÉS DE 1945	VERBO
1. Gabriela ya **había hecho** muchas cosas importantes.	________	________
2. Su padre **había abandonado** a la familia.	________	________
3. Gabriela, su hermana y su madre **habían pasado** muchas necesidades.	________	________
4. **Vivió** fuera de Chile por muchos años.	________	________
5. **Murió** en Nueva York en 1957.	________	________
6. Ningún escritor latinoamericano **había ganado** el Premio Nobel hasta ese momento.	________	________

The past perfect

- Use the past perfect, or **pluscuamperfecto** in Spanish, to refer to a past event, action, or condition that occurred prior to another past event, action, or state.

Ningún escritor latinoamericano **había ganado** el Premio Nobel de Literatura antes de Mistral.	*No Latin American writer had won the Nobel Prize for Literature before Mistral.*
Otros escritores **habían sido** nominados para el premio, pero ella lo recibió.	*Other writers had been nominated for the award, but she received it.*

- Form the past perfect with the imperfect tense of **haber** and the past participle of the main verb.

IMPERFECT OF *HABER* + PAST PARTICIPLE					
yo	**había**	nosotros/as	**habíamos**		**hablado**
tú	**habías**	vosotros/as	**habíais**	+	**comido**
Ud., él, ella	**había**	Uds., ellos/as	**habían**		**vivido**

¿Comprendes? Completa las afirmaciones con la forma del pluscuamperfecto del verbo entre paréntesis.

1. Cuando Gabriela Mistral ganó el Premio Nobel, ya ____________ (trabajar) como profesora ayudante en una escuela de su pueblo.
2. El novelista y diplomático chileno Roberto Ampuero ya __________ (escribir) muchos libros antes de ser embajador y Ministro de Relaciones Exteriores de su país.
3. Sacamos muy malas notas en el examen de la semana pasada porque no __________ (leer) el material.
4. Cuando invité a mis amigos a una manifestación en contra de la discriminación, me dijeron que ya ____________ (hacer) otros planes para esa noche.

PRÁCTICA

14-24 ¡Recuerdos!

PREPARACIÓN. Para cada afirmación, indica la acción que ocurrió cronológicamente primero (**1**) y la que ocurrió después (**2**).

MODELO **(a)** _2_ Cuando yo cumplí diez años, **(b)** _1_ ya había escuchado discusiones políticas.

1. **(a)** _____ Cuando cumplimos 17 años, **(b)** _____ mis amigos y yo ya habíamos participado en actividades políticas.
2. **(a)** _____ Cuando terminé la escuela secundaria, **(b)** _____ mis padres ya me habían comprado un carro.
3. **(a)** _____ Yo ya había trabajado y había ahorrado (*saved*) dinero **(b)** _____ cuando empecé la universidad.
4. **(a)** _____ Cuando pasó el primer mes de clases en la universidad, **(b)** _____ yo ya me había acostumbrado a todo el trabajo que tenía que hacer.
5. **(a)** _____ Mis padres pensaban que yo me había hecho más independiente **(b)** _____ cuando los visité después de algunos meses.

INTERCAMBIOS. ¿Cuáles de las acciones de **Preparación** asocias con tu experiencia personal? Comparte tus respuestas con tu compañero/a.

14-25 ¡Una familia solidaria!

PREPARACIÓN. El señor y la señora Rosales salieron temprano para el trabajo hoy. Al volver por la noche, notaron que sus hijos Carlos, Eduardo y Ruth habían hecho todo el trabajo doméstico. Túrnense para conjeturar qué había hecho cada uno.

MODELO Al salir, les dijeron a sus hijos que iban a llegar un poco tarde y les pidieron cocinar algo fácil.

E1: *Carlos había cocinado unos espaguetis para toda la familia.*
E2: *Eduardo había preparado una deliciosa ensalada.*
E3: *Y Ruth había puesto la mesa.*

1. Después del desayuno, dejaron los platos sucios en el fregadero, la cafetera sin lavar y el jugo de naranja en la mesa.
2. Antes de irse a la oficina, la señora Rosales vio que había un montón de libros de la biblioteca en la mesa del comedor, el mantel de la mesa estaba manchado (*stained*) y la cafetera estaba encendida en la cocina.
3. Cuando salía de casa, el señor Rosales notó que el garaje estaba sucio, las repisas (*shelves*) estaban desorganizadas y la bicicleta de Ruth estaba en el piso.
4. Los dormitorios y los baños de sus hijos estaban desordenados; había ropa y libros en el piso. No había jabón ni champú en la bañera.
5. Como tenía prisa, la señora Rosales olvidó mandar por correo unos cheques importantes, darle la comida al gato y sacar al perro a caminar.
6. No llevaron a la tintorería (*dry cleaner*) unas chaquetas. Las camisas del señor Rosales estaban limpias, pero alguien debía plancharlas.

INTERCAMBIOS. Conversen sobre lo que ustedes ya habían hecho antes del regreso de sus padres de sus vacaciones. Usen las expresiones de la lista u otras.

comprar comida
darles comida al perro y al gato
hacer una limpieza completa de la casa
pagar las cuentas de luz y agua
poner gasolina al auto de mis padres
recoger el correo del buzón (*mailbox*)

MODELO E1: *Cuando mis padres volvieron de sus vacaciones, yo ya había cortado el césped. ¿Y tú?*
E2: *Yo ya había…*

14-26 Una investigación.

PREPARACIÓN. Completa la tabla y dile a tu compañero/a quién(es) en tu familia ya había(n) hecho estas cosas antes de este año.

MODELO buscar trabajo en internet antes de este año
E1: *Mi hermano y yo ya habíamos buscado trabajo en internet en años anteriores. El año pasado, los dos conseguimos trabajo por internet.*
E2: *Pues, yo nunca había pensado en buscar trabajo por internet.*

Antes de este año	Sí	No	¿Quién(es)?
1. cocinar para alguien			
2. dibujar o pintar algo para alguien			
3. enviar una foto en un mensaje de texto			
4. hacer trabajo de voluntariado			
5. hablar español			
6. manejar un carro nuevo o rápido			
7. participar en una protesta			
8. ver en persona a alguien importante o famoso			
9. viajar en crucero			
10. votar en las elecciones			

INTERCAMBIOS. Hagan una encuesta para averiguar qué tres actividades de **Preparación** marcaron más personas del grupo.

Cultura

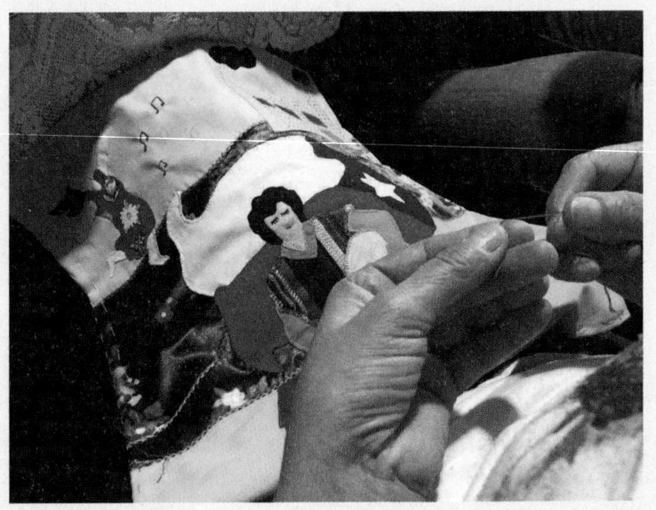

Las arpilleras: arte de protesta y resistencia Durante la dictadura militar en Chile (1973–1990), grupos de mujeres, conocidas como **arpilleristas,** comenzaron a hacer arpilleras (*patchwork pictures*) dentro y fuera del país para protestar por la violencia y la pobreza. Las arpilleristas dentro de Chile las hacían y vendían en secreto a turistas que visitaban el país. Sus obras describían el sufrimiento y la represión, pero también la esperanza de justicia y liberación. En el exilio, otras arpilleristas informaban al mundo de la desaparición y muerte de sus familiares. Sin duda, las arpilleras fueron un arte instrumental que les permitió a las arpilleristas comunicarse con el mundo fuera de Chile y mantener a sus familias durante años de mucho desempleo y violación de los derechos humanos.

Comparaciones ¿Existe un tipo de arte similar al de las arpilleras en tu comunidad o país? ¿Qué función tiene: es un arte puramente estético o también tiene una función social? ¿Alguna vez en la historia de tu país se ha utilizado el arte como instrumento de protesta o resistencia? ¿Qué tipo de arte se ha utilizado? ¿Cómo se usa o se usó?

14-27 Las mujeres y el arte de resistencia. **PREPARACIÓN.** Indiquen las experiencias probables de las arpilleristas antes del retorno a la democracia en Chile. Prepárense para explicar sus respuestas.

1. _____ Los chilenos habían vivido una dictadura de 17 años.
2. _____ Muchos chilenos habían desaparecido o habían muerto.
3. _____ Las mujeres se habían organizado para resistir al gobierno militar.
4. _____ Las arpilleristas habían creado su arte para protestar por la violencia y la pobreza.
5. _____ Las arpilleras les habían permitido a las arpilleristas comunicarse con el mundo fuera de Chile.
6. _____ Sus arpilleras se habían visto solamente en Chile.
7. _____ El mundo se había informado del sufrimiento y la represión en Chile a través de las arpilleras.
8. _____ Los turistas interesados en la política de Chile habían comprado arpilleras y habían divulgado fuera de Chile el sufrimiento de los chilenos.

INTERCAMBIOS. Respondan a las siguientes preguntas.

1. ¿Alguna vez habían escuchado ustedes la historia de las arpilleristas?
2. ¿Habían visto alguna arpillera en fotos antes de tomar esta clase de español? ¿Qué les pareció el arte de las arpilleristas?
3. ¿Cuál(es) de estos derechos habían perdido los chilenos antes del regreso de la democracia: el derecho de libre expresión, el derecho a la libertad, el derecho de libre asamblea (*assembly*), el derecho a votar? ¿Otro derecho?
4. ¿Por qué son importantes estos derechos en una democracia?

14-28 Figuras influyentes (*influential*). Hagan una breve investigación para conseguir la siguiente información sobre el personaje famoso asignado. Su investigación debe responder a estas preguntas:

1. ¿Dónde y cuándo nació (*was born*) y murió?
2. ¿Qué hechos interesantes de su vida se conocen? Indiquen dos o tres.
3. ¿Qué había hecho antes de ser famoso/a? Expliquen en detalle.

- Salvador Allende
- Simón Bolívar
- César Chávez
- Ernesto "Che" Guevara
- Víctor Jara
- Martin Luther King, hijo
- Rosa Parks
- Violeta Parra
- Eva Perón

e Situación

PREPARACIÓN. Lean la situación. Luego, compartan ejemplos de vocabulario, gramática y otra información que necesitan para desarrollar la conversación.

Role A. You are interviewing a student for your campus newspaper. Ask a) what he/she had planned to study before coming to the university; b) what other schools he/she had considered before choosing this one; and c) how his/her experience has been different from what he/she had expected.

Role B. You are a student who is being interviewed for the campus newspaper. Provide as much information to the reporter as possible, including: a) what you had done (your accomplishments) before college, b) your expectations (**lo que habías pensado**) before you entered college, and c) the reality you found when you started to study here.

	ROLE A	ROLE B
Vocabulario	Studies Extracurricular activities	Studies Extracurricular activities
Funciones y formas	Asking questions Past perfect Present perfect	Answering questions Past perfect Present perfect

INTERCAMBIOS. Practiquen la conversación, incorporando el vocabulario y las funciones de **Preparación.** Luego, represéntenla ante la clase.

MOSAICOS

ESCUCHA

Estrategia

Identify the speaker's point of view When you listen to someone or see someone talk you may identify the speaker's intention and point of view by paying attention to word choice as well as other cues, such as tone, organization of ideas, and pitch. Identifying the speaker's point of view will help you understand his/her position on the issues.

 **14-29 Preparación.** Dos amigos conversan sobre los cambios que han ocurrido en la sociedad. Escriban en la tabla un cambio que probablemente se mencionará en relación con cada una de las áreas indicadas. Luego, compartan sus ideas con la clase.

	Cuando sus padres eran muy jóvenes	Hoy en día
el uso de la tecnología en las relaciones personales		
la edad cuando las personas se casan		
las tareas domésticas		

 **14-30 Escucha.** Read the statements, and then listen to Sonia and Pablo talk about societal changes that have occurred over the past decades. Pay attention to how each one of them organizes his/her ideas, his/her choice of words, and the tone he/she uses. Then indicate whether each statement reflects Sonia's (**S**) point of view or Pablo's (**P**).

1. _____ No todos los cambios que han ocurrido en la sociedad han sido positivos.
2. _____ La tecnología ha creado dependencia.
3. _____ Por razones económicas, las personas se casan más mayores que en el pasado.
4. _____ Hoy en día la responsabilidad de los quehaceres domésticos y el cuidado de los hijos es compartida.
5. _____ Aunque la situación está cambiando, persiste la discriminación en contra de la mujer en el trabajo.
6. _____ Todas las personas merecen (*deserve*) justicia e igualdad.

Comprueba

I was able to . . .

- understand the main points and some details in a conversation about social trends.
- identify the different points of view of the participants in the conversation.

 **14-31 Un paso más.** Compartan su punto de vista sobre los siguientes asuntos.

1. ¿Es importante que las personas limiten el uso de la tecnología en su relación con otras personas? ¿Por qué?
2. ¿Qué condiciones mínimas debe cumplir una persona que desea casarse? ¿Por qué?
3. ¿Cómo se puede resolver la discriminación salarial en contra de las mujeres? Expliquen.

HABLA

Estrategia

Organize ideas to present solutions to problems When you present your ideas about how to solve a problem, organize them so that you can communicate clearly to your listeners a) what the problem is, to whom it is important, and why; b) how your proposal is to be implemented and how it addresses the problem; and c) the likely consequences of your solution. Your underlying goal is to convince your listeners of the wisdom of your approach.

14-32 Preparación. Investiguen un asunto de carácter social que les interese y cómo ha afectado a los individuos y a las comunidades en las últimas décadas. Anoten en qué consiste el asunto y su efecto en los individuos y las comunidades.

MODELO Área: *la educación*
Asunto: *costo de la educación*
Efectos: *Hoy en día, la educación cuesta más del 100% de lo que costaba en los años 90. Por eso, los jóvenes necesitan pedir préstamos* (loans)*...*

ÁREAS

1. la economía
2. la igualdad
3. la educación
4. la salud
5. la violencia doméstica / la violencia en la sociedad
6. la discriminación

14-33 Habla. Conversen con dos compañeros/as que investigaron el mismo tema que ustedes en **Preparación.** Explíquense detalladamente el problema y sus efectos. Luego, háganse preguntas. Tomen nota de las respuestas del grupo.

MODELO la falta de seguridad en las escuelas
E1: *¿Piensa que hay solución para la falta de seguridad en las escuelas?*
E2: *Sí, la solución es tener/establecer más comunicación con la administración de las escuelas para que controlen mejor la seguridad de los alumnos.*
E3: *A mí me parece que la solución es instalar máquinas en las entradas de las escuelas...*

En directo

To present a group's conclusion:

Después de hablar sobre el tema, hemos llegado a la siguiente conclusión. *After our discussion on the topic, we concluded that . . .*

Nuestro grupo cree/piensa que... *Our group thinks that . . .*

A nuestro grupo le parece que... *It seems to our group that . . .*

Para nosotros/as, el problema más serio es... *For us, the most serious issue is . . .*

To support a group's view or position:

No tenemos duda de que es el asunto/problema más serio porque... *We don't doubt that this is the most serious issue because . . .*

Si miramos/observamos... nos damos cuenta de que... *If we look at / observe . . . we realize that . . .*

Las estadísticas / La opinión de los expertos apoya(n) nuestra conclusión. *The data / Expert opinion supports our conclusion.*

 Listen to a conversation with these expressions.

Comprueba

I was able to . . .

- exchange information and ideas about a social problem and possible solutions.
- organize my ideas in a logical sequence.
- present my well-organized proposal for a course of action.

14-34 Un paso más. Preséntenle a la clase la información y conclusión a la que llegaron en la actividad **14-33.** Prepárense para defender su posición con información factual.

LEE

Estrategia

Identify the tone of a text Identifying the tone of a text is important when reading literature. A writer may use subtle irony or sarcasm to convey social criticism. Sometimes the writer adopts a traditional genre (e.g., fairy tale, fable) to present a message about contemporary life. By using animals as the main characters, authors may make their stories accessible to readers of all ages while still imparting a social or political message.

14-35 Preparación. Responde a las siguientes preguntas. Compara tus respuestas con las de tu compañero/a.

1. ¿Qué fábulas (*fables*) conoces o recuerdas de tu niñez?
2. ¿Cuáles son los elementos de las fábulas?
3. ¿Cuál es el propósito (*purpose*) de una fábula?
4. ¿Qué diferencias hay entre una mosca (*fly*) y un águila (*eagle*)? ¿Qué tienen en común?
5. Imagínate que no eres un ser humano, sino un animal. ¿Preferirías ser una mosca o un águila? ¿Por qué?

Augusto Monterroso (1921–2003) nació en Honduras de padre guatemalteco y madre hondureña, pero se crió en Guatemala y siempre se consideró guatemalteco. Por sus actividades políticas, estuvo encarcelado brevemente en 1944 pero escapó y vivió exiliado en Chile y luego en México, donde vivió hasta su muerte. Monterroso, conocido por sus relatos breves que tratan sobre temas complejos del comportamiento humano, es uno de los maestros de la minificción. Su microcuento "El dinosaurio" es considerado uno de los más breves de la literatura universal (el cuento consta de solo una oración: *Cuando despertó, el dinosaurio todavía estaba allí.*).

 **14-36 Lee.** Lee el microcuento e indica cuáles son las ventajas (**V**) y las desventajas (**D**) de ser un Águila, desde la perspectiva de la Mosca.

1. _____ volar por los Alpes
2. _____ tener alas grandes
3. _____ tener un cuerpo pesado
4. _____ tener un pico duro
5. _____ tener garras fuertes
6. _____ remontar montañas

Palabras clave	
el águila	*eagle*
las alas	*wings*
andar	*to travel*
duro/a	*hard*
las garras	*claws*
la mosca	*fly*
pesado/a	*heavy*
el pico	*beak*
soñar	*to dream*
volar	*to fly*

Comprueba

I was able to . . .

- understand the literal meaning of the story.
- understand the fly's internal conflict.
- apply the message of the story to human behavior.

LA MOSCA QUE SOÑABA QUE ERA UN ÁGUILA

Había una vez una Mosca que todas las noches soñaba que era un Águila y que se encontraba volando por los Alpes y por los Andes.

En los primeros momentos esto la volvía[1] loca de felicidad; pero pasado un tiempo le causaba una sensación de angustia, pues hallaba[2] las alas demasiado grandes, el cuerpo demasiado pesado, el pico demasiado duro y las garras demasiado fuertes; bueno, que todo ese gran aparato le impedía posarse a gusto sobre los ricos pasteles o sobre las inmundicias[3] humanas, así como sufrir a conciencia dándose topes[4] contra los vidrios[5] de su cuarto.

En realidad no quería andar en las grandes alturas o en los espacios libres, ni mucho menos. Pero cuando volvía en sí[6] lamentaba con toda el alma[7] no ser un Águila para remontar montañas, y se sentía tristísima de ser una Mosca, y por eso volaba tanto, y estaba tan inquieta, y daba tantas vueltas, hasta que lentamente, por la noche, volvía a poner las sienes[8] en la almohada.

Monterroso, Augusto. *La oveja negra y demás fábulas*. Alfaguara. México: 2a edición. 1998.

[1]*made* [2]*found* [3]*filth* [4]*running into* [5]*panes of glass* [6]*woke up* [7]*soul* [8]*head* (lit. *temples*)

 **14-37 Un paso más.** Hablen de su interpretación del microcuento. Escriban sus ideas en una lista breve y preséntenlas a la clase. Enfóquense en cómo se puede aplicar el conflicto interno de la Mosca al comportamiento (*behavior*) humano.

ESCRIBE

Estrategia

Write to spark interest To hold the interest of your reader, whether your writing is analytical or creative, these tips may prove useful.

- Plan ahead. Spend some time on online research to extend or deepen your knowledge, or to consult the ideas of others.
- Organize your information to stay focused as you write.
- Strive to vary your vocabulary.
- In creative writing, such as a description or a narrative, be aware of your perspective: Who is telling the story? Who is observing the scene?
- Make sure that you make your main point (i.e., your thesis, argument) clearly for your readers.
- Choose a title that will capture the attention and imagination of your readers.

14-38 Preparación. Lee otra vez el cuento en la actividad **14-36** y también las ideas sobre la interpretación del cuento que tu grupo escribió en la actividad **14-37.** Luego, piensa en cómo sería el cuento con el Águila de narrador. Utiliza la siguiente tabla para organizar tus ideas.

Características de la Mosca	¿Por qué quiere el Águila tener estas características?
1.	1.
2.	2.
3.	3.
4.	4.
...	...
Características del Águila	**¿Por qué está contenta el Águila de tener estas características?**
1.	1.
2.	2.
3.	3.
4.	4.
...	...

14-39 Escribe. Usando lo que escribiste sobre el Águila en la actividad **14-38** como punto de partida (*point of departure*), escribe un microcuento con este título: "El águila que soñaba que era una mosca". Comienza tus párrafos con las siguientes frases:

(Párrafo 1) Todas las noches el Águila soñaba que era una Mosca y que...
(Párrafo 2) Al principio se sentía muy feliz, porque... Pero al pensarlo más, se sentía angustiada. No quería ser una Mosca, porque...
(Párrafo 3) Al final, decidió que era mejor ser un Águila porque...

14-40 Un paso más. Lee el microcuento de tu compañero/a. Luego, háganse preguntas para descubrir el propósito de los detalles que cada uno/a incluyó. ¿Están de acuerdo con las razones de por qué el Águila prefiere ser quien es? Expliquen.

Comprueba

I was able to . . .

- write a fable using the guidance provided in the instructions.
- create a perspective, desires, and internal conflicts for the eagle.
- incorporate a message into the the story that can be applied to human behavior.

En este capítulo...

Vocabulario

La sociedad	Society
la adaptación	*adjustment, adaptation*
el analfabetismo	*illiteracy*
la brecha	*gap*
la calidad	*quality*
el cambio	*change*
el capital	*capital* (money)
el comercio	*commerce*
la condición	*condition*
la corrupción	*corruption*
el crecimiento	*growth*
el derecho	*right*
el desafío	*challenge*
el desarrollo	*development*
el desempleo	*unemployment*
el desplazamiento	*movement, displacement*
la (des)igualdad	*(in)equality*
la discriminación	*discrimination*
la diversidad	*diversity*
la emigración	*emigration*
el empleo	*employment*
la escolarización	*schooling*
la esperanza de vida	*life expectancy*
la exportación	*exports*
el factor	*factor*
el flujo	*flow*
la infraestructura	*infrastructure*
el ingreso (alto/bajo)	*(low/high) income*
la inmigración	*immigration*
la ley	*law*
el logro	*achievement*
la migración	*migration*
la mortalidad infantil	*child mortality*
la nacionalidad	*nationality*
el país de acogida	*host country*
el permiso	*permit*
la pobreza	*poverty*
el poder	*power*
la precariedad	*precariousness*
las prestaciones	*benefits*
la proximidad	*proximity*
la recuperación	*recovery*
la vejez	*old age*

Las personas	People
el/la emigrante	*emigrant*
el/la extranjero/a	*foreigner*
el/la inmigrante	*immigrant*
los datos	*data, information*
el índice	*rate*
el porcentaje	*percentage*
el promedio	*average*
la tasa	*rate*

Las descripciones	Descriptions
alfabetizado/a	*literate*
económico/a	*economic*
emergente	*emerging*
financiero/a	*financial*
laboral	*work, job*
migratorio/a	*migratory*
remunerado/a	*paid*
salarial	*salary, wage*
seguro/a	*safe*

Verbos	Verbs
desplazarse (c)	*to move, to be displaced*
disminuir (y)	*to decrease*
emigrar	*to emigrate*
frenar	*to slow down*
invertir (ie, i)	*to invest*
luchar	*to fight*
mejorar	*to improve*

Palabras y expresiones útiles	Useful words and expressions
a escala mundial	*on a global scale*
a pesar de	*in spite of*
debido a	*due to*
en vez de	*instead of*

See pages 522 and 526–527 for adverbial conjunctions.

Capítulo 15
¿Qué nos trae el futuro?

Learning Outcomes

You will be able to:

- talk about advances in science and technology
- express wishes and recommendations in the past
- hypothesize and share information about the present and the future
- express unexpected occurrences
- talk about Puerto Rico in terms of products, practices, and perspectives
- talk about technology and scientific research in Spain and Latin America

Enfoque cultural

Puerto Rico

OCÉANO ATLÁNTICO
PUERTO RICO
Arecibo
San Juan
Bosque Nacional El Yunque
Bayamón
Manatí
Guaynabo
Carolina
Trujillo Alto
Mayagüez
Cerro de Punta
CORDILLERA CENTRAL
Caguas
Humacao
Isla de Culebra
San Germán
Ponce
Guayama
Arroyo
Isla de Vieques
Cabo Rojo
Mar Caribe

San Juan, el puerto (*port*) más importante de Puerto Rico, es un centro cultural, turístico y financiero.

El Parque Nacional El Yunque sirve de laboratorio para la investigación sobre los bosques de todo el mundo.

El huracán María tocó tierra en Puerto Rico en septiembre de 2017, causando gran destrucción.

Arte hispano

El velorio del pintor puertorriqueño Francisco Oller.

Enfoque cultural

¿Qué te parece?

- En Puerto Rico se mide (*measure*) la temperatura ambiental (*atmospheric*) en grados Fahrenheit mientras que la temperatura del cuerpo se mide en grados centígrados.
- En Puerto Rico se usa el sistema monetario de Estados Unidos, pero se han mantenido los nombres de las antiguas monedas (*coins*) españolas. Un dólar se conoce como un peso y la moneda de 25 centavos es una peseta.
- En la isla hay cientos de especies de bananas. La palabra genérica para esta fruta es **guineo** porque en la época colonial las importaban del país africano Guinea. En vez de **naranja,** se usa la palabra **china** porque esta fruta se trajo de China.
- Puerto Rico participa como país independiente en los Juegos Olímpicos. Ha ganado nueve medallas: seis en boxeo, una en lucha libre, una en tenis y una en atletismo. Javier Culson, de la ciudad de Ponce, es el atleta olímpico más conocido.

La Parguera, en el pueblo de Lajas, es uno de los tres lugares de Puerto Rico donde se puede observar el fenómeno de la bioluminiscencia. Durante las noches sin luna, unos organismos microscópicos emiten una luz intensa bajo el mar. Este espectáculo de luz puede observarse desde las casas flotantes de la bahía, o desde barcos pequeños.

Desde su construcción en los años 60 hasta 2016, el Observatorio de Arecibo, en el norte de la isla, tuvo el radiotelescopio más grande del mundo. A través de este radiotelescopio se analizan datos atmosféricos y astronómicos. También se busca evidencia de la existencia de inteligencia extraterrestre. Por eso, en el mundo del cine, este observatorio se asocia frecuentemente con temas de ciencia ficción. Allí se filmaron las películas *Contact* y *GoldenEye* del famoso Agente 007.

La ciudad de Ponce, al sur de la isla, tiene una elegante arquitectura, de estilo *art nouveau* y neoclásico, que se desarrolló principalmente en el siglo XIX. Además, es un centro cultural importante con numerosos museos, ferias de artesanía y festivales de música. Entre sus múltiples tradiciones se celebra un carnaval que atrae a miles de turistas. Antes, la economía de Ponce se basaba en el cultivo de la caña de azúcar, pero hoy en día, el sector industrial es muy importante, con la manufactura de equipos eléctricos y electrónicos, instrumentos científicos y productos farmacéuticos.

Puerto Rico es la tierra de numerosos artistas: escritores, pintores, arquitectos, actores y músicos. La música de Puerto Rico, resultado de una gran mezcla de culturas, es muy variada. Uno de los géneros musicales de fusión más conocidos es el reguetón, música urbana que mezcla el reggae en español proveniente de Panamá, el hip hop y otros ritmos caribeños. Cantantes como Don Omar, Daddy Yankee y Tego Calderón, que ganó un Premio Grammy en 2015, han popularizado el reguetón en todo el mundo.

¿Cuánto sabes? Completa estas oraciones con la información correcta.

1. El puerto comercial más importante de Puerto Rico es el de __________.
2. El reguetón es una mezcla de hip hop, ____________ en español y otros ritmos caribeños.
3. Una china en Puerto Rico es una __________.
4. En Puerto Rico un peso equivale a __________ pesetas.
5. El Observatorio de Arecibo es famoso por las investigaciones sobre la vida __________ que se realizan allí.

To learn more about Puerto Rico, go online to view the *Club cultura* videos.

VOCABULARIO EN CONTEXTO

Talking about technology, science, and the environment

La tecnología en el mundo de hoy

Por la mañana temprano, Ángel, un joven puertorriqueño, **se conecta** a internet. Entra en las redes sociales para tener una idea de las últimas noticias. Luego, le **reenvía** un **tuit** a Carmen sobre la nueva película de **ciencia ficción** y **chatea** un rato con ella. Más tarde, **baja** el último *podcast* para su clase en línea y le envía a su profesor de ciencias naturales un **mensaje** con un **documento adjunto.**

Por la tarde, Lorena, la hermana de Ángel, le pide ayuda para **actualizar** una **aplicación,** mientras escucha música con sus **auriculares.** Después, Ángel entra en el blog de su amigo Juanjo para leer las últimas **novedades** sobre sus videojuegos preferidos. Allí encuentra un **enlace** que le interesa, y **sube** a la **nube** la información para **guardarla.**

Actualmente, la ciencia y la tecnología **contribuyen** a un mejor **conocimiento** del **entorno.** Las **máquinas** y computadoras usan algoritmos que superan la capacidad humana de **programar medidas** para **resolver** problemas. Es lo que se llama la **inteligencia artificial**, que ya se aplica a la medicina, a los negocios y a otras muchas áreas. Por otro lado, el **acceso** global a los recursos de internet a través de las tabletas, computadoras y otros **dispositivos móviles** hace más fluida la comunicación y facilita la **diseminación** y el **intercambio** de información.

Desde hace unos años, nuevas **carreras** están apareciendo en los catálogos de las universidades de Puerto Rico para responder a una demanda laboral que **se enfoca** en la tecnología. Son carreras como computación, bioingeniería, ciencias en **seguridad de la información, administración de redes** y **programación.** Conscientes de esta necesidad, los gobiernos actuales dan **becas** y ayudas para **promover** el estudio de las ciencias y la tecnología entre los jóvenes. Además, los cursos en línea y las **bibliotecas digitales** son ahora recursos que preparan a los estudiantes para las necesidades del futuro.

PRÁCTICA

15-1 Escucha y confirma. Escucha el anuncio radiofónico y decide si las afirmaciones son ciertas (C) o falsas (F). Corrige las oraciones falsas.

1. _____ Es un anuncio de una tienda digital.
2. _____ Según el anuncio, se puede obtener un título de maestría en línea.
3. _____ Se ofrecen clases de humanidades solamente.
4. _____ Los expertos en recursos digitales son los profesores.
5. _____ La calidad de la enseñanza (*teaching*) es más importante que la interacción.
6. _____ Los estudiantes no necesitan acceso a internet.

15-2 ¿Para qué lo usamos? Añade otro posible uso de la tecnología a cada uno de los siguientes grupos. Luego, comparen sus respuestas y añadan una acción para la que no se usa la tecnología.

1. Internet sirve para...
   - **a.** acceder a información sobre muchas disciplinas.
   - **b.** ver películas.
   - **c.** enviar felicitaciones.
   - **d.** __________

   No sirve para...
2. El correo electrónico se usa para...
   - **a.** comunicarse con otras personas.
   - **b.** enviar un documento adjunto.
   - **c.** recibir mensajes.
   - **d.** __________

   No sirve para...
3. La biblioteca digital se utiliza para...
   - **a.** encontrar enlaces.
   - **b.** bajar artículos.
   - **c.** identificar documentación.
   - **d.** __________

   No sirve para...
4. La inteligencia artificial sirve para...
   - **a.** resolver problemas financieros.
   - **b.** diagnosticar enfermedades.
   - **c.** manejar carros sin conductor (*driver*).
   - **d.** __________

   No sirve para...

Cultura

La Universidad de Río Piedras La Universidad de Puerto Rico está formada por 11 campus que se encuentran por toda la isla. El campus de Río Piedras es el más importante de todos y el que tiene mayor número de estudiantes, más de 17.000. Está situado en el centro de la zona comercial y cultural de Río Piedras, a las afueras de San Juan. El campus es fácilmente identificable desde diferentes puntos de la ciudad por su extraordinaria torre (*tower*).

Comparaciones ¿Tiene tu universidad un solo campus o más de uno? Si hay varios, ¿cuál es el más importante? ¿Cuántos estudiantes tiene? ¿Qué programas, actividades o edificios de tu universidad son los más conocidos?

15-3 Usen la tecnología. PREPARACIÓN. Usen la tecnología para preparar una presentación sobre Puerto Rico que incluya lo siguiente:

1. ubicación en un mapa de un lugar de Puerto Rico que les interese
2. descripción y tres datos que se refieran a las características físicas del lugar, la gente que vive allí y una costumbre local
3. fotos

INTERCAMBIOS. Compartan la información con la clase, incluyendo una descripción de los recursos tecnológicos que utilizaron.

MODELO *Nosotros investigamos la ciudad de Isabela. Accedimos al sitio web de la ciudad para buscar... Estas son las fotos que encontramos en...*

15-4 Una noticia. **PREPARACIÓN.** Busca una noticia que te interese en un periódico virtual de Puerto Rico. Léela y toma apuntes sobre lo esencial de la noticia.

INTERCAMBIOS. Mándales a tres personas de la clase un mensaje incluyendo un resumen de la noticia y tu opinión sobre ella.

La ciencia y el medio ambiente

La contribución de América Latina a la ciencia se ha enfocado principalmente en la biología, la agricultura y la medicina. Aunque a veces las infraestructuras y los recursos son insuficientes, algunos científicos de esta región han hecho **descubrimientos** importantes. Además, la riqueza de la flora y la fauna de la región **ha aumentado** la necesidad de **proteger** y **conservar** la naturaleza con técnicas avanzadas.

Muchos ingenieros, técnicos y científicos originarios de Puerto Rico contribuyen al desarrollo de la industria **aeroespacial** de Estados Unidos. Por ejemplo, la científica e inventora Olga González-Sanabria tuvo un papel fundamental en el desarrollo de las **baterías** de níquel e hidrógeno de larga resistencia que mantienen las estaciones eléctricas de la NASA y los **satélites** desde los que se observan los **cambios climáticos.**

En países como Chile, las ciencias del mar están muy desarrolladas. Universidades como la de Valparaíso elaboran proyectos para controlar los **vertidos** químicos y **residuales** y proteger la industria **pesquera.** La **contaminación** de los océanos es muy preocupante y algunos estudios se enfocan en **medir** el carbono orgánico que proviene de los **residuos plásticos** y su efecto sobre las bacterias **marinas.**

La **cuenca** del **río** Amazonas **cubre** un área de más de siete millones de kilómetros cuadrados (*square*), región comparable en extensión a dos terceras partes (*two-thirds*) del territorio continental de Estados Unidos. Debido a su densa vegetación **selvática,** esta zona es conocida como el pulmón del **planeta.** Hoy en día, millones de árboles se cortan en el mundo para abrir espacios de **cultivo.** La **deforestación** de nuestros bosques se considera una **pérdida** irreparable para el **medio ambiente.**

PRÁCTICA

15-5 Para confirmar.

PREPARACIÓN. Indica cuáles de los siguientes problemas se asocian con la industria pesquera (**IP**), con los bosques tropicales (**BT**) o con ambos (*both*) (**A**).

1. _____ la extensión de cultivos incontrolados
2. _____ la desertización
3. _____ la erosión
4. _____ la extinción de especies animales
5. _____ la deforestación
6. _____ la contaminación provocada por aguas residuales y sustancias químicas
7. _____ la disminución de la capa de ozono (*ozone layer*)
8. _____ la reducción de recursos marinos

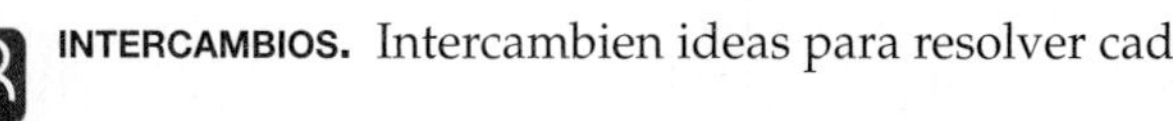

INTERCAMBIOS. Intercambien ideas para resolver cada problema.

15-6 Los adelantos (*advances*) y los cambios.

PREPARACIÓN. Haz una lista de tres adelantos científicos y tres cambios sociales que esperas que se realicen en las próximas décadas.

INTERCAMBIOS. Comparen sus listas y justifiquen la razón de los cambios que indicaron en **Preparación.** ¿Por qué ocurrirán? ¿Son cambios necesarios?

Cultura

El coquí El coquí es el nombre general para designar de manera popular un conjunto de ranas pequeñas de Puerto Rico. El nombre es una onomatopeya del sonido emitido por las ranas. Debido a los cambios medioambientales, su población ha disminuido considerablemente en los últimos años. Muchas organizaciones ecologistas siguen luchando por la protección del hábitat del coquí. Hoy en día el coquí llanero (*of the plains*) se ha convertido en símbolo nacional de Puerto Rico y está protegido bajo la Ley Federal de Especies en Peligro de Extinción (*Endangered Species*).

Conexiones Busca información sobre las causas de la destrucción del hábitat del coquí llanero. ¿Qué animales están en peligro de extinción en tu estado o región? ¿Qué hacen los grupos ecologistas y el gobierno para protegerlos?

15-7 Organizaciones ecologistas.

PREPARACIÓN. Busca información en internet sobre organizaciones como Greenpeace o el Club Sierra, cuyo propósito es proteger el medio ambiente. Escoge una de esas organizaciones y prepara un breve informe oral con la siguiente información.

1. ¿Qué objetivos tiene la organización?
2. ¿Cómo se financia?
3. ¿Quiénes trabajan o hacen voluntariado en ella?
4. ¿Cuál fue una de sus campañas recientes?
5. ¿Qué objetivos tenía la campaña?
6. ¿Cómo la realizaron?
7. ¿Cuál fue el resultado de la campaña?
8. ¿Cómo crees que podrías ayudar tú?

INTERCAMBIOS. Háganse al menos tres preguntas cada uno/a sobre la organización que escogieron.

Otros retos del futuro

Las ciudades

- Se **construirán** ciudades verticales con edificios **climatizados** por medio de **energías alternativas**, como la energía **solar** o la **eólica.** Los edificios tendrán jardines verticales **sostenibles.**
- El 90% de la población vivirá en las ciudades y se incentivará el transporte público **no contaminante.**
- Todas las basuras urbanas serán **recicladas,** los servicios serán **digitalizados** y muchos de ellos serán compartidos.

La atmósfera

- El **agujero** de la **capa de ozono** hará aumentar el número de enfermos de cáncer de piel. El aumento de los **rayos ultravioleta** también afectará a las plantas, que producirán sustancias tóxicas y serán más vulnerables a **plagas** y enfermedades.
- La industria transgénica permitirá cultivar plantas resistentes a los factores climatológicos, o **criar** animales que lleguen más rápidamente al **tamaño** deseado por el mercado y sean resistentes a las enfermedades. Pero la comercialización de estos productos manipulados genéticamente podría **poner en riesgo** la seguridad alimentaria de los consumidores vulnerables a nuevas alergias.

El mar

- El **nivel del mar** subirá por los **deshielos** debidos al **calentamiento** de la atmósfera y causará **inundaciones** y **erosión** en algunas costas, así como la **desaparición** de ciudades costeras.
- La contaminación de los mares **provocará** la **extinción** de los **bancos de peces.**

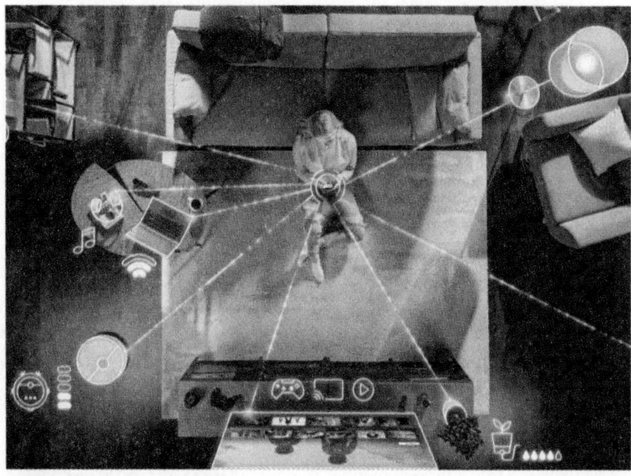

Las viviendas

- Todas las casas estarán conectadas a internet y no será necesario hacer compras presenciales. Las compras se harán siempre **virtualmente.**
- Las puertas y los aparatos electrónicos serán activados por la voz o con sensores que reconocerán a cada individuo.
- Habrá **robots** que se ocuparán de hacer la limpieza, de preparar la comida o de regar (*water*) las plantas.

El transporte

- Los trenes de alta velocidad conectarán las grandes ciudades y circularán por **rieles** suspendidos a la altura de los edificios.
- Los coches combinarán la energía eléctrica y la energía solar. Serán pequeñas **cápsulas voladoras** que podrán **despegar** y **aterrizar** verticalmente como los helicópteros.
- El tráfico aéreo de las ciudades será controlado por satélite.

La ciencia y la tecnología

- Habrá **clonaciones** de animales **extinguidos.**
- Los embriones humanos se seleccionarán **genéticamente.**
- Se implantarán **chips electrónicos** en el cerebro mediante **microcirugía.**
- Se explorarán otras energías alternativas.
- Se **repoblarán** los bosques con técnicas avanzadas para eliminar la desertización.

PRÁCTICA

15-8 Para confirmar. PREPARACIÓN. Según las fotos y textos anteriores, haz una lista de tus propias predicciones para el futuro en dos de las siguientes áreas: el transporte, la tecnología, las formas de vida, la vivienda o la planificación de las ciudades. Indica cuáles de las ideas mencionadas se discuten ya en tu comunidad.

INTERCAMBIOS. Compartan sus predicciones sobre el mundo del futuro. Luego hagan lo siguiente:

- Hablen de dos problemas específicos que existen en el mundo contemporáneo.
- Sugieran posibles soluciones para cada uno de los problemas.
- Presenten sus ideas ante la clase.

MODELO *El tráfico en las ciudades es un problema muy grande. Proponemos construir aparcamientos en las afueras de las ciudades y tener más zonas peatonales.*

15-9 El reto más serio de hoy. Preparen un informe oral sobre el reto más serio que enfrentan el mundo y el ser humano hoy, según su opinión. Describan detalladamente el problema y ofrezcan algunas soluciones.

15-10 ¡El futuro es hoy! Primero, individualmente hagan una lista de cinco cosas (aparatos, sistemas de comunicación, transporte, etc.) que existen hoy y que no existían cuando sus padres tenían la edad de ustedes. Luego, comparen sus listas y expliquen el impacto y las consecuencias de estas nuevas cosas en sus vidas.

15-11 Un viaje a lo desconocido. **PREPARACIÓN.** Planeen un viaje a un planeta habitado desconocido y expliquen con quiénes irán, qué llevarán, cuánto tiempo tardarán en llegar, qué verán allí y cómo se sentirán física y emocionalmente en este nuevo ambiente. Compartan su plan con otros dos astronautas (sus compañeros/as) para formular el mejor plan posible.

INTERCAMBIOS. De regreso del viaje al planeta desconocido, explíquenle a la clase lo que vieron e hicieron allí. Luego, escriban un párrafo sobre sus observaciones. Incluyan la siguiente información.

1. nombre y descripción del planeta
2. descripción de sus habitantes
3. descripción de sus ciudades, viviendas y medios de transporte

15-12 Los OVNIS (Objetos Voladores No Identificados).

PREPARACIÓN. Observen la imagen y contesten las preguntas.

1. ¿Qué va a pasar si llegan las cápsulas voladoras a la Tierra?
2. ¿Qué van a encontrar los extraterrestres?
3. ¿Cómo van a reaccionar los habitantes de la Tierra?

INTERCAMBIOS. Inventen una historia en la que llegan a la Tierra unos seres de otro planeta. Describan la situación, los personajes y las acciones. Añadan detalles e intercambien sus historias con otra pareja. Háganse preguntas para obtener más detalles. Usen su imaginación para escribir un párrafo sobre esa situación que compartirán con la clase.

Cultura

Agricultura sostenible Debido a la riqueza medioambiental y a la biodiversidad de la isla, Puerto Rico es un lugar apropiado para la explotación agrícola que respeta la naturaleza y el medio ambiente. En los últimos años, se ha incrementado la agricultura sostenible que cumple (*complies*) con unas normas éticas y ecológicas, con el fin de proteger los recursos naturales para las futuras generaciones.

Comparaciones ¿En qué lugares de tu comunidad puedes comprar productos cultivados usando prácticas de la agricultura sostenible? ¿Qué ventajas tienen estos productos?

15-13 El problema de la alimentación. **PREPARACIÓN.** You will listen to a short talk about the problem of feeding the world's population. Before you listen, list two problems you think the speaker may mention and two solutions you think she may provide.

ESCUCHA. First, read the following incomplete ideas. Then, as you listen, pay attention to the general idea of what is said and select the appropriate ending to each statement.

1. Los gobiernos tienen que solucionar el problema de…
   a. la agricultura tradicional.
   b. la falta de alimentos para la población.
   c. las pocas variedades de productos.
2. La tecnología y los científicos…
   a. pueden ayudar a solucionar este problema.
   b. trabajan en las islas Filipinas.
   c. desarrollan computadoras de mucha utilidad.
3. Si se aumenta la producción de arroz, los gobiernos pueden…
   a. exportarlo y ganar más dinero.
   b. alimentar a más personas.
   c. obtener variedades más nutritivas.
4. Hay que beneficiarse de los avances de la tecnología, pero también es necesario…
   a. aumentar la productividad en un 70%.
   b. conseguir alimentos básicos.
   c. preservar el medio ambiente.

Mosaico cultural

La investigación tecnológica y científica en España e Hispanoamérica

La inversión en el desarrollo de la ciencia y la tecnología se ha duplicado en los últimos diez años en España e Hispanoamérica, aunque el 91% de estas inversiones se concentran en países como España, México, Chile o Argentina. Sin embargo, otros países como Uruguay, Ecuador o Colombia están impulsando proyectos educativos para desarrollar el estudio de estas materias desde la infancia. A la vez, en América Latina se están asignando cada vez más recursos a las universidades para impulsar la investigación, retener a los científicos de talento y evitar que, como hasta ahora, muchos prefieran salir hacia Europa o Estados Unidos. A pesar de la tradicional falta de recursos, muchos inventos importantes de hispanos han tenido un impacto en el mundo: la píldora anticonceptiva (*birth control pill*) del químico mexicano Luis Miramontes, la vacuna contra la malaria del colombiano Manuel Elkin Patarroyo y el test de paternidad del venezolano Baruj Benacerraf son solo unos ejemplos.

Estos científicos tuvieron que hacer grandes esfuerzos para producir avances tan importantes. Hoy en día, los tratados (*treaties*) de comercio son buenas oportunidades para la ciencia y la tecnología porque permiten a investigadores y científicos importantes trabajar sin tantas limitaciones. La inversión extranjera, los grandes avances en la educación y los tratados de comercio comienzan a mostrar a una Latinoamérica con mucho potencial para el futuro. Gracias a los grandes proyectos de cooperación científica y tecnológica mundial disminuirán los desequilibrios sociales y aumentarán los niveles de educación, la cual es muy importante para el bienestar y el progreso de la humanidad.

El científico español Santiago Ramón y Cajal (1852–1934), pionero de la neurociencia, y Premio Nobel de Medicina en 1906

Una científica hispana trabaja en su laboratorio.

Compara

1. ¿Qué beneficios sociales trae la investigación científica? ¿Qué desventajas? En tu opinión, ¿cuáles son los avances científicos y tecnológicos más importantes de los últimos tiempos?
2. ¿Cuáles son las principales contribuciones tecnológicas de científicos de tu país para el mundo? Elabora tu respuesta.
3. ¿Qué otras aportaciones científicas y tecnológicas hispanas conoces? ¿Cómo afectará a tu comunidad el incremento de la población hispana en el futuro? ¿Crees que el rol de la comunidad hispana en tu país cambiará para el año 2040? Explica y justifica tu respuesta.

En acción

¡Cuidemos el medio ambiente!

Antes de ver

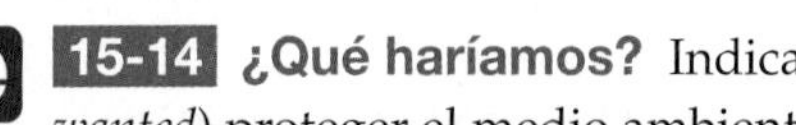

15-14 ¿Qué haríamos? Indica qué haríamos si realmente quisiéramos (*we wanted*) proteger el medio ambiente.

1. _____ Usaríamos más autos eléctricos y más energía solar.
2. _____ Aplicaríamos pesticidas a las plantas.
3. _____ Cuidaríamos más el agua.
4. _____ Dependeríamos menos de los combustibles como la gasolina.
5. _____ No compraríamos agua en botellas de plástico.
6. _____ Llevaríamos bolsas de tela al supermercado.
7. _____ Disminuiríamos el uso de los aerosoles.
8. _____ Continuaríamos la deforestación de nuestros bosques.
9. _____ Tendríamos más áreas verdes.
10. _____ Causaríamos incendios en los bosques.

Mientras ves

15-15 La tecnología y el medio ambiente. Indica si las afirmaciones son ciertas (**C**) o falsas (**F**), según el video. Corrige las falsas.

Techos (*Roofs*) verdes:

1. _____ Es un programa del gobierno de Estados Unidos para mejorar el problema de la contaminación en México.
2. _____ El principal beneficiario de este programa es la Ciudad de México.
3. _____ En la Ciudad de México hay muy pocos espacios verdes.
4. _____ En los techos y paredes de los edificios se planta vegetación nativa.

Autos eléctricos y taxis solares:

5. _____ El gobierno de California está a la vanguardia de la tecnología de autos eléctricos.
6. _____ El plan ZEV es un programa del gobierno mexicano que promueve la creación de autos con cero emisiones.
7. _____ Tesla Motors produce autos que funcionan con energía solar.
8. _____ En la Ciudad de México hay algunos taxis ecológicos.

La beca. PREPARACIÓN. Los estudiantes han trabajado todo el verano en sus proyectos cinematográficos. Ahora, debes decidir quién va a ganar la beca. Vuelve a ver los proyectos finales y decide quién es el/la ganador/a.

INTERCAMBIOS. Decidan quién debería ganar la beca. ¿Están de acuerdo? Explíquenle a la clase su selección del / de la ganador/a.

Después de ver

15-16 ¡Bienvenida sea la tecnología!

PREPARACIÓN. Selecciona un fin lógico para cada afirmación.

1. _____ Con más programas como Techos verdes…	a. habría menos emisiones de monóxido de carbono en la atmósfera.
2. _____ Para disminuir la contaminación causada por la gasolina…	b. habría más oxígeno en el medio ambiente.
3. _____ Al implementar el plan ZEV…	c. podríamos usar autobuses o taxis solares.

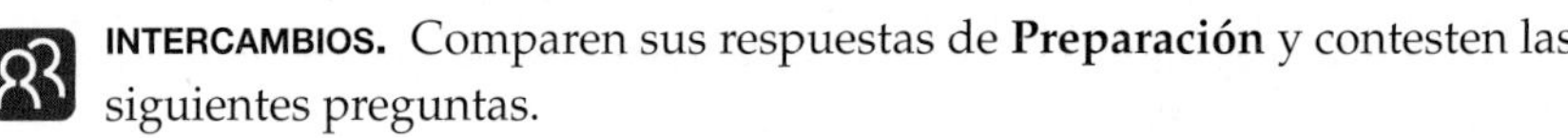

INTERCAMBIOS. Comparen sus respuestas de **Preparación** y contesten las siguientes preguntas.

1. ¿Qué otros planes o proyectos conocen ustedes para mejorar los problemas del medio ambiente?
2. ¿Quiénes deben ser los responsables de resolver los problemas del medio ambiente: los individuos, los gobiernos, las organizaciones internacionales o todos? Justifiquen sus respuestas.

FUNCIONES Y FORMAS

1 Expressing the unexpected

e **Piénsalo.** Primero, indica quién dice cada afirmación, **Carlos** o **Lorena.** Luego, indica a quién(es) se refiere el pronombre que está antes del verbo y cuál es el sujeto del verbo.

	¿QUIÉN LO DICE?	¿A QUIÉN(ES) SE REFIERE EL PRONOMBRE?	SUJETO DEL VERBO
1. **Se me rompió** la computadora.	______	me: ______________________	__________
2. ¡**Se me acabó** el tiempo!	______	me: ______________________	__________
3. **Se me olvidaron** las llaves del carro en el café.	______	me: ______________________	__________
4. **Se nos cayó** la conexión.	______	nos: ______________________	__________
5. **Se nos perdieron** temporalmente dos planos.	______	nos: ______________________	__________
6. A ellos no **se les escapa** la solución de ningún problema.	______	les: ______________________	__________

Se for unplanned occurrences

- Use **se** + *indirect object* + *verb* to express unplanned or accidental events. This construction puts the focus on the person(s) (indicated by the indirect object pronoun) who is/are affected by the action. Some verbs often used with this construction include **acabarse** (*to run out of something*), **apagarse** (*to shut off, to go out*), **descargarse** (*to lose charge, to die* [*devices*]), **descomponerse** (*to break down*), **escaparse, olvidarse** (*to forget*), **quedarse** (*to leave behind*), **quemarse** (*to burn*), and **romperse** (*to break, to tear*).

Se les apagaron las luces del carro.	*Their car headlights went out.*
A él **se le acabó** el dinero.	*He ran out of money.*
Se les descompuso el coche en la carretera.	*Their car broke down on the highway.*
¿Cómo **se te rompió** la chaqueta?	*How did your jacket get torn?*
¡Ay, perdón! **Se me olvidó** llamarte.	*Oh, sorry! I forgot to call you.*

- Use an indirect object pronoun (**me, te, le, nos, os, les**) to indicate whom the unplanned event affects. Place the pronoun between **se** and the verb. The verb always takes the third person singular or plural, depending on whether what is lost (forgotten, etc.) is singular or plural.

Se te quedó la computadora en el café.	*You left your computer at the café.*
Se me quedaron los cables en casa.	*I left my cables at home.*
Se nos descargó la tableta.	*Our tablet died.*

¿Comprendes? Completa las oraciones con el pronombre de objeto indirecto apropiado.

1. A Miguel se _____descompuso la computadora.
2. A mí se _____ perdió el teléfono móvil.
3. A Juan y Elisa se _____ olvidó comprar la comida.
4. A ti se _____ acabó la tinta (*ink*) de la impresora.
5. A Elena se _____ apagaron las luces mientras trabajaba.
6. A ustedes se _____ rompieron los platos.
7. A Luis y a mí se _____ descargó la batería del auto.
8. A los niños se _____ escaparon los perros en el parque.

PRÁCTICA

15-17 ¿Qué les pasó? Selecciona un fin lógico para cada una de las ideas.

1. _____ Hablaron con el plomero porque…
2. _____ Tuve que pedirle dinero a mi amiga porque…
3. _____ No pude llamarte por el celular porque…
4. _____ Tuvieron que llamar al electricista porque…
5. _____ Hablamos con el técnico porque…
6. _____ Llegué tarde a clase porque…
7. _____ Tomamos un taxi porque…
8. _____ El auto no enciende (*start*) porque…
9. _____ Los bomberos vinieron a la casa de mi vecino (*neighbor*) porque…

a. se nos descompuso el auto.
b. se le estaba quemando la cocina.
c. se le acabó la gasolina.
d. se me perdió la llave del coche.
e. se les inundó el baño.
f. se les cortó la luz en la casa.
g. se me quedó la tarjeta de débito en casa.
h. se me olvidó tu nuevo número de teléfono.
i. se nos rompió la computadora.

15-18 Problemas. Trabajas en un laboratorio de investigación donde hubo muchos problemas esta semana. Explícale a tu supervisor (tu compañero/a) qué pasó usando las opciones de la lista u otras.

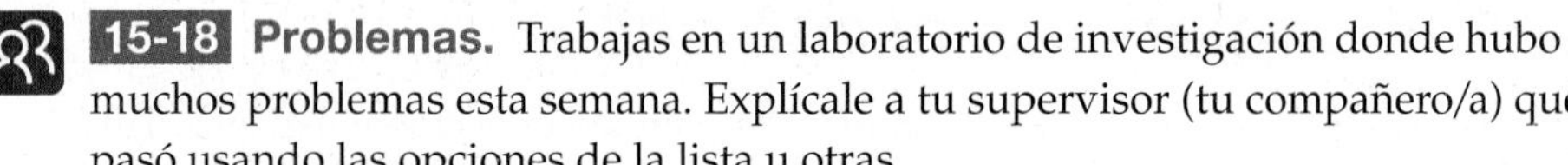

acabarse la gasolina	perderse las llaves
caerse las probetas (*test tubes*)	quedarse documentos confidenciales en un café
descomponerse la computadora	quemarse el documento
enfermarse un hijo	romperse el microscopio
olvidarse la contraseña (*password*)/fórmula	

MODELO E1: El investigador principal no pudo completar el experimento.
E1: *Se le olvidó la fórmula.*
E2: *¿Por qué se le olvidó la fórmula?*
E1: *Se le olvidó escribirla. / No tomó notas.*

1. Los científicos no pudieron hacer el experimento con las bacterias en el microscopio.
2. El director nunca falta (*misses*) al trabajo, pero ayer no fue a trabajar.
3. Los ayudantes llegaron tarde de un viaje a un laboratorio de otra ciudad.
4. La doctora Milán no pudo entrar en el laboratorio durante el fin de semana.
5. El subdirector no pudo acceder a su correo electrónico.
6. El presidente de la compañía estaba histérico cuando llegó a la oficina y se dio cuenta de lo que le había ocurrido.
7. Los estudiantes pusieron el documento con las instrucciones del experimento al lado de un mechero (*gas burner*) encendido.
8. Dos estudiantes tuvieron un pequeño accidente en el laboratorio y no pudieron hacer los experimentos.

15-19 ¡Qué mala suerte! **PREPARACIÓN.** Túrnense para narrar lo que le(s) pasó a esta(s) persona(s). Usen las expresiones de la lista y su imaginación para responder a las siguientes preguntas.

acabarse la gasolina
descomponerse el auto
olvidarse las llaves / el número del apartamento de...
quedarse las llaves dentro de...
quemarse la casa / el apartamento

- ¿Dónde estaba(n) la(s) persona(s)?
- ¿Qué le(s) ocurrió probablemente?
- ¿Qué hizo/hicieron?
- ¿Cómo se resolvió la situación?

1.

2.

3.

4.

5.

INTERCAMBIOS. Hablen sobre alguna experiencia similar a las de **Preparación.** Respondan a las siguientes preguntas y háganse otras adicionales.

1. ¿Qué te ocurrió? ¿Cuándo y dónde?
2. ¿Qué hiciste?
3. ¿Cómo se resolvió la situación?

15-20 ¡Lo que menos esperaba! **PREPARACIÓN.** Usen los verbos de la lista para contarse un imprevisto (*unexpected event*) que le ocurrió a cada uno/a de ustedes en el pasado. Háganse preguntas para obtener la mayor cantidad de información posible. Tomen notas para recordar.

acabarse	morirse
caerse	olvidarse
descargarse	quedarse
descomponerse	romperse
escaparse	

MODELO E1: *El verano pasado, se me descompuso el auto en la carretera cuando iba de vacaciones.*

E2: *¿En qué carretera se te descompuso el auto? ¿Adónde ibas? ¿Y qué hiciste? ¿Ibas solo/a?*

E1: *Iba a la playa con mis amigos por la carretera 95. Llamé al servicio de ayuda en la carretera.*

E2: *¿Y te remolcaron* (towed) *el auto a un taller mecánico?*

E1: *Sí, y afortunadamente me repararon el coche en tres horas.*

INTERCAMBIOS. Cuéntale a un/a compañero/a diferente el imprevisto de tu compañero/a de **Preparación.**

15-21 ¡Qué infortunio (*misfortune*)! Túrnense para hacer algunas especulaciones lógicas sobre qué les ocurrirá a estas personas. Usen los verbos de la lista para enfatizar el evento.

acabarse	morirse
congelarse (*to freeze*)	olvidarse
descargarse	romperse
descomponerse	terminarse
infectarse	

MODELO Tomás no carga su teléfono celular desde hace cuatro días.
A Tomás se le morirá el teléfono. / Se le descargará la batería. / Tendrá que cargarlo pronto para usarlo.

1. Juan tiene un auto muy viejo. Lo compró en 1998.
2. Mis padres compraron una nueva batería para su auto hace cuatro años.
3. Mi abuelo de 92 años tiene una memoria frágil. No recuerda nada.
4. Mis compañeros toman un examen de 50 minutos en línea. Hace 45 minutos que comenzó el examen.
5. A ti te encanta gastar dinero en restaurantes y en ropa. Pero nunca sabes lo que gastas.
6. Las computadoras del laboratorio tienen un virus. Los estudiantes tienen problemas para trabajar en ellas.
7. Sebastián y Pamela pusieron una botella de vino en el congelador hace una hora y se olvidaron.

Situación

PREPARACIÓN. Lean esta situación. Luego, compartan ejemplos de vocabulario, gramática y otra información que necesitan para desarrollar la conversación.

Role A. You have had a bad day and you call your friend to vent. Say that:

a. you forgot to set your alarm clock, so you got up late and missed your first class;
b. your car ran out of gas on the highway;
c. you left your homework for your Spanish class at home; and
d. in the cafeteria you accidentally dropped your soup and salad on your friend's backpack.

Role B. Your friend calls to complain about his/her day. Commiserate with him/her and describe what happened to you last night:

a. there was a big storm in your city and the lights went out so you could not watch your favorite TV show;
b. you decided to drive to your parents' house, but when you were leaving your apartment, both of your cats accidentally escaped; and
c. when you were walking in the dark (**oscuridad**), your wallet fell out of your pocket and you could not find it.

	ROLE A	ROLE B
Vocabulario	Time Problems at school Food	Weather Pets Personal belongings
Funciones y formas	Expressing the unexpected **Se** for unplanned occurrences Narrating The preterit and the imperfect	Expressing the unexpected **Se** for unplanned occurrences Narrating The preterit and the imperfect

INTERCAMBIOS. Practiquen la conversación, incorporando el vocabulario y las funciones de **Preparación.** Luego, represéntenla ante la clase.

2 Expressing wishes and recommendations in the past

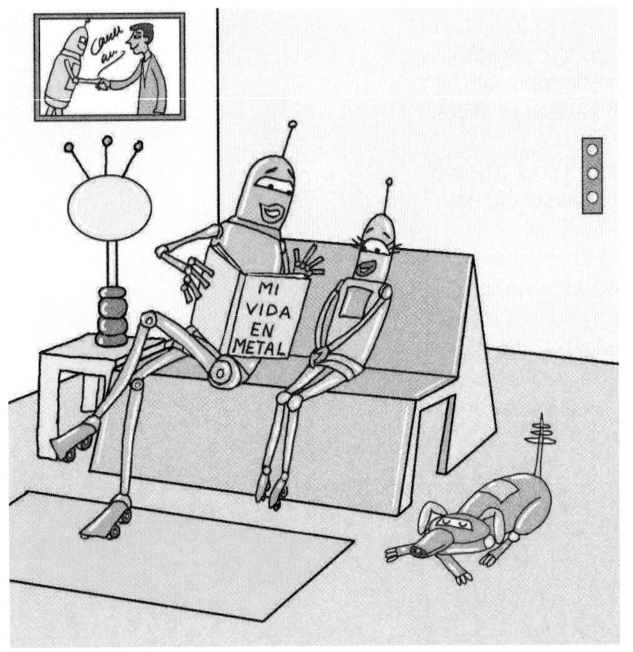

PADRE: ¿Qué quieres que **hagamos** ahora?

NIÑA: Papá, quiero que me **cuentes** un cuento.

PADRE: Muy bien, hija. Cuando mi abuelo era niño, los seres humanos querían que los robots **hicieran** todo su trabajo. Mis abuelos limpiaban la casa, preparaban la comida, hacían las tareas de los niños…

NIÑA: ¡Qué terrible, papá! Pero luego, ¿qué pasó?

PADRE: Los políticos recomendaron que los científicos **produjeran** robots más complejos. Querían que los robots **tuvieran** computadoras muy potentes (*powerful*). Los científicos temían que los robots **fueran** más inteligentes que ellos, pero los políticos insistieron en que los científicos los **construyeran** con más capacidad intelectual. Entonces…

e **Piénsalo.** Primero, indica si las siguientes oraciones se refieren a un evento en el presente/futuro o en el pasado, según la conversación entre los robots. Luego, escribe el verbo que te dio esa información.

	PRESENTE/ FUTURO	PASADO	VERBO
1. ¿Qué quieres que **hagamos** ahora?	_____	_____	__________
2. Quiero que me **cuentes** un cuento.	_____	_____	__________
3. Los seres humanos querían que los robots **hicieran** todo su trabajo.	_____	_____	__________
4. Los políticos recomendaron que los científicos **produjeran** robots más complejos.	_____	_____	__________
5. Querían que los robots **tuvieran** computadoras muy potentes.	_____	_____	__________
6. Los científicos temían que los robots **fueran** más inteligentes que ellos.	_____	_____	__________
7. Los políticos insistieron en que los **construyeran** con más capacidad intelectual.	_____	_____	__________

The imperfect subjunctive

- In previous chapters, you studied the forms and uses of the present subjunctive. Now you will study the past subjunctive, also called the imperfect subjunctive. All regular and irregular past subjunctive verb forms are based on the **ustedes/ellos/ellas** form of the preterit. Drop the **-on** preterit ending and substitute the past subjunctive endings. Note the written accent on the **nosotros/as** forms.

	HABLAR	COMER	VIVIR	ESTAR
	(hablaron)	(comieron)	(vivieron)	(estuvieron)
yo	habla**ra**	comie**ra**	vivie**ra**	estuvie**ra**
tú	habla**ras**	comie**ras**	vivie**ras**	estuvie**ras**
Ud., él, ella	habla**ra**	comie**ra**	vivie**ra**	estuvie**ra**
nosotros/as	hablá**ramos**	comié**ramos**	vivié**ramos**	estuvié**ramos**
vosotros/as	habla**rais**	comie**rais**	vivie**rais**	estuvie**rais**
Uds., ellos/as	habla**ran**	comie**ran**	vivie**ran**	estuvie**ran**

- The present subjunctive is oriented to the present or future, whereas the past subjunctive generally focuses on the past. In general, the same rules that determine the use of the present subjunctive also apply to the past subjunctive.

  HOY O MAÑANA → PRESENT SUBJUNCTIVE

  Sandra quiere comprar una computadora portátil que no **sea** muy cara.
  Sandra wants to buy a laptop that is not very expensive.

  Hablará con sus amigos para que le **den** unas recomendaciones.
  She will talk to her friends so that they can give her some recommendations.

  AYER → PAST SUBJUNCTIVE

  Sandra quería comprar una computadora portátil que no **fuera** muy cara.
  Sandra wanted to buy a laptop that was not very expensive.

  Habló con sus amigos para que le **dieran** unas recomendaciones.
  She talked to her friends so that they could give her some recommendations.

- Always use the past subjunctive after **como si** (*as if, as though*).

  Gastan dinero en aparatos electrónicos **como si fueran** millonarios.
  They spend money on electronic gadgets as though they were millionaires.

  Hablaba con la científica **como si entendiera** el problema.
  He talked with the scientist as if he understood the problem.

e **¿Comprendes?** Completa las oraciones con la forma apropiada del subjuntivo (presente o pasado) de los verbos entre paréntesis.

1. Juan me recomendó que _______ (ver) la nueva película de ciencia ficción.
2. Mi profesora quiere que nosotros _______ (usar) la tecnología en nuestras presentaciones.
3. El gobierno les pidió a los científicos que _______ (hacer) investigación sobre energías alternativas.
4. Los viajeros prefieren que los trenes _______ (ser) rápidos y puntuales.
5. Es necesario que los edificios climatizados _______ (conservar) mejor la energía.
6. Era inevitable que la contaminación de los mares _______ (afectar) a los peces.

PRÁCTICA

15-22 Cuando era niño/a. **PREPARACIÓN.** Indica lo que tus padres querían o no querían que hicieras cuando eras niño/a. Después, compara tus respuestas con las de tu compañero/a.

1. _____ Querían que yo comiera muchos vegetales y frutas.
2. _____ Querían que estudiara ciencias.
3. _____ No querían que viera programas violentos en la televisión.
4. _____ No querían que usara el teléfono móvil por la noche.
5. _____ Querían que leyera en vez de jugar videojuegos.
6. _____ Querían que me mantuviera activo/a.

INTERCAMBIOS. Indica lo que tú querías que tus padres hicieran cuando eras niño/a. Luego, compara tus respuestas con las de tu compañero/a. Añade otra opción si es necesario.

1. Para divertirme con la tecnología, …
   - **a.** yo quería que mis padres me llevaran a ver una nave espacial (*spaceship*).
   - **b.** deseaba que mis padres me dejaran jugar videojuegos muchas horas.
2. Para estar con mis amigos, …
   - **a.** yo quería que mis padres me prestaran el auto para ir al parque los fines de semana.
   - **b.** les pedía a mis padres que me permitieran pasar la noche en casa de mis amigos.
3. Para pasarlo bien los fines de semana, …
   - **a.** yo quería que mis padres me dieran más dinero.
   - **b.** insistía en que mis padres me dieran permiso de hacer fiestas en casa.
4. Para mi cumpleaños, …
   - **a.** siempre quería que mis padres me regalaran juguetes electrónicos.
   - **b.** prefería que mis padres me compraran ropa.

> **En otras palabras**
>
> Cell phones are **teléfonos móviles** or **teléfonos celulares.** The name of these devices is usually shortened to **móvil, celular,** or **cel.**

15-23 En el laboratorio. Miguel es un estudiante inteligente, pero muy distraído. Hoy hizo unos experimentos con su profesor de química en el laboratorio. ¿Qué le dijo el profesor en estas situaciones? Túrnense para dar respuestas lógicas, usando los verbos de la lista u otros.

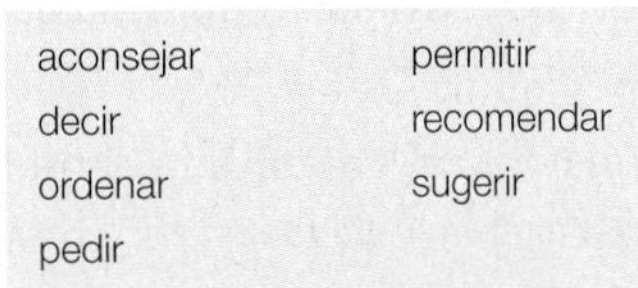

aconsejar	permitir
decir	recomendar
ordenar	sugerir
pedir	

MODELO Miguel no se puso los guantes para hacer el experimento.
El profesor le dijo que se pusiera los guantes.

1. Llegó tarde al laboratorio.
2. Escuchaba música mientras hacía un experimento.
3. Dejó una botella de alcohol cerca de una estufa.
4. No esterilizó unos instrumentos.
5. Recibió una llamada en su celular y la contestó.
6. La mesa donde Miguel trabajaba estaba muy desordenada.
7. No comparó sus resultados con los del ayudante del profesor.
8. Salió del laboratorio durante un experimento para conversar con una amiga.

15-24 Una persona arrogante. **PREPARACIÓN.** Imagínense que ustedes conocen a una persona arrogante que cree que es mejor que todos. Digan cómo se comporta esta persona en los siguientes aspectos de su vida. Pueden usar los verbos de la lista u otros.

cambiar	gastar	usar
caminar	manejar	vestirse
discutir	ser	vivir

MODELO cuando va a pie de un lugar a otro
Camina como si fuera la única persona en la calle.

1. cuando quiere comprar algo
2. cuando sale con un grupo de amigos
3. cuando habla con otras personas
4. cuando se sube a (*gets into*) su auto

INTERCAMBIOS. Ahora háganse las siguientes preguntas e informen a la clase.

1. ¿Conoces a alguna persona que sea arrogante?
2. ¿Qué hábito o comportamiento de esa persona te molesta? ¿Por qué?
3. ¿Te gustaría que esa persona cambiara? Si es así, ¿cómo te gustaría que cambiara?

15-25 Usos de la tecnología.

PREPARACIÓN. Completa las afirmaciones sobre los usos de la tecnología en el trabajo con la forma apropiada del imperfecto del subjuntivo del verbo entre paréntesis.

1. La directora quería que Carlota y Samuel ____________ (hacer) una presentación multimedia sobre los productos nuevos de la compañía.
2. Insistió en que Carlota ____________ (comenzar) con entrevistas virtuales con los clientes más importantes.
3. Quería que Samuel ____________ (incluir) unas recomendaciones para el equipo de redes sociales.
4. Los empleados preferían que las presentaciones ____________ (ser) virtuales para ahorrar tiempo.
5. La directora les dijo a los empleados de marketing que ____________ (comunicarse) con los empleados de ventas.
6. En realidad, era necesario que ____________ (haber) mejor uso de la tecnología para facilitar la comunicación en la compañía.

INTERCAMBIOS. Túrnense para dar recomendaciones sobre cómo la tecnología podría facilitar la comunicación entre sus amigos. Usen los verbos de la lista u otros.

aconsejar	es bueno/importante/mejor	querer
desear	es aconsejable/recomendable	recomendar
esperar	preferir	sugerir

MODELO los celulares
E1: *Es mejor que no miremos nuestros celulares cuando estamos con nuestros amigos en un restaurante.*
E2: *De acuerdo. Mis padres siempre quieren que conversemos cuando estamos juntos.*

1. las computadoras portátiles
2. las tabletas
3. los videojuegos
4. las aplicaciones de GPS
5. los mensajes de texto
6. las redes sociales

15-26 Una pasantía (*internship*) de verano.

PREPARACIÓN. Tania hace una pasantía en el Centro de Conservación de Manatíes de Puerto Rico. Completa el mensaje que les escribió a sus padres con la forma correcta del indicativo o del subjuntivo de los verbos entre paréntesis.

Queridos padres:

¡Qué gusto recibir su mensaje y leer sobre sus actividades! Fue muy buena idea que ustedes (1) __________ (asistir) a las competencias de tenis en Wimbledon el mes pasado. Era importante que ustedes (2) __________ (hacer) turismo también. Es verdad que ustedes (3) __________ (ser) grandes aficionados al tenis, pero también es importante que (4) __________ (conocer) lugares interesantes y que (5) __________ (divertirse) haciendo diversas actividades.

Yo también tengo noticias interesantes. Ayer el director del centro nos pidió que lo (6) __________ (acompañar) a la playa. Era necesario que todo el equipo (7) __________ (colaborar) para rescatar (*rescue*) a unos manatíes que se habían varado (*stranded*) en la arena. Al principio yo dudaba que (8) __________ (ser) posible rescatarlos, porque hacía varias horas que estaban fuera del mar. Los científicos nos dijeron que (9) __________ (trabajar) en equipos de dos, para que todos juntos (10) __________ (devolver) los manatíes al mar. Gracias a Dios, logramos rescatarlos a todos.

Reciban un fuerte abrazo de su hija,
Tania

INTERCAMBIOS. Ahora asuman el papel de los padres de Tania. Túrnense para darle consejos respecto a los siguientes temas.

MODELO trabajar mucho

E1: *Tania, te recomendamos que trabajes mucho en tu pasantía.*

E2: *Sí, es importante que aprendas mucho.*

1. conocer bien a los otros estudiantes
2. divertirse los fines de semana
3. aprender mucho español
4. dormir lo suficiente
5. protegerse del sol
6. visitar otras partes de la isla

Situación

PREPARACIÓN. Lean esta situación. Luego, compartan ejemplos de vocabulario, gramática y otra información que necesitan para desarrollar la conversación.

Role A. You are unhappy with your new digital device (cell phone, tablet, laptop, etc.). You go back to the electronics store and tell the manager:
a. your friend had recommended that you buy this device;
b. you hoped the device would be of better quality; and
c. you want to return it and expect them to give you back your money.

Role B. You are the manager of the computer department at an electronics store. A customer is unhappy with a recent purchase of a digital device and tells you why. Explain:
a. the store does not give refunds (**devolver el dinero**); but
b. you would be glad to exchange the device for a different one; and
c. you hope that the customer will like the new device.

	ROLE A	ROLE B
Vocabulario	Digital technology	Digital technology
Funciones y formas	Expressing wishes Present and past subjunctive	Expressing wishes Present and past subjunctive

INTERCAMBIOS. Practiquen la conversación, incorporando el vocabulario y las funciones de **Preparación.** Luego, represéntenla ante la clase.

3 Hypothesizing about the present and the future

MATEO: Oye, Lucía. ¿Has visto la calidad de los nuevos drones? ¡Es increíble! Son totalmente silenciosos y tan pequeños como una abeja (*bee*). **Si** la tecnología **sigue** avanzando así, pronto **serán** invisibles y **entrarán** en las casas para filmar a la gente.

LUCÍA: **Si** lo **hicieran, pondrían** en peligro (*danger*) las libertades individuales. Pero **si** la ciencia **avanza** tan rápidamente, ¿por qué no **podemos** trabajar por la paz? Yo no quiero que se perfeccione la tecnología para vigilar a la gente y controlarla, sino para protegerla.

MATEO: Tienes razón, Lucía. **Si** los jóvenes no **hacemos** nada para dar un buen uso a la tecnología, **tendremos** problemas en el futuro.

Piénsalo. Indica si las siguientes afirmaciones hechas por Mateo y Lucía indican una condición relacionada con el presente (**P**), con el futuro (**F**) o si indican una condición que es improbable (**I**) que se cumpla (*come to pass*).

1. _____ **Si** la tecnología **sigue** avanzando así, pronto **serán** invisibles y **entrarán** en las casas para filmar a la gente.
2. _____ **Si** lo **hicieran, pondrían** en peligro las libertades individuales.
3. _____ Pero **si** la ciencia **avanza** tan rápidamente, ¿por qué no **podemos** trabajar por la paz?
4. _____ **Si** los jóvenes no **hacemos** nada para dar un buen uso a la tecnología, **tendremos** problemas en el futuro.

If-clauses

- To express what happens or will happen *if* certain conditions are met, use the present indicative in the *if*-clause and the present or future indicative in the main clause.

  Si **continuamos** cortando árboles, los bosques **van a** desaparecer.
  If we continue cutting down trees, the forests will disappear.

  Si **creamos** tecnología para cuidar los recursos naturales, las generaciones futuras **tendrán** una vida mejor.
  If we create technology to protect natural resources, future generations will have a better life.

  Puedes obtener información sobre las últimas novedades tecnológicas si la **buscas** en internet.
  You can get information on the latest technology if you look for it on the internet.

- To express a condition that is unlikely or contrary to fact, use the imperfect subjunctive in the *if*-clause. Use the conditional in the main clause.

  Si **invirtieran** más dinero en el aeropuerto, el tráfico aéreo **podría** mejorar.
  If they invested more money in the airport, air traffic could improve.

  Si **usáramos** la energía solar en las casas, **bajaría** el consumo del petróleo.
  If we used solar energy in our homes, oil consumption would decrease.

e **¿Comprendes?** Completa las oraciones con el presente de indicativo o el imperfecto de subjuntivo del verbo entre paréntesis, según su grado de probabilidad.

1. Si los habitantes _________ (mantener) limpias las ciudades, será más agradable pasear por ellas.
2. Si los perros _________ (hablar), dirían que los humanos estamos locos.
3. Si el gobierno _________ (proteger) más el medio ambiente, habría menos contaminación.
4. Si los ingenieros _________ (hacer) un cohete espacial más barato, irían turistas al espacio.
5. Si nosotros _________ (tener) más imaginación y más dinero, inventaríamos una máquina para viajar en el tiempo.
6. Si los estudiantes _________ (practicar) mucho el español, aprenderán más rápidamente.

Cultura

Reforestar costas y rehabilitar dunas Puerto Rico tiene un rico patrimonio natural, con bosques, aguas termales y playas espectaculares. En la isla hay una gran diversidad de plantas y animales: unas 3.200 especies de plantas y unas 299 especies de animales vertebrados. Pero Puerto Rico también es una de las islas con mayor densidad de población del mundo. Esto ha causado problemas medioambientales, como la deforestación y la contaminación del aire, que se agravaron (*got worse*) debido a la devastación causada por los huracanes Irma y María en 2017. Varias organizaciones internacionales están cooperando para recuperar la naturaleza del impacto ecológico sufrido a causa de los huracanes. Más de 200 voluntarios han restaurado dunas y han plantado árboles nativos en ocho playas diferentes para proteger la vida silvestre de la fuerza del viento y del océano y además para aumentar la seguridad de los habitantes de la isla.

Comparaciones ¿Crees que la vulnerabilidad del patrimonio natural de Puerto Rico frente a los desastres naturales es igual a la que existe en tu comunidad? ¿Qué proyectos o medidas para proteger la naturaleza hay en tu comunidad?

PRÁCTICA

15-27 El mundo que todos queremos. Selecciona un fin lógico para completar cada idea. En algunos casos, puede haber más de una respuesta lógica. Luego, compara tus respuestas con las de tu compañero/a. Si tienen respuestas diferentes, justifíquenlas.

1. _____ Si las escuelas tuvieran más dinero, …
2. _____ Si la educación universitaria costara menos, …
3. _____ Si cuidáramos más nuestro planeta, …
4. _____ Tendríamos un mundo mejor…
5. _____ Si hubiera trenes de alta velocidad, …
6. _____ Gastaríamos menos gasolina…

a. no contaminaríamos tanto el medio ambiente.
b. todos los alumnos tendrían acceso a los laboratorios para hacer investigación.
c. si todos nos respetáramos y dialogáramos en vez de pelear (*fight*).
d. habría menos tráfico en las carreteras.
e. los jóvenes tendrían menos deudas (*debts*).
f. si usáramos el transporte público.

15-28 ¿Qué pasa si…? Túrnense para decir cuáles serán los resultados si se hacen ciertas cosas.

MODELO leer las noticias
Si leemos o miramos las noticias regularmente, sabremos qué está pasando en el mundo.

1. usar solamente tecnología para aprender otra lengua
2. inventar aparatos electrónicos desechables (*disposable*)
3. proteger los recursos naturales
4. legalizar las drogas
5. comunicarse solamente por mensajes de texto
6. construir más estaciones espaciales

15-29 ¿Cómo sería el mundo? Expliquen cómo sería el mundo si las siguientes circunstancias fueran reales. Después, compartan sus ideas con otros/as estudiantes.

1. si no hubiera teléfonos celulares
2. si los seres humanos viviéramos más de 150 años
3. si la clonación fuera legal
4. si no existieran fronteras entre los países
5. si pudiéramos viajar en autos supersónicos a todas partes
6. si toda la educación se hiciera por internet

15-30 ¿Qué haríamos? **PREPARACIÓN.** Usa tu imaginación para completar las siguientes ideas relacionadas con tu vida.

1. Si tuviera dinero suficiente para comprar un aparato tecnológicamente avanzado, ...
2. Iría a vivir a... si...
3. Si pudiera cambiar mi vida ahora, ...
4. Ayudaría más a las personas necesitadas si...
5. Si tuviera tres meses de vacaciones y dinero ilimitado, ...
6. Si tuviera que elegir entre tener una vida sencilla y feliz o ser rico/a e importante pero con pocos amigos...

INTERCAMBIOS. Túrnense para compartir sus respuestas. Háganse preguntas para obtener más detalles.

15-31 Cambios. **PREPARACIÓN.** Elige uno de los temas e identifica un problema serio. Explica por escrito por qué lo consideras un problema serio.

1. la privacidad en la era digital
2. la adicción a los dispositivos móviles
3. el transporte público
4. el costo de las necesidades básicas, como la comida y la gasolina

INTERCAMBIOS. Ahora compartan sus ideas. Explíquenles a sus compañeros/as por qué lo consideran un problema serio. Luego, entre todos, hablen sobre qué harían para reducir o solucionar cada problema.

MODELO el medio ambiente

PROBLEMA SERIO: *el uso excesivo de productos de plástico*

RAZÓN: *Usamos muchos productos de plástico y no reciclamos lo suficiente. El plástico no reciclado produce basura. Además, si se quema el plástico, se contamina el medio ambiente.*

PLAN HIPOTÉTICO: *Prohibiríamos las bolsas de plástico en las tiendas. Las personas usarían sus propias bolsas. Sería bueno también eliminar los envases* (packaging) *de plástico de los productos. Por ejemplo, en los supermercados la gente compraría fruta y vegetales sueltos* (loose). *También subiríamos el costo de las botellas de plástico para animar a todos a usar sus propias botellas.*

En directo

To ask that people request the floor before speaking:

Por favor, no interrumpas/interrumpan sin pedir la palabra. *Please, don't interrupt without requesting the floor.*

Pide/Pidan la palabra. *Request the floor.*

To request the floor:

Yo quisiera decir/añadir/explicar algo. *I would like to say/add/explain something.*

¿Podría añadir/agregar algo? *Could I add something?*

To give someone the floor:

X tiene la palabra. *X has the floor.*

Dinos lo que piensas sobre... *Tell us what you think about . . .*

Listen to a conversation with these expressions.

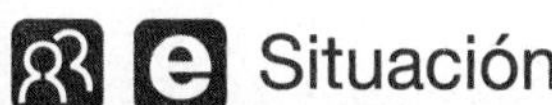

Situación

PREPARACIÓN. Lean esta situación. Luego, compartan ejemplos de vocabulario, gramática y otra información que necesitan para desarrollar la conversación.

Role A. You are a billionaire who believes that education should be radically different. You would give your local college 20 million dollars if they did the following:
a. there would be no requirements, and students could choose all of their own courses;
b. there would be no exams, only projects and papers; and
c. students would tell the faculty what courses should be taught.
Respond to the reaction of the college president.

Role B. You are a college president. A billionaire (your classmate) would donate 20 million dollars to the college if you agreed to make radical changes to the curriculum. Listen to the potential donor's proposal and respond with your hypotheses of what would happen if:
a. there were no requirements, and instead students could choose their own courses;
b. there were no exams, only projects and papers; and
c. students told the faculty what courses should be taught.

	ROLE A	ROLE B
Vocabulario	Numbers Academic policies	Numbers Academic policies
Funciones y formas	Talking about hypothetical situations The conditional The past subjunctive	Talking about hypothetical situations The conditional The past subjunctive

INTERCAMBIOS. Practiquen la conversación, incorporando el vocabulario y las funciones de **Preparación.** Luego, represéntenla ante la clase.

MOSAICOS

ESCUCHA

Estrategia

Identify the speaker's intention through the main idea and specific information
To understand what a speaker says, it is necessary to use a number of strategies. To identify the main idea, you should anticipate key concepts that may be associated with the topic and focus on phrases that signal the presentation of the main idea. Keep track of the speaker's message by organizing the information mentally as you listen. Pay attention to the speaker's verbal and nonverbal cues, such as word choice, tone, and gestures.

15-32 Preparación. Escucharán la anécdota de un paciente que fue operado de urgencia. Hablen de dos problemas de salud que requieren atención médica de urgencia. Indiquen qué provoca cada problema.

Comprueba

I was able to . . .

- understand the main events of the narrator's story.
- understand most of the details in the story.
- understand the narrator's take-away message.

15-33 Escucha. Read the statements below and then listen to the narration. For each item, select the correct options that reflect the main idea and the supporting detail. Finally, indicate the speaker's intention for sharing this information.

	Idea principal	Detalle
1. Roberto...	**a.** tuvo un accidente. **b.** sufrió un ataque al corazón. **c.** tuvo una operación en el cerebro.	La emergencia ocurrió... **a.** en la casa del paciente. **b.** en el trabajo del paciente. **c.** en la ambulancia.
2. El marcapasos (*pacemaker*)...	**a.** se usa para ayudar a los deportistas. **b.** ayudó al paciente con los latidos del corazón (*heartbeat*). **c.** es un tipo de tecnología obsoleta.	**a.** regula los latidos del corazón. **b.** facilita la operación de los pacientes. **c.** es una microcomputadora que regula la presión arterial.
3. Esta experiencia...	**a.** no afectó a Roberto para nada. **b.** le permitió a la doctora experimentar con los marcapasos. **c.** impactó fuertemente a Roberto.	**a.** ayudó a Roberto a controlar el estrés y a valorar más la vida. **b.** obligó a Roberto a dejar de trabajar. **c.** le enseñó a Roberto que debe evitar salir con amigos para no estresarse.
4. What is the speaker's intention in sharing this information? **a.** dar recomendaciones de qué hacer con un paciente que sufre un ataque al corazón **b.** informar al público sobre la última tecnología en cardiología **c.** alertar al público sobre los síntomas y los efectos devastadores del estrés		

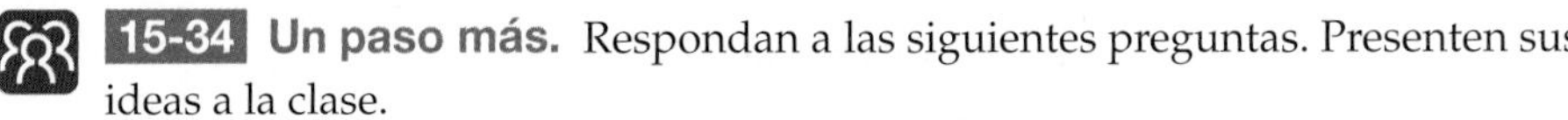

15-34 Un paso más. Respondan a las siguientes preguntas. Presenten sus ideas a la clase.

1. ¿Es común el estrés entre los estudiantes?
2. ¿Qué les causa estrés a ustedes? ¿Y a sus padres?
3. ¿De qué manera pueden controlar el estrés ustedes?
4. Una situación de emergencia ayudó a Roberto a valorar más la vida sin estrés. Hagan una lista de tres cosas (eventos, situaciones, experiencias) que pueden ayudar a una persona a aprender a valorar la vida.

HABLA

Estrategia

Use drama and humor in telling a personal anecdote You learned in **Capítulo 13** to keep your listeners interested in your story by inserting remarks to draw their attention to moments that are particularly funny, frightening, or surprising. You can use these remarks, called *evaluations*, to make your story humorous or to heighten the drama. You can also increase the drama by strategically using descriptive details to slow down the pace and thus create suspense.

15-35 **Preparación.** Lee las anécdotas y luego sigue las instrucciones para analizar las estrategias de los narradores.

"Hace dos años, durante mis vacaciones de fin de año, fui a visitar a mi abuela en San Francisco. Los dos estábamos felices de pasar unos días juntos. El sábado por la noche, abuelita me invitó a cenar en un restaurante español muy elegante, de primera clase. "Tenemos que celebrar esta hermosa ocasión", me dijo abuelita. Después de comer muy bien y beber el mejor vino que tenían, el mesero le trajo la cuenta. La cantidad era enorme para mí, un pobre estudiante. Sin embargo, no había problema, porque abuelita siempre había tenido mucho éxito en sus negocios. Abrió su bolso y se dio cuenta de (*realized*) que se le había olvidado la billetera en casa. Sin pensarlo dos veces, yo me ofrecí a pagar la cuenta con una aplicación de mi teléfono. Después, le pedí a abuelita que nos tomáramos una *selfie*. La subí inmediatamente a mi cuenta favorita en las redes sociales. En cuestión de horas, la foto se hizo viral porque al fondo aparecieron Enrique Iglesias y Pitbull cenando y conversando animadamente. Sin saberlo, abuelita y yo habíamos cenado en un restaurante con dos hispanos famosos. ¡Qué sorprendente es la vida!"

"Una tarde de verano decidí ir de incógnito a Manhattan. Iba a pasar unas horas comprando, y luego quería ver una película. Después de viajar unos 20 minutos por la carretera, se me descompuso el carro en el puente George Washington. ¡Qué feo! Había mucho tráfico y hacía un calor insoportable. A unos metros de donde se me descompuso el auto, había una señal que decía **prohibido detenerse en el puente.** Muy nerviosa, me bajé del carro, levanté el capó y revisé lo que había allí dentro. Como aparentemente no había ningún problema mecánico, volví al carro. Cuando vi que la fila de autos detrás de mí seguía aumentando y algunos choferes empezaban a tocar la bocina, se me fue el alma a los pies. De repente, se me ocurrió leer el gasómetro y me di cuenta de que el marcador de gasolina no funcionaba y que ¡se me había olvidado llenar el tanque! En ese momento, llegaron dos policías que me pidieron la licencia de conducir. Antes de dársela, traté de explicarles que era Selena Gómez. No me quisieron creer, pero por si acaso (*in case*) era verdad, me pidieron sacarse una *selfie* conmigo. Y al final, ¡me pusieron una multa altísima! Claro, como todos sabemos, en las ciudades grandes la gente nunca hace excepciones a las reglas (*bends the rules*). ¡Todos son santos!"

Lengua

Spanish has several expressions with **se** that speakers use often. Read the following and think of possible situations in which they may be used.

- **Se me puso la piel de gallina.** *I got goosebumps.*
- **Se me fue el alma a los pies.** *My heart sank.*
- **Se me fue la lengua.** *I gave myself away.*
- **Se me partió el alma.** *It broke my heart.*

1. En la primera anécdota:
   a. Identifica los adjetivos que describen el restaurante.
   b. ¿Qué palabras y frases indican que la abuela del narrador no tiene problemas económicos? Indícalas.
   c. Indica la perspectiva del narrador sobre la experiencia de comer en un restaurante elegante.
2. En la segunda anécdota:
   a. Identifica las frases que indican que la narradora es famosa.
   b. ¿Qué palabras y frases indican las emociones de la narradora? Identifícalas.
   c. Identifica las frases que indican la perspectiva de los policías.

Comprueba

I was able to . . .

- organize the events of my story in a logical sequence.
- insert descriptive elements to flesh out the events.
- use exclamations or direct quotes to make my story humorous or dramatic.

15-36 Habla. Prepara una anécdota (real o ficticia) de una experiencia personal y cuéntasela a tu grupo. Usa las expresiones de **En directo** para que tu anécdota tenga humor y un tono dramático. Cada miembro del grupo debe hacerte preguntas y consultar el segundo recuadro de **En directo** para expresar sus reacciones efectivamente.

En directo

To make your story dramatic:

¿Y qué crees/creen que pasó después? *And what do you think happened then?*

¡No vas/van a creerlo! *You're not going to believe it!*

Espera/Esperen, que todavía no has/han escuchado la mejor parte. *Wait, you still haven't heard the best part.*

To incorporate humor:

Hacía más frío/calor que... *It was colder/warmer than . . .*

Me/Nos miró con cara de... *He/She looked at me/us with an expression of . . .*

Me/Nos respondió como si... *He/She answered me/us as if . . .*

Listen to a conversation with these expressions.

En directo

To express sympathy:

¡Qué lástima! / ¡Cuánto lo siento! *I am (so) sorry.*

¡Qué triste/horrible! *How sad/horrible!*

To express happiness:

¡Qué bueno/bien! *Great!*

¡Cuánto me alegro! *I am really happy!*

To express relief after a tense situation:

¡Qué alivio! *What a relief!*

¡Por fin! *Finally!*

¡Gracias a Dios! *Thank goodness!*

Listen to a conversation with these expressions.

15-37 Un paso más. Seleccionen la anécdota más dramática o graciosa (*humorous*) de su grupo. Conviertan la anécdota en una pequeña obra de teatro y represéntenla frente a la clase.

LEE

Estrategia

Identify the narrator's perspective A narrative can be told from one of several perspectives: (a) someone who recounts his/her own experience (**narrador en primera persona** [*I*, *we*]); (b) a witness who sees and may be a part of the story (**narrador testigo** [*witness*]); or (c) a narrator who knows everything, even what the characters are thinking (**narrador omnisciente**). Sometimes readers can believe what a narrator recounts, but not always, and an unreliable narrator allows the author to blur the line between reality and fantasy. Therefore, as you read, it is important to ask yourself the following questions: Who is telling the story? Who witnesses it? Do we believe what the narrator is telling us?

Wilfredo Machado (1956–), escritor venezolano, nació en Barquisimeto en una familia numerosa de ocho hermanos. Su padre fue comerciante y viajaba constantemente por los Andes venezolanos. Su madre, que es de Carora, pueblo ligado (*connected*) a importantes tradiciones musicales de Venezuela, tuvo una gran influencia en su formación artística. De niño cantaba con su hermano en radios locales.

Comenzó a leer y a escribir desde muy joven, sin saber que esa pasión por el canto y la literatura lo llevaría (*would lead him*) a convertirse en escritor. Estudió en la Escuela de Letras de la Universidad de Los Andes.

Fue agregado cultural (*cultural attaché*) de la Embajada de Venezuela en Brasil. Escribe cuentos breves (algunos han sido traducidos a otros idiomas), poesía y novelas. Ha recibido algunas distinciones nacionales por sus cuentos breves y fábulas fantásticas, cargados (*packed*) de humor lacerante (*cutting*), parodias intertextuales y situaciones absurdas.

15-38 **Preparación.** Háganse estas preguntas acerca de sus sueños (*dreams*).

1. ¿Están relacionados tus sueños con los eventos de la vida real, o están desconectados de tus experiencias?
2. ¿Sueñas frecuentemente? ¿Recuerdas tus sueños?
3. ¿Has tenido alguna vez un sueño premonitorio, es decir, un sueño que anticipa un evento que más tarde pasa en la vida real? Da un ejemplo.

Comprueba

I was able to . . .

- identify the narrator.
- distinguish the two speakers in the dialogue.
- understand the ending.

e **15-39 Lee.** Lee el cuento "La invención del fuego". Luego, responde a las preguntas.

1. ¿Quién narra los eventos del cuento?
   _____ **a.** el hombre
   _____ **b.** la mujer
   _____ **c.** un narrador omnisciente
2. Pon en orden cronológico los eventos del cuento.
   _____ El hombre se despierta.
   _____ La mujer espera al hombre en el metro.
   _____ La mujer se sienta al lado del hombre en el metro.
   _____ El hombre se duerme.
   _____ El hombre sale de su apartamento.
   _____ La mujer le dice al hombre que su cama está ardiendo.
   _____ El hombre mira los escombros de lo que antes fue su hogar (*home*).
3. Lee otra vez el primer párrafo del cuento. Indica si las siguientes afirmaciones tienen una función narrativa (**N**) o descriptiva (**D**).
   _____ **a.** En el sueño la mujer entró en el vagón.
   _____ **b.** Vino a sentarse justo a su lado.
   _____ **c.** A esa hora la estación del metro estaba vacía.
   _____ **d.** La mujer olía al humo de mil bares.
4. ¿Quién dice las siguientes afirmaciones, el hombre (**H**), la mujer (**M**) o el narrador (**N**)?
   _____ **a.** ¿Qué estación es esta?
   _____ **b.** No sé. Es difícil reconocer las estaciones a esta hora.
   _____ **c.** Sacó un cigarrillo de su bolso y le pidió fuego.
   _____ **d.** ¿Por qué ese gran incendio sobre tu cama?
   _____ **e.** Su corazón, su vida, sus huesos olían a humo.

LA INVENCIÓN DEL FUEGO

En el sueño la mujer entró en el vagón[1] y vino a sentarse justo a su lado. A esa hora la estación del metro estaba vacía. Los trenes viajaban a gran velocidad. No daba ni siquiera tiempo de leer los carteles que desaparecían como manchas brillantes sobre el muro y que quedaban atrás sumidos[2] en la oscuridad de los túneles. Recordó que la mujer olía al humo de mil bares y al deseo de tantas preguntas sin respuesta que se habían quedado flotando en el aire turbio[3] del salón bajo la música de la orquesta. Corazón de sombra. Pensó que era un buen título para un bolero[4].

—¿Qué estación es esta? —preguntó con cierta urgencia, como si de ello dependiera su vida.

—No sé —respondió. Es difícil reconocer las estaciones a esta hora.

—¿Para dónde vas?

—Dos Caminos.

—¡Ah, eres de los indecisos[5]! —dijo con cierta ironía.

Fue en ese preciso momento que sacó un cigarrillo de su bolso y le pidió fuego.

—Yo no fumo —respondió cortésmente.

Entonces, acercándose, le susurró[6] casi al oído:
—¿Por qué ese gran incendio sobre tu cama?
Cuando despertó, el apartamento ardía[7] en llamas. Apenas tuvo tiempo de huir escaleras abajo para salvar la vida. Por instrucciones del Cuerpo de Bomberos todos los inquilinos debieron abandonar el edificio esa misma noche. Su corazón, su vida, sus huesos olían a humo. Se sentó en la acera a observar cómo las llamas iban desapareciendo entre los escombros[8]. No había nada que hacer. Cuando más tarde tomó el metro —casi al amanecer, entre obreros de la construcción y estudiantes somnolientos—, la mujer todavía estaba allí, en el mismo vagón, aguardándolo[9]. El cigarrillo apagado colgando entre los labios.

[1]*subway car* [2]*lost* [3]*murky* [4]*a type of Caribbean popular music* [5]*undecided* [6]*whispered* [7]*was burning* [8]*rubble* [9]*waiting for him*

 **15-40 Un paso más.** Respondan a las preguntas y apunten las ideas que salgan en su discusión. Presenten sus respuestas y justificaciones a la clase.

1. ¿Qué elementos del cuento pasan en el sueño? ¿Cuáles pasan en la vida real? Hagan dos listas y justifiquen sus decisiones.
2. ¿Qué pasa al final del cuento? Cuando el hombre ve a la mujer en el vagón del metro después del incendio, ¿es sueño o realidad? ¿Qué significa el cigarrillo apagado de la mujer?

ESCRIBE

Estrategia

Use imagination and humor in writing a narrative In creative writing, you can use your imagination to invent events and characters that would be impossible in real life. You can use fantasy and humor to exaggerate events and characters' behaviors to entertain your readers. To write an imaginative and humorous story, consider the following tips:

- Create situations or behaviors that differ from people's expectations.
- Use contradictions within a character to create humor. The humor will be apparent when you reveal the contradictions.
- Base your humor on situations and characterizations that will be familiar to your audience.

15-41 Preparación. Lee otra vez "La invención del fuego" en la actividad **15-39.** Luego, imagínate la perspectiva de la mujer sobre los eventos del cuento. Haz lo siguiente:

1. Escribe unas notas sobre el primer encuentro entre el hombre y la mujer: los pensamientos de la mujer cuando el hombre entra en el vagón del metro, lo que está pensando durante su conversación y el momento cuando le dice al hombre que su cama está ardiendo.
2. Usa la imaginación para crear su segundo encuentro, después del incendio. Primero, escribe unas notas sobre lo que está pensando la mujer. Luego, escribe el diálogo entre los dos.
3. Escribe unas notas sobre uno o dos posibles finales del cuento.

 **15-42 Escribe.** Desde la perspectiva de la mujer, escribe una nueva versión del cuento usando el pronombre **yo.** Usa la información que preparaste en la actividad **15-41.**

1. Explica los eventos del cuento desde tu perspectiva.
2. Indica con humor o ironía algunos aspectos de tu interacción con el hombre en los momentos clave (*key*) del cuento: cuando conversas con él por primera vez; cuando le ayudas a escaparse del incendio; y cuando vuelves a verlo a la mañana siguiente.
3. Usa tu imaginación para escribir un desenlace (*resolution*) creativo.

 **15-43 Un paso más.** Lee la narración de tu compañero/a. Hagan comparaciones para ver cómo los/las dos usaron la imaginación en sus respectivos cuentos.

Comprueba

I was able to . . .

- write a story from the perspective of one of the characters.
- mix fantasy and reality to make my story interesting.
- create a humorous situation by using contradictions or exaggerations.

En este capítulo...

Vocabulario

La ciencia y la tecnología	Science and technology
la administración de redes	network administration
el acceso	access
la aplicación	app
los auriculares	headphones
la batería	battery
la biblioteca digital	digital library
la cápsula	capsule
la carrera	professional career
el chip electrónico	electronic chip
la ciencia ficción	science fiction
la clonación	cloning
el conocimiento	knowledge
el descubrimiento	discovery
la diseminación	dispersal, dissemination
el dispositivo (móvil)	(mobile) device
el (documento) adjunto	attachment
el enlace	link
el entorno	surroundings, environment
la inteligencia artificial	artificial intelligence
el intercambio	exchange
la máquina	machine
el mensaje	message
la microcirugía	microsurgery
las novedades	updates (information, news)
la nube	cloud
la programación	programming
el riel	rail
el robot	robot
el satélite	satellite
la seguridad de la información	data security
el tuit	tweet

El medio ambiente	Environment
el agujero	hole
la atmósfera	atmosphere
el banco de peces	shoal (group of fish)
el calentamiento	warming
el cambio climático	climate change
la capa de ozono	ozone layer
la contaminación	pollution
la cuenca	(river) basin
el cultivo	farming, crops
la deforestación	deforestation
la desaparición	disappearance
el deshielo	melting
la energía (alternativa/eólica/solar)	(alternative/wind/solar) energy
la erosión	erosion
la extinción	extinction
la inundación	flood
el nivel del mar	sea level
la pérdida	loss
la plaga	plague
el planeta	planet
los rayos ultravioleta	ultraviolet (UV) rays
los residuos (plásticos)	(plastic) waste
el reto	challenge
el río	river
el vertido	spill

Las descripciones	Descriptions
aeroespacial	aerospace
climatizado/a	air-conditioned
(no) contaminante	(non)polluting
digitalizado/a	digital
extinguido/a	extinct
marino/a	marine
pesquero/a	(related to) fishing
reciclado/a	recycled
residual	(related to) waste
selvático/a	jungle
sostenible	sustainable
volador/a	flying

Verbos	Verbs
acabar(se)	to run out of something
actualizar (c)	to update
apagar(se)	to shut off; to go out
aterrizar (c)	to land (aircraft)
aumentar	to increase
avanzar (c)	to progress, to advance
bajar	to download
chatear	to chat
conectarse	to connect
conservar	to conserve
construir (y)	to build
contribuir (y)	to contribute
criar	to raise (animals)
cubrir	to cover
descargar(se)	to lose charge, to die (devices)
descomponer(se)	to break down
despegar (u)	to take off (aircraft)
enfocarse (qu)	to focus
escapar(se)	to escape, to overlook
guardar	to save
medir (i)	to measure
olvidar(se)	to forget
programar	to program
promover (ue)	to promote
proteger (j)	to protect
provocar (qu)	to cause
quedar	to leave behind
quemar(se)	to burn (down)
reenviar	to forward
repoblar (ue)	to replant
resolver (ue)	to resolve
romper(se)	to break (down); to tear
subir	to upload

Palabras y expresiones útiles	Useful words and expressions
actualmente	currently, nowadays
la beca	scholarship
genéticamente	genetically
la medida	step, measure
poner en riesgo	to put at risk
el tamaño	size
virtualmente	virtually

Appendix 1

WRITTEN ACCENTS AND WORD FORMATION IN SPANISH

Rules for Word Stress and Written Accents

The following rules are based on pronunciation.

1. If a word ends in **n**, **s**, or a vowel, the stress falls on the penultimate (second-to-last) syllable.

   ca**mi**nan **mu**chos **si**lla

2. If a word ends in a consonant other than **n** or **s**, the last syllable is stressed.

   espa**ñol** profe**sor** re**loj**

3. Words that are exceptions to the preceding rules have a written accent mark on the stressed vowel.

   per**dón** **mié**rcoles ma**má** por**tá**til **lá**piz

4. **Separation of diphthongs.** When **i** or **u** is combined with another vowel, the two vowels are pronounced as one sound (a diphthong). When each vowel sound is pronounced separately, a written accent mark is placed over the stressed vowel (either the **i** or the **u**).

   farmacia gracias día d**ú**o

Note: There are two other types of words that require written accents. The accent mark must be memorized as part of the spelling.

1. **Homonyms.** When two monosyllabic words are spelled the same, but have different meanings, a written accent is used to distinguish and differentiate meaning.

de	*of*	**dé**	*give* (formal command)
el	*the*	**él**	*he*
mas	*but*	**más**	*more*
mi	*my*	**mí**	*me*
se	*him/herself; (to) him/her/them*	**sé**	*I know; be* (formal command)
si	*if*	**sí**	*yes*
te	*(to) you*	**té**	*tea*
tu	*your*	**tú**	*you*

2. **Interrogatives and exclamations.** In questions (direct and indirect) and exclamations, a written accent is placed over the following words: **dónde, cómo, cuándo, cuál(es), quién(es), cuánto(s)/cuánta(s),** and **qué.**

   ¿De **dónde** eres? *Where are you from?*
   No sé **cuánto** cuesta el libro. *I don't know how much the book costs.*
   ¡**Qué** interesante! *How interesting!*

Word Formation in Spanish

Recognizing certain patterns in Spanish word formation can be a big help in deciphering meaning. Use the following information about word formation to help you as you read.

- **Prefixes.** Spanish and English share a number of prefixes that shade the meaning of the word to which they are attached: **inter-** (between, among); **intro/a-** (within); **ex-** (former, toward the outside); **en-/em-** (the state of becoming); **in-/a-** (not, without), among others.

inter-	interdisciplinario, interacción
intro/a-	introvertido, introspección
ex-	exponer (*expose*)
en-/em-	enrojecer (*to turn red*), empobrecer (*to become poor*)
in-/a-	inmoral, incompleto, amoral, asexual

- **Suffixes.** Suffixes and, in general, word endings will help you identify various aspects of words such as part of speech, gender, meaning, degree, etc. Common Spanish suffixes are **-ría, -za, -miento, -dad/tad, -ura, -oso/a, -izo/a, -(c)ito/a,** and **-mente.**

-ría	place where something is made and/or bought: **panadería, zapatería** (*shoe store*), **librería**
-za	feminine, abstract noun: **pobreza** (*poverty*), **riqueza** (*wealth, richness*)
-miento	masculine, abstract noun: **empobrecimiento** (*impoverishment*), **entrenamiento** (*training*)
-dad/tad	feminine noun: **ciudad** (*city*), **libertad** (*liberty, freedom*)
-ura	feminine noun: **verdura, locura** (*craziness*)
-oso/a	adjective meaning having the characteristics of the noun to which it's attached: **montañoso, lluvioso** (*rainy*)
-izo/a	adjective meaning having the characteristics of the noun to which it's attached: **rojizo** (*reddish*), **enfermizo** (*sickly*)
-(c)ito/a	diminutive form of noun or adjective: **Juanito, mesita** (*little table*), **Carmencita**
-mente	attached to the feminine form of adjective to form an adverb: **rápidamente, felizmente** (*happily*)

- **Compounds.** Compounds are made up of two words (e.g., *mailman*), each of which has meaning in and of itself: **altavoz** (*loudspeaker*) from **alto/a** and **voz; sacacorchos** (*corkscrew*) from **sacar** and **corcho.** Your knowledge of the root words will help you recognize the compound; and likewise, learning compounds can help you to learn the root words. What do you think **sacar** means?

- **Spanish–English associations.** Learning to associate aspects of word formation in Spanish with aspects of word formation in English can be very helpful. Look at the associations below.

SPANISH	ENGLISH
es/ex + consonant	*s* + consonant
estatua, extraño	*statue, strange*
gu-	*w-*
guerra, Guillermo	*war, William*
-tad/dad	*-ty*
libertad, universidad	*liberty, university*
-sión/-ción	*-sion/-tion*
tensión, emoción	*tension, emotion*

Appendix 2

VERB CHARTS

Regular Verbs: Simple Tenses

Infinitive Present Participle Past Participle	Indicative					Subjunctive		Imperative
	Present	Imperfect	Preterit	Future	Conditional	Present	Imperfect	Commands
hablar hablando hablado	hablo hablas habla hablamos habláis hablan	hablaba hablabas hablaba hablábamos hablabais hablaban	hablé hablaste habló hablamos hablasteis hablaron	hablaré hablarás hablará hablaremos hablaréis hablarán	hablaría hablarías hablaría hablaríamos hablaríais hablarían	hable hables hable hablemos habléis hablen	hablara hablaras hablara habláramos hablarais hablaran	habla (tú), no hables hable (usted) hablemos hablad (vosotros), no habléis hablen (Uds.)
comer comiendo comido	como comes come comemos coméis comen	comía comías comía comíamos comíais comían	comí comiste comió comimos comisteis comieron	comeré comerás comerá comeremos comeréis comerán	comería comerías comería comeríamos comeríais comerían	coma comas coma comamos comáis coman	comiera comieras comiera comiéramos comierais comieran	come (tú), no comas coma (usted) comamos comed (vosotros), no comáis coman (Uds.)
vivir viviendo vivido	vivo vives vive vivimos vivís viven	vivía vivías vivía vivíamos vivíais vivían	viví viviste vivió vivimos vivisteis vivieron	viviré vivirás vivirá viviremos viviréis vivirán	viviría vivirías viviría viviríamos viviríais vivirían	viva vivas viva vivamos viváis vivan	viviera vivieras viviera viviéramos vivierais vivieran	vive (tú), no vivas viva (usted) vivamos vivid (vosotros), no viváis vivan (Uds.)

Regular Verbs: Perfect Tenses

Indicative								Subjunctive			
Present Perfect		Past Perfect		Future Perfect		Conditional Perfect		Present Perfect		Past Perfect	
he has ha hemos habéis han	hablado comido vivido	había habías había habíamos habíais habían	hablado comido vivido	habré habrás habrá habremos habréis habrán	hablado comido vivido	habría habrías habría habríamos habríais habrían	hablado comido vivido	haya hayas haya hayamos hayáis hayan	hablado comido vivido	hubiera hubieras hubiera hubiéramos hubierais hubieran	hablado comido vivido

Irregular Verbs

Infinitive Present Participle Past Participle	Indicative					Subjunctive		Imperative
	Present	Imperfect	Preterit	Future	Conditional	Present	Imperfect	Commands
andar andando andado	ando andas anda andamos andáis andan	andaba andabas andaba andábamos andabais andaban	anduve anduviste anduvo anduvimos anduvisteis anduvieron	andaré andarás andará andaremos andaréis andarán	andaría andarías andaría andaríamos andaríais andarían	ande andes ande andemos andéis anden	anduviera anduvieras anduviera anduviéramos anduvierais anduvieran	anda (tú), no andes ande (usted) andemos andad (vosotros), no andéis anden (Uds.)
caer cayendo caído	caigo caes cae caemos caéis caen	caía caías caía caíamos caíais caían	caí caíste cayó caímos caísteis cayeron	caeré caerás caerá caeremos caeréis caerán	caería caerías caería caeríamos caeríais caerían	caiga caigas caiga caigamos caigáis caigan	cayera cayeras cayera cayéramos cayerais cayeran	cae (tú), no caigas caiga (usted) caigamos caed (vosotros), no caigáis caigan (Uds.)
dar dando dado	doy das da damos dais dan	daba dabas daba dábamos dabais daban	di diste dio dimos disteis dieron	daré darás dará daremos daréis darán	daría darías daría daríamos daríais darían	dé des dé demos deis den	diera dieras diera diéramos dierais dieran	da (tú), no des dé (usted) demos dad (vosotros), no deis den (Uds.)
decir diciendo dicho	digo dices dice decimos decís dicen	decía decías decía decíamos decíais decían	dije dijiste dijo dijimos dijisteis dijeron	diré dirás dirá diremos diréis dirán	diría dirías diría diríamos diríais dirían	diga digas diga digamos digáis digan	dijera dijeras dijera dijéramos dijerais dijeran	di (tú), no digas diga (usted) digamos decid (vosotros), no digáis digan (Uds.)
estar estando estado	estoy estás está estamos estáis están	estaba estabas estaba estábamos estabais estaban	estuve estuviste estuvo estuvimos estuvisteis estuvieron	estaré estarás estará estaremos estaréis estarán	estaría estarías estaría estaríamos estaríais estarían	esté estés esté estemos estéis estén	estuviera estuvieras estuviera estuviéramos estuvierais estuvieran	está (tú), no estés esté (usted) estemos estad (vosotros), no estéis estén (Uds.)
haber habiendo habido	he has ha hemos habéis han	había habías había habíamos habíais habían	hube hubiste hubo hubimos hubisteis hubieron	habré habrás habrá habremos habréis habrán	habría habrías habría habríamos habríais habrían	haya hayas haya hayamos hayáis hayan	hubiera hubieras hubiera hubiéramos hubierais hubieran	
hacer haciendo hecho	hago haces hace hacemos hacéis hacen	hacía hacías hacía hacíamos hacíais hacían	hice hiciste hizo hicimos hicisteis hicieron	haré harás hará haremos haréis harán	haría harías haría haríamos haríais harían	haga hagas haga hagamos hagáis hagan	hiciera hicieras hiciera hiciéramos hicierais hicieran	haz (tú), no hagas haga (usted) hagamos haced (vosotros), no hagáis hagan (Uds.)
ir yendo ido	voy vas va vamos vais van	iba ibas iba íbamos ibais iban	fui fuiste fue fuimos fuisteis fueron	iré irás irá iremos iréis irán	iría irías iría iríamos iríais irían	vaya vayas vaya vayamos vayáis vayan	fuera fueras fuera fuéramos fuerais fueran	ve (tú), no vayas vaya (usted) vamos, no vayamos id (vosotros), no vayáis vayan (Uds.)

Irregular Verbs (*continued*)

Infinitive Present Participle Past Participle	Indicative					Subjunctive		Imperative
	Present	Imperfect	Preterit	Future	Conditional	Present	Imperfect	Commands
oír oyendo oído	oigo oyes oye oímos oís oyen	oía oías oía oíamos oíais oían	oí oíste oyó oímos oísteis oyeron	oiré oirás oirá oiremos oiréis oirán	oiría oirías oiría oiríamos oiríais oirían	oiga oigas oiga oigamos oigáis oigan	oyera oyeras oyera oyéramos oyerais oyeran	oye (tú), no oigas oiga (usted) oigamos oíd (vosotros), no oigáis oigan (Uds.)
poder pudiendo podido	puedo puedes puede podemos podéis pueden	podía podías podía podíamos podíais podían	pude pudiste pudo pudimos pudisteis pudieron	podré podrás podrá podremos podréis podrán	podría podrías podría podríamos podríais podrían	pueda puedas pueda podamos podáis puedan	pudiera pudieras pudiera pudiéramos pudierais pudieran	
poner poniendo puesto	pongo pones pone ponemos ponéis ponen	ponía ponías ponía poníamos poníais ponían	puse pusiste puso pusimos pusisteis pusieron	pondré pondrás pondrá pondremos pondréis pondrán	pondría pondrías pondría pondríamos pondríais pondrían	ponga pongas ponga pongamos pongáis pongan	pusiera pusieras pusiera pusiéramos pusierais pusieran	pon (tú), no pongas ponga (usted) pongamos poned (vosotros), no pongáis pongan (Uds.)
querer queriendo querido	quiero quieres quiere queremos queréis quieren	quería querías quería queríamos queríais querían	quise quisiste quiso quisimos quisisteis quisieron	querré querrás querrá querremos querréis querrán	querría querrías querría querríamos querríais querrían	quiera quieras quiera queramos queráis quieran	quisiera quisieras quisiera quisiéramos quisierais quisieran	quiere (tú), no quieras quiera (usted) queramos quered (vosotros), no queráis quieran (Uds.)
saber sabiendo sabido	sé sabes sabe sabemos sabéis saben	sabía sabías sabía sabíamos sabíais sabían	supe supiste supo supimos supisteis supieron	sabré sabrás sabrá sabremos sabréis sabrán	sabría sabrías sabría sabríamos sabríais sabrían	sepa sepas sepa sepamos sepáis sepan	supiera supieras supiera supiéramos supierais supieran	sabe (tú), no sepas sepa (usted) sepamos sabed (vosotros), no sepáis sepan (Uds.)
salir saliendo salido	salgo sales sale salimos salís salen	salía salías salía salíamos salíais salían	salí saliste salió salimos salisteis salieron	saldré saldrás saldrá saldremos saldréis saldrán	saldría saldrías saldría saldríamos saldríais saldrían	salga salgas salga salgamos salgáis salgan	saliera salieras saliera saliéramos salierais salieran	sal (tú), no salgas salga (usted) salgamos salid (vosotros), no salgáis salgan (Uds.)
ser siendo sido	soy eres es somos sois son	era eras era éramos erais eran	fui fuiste fue fuimos fuisteis fueron	seré serás será seremos seréis serán	sería serías sería seríamos seríais serían	sea seas sea seamos seáis sean	fuera fueras fuera fuéramos fuerais fueran	sé (tú), no seas sea (usted) seamos sed (vosotros), no seáis sean (Uds.)
tener teniendo tenido	tengo tienes tiene tenemos tenéis tienen	tenía tenías tenía teníamos teníais tenían	tuve tuviste tuvo tuvimos tuvisteis tuvieron	tendré tendrás tendrá tendremos tendréis tendrán	tendría tendrías tendría tendríamos tendríais tendrían	tenga tengas tenga tengamos tengáis tengan	tuviera tuvieras tuviera tuviéramos tuvierais tuvieran	ten (tú), no tengas tenga (usted) tengamos tened (vosotros), no tengáis tengan (Uds.)

Irregular Verbs (*continued*)

Infinitive Present Participle Past Participle	Indicative					Subjunctive		Imperative
	Present	Imperfect	Preterit	Future	Conditional	Present	Imperfect	Commands
traer trayendo traído	traigo traes trae traemos traéis traen	traía traías traía traíamos traíais traían	traje trajiste trajo trajimos trajisteis trajeron	traeré traerás traerá traeremos traeréis traerán	traería traerías traería traeríamos traeríais traerían	traiga traigas traiga traigamos traigáis traigan	trajera trajeras trajera trajéramos trajerais trajeran	trae (tú), no traigas traiga (usted) traigamos traed (vosotros), no traigáis traigan (Uds.)
venir viniendo venido	vengo vienes viene venimos venís vienen	venía venías venía veníamos veníais venían	vine viniste vino vinimos vinisteis vinieron	vendré vendrás vendrá vendremos vendréis vendrán	vendría vendrías vendría vendríamos vendríais vendrían	venga vengas venga vengamos vengáis vengan	viniera vinieras viniera viniéramos vinierais vinieran	ven (tú), no vengas venga (usted) vengamos venid (vosotros), no vengáis vengan (Uds.)
ver viendo visto	veo ves ve vemos veis ven	veía veías veía veíamos veíais veían	vi viste vio vimos visteis vieron	veré verás verá veremos veréis verán	vería verías vería veríamos veríais verían	vea veas vea veamos veáis vean	viera vieras viera viéramos vierais vieran	ve (tú), no veas vea (usted) veamos ved (vosotros), no veáis vean (Uds.)

Stem-Changing and Orthographic-Changing Verbs

Infinitive Present Participle Past Participle	Indicative					Subjunctive		Imperative
	Present	Imperfect	Preterit	Future	Conditional	Present	Imperfect	Commands
almorzar (ue) (c) almorzando almorzado	almuerzo almuerzas almuerza almorzamos almorzáis almuerzan	almorzaba almorzabas almorzaba almorzábamos almorzabais almorzaban	almorcé almorzaste almorzó almorzamos almorzasteis almorzaron	almorzaré almorzarás almorzará almorzaremos almorzaréis almorzarán	almorzaría almorzarías almorzaría almorzaríamos almorzaríais almorzarían	almuerce almuerces almuerce almorcemos almorcéis almuercen	almorzara almorzaras almorzara almorzáramos almorzarais almorzaran	almuerza (tú), no almuerces almuerce (usted) almorcemos almorzad (vosotros), no almorcéis almuercen (Uds.)
buscar (qu) buscando buscado	busco buscas busca buscamos buscáis buscan	buscaba buscabas buscaba buscábamos buscabais buscaban	busqué buscaste buscó buscamos buscasteis buscaron	buscaré buscarás buscará buscaremos buscaréis buscarán	buscaría buscarías buscaría buscaríamos buscaríais buscarían	busque busques busque busquemos busquéis busquen	buscara buscaras buscara buscáramos buscarais buscaran	busca (tú), no busques busque (usted) busquemos buscad (vosotros), no busquéis busquen (Uds.)

Stem-Changing and Orthographic-Changing Verbs (*continued*)

Infinitive Present Participle Past Participle	Indicative					Subjunctive		Imperative
	Present	Imperfect	Preterit	Future	Conditional	Present	Imperfect	Commands
corregir (i, i) (j) corrigiendo corregido	corrijo corriges corrige corregimos corregís corrigen	corregía corregías corregía corregíamos corregíais corregían	corregí corregiste corrigió corregimos corregisteis corrigieron	corregiré corregirás corregirá corregiremos corregiréis corregirán	corregiría corregirías corregiría corregiríamos corregiríais corregirían	corrija corrijas corrija corrijamos corrijáis corrijan	corrigiera corrigieras corrigiera corrigiéramos corrigierais corrigieran	corrige (tú), no corrijas corrija (usted) corrijamos corregid (vosotros), no corrijáis corrijan (Uds.)
dormir (ue, u) durmiendo dormido	duermo duermes duerme dormimos dormís duermen	dormía dormías dormía dormíamos dormíais dormían	dormí dormiste durmió dormimos dormisteis durmieron	dormiré dormirás dormirá dormiremos dormiréis dormirán	dormiría dormirías dormiría dormiríamos dormiríais dormirían	duerma duermas duerma durmamos durmáis duerman	durmiera durmieras durmiera durmiéramos durmierais durmieran	duerme (tú), no duermas duerma (usted) durmamos dormid (vosotros), no durmáis duerman (Uds.)
incluir (y) incluyendo incluido	incluyo incluyes incluye incluimos incluís incluyen	incluía incluías incluía incluíamos incluíais incluían	incluí incluiste incluyó incluimos incluisteis incluyeron	incluiré incluirás incluirá incluiremos incluiréis incluirán	incluiría incluirías incluiría incluiríamos incluiríais incluirían	incluya incluyas incluya incluyamos incluyáis incluyan	incluyera incluyeras incluyera incluyéramos incluyerais incluyeran	incluye (tú), no incluyas incluya (usted) incluyamos incluid (vosotros), no incluyáis incluyan (Uds.)
llegar (gu) llegando llegado	llego llegas llega llegamos llegáis llegan	llegaba llegabas llegaba llegábamos llegabais llegaban	llegué llegaste llegó llegamos llegasteis llegaron	llegaré llegarás llegará llegaremos llegaréis llegarán	llegaría llegarías llegaría llegaríamos llegaríais llegarían	llegue llegues llegue lleguemos lleguéis lleguen	llegara llegaras llegara llegáramos llegarais llegaran	llega (tú), no llegues llegue (usted) lleguemos llegad (vosotros), no lleguéis lleguen (Uds.)
pedir (i, i) pidiendo pedido	pido pides pide pedimos pedís piden	pedía pedías pedía pedíamos pedíais pedían	pedí pediste pidió pedimos pedisteis pidieron	pediré pedirás pedirá pediremos pediréis pedirán	pediría pedirías pediría pediríamos pediríais pedirían	pida pidas pida pidamos pidáis pidan	pidiera pidieras pidiera pidiéramos pidierais pidieran	pide (tú), no pidas pida (usted) pidamos pedid (vosotros), no pidáis pidan (Uds.)
pensar (ie) pensando pensado	pienso piensas piensa pensamos pensáis piensan	pensaba pensabas pensaba pensábamos pensabais pensaban	pensé pensaste pensó pensamos pensasteis pensaron	pensaré pensarás pensará pensaremos pensaréis pensarán	pensaría pensarías pensaría pensaríamos pensaríais pensarían	piense pienses piense pensemos penséis piensen	pensara pensaras pensara pensáramos pensarais pensaran	piensa (tú), no pienses piense (usted) pensemos pensad (vosotros), no penséis piensen (Uds.)

Stem-Changing and Orthographic-Changing Verbs (*continued*)

Infinitive Present Participle Past Participle	Indicative					Subjunctive		Imperative
	Present	Imperfect	Preterit	Future	Conditional	Present	Imperfect	Commands
producir (zc) (j) produciendo producido	produzco produces produce producimos producís producen	producía producías producía producíamos producíais producían	produje produjiste produjo produjimos produjisteis produjeron	produciré producirás producirá produciremos produciréis producirán	produciría producirías produciría produciríamos produciríais producirían	produzca produzcas produzca produzcamos produzcáis produzcan	produjera produjeras produjera produjéramos produjerais produjeran	produce (tú), no produzcas produzca (usted) produzcamos producid (vosotros), no produzcáis produzcan (Uds.)
reír (i, i) riendo reído	río ríes ríe reímos reís ríen	reía reías reía reíamos reíais reían	reí reíste rió/rio reímos reísteis rieron	reiré reirás reirá reiremos reiréis reirán	reiría reirías reiría reiríamos reiríais reirían	ría rías ría riamos riáis/riais rían	riera rieras riera riéramos rierais rieran	ríe (tú), no rías ría (usted) riamos reíd (vosotros), no riáis/riais rían (Uds.)
seguir (i, i) (ga) siguiendo seguido	sigo sigues sigue seguimos seguís siguen	seguía seguías seguía seguíamos seguíais seguían	seguí seguiste siguió seguimos seguisteis siguieron	seguiré seguirás seguirá seguiremos seguiréis seguirán	seguiría seguirías seguiría seguiríamos seguiríais seguirían	siga sigas siga sigamos sigáis sigan	siguiera siguieras siguiera siguiéramos siguierais siguieran	sigue (tú), no sigas siga (usted) sigamos seguid (vosotros), no sigáis sigan (Uds.)
sentir (ie, i) sintiendo sentido	siento sientes siente sentimos sentís sienten	sentía sentías sentía sentíamos sentíais sentían	sentí sentiste sintió sentimos sentisteis sintieron	sentiré sentirás sentirá sentiremos sentiréis sentirán	sentiría sentirías sentiría sentiríamos sentiríais sentirían	sienta sientas sienta sintamos sintáis sientan	sintiera sintieras sintiera sintiéramos sintierais sintieran	siente (tú), no sientas sienta (usted) sintamos sentid (vosotros), no sintáis sientan (Uds.)
volver (ue) volviendo vuelto	vuelvo vuelves vuelve volvemos volvéis vuelven	volvía volvías volvía volvíamos volvíais volvían	volví volviste volvió volvimos volvisteis volvieron	volveré volverás volverá volveremos volveréis volverán	volvería volverías volvería volveríamos volveríais volverían	vuelva vuelvas vuelva volvamos volváis vuelvan	volviera volvieras volviera volviéramos volvierais volvieran	vuelve (tú), no vuelvas vuelva (usted) volvamos volved (vosotros), no volváis vuelvan (Uds.)

Appendix 3

SPANISH–ENGLISH GLOSSARY

This vocabulary includes all words and expressions presented in the text, except for proper nouns spelled the same in English and Spanish, diminutives with a literal meaning, cognates and words easily recognized because of the context, and cardinal numbers (see page 21).

The number following each entry in bold corresponds to the **capítulo** in which the word is introduced for active mastery. Non-bold numbers correspond to introduction of words for receptive use.

A

a *at, to* **P**
a escala mundial *on a global scale* **14**
a eso de... *at about . . .* **8**
a finales de... *at the end of . . .* **8**
a la derecha *(to the) right* **12**
a la izquierda *(to the) left* **12**
a la vez *at the same time* 6
a menos que *unless* **14**
a partir de *from, since, starting at* 9
a pesar de *in spite of* **14**
¿A qué hora es? *At what time is (it)?* P
a través de *through* 13
a veces *sometimes* **1**, 8; *at times* 12
el/la abogado/a *lawyer* **9**
abrazar *to hug* **4**
Abre/Abran el libro. *Open the book.* **P**
el abrigo *coat* **6**
abril *April* **P**
abrir *to open* 5
el/la abuelo/a *grandfather/grandmother* **4**
los abuelos *grandparents* **4**
abundar *to abound* **13**
aburrido/a *boring* **1**; *bored* 6
acabar(se) *to run out of something* **15**
el accesorio *accessory* **6**
el acceso *access* **15**
el aceite (de oliva) *(olive) oil* **10**
la aceituna *olive* **3**
el achiote *annatto* **10**
acompañar *to accompany* **8**
aconsejar *to advise* 5, **11**
el acontecimiento *event* 13
aconsejable *advisable* 11
acostarse (ue) *to put to bed; to go to bed; to lie down* **4**, 7
la actividad *activity* 1
el/la actor/actriz *actor/actress* **9**
la actualidad *the present time* **13**
actualizar *to update* 9, **15**
actualmente *at the present time* **9**; *currently, nowadays* **15**
la acupuntura *acupuncture* 11
la adaptación *adaptation* **13**; *adjustment, adaptation* **14**
Adelante. *Come in.* 5
el adelanto *advance* 15
además (de) *besides, in addition (to)* 1, 6, 11
el aderezo *salad dressing* **10**
adiós *goodbye* **P**
adivinar *to guess* 1
el (documento) adjunto *attachment* **15**
la administración de redes *network administration* **15**
la administración y dirección de empresas *business administration and management* **1**
admirar *to admire* 4
¿adónde? *where to?* **1**
adornar *to decorate* 8
adquirir (ie) *to acquire* 13
la aduana *customs* **12**
la aerolínea *airline* **12**
el aeroplano *airplane* 4
el aeropuerto *airport* 1, **12**
aeroespacial *aerospace* **15**
afeitarse *to shave (oneself)* **4**
afortunadamente *fortunately* 5
las afueras *outskirts* 1, **5**
la agencia de viajes *travel agency* **12**
agosto *August* **P**
agradable *nice* **2**
agradecer (zc) *to give thanks* 11
agradecido/a *grateful* 10
agregar *to add* 9, **10**
agrícola *agricultural* **9**
el/la agricultor/a *farmer* **9**
la agricultura *farming* **9**
el agua *water* **3**
el aguacate *avocado* 4, **10**
el águila *eagle* 14
el agujero *hole* **15**
ahora *now* **1**
ahorrar *to save* 9
el aire acondicionado *air conditioning* **5**
el ají *hot, spicy pepper* 10
el ajo *garlic* **10**
al (contraction of **a** + **el**) *to the* **3**
al aire libre *open-air* **6**
al carbón *grilled (on the BBQ)* 10
al fondo *in the background* **13**
al lado (de) *next to* **P**; *beside* 5
al menos *at least* 7
el ala *wing* 14
la alberca *swimming pool* 5
alcanzar (c) *to reach* 11
la alcoba *bedroom* 5
alegrarse (de) *to be glad (about)* **11**
alegre *happy, glad* **2**
la alegría *joy* **8**
alemán/alemana *German* 2
alfabetizado/a *literate* **14**
la alfombra *carpet, rug* **5**
algo/a *something* **1**; *anything* **12**
el algodón *cotton* **6**
alguien *someone, anyone* **12**
algún, alguno/a *some, any, several* 2, **12**
alguna vez *sometime, ever* **12**
algunas veces *sometimes* **12**
la alimentación *food, diet* **10**
los alimentos *food* 6
allí *there* 4
el alma *soul* 14
el almacén *department store* **6**
las almas gemelas *kindred spirits* 8
almorzar (ue) *to have lunch* **4**
el almuerzo *lunch* **3**
¿Aló? *Hello? (telephone greeting)* 3
el alojamiento *lodging* 8, 11, **12**
alquilar *to rent* 1
el alquiler *rent* **5**
alto/a *tall* **2**
altura *height, elevation, altitude* 10
el/la alumno/a *student* **1**
la amabilidad *kindness, courtesy* 9
amar *to love* **4**
amarillo/a *yellow* **2**
ambiental *atmospheric* 15
el ambiente *atmosphere* 3
la ambulancia *ambulance* 11
la amenaza *threat* 11
el/la amigo/a *friend* **P**
la amistad *friendship* 4, 6, 7, **13**
el amo/a de casa *homemaker* **9**
el amor *love* **13**
añadir *to add* 4, 7, 10
el analfabetismo *illiteracy* **14**
el analgésico *painkiller* 11
el análisis financiero *financial analysis* **1**
anaranjado/a *orange* **2**
ancho/a *wide, loose* **6**
¡Anda, anímate! *Come on, let's do it!* 3
andar *to travel* 14
el andén *platform* 12
el anillo *ring* **6**
animado/a *lively* **8**
el ánimo *mood* 5
el año *year* **P**
el Año Nuevo *New Year's Day* **8**
anoche *last night* **6**
ante(a)noche *the night before last* **6**
anteayer *the day before yesterday* **6**
el/la antepasado/a *ancestor* **8**
antes *before* 5, **8**
antes de eso *before that* 6
antes (de) que *before* **14**
el antibiótico *antibiotic* **11**
antiguo/a *ancient, old* 1, 2, 8

antipático/a *unpleasant* **2**
el/la antropólogo/a *anthropologist* 6
el anuncio *ad, advertisement* **9**; *radio announcement* 15
apagar *to extinguish, to turn off* **9**
apagar(se) *to shut off; to go out* **15**
el apagón *power outage* 9
los aparatos eléctricos *electronic devices* **5**
el apartamento *apartment* **5**
el apellido *surname* 4
el aperitivo *appetizer* 9
la aplicación *app* 12, **15**
apostar (ue) por *to bet on* 12
apoyar *to support* 7
aprender *to learn* **1**
apretado/a *busy, tight* 9
aprobar (ue) *to approve* 14
los apuntes *notes* **1**
aquel/aquella/aquello *that (over there)* 5
aquellos/aquellas *those (over there)* 5
el/la árbitro/a *umpire, referee* **7**
el árbol *tree* 4, **7**
la arcilla *clay* 13
la arena *sand* 3, 4
el arete *earring* **6**
argentino/a *Argentinian* **2**
el armario *armoire, wardrobe* **5**
la armonía *harmony* 13
el aro *earring* 6
el arpa *harp* 13
el/la arquitecto/a *architect* 5, **9**
la arquitectura *architecture* **5**
el arrecife (coralino) *(coral) reef* 6, 12
arreglar *to tidy up; to put in order* 10
arrepentirse (ie) *to regret* 7
arriesgado/a *risky* 12
el arroz *rice* **3**
el arroz chaufa *Peruvian fried rice* 10
el arte *art* P, **13**
la artesanía *handicrafts* **6**
artístico/a *artistic* 8
el asado *barbecue* 3
la asamblea *assembly* 14
asar *to roast; to grill* **10**
el ascensor *elevator* 12
el aserrín *sawdust* 8
el asiento *seat* **12**
el asiento de pasillo *aisle seat* **12**
el asiento de ventanilla *window seat* **12**
la asignatura *subject* **1**
el asistente virtual *virtual assistant* 5
asistir *to attend* **1**
el asma *asthma* **11**
la aspiradora *vacuum cleaner* **5**
el/la astronauta *astronaut* 6
el asunto *issue, topic* 9, **13**
el ataque de corazón *heart attack* 7
la atención *service* 3
atender (ie) *to look after, tend to* 9
aterrizar *to land (aircraft)* **15**
el ático *attic* 5
el atletismo *track and field* **7**
la atmósfera *atmosphere* **15**
atractivo/a *attractive* 8
atreverse *to dare* 7
el atún *tuna* **10**
aumentar *to increase, to raise* 9, 14, **15**
aún *still* 9
aunque *although, even though, even if* 8, 12, **14**
los auriculares *headphones* **15**
el auto *car* **2**
el autobús *bus* **12**
la autopista *freeway* **12**
autoritario/a *authoritarian* 9
el autorretrato *self-portrait* 8
el/la auxiliar de vuelo *flight attendant* **12**
avanzar *to progress; to advance* **15**
avergonzado/a *embarrassed* 10
averiguar *to find out* 12
las aves *poultry, fowl* **10**
el avión *plane* 11, **12**
ayer *yesterday* 6
ayudar *to help* 1, **4**
el azafrán *saffron* 10
el azúcar *sugar* 8, **10**
azul *blue* **2**

B

la bahía *bay* 11
bailar *to dance* **1**
el baile *dance* 1
bajar *to download* **15**
bajar de peso *to lose weight* 3, 10
bajarse (de) *to get off/out (of); to go down* **12**
bajo *under* 5
bajo/a *short (in stature)* **2**
el/la bailarín/bailarina *dancer* **13**
la ballena (jorobada) *(humpback) whale* 11, 12
el balón *ball* **7**
el baloncesto *basketball* 1, **7**
la bañadera *bathtub* 5
la banana *banana* **10**
bañar(se) *to bathe; to take a bath* **4**
bancario/a *banking* 12
el banco de peces *shoal (group of fish)* **15**
la bandeja *tray* 9, **10**
la bandera *flag* 2
la bañera *bathtub* **5**
el baño *bathroom* **5**
barato/a *inexpensive, cheap* **6**
la barbacoa *barbecue pit; barbecue (event)* **5**
el barco *ship, boat* **12**
barrer *to sweep* **5**
el barrio *neighborhood* **5**
el barro *mud* 13
básicamente *basically* 5
el básquetbol *basketball* **7**
bastante *rather* **P**; *enough, sufficient* 10
la basura *garbage, trash* **5**
la bata *robe* **6**
la batalla *battle* 8
el bate *bat* **7**
la batería *battery* **15**
el batido *smoothie* 10
batido/a *beaten* **10**
el baúl *trunk* **12**
el bautismo *baptism* 8
beber *to drink* **1**
la bebida *drink, beverage* **3**, **10**
la beca *scholarship* 1, **15**
el béisbol *baseball* **7**
el/la beisbolista *baseball player* P, **7**
las bellas artes *fine arts* 1
la belleza *beauty* 4
la bendición *blessing* 8
los beneficios *benefits* **9**
besar *to kiss* 4
la biblioteca *library* **1**
la biblioteca digital *digital library* **15**
el/la bibliotecario/a *librarian* **9**
bien *well* **P**
bien parecido *good-looking, handsome (male)* 2
bien/mal aparcado/a *well/badly parked* **12**
bienvenido/a *welcome* P
bilingüe *bilingual* **2**
la billetera *wallet* **6**
la biología *biology* **1**
el bistec *steak* **3**
blanco/a *white* **2**
blando/a *tender* 10
la blusa *blouse* 5, **6**
la boca *mouth* 8, 10, **11**
la boda *wedding* 3, 4, 6
la boina *beret* 6
el bol *bowl* **10**
el boleto *ticket* **12**
el bolígrafo *ballpoint pen* P
boliviano/a *Bolivian* **2**
la bolsa de aire *airbag* **12**
el bolso *purse* **6**
el/la bombero/a *firefighter* **9**
bonito/a *pretty* **2**
el bono *bonus* 9
el bordado *embroidery* 10
el borrador *eraser* **P**
el bosque *forest* 6, **9**
las botas *boots* **6**
la botella *bottle* **10**
las bragas *women's underwear* 6
el brazo *arm* 6, **11**
la brecha *gap* **14**
breve *brief* 13
el brócoli *broccoli* 11
el brote *outbreak* 11
la bruja *witch* 8
buen mozo *good-looking, handsome (male)* 2
¡Buena suerte! *Good luck!* **1**
buenas noches *good evening, good night* **P**
buenas tardes *good afternoon* **P**
¡Bueno! *Hello? (telephone greeting)* 3
bueno/a *good* **1**; *well (health); physically attractive* 6
buenos días *good morning* **P**
la bufanda *scarf* **6**
el/la burgués/burguesa *member of the wealthy (class)* 13
burlarse de *to make fun of* 7
el burro *donkey* 12
el bus *bus* **12**
buscar *to look for* **1**
la butaca *armchair* **5**
el buzón *mailbox* 14

C

el cabello *hair* **11**
la cabeza *head* 6, **11**
el cacique *chief* 15
cada *each* 4, 5, **7**
cada… horas *every . . . hours* **11**
la cadena *chain* 6
la cadera *hip* **11**
caer bien/mal *to like/dislike (a person)* **6**
caer(se) (g) *to fall* **11**
el café *coffee* 1, **3**
la cafetería *cafeteria* **1**
la caída *fall* 11
la caja *box* 5, 6
la caja fuerte *safe* **12**
el cajero automático *ATM* 9, **12**
el/la cajero/a *cashier* **9**
la calavera *skull* 8
los calcetines *socks* **6**
la calcomanía *bumper sticker* 13
la calculadora *calculator* **P**
la calefacción *heating* **5**
el calendario *calendar* P
el calentamiento *warm-up* 7; *warming* **15**
la calidad *quality* 5, **13**, **14**
caliente *hot* **3**
callado/a *quiet* **2**
la calle *street* **5**
calmarse *to calm down* 4
el calzado *footwear* 6
calzar *to wear a shoe size* 6
los calzoncillos *boxer shorts* **6**

los calzones *panties* **6**
la cama *bed* **5**
la Cámara de Representantes *Congress* 3
el/la camarero/a *server, waiter/waitress (restaurant)* **3**
el camarón *shrimp* **10**
cambiar *to change; to exchange* **6**
el cambio *change* **14**
el cambio climático *climate change* **15**
el camello *camel* 8
la camilla *stretcher* 12
caminar *to walk* **1**
el camión *truck* 5; *bus* **12**
la camisa *shirt* **6**
la camisa de manga corta *short-sleeved shirt* **6**
la camiseta *T-shirt* 2, **6**
el camisón *nightgown* **6**
el/la campeón/campeona *champion* **7**
el campeonato *championship* **7**; *tournament* 8
el/la campesino/a *farm worker* **10**
el campo *field, course (golf)* **7**; *countryside* **9**
la caña de azúcar *sugar cane* 9
canadiense *Canadian* 2
la cancha *court* **7**
la canción *song* **3**
la canela *cinnamon* 10
cansado/a *tired* **2**
cansar *to tire out* 10
el/la cantante *singer* 2, **13**
cantar *to sing* 2, **3**
el canto *song* 4
la capa de ozono *ozone layer* **15**
el capital *capital (money)* **14**
la capital *capital (city)* P
el capítulo *chapter* P
el capó *hood* **12**
la cápsula *capsule* **15**
la cara *face* **11**
cara a cara *face-to-face* 2
la caravana *earring* 6
el cargador *charger* 5
cargar *to charge* 6
cariñoso/a *affectionate* **2**
carmelita *brown* 2
el carnaval *carnival* **8**
la carne *meat* **10**
la carne de res *beef/steak* **10**
la carne molida *ground beef* **10**
la carnicería *butcher shop* **10**
caro/a *expensive* **6**
la carpeta *folder* 9
el/la carpintero/a *carpenter* **9**
la carrera *professional career* **15**
la carrera literaria *literary career* **13**
la carretera *highway* **12**
el carro *car* 2, **12**
la carroza *float (in a parade)* **8**
la carta *letter* 5
la casa *house, home* **1**
casado/a *married* **2**
casarse *to get married* **4**
la cascada *cascade, waterfall* 12
el casco *helmet* 7
casi *almost* 4
el casillero *locker* 9
castaño/a *brown* **2**
el castillo *castle* 8
la catarata *waterfall* 4
la cebolla *onion* 4, **10**
la ceja *eyebrow* **11**
la celebración *celebration* **3, 8**
el cementerio *cemetery* **8**
la cena *dinner, supper* **3**
cenar *to have dinner* **3**
Cenicienta *Cinderella* 3
el cenote *sinkhole* 8
el centro *downtown, center* **5**
el centro comercial *mall* **6**
el centro de atención al cliente *customer care center* 6
el centro de salud *clinic* **11**
la cepa *strain* 11
cerca de *close to, near* **3**
cercano/a *close* 4
el cerdo *pork* **10**
el cereal *cereal* **3**
el cerebro *brain* **11**
la cereza *cherry* **10**
cerrar (ie) *to close* **4**
el certamen *contest* 9
la cerveza *beer* **3**
el césped *lawn* **5**
el cesto *wastebasket* **P**
el/la cesto/a *basket, hoop* **7**
el ceviche *raw fish marinated in citrus juices* **3**
el champiñón *mushroom* 3
chao/chau *goodbye* **P**
la chaqueta *jacket* 4, **6**
el charango *guitar-like instrument* **13**
chatear *to chat* 3, **15**
el cheque *check* 9
chicano/a *Mexican-American* 2
la chicha morada *purple corn drink* **3**
el/la chico/a *boy/girl* **P**
el chile *hot, spicy pepper* 10
chileno/a *Chilean* **2**
la chimenea *chimney* **5**
chino/a *Chinese* 2
el chip electrónico *electronic chip* **15**
el chiste *joke* 7
la chiva *bus* 12
el/la chofer *driver* **9**
la chuleta *chop* **10**
los churros *fried dough* **10**
el ciclismo *cycling* **7**
la ciencia *science* **1, 15**
la ciencia ficción *science fiction* **15**
las ciencias naturales *natural sciences* **1**
las ciencias políticas *political science* **1**
el/la científico/a *scientist* P, **9**
Cierra/Cierren el libro. *Close the book.* **P**
cierto/a *true* P
el cilantro *cilantro* **10**
el cine *movies* 2; *movie theater* **3**
la cintura *waist* 6, **11**
el cinturón *belt* **6**
el cinturón de seguridad *seatbelt* **12**
el círculo *circle* 10
la cirugía *surgery* 11
el/la cirujano/a *surgeon* 11
la ciudad *city* P, **3**
claramente *clearly* 5
la clase *class* P
la clase turista *tourist class* **12**
clásico/a *classical* **13**
la clave *key* 15
el/la cliente/a *client* **9**
el clima *climate* 5
climatizado/a *air-conditioned* **15**
la clínica *clinic* **11**
la clonación *cloning* **15**
el clóset *closet* **5**
la cobija *blanket* 5
el cobre *copper* 14
el coche *car* 2, **12**
la cocina *kitchen* **5**; *stove* 5
cocinar *to cook* **5**
el coco *coconut* 6
codiciado/a *sought-after* 13
el codo *elbow* **11**
el cojín *cushion* 12
colar (ue) *to drain* 10
el colectivo *bus* 12
colgar (ue) *to hang* 10
el collar *necklace* **6**
colombiano/a *Colombian* **2**
el color *color* **2**
el colorido *coloring* **13**
colorido/a *colorful* 8
el comedor *dining room* **5**
el/la comentador/a de noticias *news commentator* 2
comenzar (ie) *to begin* **8**
comer *to eat* **1**
el comercio *commerce* **14**
la comida *food; meal; dinner, supper* **3**
el comienzo *beginning* **8**
el comino *cumin* 10
¿cómo? *how?/what?* **1**
¿Cómo es? *What is he/she/it like?* **P**
¿Cómo está (usted)? *How are you? (formal)* **P**
¿Cómo estás? *How are you? (familiar)* **P**
cómo no *of course* **8**
¿Cómo se dice... en español? *How do you say . . . in Spanish?* **P**
¿Cómo se escribe...? *How do you spell . . .?* **P**
¿Cómo se llama usted? *What is your name?* **P**
¿Cómo te llamas? *What is your name?* **P**
¿Cómo te va? *How is it going?* **1**
la cómoda *dresser* **5**
cómodo/a *comfortable* **6**
el/la compañero/a *partner, classmate* **P**
el/la compañero/a de cuarto *roommate* 1
la compañía *company* **9**
la compañía (de danza/teatro) *(dance/theater) company* **13**
la comparsa *troupe* **8**
compartir *to share* **3**
la competencia *competition* 1
complejo/a *complex* 5
el comportamiento *behavior* 4, 9
comprar *to buy* **1**
las compras *shopping* **6**
¿Comprenden?/¿Comprendes? *Do you understand?* **P**
comprender *to understand* **1**
la computación *computer science* **1**
la computadora *computer* **P**
la computadora portátil *laptop* **P**
común *common* 1
el comunicado de prensa *press release* 13
comunicarse *to communicate with* **4**
con *with* **1**
con anterioridad *in advance* **8**
Con mucho gusto. *With pleasure.* 1
con permiso *pardon me, excuse me* **P**
¿Con qué frecuencia? *How often?* 1
con tal (de) que *provided that* **14**
la concha *shell* 8
el concierto *concert* P
el concurso *contest* 7, 8
la condición *condition* **14**
el condimento *condiment* **10**
el/la conductor/a *driver* 15
conectarse (a) *to connect (to)* **4, 15**
confirmar *to confirm* 1
el congelador *freezer* 10
congelar(se) *to freeze* **7**
conmigo *with me* **7**
conocer(se) (zc) *to know (each other)* **3, 4**
conocido/a *well-known* **13**
el conocimiento *knowledge* **15**
el/la consejero/a *adviser* 1
el consejo *advice* 4
conservar *to conserve* **15**
la consola *control panel* 4

la consola de videojuegos *games console* 5
construir (y) *to build, to develop* 5, **7**, **15**
el consultorio *office (of doctor, dentist, etc.)* **9**
consumir *to consume* **10**
la contabilidad *accounting* 1
contactar *to network* 13
el/la contador/a *accountant* **9**
la contaminación *pollution* 12, **15**
(no) contaminante *(non)polluting* **15**
contar (ue) *to tell* 9
contemporáneo/a *contemporary* **13**
contento/a *happy, glad* 1, **2**
Contesta/Contesten, por favor. *Please answer.* **P**
contigo *with you (familiar)* **7**
contra *against* 11
contrario/a *opposing* **7**
la contraseña *password* 5, 15
el contraste *contrast* **13**
el contrato *contract* 9
contribuir (y) *to contribute* **15**
el control remoto *remote control* 4
controlar *to monitor* 4
conversador/a *talkative* **2**
conversar *to talk, to converse* **1**
convivir *to live with* 4
la copa *(stemmed) glass* **10**
el corazón *heart* **11**
la corbata *tie* **6**
el cordero *lamb* **10**
la cordillera *mountain range* 6
el corpiño *bra* 6
corregir (i, i) (j) *to correct* 6
el correo *mail* 5, 14
el correo electrónico *email* 4, 11, 14, 15
el correo expreso *overnight mail* 6
correr *to run* **1**
la corrida de toros *bullfight* 2
la corriente *current* 12
la corrupción *corruption* **14**
cortar *to cut* **9**
la cortesía *courtesy* P
la cortina *curtain* **5**
corto/a *short (in length)* **2**
la cosa *thing* **2**
cosechado/a *harvested* 5
cosechar *to harvest* **9**
la costa *coast* 6
costar (ue) *to cost* **4**
costarricense *Costa Rican* **2**
la costilla *rib* **10**
la costumbre *custom* **8**
cotidiano/a *everyday* 13
el crecimiento *growth* 5, **14**
creer *to believe* 4, **5**
la crema *cream* **10**
la crema agria *sour cream* **10**
criar *to raise (animals)* **15**
el crucero *cruise* **12**
crudo/a *raw* **10**
la crueldad *cruelty* 13
el cuaderno *notebook* **P**
la cuadra *city block* **12**
cuadrado/a *square* 15
el cuadro *picture, painting* 3, **5**
¿Cuál es la fecha? *What is the date?* **P**
¿cuál(es)? *which?* **1**
¿cuándo? *when?* **1**
¿Cuántas clases tienes? *How many classes do you have?* **1**
¿Cuánto cuesta? *How much does it cost?* **1**
¿Cuánto tiempo hace que...? *How long has it been since . . .?* 4
¿cuánto/a? *how much?* **1**
¿cuántos/as? *how many?* **1**
la Cuaresma *Lent* 6, 8
el cuarto *room; bedroom* 1, 2, **5**
cuarto/a *fourth* **5**
cubano/a *Cuban* **2**
cubista *cubist* **13**
cubrir *to cover* **15**
la cuchara *spoon* **10**
la cucharada *tablespoon* 10
la cucharita *teaspoon* **10**
el cuchillo *knife* **10**
el cuello *neck* 6, **11**
la cuenca *(river) basin* **15**
la cuenta *bead* 8
el cuento *story* **13**
el cuero *leather* **6**
el cuerpo (humano) *the (human) body* 6, **11**
cuidadosamente *carefully* 5
cuidadoso/a *thorough, careful* 9
cuidar(se) (de) *to take care (of)* **11**
Cuídate. *Take care. (informal)* 2
cultivar *to grow, to cultivate* **9**
el cultivo *farming, crops* **15**
el cumpleaños *birthday* P, **3**
cumplir *to turn (an age)* 5; *to fulfill* 7, 14
el/la cuñado/a *brother-/sister-in-law* 6
curar *to cure* **11**
el currículum *résumé* **9**
el curso *course* 1
el cuy *guinea pig* 10
cuyo/a *whose* 13

D

la danza *dance* **13**
el/la danzarín/danzarina *dancer* 8
dar *to give* 1, 4, **6**
dar una vuelta *to take a walk* **8**
darse cuenta *to realize* 12
los datos *facts* 6; *data, information* **14**
de *of, from* P, **2**
¡De acuerdo! *I agree!* 3
de color café *brown* **2**
de color entero *solid* **6**
de cuadros *plaid* **6**
de estatura mediana *average, medium height* **2**
de ida y vuelta *round-trip* **12**
de la mañana *in the morning* P
de la noche *at night* P
de la tarde *in the afternoon/evening* P
de lunares *polka-dotted* **6**
de nada *you're welcome* **P**
¡De ninguna manera! *Absolutely not!* 2
¿de quién? *whose?* **2**
de rayas *striped* **6**
debajo (de) *under* **P**
deber *should, to have to* **1**
debido a *due to* **14**
débil *weak* **2**
la década *decade* 6
el/la **decano/a** *dean* 3
décimo/a *tenth* **5**
decir (i) (g) *to say, to tell* **4**
decorar *to decorate* 10
dedicado/a *dedicated* 9
el dedo *finger* **11**
el dedo del pie *toe* **11**
la deforestación *deforestation* **15**
dejar *to leave, to quit* **9**
del (contraction of **de** + **el**) *of the* **2**
delante de *in front of* **P**
delgado/a *thin* **2**
demostrar (ue) *to show, to demonstrate* **4**
el departamento *apartment* 5
el/la dependiente/a *salesperson* 1
el deporte *sport* 1, 2, **7**
los deportes de riesgo *extreme sports* **7**
el/la deportista *athlete* 7
deprimido/a *depressed* 4, 11
la derecha *right (direction)* **12**
derecho *straight (ahead)* **12**
el derecho *law* **1**; *right* 9, **14**
derramar *to spill* 10
derretido/a *melted* 10
el desafío *challenge* **14**
desafortunado/a *unfortunate* 12
la desaparición *disappearance* **15**
desarmar *take apart* 9
desarrollado/a *developed* 11
desarrollar *to develop* **13**
el desarrollo *development* **14**
el desastre *disaster* 5
desayunar *to have breakfast* **4**
el desayuno *breakfast* **3**
descalzo/a *barefoot* 6
descansar *to rest* **3**
descargar(se) *to lose charge, to die (devices)* **15**
descomponerse (g) *to break down* **12, 15**
desconsiderado/a *inconsiderate* 11
describir *to describe* 6
la descripción *description* 5
el descubrimiento *discovery* 15
descuidado/a *careless, sloppy* 9
desde *from, since* P, **13**
desear *to want; to wish* **2**
desechable *disposable* 15
el desempleo *unemployment* 5, **14**
el desenlace *resolution* 15
desfilar *to parade; to march* **8**
el desfile *parade* 2, **8**
el deshielo *melting* **15**
la desigualdad *inequality* **14**
desleal *disloyal* 11
desnudo/a *naked* **13**
desordenado/a *messy* 5
desorganizado/a *disorganized* 2
la despedida *leave-taking* P
despedir (i, i) *to fire, lay off* 9
despedirse (i, i) *to say goodbye* **7**
despegar *to take off (aircraft)* **15**
despertarse (ie) *to wake up* **4**
el desplazamiento *movement, displacement* **14**
desplazarse *to move, to be displaced* **14**
después *after, later on* 2, **3**
después (de) que *after* **14**
destacado/a *outstanding* 8; *prominent* **13**
destapar *to uncover* 10
destrozar *to destroy* 10
destruir (y) *to destroy* **7**
la desventaja *disadvantage* 4, 5
detallista *meticulous, detail-oriented* 9
detener (ie) (g) *to stop, detain* 9
detestar *to hate, loathe* 4
detrás (de) *behind* **P**
la deuda *debt* 14
el día *day* **1**
el Día de Acción de Gracias *Thanksgiving* **8**
el Día de la Independencia de México *Mexican Independence Day* **8**
el Día de la Madre *Mother's Day* **8**
el Día de las Brujas *Halloween* **8**
el Día de los Enamorados/del Amor y de la Amistad *Valentine's Day* **8**
el Día de los Muertos/Difuntos *Day of the Dead* **8**
el Día del Padre *Father's Day* **8**
el día feriado *legal holiday* 8
el día festivo *holiday* 8
diabético/a *diabetic* 10
dibujar *to draw* 5

el dibujo *drawing* 4
el diccionario *dictionary* **1**
diciembre *December* **P**
la dictadura *dictatorship* 13
el diente *tooth* **11**
el diente de ajo *garlic clove* 10
difícil *difficult* **1**
el/la difunto/a *deceased person* **8**
¿Diga?/¿Dígame? *Hello? (telephone greeting)* 3
digitalizado/a *digital* **15**
Dile a tu compañero/a... *Tell your partner . . .* **P**
el dinero *money* **6**
el dios *god* 11
la dirección *address* P; *direction* **12**
el/la director/a *director* **13**
dirigir (j) *to direct* 13
el disco *album* **13**
la discoteca *nightclub* **1**
la discriminación *discrimination* **14**
disculparse *to apologize* **7**
discutir *to argue* 5, **7**
la diseminación *dispersal, dissemination* **15**
el/la diseñador/a *designer* 6, 7
el diseño *design* **6**
el diseño gráfico *graphic design* 1
disfrazarse *to wear a costume* **8**
disfrutar *to enjoy* 5, 6, 11
el disgusto *annoyance* 10
disminuir (y) *to decrease* **14**
disponible *available* 12
el dispositivo (móvil) *(mobile) device* 1, 4, **15**
distraído/a *distracted* 12
la distribución *layout* 5
la diversidad *diversity* 2, **14**
la diversión *fun* **3**
divertido/a *funny, amusing* **2**
divertirse (ie, i) *to have fun, enjoy* **4, 7**
divorciado/a *divorced* **4**
doblar *to fold* **5**; *to turn* **12**
doler (ue) *to hurt; to ache* **11**
el dolor *pain, ache* **11**
el dolor de estómago *stomachache* 2, 10
domingo *Sunday* **P**
dominicano/a *Dominican* P, **2**
donde *where, wherever* **14**
¿dónde? *where?* **1**
¿Dónde está...? *Where is . . .?* **P**
dorar *to brown* 10
dormir (ue) la siesta *to take a nap* **4**
dormir(se) (ue) *to sleep; to fall asleep* **4**
el dormitorio *bedroom* 5
dos terceras partes *two-thirds* 15
dos veces *twice* 3
el drama *drama* 1
la ducha *shower* **5**
duchar(se) *to give a shower to; to take a shower* **4**
el/la dueño/a *owner* 4
el dulce *candy/sweets* **10**
duradero/a *long lasting* 14
durante *during* 1, **3**
durar *to last* **8**
duro/a *hard* 14

E

la economía *economics* **1**
económico/a *economic* **14**
ecuatoriano/a *Ecuadorian* **2**
la edad *age* 2, 4, 5
el edificio *building* 1, 2, **5**
el/la ejecutivo/a *executive* **9**
el ejercicio *exercise* 2
el ejército *army* 12
él *he* **P**
el año/mes pasado *last year/month* **6**
el/la *the* **P**
el/la electricista *electrician* **9**
los electrodomésticos *appliances* **5**
el elenco *cast* 4
ella *she* **P**
ellos/as *they* **1**
emergente *emerging* 14
la emigración *emigration* 9, **14**
el/la emigrante *emigrant* **14**
emigrar *to emigrate* **14**
la empatía *empathy* 14
empezar (ie) *to begin, to start* **4**
el/la empleado/a *employee* 2, **9**
el empleo *employment* **14**
la empresa *company* **9**
el/la empresario/a *entrepreneur* 2
en *in, on* **P**
En aquellos tiempos... *In those days . . .* 8
en cambio *however* 13
en cuanto *as soon as* **14**
en efectivo *cash* **6**
En esos años... *During those years . . .* 8
en línea *online* **3**
en punto *on the dot/sharp* **P**
¿En que página? *On what page?* **P**
¿En qué puedo servirle(s)? *How may I help you?* **6**
en realidad *in fact, really* **9**
en vez de *instead of* 4, **14**
en vivo *live* **8**
enamorarse *to fall in love* 8
el encaje *lace* 13
Encantado/a. *Pleased/Nice to meet you.* **P**
encantar *to like a lot, to love* 5, **6**
encender (ie) *to start, to turn on* 15
encima de *on, on top of* **P**
encontrar (ue) *to find* **4**
el encuentro *encounter* P
la energía (alternativa/eólica/solar) *(alternative/wind/solar) energy* **15**
enero *January* **P**
enfermarse *to get sick* 7
la enfermedad *illness* 2, **11**
el/la enfermero/a *nurse* **9, 11**
enfermo/a *sick* 2, 3, **11**
el/la enfermo/a *ill/sick person* **11**
enfocarse *to focus* **15**
el enfoque *focus* 1
enfrente (de) *in front of, facing* **P**
enfriar *to chill* 10
el enlace *link* **15**
enlatado/a *canned* 10
enojado/a *angry* **2**
enojarse *to get angry* **7**
el enrutador inalámbrico *wireless router* 4, 5
la ensalada *salad* **3**
el ensayo *essay, test* 5; *rehearsal* 9
enseguida *immediately, right away* **6**
enseñar *to teach* 2
entender (ie) *to understand* **4**
enterarse *to find out, notice* 7
enterrar (ie) *to bury* 8
la **entonación** *intonation* 7
entonces *then* **8**
el entorno *surroundings, environment* **15**
entrar (en) *to go in, to enter* **6**
entre *between* **P**
entregar *to deliver* 5; *to turn in* 9
entregar a domicilio *to deliver* 3
el/la entrenador/a *coach* **7**
el entrenamiento *training* 9
el entretenimiento *entertainment* 2, 6
la entrevista *interview* 1, **9**
entrevistar *to interview* 1, 9
el envase *packaging* 15
enviar *to send* 3, 8, **9**
la envidia *envy* 13
la época *era, age* 3
el equipaje (de mano) *(carry-on) luggage* **12**
el equipo *team* 1, 2, 4, **7**
el equipo deportivo *sports equipment* **7**
la erosión *erosion* **15**
(Es) a las... *It is at . . . (time)* P
la escala *stopover* **12**
la escalera *stairs* **5**
los escalofríos *chills* 11
escapar(se) *to escape, to overlook* **15**
el escaparate *store window* **6**
la escasez *shortage* 14
la escena *scene* **13**
el escenario *stage* **13**
la esclusa *lock (of a canal)* 12
escoger (j) *to choose* 4, 10
la escolarización *schooling* **14**
el escombro *rubble* 15
esconder *to hide* 10
el escorpión *scorpion* 11
escribir *to write* **1**
el/la escritor/a *writer* P, 2, 6, **13**
el escritorio *desk* **P**
escuchar *to listen (to)* **1**
el escudo *coat of arms* 8, 9
el/la escultor/a *sculptor* **13**
la escultura *sculpture* 7, **13**
ese/esa/eso *that (adjective)* **P**; *(pronoun)* **5**
la esmeralda *emerald* 6
esos/esas *those* **5**
el espacio *space* 5
los espaguetis *spaghetti* **3**
la espalda *back* **11**
el **español** *Spanish (language)* **P**
español/a *Spanish* **1, 2**
espantoso/a *scary* 8
el espárrago *asparagus* 3
el/la **especialista** *specialist* 11
las especias *spices* **10**
la especie en peligro de extinción *endangered species* 15
el espejo *mirror* **5**
el espejo retrovisor *rearview mirror* **12**
la esperanza de vida *life expectancy* **14**
esperar *to wait for* **5, 9**; *to hope, to expect* **11**
las espinacas *spinach* **10**
el/la esposo/a *husband/wife* **2, 4**
el esqueleto *skeleton* 8
el **esquí** *skiing* **7**
esquiar *to ski* **7**
la esquina *corner* **12**
los esquís *skis* 7
está despejado *it's clear* **7**
esta noche *tonight* 3
está nublado *it's cloudy* **7**
establecer (zc) *to establish* 1
la estación *season* **P**
el estacionamiento *parking* 12
la estadía *stay* 11
el estadio *stadium* 4, 7
la estadística *statistics* 1, **14**
el estado *state* 5
el estado civil *marital status* 9
el estado libre asociado *commonwealth* 2
estar *to be* **P, 1**
estar contento/a (de) *to be happy about* **11**
estar de moda *to be fashionable* **6**
Este/a es... *This is . . .* **P**
el estereotipo *stereotype* 2
el estilo *style* **5, 13**
el estómago *stomach* **11**
estornudar *to sneeze* **11**

la estrategia *strategy* 1
el estrecho *strait* 14
estrecho/a *narrow, tight* **6**
la estrella *star* **13**
estresarse *to get stressed* 7
el/la estudiante *student* **P**
estudiar *to study* **1**
estudioso/a *studious* **1**
la estufa *stove* **5**
la estufa de leña *wood stove* 9
estupendamente *wonderfully* **8**
estupendo/a *great, wonderful* **3**
la etnia *ethnic group* 2
el euro *euro* **1**
evitar *to avoid* 2, 9, **11**
el examen *exam* **1**
examinar *to examine* **11**
excelente *excellent* **1**
la excursión *outing, trip* **12**
exhibir *to exhibit* **13**
el éxito *success* P, 4, **13**
la experiencia *experience* **9**
explicar *to explain* **6**
el/la explorador/a *explorer* 6
explotar *to exploit* **9**
la exportación *export* **9, 14**
la exposición *exhibition* 3
la extinción *extinction* **15**
extinguido/a *extinct* **15**
extrañar *to miss* 10
el/la extranjero/a *foreigner* **14**
(en) el extranjero *abroad* 4

F

la fábrica *factory* **9**
fabricar *to manufacture, to make* 10
la fábula *fable* 14
fabuloso/a *fabulous, great* **3**
fácil *easy* **1**
el factor *factor* **14**
facturar *to check (luggage)* **12**
la facultad *school, department* **1**
la falda *skirt* **6**
falso/a *false* P
la falta (de) *lack (of)* 2, 5
faltar *to miss* 15
la familia *family* **4**
la familia mixta *blended family* 4
famoso/a *famous* 4
el fantasma *ghost* 8
el/la farmacéutico/a *pharmacist* **11**
la farmacia *pharmacy* **11**
fascinar *to like a lot, to love* **6**
fastidioso/a *annoying, frustrating* 11
favorito/a *favorite* P, **1**
febrero *February* **P**
la fecha *date* **P**
felicidades *congratulations* **3**
¡Fenomenal! *Great!* 3
feo/a *ugly* **2**
fértil *fertile* **9**
el festival *festival* **8**
la festividad *festival, celebration* 8
fiable *reliable* 6
la fibra *fiber* 10
la fiebre *fever* 10, **11**
la fiesta *party* 3; *festival; holiday; celebration* **8**
¡Fíjate qué noticia! *How about that!* 3
fijo/a *fixed* 1
el fin de semana *weekend* **1**
el Fin del Año *New Year's Eve* **8**
financiero/a *financial* **14**
la finca *ranch, farm* **9**
el fiordo *fjord* 14
firmar *to sign* 9
la flauta *flute* **13**
la flecha *arrow* 5
la flor *flower* **2**
la floristería *florist* 9
flotante *floating* 3
el flujo *flow* **14**
al fondo *in the background* **13**
la forma *shape, form* P, **1, 13**
formar *to form* 1
el formulario *form* 1
fortalecer (zc) *to strengthen* 10
el fracaso *failure* **13**
fracturar(se) *to fracture, to break* **11**
el francés *French (language)* **1**
francés/francesa *French* 2
la franja *stripe* 9
la frazada *blanket* 5
frecuentemente *frequently, often* **4**
el fregadero *kitchen sink* **5**
freír (i, i) *to fry* **10**
frenar *to slow down* **14**
la frente *forehead* **11**
la fresa *strawberry* **10**
los frijoles *beans* **3, 10**
frío/a *cold* **3**
la fritada *fried food (meat)* 10
frito/a *fried* **3**
la frontera *border* 7, 14
frustrar *to frustrate* 11
la fruta *fruit* 2, **3, 10**
los fuegos artificiales *fireworks* **8**
la fuente de ingresos *source of income* **9**
fuerte *strong* **2**
la fuerza laboral *workforce* **9**
fumar *to smoke* 9, **11**
la función *function, purpose* P, 1
funcionar *to work/run* 5
el/la fundador/a *founder* 2, 6
el fútbol (americano) *soccer (football)* 1, **7**

G

las gafas *glasses* 11
las gafas de sol *sunglasses* **6**
galardonado/a *awarded* **13**
la galleta *cookie* **10**
el gallo pinto *rice and beans dish* 12
la ganancia *profit* 11
ganar *to earn* 5; *to win* 2, **7**
el garaje *garage* **5**
los garbanzos *garbanzo beans* **10**
la garganta *throat* 7, **11**
la garra *claw* 14
gastar *to spend* 3, **6**
el gasto *expense* 5
la gastronomía *gastronomy* 2
el/la gato/a *cat* **2**
gemelo/a *twin* **4**
generalmente *generally* 1, 5, **8**
genéticamente *genetically* **15**
la gente *people* **8**
la geografía *geography* P, **1**
el/la gerente (de ventas) *(sales) manager* **9**
el gimnasio *gymnasium* **1**
el/la gitano/a *gypsy* 13
la globalización *globalization* 11
el globo *balloon* 4
el/la **gobernador/a** *governor* 3
el/la gobernante *ruler* 8
el gobierno *government* 1, **11**
el golf *golf* **7**
gordo/a *fat* **2**
el gorila *gorilla* 3
la gorra *baseball cap* **6**
el gorro *hat* **6**
grabado/a *engraved* 13
grabar *to record* 13
gracias *thanks* **P**
¡Gracias a Dios! *Thank goodness!* 15
gracioso/a *humorous* 15
grados Celsius/centígrados *degrees Celsius/centigrade* 7
graduarse *to graduate* 4
grande *big* **1**
gratis *free (of charge)* 9
gratuito/a *free (of charge)* 9
grave *serious* 6, **11**
la gripe *flu* **11**
gris *gray* **2**
gritar *to shout* 8
la guagua *bus* 12
el guante *glove* **6**
la guantera *glove compartment* **12**
guapo/a *good-looking, handsome* **2**
guardar *to put away* 10; *to save* **15**
guatemalteco/a *Guatemalan* **2**
la guerra *war* 9, 13
el/la guía *guide* 4, 12
la guirnalda *garland* 8
la guitarra *guitar* **3**
el/la guitarrista *guitarist* **13**
gustar *to like, to be pleasing to* **2, 6, 11**

H

la habitación *bedroom* **5**
la habitación doble *double room* **12**
la habitación sencilla *single room* **12**
el/la habitante *inhabitant* 2
hablador/a *talkative* 2
el/la hablante *speaker* P
hablar *to speak* **1**
Hablen (sobre...). *Talk (about . . .).* **P**
Hace buen/mal tiempo. *The weather is good/bad.* **P**
hace calor *it's hot* **7**
hace fresco *it's cool* **7**
hace frío *it's cold* **7**
Hace sol. *It's sunny.* **P**
Hace un día/mes/año (que)... *It's been a day/month/year since . . .* **6**
hace viento *it's windy* **7**
hacer (g) *to do; to make* **3**
hacer cola *to stand in line* **12**
hacer malabarismos *to juggle* 9
hacer surf *to surf* **7**
hacia *toward* 7
la hamaca *hammock* 12
la hamburguesa *hamburger* **3**
la harina *flour* **10**
hasta *even* P; *until, (up) to* **13, 14**
hasta luego *see you later* **P**
hasta mañana *see you tomorrow* **P**
hasta pronto *see you soon* **P**
hay *there is, there are* **P**
la heladera *refrigerator* 5
la **heladería** *ice cream shop* 6
el helado *ice cream* **3**
el hemisferio *hemisphere* P
el herbolario *herbal shop* 11
la herencia *heredity* 2; *heritage* 4
la herida *wound* 11
el/la hermano/a *brother/sister* **4**
hermoso/a *beautiful* **8**
la herramienta *tool* 6
hervir (ie, i) *to boil* **10**
el hielo *ice* **7**
la hierba medicinal *medicinal herb* **11**
las hierbas *herbs* **10**
el hierro *iron* **9**
el higo *fig* 10

el/la hijo/a *son/daughter* **4**
los hijos *children* **4**
el/la hincha *fan* **7**
hinchado/a *swollen* 11
el hinchazón *swelling* 11
hispano/a *Hispanic* **2**
la historia *history* **1**
histórico/a *historic* 8
el hockey sobre hierba *field hockey* **7**
el hogar *home* 14
la hoja *leaf* **5**
hola *hi, hello* **P**
el hombre *man* **3**
el hombre/la mujer de negocios *businessman/businesswoman* **9**
el hombro *shoulder* **11**
la homeopatía *homeopathy* 11
hondureño/a *Honduran* **2**
la hora *hour, time* **P**
el horario *schedule* P, 1, 4
hornear *to bake* 10
el horno *oven* **5**
horroroso/a *dreadful, horrific* 8
el hospital *hospital* **11**
el hotel *hotel* **12**
hoy *today* **P**
hoy en día *nowadays* **8**
Hoy es... *Today is . . .* **P**
el hueso *bone* 8, **11**
el huevo *egg* **3**
las humanidades *humanities* **1**
el humo *smoke* 12
el hundimiento *sinking* 14
el huracán *hurricane* 5, 10

I

el idioma *language* 1
la iglesia *church* 4, 5
la igualdad *equality* **14**
Igualmente. *Likewise.* **P**
la imaginación *imagination* 5
¡Imagínate! *Imagine that!* 3
imparcial *impartial* 2
el imperio *empire* 3, 10
el impermeable *raincoat* **6**
la impresora multifuncional *multifunction printer* 5
imprevisto/a *unforeseen* 12
imprimir *to print* 10
el impuesto *tax* 9, 14
incendiarse *to catch on fire* 8
el incendio *fire* **9**
inclusivo/a *inclusive* 8
la incultura *ignorance* 13
indeciso/a *indecisive* 5
independizarse *to become independent* 5
el/la indocumentado/a *undocumented person* 9, 14
la industria textil *textile industry* **9**
el índice *rate* **14**
la infancia *childhood* 4
la infección *infection* **11**
infeccioso/a *infectious* 11
influyente *influential* 2
la informática *computer science* **1**
el informe *report* 9
el infortunio *misfortune* 15
la infraestructura *infrastructure* **14**
el/la ingeniero/a *engineer* **9**
el inglés *English (language)* **1**
el ingreso (alto/bajo) *(low/high) income* **14**
la injusticia *injustice* 13
inmediatamente *immediately* 5
(de) inmediato *immediately* 5
la inmigración *immigration* 9, **14**
el/la inmigrante *immigrant* **14**
la inmundicia *filth* 14
el inodoro *toilet* **5**
inolvidable *unforgettable* **13**
insistir (en) *to insist* **11**
el/la inspector/a de aduana *customs agent* **12**
la inteligencia artificial *artificial intelligence* **15**
el intercambio *exchange* P, 1, **15**
interesante *interesting* **1**
interesar *to interest, to matter* 1, **6**
interpretar *to perform, to play* **13**
el/la intérprete *interpreter* **9**; *performer, artist* **13**
la inundación *flood* 5, **15**
invertir (ie, i) *to invest* 14
la investigación *research* 1, 4
el invierno *winter* **P**
el/la invitado/a *guest* 4, 10
invitar *to invite* **8**
involucrado/a *involved* 9
la inyección *injection* **11**
ir *to go* **3**
ir a + ***infinitive*** *to be going to do something* 3
ir de compras *to go shopping* 4, **6**
ir de ***bowling*** *to go bowling* 7
la isla *island* 4, 11
la izquierda *left* **12**

J

el jabón *soap* **5**
jamás *never, (not) ever* **12**
el jamón *ham* **3**
japonés/japonesa *Japanese* 2
el jardín *garden* **5**
los jeans *jeans* **6**
el/la jefe/a *boss* **9**
joven *young* **2**
el/la joven *young man/woman* 1, **3**
la joya *piece of jewelry* **6**
la joyería *jewelry store* 6
jubilarse *to retire* 12
jueves *Thursday* **P**
el/la juez *judge* 7, **9**
el/la jugador/a *player* 2, **7**
jugar (ue) *to play (a game, sport)* 3, **4**
jugar (al) boliche *to go bowling* 7
jugar a los bolos *to bowl* **7**
el jugo *juice* **3**
el juguete *toy* **6**
julio *July* **P**
junio *June* **P**
juntos/as *together* **2**

K

el kétchup *ketchup* **10**

L

el labio *lip* **11**
laboral *work, job* **14**
el ladrón *robber, thief* 8, 9
el lago *lake* 5, **7**
la lámpara *lamp* **5**
la lana *wool* **6**
la langosta *lobster* **10**
lanzar *to throw* 7
el lápiz *pencil* **P**
largo/a *long* **2**
la lástima *pity, shame* **1, 11**
el latido del corazón *heartbeat* 15
el lavabo *bathroom sink* **5**
la lavadora *washing machine* 5
la lavandería *laundry room* **5**
el lavaplatos *dishwasher* 4, **5**
lavar *to wash* **4, 5**
la lección *lesson* 1
la leche *milk* **3**
la leche de coco *coconut milk* **10**
la leche desnatada *skim milk* 3
la lechuga *lettuce* **3**
la lectura *reading* P, 13
Lee. *Read.* **P**
leer *to read* **1**
legislar *to legislate* 14
la legumbre *legumes* **10**
lejano/a *distant* 4
lejos (de) *far (from)* **5**
la lengua *language* P, 1, 2, **9**
lentamente *slowly* 5
las lentejas *lentils* **10**
los lentes de contacto *contact lenses* **2**
Levanta la mano. *Raise your hand.* **P**
levantar pesas *to lift weights* **7**
levantar(se) *to raise, to lift; to get up* **4**
la ley *law* 1, **14**
la leyenda *legend* 8
la libra *pound* 10
la librería *bookstore* **1**
el libro *book* **P**
la licencia de conducir *driver's license* **12**
la licuadora *blender* 10
el lienzo *canvas* 13
el limón *lemon* 1, **10**
el limpiaparabrisas *windshield wiper* **12**
limpiar *to clean* 4, **5**
limpiar en seco *to dry clean* 6
limpio/a *clean* **5**
lindo/a *pretty, nice-looking* 2, 5
la línea aérea *airline* **12**
listo/a *smart; ready* **2**; *clever* 6
la literatura *literature* P, **1**
el litio *lithium* 13
liviano/a *light* 2
llamar(se) *to call, to be named* **4**
llamativo/a *striking* 8
llanero/a *of the plains* 15
la llanta *tire* **12**
el llapingacho *potato dish from Ecuador* 10
la llave *key* 6, 9, **12**
llegar *to arrive* **1**
llenar *to fill (out)* **9**
lleno/a *full* 3
llevar *to bring* 4; *to wear; to take* **6**
llevarse bien *to get along (with)* 4
llorar *to cry* 5, 8
llover (ue) *to rain* **7**
Llueve/Está lloviendo. *It's raining.* **P**
la lluvia *rain* **7**
lo importante *the important thing* **9**
Lo siento. *I'm sorry (to hear that).* **P**
Lo vamos a pasar muy bien. *We are going to have a good time.* 3
la localización *location* 2
el/la locutor/a *radio announcer* **9**
el logro *achievement* **14**
las luces intermitentes *flashers, hazard lights* **12**
luchar *to fight* **14**
luego *after, later* **3**
el lugar *place* **1**
el lujo *luxury* 13
la luna de miel *honeymoon* 4
lunes *Monday* **P**
la luz (las luces) *light(s)* **5, 12, 13**

M

machacado/a *crushed* 10
la madera *wood* 2, **9**

la madrastra *stepmother* **4**
la madre *mother* **4**
la madre soltera *single mother* 4
magnífico/a *great* **6**
el maíz *corn* **3, 10**
la maleta *suitcase* 6, **12**
el maletero *trunk* **12**
maligno/a *evil* 8
las mallas *tights; leggings* **6**
mal, malo/a *bad* **P;** *ill* 6
la malva *mallow* 11
la mamá *mom* **4**
mañana *tomorrow (adv.)* **P, 3**
la mañana *morning* **P**
la mancha *spot, stain* 10
mandar *to send* 4, **6**
manejar *to drive* 4, 11, **12**
la manifestación *demonstration, protest* 7
manifestarse *to show up, to appear* 11
la mano *hand* 4, 6, **11**
la manta *blanket* **5**
el mantel *tablecloth* **10**
mantener (ie) (g) *to keep; to maintain* **8**
la mantequilla *butter* **10**
la manzana *apple* 2, **10**
la manzanilla *chamomile* 11
el mapa *map* **1**
maquillarse *to put on makeup* **4**
la máquina *machine* 9, **15**
el mar *sea* **3**
la maracuyá *passion fruit* **10**
el maratón *marathon* 1, 3
maravilloso/a *marvelous* **8**
la marca *brand-name* 6; *brand* 7
el marcador *marker* **P;** *scoreboard* 5
el marcapasos *pacemaker* 15
marcar *to mark* 1; *to indicate* 9
la margarina *margarine* **10**
el marido *husband* 4
marinar *to marinate* **10**
marino/a *marine* **15**
la mariposa *butterfly* 5
los mariscos *seafood* 3; *shellfish* **10**
marrón *brown* **2**
marroquí *Moroccan* 2
martes *Tuesday* **P**
marzo *March* **P**
más *more* **1**
más allá *beyond* 11
Más alto, por favor. *Louder, please.* **P**
más de *more than* P, **8**
Más despacio, por favor. *More slowly, please.* **P**
más o menos *about, more or less* **P**
más tarde *later* **3**
más... que *more than . . .* 4, **8**
la masa *dough* 4, 10
masticar *to chew* 11
matar *to kill* 8, 13
las matemáticas *mathematics* **1**
la materia *subject* **1**
el material *material* **6**
la maternidad *motherhood* **13**
el matrimonio *marriage* **4**
el matrimonio igualitario *same-sex marriage* 4
mayo *May* **P**
la mayonesa *mayonnaise* 4, **10**
el/la mayor *the oldest* **4**
mayor *old* **2**
la mayoría *majority* 5
me encanta... *I love . . .* **3**
me gustaría... *I would like . . .* **6**
me llamo... *my name is . . .* **P**
el mechero *gas burner* 15
la media *median* 9
las medias *stockings, socks* **6**
el medicamento *medicine* 9, **11**
la medicina *medicine* **1, 11**
el/la médico/a *medical doctor* **9**
la medida *step, measure* 12, **15**
el medio ambiente *environment* 12, **15**
el medio de transporte *transportation* **12**
el medio hermano / la media hermana *half-brother/half-sister* 4
medioambiental *environmental* 12
medir (i) *to measure* **15**
la mejilla *cheek* **11**
mejor *better* P, **8**
el/la mejor *the best* **8**
mejorar *to improve* **14**
melodioso/a *melodious* 4
el melón *melon* **10**
el/la menor *the youngest* **4;** *the least* **8**
menos *less, before* **P**
menos de *less than* **8**
menos... que *less . . . than* **8**
el mensaje *message* **15**
el mensaje (de texto) *(text) message* 1
mentir (ie, i) *to lie* 11
la mentira *lie* 7
el mercado laboral *job market* 5
el mercado *market* **6**
merecer (zc) *to deserve* 8, 14
la merienda *snack, afternoon snack* 3
el mes *month* **P**
la mesa (de la computadora) *(computer) table* **P**
el mestizaje *fusion* 8, **13**
el/la mestizo/a *mixed race* 12
meter un gol *to score a goal* **7**
el metro *meter* 1; *subway* **12**
mexicano/a *Mexican* P, **2**
mezclar *to mix, to combine* 8, **10**
mi(s) *my* **P, 2**
la micro *bus* 12
la microcirugía *microsurgery* **15**
el microondas *microwave* **5**
la miel *honey* 11
el/la miembro *member* 4
mientras *while* **8;** *while, as long as* **14**
miércoles *Wednesday* **P**
la migración *migration* **14**
la migraña *migraine* 11
migratorio/a *migratory* **14**
la mina de cobre *copper mine* 9
minoritario/a *minority* 2
mirar *to look (at)* **1**
la Misa del Gallo *Midnight Mass* 8
la misma manera *the same way* 3
mismo/a *same* 1
misterioso/a *mysterious* 8
la mitad *half* 2, 5
la mochila *backpack* **P**
el/la mochilero/a *backpacker* 12
moderadamente *moderately* 10
módico/a *reasonable* 12
mojado/a *wet* 7, 10
molestar *to bother, to be bothered by* **11**
la molestia *discomfort* 11
molido/a *ground* 6, **10**
la **moneda** *currency* 3
el mono (araña) *(spider) monkey* 12
la montaña *mountain* 6
montar (en bicicleta) *to ride (a bicycle)* **1**
morado/a *purple* **2**
moreno/a *dark-haired; dark-skinned* **2**
morir (ue, u) *to die* **7**
la mortalidad infantil *child mortality* **14**
la mosca *fly* 14
la mostaza *mustard* **10**
el mostrador *counter* 11, **12**
mostrar (ue) *to show* **6**
el motor *motor* **12**
mover (ue) *to move* 5
muchas veces *often* **1**
mucho (adv.) *much, a lot* 1, **2**
Mucho gusto. *Nice to meet you.* **P**
mucho/a (adj.) *many* **2**
mudarse *to move* 5
la **mueblería** *furniture store* 6
los muebles *furniture* **5**
la muerte *death* **13**
muerto/a *dead* 6; *deceased* **8**
la mujer *woman* 3; *wife* 4
la multa *fine* **12**
el mundo *world* P, 1
la muñeca *wrist* **11**
el/la muñeco/a *doll, puppet* **8**
el mural *mural* **13**
la muralla *wall* 6
el músculo *muscle* **11**
el museo *museum* 1
la música *music* **3**
el/la musulmán/musulmana *Muslim* 1
mutuamente *mutually* 4
muy *very* **P**

N

nacer (zc) *to be born* 14
el **nacimiento** *birth* 7
la nacionalidad *nationality* **2, 14**
nada *nothing* **12**
nadar *to swim* **3**
nadie *no one, nobody* 5, **12**
naranja *orange (color)* 2
la naranja *orange* **3**
la nariz *nose* 6, **11**
narrar *to narrate* **13**
la natación *swimming* **7**
la naturaleza *nature* 4, **7**
la Navidad *Christmas* **8**
necesitar *to need* **1**
el negocio *business* 1, 6, 9
negro/a *black* **2**
el nervio *nerve* **11**
nevar (ie) *to snow* **7**
la nevera *refrigerator* 5
ni... ni *neither . . . nor* **2, 12**
nicaragüense *Nicaraguan* **2**
el nido *nest* 5
el/la nieto/a *grandson/granddaughter* **4**
los nietos *grandchildren* **4**
la nieve *snow* **7**
nigeriano/a *Nigerian* 2
ningún, ninguno/a *no, not any, none* **12**
el/la niño/a *child* **4**
el níquel *nickel* 9
el nivel *level* 11
el nivel del mar *sea level* **15**
No comprendo. *I don't understand.* **P**
No sé. *I don't know.* **P**
la Nochebuena *Christmas Eve* **8**
la Nochevieja *New Year's Eve* **8**
el nombre *name* P, 1
el **nordeste** *northeast* 4
la norma *norm, standard, regulation* 15
el **norte** *north* P, 4
norteamericano/a *North American* P, **2**
nosotros/as *we* **1**
las noticias *news* 1, **3**
las novedades *updates (information, news)* **15**
la novela *novel* **13**
el/la novelista *novelist* **13**
noveno/a *ninth* **5**

noviembre *November* **P**
el/la novio/a *fiancé(e); boyfriend/girlfriend* 2, **4**
la nube *cloud* **15**
nuestro/a *our* **2**
nuevo/a *new* **2**
el número *number* **P, 1**; *shoe size* 6
nunca *never* 1
nunca *never, (not) ever* **12**

O

o… o *either . . . or* **12**
la obra *work* 5, 12, **13**
la obra de arte *work of art* **13**
el/la obrero/a *worker* **9**
obtener (ie) (g) *to get (something)* 4
occidental *western* 11
el océano *ocean* 3
el ocio *leisure* 6; *free time* 11
octavo/a *eighth* **5**
octubre *October* **P**
la ocupación *occupation* **9**
ocupado/a *busy* 2, **4**
odiar *to hate* 4
el oeste *west* 7
la oficina *office* P, **1**
el oficio *trade* **9**
ofrecer (zc) *to offer* **9**
la ofrenda *offering* **8**
el oído *(inner) ear* **11**
Oiga, por favor. *Excuse me. (formal)* 1
¡Oigo! *Hello? (telephone greeting)* 3
oír (g) *to hear* **3**
ojalá (que)... *I/we hope (that) . . .* **11**
el ojo *eye* 2, **11**
oler (ue) (h) *to smell* 14
el olor *smell* 11, 14
olvidar(se) *to forget* 10, **15**
el omnibús *bus* 12
la oración *sentence* 4
el orden *order* P
el ordenador *computer* 1
ordenar *to tidy up* **5**
el orégano *oregano* 10
la oreja *(outer) ear* 6, **11**
el orgullo *pride* 12
el origen *origin* 2
el oro *gold* 2, 3, **6**
la orquesta *orchestra* 4
oscuro/a *dark* **2**
el oso perezoso *sloth* 6, 12
el otoño *fall* **P**
Otra vez. *Again.* **P**
otro/a *other, another* 1, 2
la oveja *sheep* **10**
¡Oye! *Hey! (informal)* 1

P

el/la paciente *patient* **11**
el padrastro *stepfather* **4**
el padre *father* **4**
el padre soltero *single father* 4
los padres *parents* **4**
pagano/a *pagan* 8
pagar *to pay (for)* 1, **6**
la página *page* 1, 4
el país *country* 1
el país de acogida *host country* **14**
el paisaje *landscape* 11, **13**
el pájaro *bird* 5, 12
la palabra *word* 1, 4
el palacio *palace* 7
pálido/a *pale* 2
las palomitas de maíz *popcorn* 10
los palos de golf *golf clubs* **7**
el pan *bread* **3, 10**
el pan dulce *bun, small cake* **10**
el pan tostado *toast* **3**
panameño/a *Panamanian* **2**
la pandilla *gang* 9
la pantalla *screen* **P**; *earring* 6
los pantalones *pants* **6**
los pantalones cortos *shorts* **6**
el pañuelo *handkerchief* **6**; *scarf* 7
la papa *potato* **3**
el papá *dad* **4**
el papalote *kite* 8
las papas fritas *French fries* **3**
la papaya *papaya* **10**
el papel *paper* 1; *role* 9
para *for, to* **1**
para que *so that* **14**
¿para qué? *why?/what for?* **1**
el parabrisas *windshield* **12**
el parachoques *bumper* **12**
el paraguas *umbrella* **6**
paraguayo/a *Paraguayan* **2**
el parapente *paragliding* **7**
el parásito *parasite* 11
pardo/a *brown* 2
parecer (zc) *to seem* 4, **6**
la pareja *couple; partner, significant other* **4**
la pareja de hecho *domestic partnership* 4
la pareja del mismo sexo *same-sex couple* 4
el parentesco *kinship* 4
el pariente *relative* **4**
el párrafo *paragraph* 4
la parrilla *grill* 10
el parque *park* 4
la parte *part* 1
participar *to participate* **1**
el partido *game, match* 4, **7**
pasado mañana *the day after tomorrow* **3**
el pasaje *ticket* **12**
el/la pasajero/a *passenger* **12**
el pasaporte *passport* **12**
pasar *to pass; to spend (time)* 1, **4**
pasar la aspiradora *to vacuum* **5**
pasarlo bien *to have a good time* 1
la Pascua *Easter* **8**
Pase/Pasen. *Come in.* 5
pasear *to take a walk, to stroll* 1, **4**
el pasillo *corridor, hall* **5**
el paso *step* 1
el pastel *cake* 5, 8; *pastry* **10**
la pastilla *pill* 9, **11**
la pata *leg, foot (of an animal)* 2
patinar *to skate* **7**
patrocinar *to sponsor* 12
el pavo *turkey* 8, **10**
la paz *peace* 13
el pecho *chest* **11**
la pechuga de pollo *chicken breast* 10
el/la pediatra *pediatrician* 11
pedir (i, i) *to ask for; to order* **3, 11**
peinar(se) *to comb (someone's hair); to comb (one's hair)* 4
pelado/a *peeled* 10
pelearse *to fight* 4, 9
la película *film, movie* 1, **3**
el peligro *danger* 8, 15
peligroso/a *dangerous* 8
pelirrojo/a *redhead* **2**
el pelo *hair* **2, 11**
la pelota *ball* **7**
el/la peluquero/a *hairdresser* **9**
la peña *club* 3
el penalti *penalty (in sports)* **7**
el pendiente *earring* 6
pensar (ie) *to think* **4**
pensar (ie) + ***infinitive*** *to plan to + verb* **4**
la pensión *guest house, hostel* 1; *boarding house* 14
peor *worse* **8**
el pepino *cucumber* **10**
pequeño/a *small* **1**
la pera *pear* **10**
perder (ie) *to lose* **7**
perderse (ie) *to get lost* **12**
la pérdida *loss* **15**
perdón *pardon me, excuse me* **P**
peregrinar *to make a pilgrimage* 11
el perejil *parsley* **10**
la pereza *laziness* 13
perezoso/a *lazy* **2**
perfectamente *perfectly* 5
¡Perfecto! *Perfect!* 3
el periódico *newspaper* 3
el/la periodista *journalist* 2, **9**
perjudicar *to harm, damage* 4
el permiso *permit* **14**
permitir *to permit; to allow* **11**
pero *but* **1**
el/la perro/a *dog* **2**
la persona *person* **P**
el personaje principal *main character* **13**
pertenecer (zc) *to belong* 4
peruano/a *Peruvian* **2**
la pesadilla *nightmare* 12
pesado/a *heavy* 14
la pescadería *fish market* **10**
el pescado *fish* **3, 10**
pesquero/a *(related to) fishing* **15**
la pestaña *eyelash* **11**
el petróleo *petroleum, oil* 4, **9**
picado/a *chopped* 10
la picadura *bite, sting* 11
picante *spicy* 8, **10**
el pico *beak* 14
el pie *foot* 2, 6, **11**
la piedra *stone* 13
la piel *skin* 11
la pierna *leg* 2, 6, **11**
la pileta *swimming pool* 5
la pimienta *pepper* **10**
el pimiento *bell pepper* **10**
la piña *pineapple* 3, **10**
el pincel de inclinación *tilt brush* 13
pintar *to paint* 13
el/la pintor/a *painter* 5, **13**
la pintura *painting* **13**
la pirámide *pyramid* 8
el/la pirata *hacker* 13
pisar *to set foot* 6
la piscina *swimming pool* **5**
la piscina termal *hot springs* 12
el piso *floor; apartment* **5**
la pista *ski slope; track (running)* **7**
pitar *to whistle* **7**
el/la piyama *pajamas* **6**
la pizarra *chalkboard* **P**
la placa *license plate* **12**
la plaga *plague* 15
planchar *to iron* **5**
el planeta *planet* 5, **15**
la planta *plant* 5, **7**
la planta baja *first floor, ground floor* **5**
el plástico *plastic* 2, 15
la plata *silver* **6**
el plátano *plantain* **10**
la platería *silversmithing* 13
el plato *plate, dish* 1, **5, 10**
la playa *beach* **1**
la plaza *plaza, square* **1**

el/la plomero/a *plumber* **9**
poblado/a *populated* 11
pobre *poor* **2**
la pobreza *poverty* 13, **14**
poco después *shortly after* **4**
el poder *power* **14**
poder (ue, u) *to be able to, can* **4**
poderoso/a *powerful* 4
¿Podría...? *Could you . . .?* **12**
el poema *poem* 1, 13
la poesía *poetry* **13**
el/la poeta *poet* **13**
polaco/a *Polish* 2
el/la policía *police officer* **9**
el poliéster *polyester* **6**
la política *politics* 2
la pollera *skirt* 6
el pollo *chicken* **3, 10**
el polvo *powder* 8
la pólvora *gunpowder* 8
el ponche *punch* 10
poner (g) *to put* **3**
poner en riesgo *to put at risk* **15**
poner la mesa *to set the table* **3**
poner una película *to show a movie* **3**
poner(se) (g) la ropa *to put one's clothes on* **4**
por *along; for; per; through* 1
Por aquel entonces... *Back then . . .* 8
por casualidad *by any chance* 12
por ciento *percent* **3**
por cierto *by the way* **9**
por ejemplo *for example* **3**
por eso *therefore, for that reason* 1; *that is why* **3**
por favor *please* **P**
por fin *finally, at last* **3**
por la mañana *in the morning* 1
por la noche *at night* 1
por la tarde *in the afternoon* 1
por lo general *in general* 1
por lo menos *at least* **3**
por otro (lado)... *on the other (hand) . . .* 11
¿por qué? *why?* **1**
por supuesto *of course* **3**
por último *finally* **4, 8**
por un lado... *on one hand . . .* 11
el porcentaje *percentage* 2, 4, **14**
la porción *portion* 10
porque *because* **1**
portugués/portuguesa *Portuguese* 2
el postre *dessert* **10**
potente *powerful* 15
practicar *to practice* **1**
practicar deportes *to practice sports* **3**
práctico/a *practical* **1**
la precariedad *precariousness* **14**
el precio *price* 3, 5, **6**
precioso/a *beautiful* **6**
preferible *preferable* 11
preferir (ie, i) *to prefer* **4**
la pregunta *question* **P**
preliminar *preliminary* P
el premio *award, prize* 6, 8, 10, **13**
la prenda *garment* 12
preocupar (se) *to worry* 10, **11**
la preparación *preparation* P
preparar(se) *to train* **7**
el preparativo *preparation* 4, **8**
presencial *in person* 13
la presentación *introduction* P
Presente. *Here.* **P**
las prestaciones *benefits* **14**
el préstamo *loan* 5, 14
prestar *to lend* **6**
el presupuesto *budget* 10
la primavera *spring* **P**
la primera clase *first class* **12**
primero/a, primer *first* P, 4, **5**
el/la primo/a *cousin* **4**
probar (ue) *to try; to taste* **10**
probarse (ue) *to try on* **6**
la probeta *test tube* 15
el problema *problem* 1, 5
la procesión *procession* **8**
el producto de belleza *beauty item* **11**
el producto lácteo *dairy product* **10**
la profesión *profession* **9**
el/la profesor/a *professor, teacher* **P**
el programa *program* 1
la programación *programming* **15**
programar *to program* **15**
prohibir *to prohibit; to forbid* **11**
el promedio *average* **14**
la promoción *promotion, advertising* 13
promover (ue) *to promote* **15**
el pronóstico del tiempo *weather forecast* 7
pronto *soon* 5
propagar *to spread* 11
la propina *tip* 9
propio/a *own* 4, **9**
el propósito *purpose* 4, 8, 11, 14
protagonizar *to star in; to have the leading role in* 10
proteger (j) *to protect* 6, **15**
protegido/a *protected* 10
la proteína *protein* 10
los proveedores de salud *healthcare providers* **11**
provocar *to cause* **15**
la próxima semana *next week* **3**
la proximidad *proximity* **14**
el próximo mes/año *next month/year* **3**
próximo/a *next* 2, 6
la prueba de esfuerzo *stress test* 11
el/la psicólogo/a *psychologist* **9**
el/la psiquiatra *psychiatrist* 11
la puerta *door* **P**
la puerta (de salida/llegada) *(departure/arrival) gate* **12**
el puerto *port* 15
puertorriqueño/a *Puerto Rican* **2**
el puesto *position* **9**; *stall, stand* **10**
el puesto de control *checkpoint* 12
el pulmón *lung* **11**
la pulsera *bracelet* **6**
el punto de ebullición *boiling point* 10
la puntualidad *punctuality* 3

Q

¡Qué aburrido! *How boring!* 1
¡Qué alivio! *What a relief!* 15
¡Qué bien! *How nice!* 3
¡Qué casualidad! *What a coincidence!* 1
¿Qué día es hoy? *What day is today?* **P**
¡Qué divertido! *How funny!* 1, 3
¿Qué fecha es? *What is the date?* **P**
¡Qué ganga! *What a bargain!* 6
¿Qué hay? *Hello? (telephone greeting)* 3
¿Qué hora es? *What time is it?* **P**
¡Qué increíble! *That's unbelievable!* 1
¡Qué interesante! *That's so interesting!* 1, 3, 8
¡Qué lástima! *What a pity!* **1**
¡Qué lata! *What a nuisance!* 3
¡Que lo pases bien! *Have fun/have a good time!* 1
¡Qué maravilla! *How wonderful!* 3
¡Que se mejore! *Feel better!* **P**
¡Qué suerte! *How lucky!* 1, 3
¿Qué tal? *What's up? What's new? (informal)* **P**
¿Qué te parece? *What do you think?* **3**
¿Qué te/le(s) pasa? *What's wrong (with you/them)?* **11**
¿Qué tiempo hace? *What's the weather like?* **P**
¡Qué triste/horrible! *How sad/horrible!* 15
¿qué? *what?* P, **1**
quedar *to fit; to be left over* **6**; *to leave behind* **15**
quejarse *to complain* **7**
quemar(se) *to burn (down)* 10, **15**
querer (ie) *to want* **4**
el queso *cheese* **3, 10**
el queso crema *cream cheese* **10**
¿Quién es...? *Who is . . . ?* **P**
¿quién(es)? *who?* P, **1**
la química *chemistry* **1**
la quinceañera *celebration for a girl's 15th birthday* 8
quinto/a *fifth* 4, 5
Quisiera... *I would like . . .* 5, **6**
quitar(se) *to take away; to take off* **4**

R

el rábano *radish* 8
el radiador *radiator* **12**
el/la radio *radio* **5**
el/la radiólogo/a *radiologist* 11
rallar *to grate* 10
rápidamente *quickly* 5
la **raqueta** *racquet* **7**
el rasgo *trait* 13
el rayo de sol *sunbeam* 8
los rayos ultravioleta *ultraviolet (UV) rays* **15**
la raza *race* 14
la razón *reason* 1, 3, 4, **5**
realista *realist* **13**
realmente *really, actually, in fact* 1, 5, **9**
la rebaja *sale* **6**
rebajado/a *marked down* **6**
rebajar *to reduce, lower (a price)* 6
la rebanada *slice* 10
rebelarse *to rebel; to revolt* 8
la recámara *bedroom* 5
la recepción *front desk* **12**
el/la recepcionista *receptionist* 11
la receta *recipe* **10**; *prescription* **11**
recetar *to prescribe* **11**
rechazar *to reject* 14
recibir *to receive* **1**
reciclado/a *recycled* **15**
recién *recently* 5
recoger (j) *to pick up* **5**
recomendar (ie) *to recommend* **11**
la recompensa *reward* 12
reconocer (zc) *to recognize; to acknowledge* 4
el reconocimiento *recognition* 7
recopilar *to compile* 14
recordar (ue) *to remember* 4, **8**
recorrer *to cover; to travel* **12**
el recuerdo *memory* **13**
la recuperación *recovery* **14**
los recursos naturales *natural resources* **9**
la red *net* **7**
las redes sociales *social media* **3**
reducir (zc) *to reduce* 11
reenviar *to forward* **15**
el refrán *proverb* 12
el refresco *soda, soft drink* **3, 10**
el refrigerador *refrigerator* **5**
el refrito *sauce made in a pan* 10
regalar *to give (a present)* **6**
el regalo *present, gift* **6**
regar (ie) *to water* 5, 9, 15
regatear *to haggle* 6
la región *region* 2
la regla *rule* 4
regular *so-so, not so great* **P**
regularmente *regularly* 5
rehusar *to refuse* 9
la reina *queen* 8

reír(se) (i,i) *to laugh* **7**
relajado/a *laid back* 2
relajante *sedative, relaxant* 11
relajarse *to relax* 7
religioso/a *religious* 8
rellenar *to fill out* 1
relleno/a *filled* 5, 10
el reloj *clock* **P**
el remedio *remedy, medicine* **11**
la remesa *remittance, money transfer* 9
remunerado/a *paid* **14**
el renacimiento *rebirth* 8
el rendimiento *performance* 9
el repertorio *repertoire* **13**
repetir (i, i) *to repeat* **4, 7**
Repite/Repitan. *Repeat.* **P**
repoblar (ue) *to replant* **15**
el repollo *cabbage* 4
la represa *dam* 13
la representación *representation* **13**
rescatar *to rescue* 12
la reseña *review* 13
la reservación *reservation* 10
reservar *to reserve* **12**
el resfriado *cold* **11**
la residencia estudiantil *dorm* **1**
residual *(related to) waste* **15**
los residuos (plásticos) *(plastic) waste* **15**
resolver (ue) *to resolve* **15**
respetar *to respect* 4
respirar *to breathe* 11
responder *to respond* **1**
responsable *responsible* **1**
la respuesta *answer* 1, 4
el restaurante *restaurant* **3**
el resultado *result* 5
el resumen *summary* 5
el reto *challenge* **15**
retratar *to portray* **13**
el retrato *portrait* **13**
la reunión *meeting, gathering* P, 1, **3**
reunirse *to get together; to gather* **8**
revelar *to reveal* 4
la revista *magazine* 2
la revista del corazón *gossip magazine* **13**
rico/a *rich, wealthy* **2**; *delicious* **3**
el riel *rail* **15**
el riesgo *risk* 12
el rincón *corner* 12
el río *river* P, 4, **15**
la riqueza *richness* 7; *riches, wealth* 15
la rivalidad *rivalry* 4
robar *to steal* 6
el robot *robot* **15**
rociar *to spray* 8
rodear *to surround* 6
la rodilla *knee* **11**
rojo/a *red* **2**
romper(se) *to break (down); to tear* **15**
la ropa *clothing, clothes* **4, 6**
la ropa interior *underwear* **6**
rosa *pink* 2
rosado/a *pink* **2**
el rotulador *marker* **P**
rubio/a *blond* **2**
la rueda *wheel* **12**
el ruido *noise* 5, 9
las ruinas *ruins* 5
la rutina *routine* 1, 4

S

sábado *Saturday* **P**
la sábana *sheet* **5**
saber *to know* **3**
el sabor *flavor* **10**
el sacacorchos *corkscrew* **10**
sacar *to take out* **5**
sacar buenas/malas notas *to get good/bad grades* **1**
el saco *blazer, suit jacket* **6**
la sal *salt* **10**
la sala *living room* **5**
la sala de espera *waiting room* **12**
salado/a *salty* 10
salarial *salary, wage* **14**
la salchicha *sausage* 10
la salida *departure* **12**
la salida de emergencia *emergency exit* **12**
salir (g) *to leave; to go out* **3**
el salmón *salmon* **10**
el salón *living room* 5
el salón de clase *classroom* **P**
la salsa de tomate *tomato sauce* **10**
la salsa picante *hot sauce* **10**
saltar *to jump* 11
la salud *health* **11**
saludable *healthy* 2, 10
el saludo *greeting* **P**
salvadoreño/a *Salvadoran* **2**
salvaje *wild* 12
la salvia *sage* 11
el sanatorio *clinic* **11**
las sandalias *sandals* **6**
el sándwich *sandwich* **3**
la sangre *blood* **11**
el satélite *satellite* **15**
el saúco *elder* 11
sazonar *to season* 10
Se fue la luz. *There was a blackout.* 8
Se me fue el alma a los pies. *My heart sank.* 15
Se me fue la lengua. *I gave myself away.* 15
Se me partió el alma. *It broke my heart.* 15
Se me puso la piel de gallina. *I got goosebumps.* 15
secar(se) *to dry (oneself)* **4, 5**
seco/a *dry* **5**
la seda *silk* **6**
la sede *headquarters* 1, 13
seguir (i, i) *to follow; to go on* **4, 7**
seguir derecho *to go straight* **12**
según *according to, as* **14**
segundo/a *second* **5**
seguramente *surely, probably, very likely* 5
la seguridad *security* 5
la seguridad de la información *data security* **15**
el seguro *insurance* 9, 11
seguro/a *safe* **14**
la selva *jungle* 5
selvático/a *jungle* **15**
la semana *week* **P**
la semana pasada *last week* **6**
la Semana Santa *Holy Week* 8
la semejanza *similarity* 4, 5, 13
la semilla *seed* **8**
el senderismo *hiking* 12
el sendero *trail, path* 12
la señal *signal* **9**
el señor (Sr.) *Mr.* **P**
la señora (Sra.) *Ms., Mrs.* **P**
la señorita (Srta.) *Ms., Miss* **P**
sensible *sensitive* P
sentarse (ie) *to sit down* **4**
el sentido común *common sense* 8
el sentimiento *feeling* 3
sentir(se) (ie, i) *to feel* **4, 7, 11**
septiembre *September* **P**
séptimo/a *seventh* **5**
ser *to be* **P, 1, 2**
ser alérgico/a *to be allergic* 11
Será un placer. *It will be a pleasure.* 8
serio/a *serious* P, 9
la servilleta *napkin* **10**
servir (i, i) *to serve* **4, 7**
sexto/a *sixth* **5**
si *if* **3**
la sidra *cider* 10
siempre *always* **1, 8, 12**
Siga/Sigan. *Come in.* 5
el siglo *century* 1, 6
significar *to mean* 4
siguiente *following* 4
la silla *chair* **P, 5**
la silla de ruedas *wheelchair* 12
el sillón *armchair* **2**
silvestre *wild* 10
el símbolo *symbol* 3, 7, **13**
simpático/a *nice, charming* **2**
simplemente *simply* 5
sin duda *without a doubt* 3
sin embargo *however, nevertheless* 5, 6, **9**
sin que *without* **14**
el síntoma *symptom* 11
sobre *on, on top of* **P**; *about* 1
el/la sobrino/a *nephew/niece* **4**
la sociedad *society* **14**
la soda *informal restaurant in Costa Rica* 12
el sofá *sofa* **5**
sofreír (i, i) *to sauté* **10**
solamente *only* 1
solicitar *to apply (for)* **9**
la solicitud *application* **9**
solo *only* **1**
soltero/a *single* **2**
solucionar *to solve* 5
la sombra *shade* **13**
el sombrero *wide-brimmed hat* **6**
sonar (ue) *to ring* 7
soñar (ue) *to dream* 14
la sopa *soup* **3**
sorprender *to surprise* 10
la sorpresa *surprise* 1, 10
el sostén *bra* **6**
sostenible *sustainable* 6, **15**
el sótano *basement* 5
su(s) *your (formal), his, her, its, their* **2**
subir *to upload* **15**
subir (a) *to get on/in(to); to go up* **12**
subir de peso *to gain weight* 3
el subtítulo *subtitle* 10
sucio/a *dirty* 4, **5**
la sudadera *sweatshirt, jogging suit* **6**
el sueldo *salary, wage* **9**
suelto/a *loose* 15
el sueño *dream* 7
el suéter *sweater* **6**
la sugerencia *suggestion* 4
sugerir (ie, i) *to suggest* 15
el sujetador *bra* 6
suministrar *to provide* 13
superar *to overcome* 14
el supermercado *supermarket* **6**
suprimir *to suppress* 14
el sur *South* P
el **sureste** *Southeast* 8
surrealista *surrealist* **13**
el sustantivo *noun* 9
susurrar *to whisper* 15

T

la tableta *tablet* **P**
tacaño/a *stingy* 11
la talla *clothing size* **6**

el taller *workshop* 8
el tamal *tamale* **3**
el tamaño *size* 6, **15**
también *also, too* 1, **2, 12**
tampoco *neither, not* **12**
tan pronto (como) *as soon as* **14**
tan… como *as . . . as* 1, **8**
tanto como *as much as (with verbs)* **8**
tanto/a… como *as much as* **8**
tantos/as… como *as many . . . as* **8**
tapar *to cover* 10
el tapiz *tapestry* 9
la tarde *afternoon* 1
tarde *late* **4**
la tarea *homework* **P**
La tarea, por favor. *Homework, please.* **P**
la tarjeta de crédito *credit card* **6**
la tarjeta de embarque *boarding pass* **12**
la tarjeta magnética *key card* **12**
la tarta de manzana *apple pie* 10
la tasa *rate* 9, **14**
la tasa de cambio *exchange rate* 8
el tatuaje *tattoo* 6
la taza *cup, mug* **10**
el té *tea* **3**
el teatro *theater* 5, **13**
el techo *roof* 14
el/la técnico/a *technician* **9**
la tecnología *technology* **15**
el tejido *weaving* 10; *fabric* 12
la tela *fabric* 2, **6**
el teleférico *cable car* 4
el teléfono (celular/móvil) *(cell) phone* P, 1, 3, 15
la televisión *television* 1
el televisor *television set* **5**
el tema *topic, theme* 4, 9, **13**
temer *to fear* **11**
el templo *temple* 5
temprano *early* **4**
tender (ie) *to hang (clothes)* **5**
el/la tendero/a *shopkeeper* **10**
el tenedor *fork* **10**
tener (ie) (g) *to have* 1, **4**
tener calor *to be hot* **5**
tener cuidado *to be careful* **5**
tener dolor de… *to have a(n) . . . ache* **11**
tener frío *to be cold* **5**
tener hambre *to be hungry* **5**
tener mala cara *to look terrible* **11**
tener miedo *to be afraid* **5**
tener muchas ganas de… *to be very excited to . . .* **8**
tener prisa *to be in a hurry* **5**
tener que + *infinitive* *to have to (do something)* **4**
tener razón *to be right* **5**
tener sed *to be thirsty* **5**
tener sueño *te be sleepy* **5**
tener suerte *to be lucky* **5**
Tengo… años. *I am . . . years old.* **2**
el tenis *tennis* **7**
el/la tenista *tennis player* 2, **7**
la tensión (arterial) *(blood) pressure* **11**
tercero/a, tercer *third* **5**
terminar *to finish* **4**
el termómetro *thermometer* **11**
la terraza *deck, balcony* **5**
el terremoto *earthquake* 5
el terreno *land* **9**
el/la testigo/a *witness* 15
textear *to text* 4
el tiburón *shark* 5
el tiempo *weather* **P**
el tiempo libre *free time* 1, **3**
la tienda *store* **6**; *tent* 12
la tienda de conveniencia *convenience store* 6
la tienda del barrio *convenience store* 6
¿Tienes/Tienen preguntas? *Do you have any questions?* **P**
la tierra *land* **9**
tímido/a *timid, shy* 8
la tina *bathtub* 5
la tinta *ink* 15
la tintorería *dry cleaner* 6
el/la tío/a *uncle/aunt* **4**
típico/a *typical* 1
el tipo *type* 5
tirar *to throw* 10
el título *title* 10; *degree* 14
la toalla *towel* **5**
el tobillo *ankle* **11**
tocar (un instrumento) *to play (an instrument)* **3**
el tocino *bacon* 10
todas las semanas *every week* **1**
todavía *still, yet* **10**
todo *everything* 12
todos los días/meses *every day/month* **1**
todos/as *everybody* **2**; *all* **12**
tomar *to take, to drink* **1**
tomar apuntes/notas *to take notes* **1**
tomar el sol *to sunbathe* **3**
el tomate *tomato* **3**
tonto/a *silly, foolish* **2**
torcer(se) (ue) *to twist* **11**
el/la torero/a *bullfighter* 2
el torneo *tournament* 2, 7
el toro *bull* **8**
la toronja *grapefruit* **10**
la torre *tower* 8, 15
la tortuga *turtle* 4, 10
la tos *cough* **11**
toser *to cough* **11**
la tostada *toast* **3**
tostar (ue) *to toast* 10
totalmente *totally* 5
trabajador/a *hardworking* **2**
trabajar *to work* **1**
el trabajo *work* 1, 2, **5, 9**
la tradición *tradition* **8**
tradicionalmente *traditionally* 5
traducido/a *translated* **13**
traducir (zc) *to translate* **7**
traer (g) *to bring* **3**
el tráfico *traffic* 12
el traje *suit* **6**
el traje de baño *bathing suit* **6**
tranquilamente *calmly* 5
tranquilo/a *calm, quiet* 5
transgénero *transgender* **13**
el transporte *transportation* **12**
el tratado *treaty* 15
el tratamiento *treatment* **11**
tratar *to try* 9; *to treat* **11**; *to deal with, to be about* **13**
trazado/a *drawn* 3
el tren *train* **12**
trigueño/a *light brown skin* 2
triste *sad* **2**
la tristeza *sadness* 13
el **triunfo** *triumph* **7**
tú *you (familiar)* **P**
tu(s) *your (familiar)* P, **2**
el tuit *tweet* **15**
turbio/a *murky* 15
el/la turista *tourist* 1, 5
Túrnense. *Take turns.* **P**

U

la ubicación *location* 4, 12
último/a *last* **8**
un poco *a little* **4**
un/una *a, an* **P**
la uña *fingernail* 13
una semana atrás *a week ago* **6**
una vez *once* **12**
único/a *only* 4
el uniforme *uniform* 7, 9
la universidad *university* **1**
uruguayo/a *Uruguayan* **2**
usar *to use* **1**
usted *you (formal)* **P**
ustedes *you (plural)* **1**
el/la usuario/a *users* 4
útil *useful* **P**
la uva *grape* 8, **10**

V

las vacaciones *vacation* 1, **3**
la vacante *opening* **9**
vacío/a *empty* 8, 10
la vacuna *vaccine* 6
el vagón *subway car* 15
la vainilla *vanilla* **10**
la vajilla *set of dishes* 10
¡Vale! *I agree!, Okay!* 3
valer (g) *to be worth* **6**
valiente *courageous, brave* 9
valioso/a *valuable* 4
el valle *valley* 4, 5
el valor *value* 4
valorar *to value* 14
los vaqueros *jeans* **6**
los vaqueros ajustados *skinny jeans* 6
variado/a *varied, assorted* P, 4
el vaso *glass* 8, **10**
Vayan a la pizarra. /Ve a la pizarra. *Go to the board.* **P**
el/la vecino/a *neighbor* 5, 11
el vegetal *vegetable* **3, 10**
vegetariano/a *vegetarian* 10
la vejez *old age* **14**
la vela *candle* **8**
la velocidad *speed* **12**
la vena *vein* **11**
el/la vendedor/a *salesperson* **9**
vender *to sell* 5, **6**
el veneno *venom* 11
venerar *to worship* 8
venezolano/a *Venezuelan* **2**
¡Venga! *Come on, let's do it!* 3
venir (ie) (g) *to come* 4
(en) venta *(for) sale* 5
la ventaja *advantage* 4, 5
la ventana *window* **P**
ver *to see* **1, 4**
el verano *summer* **P**
la verdad *truth* 7
¿verdad? *don't you?* 1
verde *green* **2**; *unripe* 6
la verdura *vegetable* **3, 10**
el vertido *spill* **15**
el vestido *dress* **6**
vestir(se) (i, i) *to dress; to get dressed* **4, 7**
el/la veterinario/a *veterinarian* 9
viajar *to travel* 3, 4, 9, **12**
el viaje *trip* 7, 8, **12**
el/la viajero/a *traveler* **12**
la vida *life* 1, 2

los videojuegos *videogames* **3**
el vidrio *glass* 2
viejo/a *old* **2**
el viento *wind* 6
viernes *Friday* **P**
el vinagre *vinegar* **10**
el vino *wine* 1, **3**
el vino blanco *white wine* **10**
el vino tinto *red wine* **10**
la violencia *violence* 13
virtualmente *virtually* **15**
visitar *to visit* 1, **4**
la vista *view* **5**
el/la viudo/a *widower/widow* 4
la vivienda *housing* **5**
vivir *to live* **1**
vivo/a *lively; alive* 6
el vocabulario *vocabulary* P
volador/a *flying* **15**
el volante *steering wheel* **12**
volar (ue) *to fly* 8, **12**
el volcán *volcano* 5, 10
el vóleibol *volleyball* **7**
el/la voluntario/a *volunteer* 4
volver (ue) *to return* **4**
vosotros/as *you (plural)* **1**
votar *to vote* 4
la voz *voice* 9, **13**
el vuelo *flight* **12**
vuestro/a *your (familiar plural)* **2**

Y

y *and* P
¿Y tú? *And you? (informal)* **P**
¿Y usted? *And you? (formal)* **P**
ya *already* 9, **10**
yo *I* **P**
el yogur *yogurt* **10**
la yuca *yucca* **3**

Z

la zanahoria *carrot* **10**
la zapatería *shoe store* 6
las zapatillas *slippers* **6**
las zapatillas de deporte *athletic shoes* **6**
los zapatos *shoes* **6**
los zapatos de tacón *high-heeled shoes* **6**
el zarcillo *earring* 6
la zona *area* **5**
la zona peatonal *pedestrian area* 10

Appendix 4

ENGLISH–SPANISH GLOSSARY

A

a little *un poco*
a week ago *una semana atrás*
a, an *un/una*
A.M. (from midnight to noon) *de la mañana*
about (approximately) *más o menos*
about (concerning) *sobre*
abroad *(en) el extranjero*
Absolutely not! *¡De ninguna manera!*
access *el acceso*
accessory *el accesorio*
to accompany *acompañar*
accountant *el/la contador/a*
accounting *la contabilidad*
to ache *doler*
ache *el dolor*
achievement *el logro*
to acknowledge *reconocer*
to acquire *adquirir*
activity *la actividad*
actor *el actor*
actress *la actriz*
actually *realmente*
acupuncture *la acupuntura*
adaptation *la adaptación*
to add *agregar, añadir*
adjustment *la adaptación*
to admire *admirar*
to advance *avanzar*
advance *el adelanto*
advantage *la ventaja*
advertisement *el anuncio*
advertising *la promoción, la publicidad*
advice *el consejo*
advisable *aconsejable*
to advise *aconsejar*
adviser *el/la consejero/a*
aerospace *aeroespacial*
affectionate *cariñoso/a*
after *después (de) que*
afternoon *la tarde*
Again. *Otra vez.*
against *contra*
age *la edad; la época*
agricultural *agrícola*
ahead of *delante de*
air conditioning *el aire acondicionado*
airbag *la bolsa de aire*
air-conditioned *climatizado/a*
airline *la aerolínea, linea aérea*
airplane *el avión*
airport *el aeropuerto*
aisle seat *el asiento de pasillo*
album *el disco*
all (of) *todos/as*
to allow *permitir*
almost *casi*
along *por*
already *ya*
also *también*
although *aunque*
altitude *la altura*
among *entre*
amusing *divertido/a*
always *siempre*
ambulance *la ambulancia*
ancestor *el/la antepasado/a*
ancient *antiguo/a*
and *y*
angry *enojado/a*
ankle *el tobillo*
annoyance *el disgusto*
annoying *fastidioso/a*
answer *la respuesta*
to answer *contestar*
anthropologist *el/la antropólogo/a*
antibiotic *el antibiótico*
another *otro/a*
anyone *alguien*
anything *algo*
apartment *el apartamento*
to apologize *disculparse*
app *la aplicación*
appetizer *el aperitivo*
apple *la manzana*
apple pie *la tarta de manzana*
appliance *el aparato*
appliances *los electrodomésticos*
application *la solicitud*
to apply (for) *solicitar*
to approve *aprobar*
April *abril*
architect *el/la arquitecto/a*
architecture *la arquitectura*
area *la zona*
Argentinian *argentino/a*
to argue *discutir*
arm *el brazo*
armchair *el sillón, la butaca*
armoire *el armario*
army *el ejército*
to arrive *llegar*
arrow *la flecha*
art *el arte*
artificial intelligence *la inteligencia artificial*
artistic *artístico/a*
as long as *mientras*
as many . . . as *tantos/as…como*
as much as *tanto/a…como*
as much as (with verbs) *tanto como*
as soon as *en cuanto; tan pronto (como)*
as . . . as *tan…como*
to ask for *pedir*
asparagus *el espárrago*
assembly *la asamblea*
assorted *variado/a*
asthma *el asma*
astronaut *el/la astronauta*
at about . . . *a eso de…*
at last *por fin*
at least *al menos, por lo menos*
at night *por la noche*
at the back *al fondo*
at the end of . . . *a finales de…*
at the present time *actualmente*
at the same time *a la vez*
at times *a veces*
At what time is (it)? *¿A qué hora es?*
athlete *el/la deportista*
athletic shoes *las zapatillas de deporte*
ATM *el cajero automático*
atmosphere *el ambiente, la atmósfera*
atmospheric *ambiental*
attachment *el (documento) adjunto*
to attend *asistir*
attic *el ático*
attractive *atractivo/a*
August *agosto*
aunt *la tía*
authoritarian *autoritario/a*
available *disponible*
average *el promedio*
average (medium) height *de estatura mediana*
avocado *el aguacate*
to avoid *evitar*
award *el premio*
awarded *galardonado/a*

B

back *la espalda*
Back then . . . *Por aquel entonces…*
backpack *la mochila*
backpacker *el/la mochilero/a*
to go backpacking *mochilear*
bacon *el tocino*
bad *mal, malo/a*
to bake *hornear*
balcony *la terraza*
ball *el balón, la pelota*
balloon *el globo*
banana *la banana*
banking *bancario/a*
baptism *el bautismo*
barbecue *el asado*
barbecue (pit/event) *la barbacoa*
barefoot *descalzo/a*
baseball *el béisbol*
baseball cap *la gorra*
baseball player *el/la beisbolista*
basement *el sótano*
basically *básicamente*
basket *el/la cesto/a*
basketball *el baloncesto, el básquetbol*
bat *el bate*
bathing suit *el traje de baño*
bathroom *el baño*
bathroom sink *el lavabo*
bathtub *la bañera*
battery *la batería*
battle *la batalla*
bay *la bahía*
to be *estar, ser*
to be able to, can *poder*
to be afraid *tener miedo*
to be allergic *ser alérgico/a*
to be born *nacer*
to be bothered by *molestar*
to be called *llamarse*
to be careful *tener cuidado*
to be cold *tener frío*

to be fashionable *estar de moda*
to be glad (about) *alegrarse (de)*
to be going to do something *ir a + infinitive*
to be happy about *estar contento/a (de)*
to be hot *tener calor*
to be hungry *tener hambre*
to be in a hurry *tener prisa*
to be left over *quedar, sobrar*
to be lucky *tener suerte*
to be right *tener razón*
to be sleepy *tener sueño*
to be thirsty *tener sed*
to be very excited . . . *tener muchas ganas de…*
to be windy *hacer viento*
to be worth *valer*
beach *la playa*
bead *la cuenta*
beak *el pico*
beans *los frijoles*
beautiful *hermoso/a, precioso/a*
beauty *la belleza*
beauty item *el producto de belleza*
to become independent *independizarse*
bed *la cama*
bedroom *el cuarto, el dormitorio, la habitación*
beef *la carne de res*
beer *la cerveza*
before *antes, antes de que*
before that *antes de eso*
to begin *comenzar, empezar*
beginning *el comienzo*
behavior *el comportamiento*
behind *detrás (de)*
to believe *creer*
bell pepper *el pimiento*
to belong *pertenecer*
belt *el cinturón*
benefits *los beneficios, las prestaciones*
beret *la boina*
beside *al lado de*
besides *además*
best *mejor*
to bet on *apostar por*
better *mejor*
beverage *la bebida*
between *entre*
beyond *más allá*
big *grande*
bilingual *bilingüe*
bird *el pájaro*
birth *el nacimiento*
birthday *el cumpleaños*
bite (insect) *la picadura*
black *negro/a*
blanket *la manta*
blazer *el saco*
blended family *la familia mixta*
blender *la licuadora*
blessing *la bendición*
blond *rubio/a*
blood *la sangre*
blouse *la blusa*
blue *azul*
board *la pizarra*
boarding house *la pensión*
boarding pass *la tarjeta de embarque*
body *el cuerpo*
to boil *hervir*
boiling point *el punto de ebullición*
Bolivian *boliviano/a*
bone *el hueso*
bonus *el bono*
book *el libro*
bookstore *la librería*
boots *las botas*
border *la frontera*
bored *aburrido/a*
boring *aburrido/a*
boss *el/la jefe/a*
to bother *molestar*
bottle *la botella*
to bowl *jugar a los bolos*
bowl *el bol*
box *la caja*
boxer shorts *los calzoncillos*
boy *el chico*
boyfriend *el novio*
bra *el sostén*
bracelet *la pulsera*
brain *el cerebro*
brand *la marca*
brand-name *de marca*
brave *valiente*
bread *el pan*
to break *romper(se), fracturar(se)*
to break down *descomponer(se)*
breakfast *el desayuno*
to breathe *respirar*
brief *breve*
to bring *llevar, traer*
broccoli *el brócoli*
brother *el hermano*
brother-in-law *el cuñado*
to brown *dorar*
brown *castaño/a, de color café, marrón*
budget *el presupuesto*
to build *construir*
building *el edificio*
bull *el toro*
bullfight *la corrida de toros*
bullfighter *el/la torero/a*
bumper *el parachoques*
bumper sticker *la calcomanía*
bun *el pan dulce*
to burn (down) *quemar(se)*
to bury *enterrar*
bus *el autobús, el bus*
business *el negocio*
Business Administration and Management *Administración y Dirección de Empresas*
businessman *el hombre de negocios*
businesswoman *la mujer de negocios*
busy *ocupado/a*
busy *apretado/a*
but *pero*
butcher shop *la carnicería*
butter *la mantequilla*
butterfly *la mariposa*
to buy *comprar*
by any chance *por casualidad*
by the way *por cierto*

C

cabbage *el repollo*
cable car *el teleférico*
cake *el pastel*
calculator *la calculadora*
calendar *el calendario*
to call *llamar*
to calm down *calmarse*
calm *tranquilo/a*
calmly *tranquilamente*
camel *el camello*
Canadian *canadiense*
candle *la vela*
candy *los dulces*
canned *enlatado/a*
canvas *el lienzo*
capital (city) *la capital*
capital (money) *el capital*
capsule *la cápsula*
car *el auto, el carro, el coche*
careful *cuidadoso/a*
carefully *cuidadosamente*
careless *descuidado/a*
carnival *el carnaval*
carpenter *el/la carpintero/a*
carpet *la alfombra*
carrot *la zanahoria*
carry-on luggage *el equipaje de mano*
cash *en efectivo*
cashier *el/la cajero/a*
cast (actors) *el elenco*
castle *el castillo*
cat *el/la gato/a*
to catch on fire *incendiarse*
to cause *provocar*
cavern *la caverna*
celebration *la celebración*
celebration for a girl's 15th birthday *la quinceañera*
cell phone *el (teléfono) celular, el (teléfono) móvil*
Celsius scale *escala Celsius*
cemetery *el cementerio*
(town) center *el centro*
century *el siglo*
cereal *el cereal*
chain *la cadena*
chair *la silla*
challenge *el desafío, el reto*
champion *el/la campeón/campeona*
championship *el campeonato*
change *el cambio*
to change *cambiar*
chaotic *cáotico/a*
chapter *el capítulo*
to charge *cargar*
charger *el cargador*
to chat *chatear*
cheap *barato/a*
check *el cheque*
to check (luggage) *facturar*
checkpoint *el puesto de control*
cheek *la mejilla*
cheese *el queso*
chemistry *la química*
cherry *la cereza*
chest *el pecho*
to chew *masticar*
chicken *el pollo*
chicken breast *la pechuga de pollo*
child *el/la niño/a*
child mortality *la mortalidad infantil*
childhood *la infancia*
Chilean *chileno/a*
to chill *enfriar*
chills *los escalofríos*
chimney *la chimenea*
Chinese *chino/a*
to choose *escoger*
chop *la chuleta*
chopped *picado/a*
Christmas *la Navidad*
Christmas Eve *la Nochebuena*
church *la iglesia*
cider *la sidra*
cilantro *el cilantro*
cinnamon *la canela*
Cinderella *Cenicienta*
circle *el círculo*
city *la ciudad*
city block *la cuadra*
class *la clase*
classical *clásico/a*
classmate *el/la compañero/a de clase*
claw *la garra*
clay *la arcilla*
to clean *limpiar*
clean *limpio/a*
clearly *claramente*

clever *listo/a*
client *el/la cliente/a*
climate *el clima*
climate change *el cambio climático*
clinic *el centro de salud, la clínica, el sanatorio*
clock *el reloj*
cloning *la clonación*
to close *cerrar*
Close the book. *Cierra/Cierren el libro.*
close to *cerca de*
closet *el clóset*
clothing *la ropa*
clothing size *la talla*
cloud *la nube*
coach *el/la entrenador/a*
coast *la costa*
coat *el abrigo*
coconut *el coco*
coconut milk *la leche de coco*
coffee *el café*
cold *el resfriado*
cold (temperature) *frío/a*
Colombian *colombiano/a*
color *el color*
colorful *colorido/a*
to comb *peinar(se)*
to combine *mezclar*
to come *venir*
Come in. *Pase(n). Adelante.*
Come on, let's do it! *¡Venga/Anda, anímate!*
comfortable *cómodo/a*
commerce *el comercio*
common *común*
common sense *el sentido común*
commonwealth *el estado libre asociado*
to communicate with *comunicar(se) con*
community *la comunidad*
company *la compañía, la empresa*
(dance/theater) company *la compañía (de danza/ teatro)*
competition *la competencia*
to compile *recopilar*
to complain *quejarse*
complex *complejo/a*
computer *la computadora*
computer science *la computación, la informática*
to concentrate *concentrarse*
concert *el concierto*
condiment *el condimento*
condition *la condición*
to confirm *confirmar*
congratulations *felicidades*
Congress *la Cámara de Representantes*
to connect *conectar(se)*
to conserve *conservar*
to construct *construir*
to consume *consumir*
contact lenses *los lentes de contacto*
contemporary *contemporáneo/a*
contest *el certamen, el concurso*
contract *el contrato*
contrast *el contraste*
to contribute *contribuir*
control panel *la consola*
convenience store *la tienda del barrio*
to converse *conversar*
to cook *cocinar*
cookie *la galleta*
copper *el cobre*
copper mine *la mina de cobre*
coral reef *el arrecife coralino*
corkscrew *el sacacorchos*
corn *el maíz*
corner *la esquina, el rincón*
to correct *corregir*
corridor *el pasillo*
corruption *la corrupción*
to cost *costar*
Costa Rican *costarricense*
cotton *el algodón*
to cough *toser*
cough *la tos*
cough syrup *el jarabe antitusivo*
Could you . . .? *¿Podría...?*
counter *el mostrador*
country *el país*
couple *la pareja*
courageous *valiente*
course *el curso*
court *la cancha*
courtesy *la cortesía*
cousin *el/la primo/a*
to cover *cubrir, tapar*
to cover (travel) *recorrer*
cream *la crema*
cream cheese *el queso crema*
credit card *la tarjeta de crédito*
crops *la agricultura*
cruelty *la crueldad*
cruise *el crucero*
crushed *machacado/a*
to cry *llorar*
Cuban *cubano/a*
cubist *cubista*
cucumber *el pepino*
to cultivate *cultivar*
cumin *el comino*
cup *la taza*
to cure *curar*
currency *la moneda*
(river) current *la corriente*
currently *actualmente*
curtain *la cortina*
custom *la costumbre*
customer care center *el centro de atención al cliente*
customs *la aduana*
customs agent *el/la insepctor/a de aduana*
to cut *cortar*
cycling *el ciclismo*

D

dad *el papá*
dairy product *el producto lácteo*
dam *la represa*
to damage *perjudicar*
to dance *bailar*
dance *el baile; la danza*
dancer *el bailarín/la bailarina, el danzarín/la danzarina*
danger *el peligro*
dangerous *peligroso/a*
to dare *atreverse*
dark *oscuro/a*
dark-haired *moreno/a*
dark-skinned *moreno/a*
data *los datos*
data security *la seguridad de la información*
date *la fecha*
daughter *la hija*
day *el día*
day after tomorrow *pasado mañana*
day before yesterday *anteayer*
Day of the Dead *el Día de los Muertos/Difuntos*
dead *muerto/a*
to deal with (be about) *tratar*
dean *decano/a*
death *la muerte*
debt *la deuda*
decade *la década*
deceased *muerto/a*
deceased person *el/la difunto/a*
December *diciembre*
deck *la terraza*
to decorate *adornar, decorar*
to decrease *disminuir*
dedicated *dedicado/a*
deforestation *la deforestación*
degree *el título*
degrees centigrade *grados centígrados*
delicious *rico/a*
to deliver (food) *entregar a domicilio*
to deliver (turn in) *entregar*
demonstration *la manifestación*
department (university unit) *el departamento, la facultad*
department store *el almacén*
departure *la salida*
depressed *deprimido/a*
to describe *describir*
description *la descripción*
to deserve *merecer*
design *el diseño*
designer *el/la diseñador/a*
desk *el escritorio*
dessert *el postre*
to destroy *destrozar, destruir*
detail-oriented *detallista*
to detain *detener*
to develop *construir, desarrollar*
developed *desarrollado/a*
development *el desarrollo*
(mobile) device *el dispositivo (móvil)*
diabetic *diabético/a*
dictatorship *la dictadura*
dictionary *el diccionario*
to die *morir*
diet *la dieta*
difficult *difícil*
digital *digitalizado/a*
digital library *la biblioteca digital*
dining room *el comedor*
dinner *la cena (evening meal), la comida (main meal)*
to direct *dirigir*
direction *la dirección*
director *el/la director/a*
dirty *sucio/a*
disadvantage *la desventaja*
disappearance *la desaparición*
disaster *el desastre*
discomfort *la molestia*
discovery *el descubrimiento*
discrimination *la discriminación*
dish (prepared food) *el plato*
dishwasher *el lavaplatos*
disloyal *desleal*
disorganized *desorganizado/a*
disposable *desechable*
dissemination *la diseminación*
distant *lejano/a*
to distract *distraer*
distracted *distraído/a*
diversity *la diversidad*
divorced *divorciado/a*
Do you have any questions? *¿Tienen/Tienes preguntas?*
Do you understand? *¿Comprenden/Comprendes?*
to do *hacer*
dog *el/la perro/a*
doll *el/la muñeco/a*
domestic partnership *la pareja de hecho*
Dominican *dominicano/a*
donkey *el burro*
don't you? *¿verdad?*
door *la puerta*
dorm *la residencia estudiantil*
double room *la habitación doble*
dough *la masa*

to download *bajar*
downtown *el centro*
to drain *colar*
drama *el drama*
to draw *dibujar*
drawing *el dibujo*
dreadful *horroroso/a*
to dream *soñar*
dream *el sueño*
dress *el vestido*
dresser *la cómoda*
to drink *beber*
drink *la bebida*
to drive *manejar*
driver *el/la chofer, el/la conductor/a*
driver's license *la licencia de conducir*
to dry *secar*
dry *seco/a*
to dry (oneself) *secar(se)*
dry clean *limpiar en seco*
dry cleaner *la tintorería*
due to *debido a*
during *durante*
During those years . . . *En esos años...*

E

each *cada*
eagle *el águila*
(outer) ear *la oreja*
(inner) ear *el oído*
early *temprano*
to earn *ganar*
earring *el arete*
earthquake *el terremoto*
Easter *la Pascua*
easy *fácil*
to eat *comer*
economic *económico/a*
economics *la economía*
Ecuadorian *ecuatoriano/a*
egg *el huevo*
eighth *octavo/a*
either . . . or *o... o*
elbow *el codo*
elder (tree) *el saúco*
electrician *el/la electricista*
electronic devices *los aparatos eléctricos*
electronic chip *el chip electrónico*
elevator *el ascensor*
embarrassed *avergonzado/a*
embroidery *el bordado*
emerald *la esmeralda*
emergency exit *la salida de emergencia*
emerging *emergente*
emigrant *el/la emigrante*
to emigrate *emigrar*
emigration *la emigración*
empathy *la empatía*
empire *el imperio*
employee *el/la empleado/a*
employment *el empleo*
empty *vacío/a*
encounter *el encuentro*
endangered species *la especie en peligro de extinción*
(alternative/wind/solar) energy *la energía (alternativa/eólica/solar)*
engineer *el/la ingeniero/a*
English *el inglés*
engraved *grabado/a*
to enjoy *disfrutar*
enormous *enorme, inmenso*
enough *bastante*
to enter *entrar*
entertainment *el entretenimiento*
entrepreneur *el/la empresario/a*
environment *el medio ambiente*
environmental *medioambiental*
envy *la envidia*
(in)equality *la (des)igualdad*
era *la época*
eraser *el borrador*
erosion *la erosión*
to escape *escapar(se)*
essay *el ensayo*
to establish *establecer*
ethnic group *la etnia*
even *hasta*
event *el acontecimiento*
ever *alguna vez*
everyday *cotidiano/a*
every day/month *todos los días/meses*
every . . . hours *cada... horas*
everybody *todos/as, todo el mundo*
everything *todo*
every week *todas las semanas*
evil *maligno/a*
exam *el examen*
to examine *examinar*
excellent *excelente*
to exchange *cambiar*
exchange *el intercambio*
exchange rate *la tasa de cambio*
Excuse me. *con permiso, perdón*
executive *el/la ejecutivo/a*
exercise *el ejercicio*
exhausted *cansado/a*
to exhibit *exhibir*
exhibition *la exposición*
expense *el gasto*
expensive *caro/a*
experience *la experiencia*
to explain *explicar*
to exploit *explotar*
explorer *el/la explorador/a*
export *la exportación*
extinct *extinguido/a*
extinction *la extinción*
to extinguish *apagar*
extreme sports *los deportes de riesgo*
extroverted *extrovertido/a*
eye *el ojo*
eyebrow *la ceja*
eyelash *la pestaña*

F

fable *la fábula*
fabric *la tela*
fabulous *fabuloso/a*
face *la cara*
face-to-face *cara a cara*
factor *el factor*
facts *los datos*
failure *el fracaso*
to fall *caer(se)*
fall *la caída*
fall (autumn) *el otoño*
to fall asleep *dormirse*
to fall in love *enamorarse*
false *falso/a*
family *la familia*
famous *famoso/a*
fan *el/la hincha*
far (from) *lejos (de)*
farm *la finca*
farm worker *el/la campesino/a*
farming *la agricultura*
fat *gordo/a*
father *el padre*
Father's Day *el Día del Padre*
favorite *favorito/a*
to fear *temer*
February *febrero*
to feel *sentir(se)*
to feel sorry *sentir*
feeling *el sentimiento*
fertile *fértil*
festival *el festival, la festividad*
fever *la fiebre*
fiancé *el novio*
fiancée *la novia*
fiber *la fibra*
field *el campo*
field hockey *el hockey sobre hierba*
field *el campo*
fifth *quinto/a*
fig *el higo*
to fight *luchar, pelearse*
to fill (out) *llenar*
filled *relleno/a*
film *la película*
filth *la inmundicia*
finally *por último; por fin*
Finally! *¡Por fin!*
financial *financiero/a*
financial analysis *el análisis financiero*
to find *encontrar*
to find out *averiguar*
fine *la multa*
fine arts *las bellas artes*
finger *el dedo*
fingernail *la uña*
to finish *terminar*
fire *el incendio*
to fire *despedir*
firefighter *el/la bombero/a*
firewood *la leña*
fireworks *los fuegos artificiales*
first *primer, primero/a*
first class *la primera clase*
first floor *la planta baja*
fish *el pescado*
(related to) fishing *pesquero/a*
fish market *la pescadería*
to fit *quedar*
fixed *fijo/a*
flag *la bandera*
flashers *las luces intermitentes*
flavor *el sabor*
flight *el vuelo*
flight attendant *el/la auxiliar de vuelo*
float (in a parade) *la carroza*
floating *flotante*
flood *la inundación*
floor *el piso*
florist *la floristería*
flour *la harina*
flow *el flujo*
flu *la gripe*
flute *la flauta*
to fly *volar*
fly *la mosca*
flying *volador/a*
to focus *concentrarse, enfocarse*
focus *el enfoque*
folder *la carpeta*
to follow *seguir*
following *siguiente*
food *la comida*
foolish *tonto/a*
foot *el pie*
football (American) *el fútbol americano*
footwear *el calzado*
for *por, para*
for example *por ejemplo*
forehead *la frente*
foreigner *el/la extranjero/a*
forest *el bosque*
to forget *olvidar(se)*
fork *el tenedor*

to form *formar*
form (to fill out) *el formulario*
fortunately *afortunadamente*
to forward *reenviar*
founder *el/la fundador/a*
fourth *cuarto/a*
fowl *las aves*
to fracture *fracturar(se)*
free (of charge) *gratis, gratuito/a*
free time *el tiempo libre, el ocio*
freeway *la autopista*
to freeze *congelar(se)*
freezer *el congelador*
French *el francés*
French (adj.) *francés/francesa*
French fries *las papas fritas*
frequently *frecuentemente*
Friday *viernes*
fried *frito/a*
fried dough *los churros*
fried food (meat) *la fritada*
fried rice *el arroz chaufa*
friend *el/la amigo/a*
friendship *la amistad*
from *a partir de, desde*
front desk *la recepción*
fruit *la fruta*
to frustrate *frustrar*
frustrating *fastidioso/a*
to fry *freír*
to fulfill *cumplir*
full *lleno/a*
fun *la diversión*
function *la función*
funny *divertido/a*
furious *furioso/a*
furniture *los muebles*
furniture store *la mueblería*
fusion *el mestizaje*

G

to gain weight *subir de peso*
game *el partido*
games console *la consola de videojuegos*
gang *la pandilla*
gap *la brecha*
garage *el garaje*
garbage *la basura*
garbanzo beans *los garbanzos*
garden *el jardín*
garland *la guirnalda*
garlic *el ajo*
garlic clove *el diente de ajo*
garment *la prenda*
gas burner *el mechero*
gastronomy *la gastronomía*
(departure/arrival) gate *la puerta (de salida/llegada)*
to gather (in a group) *reunirse*
gathering *la reunión*
generally *generalmente*
genetically *genéticamente*
geography *la geografía*
German *alemán/alemana*
to get (something) *obtener*
to get along (with) *llevarse bien*
to get angry *enojarse*
to get dressed *vestirse*
to get together *reunirse*
to get good/bad grades *sacar buenas/malas notas*
to get lost *perderse*
to get married *casarse*
to get sick *enfermarse*
to get stressed *estresarse*
ghost *el fantasma*
gift *el regalo*
girl *la chica*
girlfriend *la novia*
to give *dar*
to give (a present) *regalar*
to give (someone) a bath *bañar*
to give thanks *agradecer*
glad *alegre, content/a*
glass *el vidrio*
(drinking) glass *el vaso*
(stemmed) glass *la copa*
glasses *las gafas*
globalization *la globalización*
glove *el guante*
glove compartment *la guantera*
to go *ir*
to go bowling *jugar a los bolos*
to go in *entrar (en)*
to go on *seguir*
to go out *salir*
to go out (electricity) *apagarse*
to go shopping *ir de compras*
to go straight *seguir derecho*
to go to bed *acostarse*
Go to the board. *Ve/Vayan a la pizarra.*
god *el dios*
gold *el oro*
golf *el golf*
golf clubs *los palos de golf*
golf course *el campo de golf*
good *bueno/a*
good afternoon *buenas tardes*
good day *buenos días*
Good luck! *¡Buena suerte!*
good morning *buenos días*
good night *buenas noches*
goodbye *adiós, chao/chau*
good-looking *guapo/a*
gorilla *el gorila*
government *el gobierno*
governor *gobernador/a*
to graduate *graduarse*
granddaughter *la nieta*
grandfather *el abuelo*
grandmother *la abuela*
grandson *el nieto*
grape *la uva*
grapefruit *la toronja*
graphic design *el diseño gráfico*
to grate *rallar*
grateful *agradecido/a*
gray *gris*
great *estupendo/a, fabuloso/a, magnífico/a*
green *verde*
greeting *el saludo*
to grill *asar*
grill *la parrilla*
grilled (on the BBQ) *al carbón*
ground *molido/a*
ground beef *la carne molida*
ground floor *la planta baja*
to grow (cultivate) *cultivar*
growth *el crecimiento*
Guatemalan *guatemalteco/a*
to guess *adivinar*
guest *el/la invitado/a*
guest house *la pensión*
guide *el/la guía*
guinea pig *el cuy*
guitar *la guitarra*
guitarist *el/la guitarrista*
gunpowder *la pólvora*
gymnasium *el gimnasio*
gypsy *el/la gitano/a*

H

hacker *el/la pirata*
to haggle *regatear*
hair *el cabello, el pelo*
hairdresser *el/la peluquero/a*
half *la mitad*
half-brother *el medio hermano*
half-sister *la media hermana*
Halloween *el Día de las Brujas*
ham *el jamón*
hamburger *la hamburguesa*
hammock *la hamaca*
hand *la mano*
handicrafts *la artesanía*
handkerchief *el pañuelo*
handsome (male) *bien parecido, buen mozo*
to hang *colgar*
to hang (clothes) *tender*
happy *contento/a, alegre*
hard *duro/a*
hardworking *trabajador/a*
to harm *perjudicar*
harmful *perjudicial*
harmony *la armonía*
harp *el arpa*
to harvest *cosechar*
harvested *cosechado/a*
hat *el gorro, el sombrero*
to hate *odiar, detestar*
to have *tener*
to have (do something) *tener que + infinitive*
to have a good time *pasarlo bien, divertirse*
to have a(n)... ache *tener dolor de...*
to have breakfast *desayunar*
to have dinner *cenar*
to have fun *divertirse*
Have fun/Have a good time! *¡Que lo pases bien!*
to have lunch *almorzar*
to have to *deber*
hazard lights *las luces intermitentes*
he *él*
head *la cabeza*
headphones *los auriculares*
headquarters *la sede*
health *la salud*
healthcare providers *los proveedores de salud*
healthy *saludable*
to hear *oír*
heart *el corazón*
heart attack *el ataque de corazón*
heartbeat *el latido del corazón*
heating *la calefacción*
heavy *pesado/a*
height *la altura*
hello (greeting) *hola*
Hello? (telephone greeting) *¿Aló?*
helmet *el casco*
to help *ayudar*
hemisphere *el hemisferio*
herbal shop *el herbolario*
herbs *las hierbas*
Here (present). *Presente.*
heritage *la herencia*
Hey! (informal, to a friend) *¡Oye!*
hi *hola*
to hide *esconder*
high-heeled shoes *los zapatos de tacón*
highway *la carretera*
hiking *el senderismo*
hip *la cadera*
Hispanic *hispano/a*
historic *histórico/a*
history *la historia*
hole *el agujero*
holiday *el día festivo*
Holy Week *la Semana Santa*
home *el hogar*
homemaker *el amo/a de casa*
homeopathy *la homeopatía*
homework *la tarea*

Honduran *hondureño/a*
honey *la miel*
honeymoon *la luna de miel*
hood *el capó*
(basketball) hoop *la canasta, la cesta*
to hope for *esperar*
Hope you get better! *¡Que se mejore!*
horrific *horroroso/a*
hospital *el hospital*
host country *el país de acogida*
hostel *el hostal, la pensión*
hot *caliente*
hot sauce *la salsa picante*
hot, spicy pepper *el ají, el chile*
hotel *el hotel*
hour *la hora*
house *la casa*
housing *la vivienda*
How about that! *¡Fíjate qué noticia!*
How boring! *¡Qué aburrido!*
How do you say... in Spanish? *¿Cómo se dice... en español?*
How do you spell . . .? *¿Cómo se escribe...?*
How funny! *¡Qué divertido!*
How is it going? *¿Cómo te va?*
How long has it been since. . .? *¿Cuánto tiempo hace que...?*
How lucky! *¡Qué suerte!*
How many classes do you have? *¿Cuántas clases tienes?*
how many? *¿cuántos/as?*
How may I help you? *¿En qué puedo servirle(s)?*
How much is it? *¿Cuánto cuesta?*
how much? *¿cuánto/a?*
How nice! *¡Qué bien!*
How often? *¿Con qué frecuencia?*
How sad/horrible! *¡Qué triste/horrible!*
How wonderful! *¡Qué maravilla!*
how? *¿cómo?*
however *en cambio, sin embargo*
to hug *abrazar*
humanities *las humanidades*
humorous *gracioso/a*
hurricane *el huracán*
to hurt (feel pain) *doler*
husband *el esposo*

I

I *yo*
I am . . . years old. *Tengo... años.*
I don't know. *No sé.*
I don't understand. *No comprendo.*
I gave myself away. *Se me fue la lengua.*
I got goosebumps. *Se me puso la piel de gallina.*
I love . . . *Me encanta...*
I would like . . . *Me gustaría...; Quisiera...*
I/we hope (that) . . . *Ojalá (que)...*
ice *el hielo*
ice cream *el helado*
ice cream shop *la heladería*
if *si*
ignorance *la incultura*
illiteracy *el analfabetismo*
illness *la enfermedad*
I'm sorry (to hear that). *Lo siento.*
imagination *la imaginación*
Imagine that! *¡Imagínate!*
immediately *inmediatamente, de inmediato, enseguida*
immense *inmenso/a*
immigrant *el/la inmigrante*
immigration *la inmigración*
impartial *imparcial*
to improve *mejorar*
in addition to *además de*
in advance *con anterioridad*
in fact *en realidad, realmente*
in front of (facing) *enfrente de*
in general *por lo general*
in order (to) *para*
in person *presencial*
in spite of *a pesar de*
in the afternoon *por la tarde*
in the background *al fondo*
in the morning *por la mañana*
in the same way *de la misma manera*
In those days . . . *En aquellos tiempos...*
inclination *la tendencia*
inclusive *inclusivo/a*
income *el ingreso*
inconsiderate *desconsiderado/a*
to increase *aumentar*
indecisive *indeciso/a*
to indicate *marcar, señalar*
inexpensive *barato/a*
infection *la infección*
infectious *infeccioso/a*
influential *influyente*
information *los datos, la informacion*
information technology *la informática*
infrastructure *la infraestructura*
inhabitant *el/la habitante*
injection *la inyección*
injustice *la injusticia*
ink *la tinta*
to insist *insistir (en)*
instead of *en vez de*
insurance *el seguro*
to interest (be interested in) *interesar*
interesting *interesante*
interpreter *el/la intérprete*
to interview *entrevistar*
interview *la entrevista*
intonation *la entonación*
introduction *la presentación*
to invest *invertir*
to invite *invitar*
involved *involucrado/a*
to iron *planchar*
iron (metal) *el hierro*
ironic *irónico/a*
irresponsible *irresponsable*
island *la isla*
issue *el asunto*
It broke my heart. *Se me partió el alma.*
It has been a day/month/year since . . . *hace un día/mes/año (que)…*
It is at . . . (time) *(Es) a las...*
It will be a pleasure. *Será un placer.*
it's been (time expression) since . . . *hace (+ expresión de tiempo) que…*
it's clear *está despejado*
it's cloudy *está nublado*
it's cool *hace fresco*
it's raining *llueve / está lloviendo*
it's sunny *hace sol*
it's windy *hace viento*

J

jacket *la chaqueta, el saco (suit)*
January *enero*
Japanese *japonés/japonesa*
jeans *los jeans, vaqueros*
jewelry (piece of) *la joya*
jewelry store *la joyería*
job market *el mercado laboral*
joke *el chiste*
journalist *el/la periodista*
joy *la alegría*
judge *el/la juez*
to juggle *hacer malabarismos*
juice *el jugo*
July *julio*
to jump *saltar*
June *junio*
jungle *la selva*
jungle (adj.) *selvático/a*
junk food *la comida basura*

K

to keep *guardar, mantener*
ketchup *el kétchup*
key *la llave*
key card *la tarjeta magnética*
to kill *matar*
kindness *la amabilidad*
kindred spirits *las almas gemelas*
kinship *el parentesco*
to kiss (each other) *besar(se)*
kitchen *la cocina*
kitchen sink *el fregadero*
kite *el papalote, cometa*
knee *la rodilla*
knife *el cuchillo*
to know *conocer, saber*
knowledge *el conocimiento*

L

lace *el encaje*
lack *la falta*
ladies' underwear *las bragas*
laid back *relajado/a*
lake *el lago*
lamb *el cordero*
lamp *la lámpara*
land *el terreno, la tierra*
to land (aircraft) *aterrizar*
landscape *el paisaje*
language *el idioma, la lengua*
laptop *la computadora portátil*
to last *durar*
last *último/a*
last night *anoche*
last week *la semana pasada*
last year/month *el año/mes pasado*
late *atrasado/a, tarde*
later *más tarde, después, luego*
to laugh *reírse*
laundry room *la lavandería*
law *el derecho (area of study); la ley (legislation)*
lawn *el césped*
lawyer *el/la abogado/a*
to lay off *despedir*
layout *la distribución*
laziness *la pereza*
lazy *perezoso/a*
leaf *la hoja*
to learn *aprender*
leather *el cuero*
to leave *salir*
to leave (something) behind *quedar*
leavetaking *la despedida*
left *la izquierda*
leg *la pierna (person); la pata (animal, furniture)*
legal holiday *el día feriado*
legend *la leyenda*
leggings *las mallas*
to legislate *legislar*
leisure time *el ocio*
lemon *el limón*
to lend *prestar*
Lent *la Cuaresma*
lentils *las lentejas*
less *menos*
less than *menos de*
less . . . than *menos... que*

lesson *la lección*
letter *la carta*
lettuce *la lechuga*
level *el nivel*
librarian *el/la bibliotecario/a*
library *la biblioteca*
license plate *la placa*
to lie *mentir*
lie *la mentira*
life *la vida*
life expectancy *la esperanza de vida*
to lift *levantar*
to lift weights *levantar pesas*
light *liviano/a*
light brown skin *trigueño/a*
light(s) *la luz (las luces)*
to like (a lot) *gustar (encantar, fascinar)*
to like/dislike (a person) *caer bien/mal*
Likewise. *Igualmente.*
to limit *limitar*
link *el enlace*
lip *el labio*
to listen *escuchar*
literary career *la carrera literaria*
literate *alfabetizado/a*
literature *la literatura*
to live *vivir*
live *en vivo*
to live with *convivir*
lively *animado/a, vivo/a*
living room *la sala*
loan *el préstamo*
to loathe *detestar*
lobster *la langosta*
location *la localización, la ubicación*
lock *la esclusa (boats); la cerradura (door)*
locker *el casillero*
lodging *el alojamiento*
long *largo/a*
long lasting *duradero/a*
to look (at) *mirar*
to look after *atender*
to look for *buscar*
to look terrible *tener mala cara*
loose (clothing) *ancho/a*
to lose *perder*
to lose charge (devices) *descargarse*
to lose weight *bajar de peso*
loss *la pérdida*
Louder, please. *Más alto, por favor.*
to love *amar, querer*
love *el amor*
to lower (a price) *rebajar*
luggage *el equipaje*
lunch *el almuerzo*
lung *el pulmón*
luxury *el lujo*

M

machine *la máquina*
magazine *la revista*
mail *el correo*
mailbox *el buzón*
main character *el personaje principal*
to maintain *mantener*
majority *la mayoría*
to make *hacer; manufacturar*
to make a pilgrimage *peregrinar*
to make fun of *burlarse de*
mall *el centro comercial*
man *el hombre*
(sales) manager *el/la gerente (de ventas)*
to manufacture *fabricar*
many *muchos/as*
map *el mapa*
marathon *el maratón*
to march (parade) *desfilar*
March *marzo*
margarine *la margarina*
to marinate *marinar*
marine *marino/a*
marital status *el estado civil*
to mark *marcar*
marked down *rebajado/a*
marker *el marcador, el rotulador*
market *el mercado*
marriage *el matrimonio*
married *casado/a*
marvelous *maravilloso/a*
match (sports) *el partido*
materialistic *materialista*
mathematics *las mátematicas*
May *mayo*
mayonnaise *la mayonesa*
meal *la comida*
to mean *significar*
to measure *medir*
meat *la carne*
mechanism *el dispositivo*
median *la media*
medical doctor *el/la médico/a*
medicinal herb *la hierba medicinal*
medicine *el medicamento, la medicina*
to meet *conocer*
meeting *la reunión*
melodious *melodioso/a*
melon *el melón*
to melt *derretirse*
melted *derretido/a*
melting *el deshielo*
member *el/la miembro*
memory *el recuerdo*
(text) message *el mensaje (de texto)*
messy *desordenado/a*
meter *el metro*
meticulous *detallista*
Mexican *mexicano/a*
Mexican Independence Day *el Día de la Independencia de México*
microsurgery *la microcirugía*
microwave *el microondas*
Midnight Mass *la Misa del Gallo*
migraine *la migraña*
migration *la migración*
migratory *migratorio/a*
milk *la leche*
million *millón*
minority *minoritario/a (adj.), la minoría*
mirror *el espejo*
misfortune *el infortunio*
to miss *extrañar, faltar*
to mix *mezclar*
moderately *moderadamente*
mom *la mamá*
Monday *lunes*
money *el dinero*
money transfer *la remesa*
month *el mes*
mood *el ánimo*
more *más*
more than *más de*
more than . . . *más... que*
more . . . *más + adjective*
more or less *más o menos*
morning *la mañana*
Moroccan *marroquí*
mother *la madre*
motherhood *la maternidad*
Mother's Day *el Día de la Madre*
motor *el motor*
mountain *la montaña*
mountain range *la cordillera*
mouth *la boca*
to move *mover, mudarse*
movie *la película*
movies *el cine*
Mr. *el señor (Sr.)*
Ms., Miss *la señorita (Srta.)*
Ms., Mrs. *la señora (Sra.)*
much *mucho (adv.), mucho/a (adj.)*
mud *el barro*
mug *la taza*
multifunction printer *la impresora multifuncional*
mural *el mural*
murky *turbio/a*
muscle *el músculo*
museum *el museo*
mushroom *el champiñón*
music *la música*
Muslim *el/la musulmán/musulmana*
mustard *la mostaza*
mutually *mutuamente*
my *mi(s)*
My heart sank. *Se me fue el alma a los pies.*
My name is . . . *Me llamo...*
mysterious *misterioso/a*

N

naked *desnudo/a*
name *el nombre*
napkin *la servilleta*
to narrate *narrar*
narrow *estrecho/a*
nationality *la nacionalidad*
natural resources *los recursos naturales*
nature *la naturaleza*
near *cerca (de)*
nearby *cercano*
neck *el cuello*
necklace *el collar*
to need *necesitar*
neighbor *el/la vecino/a*
neighborhood *el barrio*
neither *niguno/a de los/las dos*
neither *tampoco*
neither . . . nor *ni... ni*
nephew *el sobrino*
nerve *el nervio*
nervous *nervioso/a*
nest *el nido*
net *la red*
to network *contactar*
network administration *la administración de redes*
never *nunca, jamás*
nevertheless *sin embargo*
new *nuevo/a*
New Year's Day *el Año Nuevo*
New Year's Eve *la Nochevieja, el Fin del Año*
news *las noticias*
news commentator *el/la comentador/a de noticias*
newspaper *el periódico*
next *próximo/a*
next month/year *el próximo mes/año*
next to *al lado de*
next week *la próxima semana*
Nicaraguan *nicaragüense*
nice (person) *agradable, simpático/a*
Nice to meet you. *Mucho gusto. / Encantado/a.*
niece *la sobrina*
night *la noche*
night before last *anteanoche*
nightclub *la discoteca*
nightgown *el camisón*
nightmare *la pesadilla*
ninth *noveno/a*
nobody *nadie*
noise *el ruido*
none *ningún, ninguno/a*

norm *la norma*
north *el norte*
North American *norteamericano/a*
northeast *el nordeste*
nose *la nariz*
notes *los apuntes*
notebook *el cuaderno*
nothing *nada*
to notice *enterarse*
noun *el sustantivo*
novel *la novela*
novelist *el/la novelista*
November *noviembre*
now *ahora*
nowadays *hoy en día, actualmente*
number *el número*
nurse *el/la enfermero/a*

O

occupation *la ocupación*
ocean *el océano*
October *octubre*
of course *cómo no, por supuesto*
of the (contraction of *de + el*) *del*
of the plains *llanero/a*
to offer *ofrecer*
offering *la ofrenda*
office *la oficina*
office (of doctor, dentist, etc.) *el consultorio*
often *muchas veces, frecuentemente*
oil *el aceite; el petróleo*
old *viejo/a, mayor*
old age *la vejez*
oldest *mayor*
olive *la aceituna*
on a global scale *a escala mundial*
on one hand . . . *por un lado...*
on the dot, sharp (time) *en punto*
on the other (hand) . . . *por otro (lado)...*
on top of *encima (de)*
On what page? *¿En que página?*
once *una vez*
onion *la cebolla*
online *en línea*
only *solamente, solo*
to open *abrir*
Open the book. *Abre/Abran el libro.*
open-air *al aire libre*
opening *la vacante*
opposing *contrario/a*
optimistic *optimista*
orange (color) *anaranjado/a, naranja*
orange (fruit) *la naranja*
orchestra *la orquesta*
order *el orden*
oregano *el orégano*
origin *el origen*
other *otro/a*
our *nuestro/a*
outbreak *el brote*
outing *la excursión*
outskirts *las afueras*
outstanding *destacado/a*
oven *el horno*
to overcome *superar*
overnight mail *el correo expreso*
own *propio/a*
owner *el/la dueño/a*
ozone layer *la capa de ozono*

P

P.M. (from nightfall to midnight) *de la noche*
P.M. (from noon to nightfall) *de la tarde*
pacemaker *el marcapasos*
packaging *el envase*
pagan *pagano/a*
page *la página*
paid (work) *remunerado/a*
pain *el dolor*
to paint *pintar*
painter *el/la pintor/a*
painting *la pintura*
pajamas *el/la piyama*
palace *el palacio*
pale *pálido/a*
painkiller *el analgésico*
Panamanian *panameño/a*
pantry *la despensa*
pants *los pantalones*
papaya *la papaya*
paper *el papel*
parade *el desfile*
paragliding *el parapente*
paragraph *el párrafo*
Paraguayan *paraguayo/a*
parasite *el parásito*
pardon me *con permiso, perdón*
parents *los padres*
parking *el estacionamiento*
parsley *el perejil*
part *la parte, el papel (in a play)*
to participate *participar*
partner *el/la compañero/a; la pareja (relationship)*
party *la fiesta*
to pass *pasar*
passenger *el/la pasajero/a*
passion fruit *la maracuyá*
passive *pasivo/a*
passport *el pasaporte*
password *la contraseña*
path *el sendero*
patient *el/la paciente*
to pay (for) *pagar*
peace *la paz*
pear *la pera*
pedestrian area *la zona peatonal*
pediatrician *el/la pediatra*
peeled *pelado/a*
pen *el bolígrafo*
penalty (in sports) *el penalti*
pencil *el lápiz*
people *la gente*
pepper *la pimienta*
per *por*
percent *por ciento*
percentage *el porcentaje*
perfectionist *perfeccionista*
perfectly *perfectamente*
to perform (act) *interpretar*
performance *el rendimiento*
permit *el permiso*
to permit *permitir*
person *la persona*
personality *la personalidad*
Peruvian *peruano/a*
pessimistic *pesimista*
petroleum *el petróleo*
pharmacist *el/la farmacéutico/a*
pharmacy *la farmacia*
photograph *la fotografía*
to pick up *recoger*
picture, painting *el cuadro*
pill *la pastilla*
pineapple *la piña*
pink *rosado/a*
pity *la lástima*
place *el lugar*
plague *la plaga*
plaid *de cuadros*
to plan *pensar + infinitive*
plane *el avión*
planet *el planeta*
plant *la planta*
plantain *el plátano*
plastic *el plástico*
plate *el plato*
platform (transportation) *el andén*
to play (a game, sport) *jugar*
to play (an instrument) *tocar*
player *el/la jugador/a*
plaza *la plaza*
please *por favor*
Please answer. *Contesta/Contesten, por favor.*
Pleased/Nice to meet you. *Encantado/a.*
plumber *el/la plomero/a*
poem *el poema*
poet *el/la poeta*
poetry *la poesía*
police officer *el/la policía*
Polish *polaco/a*
political science *las ciencias políticas*
politics *la política*
polka-dotted *de lunares*
(non)polluting *(no) contaminante*
pollution *la contaminación*
polyester *el poliéster*
poor *pobre*
popcorn *las palomitas de maíz*
populated *poblado/a*
pork *el cerdo*
port *el puerto*
portion *la porción*
portrait *el retrato*
to portray *retratar*
Portuguese *portugués/portuguesa*
potato *la papa*
poultry *las aves*
pound *la libra*
poverty *la pobreza*
powder *el polvo*
power *el poder*
power outage *el apagón*
powerful *poderoso/a, potente*
practical *práctico/a*
to practice (sports) *practicar (deportes)*
precariousness *la precariedad*
predator *el predador*
to prefer *preferir*
preferable *preferible*
preliminary *preliminar*
preparation *la preparación, el preparativo*
to prescribe *recetar*
present *el regalo*
present time *la actualidad*
press release *el comunicado de prensa*
(blood) pressure *la tensión (arterial)*
prestigious *prestigioso/a*
pretty *bonito/a*
pretty (female) *linda*
price *el precio*
pride *el orgullo*
to print *imprimir*
prize *el premio*
probably *probablemente*
problem *el problema*
procession *la procesión*
to produce *producir*
profession *la profesión*
professional career *la carrera*
professor, teacher *el/la profesor/a*
profit *la ganancia*
to program *programar*
program *el programa*
programming *la programación*
to progress *avanzar*
to prohibit, forbid *prohibir*
to promote *promover*
promotion *la promoción*
to protect *proteger*

protected *protegido/a*
protein *la proteína*
protest *la manifestación*
proverb *el refrán*
to provide *suministrar*
provided that *con tal (de) que*
proximity *la proximidad*
psychiatrist *el/la psiquiatra*
psychologist *el/la psicólogo/a*
Puerto Rican *puertorriqueño/a*
punch (beverage) *el ponche*
punctuality *la puntualidad*
puppet *el/la muñeco/a*
purple *morado/a*
purpose *el propósito, la función*
purse *el bolso*
to put *poner*
to put at risk *poner en riesgo*
to put on makeup *maquillarse*
to put one's clothes on *ponerse la ropa*
to put to bed *acostar*
pyramid *la pirámide*

Q

quality *la calidad*
queen *la reina*
question *la pregunta*
quickly *rápidamente*
quiet *callado/a, tranquilo/a*
to quit (doing something) *dejar*

R

race *la raza*
racquet *la raqueta*
radiator *el radiador*
radio *el/la radio*
radio/TV announcer *el/la locutor/a*
radio/TV announcement *el anuncio*
radiologist *el/la radiólogo/a*
radish *el rábano*
rail *el riel*
to rain *llover*
rain *la lluvia*
raincoat *el impermeable*
to raise (animals) *criar*
Raise your hand. *Levanta la mano.*
to raise *levantar*
ranch *la finca*
rate *el índice, la tasa*
rather *bastante*
raw *crudo/a*
to reach *alcanzar*
to read *leer*
Read. *Lee.*
reading *la lectura*
ready *listo/a*
realist *realista*
to realize *darse cuenta*
really *realmente*
rearview mirror *el espejo retrovisor*
reason *la razón*
reasonable *módico/a*
to rebel *rebelarse*
rebirth *el renacimiento*
to receive *recibir*
recently *recién*
receptionist *el/la recepcionista*
recipe; prescription *la receta*
recognition *el reconocimiento*
to recognize *reconocer*
to recommend *recomendar*
to record *grabar*
recovery *la recuperación*
recycled *reciclado/a*
red *rojo/a*
redhead *pelirrojo/a*
to reduce *reducir*
to reduce (a price) *rebajar*
reef *el arrecife*
referee *el/la árbitro/a*
refrigerator *el refrigerador*
to refuse *rehusar*
region *la región*
to regret *arrepentirse*
regularly *regularmente*
rehearsal *el ensayo*
to reject *rechazar*
relative *el pariente*
to relax *relajarse*
reliable *fiable*
religious *religioso/a*
remedy *el remedio*
to remember *recordar*
remittance *la remesa*
remote *el mando*
to rent *alquilar*
rent *el alquiler*
to repeat *repetir*
Repeat. *Repite/Repitan.*
repertoire *el repertorio*
to replant *repoblar*
report *el informe*
representation *la representación*
to rescue *rescatar*
research *la investigación*
reservation *la reservación*
to reserve *reservar*
resolution *el desenlace*
to resolve *resolver*
to respect *respetar*
to respond *responder*
responsible *responsable*
to rest *descansar*
restaurant *el restaurante*
result *el resultado*
résumé *el currículum*
to retire *jubilarse*
to return *volver*
to reveal *revelar*
review *la reseña*
to revolt *rebelarse*
reward *la recompensa*
rib *la costilla*
rice *el arroz*
rich *rico/a*
to ride (a bicycle) *montar (en bicicleta)*
right (direction) *la derecha*
right? *¿verdad?*
right away *enseguida, inmediatamente*
rights *los derechos*
to ring *sonar*
ring *el anillo*
risk *el riesgo*
risky *arriesgado/a*
rivalry *la rivalidad*
river *el río*
to roast *asar*
robber *el ladrón*
robe *la bata*
robot *el robot*
role (acting) *el papel*
romantic *romántico/a*
roof *el techo*
room *el salón, la sala, el cuarto*
roommate *el/la compañero/a de cuarto*
round-trip *de ida y vuelta*
router *el enrutador*
routine *la rutina*
rubble *el escombro*
rug *la alfombra*
ruins *las ruinas*
rule *la regla*
ruler *el/la gobernante*
to run *correr*
to run out of something *acabar(se)*
running of the bulls *el encierro*

S

sad *triste*
sadness *la tristeza*
safe *la caja fuerte*
safe *seguro/a*
saffron *el azafrán*
sage *la salvia*
salad *la ensalada*
salad dressing *el aderezo*
salary *el sueldo*
sale *la rebaja*
(for) sale *(en) venta*
salesperson *el/la dependiente/a, el/la vendedor/a*
salmon *el salmón*
salt *la sal*
salty *salado/a*
Salvadoran *salvadoreño/a*
same *el/la mismo/a*
same-sex couple *la pareja del mismo sexo*
same-sex marriage *el matrimonio igualitario*
sand *la arena*
sandals *las sandalias*
sandwich *el sándwich*
satellite *el satélite*
Saturday *sábado*
sausage *la salchicha*
to sauté *sofreír*
to save *ahorrar*
sawdust *el aserrín*
to say goodbye *despedirse*
to say *decir*
scarf *la bufanda (winter), el pañuelo*
scary *espantoso/a*
scene *la escena*
schedule *el horario*
scholarship *la beca*
school (university unit) *la facultad*
schooling *la escolarización*
science *la ciencia*
science fiction *la ciencia ficción*
scientist *el/la científico/a*
to score a goal *meter un gol*
scoreboard *el marcador*
scorpion *el escorpión*
screen *la pantalla*
sculptor *el/la escultor/a*
sculpture *la escultura*
sea *el mar*
sea level *el nivel del mar*
seafood *los mariscos*
to season *sazonar*
season *la estación*
seat *el asiento*
seatbelt *el cinturón de seguridad*
second *segundo/a*
secure *seguro/a*
security *la seguridad*
sedative *el relajante*
to see *ver*
see you later *hasta luego*
see you soon *hasta pronto*
see you tomorrow *hasta mañana*
seed *la semilla*
to seem *parecer*
self-portrait *el autorretrato*
to sell *vender*
to send *enviar, mandar*
sensitive *sensible*
sentence *la oración*
September *septiembre*
serious *grave, serio/a*

to serve *servir*
server (restaurant) *el/la camarero/a*
service *la atención*
to set foot *pisar*
set of dishes *la vajilla*
to set the table *poner la mesa*
seventh *séptimo/a*
several *algunos/as*
shade *la sombra*
shape, form *la forma*
to share *compartir*
shark *el tiburón*
to shave *afeitarse*
she *ella*
sheep *la oveja*
sheet *la sábana*
shell *la concha*
shellfish *los mariscos*
ship, boat *el barco*
shirt *la camisa*
shoe size *el número*
shoe store *la zapatería*
shoes *los zapatos*
shopkeeper *el/la tendero/a*
shopping *las compras*
short *corto/a length), bajo/a (stature)*
shortage *la escasez*
shortly after *poco después*
shorts *los pantalones cortos*
short-sleeved shirt *la camisa de manga corta*
should *deber*
shoulder *el hombro*
to shout *gritar*
to show *mostrar, demostrar*
to show a movie *poner una película*
shower *la ducha*
shrewd *calculador/a*
shrimp *el camarón*
to shut off *apagar(se)*
shy *tímido/a*
sick *enfermo/a*
to sign *firmar*
signal *la señal*
silk *la seda*
silly *tonto/a*
silver *la plata*
silversmithing *la platería*
similarity *la semejanza*
simply *simplemente*
since *desde*
to sing *cantar*
singer *el/la cantante*
single *soltero/a*
single room *la habitación sencilla*
sinking *el hundimiento*
sister *la hermana*
sister-in-law *la cuñada*
to sit down *sentarse*
Sit down. *Siéntate.*
sixth *sexto/a*
size *el tamaño*
to skate *patinar*
skeleton *el esqueleto*
to ski *esquiar*
ski slope *la pista*
skiing *el esquí*
skim milk *la leche desnatada*
skin *la piel*
skinny jeans *los vaqueros ajustados*
skirt *la falda*
skis *los esquís*
skull *la calavera*
to sleep *dormir*
slice *la rebanada*
slippers *las zapatillas*
sloppy *descuidado/a*
sloth *el oso perezoso*
to slow down *frenar*
slowly *lentamente*
small *pequeño/a*
smart *listo/a*
to smell *oler*
smell *el olor*
to smoke *fumar*
smoke *el humo*
smoothie *el batido*
snack *la merienda*
to sneeze *estornudar*
to snow *nevar*
snow *la nieve*
so that *para que*
soap *el jabón*
soccer *el fútbol*
social media *las redes sociales*
society *la sociedad*
socks *los calcetines*
soda *el refresco*
sofa *el sofá*
soft drink *el refresco*
solid *de color entero*
to solve *solucionar*
some *algunos/as*
someone *alguien*
something *algo*
sometime *alguna vez*
sometimes *a veces*
son *el hijo*
song *la canción, el canto*
soon *pronto*
sought-after *codiciado/a*
soul *el alma*
soup *la sopa*
sour cream *la crema agria*
source of income *la fuente de ingresos*
south *el sur*
southeast *el sureste*
space *el espacio*
spaghetti *los espaguetis*
Spanish *español/a*
to speak *hablar*
speaker *el/la hablante*
specialist *el/la especialista*
speed *la velocidad*
to spend *gastar*
to spend (time) *pasar*
spices *las especias*
spicy *picante*
to spill *derramar*
spill *el vertido*
spinach *las espinacas*
to sponsor *patrocinar*
spoon *la cuchara*
sport *el deporte*
sports equipment *el equipo deportivo*
spot *la mancha*
to spray *rociar*
to spread *propagar*
spring *la primavera*
square (in a city) *la plaza*
stadium *el estadio*
stage *el escenario*
stairs *la escalera*
stall (market) *el puesto*
stand (market) *el puesto*
to stand in line *hacer cola*
to stand up *levantarse*
star *la estrella*
to star in *protagonizar*
to start *comenzar, empezar*
starting at *a partir de*
state *el estado*
statistics *la estadística*
stay *la estadía*
steak *el bistec*
to steel *robar*
steering wheel *el volante*
step *el paso*
stepfather *el padrastro*
stepmother *la madrastra*
stereotype *el estereotipo*
still *aún*
stingy *tacaño/a*
stockings *las medias*
stomach *el estómago*
stomachache *el dolor de estómago*
stone *la piedra*
to stop *detener*
stopover *la escala*
store *la tienda*
store window *el escaparate*
story *el cuento*
stove *la estufa*
strain *la cepa*
strait *el estrecho*
strategy *la estrategia*
strawberry *la fresa*
street *la calle*
to strengthen *fortalecer*
stress test *la prueba de esfuerzo*
stretcher *la camilla*
striking *llamativo/a*
stripe *la franja*
striped *de rayas*
strong *fuerte*
student *el/la alumno/a, el/la estudiante*
studious *estudioso/a*
to study *estudiar*
style *el estilo*
subject *la asignatura, la materia*
subtitle *el subtítulo*
subway *el metro*
subway car *el vagón*
success *el éxito*
sufficient *bastante*
sugar *el/la azúcar*
sugar cane *la caña de azúcar*
to suggest *sugerir*
suggestion *la sugerencia*
suit *el traje*
suitcase *la maleta*
summary *el resumen*
summer *el verano*
to sunbathe *tomar el sol*
sunbeam *el rayo de sol*
Sunday *domingo*
sunglasses *las gafas de sol*
supermarket *el supermercado*
supper *la cena*
to support *apoyar*
to suppress *suprimir*
surely *seguramente*
to surf *hacer surf*
surgeon *el/la cirujano/a*
surgery *la cirugía*
surname *el apellido*
to surprise *sorprender*
surprise *la sorpresa*
surrealist *surrealista*
to surround *rodear*
surroundings *el entorno*
sustainable *sostenible*
sweatshirt *la sudadera*
sweater *el suéter*
to sweep *barrer*
sweets *los dulces*
swelling *la hinchazón*
to swim *nadar*
swimming *la natación*
swimming pool *la piscina*
swollen *hinchado/a*

symbol *el símbolo*
symptom *el síntoma*

T

table *la mesa*
tablecloth *el mantel*
tablespoon *la cucharada*
tablet *la tableta*
to take *tomar; llevar*
to take a bath *bañarse*
to take a nap *dormir la siesta*
to take a shower *ducharse*
to take a walk *dar una vuelta, pasear*
take apart *desarmar*
to take away *quitar*
Take care. (informal) *Cuídate.*
to take care (of) *cuidar(se) (de)*
to take notes *tomar apuntes/notas*
to take off (aircraft) *despegar*
to take off (clothing) *quitarse*
to take out *sacar*
Take turns. *Túrnense.*
Talk (about . . .) *Hablen (sobre...)*
talkative *conversador/a, hablador/a*
tall *alto/a*
tamale *el tamal*
tapestry *el tapiz*
tattoo *el tatuaje*
tax *el impuesto*
tea *el té*
to teach *enseñar*
team *el equipo*
to tear *romper(se)*
teaspoon *la cucharita*
technician *el/la técnico/a*
technology *la tecnología*
teeth *los dientes*
television *la televisión*
television set *el televisor*
to tell *contar, decir*
Tell your partner . . . *Dile a tu compañero/a...*
temple *el templo*
tendency *la tendencia*
tender *blando/a*
tennis *tenis*
tennis player *el/la tenista*
tent *la tienda*
tenth *décimo/a*
test *el examen, la prueba*
test tube *la probeta*
to text *textear*
textile industry *la industria téxtil*
Thank goodness! *¡Gracias a Dios!*
thanks *gracias*
Thanksgiving *el Día de Acción de Gracias*
that *ese/esa/eso*
that (over there) *aquel/aquella/aquello*
That's so interesting! *¡Qué interesante!*
That's unbelievable! *¡Qué increíble!*
the *el/la*
The weather is good/bad. *Hace buen/mal tiempo.*
theater *el teatro*
theme *el tema*
then *entonces, luego*
there *allí*
there is/are *hay*
There was a blackout. *Se fue la luz.*
therefore *por eso*
thermometer *el termómetro*
they *ellos/as*
thief *el ladrón*
thin *delgado/a*
to think *pensar*
third *tercer, terecero/a*
this *este/a*
thorough *cuidadoso/a*
those *esos/as*
those (over there) *aquellos/as*
thousand *mil*
threat *la amenaza*
throat *la garganta*
through *a través de, por*
to throw *tirar, lanzar*
Thursday *jueves*
ticket *el billete, el boleto, el pasaje*
to tidy up *ordenar, arreglar*
tie *la corbata*
tight *apretado/a*
tights *las mallas*
time (clock) *la hora*
timid *tímido/a*
tip *la propina*
tire *la llanta*
to tire *cansar*
tired *cansado/a*
title *el título*
to toast *tostar*
toast *el pan tostado/la tostada*
today *hoy*
toe *el dedo del pie*
together *juntos/as*
toilet *el inodoro*
tomato *el tomate*
tomato sauce *la salsa de tomate*
tomorrow *mañana*
tonight *esta noche*
too *también*
too much *demasiado/a*
tool *la herramienta*
tooth *el diente*
topic *el asunto, el tema*
totally *totalmente*
tourist *el/la turista*
tourist class *la clase turista*
tournament *el torneo, el campeonato*
toward *hacia*
because *porque*
towel *la toalla*
tower *la torre*
toy *el juguete*
track (running) *la pista*
track and field *el atletismo*
trade *el oficio*
tradition *la tradición*
traditionally *tradicionalmente*
traffic *el tráfico*
trail *el sendero*
to train *prepararse*
train *el tren*
training *el entrenamiento*
trait *el rasgo*
transgender *transgénero*
to translate *traducir*
trash *la basura*
translated *traducido/a*
transportation *el medio de transporte, el transporte*
to travel *viajar*
travel agency *la agencia de viajes*
traveler *el/la viajero/a*
tray *la bandeja*
to treat *tratar*
treatment *el tratamiento*
treaty *el tratado*
tree *el árbol*
trip *el viaje, la excursión*
triumph *el triunfo*
troupe *la comparsa*
truck *el camión*
true *cierto*
trunk *el baúl, el maletero*
truth *la verdad*
to try *probar (test out); tratar (make effort)*
to try on *probarse*
T-shirt *la camiseta*
Tuesday *martes*
tuna *el atún*
turkey *el pavo*
to turn *doblar*
to turn (an age) *cumplir*
to turn off *apagar*
turtle *la tortuga*
tweet *el tuit*
twice *dos veces*
twin *gemelo/a*
to twist *torcer*
two-thirds *dos terceras partes*
type *el tipo*
typical *típico/a*

U

ugly *feo/a*
ulcer *la úlcera*
ultraviolet (UV) rays *los rayos ultrovioleta*
umbrella *el paraguas*
umpire *el/la árbitro/a*
uncle *tío*
to uncover *destapar*
under *bajo, debajo (de)*
to understand *comprender, entender*
underwear *la ropa interior*
undocumented *indocumentado/a*
unemployment *el desempleo*
unforeseen *imprevisto/a*
unforgettable *inolvidable*
unfortunate *desafortunado/a*
uniform *el uniforme*
university *la universidad*
unless *a menos que*
unpleasant *antipático/a*
until *hasta*
to update *actualizar*
updates (information, news) *las novedades*
to upload *subir*
Uruguayan *uruguayo/a*
to use *usar*
useful *útil*
user *el/la usuario/a*

V

vacation *las vacaciones*
vaccine *la vacuna*
to vacuum *pasar la aspiradora*
vacuum cleaner *la aspiradora*
Valentine's Day *el Día de los Enamorados/del Amor y de la Amistad*
valley *el valle*
valuable *valioso/a*
to value *valorar*
value *el valor*
vanilla *la vainilla*
varied *variado/a*
vegetable *el vegetal/la verdura*
vegetarian *vegetariano/a*
vein *la vena*
Venezuelan *venezolano/a*
venom *el veneno*
very *muy*
veterinarian *el/la veterinario/a*
videogames *los videojuegos*
view *la vista*
vinegar *el vinagre*
violence *la violencia*
virtual assistant *el asistente virtual*
virtually *virtualmente*
to visit *visitar*
vocabulary *el vocabulario*
voice *la voz*
volcano *el volcán*

volleyball *el vóleibol*
volunteer *el/la voluntario/a*
to vote *votar*

W

wage *el sueldo*
waist *la cintura*
to wait for *esperar*
waiter *el camarero*
waiting room *la sala de espera*
waitress *la camarera*
to wake up *despertarse*
to walk *caminar*
wall *la muralla*
wallet *la billetera*
to want *querer, desear*
war *la guerra*
wardrobe (furniture) *elarmario*
warm-up *el calentamiento*
to wash *lavar(se)*
washer *la lavadora*
waste (plastic) *los residuos (plásticos)*
waste (related to) *residual*
wastebasket *el cesto*
to water *regar*
water *el agua*
waterfall *la catarata, la cascada*
we *nosotros/as*
weak *débil*
wealth *la riqueza*
wealthy *rico/a*
to wear a costume *disfrazarse*
to wear a shoe size *calzar*
to wear *llevar*
weather *el tiempo*
weather forecast *el pronóstico del tiempo*
weaving *el tejido*
wedding *la boda*
Wednesday *miércoles*
week *la semana*
weekend *el fin de semana*
well (health) *bien*
well/badly parked *bien/mal aparcado/a*
welcome *bienvenido/a*
well *bien*
well-known *conocido/a*
west *el oeste*
western *occidental*
wet *mojado/a*
what? (ask for clarification) *¿cómo?*
What a bargain! *¡Qué ganga!*
What a coincidence! *¡Qué casualidad!*
What a nuisance! *¡Qué lata!*
What a pity! *¡Qué lástima!*
What a relief! *¡Qué alivio!*
What day is today? *¿Qué día es hoy?*
What do you think? *¿Qué te parece?*
what for? *¿para qué?*
What is he/she/it like? *¿Cómo es?*
What is the date? *¿Cuál es la fecha?*
What time is it? *¿Qué hora es?*
What? *¿Perdón?/¿Qué?*
What's the weather like? *¿Qué tiempo hace?*
What's up? (familiar) *¿Qué tal?*
What's wrong (with you/them)? *¿Qué te/le(s) pasa?*
wheel *la rueda*
wheelchair *la silla de ruedas*
when? *¿cuándo?*
where (to)? *¿(a)dónde?*
Where is . . .? *¿Dónde está...?*
where? *¿dónde?*
which? *¿cuál(es)?*
while *mientras*
to whisper *susurrar*
to whistle *pitar*
white *blanco/a*
Who is . . .? *¿Quién es...?*
who? *¿quién(es)?*
whose *cuyo/a*
whose? *¿de quién?*
why? *¿por qué?*
why?/what for? *¿para qué?*
wide *ancho/a*
wide-brimmed hat *sombrero*
widow *la viuda*
widower *el viudo*
wife *la esposa*
wild *salvaje, silvestre*
to win *ganar*
wind *el viento*
window *la ventana*
window seat *el asiento de ventanilla*
windshield *el parabrisas*
windshield wiper *el limpiaparabrisas*
wine *el vino*
wing *el ala*
winter *el invierno*
wireless *inalámbrico/a*
to wish *desear*
witch *la bruja*
with me *conmigo*
With pleasure. *Con mucho gusto.*
with you (familiar) *contigo*
without *sin (que)*
without a doubt *sin duda*
witness *el/la testigo/a*
woman *la mujer*
wonderful *estupendo/a*
wonderfully *estupendamente*
wood *la madera*
wool *la lana*
word *la palabra*
to work *trabajar*
work *el trabajo*
work of art *la obra de arte*
work-related *laboral*
to work (run) *funcionar*
worker *el/la obrero/a*
workforce *la fuerza laboral*
to worry *preocuparse*
workshop *el taller*
world *el mundo*
worse *peor*
to worship *venerar*
wound *la herida*
wrist *la muñeca*
to write *escribir*
writer *el/la escritor/a*

Y

year *el año*
yellow *amarillo/a*
yesterday *ayer*
yet *todavía*
yogurt *el yogur*
you (familiar) *tú*
you (formal) *usted*
you (plural) *ustedes*
you (plural) *vosotros/as*
young *joven*
young man/woman *el/la joven*
youngest *menor*
your (familiar plural) *vuestro/a*
your (familiar) *tu*
your (formal), his, her, its, their *su*
you're welcome *de nada*
yucca *la yuca*

Text & Photo Credits

TEXT CREDITS

Capítulo 1

p. 59: Universidad de Salamanca School of Languages, http://www.usal.es/cursos-idiomas. Courtesy of Universidad de Salamanca. Creative Commons Attribution 4.0 International Public License. https://creativecommons.org/licenses/by/4.0/

Capítulo 13

p. 505: "Poema al No" by Gloria Fuertes. From *Me crece la barba: Poemas para mayores y menores*. Penguin Random House Grupo Editorial España, 2017. Used with permission of Herederas de Gloria Fuertes.

Capítulo 14

p. 541: Monterroso, Augusto. "La mosca que soñaba que era un águila." *EL PARAÍSO IMPERFECTO: ANTOLOGÍA TÍMIDA*. Debolsillo, 2013. Print. Used by permission of International Editors Company, S. L.

Capítulo 15

p. 576: Wilfredo Machado. "La invención del fuego." Used with permission.

PHOTO CREDITS

Cover: 1001nights/Getty Images

Capítulo preliminar

p. 2: Agência Brasil, CC BY 3.0 BR; **p. 3:** TL Don/AdobeStock; **p. 3:** ML kanuman/AdobeStock; **p. 3:** MR Tomas/AdobeStock; Garcia, **p. 3:** B Scherezade. "Island of many Gods I." Used by permission.; **p. 4:** TL Basso Cannarsa/Opale/Alamy Stock Photo; **p. 4** BL Keith Allison from Hanover, MD, USA, CC BY-SA 2.0; **p. 4** TL Chairman of the Joint Chiefs of Staff from Washington D.C, United States, CC BY 2.0; **p. 4** TC UNED Universidad Nacional de Educación a Distancia, CC BY 2.0; **p. 7:** T Monkey Business/AdobeStock; **p. 7** C AntonioDiaz/AdobeStock; **p. 7** B dglimages/AdobeStock; **p. 8** twinsterphoto/AdobeStock; **p. 11:** Africa Studio/AdobeStock; **p. 13:** C Jitka Laníková/AdobeStock; **p. 13** BL BC wektorygrafika/AdobeStock; **p. 13** BL BC Andrii/AdobeStock (multiple entries); **p. 16:** Ardfern, CC BY-SA 4.0; **p. 17:** TL SergeyCash/AdobeStock; **p. 17:** TC sarayutsridee/AdobeStock; **p. 19:** YummyBuum/AdobeStock

Capítulo 1

p. 28: peizais/AdobeStock; **p. 29:** TR JFL Photography/AdobeStock; **p. 29:** ML exclusive-design/AdobeStock; **p. 29:**MR Jenifoto/AdobeStock; **p. 19:** Bildarchiv Monheim GmbH; **p. 30:** TL akulamatiau/AdobeStock; **p. 30:** TR Jan Kranendonk/AdobeStock; **p. 30:** BL Sonia Oviedo/AdobeStock; **p. 30:** BR Arcady/AdobeStock; **p. 31:** TL LingroLearning; **p. 31:** BR LingroLearning; **p. 33:** TR LingroLearning; **p. 34:** Alfonsodetomas/AdobeStock; **p. 36:** Tyler Olson/AdobeStock; **p. 37:** Svitlana/AdobeStock; **p. 39:** TR fxegs/AdobeStock; **p. 39:** ML Miguel Domínguez Muñoz/AdobeStock; **p. 39:** BR franco lucato/AdobeStock; **p. 41:** Monkey Business/AdobeStock; **p. 43:** Pablo Cuadra / Stringer; **p. 49:** bramgino/AdobeStock; **p. 59:** Stockbroker/AdobeStock

Capítulo 2

p. 62: EFStock/AdobeStock; **p. 63:** TR Fotoluminate LLC/AdobeStock; **p. 63:** ML Christian Hinkle/AdobeStock; **p. 63:** MR Ryan Rahman/AdobeStock; **p. 63:** B Michele and Tom Grimm; **p. 64:** MR WENN Rights Ltd/Alamy Stock Photo; **p. 64:** MC User:Alisa Valdes, CC BY-SA 3.0, via Wikimedia Commons; **p. 64:** ML Gage Skidmore, CC BY-SA 2.0, via Wikimedia Commons; **p. 64:** TR Gilbert Carrasquillo / Contributor; **p. 65:** TL antoniosantosc/AdobeStock; **p. 65:** ML michaelheim/AdobeStock; **p. 65:** MR iuricazac/AdobeStock; **p. 65:** BL Cookie Studio/AdobeStock; **p. 65:** BR Krakenimages.com//AdobeStock; **p. 69:** TL David L/peopleimages.com//AdobeStock; **p. 69:** TR Vladimir/AdobeStock; **p. 69:** BL Andy Dean'/AdobeStock; **p. 69:** BR Prostock-studio/AdobeStock; **p. 70:** P. 70: TL Andres.Arranz, CC BY 2.5 <https://creativecommons.org/licenses/by/2.5>, via Wikimedia Commons; p. 70: TR Ralph Arvesen, CC BY 2.0 https://creativecommons.org/licenses/by/2.0, via Wikimedia Commons; **p. 73:** TR illustrissma/AdobeStock; **p. 73:** BL dgmata/AdobeStock; **p. 73:** BR Max/AdobeStock; **p. 77:** IanGibson/AdobeStock; **p. 79:** TL DoD News Features, CC BY 2.0 https://creativecommons.org/licenses/by/2.0; **p. 79:** TR Valder Beebe Show, CC BY 3.0 https://creativecommons.org/licenses/by/3.0, via Wikimedia Commons; **p. 79:** BL EricEnfermero, CC BY-SA 3.0 https://creativecommons.org/licenses/by-sa/3.0, via Wikimedia Commons; **p. 79:** BR Larry D. Moore, CC BY 4.0 https://creativecommons.org/licenses/by/4.0, via Wikimedia Commons; **p. 80:** Lunchbox LP, CC BY 2.0 https://creativecommons.org/licenses/by/2.0, via Wikimedia Commons; **p. 87:** MonkeyBusiness/AdobeStock; **p. 91:** shurkin_sun/AdobeStock

Capítulo 3

p. 102: Alisha/AdobeStock; **p. 101:**TR Alexander Sánchez/AdobeStock; **p. 101:** ML Sona/AdobeStock; **p. 101:** MR Leckerstudio/AdobeStock; **p. 101:** BC Art Collection 4/Alamy Stock Photo; **p. 102:** TR Jarmo V/AdobeStock; **p. 102:** ML Pilar, CC BY-SA 4.0 https://creativecommons.org/licenses/by-sa/4.0, via Wikimedia Commons; **p. 102:**BR lblinova/AdobeStock; **p. 103:** TL Cristophercruzfoto/AdobeStock; **p. 103:** TR NDABCREATIVITY/AdobeStock; **p. 103:** BL undrey/AdobeStock; **p. 103:** BR bernardbodo/AdobeStock; **p. 106:** TL Rido/AdobeStock; **p. 106:** BL Krakenimages.com/AdobeStock; **p. 107:** Grant Hindsley/Associated Press; **p. 108:** Hreinn Gudlaugsson, CC BY-SA 4.0 https://creativecommons.org/licenses/by-sa/4.0, via Wikimedia Commons; **p. 109:**TR hansgeel/AdobeStock; **p. 109:** ML motionshooter/AdobeStock; **p. 109:** MR Ibenk.88/AdobeStock; **p. 109:** BL volff/AdobeStock; **p. 109:** BR uckyo/AdobeStock; **p. 110:** AntAlexStudio/AdobeStock; **p. 111:** Andrey Starostin/AdobeStock; **p. 112:** TR EFStock/AdobeStock; **p. 112:** BR Santa001/AdobeStock; **p. 114:** bnenin/AdobeStock; **p. 115:** TL Grace/AdobeStock; **p. 115:** TR Daniel Prudek/AdobeStock; **p. 115:** BL Oscar Pinto Sánchez/AdobeStock; **p. 115:** BR Astarot/AdobeStock; **p. 131:** Andre Luis, CC BY-SA 3.0 https://creativecommons.org/licenses/by-sa/3.0, via Wikimedia Commons

Capítulo 4

p. 138: Monkey Business/AdobeStock; **p. 139:** TR JoslsaacAdobeStock; **p. 139:** ML ccsoler/AdobeStock; **p. 139:** MR Ramn/AdobeStock; **p. 139:** BR José Toro Moreno, Public domain, via Wikimedia Commons; **p. 140:** TR Natalia Kuzmina/AdobeStock; **p. 140:** ML Elvis/AdobeStock; **p. 140:** MR Clara/AdobeStock; **p. 140:** BL Paitoon/AdobeStock; **p. 141:** TL Framestock/AdobeStock; **p. 141:** TR Minas Panagiotakis/Getty Images; **p. 141:** BL Daniel Benavides from Austin, TX, CC BY 2.0 https://creativecommons.org/licenses/by/2.0, via Wikimedia Commons; **p. 141:** BR Anna Hult, CC BY 3.0 https://creativecommons.org/licenses/by/3.0, via Wikimedia Commons; **p. 145:** (Original uploader= Raystorm), CC BY-SA 3.0 http://creativecommons.org/licenses/by-sa/3.0/, via Wikimedia Commons; **p. 148:** TR Steve MORT/AFP/Getty Images; **p. 148:** BR Jose R. Aguirre/Cover/Getty Images; **p. 151:** Alice Nerr/AdobeStock; **p. 153:** Monkey Business/AdobeStock; **p. 160:** StratfordProductions/AdobeStock; **p. 169:** zinkevych/AdobeStock; **p. 169:** Iaroslava Zolotko/AdobeStock

Capítulo 5

p. 172: Jahman/AdobeStock; **p. 173:** TR Tobias/AdobeStock; **p. 173:** ML APstudio/AdobeStock; **p. 173:** MR Erick/AdobeStock; **p. 173:** BC Xenomanes/AdobeStock; **p. 174:** BR LUISVILLEDA/AdobeStock; **p. 174:** TL Wim/AdobeStock; **p. 174:** TR dlrz4114/AdobeStock; **p. 174:** BL Presidencia El Salvador from San Salvador, El Salvador, América Central, CC0, via Wikimedia Commons; **p. 175:** mehdi33300/AdobeStock; **p. 183:** TR Mateo Caballero/AdobeStock; **p. 183:** BL Angela Meier/AdobeStock; **p. 187:** TR New Africa/AdobeStock; **p. 187:** ML auremar/AdobeStock; **p. 187:** MC Ann Rodchua/AdobeStock; **p. 187:** MR michaeljung/AdobeStock; **p. 187:** BL PR Image Factory/AdobeStock; **p. 187:** BC NDABCREATIVITY/AdobeStock; **p. 187:** BR Rebecca Capell/AdobeStock; **p. 188:** TL Pavel Losevsky/AdobeStock; **p. 188:** BL Solarisys/AdobeStock; **p. 188:** BC Djavan Rodriguez/AdobeStock; **p. 188:** BR DavidA/AdobeStock; **p. 193:** Sidekick/AdobeStock; **p. 193:** juanpablo/AdobeStock; **p. 193:** WavebreakmediaMicro/AdobeStock; **p. 202:** Nils/AdobeStock; **p. 207:** Monkey Business/AdobeStock

Capítulo 6

p. 210: anamejia18/AdobeStock; **p. 211:** TR alexmillos/AdobeStock; **p. 211:** ML doleesi/AdobeStock; **p. 211:** MR FABIAN PONCE GARCIA/AdobeStock; **p. 211:** BC Casimiro Eilden, CC BY-SA 3.0 http://creativecommons.org/licenses/by-sa/3.0/, via Wikimedia Commons; **p. 212:** ML camaralucida1/AdobeStock; **p. 212:** TR Ulf Andersen/Hulton Archive/Getty Images; **p. 212:** BL Danny Ye/AdobeStock; **p. 212:** BR snaptitude/AdobeStock; **p. 213:** TL Brian/AdobeStock; **p. 213:** ML Rafael Prendes/AdobeStock; **p. 213:** MR EEIM, CC BY-SA 3.0 https://creativecommons.org/licenses/by-sa/3.0, via Wikimedia Commons; **p. 221:** Mauricio Toro/AdobeStock; **p. 225:** TR Monkey Business/AdobeStock; **p. 225:** BL Spectral-Design/AdobeStock; **p. 225:** BC AntonioDiaz/AdobeStock; **p. 225:** BR AntonioDiaz/AdobeStock; **p. 229:** Alejandro Macias Duque, CC BY-SA 4.0 https://creativecommons.org/licenses/by-sa/4.0, via Wikimedia Commons; **p. 233:** TR PRASERT/AdobeStock; **p. 223:** BL kiuikson/AdobeStock; **p. 223:** BC Victoria Chudinova/AdobeStock; **p. 223:** BC (JLco) Julia Amaral/AdobeStock; **p. 223:** BR Ami-Lou W/peopleimages.com/AdobeStock; **p. 240:** TL raquelm./AdobeStock; **p. 240:** TR Benedict/AdobeStock; **p. 240:** BL R.M. Nunes/AdobeStock; **p. 240:** BR Yeselly/AdobeStock

Capítulo 7

p. 249: TR Ada/AdobeStock; **p. 249:** MR Kushnirov Avraham/AdobeStock; **p. 249:** BR Zurbaran Galeria/SuperStock; **p. 249:** BL Dale Mitchell/AdobeStock; **p. 250:** TR Pedro/AdobeStock **p. 250:** MR atosan/AdobeStock; **p. 250:** TR Pedro/AdobeStock; **p. 250:** ML Damián Basante/AdobeStock; **p. 250:** BR Brastock Images/AdobeStock; **p. 251:** TL Tasnim News Agency, CC BY 4.0 https://creativecommons.org/licenses/by/4.0, via Wikimedia Commons; **p. 251:** ML D. Benjamin Miller, CC0, via Wikimedia Commons; **p. 251:** BL Harpagornis, CC BY-SA 4.0 https://creativecommons.org/licenses/by-sa/4.0, via Wikimedia Commons; **p. 252:** Tasnim News Agency, CC BY 4.0 https://creativecommons.org/licenses/by/4.0, via Wikimedia Commons; **p. 259:** TR El Gráfico, Public domain, via Wikimedia Commons; **p. 259:** BR Argentina.gob.ar, CC BY 4.0 https://creativecommons.org/licenses/by/4.0, via Wikimedia Commons; **p. 281:** TR CapturandoKilometros/AdobeStock; **p. 281:** BL Sandro Halank, Wikimedia Commons, CC BY-SA 4.0, CC BY-SA 4.0 https://creativecommons.org/licenses/by-sa/4.0, via Wikimedia Commons.

Capítulo 8

p. 284: Fernando/AdobeStock; **p. 285:** TR Dorothy Alexander/Alamy Live News/Alamy Stock Photo; **p. 285:** ML Nido Huebl/AdobeStock; **p. 285:** MR Jose Ignacio Soto/AdobeStock; **p. 285:** BC Archivart/Alamy Stock Photo; **p. 286:** TR anitasstudio/AdobeStock; **p. 286:** MR Michele/AdobeStock; **p. 286:** ML Kirk Fisher/AdobeStock; **p. 286:** BR Octavio Alonso Maya …, CC BY-SA 3.0 https://creativecommons.org/licenses/by-sa/3.0, via Wikimedia Commons; **p. 287:** TL Richard Ellis/Alamy Stock photo; **p. 287:** ML Wojciech Kuziów/AdobeStock; **p. 287:** MR Curioso.Photography/AdobeStock; **p. 288:** TL Keren Su/China Span/Alamy Stock Photo; **p. 288:** TR Fotos 593/AdobeStock; **p. 288:** BR ezioman, CC BY 2.0 https://creativecommons.org/licenses/by/2.0, via Wikimedia Commons; **p. 290:** TR Olena/AdobeStock; **p. 290:** ML by213/AdobeStock; **p. 290:** MC Hanna Syvak/AdobeStock; **p. 290:** MC tynyuk/AdobeStock; **p. 290:** BL Konstantin/AdobeStock; **p. 290:** BC kayteedesign/AdobeStock; **p. 290:** BR zlata_titmouse/AdobeStock; **p. 291:** Richard Ellis/Alamy Stock Photo; **p. 293:** Scott Griessel/AdobeStock; **p. 294:** Manoro82, CC BY-SA 4.0 https://creativecommons.org/licenses/by-sa/4.0, via Wikimedia Commons; **p. 296:** TR el heraldo, Public domain, via Wikimedia Commons; **p. 296:** BL Bruno adrian/AdobeStock; p. 304: TL Foxy_A/AdobeStock; **p. 304:** ML Felix Pergande/AdobeStock; **p. 304:** MR Daniel Ernst/AdobeStock; **p. 304:** BC Monkey Business/AdobeStock; **p. 308:** John & Lisa Merrill/Danita Delimont/AdobeStock; **p. 309:** TR José Guadalupe Posada, Public domain, via Wikimedia Commons; **p. 309:** BL Peter/AdobeStock; **p. 309:** BR Gstudio/AdobeStock; **p. 310:** TL Gage Skidmore, CC BY-SA 3.0 https://creativecommons.org/licenses/by-sa/3.0, via Wikimedia Commons; **p. 310:** TR Dominick D, CC BY-SA 2.0 https://creativecommons.org/licenses/by-sa/2.0, via Wikimedia Commons; **p. 314:** Kavalenkava/AdobeStock; **p. 323:** TR AlejandroLinaresGarcia, CC BY-SA 3.0 https://creativecommons.org/licenses/by-sa/3.0, via Wikimedia Commons; **p. 323:** BL Belikova Oksana/AdobeStock.

Capítulo 9

p. 326: jesuschurion57/AdobeStock; **p. 327:** TR Simon Dannhauer/AdobeStock; **p. 327:**ML Ingo Bartussek/AdobeStock; **p. 327:** MR David/AdobeStock; **p. 327:** BC Pedro Rafael Gonzalez Chavajay "CAFE" 1991 Arte Maya Tz'utuhil; **p. 328:** TR Byron Ortiz/Shutterstock; **p. 328:** ML Tyler/AdobeStock; **p. 328:** BL bruno/AdobeStock; **p. 328:** MR Carlos Rodriguez/ANDES, CC BY-SA 2.0 https://creativecommons.org/licenses/by-sa/2.0, via Wikimedia Commons; **p. 329:** TL S J Lievano/AdobeStock; **p. 329:** ML Crisma/AdobeStock; **p. 329:** BL Fernanda/AdobeStock; **p. 331:** TL Drazen/AdobeStock; **p. 331:** TR Prostock-studio/AdobeStock; **p. 331:** ML Rido/AdobeStock; **p. 331:** MR puhimec/AdobeStock; **p. 331:** BL sarawut/AdobeStock; **p. 331:** BR Jacob Lund/AdobeStock; **p. 334:** Drazen/AdobeStock; **p. 337:** TL Yakov/AdobeStock; **p. 337:** BR zwiebackesser/AdobeStock; **p. 337:** BL Laurent Bélanger, CC BY-SA 4.0 https://creativecommons.org/licenses/by-sa/4.0, via Wikimedia Commons; **p. 361:** DC Studio/AdobeStock

Capítulo 10

p. 364: Fotos 593/AdobeStock; **p. 365:** TR Kseniya Ragozina/AdobeStock; **p. 365:** ML Photofollies/AdobeStock; **p. 365:** MR ecuadorquerido/AdobeStock; **p. 365:** BC Vicente Albán, Public domain, via Wikimedia Commons; **p. 366:** TR Fotos 593/AdobeStock; **p. 366:** CL Kevin Oke Photograph/AdobeStock; **p. 366:** TL DEVIKA PRODUCTION/AdobeStock; **p. 366:** CR SL-Photography/AdobeStock; **p. 367:** TL Ricardo/AdobeStock; **p. 367:** TR Iryna/AdobeStock; **p. 367:** BL ecuadorquerido/AdobeStock; **p. 367:** BC atschki/AdobeStock; **p. 367:** BR grsphoto/AdobeStock; **p. 368:** Alexmegapixel/AdobeStock; **p. 372:** David/AdobeStock; **p. 373:** TR Patricio/AdobeStock; **p. 373:** BR OleksandrZastrozhnov/AdobeStock; **p. 377:** TL Joshua Resnick/AdobeStock; **p. 377:** TR Lukas Gojda/AdobeStock; **p. 377:** BL whitestorm/AdobeStock; **p. 377:** BR Vladislav Noseek/AdobeStock; **p. 381:** U.S. Embassy Kyiv Ukraine, Public domain, via Wikimedia Commons; **p. 388:** SL-Photography/AdobeStock; **p. 393:** Carlos Gamero/AdobeStock; **p. 393:** exclusive-design/AdobeStock

Capítulo 11

p. 396: Don Johnston/age fotostock/Alamy Stock Photo; **p. 397:** TL Daniel Avram/AdobeStock; **p. 397:** ML Nikolay N. Antonov/AdobeStock; **p. 397:** MR ValentinValkov/AdobeStock; **p. 397:** BC ACTIVE MUSEUM/Alamy Stock Photo; **p. 398:** TR Garry Knight, CC BY-SA 2.0 https://creativecommons.org/licenses/by-sa/2.0, via Wikimedia Commons; **p. 398:** ML kmiragaya/AdobeStock; **p. 398:** MR Ji-Elle, CC BY-SA 4.0 https://creativecommons.org/licenses/by-sa/4.0, via Wikimedia Commons; **p. 398:** BL vaclav/AdobeStock; **p. 399:** TL CHLOE HALL/Alamy Stock Photo; **p. 399:** BL Philippe Prudhomme/AdobeStock; **p. 399:** TR nenetus/AdobeStock; **p. 399:** BR beats_/AdobeStock; **p. 402:** TL bonnintorino/AdobeStock; **p. 402:** TR opolja/AdobeStock; **p. 407:** Diego Cervo/AdobeStock; **p. 407:** James Quine/Alamy Stock Photo; **p. 409:** D Lahoud/peopleimages.com/AdobeStock; **p. 416:** Giongi63/AdobeStock; **p. 418:** Jos/AdobeStock; **p. 422:** Syda Productions/AdobeStock; **p. 426:** Achirra, CC BY-SA 3.0 https://creativecommons.org/licenses/by-sa/3.0, via Wikimedia Commons; **p. 432:** Songwut Pinyo/AdobeStock;

Capítulo 12

p. 436: Jakub/AdobeStock; **p. 437:** TR julieta/AdobeStock; **p. 437:** ML Matthew/AdobeStock; **p. 437:** MR Simon Dannhauer/AdobeStock; **p. 437:** BC John Nakata/AdobeStock; **p. 438:** TR Leonel/AdobeStock; **p. 438:** ML diegograndi/AdobeStock; **p. 438:** MR Djavan Rodriguez/AdobeStock; **p. 438:** BL slowmotiongli/AdobeStock; **p. 439:** TL Matyas Rehak/AdobeStock; **p. 439:** TR Gian/AdobeStock; **p. 439:** BC Aastels/AdobeStock; **p. 440:** Ivan/AdobeStock; **p. 441:** Monkey Business/AdobeStock; **p. 443:** Mediteraneo/AdobeStock; **p. 448:** TR hh oldman, CC BY 3.0 https://creativecommons.org/licenses/by/3.0, via Wikimedia Commons; **p. 448:** BL Stefan/AdobeStock; **p. 450:** robert lerich/AdobeStock; **p. 452:** Galyna Andrushko/AdobeStock; **p. 453:** Jgz/AdobeStock; **p. 471:** BL Tony Northrup/AdobeStock; **p. 471:** TR Ivan Kuzmin/AdobeStock;

Capítulo 13

p. 474: Tasmita Gz, CC BY-SA 3.0 https://creativecommons.org/licenses/by-sa/3.0, via Wikimedia Commons; **p. 475:** TL JackF/AdobeStock; **p. 475:** ML Marcio Dufranc/AdobeStock; **p. 475:** MR b201735/AdobeStock; **p. 475:** BC DeAgostini/Getty Images; **p. 476:** TR Herland/AdobeStock; **p. 476:** BL daboost/AdobeStock; **p. 476:** BC rpbmedia/AdobeStock; **p. 476:** BR Anna/AdobeStock; **p. 477:** TL FF MM, CC BY-SA 3.0 https://creativecommons.org/licenses/by-sa/3.0, via Wikimedia Commons; **p. 477:** TR Eneas De Troya, CC BY 2.0 https://creativecommons.org/licenses/by/2.0, via Wikimedia Commons; **p. 477:** MC Gabriela_Mistral-01.jpg: Unknown authorUnknown authorderivative work: PRA, Public domain, via Wikimedia Commons; **p. 477:** MR Pedro J Pacheco, CC BY-SA 4.0 https://creativecommons.org/licenses/by-sa/4.0, via Wikimedia Commons; **p. 480:** TL Diego Velázquez, Public domain, via Wikimedia Commons; **p. 480:** MR Francisco Goya, Public domain, via Wikimedia Commons; **p. 480:** BL Antonio Campoy from Madrid, España, CC BY 2.0 https://creativecommons.org/licenses/by/2.0, via Wikimedia Commons; **p. 481:** TL Peter Barritt/SuperStock; **p. 481:** BR See Less/AdobeStock; **p. 482:** TR Arnal, Enrique; **p. 482:** TL Frank and Frances Carpenter Collection, Public domain, via Wikimedia Commons; **p. 482:** BL Diego Velázquez, Public domain, via Wikimedia Commons; **p. 482:** BR Diego Velázquez, Public domain, via Wikimedia Commons; **p. 483:** TL ElEditordelaSelva, CC BY-SA 4.0 https://creativecommons.org/licenses/by-sa/4.0, via Wikimedia Commons; **p. 483:** TC Xalo/AdobeStock; **p. 483:** MC Danilo Moroni/Alamy Stock Photo; **p. 483:** TR Walmart Stores, CC BY 2.0 https://creativecommons.org/licenses/by/2.0, via Wikimedia Commons; **p. 483:** BL tilialucida/AdobeStock; **p. 483:** MR VALERIO R.N./AdobeStock; **p. 483:** BR Serhii Shcherbakov/AdobeStock; **p. 484:** Demian/AdobeStock; **p. 486:** TR Julia Sumangil, CC BY-SA 4.0 https://creativecommons.org/licenses/by-sa/4.0, via Wikimedia Commons; **p. 486:** BL Pedro Szekely from Los Angeles, USA, CC BY-SA 2.0 https://creativecommons.org/licenses/by-sa/2.0, via Wikimedia Commons; **p. 493:** Michele Molinari/Alamy Stock Photo; **p. 494:** Provisualstock.com; **p. 505:** Ana Rojo, CC BY 2.0 https://creativecommons.org/licenses/by/2.0, via Wikimedia Commons;

Capítulo 14

p. 508: Heiner Heine/imageBROKER/Alamy Stock Photo; **p. 509:** TL Delphotostock/AdobeStock; **p. 509:** TR progat/AdobeStock; **p. 509:** MR Jose Luis Stephens/AdobeStock; **p. 509:** BR Fernando Lavoz/NurPhoto via Getty Images; **p. 510:** TR gydyt0jas/AdobeStock; **p. 510:** ML Tozzer/AdobeStock; **p. 510:** BL CarlosAugusto/AdobeStock; **p. 510:** MR Noradoa/AdobeStock; **p. 511:** TL Jorge Urrutia/Wirestock/AdobeStock; **p. 511:** ML Marcos/AdobeStock; **p. 511:** BL Hencer Olivia/AdobeStock; **p. 514:** Gianni Muratore/Alamy Stock Photo; **p. 516:** Nina Lawrenson/peopleimages.com/AdobeStock; **p. 519:** TR AJR_photo/Shutterstock; **p. 519:** BL Toniflap/AdobeStock; **p. 521:** F Armstrong Photo/AdobeStock; **p. 536:** ampueroleonardo/Getty Images; **p. 540:** MOISES CASTILLO/Associated Press

Capítulo 15

p. 544: OnePixel/AdobeStock; **p. 545:** TR Nancy Pauwels/AdobeStock; **p. 545:** ML Tomek/AdobeStock; **p. 545:** MR Mike Mareen/AdobeStock; **p. 545:** BC Gotay de Anderson, Zulia; **p. 546:** TR Bill/AdobeStock; **p. 546:** BL Andrey/AdobeStock; **p. 546:** BC Noradoa/AdobeStock; **p. 546:** BR Ventura Mendoza, CC BY 2.0 https://creativecommons.org/licenses/by/2.0; **p. 547:** TL Gorodenkoff/AdobeStock; **p. 547:** TR AntonioDiaz/AdobeStock; **p. 547:** BL pinkeyes/AdobeStock; **p. 547:** BR solraknauj/AdobeStock; **p. 548:** Klodien/AdobeStock; **p. 549:** TL PhotoSpirit/AdobeStock; **p. 549:** TR Kim Warden/AdobeStock; **p. 549:** BL Richard Carey/AdobeStock; **p. 549:** BR simanlaci/AdobeStock; **p. 550:** ondreicka/AdobeStock; **p. 551:** TL Elias Bitar/AdobeStock; **p. 551:** TR Edijs Palens/AdobeStock; **p. 551:** BL AlivePhoto/AdobeStock; **p. 551:** BR Gorodenkoff/AdobeStock; **p. 552:** TL 3D Motion/AdobeStock; **p. 552:** TR Riko Best/AdobeStock; **p. 553:** DM7/AdobeStock; **p. 555:** TR Original photo is anonymous although published by the Associated Press; **p. 555:** BL Gorodenkoff/AdobeStock; **p. 559:** TL Galina/AdobeStock; **p. 559:** TC romankosolapov/AdobeStock; **p. 559:** BL torwaiphoto/AdobeStock; **p. 559:** TR Katherine Welles/AdobeStock; **p. 559:** BR Shi/AdobeStock; **p. 569:** Sheryl Chapman/Shutterstock; **p. 575:** Courtesy of Rafael Machado.

Communicative Functions and Learning Strategies Index

Index

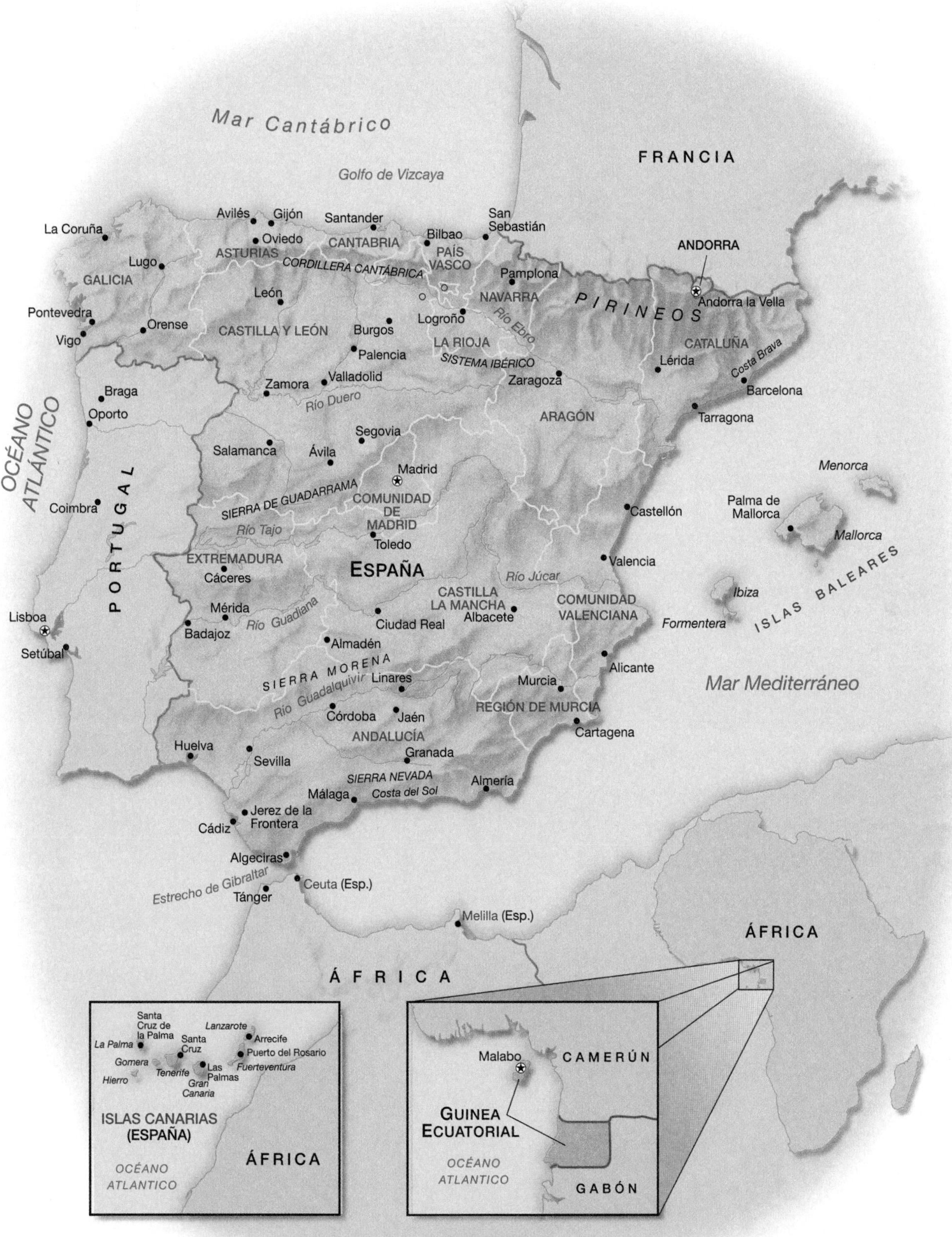

España y África

México, América Central y el Caribe

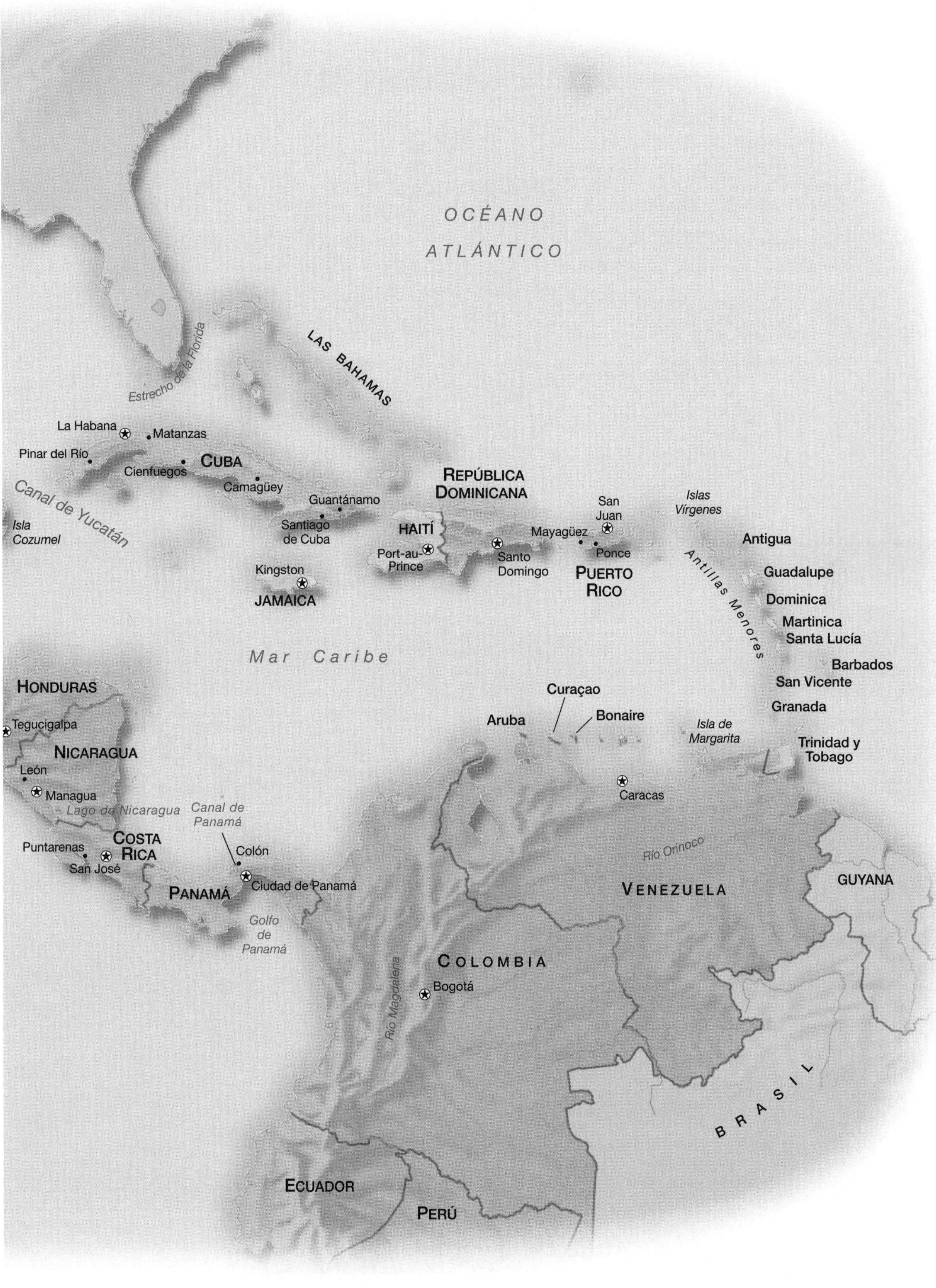

OCÉANO
ATLÁNTICO
Estrecho de la Florida
LAS BAHAMAS
La Habana
Matanzas
Pinar del Río
CUBA
Cienfuegos
Camagüey
Canal de Yucatán
Isla Cozumel
Guantánamo
Santiago de Cuba
REPÚBLICA DOMINICANA
HAITÍ
Port-au-Prince
Santo Domingo
Mayagüez
San Juan
Ponce
PUERTO RICO
Islas Vírgenes
Antigua
Guadalupe
Dominica
Martinica
Santa Lucía
Barbados
San Vicente
Granada
Antillas Menores
Kingston
JAMAICA
Mar Caribe
HONDURAS
Tegucigalpa
NICARAGUA
León
Managua
Lago de Nicaragua
Canal de Panamá
COSTA RICA
Puntarenas
San José
Colón
Ciudad de Panamá
PANAMÁ
Golfo de Panamá
Curaçao
Aruba
Bonaire
Isla de Margarita
Trinidad y Tobago
Caracas
Río Orinoco
VENEZUELA
GUYANA
COLOMBIA
Bogotá
Río Magdalena
BRASIL
ECUADOR
PERÚ

América del Sur